THE COLLECTED WRITINGS OF
T. E. HULME

The
Collected Writings of
T. E. Hulme

Edited by

Karen Csengeri

CLARENDON PRESS · OXFORD

1994

Oxford University Press, Walton Street, Oxford OX2 6DP
Oxford New York
Athens Auckland Bangkok Bombay
Calcutta Cape Town Dar es Salaam Delhi
Florence Hong Kong Istanbul Karachi
Kuala Lumpur Madras Madrid Melbourne
Mexico City Nairobi Paris Singapore
Taipei Tokyo Toronto

Oxford is a trade mark of Oxford University Press

Published in the United States
by Oxford University Press Inc., New York

© Karen Csengeri 1994

British Library Cataloguing in Publication Data
Data available

Library of Congress Cataloging in Publication Data
Hulme, T. E. (Thomas Ernest), 1883–1917.
[Works. 1994]
The collected writings of T.E. Hulme / edited by Karen Csengeri.
"A bibliography of Hulme's works": p.
Includes bibliographical references (p.) and index.
1. Philosophy. 2. Aesthetics. 3. Literature—Philosophy.
4. Political science—Philosophy. I. Csengeri, Karen. II. Title.
B1646.H82 1994   192—dc20   93-43811
ISBN 0–19–811234–3

1 3 5 7 9 10 8 6 4 2

Typeset by Best-set Typesetter Ltd., Hong Kong
Printed in Great Britain
on acid-free paper by
Bookcraft Ltd.,
Midsomer Norton, Bath

ACKNOWLEDGEMENTS

I am indebted to Hulme's previous editors: Herbert Read, Samuel Hynes, Michael Roberts, and Alun R. Jones. Most of the essays in *Speculations* (London, 1924) might well have been lost had it not been for Herbert Read. Samuel Hynes did a similar service in preserving Hulme's 'Diary from the Trenches', and I should like to thank him and the University of Minnesota Press for allowing me to reprint the 'Diary' from *Further Speculations*, edited by Hynes (Minneapolis, 1955). He also did much to establish the Hulme canon, as did Michael Roberts, Alun R. Jones, and Wallace Martin. Special thanks are due to Martin, who was the first person to insist upon the developing nature of Hulme's thought. I am also grateful to Ian H. C. Fraser and the Keele University Library for the manuscript of Hulme's 'Notes on Language and Style' and for the typescript of 'A Lecture on Modern Poetry'.

Thanks are also due to M. G. Underwood and the Master, Fellows, and Scholars of St John's College, Cambridge, for correspondence relating to Hulme's two periods of study at St John's; Newcastle High School for access to information regarding Hulme's activities at the school; the Harry Ransom Humanities Research Center, University of Texas, Austin, for correspondence between Hulme and F. S. Flint; Giuseppe Cardillo of the Istituto Italiano di Cultura and the Biblioteca Universitaria de Bologna for information on the 1911 Philosophical Congress at Bologna; Donald Davies of *Nature* for information regarding Hulme's report on the 1911 Congress; Michel Gudin of the Odéon Théâtre, Paris, and Claude Philippon of the Bibliothèque Nationale for information relating to the date of Hulme's 'Romanticism and Classicism'; Donald Gallup for information on Hulme's 'German Chronicle' for Harold Monro's *Poetry and Drama*; Ronald Schuchard for the dating of Hulme's 'Lecture on Modern Poetry'; Ann and Robert Hulme and Major F. R. Blackah of the Royal Marines for information on Hulme's military career; and the late Frank Ogden for generously placing the Hulme–Ogden correspondence at my disposal.

I should also like to thank Pierrette Frickey and Timothy Scanlan for their help with the French translations and Kenneth Sapp for his help with the German. For her untiring help in obtaining library materials, I am indebted to Nancy Farmer of the Irvine Sullivan Ingram Library at West Georgia College (Carrollton, Georgia). Special thanks are also due to Michael Nichols for his help in proof-reading a good portion of my typing and to Noel Stock, who sparked my original interest in Hulme by his continued insistence on Hulme's special importance.

I am, in addition, grateful to West Georgia College for awarding me a Faculty Research Grant, which helped pay a good part of the expenses of the project.

CONTENTS

INTRODUCTION

I

The early twentieth-century English poet, critic, and philosopher T. E. Hulme (1883–1917) wrote two or three poems that have been described deservedly by T. S. Eliot as among the most beautiful short poems in the English language. Had he done nothing more, this alone would make Hulme worth remembering. But he also played an important role in the literary and cultural history of his time as critic and philosopher. He preceded his friend Ezra Pound in imagist theory, helped to introduce Henri Bergson's philosophy into England and America, was one of the first English critics to write about modern painting and sculpture, and helped to form T. S. Eliot's ideas about classicism and original sin. He also, from quite early in his career, began to sketch out ideas that are remarkably similar to those developed later by Ludwig Wittgenstein.

Yet, for all this, and despite the fact that his influence has time and again been acknowledged, Hulme is one of the most misunderstood figures in twentieth-century letters.

The problem with his position and reputation is not due to neglect. There has always been a good deal of discussion of him and his ideas, since his first foray into print in 1909.[1] Everyone seems to have agreed that he had considerable influence on his own time and in the years that followed, and was in some ways important. But the precise nature of his thought seems never to have been understood.

Much of the confusion centres on his role as forerunner of the twentieth-century movement towards classicism—a movement which barely materialized, yet in another sense may be said to have held the stage for a decade or more as an idea or ideal, particularly through Eliot, or Eliot as others wanted to see him. While most critics acknowledge Hulme as a forerunner, a number of them, in so doing, dismiss him as no more than a disguised romantic who, they claim, practised romanticism even as he preached against it. While there may be some truth to this claim—for there is perhaps something romantic about Hulme's attempts to bring about a new classicism—a good part of the criticism has arisen from ignorance of the chronology of Hulme's writings, an ignorance that goes

---

[1] For a detailed listing of works published about Hulme between 1909 and 1984, see K. E. Csengeri, 'T. E. Hulme: An Annotated Bibliography of Writings about Him', *English Literature in Transition*, 29/4 (1986), 388–428.

back to the arrangement, by Herbert Read, of Hulme's posthumous book *Speculations* (1924). Not only are the essays in that book not dated, but the chronological order is for the most part backwards. The book begins with Hulme's 'Humanism and the Religious Attitude', which is in fact an edited version of his last philosophical writing, published in 1915–16. In it he attempts to draw together a number of ideas in which he had come to believe during the previous decade, including those he associated with classicism and original sin. So what the reader gets in the opening essay of the book is something like a distillation of his life's work, in what can easily be, for the unwary reader, a deceptively straightforward prose. As we move through the book, we are moving backwards through Hulme's life, until, with the final piece, 'Cinders', we are reading some of his earliest work, begun in 1906–7. And even the reader who is aware of the backward nature of the chronology can easily assign too much importance to the essays on Bergson, which begin half-way through and take up nearly a quarter of the book. Seen thus, with no editorial indication to the contrary, the French philosopher may seem to be the centre-piece of Hulme's intellectual life, instead of simply an important step on the way to the extremely individual views of his later work.

Following Read, and not bothering to check dates for themselves, most Hulme critics up to now have assumed that Hulme's enthusiasm for classicism came at the same time as, or even before, his enthusiasm for Bergson. This mistaken assumption has resulted over the years in a plethora of books and articles which criticize Hulme for being inconsistent and for speaking against romanticism even while practising it.[2] A few sympathetic critics have tried to resolve Hulme's 'conflicting' beliefs or show how his contradictions are 'meaningful' and may even be seen as symbolizing the contradictions in modern poetry.[3]

But the matter is simpler than this. As a young man of 24, Hulme

---

[2] e.g. Michael Roberts, *T. E. Hulme* (London, 1938, 1982); Kathleen Nott, *The Emperor's Clothes* (London, 1953); Frank Kermode, *Romantic Image* (London and New York, 1957); Alun R. Jones, *The Life and Opinions of T. E. Hulme* (London and Boston, 1960); and Miriam Hansen, 'T. E. Hulme, Mercenary of Modernism, or, Fragments of Avantgarde Sensibility in Pre-World War I Britain', *ELH* 47/2 (Summer 1980), 355–85. Not all critics have seen Hulme's writing as contradictory. Wallace Martin was the first to point out the developing nature of Hulme's thought in *'The New Age' under Orage* (Manchester, 1967). More recently, Patricia Rae has tried to settle the question by claiming that Hulme 'was above all a pragmatist'. See 'The Aesthetics of Comfort: Hulme's Pragmatism and Contemporary Criticism', *English Studies in Canada*, 15/1 (Mar. 1989), 48–65.

[3] Roberts, *T. E. Hulme*; Murray Krieger, 'The Ambiguous Anti-Romanticism of T. E. Hulme', *ELH* 20 (Dec. 1953), 300–14; and Ronald Primeau, 'On the Discrimination of Hulme: Towards a Theory of the "Anti-Romantic" Romanticism of Modern Poetry', *Journal of Modern Literature*, 3/5 (July 1974), 1104–22.

accepted Bergson because Bergson seemed to provide a sound philosophical way out of the nightmare of nineteenth-century materialism
and mechanism. In 1909, when he was 26, Hulme began a three-year
stint of writing about Bergson—expounding, defending, and commenting as a disciple. In 1911, while still a follower of Bergson, he began to
have doubts, and sought to leave behind those elements that seemed
to conflict with his own emerging philosophy of 'classicism'. He ceased
to write about Bergson in 1912, and by 1914 was no longer a Bergsonian, though some traces of the earlier philosophy may still have clung
to him.

In all this, I would claim for Hulme a general consistency of intellectual
development. The turns and changes that occurred in his thought in the
years 1909–12 make sense as we follow them. They are the natural
changes that take place in any acute, enquiring mind as it learns and
advances.

II

Hulme was born on 16 September 1883 in Staffordshire, England. His
father was a gentleman-farmer who later went into the ceramic transfer
business. Hulme attended Newcastle High School for boys, where he
seems to have been an ideal student, doing well in his studies and winning
many of the school's mathematics and science prizes; he was also active in
several of the school's clubs, including the debating society. His mathematics teacher, A. Garside Pickford, recommended him to his Alma
Mater, St John's College, Cambridge, and Hulme won a Mathematics
Exhibition to the college. But once on his own, away from the strict
Victorian upbringing of his family, Hulme became, like many young
people, rebellious; and his idleness and prankish behaviour got him sent
down. He subsequently enrolled for a short time at the University of
London, but left in 1906, without taking a degree, and set sail for Canada,
where he travelled across the country, working on the railways and also
on farms and in timber mills.

This trip to Canada was a turning-point in Hulme's life; it gave him
'lots of ideas and experience', he said in a letter to his maiden aunt, Alice
Pattinson. One idea he seems to have gathered from his Canadian travels
is a that of the world as a plurality, an ash heap of cinders, which no single
theory could comprehend. 'The flats of Canada', he wrote, 'are incomprehensible on any single theory.' And again, 'Travel is education in
cinders. . . . The road leading over the prairie, at dusk, with the half-
breed.' These notes and others expressing this idea are recorded in
'Cinders', an assortment of observations on the nature of truth, know-

ledge, the world, and language. Though begun in 1906–7 and added to in the years following, they were not published in his lifetime. After Hulme's death, Herbert Read collected and published them, first in the London weekly journal the *New Age*, in 1922, and then two years later in *Speculations*.

'Cinders' is interesting for a number of reasons. First, it makes clear the everyday basis of the 'nominalism' that underlies a good deal of Hulme's work. Secondly, it presents for the first time themes which appear throughout his writings, such as his belief concerning the danger of equating language with reality and his ideas about the influence of prejudice on belief. Thirdly, 'Cinders' is interesting intrinsically: it offers, as Hulme noted in his 'Preface' to the work, a 'new kind of food to tickle the palate'. Though most of the ideas are not new to philosophy, they have here their own particular grain, which is unmistakably Hulme's.

Altogether, the notes present a consistent nominalistic view in which the world is seen as a plurality: 'There is a difficulty in finding a comprehensive scheme of the cosmos, because there is none. The cosmos is only *organised* in parts; the rest is cinders.' He said that men were for ever inventing theories to unify the world. The mythologists, for example, made it a woman or an elephant. The scientists later made fun of the mythologists; but they themselves turned the world into the likeness of a mechanical toy. He insisted that these theories of the world, 'which satisfy and are then thrown away, one after the other, develop *not* as successive approximations to the truth, but like successive thirsts, to be satisfied at the moment, and not evolving to one great Universal Thirst'.

He thought, however, that these analogies had a practical purpose: they helped us along, and gave us a feeling of power over the chaos. The danger lay in thinking that they showed us the truth. Language, according to Hulme, had become a disease: 'Symbols are picked out and believed to be realities,' when they are in fact 'merely counters . . . to be moved about on a board for the convenience of the players.' One must not mistake, he said, the analogies for the real things they stand for. Language is merely a 'manufactured chess-board laid on a cinder-heap', a kind of 'gossamer web, woven between the real things'; it is not the reality. What lay behind a philosopher's scheme was simply prejudice. All a writer's generalizations and truths could be traced, Hulme claimed, 'to the personal circumstances and prejudices of his class, experience, capacity and body'.

Only two of the jottings seem not quite to fit Hulme's 'nominalism'. He was bothered by what he saw in the microscope. The things revealed under it seemed already to be in some kind of order; this world did not appear as merely a heap of cinders: '*But* the microscope. Things revealed, not created, but there before, and *also* seem to be in an order.' Also, he believed man's motives to be fixed: 'In opposition to Socialism and Utopian schemes comes the insistence on the fact of the unalterability of motives. Motives are the only unalterable and fixed things in the world.' Both these points continued to exercise his mind, and he returned to them later.

Hulme also introduced into 'Cinders' two themes relating to literature, themes he would likewise elaborate on later. One had to do with the use of definite and personal words, the other with poetry as an affair of the body. Both themes followed from his nominalism. If reality could not be captured in abstractions and generalizations, the way to capture it was by the use of definite and personal words. Doing this somehow brought us nearer to the realm of the physical world. It was from this philosophical background, I think, that he developed his ideas about the writing of poetry.

In the spring of 1907 Hulme returned from Canada to England; but he soon crossed to Brussels, where he taught English for a year, probably at a Berlitz school, and practised his languages. While teaching in Brussels, he worked out some of the ideas on language expressed in 'Notes on Language and Style'. Like 'Cinders', the 'Notes' are not a polished work, but a collection of jottings, and were not published in Hulme's lifetime. In general, they reflect the same view of the world as 'Cinders', and contain some of the same themes: all theories are toys; language is not equivalent to reality; a writer's beliefs reflect his prejudices, rather than universal truth. But in 'Notes' the themes are brought to bear upon the subject of language and style.

Hulme's claim that language is different from reality is dealt with in his discussion of the difference between the language of prose and that of poetry. According to him, 'We replace meaning (i.e. *vision*) by words. These words fall into well-known patterns, i.e. into certain well-known phrases which we accept without thinking of their meaning, just as we do the x in algebra.' What we get, then, are words divorced from any real vision, as in rhetoric and expository prose. Opposed to this was what he called 'literary expression'. Here, 'Each *word* must be an image *seen*, not a counter.' Hulme went on to say that with perfect style, each sentence would be 'a lump, a piece of clay, a vision seen'. A man could not write, he claimed, 'without seeing at the same time a visual signification before his eyes'. It was this image which preceded the writing and made it firm. The literary man, he said, was he who found 'subtle analogies for the ordinary street feelings' which he experienced. And this led, according to Hulme, 'to the differentiation and importance of those feelings. . . .

Hence the sudden joy these produce in the reader when he remembers a half-forgotten impression.'

Hulme was aware that the translation of physical vision into language is not easy; that there is an 'extraordinary difficulty in shaping any material, in moving from the idea to the matter'. He tried to work out just how a poem is created, and considered two possibilities. According to the first, the poet had an emotion which he then found language to express, gradually building up a poem. According to the second, language had a more positive role to play. For even while the poet was engaged in writing his poem, the language he was using, according to this second theory, took a hand in transforming and developing the ideas and emotions he was trying to express: 'the very act of trying to find a form to fit the separate phrases into, itself leads to the creation of new images hitherto not felt by the poet. In a sense the poetry writes itself.' It is interesting to note that T. S. Eliot also took this second view of language in *The Use of Poetry and the Use of Criticism* and in one or two of his later essays.

In addition to his reflections on language in literature, Hulme gave some thought to the nature of language itself. He concluded, as Wittgenstein was to do, that language and meaning are not logical: 'Phrases have meaning for no reason, cf. with nature of truth. . . . Language does not naturally come with meaning.' He also spoke of the necessity of seeing sentences as units: an inkling perhaps of the idea that words take their meaning from their context.

But Hulme's travels abroad gave rise to more than these philosophical ruminations: they gave him a desire to write poetry. The 'first time I ever felt the necessity or inevitableness of verse, was', he said in his 1908 'Lecture on Modern Poetry', 'in the desire to reproduce the peculiar quality of feeling which is induced by the flat spaces and wide horizons of the virgin prairie of western Canada'. He went on in the lecture to describe his efforts to find poetic models for certain impressions that he wanted to fix in verse. He could not, he said, find any that seemed exactly suitable until he came to read French *vers libre*. He seems, in fact, to have read a number of French poets and aestheticians of the time, and the influence of some of their ideas can be seen in various statements on poetry that he made in 1908–9.[4]

---

[4] For a detailed discussion of Hulme's borrowings from the French, see Wallace Martin, 'The Sources of the Imagist Aesthetic', *PMLA* 85/2 (Mar. 1970), 196–204; K. E. Csengeri, 'T. E. Hulme's Borrowings from the French', *Comparative Literature*, 34/1 (Winter 1982), 16–27; and Patricia Rae, 'T. E. Hulme's French Sources: A Reconsideration', *Comparative Literature*, 41/1 (Winter 1989), 69–99.

After he returned to London from Brussels, he began to put into practice the various ideas about poetry which he had formed from his reading and travels of the previous few years. He started to write poetry; and eager to exchange ideas with others, he joined a group of enthusiasts known as the Poets' Club, delivering his 'Lecture on Modern Poetry' to them in November 1908.[5]

The lecture was an appeal for a new start in the writing of English poetry, based on the assumption, gathered from his interest in the French *vers libre* movement, that there is an intimate connection between verse forms and poetic activity. The old models, he claimed, no longer reflected the modern spirit:

philosophers no longer believe in absolute truth. We no longer believe in perfection, either in verse or in thought, we frankly acknowledge the relative. . . . Instead of these minute perfections of phrase and words, the tendency will be rather towards the production of a general effect; this of course takes away the predominance of metre and a regular number of syllables as the element of perfection in words.

He described the new verse as 'impressionistic'. Moved by a certain landscape, for example, the poet selected from it certain images which, when placed in juxtaposition in separate lines, served to suggest and evoke the state he felt. To this impressionistic poetry, regular metre was, he thought, 'cramping, jangling, meaningless, and out of place'. He was not, however, advocating a mindless free verse. The sort of thing he was looking for was, he said, 'a delicate and difficult art' in which the rhythm had to be fitted to the idea. And he went on to claim that much that was already being written under the name 'free verse' was really prose.

To answer the question of whether verse without regular metre is poetry, Hulme returned to the distinction he had made in 'Notes on Language and Style' between direct and indirect language. But now, in the 'Lecture', he drew it out further. Direct language, he said, is poetry: it is direct because it deals in images. Through images the poet is able to communicate his feelings directly:

This new verse resembles sculpture rather than music; it appeals to the eye rather than to the ear. . . . It builds up a plastic image which it hands over to the reader, whereas the old art endeavoured to influence him physically by the hypnotic effect of rhythm.

---

[5] Ronald Schuchard has shown that Hulme's opening remark criticizing a reviewer in the *Saturday Review* probably refers to an unsigned review of five books in the issue of 14 Nov. 1908. See Ronald Schuchard, ' "As Regarding Rhythm": Yeats and the Imagists', in *Yeats: An Annual of Critical and Textual Studies*, vol. 2 (Ithaca, NY, and London, 1984), 213 n. 11.

In early 1909 Hulme dropped away from the Poets' Club, and in
February or March began meeting at the Café Tour d'Eiffel with another
group of poets that included F. S. Flint, Edward Storer, F. W. Tancred,
Joseph Campbell, and Florence Farr. The young American poet Ezra
Pound was introduced to the group on 22 April 1909. What brought
them together was, according to Flint's 1915 'History of Imagism', a
dissatisfaction with the way in which English poetry was being written.[6]
Among the members of the group, Flint recalled, there was 'a lot of talk
and practice', particularly 'of what we called the Image'. The group,
which Hulme called the 'Secession Club' and Pound later referred to as
the 'School of Images' and the 'forgotten school of 1909', continued to
meet regularly on Thursday evenings for several months. Hulme published four poems in the two anthologies brought out by the Poets' Club
in 1909. After that he seems to have lost interest in writing poetry and
turned instead to a more serious study of philosophy.

III

His change of direction was due largely to his enthusiasm for Henri
Bergson, who affected his ideas not only about poetry, but also about
knowledge, truth, and the world in general. Hulme appears to have first
read Bergson in 1907.[7] He described the reasons for his enthusiasm for the
French philosopher four years later, in the *New Age* of 23 November
1911. He saw Bergson, he said, as a possible answer to the mechanistic
theory so prevalent in philosophy and science at the time:

It isn't simply a question of what you would like to win. It is a matter simply of
the recognition of forces. If you are candid with yourself you find, on examining
your own state of mind, that you are forcibly, as it were, carried on to the
materialist side.

It is from this frank recognition of forces that comes my excitement about
Bergson. I find, for the first time, this force which carries me on willy-nilly to the
materialist side, balanced by a force which is, as a matter of actual fact, apart from
the question of what I want, able to meet on equal terms the first force.

Explaining further, in a lecture on Bergson in 1911, Hulme said that
Bergson endeavoured to prove

that we seem inevitably to arrive at the mechanistic theory simply because the
intellect, in dealing with a certain aspect of reality, distorts it in that direction. It
can deal with matter but it is absolutely incapable of understanding life. In

---

[6] *Egoist*, 2 (1 May 1915), 70–1. Flint also discusses the group's activities in 'The
"Ripostes" of Ezra Pound with "The Complete Poetical Works" of T. E. Hulme', *Poetry
and Drama*, 1 (Mar. 1913), 61.

[7] Martin, *'The New Age' under Orage*, 137 n. 2.

explaining vital phenomena it only distorts them, in exhibiting them as very complex mechanical phenomena.

Hulme's early enthusiasm for Bergson was such that he launched into literary journalism with an article called 'The New Philosophy'. It appeared in the *New Age* for 1 July 1909. In it Hulme pointed out that whereas others had attacked rationalism, only Bergson had developed a complete system to justify such an attack. He went on to claim that Bergson's philosophy was more than a mere revival of nominalism and a reaction against the abuse of conceptualism. For Bergson did not stop at declaring the impossibility of logical systems to comprehend reality; he went on to posit a solution to the dilemma. Bergson alleged that we could grasp 'mobile reality . . . by means of that *intellectual sympathy* which we call intuition'.

Hulme continued in his role as expositor of Bergson's ideas in England for the next two and a half years, writing some twenty articles on him for the *New Age*, compiling the bibliography appended to F. L. Pogson's translation of *Essai sur les données immédiates de la conscience*, and himself translating, with the help of his friends F. S. Flint and Ethel Kibblewhite, Bergson's *Introduction à la métaphysique*, which was published in 1912 as *An Introduction to Metaphysics*. In addition, he delivered a series of four lectures on Bergson in London between 23 November and 14 December 1911 and another at Girton College, Cambridge, on 26 February 1912. The London lectures were later collected by Herbert Read and published in *Speculations* as 'The Philosophy of Intensive Manifolds'. Bergson himself was so pleased with Hulme's studies that he wrote a letter of recommendation for him when Hulme applied for readmission to St John's College, Cambridge, in 1912. The letter was full of the highest praise, and predicted that Hulme would produce interesting and important works in the field of philosophy in general and the philosophy of art in particular:

Je me fais un plaisir de certifier que je considère Mr. T. E. Hulme comme un esprit d'une grande valeur. Il apporte, à l'étude des questions philosophiques, de rares qualités de finesse, de vigueur, et de pénétration. Ou je me trompe beaucoup, ou il est destiné à produire des oeuvres intéressantes et importantes dans le domaine de la philosophie en général, et plus particulièrement peut-être dans celui de la philosophie de l'art.

At this point, it might be well to examine more closely the nature of Bergson's importance for Hulme. In the *New Age* of 26 October 1911, Hulme made it clear that he did not see Bergson as having presented anything entirely new to philosophy; indeed, he did not think that such newness was possible:

I believe . . . that there is nothing absolutely new in either the problem or the solution of it which I am about to describe in Bergson. In substance the problem and its solution are the same in every generation. Every philosopher must deal with an old problem, and must escape from it by an equally world-old solution. It is impossible at this time of day to take up an absolutely new attitude towards the cosmos and its persistent problems.

What Bergson had done that set him apart was to provide a refutation of mechanism 'in the dialect of the time'. Thus, it was not that Hulme thought Bergson 'right' in any absolute sense, but rather that he offered a view of the world which could meet 'on equal terms' the mechanistic explanation of the world.

Further, Hulme claimed that what made Bergson popular was not what made him important for philosophy. The public was attracted, he said in the *New Age* of 3 August 1911, to Bergson's conclusions; but his real importance lay rather in his method, his theory of intensive manifolds:

the real importance of Bergson lies in pure philosophy, lies in his method, lies in the category he works with, that of intensive manifolds, yet the conclusion to which the application of his method leads him, that of the dualism of soul and body, is precisely the conclusion which most people seek. It is nice for the timid to be assured on thoroughly respectable authority that there is a chance of immortality and that they have free will.

IV

The year 1911 saw a new turn in Hulme's career. Although he was still busy explaining and defending Bergson, he became interested in political theory. This may have been due, in part at least, to political developments taking place in England at the time, developments which finally resulted in the passage by Parliament in late 1911 of resolutions limiting the powers of the House of Lords. In the clash between the Liberals and the Conservatives, Hulme sided with the Conservatives. But he did not engage in day-to-day political writing; he wrestled instead with political theory. Some of the themes he discussed—such as the constancy of human nature and the effect of prejudice on belief—had been introduced as early as 'Cinders', but now he developed them with respect to current politics.

He began with 'A Note on the Art of Political Conversion', published in three parts from 22 February to 8 March 1911 in the London political journal the *Commentator*, under the pseudonym Thomas Gratton (Gratton Hall being the name of his birthplace). In it he elaborated on the theme that belief in political matters is largely emotional and non-rational in character. He claimed that no idea, by itself, could produce a change in belief; rather, all conviction was based on emotion. While this had been recognized with respect to the masses—in such books as Gustave Le Bon's *The Crowd* and Graham Wallas's *Human Nature in Politics*—it had not, Hulme said, been recognized in the case of intellectuals. But they were as emotional as the rest: 'We may be under the delusion that we are deciding a question from purely rational motives, but we never are.'

In a supplement to the series, on 19 April, Hulme tried to account for the Conservative Party's lack of popularity among intellectuals. He claimed that just as poetry or philosophy needed to 'clothe itself in a different set of catch-words in each generation', so did political theory. The problem with the Conservative Party in England was that it had not yet worked out a new set of catchwords: 'That and nothing else is the cause of the landslide amongst the intellectuals to the Socialist side.' The 'most pressing need' of Conservatism was a set of writers who could 'make our faith living by giving it a fresh expression'. This, he claimed, was being done in France by the group of writers known as *L'Action française*; and Hulme predicted that conservatism would come to power there.

This supplement appeared while Hulme was attending the 1911 International Philosophical Congress in Bologna. On his return journey to England, he stopped in Paris to visit the literary critic Pierre Lasserre, who was then a leading figure in *L'Action française*. Lasserre had attacked Bergson; and since Hulme, who was still an ardent supporter of Bergson, found himself agreeing with the anti-romantic ideas in Lasserre's two books *La Morale de Nietzsche* and *Le Romantisme français*, he wanted to find out if there was any real inconsistency in liking them both. The meeting with Lasserre proved to be important, for Lasserre endeavoured to prove to Hulme that Bergson 'was nothing but the last disguise of romanticism'. Lasserre claimed that if Bergson's theory of real time were applied to politics, it would mean that there was a continual progress for mankind. And this was contrary to the conservative position. In his description of the meeting in the *New Age* for 9 November 1911, Hulme said that if he thought Lasserre were right, he would be compelled to change his views considerably.

This was probably the main intellectual factor that helped to change Hulme's mind about Bergson. The concomitant emotional factor emerged at the four lectures given by Bergson at University College, London, between 20 and 28 October 1911. The lectures proved to be a trying experience for Hulme. In an article in the *New Age* of 2 November 1911, he explained that he had been told beforehand that the lectures were to be for advanced students only, but that when he got to the hall, he found it filled with several hundred people. He was dismayed. His mind began at once, almost unconsciously, to feel that 'what these people thought about Bergson was entirely wrong'. More than that, he came to think that Bergson himself must be wrong. What these people agreed on could not, he thought, be right: 'It is not in the nature of truth to be grasped so easily or so enthusiastically.' He found all this profoundly disturbing, not so much because it destroyed a particular set of fixed beliefs, but because it seemed to destroy the possibility of any 'fixed' belief whatever: 'If the mere accidental fact that several hundred people share your belief destroys it automatically, then obviously the phrase "fixed belief" can never have the meaning we generally attribute to it.'

Hulme found the lectures disappointing too. In an article in the *Westminster Gazette* of 18 November, he said that Bergson merely repeated in popular form ideas which he had previously expressed more seriously, ideas which he had expressed so often that he had to a certain extent 'made them external to himself'. Even Bergson's manner of delivery disappointed Hulme; it seemed 'not at all characteristic'.

Hulme was never able to reconcile fully the beliefs he expressed in his political writings with those of Bergson; rather, he became more and more interested in *L'Action française*, particularly in the group's leading thinkers, Charles Maurras and Lasserre. In a letter dated 27 November 1911 to his friend C. K. Ogden, editor of the *Cambridge Magazine*, Hulme said that Maurras and Lasserre were the two best of the group: 'You will find them both extremely interesting if you sympathise with their point of view, a very precise and lucid Anti-Romanticism.' He was also very much taken with Georges Sorel. At the root of Sorel's beliefs was, he said in the preface he wrote for his translation of Sorel's *Reflections on Violence* (1916), a conviction that man was by nature bad or limited and consequently could only accomplish anything of value by disciplines—ethical, heroic, or political. Sorel was an absolutist in ethics, and spoke contemptuously of modernism and progress. His anti-romantic sentiment gave him a common bond with *L'Action française*. In his letter to Ogden, Hulme spoke of his plans to write about *L'Action française* and Sorel.

It was the development of these interests, the turning of his conservative views in a new direction, that finally led Hulme to reject Bergson's philosophy. In the *New Age* of 9 December 1915, he mentioned what had probably been the deciding factor in that rejection—Bergson's confusion of biology and theology. For while Bergson's philosophy recognized the difference between the mechanical and the vital, it ignored the difference between the vital and the moral:

Having made this immense step away from materialism, it believes itself adequately equipped for a statement of all the *ideal* values. It does not distinguish different levels of the non-material. All that is non-material, must it thinks be *vital*.

The momentum of its escape from mechanism carries it on to the attempt to restate the whole of religion in terms of vitalism. This is ridiculous. Biology is not theology, nor can God be defined in terms of 'life' or 'progress'.

V

Hulme turned 28 on 16 September 1911. The year 1912 saw him moving towards his third and final philosophical position. We can date the beginning of this stage fairly exactly. On 25 February 1912 he delivered a lecture entitled 'Anti-Romanticism and Original Sin' to the Heretics at Cambridge. It was, so far as I can tell, the first occasion on which he discussed publicly his beliefs concerning original sin. C. K. Ogden summarized his lecture in the *Cambridge Magazine* of 9 March:

Mr. T. E. Hulme . . . energetically declared his distaste for all Progressives from Rousseau to H. G. Wells. He emphasized the importance of much repetition of certain words—words of power—in the formation of prejudice and ideas, and the general clouding of our judgment. Repeat the word 'Progress' often enough and it is easy to delude oneself into denying the truths of the doctrine of Original Sin amidst the mess of hypothetical Utopias, which ignore the principle of the constancy of Man.

The text of Hulme's talk has been lost, but from Ogden's description, it may have been a version of 'A Tory Philosophy', which he published in the *Commentator* in the spring of 1912. In this, Hulme claimed that there were two basic temperaments in man, each with its own set of prejudices and sentiments, and that these lay behind opposing attitudes in everything from politics to art. He named them 'romantic' and 'classical'. The 'classical' point of view maintained that man was by his very nature limited and incapable of attaining any kind of perfection, because, either by nature as a result of original sin or as the result of evolution, he had within him certain antinomies. There was a war of instincts going on inside him, Hulme said, and man's condition would always be one of struggle and limitation. The best results could be achieved only as a result of discipline. Moreover, man being by nature constant, the kind of discipline which would get the best out of him and which was necessary for him, remained much the same in every generation. The classical attitude had, then, a great respect for the past and for tradition, not for sentimental reasons, but on purely rational grounds, Hulme said. It did not expect anything radically new, and did not believe in any real progress. The 'romantic' point of view was the exact opposite. It maintained that man was by nature good, and that so far he had been prevented from exhibiting his 'wonderful' qualities by the very restrictions of order and discipline that the classical view praised. One or other of these two assumptions, Hulme claimed, underlay man's every opinion.

In the last two instalments of the series, he tried to define his 'Tory' point of view a little more precisely. It did not mean, he said, that man did not change at all. Man was capable of a certain kind of progress: he had built up science and civilization, for example. But the progress here was 'one of accumulation' rather than alteration in capacity.

Hulme applied this theme of romanticism versus classicism to poetry in a lecture delivered on 15 July 1912 at Clifford's Inn Hall, London. The lecture was organized in connection with Harold Monro's newly formed *Poetry Review*, and was entitled 'The New Philosophy of Art as Illustrated in Poetry'. It appears to have been a version of the essay published in *Speculations* as 'Romanticism and Classicism'.[8] The kind of verse a poet wrote depended, Hulme said, on which of the two temperaments he had. The romantic poet thought man infinite, and he continually talked about flights into infinity; his poetry was characterized by vagueness and a sloppiness of emotion. The classical poet, on the other hand, never forgot the finiteness, the limitations, of man; his poetry was dry and hard; even in his most imaginative flights there was always a holding back, a 'reservation'.

Hulme, needless to say, detested much of what is loosely termed 'romantic' verse, and in its place wanted to see poetry which was dry and hard. 'The great aim', he said, 'is accurate, precise and definite description.' He predicted that the romantic movement was nearing its end and that a new classical period would follow, with poetry that was cheerful, dry, and sophisticated.

Hulme eventually went on to apply these ideas to the fine arts as well, following a trip to Germany in the autumn of 1913 to attend the Kongress für Ästhetik und Allgemeine Kunstwissenschaft held in Berlin from 7 to 9 October. The highlight of the Congress for Hulme was a lecture given by Wilhelm Worringer. Entitled 'Entstehung und Gestaltungsprinzipien in der Ornamentik', it was on the origins and development of ornament in art. Worringer explained the geometrical character of ancient ornament, and discussed how objects from nature came to be used in ornament until an organic regularity eventually replaced the former geometrical regularity. He claimed that this occurred when people lost sight of the original religious significance of the ornament. Five years earlier, in 1908, Worringer had published *Abstraktion und Einfühlung*, in which he discussed in greater detail the causes of, and differences between, geometrical and naturalistic art. He distinguished two poles of

---

[8] This undated essay is generally treated as if written in either 1909 or 1914, but internal evidence strongly suggests late 1911 or 1912. See my introductory note to 'Romanticism and Classicism'.

'artistic volition', one being the 'urge for empathy', the other the 'urge to abstraction'. The precondition for the 'urge for empathy' was a satisfaction with the world and a sense of being at home in it. The 'urge to abstraction', on the other hand, resulted from the belief that the world was bewildering and unfathomable. He went on to say that individual peoples were, in consequence of what he called their 'innate structure', predisposed more towards one or the other and that this predisposition led to the production of completely different kinds of art. Those peoples who found delight in organic forms produced a naturalistic art, while those possessing the 'urge to abstraction' tried to purify objects of their dependence on life and created a geometric or abstract art. The stylistic peculiarities of Egyptian and Byzantine art were, he maintained, due not to a lack of ability, but to an inner need for abstraction, which was different from the need for empathy that had given birth to the art of the Renaissance.

It is not clear when or how Hulme first heard of Worringer; but it may have been earlier than the Berlin Congress. For although he was readmitted to Cambridge in the spring of 1912, Hulme was not able to return to continue his studies in the autumn of that year, but was forced instead to flee the country, to avoid possible prosecution by an enraged father who claimed that Hulme had tried to seduce his 16-year-old daughter. Hulme travelled to Germany, planning to return to Cambridge in January 1913; but in fact he never returned there. During his stay in Germany in late 1912 and early 1913, he met Rupert Brooke, and, judging from letters written by both men, Hulme seems to have been acquainted by then with writings by Theodor Lipps and Johannes Volkelt, both of whom were discussed by Worringer.[9]

Whenever it was that Hulme first became acquainted with Worringer, he was by the end of 1913 very much influenced by him, and through him became interested in the visual arts—particularly in the geometrical art of Byzantine mosaics and the new avant-garde art that was just then emerging in England. He saw Worringer's distinction between vital and geometrical art as similar, I think, to the distinction he himself had made between the romantic and classical points of view in politics and literature.

As in the case of his earlier enthusiasm for Bergson, Hulme's new interest led him to write immediately a number of articles on the subject. He not only discussed such contemporary artists as Jacob Epstein, Henri Gaudier-Brzeska, Wyndham Lewis, and David Bomberg, but tried to

---

[9] Hulme included Lipps and Volkelt in an undated outline which he drew up for a book on 'Modern Theories of Art'. See *Speculations*, 261–4.

explain the philosophy behind the new art. Probably his clearest statements were made in a lecture entitled 'The New Art and Its Philosophy'[10]
which he delivered on 22 January 1914 to the Quest Society, a London
group run by G. R. S. Mead and devoted to Gnosticism, Theosophy, the
pagan mystery religions, and the arts. Following Worringer, Hulme
claimed that there were two kinds of art, which were absolutely distinct
in kind from one another; he called one 'geometrical', the other 'vital', or
'organic'. He claimed that the new geometrical art of his own time was
different in kind from the Renaissance art preceding it and akin to
(though not the same as) the geometrical art of the past. He went on to
predict that this change from a vital to a geometrical art would be
accompanied by a change in sensibility, a change in general attitude; and
that this new attitude would differ in kind from the humanism which had
prevailed from the Renaissance to the present. He did not try to describe
this new attitude in any detail, however, because he recognized that
current language and underlying assumptions would prevent clear discussion of the new sensibility, which would require a new way of looking
and describing.

VI

When the First World War broke out in August 1914, Hulme enlisted in
the Army as a private. In December his company was sent to the
Continent, and during the next several months he wrote a series of letters
detailing his experiences in the trenches. Collected and published by
Samuel Hynes in 1955 in *Further Speculations* as 'Diary from the Trenches',
the letters give a vivid account of trench warfare, as well as Hulme's
growing disillusionment with the war. For in the trenches Hulme experienced the world as he had described it in 'Cinders'. Of his experiences
on his way to the trenches from a rest camp, he wrote:

It's really like a kind of nightmare, in which you are in the middle of an enormous
saucer of mud with explosions & shots going off all round the edge, a sort of
fringe of palm trees made of fireworks all round it.

And in another letter he said:

In reality there is nothing picturesque about it. It's the most miserable existence
you can conceive of. I feel utterly depressed at the idea of having to do this for
48 hours every 4 days. . . . The boredom & discomfort of it, exasperate you to the
breaking point.

    In April 1915 Hulme was wounded and sent home to hospital; he did
not return to the fighting until 1916, when he was granted a commission

---

[10] This lecture was published in *Speculations* as 'Modern Art and Its Philosophy'.

as temporary second lieutenant in the Royal Marines Artillery. But while he was at home recuperating from his wounds and trying, with the help of Edward Marsh, to get his commission, he took up the subject of the war in a series of 'War Notes', which appeared weekly in the *New Age* from 11 November 1915 to 2 March 1916. Some of the notes deal with strategy and technical aspects, but many of them revolve around his disagreement with the pacifists on the importance of defeating Germany.

Hulme was very much opposed to the pacifism of his day, but not because he liked or was enjoying the war. In a letter to A. R. Jones in 1956, D. L. Murray, a friend and former fellow member of the Aristotelian Society, recalled meeting Hulme in the Café Royal, London, in 1916. Hulme's original enthusiasm had by then worn off, Murray said, but added that 'Hulme would have been the last man to allow his personal discomforts or disillusionments to affect his philosophy'.[11] Hulme shared the widespread belief at the time that victory by the Allies was somehow essential for the future of Europe. In his words, 'we are fighting to preserve the liberties of Europe; which are in fact in danger, and can only be preserved by fighting.' The pacifists, he maintained, held on to the romantic assumption that there was some inevitable progress which would eventually lead all nations, including Germany, to democracy. But this was not so, Hulme insisted: 'the mind of Germany is neither Liberal, nor even Liberalising, that is, disposed to become Liberal.'

Hulme's attitude towards Germany was based in large part on his reading during this time of books by such prominent German writers as Max Scheler and Werner Sombart. In *Helden und Händler*, a book which Hulme described as one of the most important German books on the war, Sombart praised the German conception of the State as omnipotent, and said that militarism was the German spirit itself. War, Sombart said, was an unavoidable accompaniment to all State life. Hulme was also bothered by philosopher Max Scheler's claim that the main object of the war was the creation for the first time of a 'solidarist Continental Europe' under German military leadership. He was bothered because, as he said, Scheler was 'not a sensational journalist, or a military writer like Bernhardi, but one of the most intelligent of the younger German philosophers, and one who, moreover, belongs to the school that is beginning to have the greater influence on this generation of students'.

The fact that in wartime Hulme went out of his way to read what was published in the enemy camp is, as J. Kamerbeek has pointed out, 'a remarkable fact in itself'.[12] It suggests, once again, his integrity of mind

---

[11] Letter in the Brynmor Jones Library, University of Hull.

[12] J. Kamerbeek, 'T. E. Hulme and German Philosophy: Dilthey and Scheler', *Comparative Literature*, 21/3 (Summer 1969), 193–212.

and relentless striving to get to the bottom of the matter at hand. Hulme was not a violent man who liked war just for the sake of it, as he was sometimes been characterized. If he supported the Allies' endeavours, it was because he thought that their actions against Germany were, as he said, necessary to preserve the freedom of the rest of Europe.

It was over the question of pacifism that Hulme engaged in a dispute with Bertrand Russell in the *Cambridge Magazine*, where, between 22 January and 4 March 1916, he published an edited version of his *New Age* 'War Notes'. The dispute arose from a series of lectures that Russell was giving in London on 'Principles of Social Reconstruction'.[13] In them Russell claimed that all human action sprang from either impulse or desire, impulse playing the larger role. Man's impulses could be either creative (leading to works of art or scientific achievements) or destructive (resulting in war). Russell believed that man was naturally good, and that the impulses that resulted in injury to others were due to thwarted growth; that if man were left to grow unimpaired, his self-respect would remain intact, and he would not then regard others as his enemies, but would live in peace. The world was at war, he said, because individuals were hampered by institutions. And the lectures dealt with ways in which education, economics, the State, marriage, and religion could be altered to give man freedom to develop his potential and live in peace.

Hulme attended one of Russell's lectures, and in the *New Age* of 3 February and the *Cambridge Magazine* of 5 February he objected to Russell's contention that blind impulse was the real cause of the war. While he recognized, he said, that impulse played a part in one's attitudes and views, nevertheless his support of the war was based on reason, not impulse; and the reason he disagreed with Russell and the other pacifists was because his scale of values was different from theirs. Russell's values were, he claimed, those 'first made prominent by Rousseau, and the romantic movement'. But there was nothing inevitable about them; they were simply part of one particular ideology or way of looking at the world. Nor was there a necessary connection, he maintained, between Russell's ideology and the democratic movement. 'It is quite possible', Hulme said, 'for a democrat to deny all the ideals on which Mr. Russell's principles are based.'

The dispute between Russell and Hulme continued for the next several weeks, but was never resolved. The two men held opposing assumptions about the nature of man which could not be reconciled.

[13] The lectures were later published as a book, *Principles of Social Reconstruction* (London, 1916).

One of the main complaints that Hulme brought against Russell and the other pacifists was that they refused even to consider the arguments of people like himself who supported the war. Hulme saw this refusal as one more example of the influence of prejudice on belief, an issue which he had already taken up in several earlier 'War Notes'. On 9 December 1915, for example, he had pointed out how often we decide an issue on a priori grounds without it ever occurring to us to examine the issue as a fact requiring investigation. On 23 December he had claimed further that 'A man's desire will always lead him to the facts he wishes to find'. Generally, he said, we do not even perceive facts that conflict with our own preconceived ideas and prejudices. On 27 January 1916, Hulme had insisted that 'Truth is still truth, even if it comes from the gutter', and on 10 February reminded his readers that 'many false reasons can be given for true things. The two should be carefully distinguished.'

VII

While Hulme was writing his 'War Notes', he was also writing on Georges Sorel. His translation of Sorel's *Réflexions sur la violence* had been published in the USA in November 1914 by W. B. Heubsch of New York, without any introduction or preface. At the time of publication, Hulme was in a training camp in England, waiting to be sent to France. The book was reviewed in a number of American newspapers and magazines, but does not appear to have made much of a mark. In the autumn of 1915, Hulme wrote a preface for the proposed London edition, in an attempt to clear up some of the misunderstandings about Sorel that were prevalent, he claimed, even among those sympathetic to his work.

The English edition was published in March 1916 by George Allen & Unwin, and included a slightly altered version of the preface which Hulme had published in the *New Age* of 14 October 1915. It was reviewed in the *Times Literary Supplement* of 16 March 1916:

We agree with Mr. Hulme that he [Sorel] is a remarkable Socialist writer. He has two qualities—originality and modesty—which are exceedingly rare among Socialists since Marx. . . . He is suggestive and stimulating, as an acute, sincere, and independent mind must be; but he has no system to offer.

The 28-year-old T. S. Eliot, only just beginning (with the help of Ezra Pound and Bertrand Russell) to find his feet in literary London, reviewed the book for the July 1917 issue of the American philosophical journal the *Monist*. He saw the book as 'a very acute and disillusioned commentary' on nineteenth-century Socialism and the politics of French democracy over the previous quarter of a century. One aspect that caught his eye was its attitude to romanticism: 'it expresses that violent and bitter reaction against romanticism which is one of the most interesting phenomena of our time. As an historical document, Sorel's *Reflections* gives, more than any other book that I am acquainted with, an insight into what Henri Gheon calls "our directions".' After commenting on Sorel's hatred of middle-class socialism, Eliot went on to discuss the basis of Sorel's thought:

His motive forces are ideas and feelings which never occur to the mind of the proletariat, but which are highly characteristic of the present-day intellectual. At the back of his mind is a scepticism which springs from Renan, but which is much more terrible than Renan's. For with Renan and Saint-Beuve scepticism was still a satisfying point of view, almost an esthetic pose. And for many of the artists of the eighties and nineties the pessimism of decadence fulfilled their craving for an attitude. But the scepticism of the present, the scepticism of Sorel, is a torturing vacuity which has developed the craving for belief.

And so, disgusted with modern civilization, Sorel looked forward to a new culture that might spring from the struggle of the revolutionary trade unions against the employers and the State. He was, according to Eliot:

representative of the present generation, sick with its own knowledge of history, with the dissolving outlines of liberal thought, with humanitarianism. He longs for a narrow, intolerant, *creative* society with sharp divisions. He longs for the pessimistic, classical view. And this longing is healthy. But to realize his desire he must betake himself to very devious ways. . . . It is not surprising that Sorel has become a Royalist.

The review concluded with these words on the translator: 'Mr. Hulme is also a contemporary. The footnotes to his introduction should be read.' The footnotes,[14] like the introduction itself, dealt largely with romanticism and classicism and the 'religious attitude':

Romanticism confuses both human and divine things by not clearly separating them. The main thing with which it can be reproached is that it blurs the clear outlines of human relations—whether in political thought or in the treatment of sex in literature, by introducing into them the Perfection that properly belongs only to the non-human.

Humanism thus really contains the germs of the disease that was bound to come to its full evil development in Romanticism.

---

[14] It is interesting to note Hulme's view on equality in one of these notes. In an attempt to differentiate Sorel's from other attacks on the democratic ideology, Hulme says: 'Some of these [attacks] are merely dilettante, having little sense of reality, while others are really vicious, in that they play with the idea of inequality. No theory that is not fully moved by the conception of justice asserting the equality of men, and which cannot offer something to all men, deserves or is likely to have any future.'

But even more important to Eliot, perhaps, than Hulme's playing off of classicism against romanticism was his sharp focus on original sin. Man was by nature bad or limited, and consequently could only accomplish anything of value by disciplines, ethical, heroic, or political: 'In other words', Hulme wrote, 'it [classicism] believes in Original Sin.'

Eliot began to deal with these same ideas almost immediately, beginning with his 'Six Lectures on Modern French Literature', delivered as an Oxford University extension lecturer at Ilkley, Yorkshire, from 3 October to 12 December 1916. The first lecture, called 'What is Romanticism?', was devoted largely to Rousseau; the second was entitled 'The Reaction against Romanticism'; the other lectures went on to discuss royalism and socialism, the 'tendency of the French intellectual to return to orthodox Christianity', and 'Questions for the Future'. Among the books recommended by Eliot in the syllabus published by Oxford in 1916 were Hulme's translations of Sorel's *Reflections on Violence* and Bergson's *Introduction to Metaphysics*. In his syllabus description of the second lecture, 'The Reaction against Romanticism', Eliot said: 'The classicist point of view has been defined as essentially a belief in Original Sin.'

It is still not sufficiently understood that Hulme and Eliot had much more in common with one another intellectually than with any of the other modernists. Despite differences in background, both men were closely connected with the main problems of knowledge and scepticism in the twentieth century. Eliot, from the time of his graduate studies at Harvard, had been familiar with the work of Bergson, Meinong, and Moore and with the logic of Peirce, Peano, Frege, and Russell. He had even, in Professor Josiah Royce's seminar of 1914, examined Durkheim with the aid of Ernst Mach's distinction between explanation and description, claiming that description was the more sophisticated and important of the two. He pursued the matter still further in his Harvard dissertation on Bradley (completed in 1916), noting therein that even description was ultimately something of an 'interpretation'.

Hulme followed Moore, Meinong, and Husserl, as well as Bergson, without ever giving up his original idea of discontinuity and 'cinders'. He was also aware of some, at least, of Russell's work in logic and mathematics. 'The great aim', he wrote in 'Romanticism and Classicism', 'is accurate, precise and definite description. The first thing is to recognize how extraordinarily difficult this is.' This was at the time when Wittgenstein was starting out on his intellectual voyage, under the influence of Mach and Frege, and studying under Moore and Russell. Years later, in the *Philosophical Investigations*, Wittgenstein wrote: 'We must do away with all *explanation*, and description alone must take its place.'

This is in no sense to put Hulme or Eliot, as philosophers, on the same plane as Wittgenstein. But the connection which Hulme and Eliot alone among the 'modernists' in English literature shared with men on the frontiers of twentieth-century philosophy and logic, is, I think, undeniable. Eliot met Russell, and was noticed by him as being a cut above the ordinary, in 1914, at the very time when Russell was announcing at Harvard the 'vitally important discoveries not yet published . . . of my friend Mr. Ludwig Wittgenstein'.[15] Hulme's posthumous book *Speculations* was published in 1924, in Kegan Paul's International Library of Psychology, Philosophy, and Scientific Method, a series edited by C. K. Ogden. It was Ogden who translated Wittgenstein's *Tractatus Logico-Philosophicus* and published it (with an introduction by Russell) in the same series just two years before *Speculations*.

VIII

It was during his recuperation in London in 1915–16, while he was writing his 'War Notes', that Hulme also composed what would be his final philosophical thoughts. They were published in the *New Age* in seven instalments, from 2 December 1915 to 10 February 1916, under the heading 'A Notebook'. An abridged version was later published in *Speculations* as 'Humanism and the Religious Attitude'. In this series Hulme brought together thoughts he had been articulating over the past decade: his ideas on discontinuity and 'cinders'; his theory that all beliefs and convictions are based on unconscious assumptions about the world and the nature of man; the differences between romanticism and classicism; and his acceptance of the idea of original sin. Much reading and thought went into this work. He gathered ideas from the works of Bergson, Husserl, Nietzsche, Dilthey, Pascal, Meinong, Lévy-Bruhl, and G. E. Moore. (Of Moore he said: 'the only philosophical movement of any importance in England, is that which is derived from the writings of Mr. G. E. Moore.') But Hulme did not merely construct a mosaic from the works of these writers. He used their ideas to achieve his own end, putting the borrowed materials into his own context, which was different from any of theirs.

He began the series by denying that there was a continuous line of evolution from the animal kingdom to man. There was, he maintained, an absolute difference between man and the animals: 'It is impossible to completely explain the nature of man, as a complex development out of

---

[15] Bertrand Russell, *Our Knowledge of the External World as a Field for Scientific Method in Philosophy* (1914; Chicago and London, 1915), p. vii.

the animal world.' He expanded this theme in the following instalments by claiming that there were three regions of reality separated from one another by absolute discontinuities or chasms: (1) the inorganic world of mathematical and physical science; (2) the organic world dealt with by biology, psychology, and history; and (3) the world of ethical and religious values. One of the nineteenth century's main 'achievements', he said, had been in getting rid of all sense of these discontinuities. As a result, we tended to think that there were only *apparent* discontinuities in nature, and that further investigation would reveal an underlying continuity. But this was not so: the discontinuities, Hulme claimed, were real.

Most errors in various subjects resulted from our failure to recognize these chasms. One such error was the mechanistic view of the world: this resulted, he said, from ignoring the chasm between the inorganic and the organic. Another error, which led to Romanticism in literature and Modernism in religion, came from not recognizing the chasm between the organic and the world of ethics. A few philosophers, such as Nietzsche, Dilthey, and Bergson, had seen the chasm between the organic and the inorganic, and had thus combated the mechanists. But no philosopher since the Renaissance had seen the chasm separating biology from ethical or religious values. In this sense there was a 'family resemblance' between all philosophies since that time.

To explain this 'family resemblance', Hulme went on to say that philosophy as generally propounded was not pure philosophy. It was a mixture; there was a scientific element, but mixed in with it a personal element concerned with such matters as the nature and destiny of man and his place in the universe. The technical equipment of the scientific element had been used by philosophers, according to Hulme, 'to disintegrate the solid structure of the world as it appears to common sense'. What the philosopher then did was to present us with a reconstructed world which satisfied, or conformed to, his personal standards or canons—his *Weltanschauung*. It was in this *Weltanschauung*, this particular view of the relation of man to existence, that all philosophers since the Renaissance were in agreement. They had all accepted an uncritical humanism in which man was seen as naturally good, a reservoir of possibilities. All had failed to recognize, Hulme said, the discontinuity between the organic and the ethical; they had introduced into human things the perfection that belonged properly only to the divine. This humanistic attitude had become dominant in the Western world with the Renaissance, and had lasted to the present day.

But there were, Hulme maintained, many possible 'canons of satisfaction' besides humanism. One of them, opposed to the humanistic conception of man, was the religious attitude:

It would perhaps have been better to have avoided the word religious, as that to
the 'emancipated' man at once suggests something exotic, or mystical, or some
sentimental reaction. I am not, however, concerned so much with religion, as
with the attitude, the 'way of thinking,' the categories, from which a religion
springs, and which often survive it. While this attitude tends to find expression in
myth, it is independent of myth; it is, however, much more intimately connected
with dogma. . . . I want to emphasise that this attitude is a possible one for the
'emancipated' and 'reasonable' man at this moment. I use the word religious,
because as in the past the attitude has been the source of most religions, the word
remains convenient.

This attitude separated biology from the world of ethics, and was based
on a belief in absolute values that were not relative to human desires and
feelings. And in the light of these values man was judged to be limited and
imperfect: he was tainted by original sin. Although he might occasionally
accomplish acts which partook of perfection, Hulme said, he could never
himself be perfect: 'As man is essentially bad, he can only accomplish
anything of value by discipline—ethical and political. Order is thus not
merely negative, but creative and liberating. Institutions are necessary.'
This *Weltanschauung* had prevailed in the Egyptian and Byzantine empires
and during the Middle Ages in Western Europe, and would in some
form, Hulme predicted, replace the humanistic attitude of his own day.
    The differences between these two attitudes towards man could be
seen most clearly, Hulme claimed, in the art they had given rise to.
Renaissance art was a 'vital' art; it depended on pleasure in the reproduction of human and natural forms. Byzantine art was the exact opposite of
this. There was nothing vital in it; there was rather a searching after a
perfection and a rigidity which vital things could never have, a use of
form that was almost geometrical.
    In the final instalment of the series (10 February 1916), Hulme again
took up the idea of 'frameworks', which he had invoked in earlier
writings, and applied it to the matter at hand. A framework was not
something reached or achieved by reasoning; it was, rather, he said,
simply there, something taken for granted—such as our conception of
the nature of man; and it had the effect of limiting our thinking and even
influencing how we perceived facts. Our unconsciousness of these frameworks led us to suppose that the judgements of value founded on them
were natural and inevitable; and this in turn made it difficult for anyone
in the humanist tradition to look at the religious attitude as anything but
a sentimental survival. It was important for us to see that the religious
attitude was a real attitude, possible for us today: 'To see this is a kind of
conversion. It radically alters our physical perception almost; so that the
world takes on an entirely different aspect.'

His insistence on an absolute discontinuity between the biological and the ethical is interesting, because it anticipates later statements by Wittgenstein—in the final pages of the *Tractatus* and in a letter he wrote to his friend Ludwig Ficker, in explanation of the *Tractatus* before it was published:

The book's point is an ethical one. I once meant to include in the preface a sentence which is not in fact there now, but which I will write out for you here, because it will perhaps be a key to the work for you. What I meant to write, then, was this: My work consists of two parts: the one presented here plus all that I have *not* written. And *it is precisely this second part that is the important one.* My book draws limits to the sphere of the ethical from the inside as it were, and I am convinced that this is the ONLY rigorous way of drawing those limits.[16]

Both Hume and Wittgenstein were in a sense philosophic amateurs, for whom philosophy was not a discipline or an academic subject—a question of weighing opinions and seeking a middle ground—but ultimately a personal thing. Both were men in whom intellectual power was linked with great passion. And the source of much of that passion was fear that the modern world, carrying with it a scientific and philosophical baggage from the Victorian past, was trying to merge the sphere of values with that of science. To allow the two to be merged could only lead to the destruction of the ethical: destruction of the only thing, in other words, which for them could give human life a value.

'A Notebook' and 'War Notes' were Hulme's last writings. On 20 March 1916 he received his commission in the Royal Marines Artillery. He was killed in battle the following year, on 28 September 1917.

IX

Looking back over Hulme's career, we can see the developing nature of his thought. His early belief that abstract logic could not explain reality led him to Bergson, whose philosophy seemed for a time to provide the answers to his questions. But when these ideas came into conflict with his developing anti-romanticism, he began to lose interest in Bergson. He gradually worked out his own ideas about man, which he described first as the 'classical' point of view, and later as the 'religious attitude'.[17] It is interesting to note that in spite of these developments and

---

[16] Letter in Ludwig Wittgenstein, *Briefe an Ludwig von Ficker*, ed. G. H. von Wright (Salzburg, 1969). This English version is taken from A. Janik and S. Toulmin, *Wittgenstein's Vienna* (New York, 1973), 192.

[17] Michael Levenson, in his *Genealogy of Modernism* (Cambridge, 1984), claims that Hulme, under the influence of Husserl and Moore, 'moved to a new attitude which found

changes of mind, the idea underlying his first work, 'Cinders', was still present even in his last work; to the very end he clung to the idea of discontinuity.

What is most impressive about Hulme is, I think, his intellectual honesty. He was a man passionately searching for truth. When one path proved a dead end, he tried another; he was not afraid to admit that he had made a mistake. Probably the clearest, though not the only, illustration of his facing of difficulties is in his description of his meeting with Pierre Lasserre in 1911, where he publicly wondered if there was any inconsistency in his support of both Bergson and anti-romanticism.

Hulme was aware too of the tenuousness of human knowledge. In one of his 1911 *Commentator* articles, for example, he spoke of how all of us, himself included, see the world through coloured spectacles, often without our even being aware of the existence of the distorting glass. Three years later, in his lecture on 'The New Art and Its Philosophy', he talked about the impossibility of describing in any detail what the future 'classical attitude' would be like, because 'one's mind is so soaked in the thought and language' of one's own time.

While it would be false to claim that Hulme is a major figure in twentieth-century literature, it is not misleading to say that he is one of those minor figures who, by dint of special qualities, gains for himself a place not too far away from the major figures of the time. Hulme, like Eliot, knew something of the crisis that had been reached in human thought and the problems of knowledge. Clearly he was not as well informed as Eliot on some of the technical aspects; yet Hulme can be deceptive. He worked hard to reduce previously complicated ideas to clear, simple sentences, with the result that such technical matters as he was familiar with have been reduced in his articles to straightforward analogies. What is remarkable is that he was prepared to face the possibility that man knows much less than he likes to think he does.

classicism as unsatisfactory as romanticism'. This new attitude of Hulme's was, he says, 'anti-humanism'. Levenson is right in finding Moore and Husserl in Hulme's final pages, but wrong in claiming that Hulme's 'anti-humanism' is different from his 'classicism'. The anti-humanist attitude (according to which man is not the measure of things) was already established in the two 1912 essays 'Romanticism and Classicism' and 'A Tory Philosophy'. For Hulme, a 'classical' poet or artist was one who had the right attitude towards man: what he later called the 'religious attitude'. When Hulme used the word 'classical' in 1914 in his lecture 'The New Art and Its Philosophy', he was not using it in his own special, restricted sense, but only as the accepted, vague term of art history, meaning 'the art of ancient Greece'. Levenson has confused these two quite different and distinct uses of the word 'classical'.

X

Hulme published no books of his own, and no collection or selection of essays was published during his lifetime. His reputation has rested on the selections of his work published posthumously in *Speculations* (1924) and *Further Speculations* (1955). But although both books have been valuable in preserving and making available a good portion of his writings, they have also helped to propagate an incomplete, and even inaccurate, picture of his thought. First of all, several significant essays were not included in either volume. Neither contains, for example, any of his pieces critical of Bergson; yet these are essential for a full understanding of his interest in the French philosopher. It is only by reading all the Bergson essays that one can see how and why Hulme's views developed and changed. Then again, neither volume includes any of his political essays from the *Commentator*. One of these essays, 'A Tory Philosophy', was reprinted in A. R. Jones's *The Life and Opinions of T. E. Hulme* (1960), but none of the other political essays has appeared since 1911. Not only do they represent a step in the development of Hulme's thought, but they contain a number of acute observations on perception, emotion, and the nature of belief that deserve preservation.

But the problem does not end with these and other omissions. Some of what has been printed in collections is incomplete or inaccurate. The most important piece among these works is Hulme's well-known essay, 'Humanism and the Religious Attitude'. The *Speculations* version, the only version with which most of Hulme's readers have been acquainted over the past seventy years, was put together, as already pointed out, from the series of articles which Hulme published in *New Age* in 1915–16 under the title 'A Notebook'. Herbert Read not only added his own title, but left out one entire instalment of the series and reworded some passages to make the whole piece more coherent and organic. This polish obscures the 'cindery' aspect of the work, which Hulme intended. In spite of developments and changes of mind during the course of his career, the idea underlying his first work, 'Cinders', is still present even in this last essay. To gloss over the disjunctions in these his final philosophical pages is to falsify his thought.

The present edition is the first more or less complete collection of Hulme's work. It consists of all his extant articles, reviews, and lectures, his two early unfinished works, 'Cinders' and 'Notes on Language and Style', the six poems he saw published during his lifetime and two others later found among his papers and published by Michael Roberts. I have restored 'Humanism and the Religious Attitude' to its original form and title, and I have also added material left out of the published versions of 'Cinders' and 'Notes on Language and Style'.

Thirteen of the works included in the volume have never before been collected. At least one of them—Hulme's report for *Nature* on the 1911 Philosophical Congress at Bologna—has, in fact, only fairly recently been identified as being by Hulme. Other previously uncollected essays include Hulme's political essays in the *Commentator*, sundry essays on Bergson, and his lengthy series of 'War Notes'.

Not included in the edition are Hulme's letters to the editor, which, while interesting biographically, are topical pieces lacking significance outside their original context; Hulme's cursory preface to his translation of Bergson's *Introduction to Metaphysics*; and the scattered quotations and fragments from his manuscripts that have been published posthumously. These omissions are listed with asterisks following them in Hulme's bibliography at the back of the volume.

The edition begins with Hulme's poetry. The prose works which follow are arranged according to subject, but the order also roughly reflects Hulme's intellectual development. Publication details for all the works will be found on each title-page and in the bibliography.

Hulme had his own idiosyncrasies as a writer. The reader should note that ellipses and asterisks appearing throughout this edition are Hulme's, and do not signify material omitted by me. I have corrected only a handful of misspellings and misprints.

Poetry

[Hulme published six poems in his lifetime. 'A City Sunset' and 'Autumn' were first published in Jan. 1909 in *For Christmas MDCCCCVIII*, the first book of poetry put out by the Poets' Club, London. In Dec. 1909 'The Embankment' and 'Conversion' were published in the Club's second volume of verse, entitled *The Book of the Poets' Club*. Three of these poems— 'Autumn', 'The Embankment', and 'Conversion'—and two others—'Mana Aboda' and 'Above the Dock'—were published as 'The Complete Poetical Works of T. E. Hulme' in 1912, first in the *New Age* (here after *NA*) of 25 Jan. and later that year in Ezra Pound's *Ripostes*. In 1938 Michael Roberts published, as an appendix to his book *T. E. Hulme*, three poems which he had found among Hulme's paper: 'The Man in the Crow's Nest', 'Susan Ann and Immortality', and a somewhat different version of 'A City Sunset' from that originally published.

The six poems that Hulme saw published are reproduced here in the final versions printed during his lifetime; the two new poems are taken from Roberts. In addition, Hulme left behind fragments and drafts of other unpublished poems. These have since been collected and published in *Further Speculations*, ed. Samuel Hynes (Minneapolis, 1955) (hereafter *FS*), and in Alun R. Jones, *The Life and Opinions of T. E. Hulme* (London and Boston, 1960).]

Autumn[1]

A touch of cold in the Autumn night—
I walked abroad,
And saw the ruddy moon lean over a hedge
Like a red-faced farmer.
I did not stop to speak, but nodded,
And round about were the wistful stars
With white faces like town children.

Mana Aboda[2]

Beauty is the marking-time, the stationary vibration, the feigned ecstasy of an arrested impulse unable to reach its natural end.

Mana Aboda, whose bent form
The sky in archèd circle is,
Seems ever for an unknown grief to mourn.
Yet on a day I heard her cry:
'I weary of the roses and the singing poets—
Josephs all, not tall enough to try.'

Above the Dock[3]

Above the quiet dock in mid night,
Tangled in the tall mast's corded height,
Hangs the moon. What seemed so far away
Is but a child's balloon, forgotten after play.

The Embankment[4]

(The fantasia of a fallen gentleman on a cold, bitter night)

Once, in finesse of fiddles found I ecstasy,
In the flash of gold heels on the hard pavement.
Now see I
That warmth's the very stuff of poesy.
Oh, God, make small
The old star-eaten blanket of the sky,
That I may fold it round me and in comfort lie.

Conversion[5]

Lighthearted I walked into the valley wood
In the time of hyacinths,
Till beauty like a scented cloth

Cast over, stifled me. I was bound
Motionless and faint of breath
By loveliness that is her own eunuch.
Now pass I to the final river
Ignominiously, in a sack, without sound,
As any peeping Turk to the Bosphorus.

A City Sunset[6]

Alluring, Earth seducing, with high conceits
is the sunset that reigns
at the end of westward streets. . . .
A sudden flaring sky
troubling strangely the passer by
with visions, alien to long streets, of Cytharea
or the smooth flesh of Lady Castlemaine. . . .
A frolic of crimson
is the spreading glory of the sky,
heaven's jocund maid
flaunting a trailed red robe
along the fretted city roofs
about the time of homeward going crowds
—a vain maid, lingering, loth to go. . . .

The Man in the Crow's Nest[7]

Strange to me sounds the wind that blows
By the masthead in the lonely night.
Maybe 'tis the sea whistling—feigning joy
To hide its fright
Like a village boy
That, shivering, past the churchyard goes.

Susan Ann and Immortality[8]

Her head hung down
Gazed at earth, finally keen,
As the rabbit at the stoat,
Till the earth was sky,
Sky that was green,
And brown clouds passed
Like chestnut leaves along the ground.

Early Works

Cinders

[According to Herbert Read's introduction to *Speculations*, 'Cinders' was a collection of notes and observations for a work which was to be Hulme's 'personal philosophy, cast into an allegorical form perhaps analogous to Nietzsche's *Zarathustra*' (p. xiv). Begun in 1906–7 and added to in the years following, the notes were never given any final form; nor were they published during Hulme's lifetime. The manuscript is now lost. What remain are the two posthumously published versions which Read, as editor, 'pruned . . . a good deal' (letter from Read to C. K. Ogden, 16 Apr. 1923). The first, published under the title 'The Note-Books of T. E. Hulme', appeared in *NA* in four instalments in 1922 (19, 26 Jan., 9, 16 Feb.). Read gave the collection Hulme's own title, 'Cinders', when he included it in *Speculations* (hereafter *S*) two years later. The two versions differ slightly in content and organization; and while the *S* version is more complete, each includes material not in the other. The version reproduced here incorporates notes from both *NA* and *S* versions.]

For the Preface.[1]

The history of philosophers we know, but who will write the history of the philosophic amateurs and readers? Who will tell us of the circulation of Descartes, who read the book and who understood it? Or do philosophers, like the mythical people on the island, take in each other's washing? For I take it, a man who understands philosophy is inevitably irritated into writing it. The few who have learnt the jargon must repay themselves by employing it. A new philosophy is not like a new religion—a thing to be merely thankful for and accepted mutely by the faithful. It is more of the nature of food thrown to the lions; the pleasure lies in the fact that it can be devoured. It is food for the critics, and all readers of philosophy, I take it, are critics, and not faithful ones waiting for the new gospel. With this preface I offer my new kind of food to tickle the palate of the connoisseurs.

A SKETCH OF A NEW WELTANSCHAUUNG
(1906–7)

I. In spite of pretensions to absolute truth, the results of philosophy are always tested by the effects, and by the judgments of other philosophers.

There is always an appeal to a circle of people. The same is true of values in art, in morals. A man cannot stand alone on absolute ground, but always appeals to his fellows.

II. Therefore it is suggested that there is no such thing as an absolute truth to be discovered. All general statements about truth, etc., are in the end only amplifications of man's appetites.

The ultimate reality is a circle of persons, *i.e.* animals who communicate.

There is a kind of gossamer web, woven between the real things, and by this means the animals communicate. For purposes of communication they invent a symbolic language. Afterwards this language, used to excess, becomes a disease, and we get the curious phenomena of men explaining themselves by means of the gossamer web that connects them. Language becomes a disease in the hands of the counter-word mongers. It must constantly be remembered that it is an invention for the convenience of men; and in the midst of Hegelians who triumphantly explain the world as a mixture of 'good' and 'beauty' and 'truth', this should be remembered. What would an intelligent animal (without the language disease), or a carter in the Leek road, think of it all?

Symbols are picked out and believed to be realities. People imagine that all the complicated structure of the world can be woven out of 'good' and 'beauty'. These words are merely counters representing vague groups of things, to be moved about on a board for the convenience of the players.

III. Objection might be taken that this makes man the measure of the world, and that after all he is only an animal, who came late, and the world must be supposed to have existed before he evolved at all. The reply to this is as follows:

(i) Analogy of courage and capacity. Courage in the Wild West requires capacities different from those it requires in the city. But the phenomena are the same: A non-muscular man is inevitably physically a coward.

(ii) The mental qualities of men and animals are common, though they are realised by different means—of the cat at night walking by Marylebonne Station.

(iii) These qualities—*e.g.* the common return to egoism, the roundness of the world, the absence of all infinitude, the denial of all Utopias—are extended to the ultimate nature of the world.

(iv) These qualities extend to the amœba and the inorganic world.

(v) It is these qualities with which the world is measured in I.

(vi) Hence in a sense 'Man is the measure of all things' and man (egoism) *has always existed and always will exist.*

IV. Just as no common purpose can be aimed at for the conflicting purposes of real people, *so* there is no common purpose in the world.
The world is a plurality.
A unity arrived at by stripping off essentials is not a unity. Compound is not an inner reality.

V. This plurality consists in the nature of an ash-heap. In this ash-pit of cinders, certain ordered routes have been made, thus constituting whatever unity there may be—a kind of manufactured chess-board laid on a cinder-heap. Not a real chess-board impressed on the cinders, but the gossamer world of symbolic communication already spoken of.

CINDERS

There is a difficulty in finding a comprehensive scheme of the cosmos, because there is none. The cosmos is only *organised* in parts; the rest is cinders.

Death is a breaking up into cinders. Hence partial truth of the old Greek conception of Hades (a place of less organisation and *no* happiness).

Many necessary conditions must be fulfilled before the counters and the chess-board can be posed elegantly on the cinders. Illness and death easily disturb and give falls from this condition. Perhaps this is an illustration of Nietzsche's image of the tight-rope walker. When all is arranged the counters are moved about. This is happiness, moving to enthusiastic conclusions, the musical note, perhaps Art. But it must be largely artificial. (Art prolongs it, and creates it by blur.)

The floating heroic world (built up of moments) and the cindery reality—can they be made to correspond to some fundamental constitution of the world? (An antithesis much more deep than the one which analyses all realities into forms of egoism. This latter only a particular case of the general law.)

The *absolute* is to be described not as perfect, but if existent as essentially imperfect, chaotic, and cinder-like. (Even this view is not ultimate, but merely designed to satisfy temporary human analogies and wants.)

World is indescribable, that is, not reducible to counters; and particularly it is impossible to include it all under one large counter such as 'God' or 'Truth' and the other verbalisms, or the disease of the symbolic language.

Cinders can never be counters except for certain practical purposes (good enough)—cf. rail lines and chess-board. The treatment of the soul as the central part of the nominalist position. Their habit of regarding it as a kind of round counter all red, which survives *whole* in all its redness and roundness (the redness as the character), a counter-like *distinct* separate entity, just as *word* itself is.

Why is it that London looks pretty by night? Because for the general cindery chaos there is substituted a simple ordered arrangement of a finite number of lights.

The two complementary phenomena: that each wash is a line, and that each line is a wash.

That the world is finite (atomism: there are no infinitudes except in art) and that it is yet an infinitude of cinders (there is no finite law encompassing all).

This new view may perhaps be caricatured by saying that the bad is fundamental, and that the good is artificially built up in it and out of it, like oases in the desert, or as cheerful houses in the storm.

(Two parts: 1—All cinders; 2—the part built up. So the question: How far built up and how far given us? The question of the pliability of the world.)

All is flux. The moralists, the capital letterists, attempt to find a framework outside the flux, a solid bank for the river, a pier rather than a raft. Truth is what helps a particular sect in the general flow.

School children at a fountain (moved mechanically by thirst) to some-one looking down from above, appear as a pure instinctive mechanical act. Cf. ants—we are unable to ascertain the subtler reasons which move them. They all look alike. Hence Humpty-Dumpty's remark about human faces is seen to be the foundation of all science and all philosophy.
Only in the fact of consciousness is there a unity in the world. Cf. Oxford Street at 2 a.m. All the mud, endless, except where bound together by the spectator.

Unity is made in the world by drawing squares over it. We are able to get along these at any rate—cf. railway line in desert. (Always the elusive as seen in maps. *Ad infinitum.*)
The squares include cinders—always cinders.
No unity of laws, but merely of the sorting machine. Cf. Gaultier.[2]

Formerly, one liked theories because they reduced the world to a single principle. Now the same reason disgusts us. The flats of Canada are incomprehensible on any single theory. The world only comprehensible on the cinder theory.

The same old fallacy persists—the desire to introduce a unity in the world: (1) The mythologists made it a woman or an elephant; (2) the scientists made fun of the mythologists, but themselves turned the world into the likeness of a mechanical toy. They were more concerned with models than with woman (woman troubled them and hence their particular form of anthropomorphism). One analogy is as good as another. The truth remains that the world is not any unity, but a house in the cinders (outside in the cold, primeval).

Contrast the Pythagorean ecstasies in the numbers 3 and 7. The cinder is the opposite prejudice. I am immediately up in arms if a book says a subject can be divided into three separate parts.

Most of our life is spent in buttoning and unbuttoning. Yes, quite so. This fact can be welcomed as fitting in with the general theory.

The unity of Nature is an extremely artificial and fragile bridge, a garden net.

The covers of a book are responsible for much error. They set a limit round certain convenient groups of ideas, when there are really no limits.

The aim of science and of all thought is to reduce the complex and inevitably disconnected world of grit and cinders to a few ideal counters, which we can move about and so form an ungritlike picture of reality— one flattering to our sense of power over the world.

In the end this is true too of mathematics, though at first it appears as a more complex symbolism. The conclusion of all mathematics is: that one counter stands in a certain relation to another. That counter may be a simple number or an elliptic integral, but the final effect is the same. (All mathematics is deducible from numbers, which are nothing but counters.)

There is an *objective* world (?), a chaos, a cinder-heap. Gradually cases have been built up. Egos have grown as organised trees.

So not *idealist*, as that assumes that there is nothing but a fixed number of persons, and without them nothing. (So the Real New Realism is something beyond names. World can't be 0 because 0 is opposed to human psychology.)

A landscape, with occasional oases. So now and then we are moved— at the theatre, action, a love. But mainly deserts of dirt, ash-pits of the cosmos, grass on ash-pits. No universal ego, but a few definite persons gradually built up.

Nature as the accumulation of the memories of man.

Certain groups of ideas as huts for men to live in. The Act of Creation.

Truth is always seen to lie in a compromise. All clear cut ideas turn out to be wrong. Analogy to real things, which are artificially picked out of the general lava flow of cinders.

Cf. the wandering attention in the library. Sometimes one seems to have definite clear cut moments, but not afterwards.

I. Nature. Scenery as built up by man. Oases in the desert of grit.
II. Extended to the whole of the world.
III. *But* the microscope. Things revealed, not created, but there before, and *also* seem to be in an order.
IV. Before man other powers created in the struggle.
V. So man was gradually built up, and man's world was gradually built up at the same time.

Evolution of colour; dim perception of it in the amœba; evolved—the whole modern world of colour built up from this; gradually made more counter-like and distinct.

There is no inevitable order into which ideas must be shifted.

We live in a room, of course, but the great question for philosophy is: how far have we decorated the room, and how far was it made before we came? Did we merely decorate the room, or did we make it from chaos? The laws of nature that we certainly do find—what are they?

In an organised city it is not easy to see the cinder element of earth—all is banished. But it is easy to see it psychologically. What the Nominalists call the grit in the machine, I call the fundamental element of the machine.

Properly to estimate the true purpose of absolute philosophy, it should be realised as reducing everything to number, the only rational and logical solution from the point of view that dares to conceive relation as of more importance than the persons related.

The eyes, the beauty of the world, have been organised out of the fæces. Man returns to dust. So does the face of the world to primeval cinders.

A girl's ball-dress and shoes are symbolic of the world organised (in counters) from the mud. Separate from contact.

Only the isolated points seem to have any value, so how can the world be said to be designed? Rather we may say that gradually certain points are being designed.

Taken *mystically*—then all peculiarities of the human organism must have their counterpart in the construction of the world.

E.g.—Illness and a reversion to chaos.

Man is the chaos highly organised, but liable to revert to chaos at any moment. Happiness and ecstasy at present unstable. Walking in the street, seeing pretty girls (all chaos put into the drains: not seen) and wondering what they would look like ill. Men laughing at a bar—but wait till the fundamental chaos reveals itself.

The two moods in life. (i) Ill in bed, toothache, W.C. in the Atlantic—the disorganised, withdrawn-into-oneself mood. (ii) Flying along in the wind (wind in the hair, on a motor bus). *Or* evolving a new theory. The impersonal feeling.

Ennui and disgust, the sick moments—not an occasional lapse or disease, but the fundamental ennui and chaos out of which the world has been built, and which is as necessary to it as the listeners are to intellectuals. The old world order of queens and pawns.

The apparent scientific unity of the world may be due to the fact that man is a kind of sorting machine.

'I must tell someone' as the final criterion of philosophy, the *raison d'être* of the human circle symbol.

The sick disgusting moments are part of the fundamental cinders—primeval chaos—the dream of impossible chaos.

The absolute is invented to reconcile conflicting purposes. But these purposes are necessarily conflicting, even in the nature of Truth itself. It is so absurd to construct an absolute which shall at each moment just manage by artificial gymnastics to reconcile these purposes.

Philosophical syntheses and ethical systems are only possible in arm-chair moments. They are seen to be meaningless as soon as we get into a bus with a dirty baby and a crowd.

Note the fact that all a writer's generalisations and truths can be traced to the personal circumstances and prejudices of his class, experience, capacity and body. This, however, is not an instance of error or hypocrisy. There is no average or real truth to be discerned among the different fronts of prejudice. Each is a truth in so far as it satisfies the writer.

We must judge the world from the status of animals, leaving out 'Truth', etc.

Animals are in the same state that men were before symbolic language was invented.

Philosophy is about people in clothes, not about the soul of man.

The fixed order of the world is woven in a gigantic way by the acts of men and animals.

The world lives in order to develop the lines on its face.

These little theories of the world, which satisfy and are then thrown away, one after the other, develop *not* as successive approximations to the truth, but like successive thirsts, to be satisfied at the moment, and not evolving to one great Universal Thirst.

Through all the ages, the conversation of ten men sitting together is what holds the world together.

Never think in a book: here are Truth and all the other capital letters; but think in a theatre and watch the audience. Here is the reality, here are human animals. Listen to the words of heroism and then at the crowded husbands who applaud. All philosophies are subordinate to this. It is not a question of the unity of the world and men afterwards put into it, *but* of human animals, and of philosophies as an elaboration of their appetites.

The importance of the circle of people. Sailors telling tales. Sailors looking at a map—it exists in all their minds.

Words.
Heaven as the short summary paradise of words.

The ideal of knowledge: all cinders reduced to counters (words); these counters moved about on a chess-board, and so all phenomena made obvious.

Something is always lost in generalisation. A railway leaves out all the gaps of dirt between. Generalisations are only means of getting about.

Cf. the words love, sex, nude, with the actual details.

I hate more than anything the vague long pretentious words of Wells—'indefinable tendency in events', etc., etc.

Always seek the hard, definite, personal word.

The real levelheadedness: to be able to analyse a pretty girl at first sight, not to be intoxicated with clothes, to be able to imagine the effect of dipping in water—this is what one must be able to do for words, and for all embracing philosophies. We must not be taken in by the arm-chair moments.

The World is Round.

Disillusionment comes when it is recognised that all heroic actions can be reduced to the simple laws of egoism. But wonder can even then be found in the fact that there *are* such *different* and *clear-cut* laws and egoisms and that they have been created out of the chaos.

The pathetic search for the *different* (Cf. Gide). Where shall they find it? Never found in sex. All explored sex is the same.

World as finite, and so no longer any refuge in infinities of grandeur.

Atomism.

Resolution of apparent flexibility and continuity into atomic structure. Oratory and fluency mean a collection of phrases at fingers' ends. This seen in Hyde Park, the young men, Christian preachers.

Escapes to the infinite:

(i) Art, blur, strangeness, music.
(ii) Sentimentality.

The sentimental illusion of a man (invalid) who takes pleasure in resting his head in a woman's lap—it is a deliberate act, work on her part. While he may feel the sentimental escape to the infinite, she has to be uncomfortable and prosaic.

All experience tends to do away with all sentimental escapes to the infinite, but at the same time to provide many deliberated, observed, manufactured, artificial, spectacular, poised for seeing continuities and patterns.

The universal conspiracy: other people unconsciously provide the sentimental spectacle in which you luxuriate. The world *is* nothing more or less than a stage.

There may be an attitude which sees that most things are illusions, that experience is merely the gradual process of disillusionment, that the new as well as the old ideals turn out to be partial, non-continuous or infinite, but then in face of this decides that certain illusions or moods are pleasurable and exhilarating, and deliberately and knowingly encourages them. A judicious choice of illusions, leading to activities planned and carried out, is the only means of happiness, *e.g.* the exhilaration of regarding life as a procession or a war.

In opposition to Socialism and Utopian schemes comes the insistence on the fact of the unalterability of motives. Motives are the only unalterable and fixed things in the world. They extend to the animal kingdom. They are the only *rock*: physical bases change. They are more than *human* motives: they are the constitution of the world.

That great secret which all men find out for themselves, and none reveal—or if they do, like Cassandra, are not believed—that the world is round. The young man refuses to believe it.

For discussion.

    (i) How far the pretensions of science are true. How far there are such things as non-laws.
    (ii) The nature of truth.
    (iii) Laplace's fallacy. It is not in the nature of the world to be calculated; the future is variable.

Refuse World as a unit and take Person (in flight from the word fallacy).

But why person? Why is the line drawn exactly there in the discussion of counter words?

We are becoming so particular in the choice of words and the rejection of symbolism that we are in danger of *forgetting* that the world does really exist.

The truth is that there are no ultimate principles, upon which the whole of knowledge can be built once and for ever as upon a rock. But there are an infinity of analogues, which help us along, and give us a feeling of power over the chaos when we perceive them. The field is infinite and herein lies the chance for originality. Here there are some new things under the sun. (Perhaps it would be better to say that there are some new things under the moon, for here is the land pre-eminently of shadows, fancies and analogies.)

Danger: one must recognise thought's essential independence of the imagery that steadies it. Subtle associations which familiar images recall are insinuated into the thought.

Though perhaps we do not realise it, we are still governed by the analogy, by which spirit was first compared to the wind. The contrast the same as the one between the little box and space, between the court and cinders—that between the one that thinks of a man as an elaborately built-up pyramid, a constructed elaboration, easily upset and not flexible, only functioning in one direction, the one in which he was made, and the other that considers him as a flexible essence, a spirit, like a *fluid*.

We can all see that there is an eternal flexibility in the most obviously constituted man, but we realise the contrast best when looking at a tailor's model of a man in dress, whose limbs move and flex.

In the problem of ghosts which bend and flex lies the whole difference between the two world philosophies—

I. Flexible essence.
II. Built up stuff.

Philosophical Jargon.

There is this consoling thought, supporting us while wandering in the wilderness of which the priests alone pretend they have the secret. In all other uses of language, no matter for what purpose, the analogies used are quite simple, and even can be replaced, leaving the idea behind them just as real. The analogies a man uses to represent a state of soul, though personal, can be replaced, to produce almost the same effect. *No one* mistakes the analogies for the real thing they stand for.

The Dancer.

Dancing to express the organisation of cinders, finally emancipated (cf. bird).

I sat before a stage and saw a little girl with her head thrown back, and a smile. I knew her, for she was the daughter of John of Elton.

But she smiled, and her feet were not like feet, but . . . . . [*sic*].

Though I knew her body.

All these sudden insights (*e.g.* the great analogy of a woman compared to the world in Brussels)—all of these start a line, which seems about to unite the whole world logically. But the line stops. There is no unity. All logic and life are made up of tangled ends like that.

Always think of the fringe and of the cold walks, of the lines that lead nowhere.

Mind and Matter.

Realise that to take *one* or the *other* as absolute is to perpetrate the same old counter fallacy; both are mixed up in a cindery way and we extract them as counters.

Mathematics takes one group of counters, abstracts them and makes them absolute, down to Matter and Motion.

That *fringe of cinders* which bounds any ecstasy.

The tall lanky fellow, with a rose, in a white moonlit field. But where does he sleep?

All heroes, great men, go to the outside, away from the Room, and wrestle with cinders.

And cinders become the Azores, the Magic Isles.

A house built is then a symbol, a Roman Viaduct; but the walk there and the dirt—this must jump right into the mind also.

Aphra's[3] *Finger.*

There are moments when the tip of one's finger seems raw. In the contact of it and the world there seems a strange difference. The spirit lives on that tip and is thrown on the rough cinders of the world. All philosophy depends on that—the state of the tip of the finger.

When Aphra had touched, even lightly, the rough wood, this wood seemed to cling to his finger, to draw itself backward and forward along it. The spirit returned again and again, as though fascinated, to the luxurious torture of the finger.

Rules.

The prediction of the stars is no more wonderful, and no more accurate, than the prediction of another person's conduct. There is no last refuge here for the logical structure of the world.

The phenomenon we study is not the immense world in our hand, but certain little observations we make about it. We put these on a table and look at them.

We study little chalk marks on a table (chalk because that shows the cindery nature of the division we make) and create rules near enough for them.

If we look at a collection of cinders from all directions, in the end, we are bound to find a shadow that looks regular.

The attempt to get a common element in personality, *i.e.* the old attempt to get a unity. Abstract an element and call that a fundamental.

The inner spirit of the world is miles and miles of ploughed fields.

Never speak of 'my unconquerable soul', or of any vulgarism of that sort. But thank God for the long note of the bugle, which moves all the world bodily out of the cinders and the mud.

There is only one *art* that moves me: architecture.

French.

The exact fault which is typical of French books: The taking of a few opinions, a few epigrams, a few literary *obiter dicta*, and arranging them symmetrically, finding a logical order, an underlying principle where there is one, and calling the whole a science.

I shall call my philosophy the 'Valet to the Absolute'. The Absolute not a hero to his own valet.

All these various little notes will never combine because in their nature they cannot. The facts of Nature are solid enough, but Man is a weather-cock standing in the middle, looking first at one part and then at another. A little idea in one sentence appears to contain a whole new world philosophy. So it does. But then a world philosophy is only a certain direction, N. or S. It is quite easy to change this direction. Hence the astonishing power that philosophers appear to have at the summit of the sciences. Buy a book obviously literary, by an amateur, made of light combinations of words. It seems to change the world, but nothing is further from the truth. It just turns the weathercock to a new direction. The philosophic faculty is quite irresponsible, the easiest moving thing in nature, and quite divorced from nature.

So be sceptical of the first enthusiasm that a new idea gives.

The Eagle's eye.

The ruling analogy, which is quite false, must be removed. It is that of the eagle's eye. The metaphysician imagines that he surveys the world as with an eagle's eye. And the farther he flies, the 'purer' his knowledge becomes.

Hence we can see the world as pure geometry, and can make out its dividing lines.

But the eye is in the mud, the eye *is* mud.

Pure seeing of the whole process is impossible. Little fancies help us along, but we never get pure disinterested intellect.

Space.

I. Admitted the pragmatic criterion of any analogy that makes for clearness.
II. Now *space* is essential to clearness. A developed notion, perhaps, but now essential.
III. The idealists analyse space into a mode of arranging sensations. But this gives us an unimaginable world existing all at a point.
IV. Why not try the reverse process and put all ideas (purely mental states) into terms of *space* (cf. landscape thinking)?

The sense of reality is inevitably connected with that of *space* (the world existing before us).

Truths don't exist before we invent them. They respond to man's need of economy, just as beliefs to his need of faith.

The fountain turned on. It has a definite geometrical shape, but the shape did not exist before it was turned on. Compare the arguments about the pre-existence of the soul.

But the little pipes are there before, which give it that shape as soon as the water is turned on.

The water is the same though the geometrical figures of different fountains differ.

By analogy we may perhaps claim that there is no such thing as a personal soul. The personality of the soul depends on the bodily frame which receives it, *i.e.* on the shape of the pipes.

The soul is a spirit certainly, but undifferentiated and without personality. The personality is given by the bodily frame which receives and shapes it.

Ritual and Sentiment.

Sentiment cannot easily retire into itself in pure thought; it cannot live and feed on itself for very long. In wandering, thought is easily displaced by other matters. So that the man who deliberately sets himself the task of thinking continuously of a lover or dead friend has an impossible task. He is inevitably drawn to some form of ritual for the expression and outflow of the sentiment. Some act which requires less concentration, and which at an easy level fulfils his obligations to sentiment, which changes a morbid feeling into a grateful task and employment. Such as pilgrimages to graves, standing bareheaded and similar freaks of a lover's fancy. The same phenomena can be observed in religion. A man cannot deliberatcly make up his mind to think of the goodness of God for an hour, but he can perform some ritual act of admiration whether it be the offering of a sacrifice or merely saying amen to a set prayer. Ritual tends to be constant, even that seeming exception the impromptu prayers of a Non-conformist minister are merely the stringing together in accidental order of set and well-known phrases and tags. The burning of candles to the Virgin if only one can escape from some danger. The giving of a dinner, or getting drunk in company as a celebration—a relief from concentrated thinking.

Body.

In Tube lift hearing the phrase 'fed up', and realising that all our analogies spiritual and intellectual are derived from purely physical acts.

Nay more, all attributes of the absolute and the abstract are really nothing more (in so far as they mean anything) but elaborations of simple passions.

All poetry is an affair of the body—that is, to be real it must affect body.

Action.

Teachers, university lecturers on science, emancipated women, and other spectacled anæmics attending the plays at the Court Theatre remind me of disembodied spirits, having no body to rest in. They have all the intellect and imagination required for high passion, but no material to work on. They feel all the emotions of jealousy and desire, but these leading to no action remain as nothing but petty motives. *Passion is action* and without action but a child's anger.

They lack the bodies and the daggers. Tragedy never sits steadily on a chair, except in certain vague romantic pictures which are thus much affected (as real tragedy) by the moderns and the sedentary. Just as sentiment and religion require expression in ritual, so tragedy requires action.

Jealousy, desire to kill, desire for strong arms and knives, resolution to shake off social convention and to do it.

The knife order.

Why grumble because there is no end discoverable in the world? There is no end at all except in our own constructions.

Necessity of distinguishing between a vague philosophic statement that 'reality always escapes a system', and the definite cinder, felt in a religious way and being a criterion of nearly all judgment, philosophic and æsthetic.

No Geist without ghost.

This is the only truth in the subject.

Is there here a possible violation of the cinder principle; an escape back to the old fallacy? But without some definite assertion of this kind. . . . Some definite crossing beyond is necessary to escape poetic overstatement, to relieve us.

Philosophy.

The strange quality, shade of feeling, one gets when with a few people alone in a position a little separated from the world—a ship's cabin, the last 'bus.

If all the world were destroyed and only these left. . . . That all the gods, all the winged words—love, etc.—exist *in them*, on that fluid basis.

To frankly take that fluid basis and elaborate it into a solidity: That the gods do not exist horizontally in space, but somehow vertically in the isolated fragment of the tribe. There is another form of space where gods, etc., do exist concretely.

Smoothness.
   Hate it.
   This is the obsession that starts all my theories.
   Get other examples, other facets of the one idea.
   Build them up by the catalogue method

   (I) in science;
   (II) in sex;
   (III) in poetry.

Analogy.
   I look at the reality, at London stream, and dirt, mud, power, and then I think of the pale shadowy analogy that is used without thinking by the automatic philosophers, the 'stream of time'. The people who treat words without reverence, who use analogies without thinking of them: let us always remember that solid real stream and the flat thin voice of the metaphysician, '*the stream of time*'.

   Extended clay. Looking at the Persian Gulf on a map and imagining the mud shore at night.
   Pictures of low coasts of any country. We are all just above the sea.
   Delight in perceiving the real cinder construction in a port. Upon mud as distinct from the clear-cut harbour on the map.
   Travel is education in cinders; the merchants in Hakluyt, and the difference in song. (When we are all gathered together and when we are in a book.)
   The road leading over the prairie, at dusk, with the half-breed. Travel helps one to discover the undiscovered portions of one's own mind. Scenes like the red dance leap to the centre of the mind there to synthesize what before was perhaps unknown.
   Must see these different manifestations of the cinders; otherwise we cannot work the extended clay.

   A melancholy spirit, the mind like a great desert lifeless, and the sound of march music in the street, passes like a wave over the desert, unifies it, but then goes.

Notes on Language and Style

[This collection of notes—jotted down in Hulme's hand on over 100 sheets of paper in *c*.1907—is now housed at the University of Keele Library. Although there are several pages of tentative outlines by Hulme, the material was never put into final form or published during his lifetime. After Hulme's death, Herbert Read published about half the collection, first in July 1925, in T. S. Eliot's journal, the *Criterion*, and then in 1929, in the University of Washington Chapbook series. Michael Roberts published a more complete version in 1938 in *T. E. Hulme*, and Samuel Hynes reprinted the Roberts version in *FS* (1955). The version reproduced here generally follows the order in Roberts, but the individual notes have been restored to the more fragmentary, disjointed form in which Hulme left them. Also, a few notes have been emended where there was some variation from the Hulme manuscript. Titles which seem to have been added by Read or Roberts are enclosed in square brackets.]

[NOTES FOR A] PREFACE

I believe that while the world cosmically cannot be reduced to unity as science proclaims (in the postulate of uniformity), yet on the contrary poetry can. At least its methods follow certain easily defined routes. (Anyone can be taught how to use poetry.)

Real work, history and scientific researches, the accidental, the excrescences, like digging, and necessary just as digging is. Poetry the permanent humanity, the expression of man freed from his digging, digging for poetry when it is over.

[CLUMSINESS OF PROSE—RELATION OF LANGUAGE AND THE IDEA EXPRESSED]

Analysis of the attitude of a man reading an argument

(i) Compare in algebra, the real things are replaced by symbols. These symbols are manipulated according to certain laws which are independent of their meaning.

N.B. At a certain point in the proof we cease to think of x as having a meaning and look upon it as a mere counter to be manipulated.

(ii) An analogous phenomenon happens in reasoning in language. We replace meaning (i.e. *vision*) by words. These words fall into well-known patterns, i.e. into certain well-known phrases which we accept without thinking of their meaning, just as we do the x in algebra.

But there is a constant movement above and below the line of meaning (representation).[1] And this is used in dialectical argument. At any stage we can ask the opponent to show his hand, that is to turn all his *words* into visions, in realities we can see.

[Seeing 'solid' things]

One facet of the idea may be expressed in this way. Refer back to note on the use of x in arithmetic and its analogy in expression.

Habitually we may say that the reader takes words as x *without* the meaning attached.

Aphra sees each word with an image sticking on to it, never a flat word passed over a board like a counter.

Perhaps the nearest analogy is the hairy caterpillar. Taking each segment of his body as a word, the hair on that segment is the vision the poet sees behind it.

It is difficult to do this, so that the poet is forced to use new analogies, and especially to construct a plaster model of a thing to express his emotion at the sight of the vision he sees, his wonder and ecstasy. If he employed the ordinary word, the reader would only see it as a segment, with no hair, used for getting along. And without this clay, spatial image, he does not feel that he has expressed at all what he sees.

The ordinary caterpillar for crawling along from one position to another.

The hairy one for beauty, to build up a solid vision of realities.

All emotion depends on real solid vision or sound. It is physical.

But in *rhetoric* and expositional prose we get words divorced from any real vision.

Rhetoric and emotion—here the connection is different.

So perhaps literary expression is from *Real to Real* with all the intermediate forms keeping their *real* value.

In expositional reasoning, the intermediate terms have only counter value.

Give an example of *counter* prose (boy's letter to paper).

Watching a class: the difference between their attitude to geography and that to mathematics. Probably having only spatial imagination, the geography is quite clear and comprehensible. If the mathematics could be got into the same flat form upon a map, with only relative distances to be observed, then their difficulties would vanish.

This suggests that the type of all reasoning is that of arranging counters on the flat, where they can be moved about, without the mind having to think in any involved way. (cf. this with note in the old book,[2] about chess-board.)

The ideal of modern prose is to be all counters, i.e. to pass to conclusions without thinking.

Visual Poetry

Each *word* must be an image *seen*, not a counter.

That dreadful feeling of cheapness when we contemplate the profusion of words of modern prose.

The true ideal—the little statue in Paris.

The contrast between (i) a firm simple prose, creating in a definite way a fairy story, a story of simple life in the country (in the old country). Here we have the microcosm of poetry. The pieces picked out from which it comes. Sun and sweat and all of them. Physical life and death fairies. And (ii) on the other hand, genteel poetry like Shelley's, which refers in elaborate analogies to the things mentioned in (i).

Gibbering ghosts and Morris's tales seem *real*, as (i). Transmigration of souls seems a drawing-room thrill, compounded of good-will and long words.

Style

With perfect style, the solid leather for reading, each sentence should be a lump, a piece of clay, a vision seen; rather, a wall touched with soft fingers.

Never should one feel light vaporous bridges between one solid sense and another. No bridges—all solid: then never exasperated.

A man cannot write without seeing at the same time a visual signification before his eyes. It is this image which precedes the writing and makes it firm.

The piece from Morris as an example of poetry always being a solid thing. Seen but not words.

Criticism

Rising disgust and impatience with the talking books, e.g. Lilly[3] and the books about Life, Science, and Religion. All the books which seem to be the kind of talk one could do if one wished.

Rather choose those in old leather, which are *solid*.

Here the man did not talk, but saw solid, definite things and described them.

Solidity a pleasure.

It is seeing the real clay, that men in an agony worked with, that gives pleasure. To read a book which is *real clay* moulded by fingers that had to mould something, or they would clutch the throat of their maddened author. *No* flowing on of words, but tightly clutched tense fingers leaving marks in the clay.

These are the only books that matter—and where are they to be found?

Style short, being forced by the coming together of many different thoughts, and generated by their contact. Fire struck between stones.

[*Mechanism of Creation*]

Get rid of the idea that out of vacuo can come writing.

Generally following certain practical ends, we throw out writing—comes out as the one in the many.

Not as a pure intellectual machine.

A cindery thing done, not a pure thought made manifest in some counter-like way.

The idea is nothing: it is the holding on to the idea, through the absolutely transforming influence of putting it into definiteness. The holding on through waves.

That extraordinary difficulty in shaping any material, in moving from the idea to the matter. Seen even in simple matters like going to the tailor's. The difference between the idea and the choice. Material is never plastic.

The extraordinary difficulty of the living material.

Seen in everything, even in railway meetings, in people, in everything. Write essay on it.

The resistance of the ὕλη ἐνεργής.[4]

The process of invention is that of gradually making solid the castles in the air.

Self-delusion

    (i) Whence comes the excitement, the delusion of thinker's creation?

    (ii) All inventions spring from the *idea*, e.g. Flaubert and the *purple* bases of Madame Bovary.

    (iii) I have a *central* idea like that quite *unworked* out into detail.

I see a book *worked out* from the same central idea and I unconsciously imagine that I have worked it out myself, and that I could
easily have been the author.

t in the working out is required the multiplicity of detail that
ck. The central idea is nothing.

come to think that all expression is vulgar, that only the
d and silent . . .

logies]

w phrases made in poetry, tested, and then employed in prose.
poetry they are all glitter and new coruscation, in prose useful
not noticed.
se a museum where all the old weapons of poetry kept.
try always the advance guard in language. The progress of
guage is the absorption of new analogies. (Scout, so nearest to
and real basic condition of life.)

(I)
are only means of subduing the reader.

putting in the 'finer touches', it expresses what I mean by the
refinement of language.

But the damnable thing is that if I use that phrase to another person, it
produces no equal effect on him. It is one of the rounded counters of
language and so has the least possible meaning. What to me is an entirely
physical thing, a real clay before me, moulded, an image, is when used
nothing but an expression like 'in so far, etc.'.

The pity is that in this all the *meaning* goes.

A word to me is a board with an image or statue on it.

When I pass the word, all that goes is the board, the statue remains in
my imagination.

Transfer physical to language

Dome of Brompton in the mist.

Transfer that to art. Dead things not men as the material of art.
Everything for art is a thing in itself, cf. the café at Clapham as a thing in
itself.

And the words moved until they became a dome, a solid, separate
world, a dome in a mist, a thing of terror beyond us, and not of us.
Definite heaven above worshippers, incense hides foundations. A definite
force majeure (all the foundations of the scaffolding are in us, but we want

an illusion, falsifying us, something independent of foundations). A long pillar.

Aphra took the words, and they grew into a round smooth pillar and the child wondered and the merchant caused.

Putting a few bricks together to imitate the shape of a dome, but the mist effect, the transformation in words, has the art of pushing it through the door.

Example of Plastic Imagination

The two tarts walking along Piccadilly on tiptoe, going home, with hat on back of head. Worry until could find the exact model analogy that will reproduce the extraordinary effect they produce.

Could be done at once by an artist in a blur.

The air of absolute detachment, of being things in themselves. Objects of beauty with the qualification as the basis of it. Disinterestedness, as though saying: We may have evolved painfully from the clay, and be the last leaf on a tree. But now we have cut ourselves away from that. We are things-in-themselves. We exist out of time.[5]

Language (I)

(i) Delightful sensation of power in looking at it, as a vehicle, a machine whose ages we can see. The relics of the extravagant fancies and analogies of dead and forgotten poets.

Regard each word as a picture, then a succession of pictures. Only the dead skeleton remains. We cut the leaves off. When the tree becomes a mast, the leaves become unnecessary. But now only the thick lines matter, and the accompanying pictures are forgotten.

(ii) An agricultural implement. Philosophy expressed in farmer's language. All the predominant metaphors are naturally agricultural, e.g. field of thought, flood, stream. Keep present in mind when we look at nature, the curious place of language which is founded on it and *subordinate* to it. When I see a stream now (such as Waterloo Bridge) I imagine it carrying down with it the impermeable language and the *begriffe*[6] of philosophy.

If only the making and fixing of words had begun in the city stage in the evolution of society and not in the nomadic.

(But ideas expressed would have been the same. So thought and language not identical.)

Language (II)

The fallacy that language is logical, or that meaning is. Phrases have meaning for no reason, cf. with nature of truth.

(i) The metaphysical theory. Watching a woman in the street. Is the idea expressed anything like so——

(ii) The idea is just as real as a landscape and there is the same difficulty in getting it on to paper.

Each word is a different twist to it. Something added.

Each of the 50 possible sentences that will express it changes its character.

(iii) Another question: growing conviction of the Solidity of Ideas, as opposed to language.

Very often the idea, apart from the analogy or metaphor which clothes it, has no existence.

That is, by a subtle combination of allusions we have artificially built up in us an idea, which apart from these, cannot be got at.

As if a man took us on a rocky path and said look—and we saw the view. i.e. the analogy is the thing, not merely decoration.

i.e. there is no such thing as.

Language (III)

Large clumsy instrument.

Language does not naturally come with meaning. Ten different ways of forming the same sentence. Any style will do to get the meaning down (without childish effect). There is *no* inevitable simple style as there ought to be.

Language a cumbrous growth, a compound of old and new analogies. Does this apply to thought? Is there *no* simple thought, but only styles of thought?

Poetry is neither more nor less than a mosaic of words, so great exactness required for each one.

Language (IV)

(i) Thought is prior to language and consists in the simultaneous presentation to the mind of two different images.

(ii) Language is only a more or less feeble way of doing this.

(iii) All the connections in language, this term including not only prepositions, but all phrases (ready made), which only indicate the precise relation or attitude or politeness between the two simultaneously presented images.

(iv) Connect this with the old scorn, denoted by the black edge theory, cf. *Rue de la limite*. And hence see the solution of the difficulty, and the use of words for literary purposes, always inferior.

Thought

As merely the discovery of new analogies, when useful and sincere, and not mere paradoxes.

The things bring a kind of going straight, write them as analogy and call it literature, cf. marching in step, the great procession (analogy of creative and sexual pleasure).

Creation

Thought is the joining together of new analogies, and so inspiration is a matter of an accidentally seen analogy or unlooked-for resemblance. It is therefore necessary to get as large as possible change in sense impressions, cf. looking in shop windows, and war-game. The more change of shapes and sights there is the more chance of inspiration. Thoughts won by walking.

Fertility of invention means: remembrance of accidental occurrences *noted* and arranged. (Cf. detective stories.)

Expression (II)

Think of sitting at that window in Chelsea and seeing the chimneys and the lights in the dusk.

And then imagine that by contemplation this will transfer itself bodily onto paper.

This is the direct opposite of literature, which is never an absorption and meditation.

But a deliberate choosing and working-up of analogies. The continued close, compressed effort.

The demand for clear logical expression is impossible, as it would confine us to the use of flat counter-images only.

If you only admit that form of manipulating images as good, if you deny all the other grasps, hands, for the cinders, all solid images, all patterns, then you can be clear, but not otherwise.

Expression (III)

(i) People who think, pen in hand. Like people who write at twenty, for *Eton College Chronicle*. Writers first, and then afterwards perhaps find thought.

(ii) Think in air. And then years afterwards acquire knack of writing.

Expression (IV)

The chessboard of language expression, where the two players put down counters one after the other. And the player who became interested in the pieces themselves and carved them, and gazed at them in a kind of ecstasy.

Humour and Expression

A joke analysed and viewed as the decadent form into which all forms of literary expression can be shown to pass by degeneration of function (a suitable analogy for this).

(i) The surprise at the end. Resembles novel building.
(ii) Analogies in poetry, like the likenesses of babies, to be taken half seriously, with a smile.

[CONTEMPT FOR LANGUAGE]

Black Border

Enlightenment when first see that literature is not a vision, but a voice, or a line of letters in a black border.

Vision the sight of the quaint shadows in things, of the lone trees on the hill, and the hills in life; not the deed, but the shadow cast by the deed.

The art of literature consists exactly in this *passage from the Eye to the Voice*. From the wealth of nature to that *thin* shadow of words, that gramophone. The Readers are the people who *see* things and want them expressed. The author is the Voice, or the conjuror who does tricks with that curious rope of letters, which is quite different from real passion and sight.

The Prose writer drags meaning along with the rope.

The Poet makes it stand on end and hit you.

All literature as accident, a happy escape from platitude.

Nothing new under the sun.

Literature like pitching, how to throw phrases about, to satisfy a demand.

An exercise for the time being, no eternal body of knowledge to be added to.

So learn phrases 'ringed with gold', 'in a lens', etc.

To excite certain mild feelings of delight in the reader, to produce a pleasant warm feeling in the brain as phrases run along.

[Prose]

A sentence and a worm are the most stupid of animals and the most difficult to teach tricks.

Tendency to crawl along requires genius, music to make them stand up (snake charmer).

The dreadful limitations of all—so many lines. So many images enclosed in a black border.

The uncomfortable vision of all prose as merely a line of string lying on a paper. The impossibility of getting mystery into that.

Must invent new method to do that.

Words seen as physical thing like a piece of string. e.g. walking on dark boulevard. Girl hidden in trees passes on other side. How to get this.

Always a border round, to isolate the sentence as a thing in itself, a living worm to be taught tricks.

Words

In thinking of the uselessness of words, coming between.

The residue left when each long word employed.

But different for description of emotions. Here exactly what is the new role of words.

Perhaps here the structure can be described as emotion essentially. A personal thing (though of itself in words).

[FACILITY IN MANIPULATION]

[*Phrases*]

Two people sitting talking at table.

Delight in having counters ready to hand. (French.)

Must not be taught how to *make* counters but a list of them.

(i) Collection of phrases. Words fit in and out of phrases. A *cadre* for grammar.

Impossibility of grammar because can't think of end of sentence first.

Learn list of sentences then fix grammar for them as do in English. Get grammar by ear.

(ii) No language but collection of phrases, but phrases on *different* subjects.

One wanders as over a country. No fixed guide for everything.

Start Good morning.

(iii) All one tense for past. *Je suis allé.*

Sentences

As units.

Each separated in one line in order to get effect and to analyse.

Given a large *vocabulary of sentence units*, not of words, we are fluent and can express what we want.

For practice. Write all sentences separately.

Model sentences learnt perfectly. Perhaps 3 or 4 in each Berlitz lesson.

Gradually get a definite *armoury* of sentences which will help you and be sufficient to you in conversation.

Phrases the oil without which all previous knowledge useless.

Physical need some people have to be able to make a comment, to exchange comments. Hence proverbs are the most popular authors. cf. with reading in W.C.

Never, never, never a simple statement. It has no effect. Always must have analogies, which make an other-world, through-the-glass effect, which is what I want.

Danger that when all these notes are arranged, the order will kill them in commonplace. When isolated at least there is hope they suggest great unities, which I am at any rate at present quite unable to carry out.

All theories of how to teach a language, all in the air, all null and void, if *each day* you do not learn at your finger's-ends some new phrases.

One *new word* and ten phrases as to how to employ it.

Reading gives knowledge only of roots.

Speaking and *list* method gives word in all its practical uses.

Each night. What new phrases. What new *cadres* for the word I already know?

Question of preposition etc. at end of sentence. *Il le faut le faire payer.* Do we think of end first?

In learning foreign language and teaching your own, learn how little is your knowledge of your own. Hesitating for a phrase in your own language. Very few of us learn all the *possible phrases* in our own language, and we must have them all at the tips of our fingers to write well.

So adapt same method to *English.*

Read and Read, and copy the phrases like the one about 'microscopic detail magnified'.

Language (French)

Living language is a house.

School grammar is book telling you how to build one (if had time).

First more useful when rain stops.

School grammar is learning at *lowest* level.

Can retire from the work of memory into one single rule, like spider out of sight, but cannot return quickly to speak.

[THE IMAGINARY WORLD AND
A STANDARD OF MEANING]

Imaginary World (Relation to World)
Literature always possible.
Compared with peasant, it only deals with imaginary world.
Even my attempt to get to reality (no long words) is in the end only another adjustment of the imaginary toy.
Fields left unaltered.
Literary people work in imaginary land which all of us carry about in desert moments.

Analogy
Not sufficient to find analogies.
It is necessary to find those that add something to each, and give a sense of wonder, a sense of being united in another mystic world.

The Standard
One must have something to overawe the *reader*. The fact outside him, e.g. in boasting. Take case of '*Oh, Richard, oh mon roi*'.

Expression
All literature and poetry is life seen in a mirror; it must be absolutely removed from reality, and can never be attained.

The exact relation between the expression and the inside image:
  (i) Expression obviously partakes of the nature of cinders, cf. Red girl dancing.
  (ii) But on the other hand, vague hell image common to everybody makes an infinite of limited *hard* expression.

> Over a large table, smooth, he leaned in ecstasies,
> In a dream.
> He had been to woods, and talked and walked with trees
> Had left the world
> And brought back round globes and stone images
> Of gems, colours, hard and definite.
> With these he played, in a dream,
> On the smooth table.

(cf. the red dancer in his head.)

Expression (Metaphysical)
A red dancer on the stage.
A built-up complex of cinders so not due to any primeval essence.

Cinders as foundations for (i) philosophy (ii) aesthetics.

The old controversy as to which is greater, the mind or the material in art.

Each dancer on the stage with her effects and her suggestions of intensity of meaning which are not possible, is not herself (that is a very cindery thing) but a synthesized state of mind in me. The red moving figure is a way of grouping some ideas together, just as powerful a means as the one called logic which is only an analogy to *counter-pushing*.

This can be considered more seriously. A picture like this, the cosmic dance, fading away into the margin (this the basis of all art), not [this][7] which gives the limitations, the furniture, etc.

Must be imaginary world. Trick it out with fancies. Analogies must be substituted for what suggests something, a cloud of fancies, e.g. Waterloo Bridge in the early morning.

The only intellectual pleasure in recognising old friends.

   (i) At a race. Look first and see the horses in the paper described. Then excited about result.
  (ii) Picture gallery. (a) recognition of *names*. (b) progress to recognition of characteristics. Galleries full of strange names no interest.
 (iii) Climate and landscape. The only pleasure in comparison, e.g. Waterloo Bridge and Canada by the river in the morning.

Ideal

Typical phenomena—the yellow girl leaning from the window in the morning. The Baptist meeting seen through the drawing-room window in the evening.

For the first, if it reminds me of an expressible vague something, I must first have been educated into the idea that there was such a vague something.

Observe this something is quite different to the emotional crises of ordinary people when they speak of love and hate.

There must be something on which we can hang our hat.

Better something on which, when for a surging moment we have a feeling (really the cinders drunk for a minute) there must be something to which we can *refer* it.

Literature as the building-up of this *state of reference*. Must avoid the word, the Ideal, like a plague, for it suggests easy comprehension where there is no easy comprehension.

It is used by Baptist young men to mean quite other things, it has *moral* contamination.

Ideas Staged

In a sense all ideals must be divorced, torn away from the reality where we found them and put on a stage. They must appear separate and far from all dirt and laughter at their low and common relations. They must be posed and moved dramatically, and above all their gestures must express their emotions. This is the art of literature, the making of this *other* world.

They must wear high-heeled shoes which make them appear free movers, and not sprung from that low thing Earth. The separation of the high heel and the powdered face is essential to all emotions, in order to make a work of art.

[*Intensity of Meaning*]

'By thine agony and bloody sweat.' By common effort, all this many times repeated, gives an *intensity of meaning*.

This 'intensity of meaning' is what is sought for.

Christian Mystics and Physical Expression

Read them as analogous with own temper.

For the expression of states of soul by elaborate physical landscape analogies, cf. my own walking in the evening by the Thames. Also the Neo-Platonic philosophers.

It is the physical analogies that hold me, true kindred spirits in that age, in own poetry, not the *vain* decorative and verbal images of the ordinary poets.

Feminine Form

The beauty of the feminine form, which came to be looked upon even by the halest of the four, as a typical vesture or symbol of Beauty herself, and perhaps also as the 'sovran shrine' of Melancholy.

Rossetti saw the spiritual element in face and form, and desired the spirit through his desire of the body, and at last did not know the one desire from the other, and pressed on, true mystic as he was, in ever-narrowing circles, to some third thing that seemed to lie behind both desires.

'Soul is form and doth the body make.'

Eye blur

Tennyson seems to have waited for his expression to come to him—to have brooded before a scene with its orchestra of sounds, in a kind of intense passiveness—until the thing beheld *became greatly different from what it was at any other moment or to any other man.*

DWELLING ON A POINT

Perhaps the difficulty that is found in expressing an idea, in making it long, in dwelling on it, by means of all kinds of analogy, has its roots in the nature of ideas and thought itself.

Dancing as the art of prolonging an idea, lingering on a point.

This clearly seen gives the relation between the author's and the reader's position. Both can see the points (as visions in their heads). e.g. Moore's hypostatization of the ideas as real. But I am quite unable to dwell on this point at the length of ten pages.

The author is the man who dwells on a point for the edification of the reader, and for his pleasure, thus prolonging the pleasure and luxury of thought in the mind of the reader.

Method: (i) quotation; (ii) analogies from all possible subjects.

The art of *dwelling on, drunken* ecstasy on one point.
Whole essence of poetry.

Gradually one learns the art of dwelling on a point, of decorating it, of transforming it, until it produces in the reader the sense of novelty.

Write down examples:

(i) Prose—of making a tremendous deal out of a point which can be noted down in one sentence. But perhaps the sentence only represents it to the writer. To get the same effect on the reader as it produces on him, he must work it up into a froth, like stirring eggs.

(ii) Dwelling on a point in poetry. The main function of analogy in poetry is to enable one to dwell and linger upon a point of excitement. To achieve the impossible and convert a point into a line. This can only be done by having ready-made lines in our heads, and so getting at the result by analogy.

The inner psychology of a poet at such a creative moment is like that of a drunkard who pushes his hand forward along a table, with an important gesture, and remains there pondering over it. In that relaxing gesture of pushing comes the inner psychology of all these moments.

[READER AND WRITER]

Personal

The popular idea of poet as in communion with the infinite, cf. account of Yeats walking in the woods, but remember Tennyson and his hair. (The deed and poem always greater than the man.)

The rubbish that authors write in their casual moments, when they talk. We haven't heard the kind of interview Shelley and Keats would have given.

Reason why Whitman did not go to the gold fields and become a frontiersman actually, his hatred of the particular, and desire to be the average American citizen, desire to find romance even in Brooklyn. Often at theatre, and a journalist and carpenter. When had made money would go for long holidays in the woods and by the sea. Always seen on bus-tops.

The bodily activity and position most favourable to thought requires coolness, comfort, and a table, a strenuous effort.
Can't think without words or pencil.

Object and Readers of Poetry
Poetry after all for the amusement of bankers and other sedentary arm-chair people in after-dinner moods. No other. (Not for inspiration of progress.)
(For one person in a thousand hence uselessness of school teaching.)
So no infinite nobleness and function about that.

Impossible to learn anything new in ideas from a book. Must be there beforehand, then joy in recognising it. But every book read is in some sense a disappointment, something you had previously found out for yourself.

Entirely modern view of poet as something greater than a statesman, cf. Frederic the Great.
In old days merely to amuse warrior and after banquet.

(i) amuse banker.
(ii) for use of clerks in love to send to sweethearts.
(iii) temporary moods (in theatres) of cultivated artificial people.
(iv) songs of war.

Author and Reader
Just as Aristotle asserts that Matter the unlimited contains Forms embedded in it, and that they are not thrust upon it from some ideal world, so all the effects that can be produced by the literary man (here assuming his apprenticeship and marshalling of isolated moments to produce a mystic separation, aided by old metaphors), are to be found dormant, unused in the reader, and are thus awakened.

[*The Reader*]

The new art of the Reader. (i) The relation between banker and poetry. (ii) Sympathy with reader as brother, as *unexpressed* author.

Literature a method of sudden arrangement of commonplaces. The *suddenness* makes us forget the commonplace.

Complete theory, what was thought, in the old book, of relations between the poet and the reader seen suddenly at a glance in listening to boys going home from music-hall whistling a song. Chelsea Palace.

Here a new way (a mental dance) found for them of synthesizing certain of their own emotions. (Even so with personal psychological poetry, mere putting down is for the reader a form of expression.)

Always seek the causes of these phenomena in their lowest elements— their lowest terms, i.e. literati in Chelsea.

[*The Writer*]

The effort of the literary man to find subtle analogies for the ordinary street feelings he experiences, leads to the differentiation and importance of those feelings. What would be unnoticed by others, and is nothing when not labelled becomes an important emotion. A transitory artificial impression is deliberately cultivated into an emotion and written about. Reason here creates and modifies an emotion, e.g. standing at street corners. Hence the sudden joy these produce in the reader when he remembers a half-forgotten impression. 'How true!'

What is the difference between people who can write literature and people who can merely appreciate it. The faculty of disillusionment and cynicism, of giving the show away, possessed by readers. What is the necessary quality for creation?

Literary man always first completely disillusioned and then deliberately and purposely creative of illusions.

A writer always a feeble, balanced, artificial kind of person. The mood is cultivated feeling all the time.

The vibrant and tense fingers, drawing up rhythm, which one knows could be broken at any moment by anyone coming into the room.

Do these doubts, as to authors, vitiate in any way the work they produce?

Poetry not for others, but for the poet. Nature infinite, but personality finite, rough, and incomplete. Gradually built up.

Poet's mood vague and passes away, indefinable. The poem he makes selects, builds up, and makes even his own mood more definite to him. Expression builds up personality.

The life of the literary man being always aiming at the production of these artificial deliberate poises in himself, and so at the creation of his own chess-board.

But what of the relation of this to ordinary life and people? They have their own hereditary (sentimental) chess-boards, which remain the same until changed by the survival of some of those of the literary man. The earnest striving after awkward and new points of view, such as that from a balloon, the useful seen from the non-useful attitude.

Literature as red counters moving on a chess-board, life as gradual shifting of cinders, and occasional consciousness.

Unfortunately can now see the trick, can see the author working his counters for the peroration. So very few more possible enthusiasms left. Grit and toothache still to be in any heaven or Utopia.

Literature as entirely the deliberate standing still, hovering and thinking oneself into an artificial view, for the moment, and not effecting any real actions at all. Sunsets no consolation in harvest-field. (Lovers' sentimental fancies in letters.)

A POEM

It was formerly my idea that a poem was made somewhat as follows. The poet, in common with many other people, occasionally experienced emotions which strangely moved him. In the case of the greengrocer this was satisfied by reading Tennyson and sending the lines he seemed to have experienced to his beloved. The poet on the contrary tried to find new images to express what he felt. These lines and vague collections of words he gradually built up into poems. But this I now see to be wrong; the very act of trying to find a form to fit the separate phrases into, itself leads to the creation of new images hitherto not felt by the poet. In a sense the poetry writes itself. This creation by happy chance is analogous to the accidental stroke of the brush which creates a new beauty not previously consciously thought of by the artist.

The form of a poem is shaped by the intention, vague phrases containing ideas which at past moments have strongly moved us. As the purpose of the poem is narrative or emotional the phrases become altered. The choice of a form is as important as the individual pieces and scraps of emotion of which the poem is made up. In the actual making accidental phrases are hit upon. Just as musician in striking notes on piano comes across what he wants, the painter on the canvas, so the poet not only gets the phrases he wants, but even from the words gets a *new* image.

Creative effort means *new* images. (Lobster and me.) The accidental discovery of effect, not conscious intellectual endeavour for it.

The theory that puts all phrases in a box and years later starts to arrange *all wrong*.

Don't.

Start creating *at once*, and in this very process new ideas spring up, accidentally.

So *condemn* card system, red tape leads to nothing.

The living method of arranging at once in temporary note-books.

[CROWDS]

Drama

The effect produced by multitude (i) one by one as they left the hall; (ii) policemen's dance.

Actors can add to a comedy. All gestures unreal, but add to comedy and subtract and annoy in tragedy.

Music

Fortuitous assemblage of noises.

The mechanical model, music seen for an instant once during a hymn as smooth rolling.[8]

Conductor's baton and foundation in body rhythm.

Music in its power of seeming to hold an audience or crowd together into an organism. When plays low in park the atmosphere seems to fall to pieces and crowd becomes units again. Cf. Band and Bard.

Sound a fluid beaten up by conductor.

Breaking of waves. Listening is like the motion in a ship.

Big Crowds

(i) Not found in streets which are routes, except in those which are meeting-places, as Oxford Street.
(ii) The old market-places, the gymnasia of the Greeks, Plato, and the pretty youths.
(iii) Churches and theatres to catch the prolific mood. Davidson and railway stations.
(iv) Secular churches in street, to sit, rest and look.

[BEAUTY, IMITATION, AND ECSTASY]

Tradition

Poetry always founded on tradition.

So light-haired woman with upturned face in Regent Street.

A bright moon in dark sky over Paddington.

All books, history, etc., after all only a record of the opinions of a class, the artificial moments and poses of literary men.

The other classes and little worlds inarticulate (cf. villages).

When artistic impressions of miners and artisans seen (Millet) they do not in any way have anything to do with the emotions of the miner, do not in any way dignify his life. Are only blurs in light and shade. There is no *depth* in the mirror.

Poetry as neither more or less than a nuance of words, so great exactness required of each one.

Art a point of view like literature, a selection.

Beauty

Art creates beauty (not art copies the beauty in nature: beauty does not exist by itself in nature, waiting to be copied, only organised pieces of cinders). Origin of this view, course of etchings has made cranes and chimneys at night seem beautiful.

Landscape makes the ordinary man think pieces of wood beautiful. 'Just like a picture.'

So one purpose of art to make people like the merely healthy. Necessary to correct false bias in favour of guilt. Plain steel. (Should make all art seem beautiful.)

Beauty is usefulness seen from another point (cf. distant railway line, *not* the one you yourself are on).

Point of view above, bird's eye, because *New*.

The waiting engine in the trees, *one* line, red light, like animal waiting to kill.

Culture seeks romantic in far regions.

Seeks passions and tragedies in peasants. Tolstoy.

Then sees it in prostitutes.

Why not abandon it all and take supernatural for art.

Whitman had a theory that every object under the sun comes within the range of poetry.

But he was too early in the day.

No use having a theory that motor-cars are beautiful, and backing up this theory by working up emotion not really felt.

Object must cause the emotion before poem can be written. Whitman's theory, that everything in America must be glorious, was his snare, because it was only a theory.

Minor poets, with their romantic jewels, make same mistake from other side—a lost poetic content. Lexicon of beautiful is elastic, but walla-walla not yet poetically possible.

Continual effort necessary to think of things as they are, the constraint necessary to avoid great tendencies to use big words and common phrases without meaning. Cf. Nietzsche and his ambition to say everything in a paragraph.

Imitation

Tendency to begin a tale 'It began in the E. M. restaurant' and similarly in poems. The imitation makes one imagine that one is producing stuff of the same calibre and the same effect on other people.

Stupid little poems about flowers and spring, imitations. No *new* emotion in them. Or the infinitely fascinating man (fiction), cf. G. Moore's novels, the infinitely beautiful woman.

Poetasters write in metre because poets have done so, poets because singing, not talking, is the obvious mode of expressing ecstasy. Whitman went wrong through deficiency of selective process. Even Turner had to shroud his railway train in vapour.

What is the exact difference which would be produced if chess or cinders were stated by Andrew Lang. How is the childishness made to disappear? Perhaps they don't state a thing baldly but hint at rounder and counter-like figures behind it.

People anxious to be literary men think there is no work, just as haymaking—but just as monotonous grinding it out. Concerned in the field with ecstasy, but the pains of birth and parturition are sheets and sheets of paper.

W. B. Yeats attempts to ennoble his craft by strenuously believing in supernatural world, race-memory, magic, and saying that symbols can recall these where prose couldn't. This an attempt to bring in an infinity again.

Truth that occasionally have moments of poetic feelings in W.C. and other places, banging of doors, etc.

The beauty of London only seen in detached and careful moments, never continuously, always a conscious ·effort. On top of a bus, or the sweep of the avenue in Hyde Park. But to appreciate this must be in some manner detached, e.g. wearing workmen's clothes (when not shabby but different in kind) then opportunity for conscious reflection. It is the stranger that sees the romantic and the beautiful in the commonplace, cf. in New York, or in strange city, detached and therefore able to see beauty and romance.

Moments of enthusiasm due to a selection seen as a possible *continuously* happy future.

All attempts at beauty necessarily consciously made, open to reaction of the man who talks of 'nature', etc.

Life as a rule tedious, but certain things give us sudden lifts.

Poetry comes with the jumps, cf. love, fighting, dancing. The moments of ecstasy.

Literature, like memory, selects only the vivid patches of life. The art of abstraction. If literature (realistic) did really resemble life, it would be interminable, dreary, commonplace, eating and dressing, buttoning, with here and there a patch of vividness. Zola merely selects an interesting group of sordid pieces.

Life composed of exquisite moments and the rest shadows of them.

The *gaps*—hence chess.

Drink

They followed the road with the knowledge that they were soaring along in a supporting medium, possessed of original and profound thoughts, themselves and surrounding nature forming an organism of which all the parts harmoniously and joyously interpenetrate each other.

Heroes occasionally, drink influence only for a time like effect of church or music.

The literary man deliberately perpetrates a hypocrisy, in that he fits together his own isolated moments of ecstasy (and generally deliberate use of big words without personal meaning attached) and presents them as a picture of higher life, thereby giving old maids a sense of superiority to other people and giving mandarins the opportunity to talk of 'ideals'. Then makes attempt to justify himself by inventing the soul and saying that occasionally the lower world gets glimpses of this, and that inferentially he is the medium. As a matter of fact being certain moments of ecstasy perhaps brought on by drink. Surely obvious that drink and drugs have nothing to do with a higher world (cf. Q. and his little safe yacht, a kind of mechanical ladder to the soul world).

All theories as toys.

Literary
Criticism

A Lecture on Modern Poetry

[Probably presented to the Poets' Club, London, in Nov. 1908. Although the lecture is undated, Ronald Schuchard has shown that Hulme's opening criticism probably refers to an unsigned review of five recent poetry books in the *Saturday Review* of 14 Nov. 1908. See '"As Regarding Rhythm": Yeats and the Imagists', in *Yeats: An Annual of Critical and Textual Studies*, vol. 2 (1984). The lecture was never published during Hulme's lifetime. The typescript, with corrections in Hulme's hand, is at the University of Keele Library, and is the source of this version. Except for some minor differences in punctuation and spelling, it is virtually the same as the versions published in Roberts, *T. E. Hulme*, and in *FS* 67–76.]

I want to begin by a statement of the attitude I take towards verse. I do that in order to anticipate criticism. I shall speak of verse from a certain rather low but quite definite level and I think that criticism ought to be confined to that level. The point of view is that verse is simply and solely the means of expression. I will give you an example of the position exactly opposite to the one I take up. A reviewer writing in *The Saturday Review* last week spoke of poetry as the means by which the soul soared into higher regions and as a means of expression by which it became merged into a higher kind of reality. Well, that is the kind of statement that I utterly detest. I want to speak of verse in a plain way as I would of pigs: that is the only honest way. The President[1] told us last week that poetry was akin to religion. It is nothing of the sort. It is a means of expression just as prose is and if you can't justify it from that point of view it's not worth preserving.

I always suspect the word soul when it is brought into discussion. It reminds me of the way that the medieval scientists spoke of God. When entirely ignorant of the cause of anything they said God did it. If I use the word soul, or speak of higher realities, in the course of my speech, you will know that at that precise point I didn't know of any real reason and was trying to bluff you. There is a tremendous amount of hocus pocus about most discussions of poetry. Critics attempting to explain technique make mysterious passes and mumble of the infinite and the human heart, for all the world as though they were selling a patent medicine in the market-place.

There are two ways in which one can consider this. The first as a difficulty to be conquered, the second as a tool for use. In the first case we look upon poets as we look upon pianists, and speak of them as masters of verse. The other way is to consider it merely as a tool which we want to use ourselves for definite purposes. One daily paper compared us to the Mermaid Club but we are not. We are a number of modern people, and verse must be justified as a means of expression for us. I have not a catholic taste but a violently personal and prejudiced one. I have no reverence for tradition. I came to the subject of verse from the inside rather than from the outside. There were certain impressions which I wanted to fix. I read verse to find models but I could not find any that seemed exactly suitable to express that kind of impression, except perhaps a few jerky rhythms of Henley,[2] until I came to read the French *vers-libre*, which seemed to exactly fit the case.

So that I don't want any literary criticism, that would be talking on another level. I don't want to be killed with a bludgeon and references to Dante, Milton and the rest of them.

The principle on which I rely in this paper is that there is an intimate connection between the verse form and the state of poetry at any period. All kinds of reasons are given by the academic critics for the efflorescence of verse at any period. But the true one is very seldom given. It is the invention or introduction of a new verse form. To the artist the introduction of a new art form is, as Moore says, like a new dress to a girl; he wants to see himself in it. It is a new toy. You will find the burst of poetic activity at the time of Elizabeth put down to the discovery of America. The discovery of America had about as much effect on the Courtier poets at that time as the discovery of a new asteroid would have had on the poetic activity of Swinburne. The real reason was, I take it, that the first opportunity was given for the exercise of verse composition by the introduction of all kinds of new matter and new forms from Italy and France.

It must be admitted that verse forms like manners and like individuals develop and die. They evolve from their initial freedom to decay and finally to virtuosity. They disappear before the new man, burdened with the thought more complex and more difficult to express by the old name. After being too much used their primitive effect is lost. All possible tunes have been played on the instrument. What possibility is there in that for the new men, or what attraction? It would be different if poetry like acting and dancing were one of the arts of which no record can be kept, and which must be repeated for each generation. The actor has not to feel the competition of the dead as the poet has. Personally I am of course in favour of the complete destruction of all verse more than twenty years old. But that happy event will not I am afraid take place until Plato's desire has been realised and a minor poet has become dictator. Meanwhile it is necessary to realise that as poetry is immortal it is differentiated from those arts which must be repeated. I want to call attention to this point—it is only those arts whose expression is repeated every generation that have an immutable technique. Those arts like poetry, whose matter is immortal, must find a new technique each generation. Each age must have its own special form of expression, and any period that deliberately goes out of it is an age of insincerity.

The latter stages in the decay of an art form are very interesting and worth study because they are peculiarly applicable to the state of poetry at the present day. They resemble the latter stages in the decay of religion when the spirit has gone and there is a meaningless reverence for formalities and ritual. The carcass is dead and all the flies are upon it. Imitative poetry springs up like weeds, and women whimper and whine of you and I alas, and roses, roses all the way. It becomes the expression of sentimentality rather than of virile thought.

The writers who would be able to use the old instrument with the old masters refuse to do so for they find it inadequate. They know the entirely empirical nature of the old rules and refuse to be cramped by them.

It is at these periods that a new art form is created; after the decay of Elizabethan poetic drama came the heroic couplet, after the decay of the couplet came the new lyrical poetry that has lasted till now. It is interesting to notice that these changes do not come by a kind of natural progress of which the artist himself is unconscious. The new forms are deliberately introduced by people who detest the old ones. Modern lyrical verse was introduced by Wordsworth with no pretence of it being a natural progress; he announced it in good set terms as a new method.

The particular example which has most connection with what I have to say is that of the Parnassian school about 1885: itself beginning as a reaction from romanticism, it has come rapidly to decay; its main principle of an absolute perfection of rhyme and form was in harmony with the natural school of the time. It was a logical form of verse, as distinct from a symbolical one. There were prominent names in it, Monde,[3] Prudhomme,[4] etc., but they were not very fertile; they did not produce anything of great importance; they confined themselves to repeating the same sonnet time after time, their pupils were lost in a state of sterile feebleness.

I wish you to notice that this was not the kind of unfortunate accident which has happened by chance to a number of poets. This check to the Parnassian school marked the death of a particular form of French poetry

which coincided with the birth and marvellous fertility of a new form.
With the definite arrival of this new form of verse in 1880 came the
appearance of a band of poets perhaps unequalled at any one time in the
history of French poetry.

The new technique was first definitely stated by Kahn.[5] It consisted in
a denial of a regular number of syllables as the basis of versification. The
length of the line is long and short, oscillating with the images used by the
poet; it follows the contours of his thoughts and is free rather than regular;
to use a rough analogy, it is clothes made to order, rather than ready-
made clothes. This is a very bald statement of it and I am not concerned
here so much with French poetry as with English. The kind of verse I
advocate is not the same as *vers-libre*, I merely use the French as an
example of the extraordinary effect that an emancipation of verse can
have on poetic activity.

The ancients were perfectly aware of the fluidity of the world and of
its impermanence; there was the Greek theory that the whole world was
a flux. But while they recognised it they feared it and endeavoured to
evade it, to construct things of permanence which would stand fast in this
universal flux which frightened them. They had the disease, the passion,
for immortality. They wished to construct things which should be proud
boasts that they, men, were immortal. We see it in a thousand different
forms. Materially in the pyramids, spiritually in the dogmas of religion
and in the hypostatised ideas of Plato. Living in a dynamic world they
wished to create a static fixity where their souls might rest.

This I conceive to be the explanation of many of the old ideas on
poetry. They wish to embody in a few lines a perfection of thought. Of
the thousand and one ways in which a thought might roughly be
conveyed to a hearer there was one way which was the perfect way,
which was destined to embody that thought to all eternity, hence the
fixity of the form of poem and the elaborate rules of regular metre. It was
to be an immortal thing and the infinite pains taken to fit a thought into
a fixed and artificial form are necessary and understandable. Even the
Greek name ποίημα[6] seems to indicate the thing created once and for all,
they believed in absolute duty as they believed in absolute truth. Hence
they put many things into verse which we now do not desire to, such as
history and philosophy. As the French philosopher Guyau[7] put it, the
great poems of ancient times resembled pyramids built for eternity where
people loved to inscribe their history in symbolic characters. They believed they could realise an adjustment of idea and words that nothing
could destroy.

Now the whole trend of the modern spirit is away from that, philosophers no longer believe in absolute truth. We no longer believe in

perfection, either in verse or in thought, we frankly acknowledge the relative. We shall no longer strive to attain the absolutely perfect form in poetry. Instead of these minute perfections of phrase and words, the tendency will be rather towards the production of a general effect; this of course takes away the predominance of metre and a regular number of syllables as the element of perfection in words. We are no longer concerned that stanzas shall be shaped and polished like gems, but rather that some vague mood shall be communicated. In all the arts, we seek for the maximum of individual and personal expression, rather than for the attainment of any absolute beauty.

The criticism is sure to be made, what is this new spirit, which finds itself unable to express itself in the old metre? Are the things that a poet wishes to say now in any way different to the things that former poets say? I believe that they are. The old poetry dealt essentially with big things, the expression of epic subjects leads naturally to the anatomical matter and regular verse. Action can best be expressed in regular verse, e.g., the Ballad.

But the modern is the exact opposite of this, it no longer deals with heroic action, it has become definitely and finally introspective and deals with expression and communication of momentary phrases in the poet's mind. It was well put by Mr. G. K. Chesterton in this way—that where the old dealt with the Siege of Troy, the new attempts to express the emotions of a boy fishing. The opinion you often hear expressed, that perhaps a new poet will arrive who will synthesise the whole modern movement into a great epic, shows an entire misconception of the tendency of modern verse. There is an analogous change in painting, where the old endeavoured to tell a story, the modern attempts to fix an impression. We still perceive the mystery of things, but we perceive it in entirely a different way—no longer directly in the form of action, but as an impression, for example Whistler's pictures. We can't escape from the spirit of our times. What has found expression in painting as Impressionism will soon find expression in poetry in free verse. The vision of a London street at midnight with its long rows of light, has produced several attempts at reproduction in verse, and yet the war produced nothing worth mentioning, for Mr. Watson[8] is a political orator rather than a poet. Speaking of personal matters, the first time I ever felt the necessity or inevitableness of verse, was in the desire to reproduce the peculiar quality of feeling which is induced by the flat spaces and wide horizons of the virgin prairie of western Canada.

You see that this is essentially different to the lyrical impulse which has attained completion and I think once and forever in Tennyson, Shelley and Keats. To put this modern conception of the poetic spirit, this tentative and half-shy manner of looking at things, into regular metre is like putting a child into armour.

Say the poet is moved by a certain landscape, he selects from that certain images which put into juxtaposition in separate lines serve to suggest and to evoke the state he feels. To this piling-up and juxtaposition of distinct images in different lines, one can find a fanciful analogy in music. A great revolution in music when for the melody that is one-dimensional music was substituted harmony which moves in two. Two visual images form what one may call a visual chord. They unite to suggest an image which is different to both.

Starting then from this standpoint of extreme modernism, what are the principal features of verse at the present time? It is this: that it is read and not chanted. We may set aside all theories that we read verse internally as mere verbal quibbles. We have thus two distinct arts. The one intended to be chanted, and the other intended to be read in the study. I wish this to be remembered in the criticisms that are made on me. I am not speaking of the whole of poetry, but of this distinct new art which is gradually separating itself from the older one and becoming independent.

I quite admit that poetry intended to be recited must be written in regular metre, but I contend that this method of recording impressions by visual images in distinct lines does not require the old metric system.

The older art was originally a religious incantation; it was made to express oracles and maxims in an impressive manner, and rhyme and metre were used as aids to the memory. But why, for this new poetry, should we keep a mechanism which is only suited to the old?

The effect of rhythm, like that of music, is to produce a kind of hypnotic state, during which suggestions of grief or ecstasy are easily and powerfully effective, just as when we are drunk all jokes seem funny. This is for the art of chanting, but the procedure of the new visual art is just the contrary. It depends for its effect not on a kind of half sleep produced, but on arresting the attention, so much so that the succession of visual images should exhaust one.

Regular metre to this impressionist poetry is cramping, jangling, mean-ingless, and out of place. Into the delicate pattern of images and colour it introduces the heavy, crude pattern of rhetorical verse. It destroys the effect just as a barrel organ does, when it intrudes into the subtle interwoven harmonies of the modern symphony. It is a delicate and difficult art, that of evoking an image, of fitting the rhythm to the idea, and one is tempted to fall back to the comforting and easy arms of the old, regular metre, which takes away all the trouble for us.

The criticism is sure to be made that when you have abolished the regular syllabled line, as the unit of poetry, you have turned it into prose.

Of course this is perfectly true of a great quantity of modern verse. In fact one of the great blessings of the abolition of regular metre would be that it would at once expose all this sham poetry.

Poetry as an abstract thing is a very different matter, and has its own life, quite apart from metre as a convention.

To test the question of whether it is possible to have poetry written without a regular metre I propose to pick out one great difference between the two. I don't profess to give an infallible test that would enable anyone to at once say 'This is, or is not, true poetry', but it will be sufficient for the purposes of this paper. It is this: that there are, roughly speaking, two methods of communication, a direct, and a conventional language. The direct language is poetry, it is direct because it deals in images. The indirect language is prose, because it uses images that have died and become figures of speech.

The difference between the two is, roughly, this: that while one arrests your mind all the time with a picture, the other allows the mind to run along with the least possible effort to a conclusion.

Prose is due to a faculty of the mind, something resembling reflex action in the body. If I had to go through a complicated mental process each time I laced my boots, it would waste mental energy; instead of that, the mechanism of the body is so arranged that one can do it almost without thinking. It is an economy of effort. The same process takes place with the images used in prose. For example, when I say that the hill was clad with trees, it merely conveys the fact to me that it was covered. But the first time that expression was used was by a poet, and to him it was an image recalling to him the distinct visual analogy of a man clad in clothes; but the image has died. One might say that images are born in poetry. They are used in prose, and finally die a long lingering death in journalists' English. Now this process is very rapid, so that the poet must continually be creating new images, and his sincerity may be measured by the number of his images.

Sometimes, in reading a poem, one is conscious of gaps where the inspiration failed him, and he only used metre of rhetoric. What happened was this: the image failed him, and he fell back on a dead image, that is prose, but kept an effect by using metre. That is my objection to metre, that it enables people to write verse with no poetic inspiration, and whose mind is not stored with new images.

As an example of this, I will take the poem which now has the largest circulation. Though consisting of only four verses it is six feet long. It is posted outside the Pavilion Music-hall. We instinctively shudder at these clichés or tags of speech. The inner explanation is this: it is not that they are old, but that being old they have become dead, and so evoked no image. The man who wrote them not being a poet, did not see anything definitely himself, but imitated other poets' images.

This new verse resembles sculpture rather than music; it appeals to the eye rather than to the ear. It has to mould images, a kind of spiritual clay, into definite shapes. This material, the ὕλη[9] of Aristotle, is image and not sound. It builds up a plastic image which it hands over to the reader, whereas the old art endeavoured to influence him physically by the hypnotic effect of rhythm.

One might sum it all up in this way: a shell is a very suitable covering for the egg at a certain period of its career, but very unsuitable at a later age. This seems to me to represent fairly well the state of verse at the present time. While the shell remains the same, the inside character is entirely changed. It is not addled as a pessimist might say, but has become alive, it has changed from the ancient art of chanting to the modern impressionist, but the mechanism of verse has remained the same. It can't go on doing so. I will conclude, ladies and gentlemen, by saying, the shell must be broken.

[Review of Tancrède de Visan's]
L'Attitude du lyrisme contemporain

[First published in NA 9/17 (24 Aug. 1911), 400–1.]

This is an extremely good and an extremely interesting book. I recommend those who either know nothing of modern French poetry or who, knowing something, want their knowledge systematised, to buy it at once. (True inwardness of movement.)

I confess that its goodness was a surprise to me. When I first picked it up I saw that it was a collection of essays on all the poets that one has known about for some time. The names on the cover—Verhaeren, De Régnier, Mockel, Paul Fort, Maeterlinck, and Vielé-Griffin seem just the same as those in Beaunier's book, 'La Poésie Nouvelle',[1] that I read some five or six years ago. There were no new names. I found this to be an illustration of one of my favourite theories—that French verse, after a short period of great interest, the most vital that had occurred for centuries, had now arrived at comparative stagnation, and had been succeeded by a period during which French philosophy, also for the first time for centuries, was to dominate Europe.

However, when I commenced to read the book I found it vastly different to what I had expected. It is not a mere collection of disconnected, though intelligent, essays on the fashionable moderns that we all of us know, the kind of thing which any literary man who is in the know can turn out at his leisure, but is really a definitely-thought-out attempt to exhibit all these poets as particular manifestations of the same general current of ideas.

It starts out from this thesis. That there is in each generation what Taine called a 'temperature morale', which is to be found at the same epoch in all the different orders of mental activity, and which constitutes 'l'état général de l'esprit de moeurs environnantes'. To any tendency of poetry at a given time there is a corresponding tendency of philosophy. The psychology of one of Corneille's heroes corresponds to the pure Cartesian doctrine. To the Positivism of Comte and Littré[2] corresponds in literature the spread of naturalism and the 'Parnasse'. The criticism of Taine, the poetry of Leconte de Lisle, the novels of Flaubert, the painting of Courbet, all live in one common atmosphere..The question then arises, what similar parallelism holds good of modern French literature and philosophy—Monsieur De Visan's book is a reasoned attempt to prove that the spirit which finds expression in the Symboliste movement in poetry is the same as that represented by Bergson in philosophy.

They are both reactions against the definite and the clear, not for any preference for the vague as such, not for any mere preference for sentiment, but because both feel, one by a kind of instinctive, unconscious process and the other as the result of reasoning, that the clear conceptions of the intellect are a definite distortion of reality. Bergson represents a reaction against the atomic and rational psychology of Taine and Spencer, against the idea that states of mind can be arrived at by the summation of more elementary states. He asserts the mental states from a continuous and unanalysable state of flux which cannot from its nature be ever represented clearly by the intellect, but must be seized by a process of intuition. The Symbolist reaction against the Parnasse is exactly the same reaction in a different region of thought. For what was the Parnassian attitude? It was an endeavour always to keep to accurate description. It was an endeavour to create poetry of 'clear' ideas. They employed always clear and precise descriptions of external things and strove by combinations of such 'atoms of the beautiful' to manufacture a living beauty. To the Symbolists this seems an impossible feat. For life is a continuous and unanalysable curve which cannot be seized clearly, but can only be felt as a kind of intuition. It can only be got at by a kind of central vision as opposed to analytic description, this central vision expressing itself by means of symbols. M. Visan would then define Symbolism as an attempt by means of successive and accumulated images to express and exteriorise such a central lyric intuition. This is the central idea of the book, and the working of it out in the detailed study of the poets of the movement is extremely well done. It is very interesting to see how a complex thought like that of Bergson should be unconsciously anticipated and find a tentative expression in a purely literary movement.

One amusing expression should be noted. He gives an interesting description of the eager little sets of students who used to attend Bergson's lectures at the Collège de France, and contrasts it with the present-day, when it is impossible to find a seat and the hall is overpowered by the feathers and 'blasphemous scents' of women.

Romanticism and Classicism

[This seems to have been prepared as either a lecture or a paper,
and was not published during Hulme's lifetime. Critics usually
treat it as if written in either 1909 or 1914, but internal evidence
strongly suggests a date of late 1911 or early 1912. In it Hulme
refers to René Fauchois' series of lectures on Racine at the
Odéon Théâtre (Paris) in autumn 1910. The lectures were
scheduled to precede the matinée performances of Racine's
Iphigénie en Aulide. Records of the Odéon show that it was at the
second of these lectures, on 3 Nov. 1910, that the rioting of
which Hulme speaks broke out, at the instigation of the
'camelots du roi' of *L'Action française*. Later lectures were re-
scheduled for after the performances, so that those who did not
wish to hear them could leave. If, as Hulme says, his essay was
written 'about a year' later, the date of it would be late 1911 or
early 1912. The essay is very possibly the lecture Hulme delivered on 15 July 1912, at Clifford's Inn Hall, London. No other
text for that lecture has as yet been identified. The source of the
text reproduced here is *S* 113–40.]

I want to maintain that after a hundred years of romanticism, we are in
for a classical revival, and that the particular weapon of this new classical
spirit, when it works in verse, will be fancy. And in this I imply the
superiority of fancy—not superior generally or absolutely, for that would
be obvious nonsense, but superior in the sense that we use the word good
in empirical ethics—good for something, superior for something. I shall
have to prove then two things, first that a classical revival is coming, and,
secondly, for its particular purposes, fancy will be superior to imagination.

So banal have the terms Imagination and Fancy become that we
imagine they must have always been in the language. Their history as two
differing terms in the vocabulary of criticism is comparatively short.
Originally, of course, they both mean the same thing; they first began to
be differentiated by the German writers on æsthetics in the eighteenth
century.

I know that in using the words 'classic' and 'romantic' I am doing a
dangerous thing. They represent five or six different kinds of antitheses,
and while I may be using them in one sense you may be interpreting
them in another. In this present connection I am using them in a perfectly
precise and limited sense. I ought really to have coined a couple of new

words, but I prefer to use the ones I have used, as I then conform to the practice of the group of polemical writers who make most use of them at the present day, and have almost succeeded in making them political catchwords. I mean Maurras, Lasserre and all the group connected with *L'Action Française.*[1]

At the present time this is the particular group with which the distinction is most vital. Because it has become a party symbol. If you asked a man of a certain set whether he preferred the classics or the romantics, you could deduce from that what his politics were.

The best way of gliding into a proper definition of my terms would be to start with a set of people who are prepared to fight about it—for in them you will have no vagueness. (Other people take the infamous attitude of the person with catholic tastes who says he likes both.)

About a year ago, a man whose name I think was Fauchois gave a lecture at the Odéon on Racine, in the course of which he made some disparaging remarks about his dullness, lack of invention and the rest of it. This caused an immediate riot: fights took place all over the house; several people were arrested and imprisoned, and the rest of the series of lectures took place with hundreds of gendarmes and detectives scattered all over the place. These people interrupted because the classical ideal is a living thing to them and Racine is the great classic. That is what I call a real vital interest in literature. They regard romanticism as an awful disease from which France had just recovered.

The thing is complicated in their case by the fact that it was romanticism that made the revolution. They hate the revolution, so they hate romanticism.

I make no apology for dragging in politics here; romanticism both in England and France is associated with certain political views, and it is in taking a concrete example of the working out of a principle in action that you can get its best definition.

What was the positive principle behind all the other principles of '89? I am talking here of the revolution in as far as it was an idea; I leave out material causes—they only produce the forces. The barriers which could easily have resisted or guided these forces had been previously rotted away by ideas. This always seems to be the case in successful changes; the privileged class is beaten only when it has lost faith in itself, when it has itself been penetrated with the ideas which are working against it.

It was not the rights of man—that was a good solid practical war-cry. The thing which created enthusiasm, which made the revolution practically a new religion, was something more positive than that. People of all classes, people who stood to lose by it, were in a positive ferment about the idea of liberty. There must have been some idea which enabled them to think that something positive could come out of so essentially negative a thing. There was, and here I get my definition of romanticism. They had been taught by Rousseau that man was by nature good, that it was only bad laws and customs that had suppressed him. Remove all these and the infinite possibilities of man would have a chance. This is what made them think that something positive could come out of disorder, this is what created the religious enthusiasm. Here is the root of all romanticism: that man, the individual, is an infinite reservoir of possibilities; and if you can so rearrange society by the destruction of oppressive order then these possibilities will have a chance and you will get Progress.

One can define the classical quite clearly as the exact opposite to this. Man is an extraordinarily fixed and limited animal whose nature is absolutely constant. It is only by tradition and organisation that anything decent can be got out of him.

This view was a little shaken at the time of Darwin. You remember his particular hypothesis, that new species came into existence by the cumulative effect of small variations—this seems to admit the possibility of future progress. But at the present day the contrary hypothesis makes headway in the shape of De Vries's[2] mutation theory, that each new species comes into existence, not gradually by the accumulation of small steps, but suddenly in a jump, a kind of sport, and that once in existence it remains absolutely fixed. This enables me to keep the classical view with an appearance of scientific backing.

Put shortly, these are the two views, then. One, that man is intrinsically good, spoilt by circumstance; and the other that he is intrinsically limited, but disciplined by order and tradition to something fairly decent. To the one party man's nature is like a well, to the other like a bucket. The view which regards man as a well, a reservoir full of possibilities, I call the romantic; the one which regards him as a very finite and fixed creature, I call the classical.

One may note here that the Church has always taken the classical view since the defeat of the Pelagian heresy[3] and the adoption of the sane classical dogma of original sin.

It would be a mistake to identify the classical view with that of materialism. On the contrary it is absolutely identical with the normal religious attitude. I should put it in this way: That part of the fixed nature of man is the belief in the Deity. This should be as fixed and true for every man as belief in the existence of matter and in the objective world. It is parallel to appetite, the instinct of sex, and all the other fixed qualities. Now at certain times, by the use of either force or rhetoric, these instincts have been suppressed—in Florence under Savonarola, in Geneva under Calvin, and here under the Roundheads. The inevitable result of such a process is that the repressed instinct bursts out in some abnormal direction. So with religion. By the perverted rhetoric of Rationalism, your natural instincts are suppressed and you are converted into an agnostic. Just as in the case of the other instincts, Nature has her revenge. The instincts that find their right and proper outlet in religion must come out in some other way. You don't believe in a God, so you begin to believe that man is a god. You don't believe in Heaven, so you begin to believe in a heaven on earth. In other words, you get romanticism. The concepts that are right and proper in their own sphere are spread over, and so mess up, falsify and blur the clear outlines of human experience. It is like pouring a pot of treacle over the dinner table. Romanticism then, and this is the best definition I can give of it, is spilt religion.

I must now shirk the difficulty of saying exactly what I mean by romantic and classical in verse. I can only say that it means the result of these two attitudes towards the cosmos, towards man, in so far as it gets reflected in verse. The romantic, because he thinks man infinite, must always be talking about the infinite; and as there is always the bitter contrast between what you think you ought to be able to do and what man actually can, it always tends, in its later stages at any rate, to be gloomy. I really can't go any further than to say it is the reflection of these two temperaments, and point out examples of the different spirits. On the one hand I would take such diverse people as Horace, most of the Elizabethans and the writers of the Augustan age, and on the other side Lamartine, Hugo, parts of Keats, Coleridge, Byron, Shelley and Swinburne.

I know quite well that when people think of classical and romantic in verse, the contrast at once comes into their mind between, say, Racine and Shakespeare. I don't mean this; the dividing line that I intend is here misplaced a little from the true middle. That Racine is on the extreme classical side I agree, but if you call Shakespeare romantic, you are using a different definition to the one I give. You are thinking of the difference between classic and romantic as being merely one between restraint and exuberance. I should say with Nietzsche that there are two kinds of classicism, the static and the dynamic. Shakespeare is the classic of motion.

What I mean by classical in verse, then, is this. That even in the most imaginative flights there is always a holding back, a reservation. The classical poet never forgets this finiteness, this limit of man. He remembers always that he is mixed up with earth. He may jump, but he always returns back; he never flies away into the circumambient gas.

You might say if you wished that the whole of the romantic attitude seems to crystallise in verse round metaphors of flight. Hugo is always flying, flying over abysses, flying up into the eternal gases. The word infinite in every other line.

In the classical attitude you never seem to swing right along to the infinite nothing. If you say an extravagant thing which does exceed the limits inside which you know man to be fastened, yet there is always conveyed in some way at the end an impression of yourself standing outside it, and not quite believing it, or consciously putting it forward as a flourish. You never go blindly into an atmosphere more than the truth, an atmosphere too rarefied for man to breathe for long. You are always faithful to the conception of a limit. It is a question of pitch; in romantic verse you move at a certain pitch of rhetoric which you know, man being what he is, to be a little high-falutin. The kind of thing you get in Hugo or Swinburne. In the coming classical reaction that will feel just wrong. For an example of the opposite thing, a verse written in the proper classical spirit, I can take the song from Cymbeline beginning with 'Fear no more the heat of the sun'. I am just using this as a parable. I don't quite mean what I say here. Take the last two lines:

> 'Golden lads and girls all must,
> Like chimney sweepers come to dust.'

Now, no romantic would have ever written that. Indeed, so ingrained is romanticism, so objectionable is this to it, that people have asserted that these were not part of the original song.

Apart from the pun, the thing that I think quite classical is the word lad. Your modern romantic could never write that. He would have to write golden youth, and take up the thing at least a couple of notes in pitch.

I want now to give the reasons which make me think that we are nearing the end of the romantic movement.

The first lies in the nature of any convention or tradition in art. A particular convention or attitude in art has a strict analogy to the phenomena of organic life. It grows old and decays. It has a definite period of life and must die. All the possible tunes get played on it and then it is exhausted; moreover its best period is its youngest. Take the case of the extraordinary efflorescence of verse in the Elizabethan period. All kinds of reasons have been given for this—the discovery of the new world and all the rest of it. There is a much simpler one. A new medium had been given them to play with—namely, blank verse. It was new and so it was easy to play new tunes on it.

The same law holds in other arts. All the masters of painting are born into the world at a time when the particular tradition from which they start is imperfect. The Florentine tradition was just short of full ripeness when Raphael came to Florence, the Bellinesque was still young when Titian was born in Venice. Landscape was still a toy or an appanage of figure-painting when Turner and Constable arose to reveal its independent power. When Turner and Constable had done with landscape they left little or nothing for their successors to do on the same lines. Each field of artistic activity is exhausted by the first great artist who gathers a full harvest from it.

This period of exhaustion seems to me to have been reached in romanticism. We shall not get any new efflorescence of verse until we get a new technique, a new convention, to turn ourselves loose in.

Objection might be taken to this. It might be said that a century as an organic unity doesn't exist, that I am being deluded by a wrong metaphor, that I am treating a collection of literary people as if they were an organism or state department. Whatever we may be in other things, an objector might urge, in literature in as far as we are anything at all—in as far as we are worth considering—we are individuals, we are persons, and as distinct persons we cannot be subordinated to any general treatment. At any period at any time, an individual poet may be a classic or a romantic just as he feels like it. You at any particular moment may think that you can stand outside a movement. You may think that as an individual you observe both the classic and the romantic spirit and decide from a purely detached point of view that one is superior to the other.

The answer to this is that no one, in a matter of judgment of beauty, can take a detached standpoint in this way. Just as physically you are not born that abstract entity, man, but the child of particular parents, so you are in matters of literary judgment. Your opinion is almost entirely of the literary history that came just before you, and you are governed by that whatever you may think. Take Spinoza's example of a stone falling to the ground. If it had a conscious mind it would, he said, think it was going to the ground because it wanted to. So you with your pretended free judgment about what is and what is not beautiful. The amount of freedom in man is much exaggerated. That we are free on certain rare occasions, both my religion and the views I get from metaphysics convince me. But many acts which we habitually label free are in reality automatic. It is quite possible for a man to write a book almost automatically. I have read several such products. Some observations were recorded more than twenty years ago by Robertson[4] on reflex speech, and he found that in certain cases of dementia, where the people were quite unconscious so far as the exercise of reasoning went, that very intelligent answers were given to a succession of questions on politics and such matters. The meaning of these questions could not possibly have been understood. Language here acted after the manner of a reflex. So that certain extremely complex mechanisms, subtle enough to imitate beauty, can work by themselves—I certainly think that this is the case with judgments about beauty.

I can put the same thing in slightly different form. Here is a question of a conflict of two attitudes, as it might be of two techniques. The critic, while he has to admit that changes from one to the other occur, persists in regarding them as mere variations to a certain fixed normal, just as a pendulum might swing. I admit the analogy of the pendulum as far as movement, but I deny the further consequence of the analogy, the existence of the point of rest, the normal point.

When I say that I dislike the romantics, I dissociate two things: the part of them in which they resemble all the great poets, and the part in which they differ and which gives them their character as romantics. It is this minor element which constitutes the particular note of a century, and which, while it excites contemporaries, annoys the next generation. It was precisely that quality in Pope which pleased his friends, which we detest. Now, anyone just before the romantics who felt that, could have predicted that a change was coming. It seems to me that we stand just in the same position now. I think that there is an increasing proportion of people who simply can't stand Swinburne.

When I say that there will be another classical revival I don't necessarily anticipate a return to Pope. I say merely that now is the time for such a revival. Given people of the necessary capacity, it may be a vital thing; without them we may get a formalism something like Pope. When it does come we may not even recognise it as classical. Although it will be classical it will be different because it has passed through a romantic period. To take a parallel example: I remember being very surprised, after seeing the Post Impressionists, to find in Maurice Denis's account of the matter that they consider themselves classical in the sense that they were trying to impose the same order on the mere flux of new material provided by the impressionist movement, that existed in the more limited materials of the painting before.

There is something now to be cleared away before I get on with my argument, which is that while romanticism is dead in reality, yet the critical attitude appropriate to it still continues to exist. To make this a little clearer: For every kind of verse, there is a corresponding receptive attitude. In a romantic period we demand from verse certain qualities. In a classical period we demand others. At the present time I should say that this receptive attitude has outlasted the thing from which it was formed. But while the romantic tradition has run dry, yet the critical attitude of mind, which demands romantic qualities from verse, still survives. So that

if good classical verse were to be written to-morrow very few people
would be able to stand it.

I object even to the best of the romantics. I object still more to the
receptive attitude. I object to the sloppiness which doesn't consider that
a poem is a poem unless it is moaning or whining about something or
other. I always think in this connection of the last line of a poem of John
Webster's which ends with a request I cordially endorse:

'End your moan and come away.'[5]

The thing has got so bad now that a poem which is all dry and hard, a
properly classical poem, would not be considered poetry at all. How
many people now can lay their hands on their hearts and say they like
either Horace or Pope? They feel a kind of chill when they read them.

The dry hardness which you get in the classics is absolutely repugnant
to them. Poetry that isn't damp isn't poetry at all. They cannot see that
accurate description is a legitimate object of verse. Verse to them always
means a bringing in of some of the emotions that are grouped round the
word infinite.

The essence of poetry to most people is that it must lead them to a
beyond of some kind. Verse strictly confined to the earthly and the
definite (Keats is full of it) might seem to them to be excellent writing,
excellent craftsmanship, but not poetry. So much has romanticism de-
bauched us, that, without some form of vagueness, we deny the highest.

In the classic it is always the light of ordinary day, never the light that
never was on land or sea. It is always perfectly human and never exaggerated: man is always man and never a god.

But the awful result of romanticism is that, accustomed to this strange
light, you can never live without it. Its effect on you is that of a drug.

There is a general tendency to think that verse means little else than the
expression of unsatisfied emotion. People say: 'But how can you have
verse without sentiment?' You see what it is: the prospect alarms them.
A classical revival to them would mean the prospect of an arid desert and
the death of poetry as they understand it, and could only come to fill the
gap caused by that death. Exactly why this dry classical spirit should have
a positive and legitimate necessity to express itself in poetry is utterly
inconceivable to them. What this positive need is, I shall show later. It
follows from the fact that there is another quality, not the emotion
produced, which is at the root of excellence in verse. Before I get to this
I am concerned with a negative thing, a theoretical point, a prejudice that
stands in the way and is really at the bottom of this reluctance to
understand classical verse.

It is an objection which ultimately I believe comes from a bad metaphysic of art. You are unable to admit the existence of beauty without the infinite being in some way or another dragged in.

I may quote for purposes of argument, as a typical example of this kind of attitude made vocal, the famous chapters in Ruskin's *Modern Painters*, Vol. II, on the imagination. I must say here, parenthetically, that I use this word without prejudice to the other discussion with which I shall end the paper. I only use the word here because it is Ruskin's word. All that I am concerned with just now is the attitude behind it, which I take to be the romantic.

'Imagination cannot but be serious; she sees too far, too darkly, too solemnly, too earnestly, ever to smile. There is something in the heart of everything, if we can reach it, that we shall not be inclined to laugh at. . . . Those who have so pierced and seen the melancholy deeps of things, are filled with intense passion and gentleness of sympathy.' (Part III, Chap. III, § 9)

'There is in every word set down by the imaginative mind an awful undercurrent of meaning, and evidence and shadow upon it of the deep places out of which it has come. It is often obscure, often half-told; for he who wrote it, in his clear seeing of the things beneath, may have been impatient of detailed interpretation; for if we choose to dwell upon it and trace it, it will lead us always securely back to that metropolis of the soul's dominion from which we may follow out all the ways and tracks to its farthest coasts.' (Part III, Chap. III, § 5)

Really in all these matters the act of judgment is an instinct, an absolutely unstateable thing akin to the art of the tea taster. But you must talk, and the only language you can use in this matter is that of analogy. I have no material clay to mould to the given shape; the only thing which one has for the purpose, and which acts as a substitute for it, a kind of mental clay, are certain metaphors modified into theories of æsthetic and rhetoric. A combination of these, while it cannot state the essentially unstateable intuition, can yet give you a sufficient analogy to enable you to see what it was and to recognise it on condition that you yourself have been in a similar state. Now these phrases of Ruskin's convey quite clearly to me his taste in the matter.

I see quite clearly that he thinks the best verse must be serious. That is a natural attitude for a man in the romantic period. But he is not content with saying that he prefers this kind of verse. He wants to deduce his opinion like his master, Coleridge, from some fixed principle which can be found by metaphysic.

Here is the last refuge of this romantic attitude. It proves itself to be not an attitude but a deduction from a fixed principle of the cosmos.

One of the main reasons for the existence of philosophy is not that it enables you to find truth (it can never do that) but that it does provide you a refuge for definitions. The usual idea of the thing is that it provides you with a fixed basis from which you can deduce the things you want in æsthetics. The process is the exact contrary. You start in the confusion of the fighting line, you retire from that just a little to the rear to recover, to get your weapons right. Quite plainly, without metaphor this—it provides you with an elaborate and precise language in which you really can explain definitely what you mean, but what you want to say is decided by other things. The ultimate reality is the hurly-burly, the struggle; the metaphysic is an adjunct to clear-headedness in it.

To get back to Ruskin and his objection to all that is not serious. It seems to me that involved in this is a bad metaphysical æsthetic. You have the metaphysic which in defining beauty or the nature of art always drags in the infinite. Particularly in Germany, the land where theories of æsthetics were first created, the romantic æsthetes collated all beauty to an impression of the infinite involved in the identification of our being in absolute spirit. In the least element of beauty we have a total intuition of the whole world. Every artist is a kind of pantheist.

Now it is quite obvious to anyone who holds this kind of theory that any poetry which confines itself to the finite can never be of the highest kind. It seems a contradiction in terms to them. And as in metaphysics you get the last refuge of a prejudice, so it is now necessary for me to refute this.

Here follows a tedious piece of dialectic, but it is necessary for my purpose. I must avoid two pitfalls in discussing the idea of beauty. On the one hand there is the old classical view which is supposed to define it as lying in conformity to certain standard fixed forms; and on the other hand there is the romantic view which drags in the infinite. I have got to find a metaphysic between these two which will enable me to hold consistently that a neo-classic verse of the type I have indicated involves no contradiction in terms. It is essential to prove that beauty may be in small, dry things.

The great aim is accurate, precise and definite description. The first thing is to recognise how extraordinarily difficult this is. It is no mere matter of carefulness; you have to use language, and language is by its very nature a communal thing; that is, it expresses never the exact thing but a compromise—that which is common to you, me and everybody. But each man sees a little differently, and to get out clearly and exactly what he does see, he must have a terrific struggle with language, whether it be with words or the technique of other arts. Language has its own special nature, its own conventions and communal ideas. It is only by a concentrated effort of the mind that you can hold it fixed to your own purpose. I always think that the fundamental process at the back of all the arts might be represented by the following metaphor. You know what I call architect's curves—flat pieces of wood with all different kinds of curvature. By a suitable selection from these you can draw approximately any curve you like. The artist I take to be the man who simply can't bear the idea of that 'approximately'. He will get the exact curve of what he sees whether it be an object or an idea in the mind. I shall here have to change my metaphor a little to get the process in his mind. Suppose that instead of your curved pieces of wood you have a springy piece of steel of the same types of curvature as the wood. Now the state of tension or concentration of mind, if he is doing anything really good in this struggle against the ingrained habit of the technique, may be represented by a man employing all his fingers to bend the steel out of its own curve and into the exact curve which you want. Something different to what it would assume naturally.

There are then two things to distinguish, first the particular faculty of mind to see things as they really are, and apart from the conventional ways in which you have been trained to see them. This is itself rare enough in all consciousness. Second, the concentrated state of mind, the grip over oneself which is necessary in the actual expression of what one sees. To prevent one falling into the conventional curves of ingrained technique, to hold on through infinite detail and trouble to the exact curve you want. Wherever you get this sincerity, you get the fundamental quality of good art without dragging in infinite or serious.

I can now get at that positive fundamental quality of verse which constitutes excellence, which has nothing to do with infinity, with mystery or with emotions.

This is the point I aim at, then, in my argument. I prophesy that a period of dry, hard, classical verse is coming. I have met the preliminary objection founded on the bad romantic æsthetic that in such verse, from which the infinite is excluded, you cannot have the essence of poetry at all.

After attempting to sketch out what this positive quality is, I can get on to the end of my paper in this way: That where you get this quality exhibited in the realm of the emotions you get imagination, and that where you get this quality exhibited in the contemplation of finite things you get fancy.

In prose as in algebra concrete things are embodied in signs or counters which are moved about according to rules, without being visualised at all in the process. There are in prose certain type situations and arrangements of words, which move as automatically into certain other arrangements as do functions in algebra. One only changes the X's and the Y's back into physical things at the end of the process. Poetry, in one aspect at any rate, may be considered as an effort to avoid this characteristic of prose. It is not a counter language, but a visual concrete one. It is a compromise for a language of intuition which would hand over sensations bodily. It always endeavours to arrest you, and to make you continuously see a physical thing, to prevent you gliding through an abstract process. It chooses fresh epithets and fresh metaphors, not so much because they are new, and we are tired of the old, but because the old cease to convey a physical thing and become abstract counters. A poet says a ship 'coursed the seas' to get a physical image, instead of the counter word 'sailed'. Visual meanings can only be transferred by the new bowl of metaphor; prose is an old pot that lets them leak out. Images in verse are not mere decoration, but the very essence of an intuitive language. Verse is a pedestrian taking you over the ground, prose—a train which delivers you at a destination.

I can now get on to a discussion of two words often used in this connection, 'fresh' and 'unexpected'. You praise a thing for being 'fresh'. I understand what you mean, but the word besides conveying the truth conveys a secondary something which is certainly false. When you say a poem or drawing is fresh, and so good, the impression is somehow conveyed that the essential element of goodness is freshness, that it is good because it is fresh. Now this is certainly wrong, there is nothing particularly desirable about freshness *per se*. Works of art aren't eggs. Rather the contrary. It is simply an unfortunate necessity due to the nature of the language and technique that the only way the element which does constitute goodness, the only way in which its presence can be detected externally, is by freshness. Freshness convinces you, you feel at once that the artist was in an actual physical state. You feel that for a minute. Real communication is so very rare, for plain speech is unconvincing. It is in this rare fact of communication that you get the root of æsthetic pleasure.

I shall maintain that wherever you get an extraordinary interest in a thing, a great zest in its contemplation which carries on the contemplator to accurate description in the sense of the word accurate I have just analysed, there you have sufficient justification for poetry. It must be an intense zest which heightens a thing out of the level of prose. I am using contemplation here just in the same way that Plato used it, only applied to a different subject; it is a detached interest. 'The object of æsthetic contemplation is something framed apart by itself and regarded without memory or expectation, simply as being itself, as end not means, as individual not universal.'

To take a concrete example. I am taking an extreme case. If you are walking behind a woman in the street, you notice the curious way in which the skirt rebounds from her heels. If that peculiar kind of motion becomes of such interest to you that you will search about until you can get the exact epithet which hits it off, there you have a properly æsthetic emotion. But it is the zest with which you look at the thing which decides you to make the effort. In this sense the feeling that was in Herrick's mind when he wrote 'the tempestuous petticoat'[6] was exactly the same as that which in bigger and vaguer matters makes the best romantic verse. It doesn't matter an atom that the emotion produced is not of dignified vagueness, but on the contrary amusing; the point is that exactly the same activity is at work as in the highest verse. That is the avoidance of conventional language in order to get the exact curve of the thing.

I have still to show that in the verse which is to come, fancy will be the necessary weapon of the classical school. The positive quality I have talked about can be manifested in ballad verse by extreme directness and simplicity, such as you get in 'On Fair Kirkconnel Lea'. But the particular verse we are going to get will be cheerful, dry and sophisticated, and here the necessary weapon of the positive quality must be fancy.

Subject doesn't matter; the quality in it is the same as you get in the more romantic people.

It isn't the scale or kind of emotion produced that decides, but this one fact: Is there any real zest in it? Did the poet have an actually realised visual object before him in which he delighted? It doesn't matter if it were a lady's shoe or the starry heavens.

Fancy is not mere decoration added on to plain speech. Plain speech is essentially inaccurate. It is only by new metaphors, that is, by fancy, that it can be made precise.

When the analogy has not enough connection with the thing described to be quite parallel with it, where it overlays the thing it described and there is a certain excess, there you have the play of fancy—that I grant is inferior to imagination.

But where the analogy is every bit of it necessary for accurate description in the sense of the word accurate I have previously described, and your only objection to this kind of fancy is that it is not serious in the effect it produces, then I think the objection to be entirely invalid. If it is sincere in the accurate sense, when the whole of the analogy is necessary to get out the exact curve of the feeling or thing you want to express—there you seem to me to have the highest verse, even though the subject be trivial and the emotions of the infinite far away.

It is very difficult to use any terminology at all for this kind of thing. For whatever word you use is at once sentimentalised. Take Coleridge's word 'vital'. It is used loosely by all kinds of people who talk about art, to mean something vaguely and mysteriously significant. In fact, vital and mechanical is to them exactly the same antithesis as between good and bad.

Nothing of the kind; Coleridge uses it in a perfectly definite and what I call dry sense. It is just this: A mechanical complexity is the sum of its parts. Put them side by side and you get the whole. Now vital or organic is merely a convenient metaphor for a complexity of a different kind, that in which the parts cannot be said to be elements as each one is modified by the other's presence, and each one to a certain extent is the whole. The leg of a chair by itself is still a leg. My leg by itself wouldn't be.

Now the characteristic of the intellect is that it can only represent complexities of the mechanical kind. It can only make diagrams, and diagrams are essentially things whose parts are separate one from another. The intellect always analyses—when there is a synthesis it is baffled. That is why the artist's work seems mysterious. The intellect can't represent it. This is a necessary consequence of the particular nature of the intellect and the purposes for which it is formed. It doesn't mean that your synthesis is ineffable, simply that it can't be definitely stated.

Now this is all worked out in Bergson, the central feature of his whole philosophy. It is all based on the clear conception of these vital complexities which he calls 'intensive' as opposed to the other kind which he calls 'extensive', and the recognition of the fact that the intellect can only deal with the extensive multiplicity. To deal with the intensive you must use intuition.

Now, as I said before, Ruskin was perfectly aware of all this, but he had no such metaphysical background which would enable him to state definitely what he meant. The result is that he has to flounder about in a series of metaphors. A powerfully imaginative mind seizes and combines at the same instant all the important ideas of its poem or picture, and while it works with one of them, it is at the same instant working with and modifying all in their relation to it and never losing sight of their bearings on each other—as the motion of a snake's body goes through all parts at once and its volition acts at the same instant in coils which go contrary ways.

A romantic movement must have an end of the very nature of the thing. It may be deplored, but it can't be helped—wonder must cease to be wonder.

I guard myself here from all the consequences of the analogy, but it expresses at any rate the inevitableness of the process. A literature of wonder must have an end as inevitably as a strange land loses its strangeness when one lives in it. Think of the lost ecstasy of the Elizabethans.

'Oh my America, my new found land,' think of what it meant to them and of what it means to us. Wonder can only be the attitude of a man passing from one stage to another, it can never be a permanently fixed thing.

German Chronicle

[Written during a visit to Germany in the autumn of 1913 and
published in *Poetry and Drama*, 2 (June 1914), 221–8.]

Prefatory Note.—How do I take my duties as a chronicler? Rather lightly
perhaps. My tale will be rather haphazard. I do not intend to make a
careful *inventory* of current literature, either by honestly tasting everything, or by collecting current opinions. I shall make no special effort. I
shall not read anything on your behalf that I should not naturally have
read for my own amusement. I intend merely to give an account of the
things which reach me naturally, as I sit nightly gossiping at the Café des
Westens (the Café Royal[1] of Berlin, immortalised by Rupert Brooke's
poem[2]). I am actually on the spot. I walk down Tauenzienstrasse in the
afternoon. I know many of the people I have to write about. I daily
contemplate the Kaiser Wilhelm Gedächtniskirche (so frequently mentioned in modern verse), and derive certain advantages from this physical
fact. This is the extent of my superiority. I make no claim to judicial
estimate of tendencies, but humbly communicate the 'latest thing'—quite
a useful function when you remember that by the ordinary channels of
print it takes twenty years for an idea to get from one country to another,
while even a hat takes six months.

After all, it is time that German had this kind of treatment. It has been
written about by people who felt that the literature of the country was a
phenomenon of the same kind as its rainfall or its commerce, and
deserved periodical notice and report. Careful chronicles of this kind put
the whole situation in an entirely wrong perspective. You have to
mention writers whom the native never considers.

Nobody seems to have written about German for fun. The natural
motive for such writing, the fact that you have discovered something exciting and want to communicate your excitement, seems to
have been entirely lacking here. It seems rather as if men who at some
trouble to themselves had learnt German, had looked round for suitable means of revenging themselves on others who had not had that
trouble. French, on the contrary, has been written about by people who
possessed the curious characteristic of insisting on reading only what
amused them.

One can account for the fact that this type of enthusiastic amateur does not write about German, by a rather curious reason. It lies in a certain difference between the two literatures, which makes the one more easily accessible to the amateur of this kind than the other. Every speech is at once a language serving the purposes of the will, expressing intimate desires and commands, and at the same time a language expressing thoughts by a sequence of concepts. The second aspect of a language can be readily grasped by a foreigner who has learned the language in the usual literary way. The first, depending as it does on the emotional values attaching to simple words, can only be appreciated when one has oneself used the language as a weapon of daily abuse. The qualitites inherent in this direct use of speech cannot be deliberately learnt. Here comes the point I am trying to make clear. Both French and German are in an equal degree used for these two purposes. But as far as literature itself is concerned, I should be inclined to assert that while the qualities of French literature are to be found in the use of language as a sequence of concepts, the essential qualities of German literature depend on its more homely use as a language of will and emotion.

While the essential qualities of French literature are thus easily seizable by a foreigner who has learnt the language in the usual way—*i.e.*, as a descriptive conceptual language—those of German are not. It may seem rather paradoxical, in view of the qualities of German as a philosophical language, to assert it is less a conceptual language than French. I am not, however, speaking of the languages in general, but only of the qualities they exhibit in literature. If one is not studying 'comparative literature', but just reading foreign literature in the spirit in which one reads one's own, one is apt, for this reason, at first to be repelled by German. It does not lie open at once as French does. It is only when one comes across the old peasant poems and song in dialect, which exhibit prominently of course the qualities of a speech as a 'language of will', that one begins to appreciate it. Then one begins also to recognise these qualities in classical German literature and find it more bearable. One sees it most familiarly in the extraordinary homeliness and solidity of certain parts of Goethe.

These, I repeat again, are qualities which cannot be appreciated by the literary amateur who has learnt German as he has learnt French.

*　　*　　*

To turn now to contemporary German verse. A consideration of its immediate past is of some importance. Its roots do not go very deep. One should always bear in mind that German literature had no important Victorian period. Between the classical period of 1780–1830 and the moderns lies a gap. I am quite aware that this is an exaggeration, and that anyone who has ever read a manual of German literature could supply a continuous list of names stretching from one period to the other. But that would not affect the truth of what I assert. If you read Nietzsche's denunciation of German literature about 1870 you will see what is meant. It is only when one realises the state of German literature at that time that his denunciations become comprehensible. I point this out because it does seem to me to be important. The literary cabaret I speak of later commenced by a reading of these passages from Nietzsche's 'What the Germans lack'.[3] This is not a mere dead fact from history, but throws light on the present.

The roots of the present lie only thirty years back. They resemble strawberry runners, springing from a mother root—in this case situated in Paris, Norway and elsewhere. The history of this period divides naturally into three decades. In 1880 comes the beginning of the modern period with the influence of Zola, Ibsen and Tolstoi. A few years later come the German names Conrad,[4] Hauptmann and Hart.[5] About 1892 you get a new tendency showing itself, 'Los von Naturalismus'.[6] The principal names of this generation are Liliencron[7] and Dehmel;[8] Stephan Georg, Max Dauthendey,[9] and Hofmannsthal, the group associated with *Blätter für die Kunst*;[10] Mombert,[11] Peter Hille,[12] Bierbaum,[13] Falke,[14] and Arno Holz,[15] who perhaps belongs to the previous generation. From 1900 till 1910 you get another change. Naturalism is quite dead—but no formula can be given to describe this period. Carl Spitteler[16] does not, properly speaking, belong to this generation, but I put him here because it was only at this time that his poems began to be read. The best poet of the period seems to me to be undoubtedly Rainer Maria Rilke. Other names are Schaukal,[17] Eulenberg,[18] and, among those who are not, properly speaking, poets, Wedekind, Heinrich, and Thomas Mann; Paul Ernst,[19] Loublinski,[20] and 'the Neo-Classical Movement', of which I hope to say more later.

The generation that I am to write about is the one since this.

Before doing this, however, I should like to interpolate a list of papers and reviews where new work may be found: *Pan*, 6d. weekly, published by Cassirer, very lively indeed; *Die weissen Blätter*, a 2/- monthly, which, at present at any rate, includes some of the best of the younger men; *Der neue Rundschau*, a 2/- monthly something like the *English Review*; *Der Sturm*,[21] a 4d. fortnightly, in reality a Futurist and Cubist art-paper, but always containing verse of Futurist type, well worth taking in; *Aktion*,[22] a 2d. weekly, publishing good modern verses; *Der lose Vogel*; and finally two 3d. weeklies something like *The Academy*, *Das literarishe Echo* and *Der Gegenwart*.

*   *   *

I can only give certain haphazard impressions of this last generation. Someone is sure to say that I have mistaken a small clique for contemporary poetry, but I take the risk. I attempt to give only my impressions. I attended a meeting of the 'Cabaret Gnu'. This takes place every month in a Café. The Cabaret has a president who calls on various poets to get up and read their poems. All do so without any diffidence whatever, and with a certain ferocity. It is all much pleasanter than a reading here, for having paid to go in, you are free to talk and laugh if the poem displeases you. Moreover, the confidence and the ferocity of the poets is such that you do not feel bound to encourage them. To anyone accustomed to ordinary German, the language is very surprising. Very short sentences are used, sometimes so terse and elliptical as to produce a blunt and jerky effect. It does not send you to sleep like the diffuse German of the past, but is, on the other hand, so abrupt that the prose itself at times almost resembles Futurist verse. The result is not always happy, but it is clear that a definite attempt is being made to use the language in a new way, an attempt to cure it of certain vices. That this reaction is a conscious one is shown, I suppose, by the opening reading of the passage from Nietzsche I have mentioned above. One feels that the language is passing through a period of experiment. Whether this is a local and unimportant fashion, or whether something will come of it, one cannot of course say. But there it is, an undoubted fact. The same reaction against softness and diffusiveness seems to me to be observable in the verse as in the prose.

As conveniently representing this present generation of poets, I take the anthology *Der Kondor* (edited by Kurt Hiller,[23] published by Weissbach in Heidelberg, 1912). I might compare it with the Georgian Anthology.[24] Though it has shown no signs yet of passing from edition to edition, like its remarkable English prototype, it yet attracted a certain amount of notice and criticism. Whatever its merits may be, it does represent the literary group with the greatest amount of life in it at the present moment. The editor, Kurt Hiller, was the conductor of the Cabaret Gnu I mentioned above.

The editor writes a short preface. Protesting in the first place against certain influences from which he imagines the present generation must make itself free—Stephan Georg and his school—the aristocratic view of art, 'we ourselves understand the value of strict technique, but we reject Hochnäsigkeit[25] as the constitutive principle of poetry.'

Secondly, he protests against those who mistake a metaphysical and pantheistic sentimentality for poetry.

Der Kondor then is to be a manifesto, a Dichter Sezession, 'a rigorous collection of radical strophes. It is to include only those verse writers who can be called artists. It is to give a picture of all the artists of a generation.' The eldest were born at the end of the 70's, and the youngest in 1890. In the opinion of the editor it includes the best verse that has been written in German since Rilke.

To turn now to the verse itself, I obviously cannot give any detailed criticism of the fourteen poets included.[26] I propose, therefore to quote one or two and then give my general impression.

Take first Ernst Blass,[27] whose book *Die Strassen komme ich entlang geweht*, has appeared with the same publisher as *Der Kondor* itself. I quote his 'Sonnenuntergang':

> Noch träum ich von den Ländern, wo die roten
> Palastfassaden wie Gesichter stieren
> Der Mond hängt strotzend.
> Weiss er von den Toten?
> Ich gehe an dem weichen Strand spazieren.
> Schräg durch Bekannte. (Schrieen nicht einst Löwen?)
> Vom Kaffeegarten kommt Musike her.
> Die grosse Sonne fährt mit seidnen Möwen.
> Über das Meer.[28]

Else Lasker-Schüler,[29] the best known of those included in the volume, in reality belongs to a slightly earlier generation. Some of her poems, for example, are translated in *Contemporary German Poetry* (Walter Scott, 1/-). She is a very familiar figure in the Café des Westens; her short hair, extraordinary clothes and manly stride are easily recognisable in the neighbourhood of Kurfürstendamm. Her prose, however, is extremely feminine, and anyone who is interested in gossip about the poets of this generation will find *Mein Herz* amusing. (It is put in the form of letters addressed to her former husband, Herwath Walden, the editor of the Futurist paper, *Der Sturm*.)

Ein Alter Tibetteppich

> Deine Seele, die die meine liebet,
> Ist verwirkt mit ihr im Teppichtibet,
>
> Strahl in Strahl, verliebte Farben,
> Sterne, die sich himmellang umwarben.
>
> Unsere Füsse ruhen auf der Kostbarkeit
> Maschentausendabertausendweit.
>
> Süsser Lamasohn auf Moschuspflanzenthron
> Wie lange küsst dein Mund den meinen wohl
> Und Wang die Wange buntgeknüpfte Zeiten schon?[30]

Then Georg Heym,[31] who can be compared to Richard Middleton,[32] in that he died young, leaving behind a volume of verse and some short stories:

> Beteerte Fässer rollten von den Schwellen
> Der dunklen Speicher auf die hohen Kähne.
> Die Schlepper zogen an. Des Rauches Mähne
> Hing russig nieder auf die öligen Wellen.
>
> Zwei Dampfer kamen mit Musikkapellen.
> Den Schornstein kappten sie am Brückenbogen.
> Rauch, Russ, Gestank lag auf den schmutzigen Wogen
> Der Gerbereien mit den braunen Fellen.
>
> In allen Brücken, drunter uns die Zille
> Hindurchgebracht, ertönten die Signale
> Gleichwie in Trommeln wachsend in der Stille.
>
> Wir liessen los und trieben im Kanale
> An Gärten langsam hin. In dem Idylle
> Sahn wir der Riesenschlote Nachtfanale.[33]

Arthur Drey's 'Kloster':[34]

> Und Mauern stehen ohne sich zu rühren
> Wir graue Fäuste, die im Wind erfrieren,

like several other poems in the volume, illustrates the use, which has now become epidemic, of the word *Und* at the beginning of every other line (derived probably from Hugo von Hofmannsthal's well-known 'Ballade des Äusseren Lebens').

From René Schickele's 'Auf der Friedrichstrasse bei Sonnenuntergang':[35]

> An der Ecke steht ein Mann
> Mit verklärtem Gesicht.
> Du stösst ihn an,
> Er merkt es nicht.
>
> Starrt empor mit blassem Blick,
> Schlaff die Arme herunter.
> Tiefer gestaltet sich sein Geschick
> Und der Himmel bunter.[36]

I have no space to quote any more, but I give the names of the other poets and their books: Franz Werfel,[37] *Der Weltfreund* and *Wir Sind*; Alfred Lichtenstein,[38] *Dämmerung*; Max Brod,[39] *Tagebuch in Versen*; Schickele, *Weiss und Rot*,[40] published by Paul Cassirer; Grossberger,[41] *Exhibitionen*, published by Meister, Heidelberg.

The group has to a certain extent divided. Kurt Hiller is writing for *Die weissen Blätter*, a review which commenced last autumn, while Kronfeld[42] told me when I saw him that he and Ernst Blass were starting a new review this spring, of which I hope to say something in my next chronicle.[43]

As to my general impression of the whole group. First of all must be placed to their credit the fact that none of the poems can be described as pretty. They are not then sentimentally derivative, they are the product of some constructive intelligence, but I doubt whether this intelligence is one making for poetry. I doubt it, because the poems are so recognisably those which intelligent people would write.

To explain in more detail, I assume that the sensibility of the poet is possessed by many who themselves are not poets. The differentiating factor is something other than their sensibility. To simplify matters then, suppose a poet and an intelligent man both moved in exactly the same way by some scene; both desire to express what they feel; in what way does the expression differ? The difficulty of expression can be put in an almost geometrical way. The scene before you is a picture in two dimensions. It has to be reduced to verse, which being a line of words has only one dimension. However, this one-dimensional form has other elements of rhythm, sound, etc., which form as it were an emotional equivalent for the lost dimension. The process of transition from the one to the other in the case of the poet is possibly something of this kind. First, as in the case of all of us, the emotional impression. Then probably comes *one* line of words, with a definite associated rhythm—the rest of the poem follows from this.

Now here comes the point. This first step from the thing clearly 'seen' to this almost blind process of development in verse, is the characteristic of the poet, and the step which the merely intelligent man cannot take. He sees 'clearly' and he must construct 'clearly'. This obscure mixture of description and rhythm is one, however, which cannot be *constructed* by a rational process, *i.e.*, a process which keeps all its elements clear before its eyes all the time.

The handicap of the intelligent man who is not a poet is that he cannot trust himself to this obscure world from which rhythm springs. All that he does must remain 'clear' to him as he does it. How does he then set about the work of composition? All that he can do is to mention one by one the elements of the scene and the emotions it calls up. I am moved in a certain way by a dark street at night, say. When I attempt to express this mood, I make an inventory of all the elements which make up that mood. I have written verse of that kind myself, I understand the process. The result is immediately recognisable. Qualities of sincere first-hand observation may be constantly shown, but the result is not a poem.

The Germans I have been writing about seem to me to be in this position. The qualities they display are destined rather to alter German prose than to add to its poetry.

Bergson

The New Philosophy

[First published in *NA* 5/10 (1 July 1909), 198–9. This essay-review of William James, *A Pluralistic Universe* (London, 1909) was Hulme's first published article.]

This last book of Mr. James's is in one way the most important that has yet appeared in the much-advertised English pragmatic movement; not, however, for the definite constructive philosophy it contains, but for a confession of great significance. It marks the end of a little comedy. For several years Mr. F. C. S. Schiller has implored Mr. James to write the complete metaphysic of pragmatism, 'he alone could do it.' Mr. James has returned the compliment. At last, however, he has discovered what some of us knew already—that the thing had already been done, and in a way which required no re-doing. He has discovered Bergson. The twenty years required for an idea to cross the Channel are fulfilled, and now we shall hear of nothing but Bergson.

In Chapter V James describes in detail the problem which he himself originated in his 'Principles of Psychology'—the difficulty of explaining on an intellectualist basis the compounding of different states of consciousness. In a personal way which is very engaging, he tells how he struggled with the problem for years, covering hundreds of sheets of paper with notes, memoranda, and discussions with himself over the difficulty. 'The struggle was in vain; I found myself in an impasse. I have now to confess that I should not have been emancipated, should not have thrown logic out of the deeper regions of philosophy, to take its rightful place in simple human practice, if I had not been influenced by Bergson.'[1]

He becomes almost lyrical in expressing his relief at the defeat of the old intellectualist philosophy, which only marked time, perpetually bringing the same objections and urging the same answers. 'Open Bergson and new horizons loom on every page you read. It is like the breath of the morning and the song of birds. It tells of reality itself, instead of merely reiterating what dusty-minded professors have written about what previous professors have thought.'[2]

No admission could be more thorough—one half of the book is devoted to its justification—yet such is the peculiar quality of English critics that in none of the reviews I have yet read is Bergson even mentioned.

Bergson gives a complete system to justify the vague anti-intellectualist sentiment that James has always felt. Others have attacked rationalism, but his is the only radical attack, the only attack which concedes nothing; Rationalism here being taken to mean the abuse of the power of translating the flux of immediate experience into a conceptual order. The antithesis here understood I always image roughly for myself in humble metaphors. On the one hand the complicated, intertwined, inextricable flux of reality, on the other the constructions of the logical intellect, having all the clearness and 'thinness' of a geometrical diagram. To use another metaphor, on the one hand a kind of chaotic cinder heap, on the other a chess-board. In the latter, movement is from one square to another, always definite, always just so; in the other it is indefinite. The first is an analogy for the world of sensation—the many; the other for the constructs of the intellect. I always figure the main Bergsonian position in this way: conceiving the constructs of logic as geometrical wire models and the flux of reality as a turbulent river such that it is impossible with any combination of these wire models, however elaborate, to make a model of the moving stream; not emphasising here the fact of change in the stream, but the impossibility of seizing it fully in the spare framework of intellectual formula. You cannot hold water in a wire cage, however minute the mesh.

The intellectualist asserts that the apparently rough contradictory constituents of the flux are in reality of the nature of logical concepts. In Socrates and Plato this took the form of an assertion that reality consisted of essences or 'ideas', which could be discovered by definition. This is the beginning of intellectualism in the vicious sense of the term. It survives at the present time in science, where the 'ideas' have become relations or laws. Kant slightly curtailed its pretensions to define reality 'an sich', but only partly. The first radical attack came from Nietzsche. (The metaphysical part of Nietzsche, generally neglected, is really the root of all his views.) But what he felt too deeply to express, except in a rhapsodical way, Bergson says with extraordinary clearness. There is, however, here no question of influence, I only draw a parallel. It would seem more in the Nietzschean spirit, and it happens also to be true, that the effective way of getting an insight into the obscurer part of his work is not to compare him with the philosophers who came before, like Schopenhauer, but to Bergson, who came after. (I commend this to young Italians who give dull lectures on Nietzsche, seizing all points but the essential.)

To state that in Bergson we have a revival of Nominalism and a reaction against the abuse of Conceptualism is to put the matter too generally; it does not state the particular method of this reaction, in which lies his extreme originality. The antithesis between the flux of sensation and the stable order of concepts is older than Plato, but Bergson further analyses and defines each term of the antithesis until a new philosophy arises. On the other hand he gives a genetic account of the intellect, asserting that in evolution it grew up as an annex to action, destined specially to deal with matter. Hence the geometrical character of logic; our concepts are formed in the image of solids, stable things, and so are unable to deal with life. The way in which the intellect represents the flux, the 'devenir',[3] may be compared to the way in which a cinematograph represents movement. A series of static sections are taken, none of which expresses movement; as a science develops, the sections will get closer together, the imitation will be better, but it will never represent the simple motion itself. By a series of models the intellect itself endeavours to copy the intertwined, unseizable flux. But to understand the flux by concepts is to arrest its movement. There is more in movement than in the successive positions traversed. This is very near to Nietzsche's statement: 'What can be conceived is necessarily a fiction.' 'La connaissance et le devenir s'excluent.'[4]

The exact nature of the other term of the antithesis, the flux which constitutes reality, is analysed by Bergson in an account of the nature of perception. Ordinary perception is in a great part intellectualised. We break the flux of sensible reality into 'things'. Here arises the difficulty any intellectualist system has in finding a unity. But there is an absolute perception, uninfluenced by the superimposed 'cadres' of intellect and memory. This is the 'immédiatement donnée'.[5] This is the only absolute with which philosophy can legitimately deal.

Most of the antinomies of metaphysics come from the fact that we apply to the disinterested knowledge of the real the processes which we use for practical ends. Logic has use in human life, but it has not that of making us theoretically acquainted with the essential nature of reality. Reality, immediacy, exceed our logic, overflow and surround it—reality is non-rational in its constitution. Thought only deals with surfaces, it cannot imitate the 'thickness' of experience. Reality has a fulness of content that no conceptual description can equal. What method, then, is philosophy to adopt? Here comes the positive constructive part of Bergson, as distinguished from the destructive criticism of intellectualism.

'Philosopher consiste à invertir le direction habituelle du travail de la pensée.'[6] Our intelligence must follow the inverse method. It can instal itself in the flux of reality by means of that intellectual sympathy that one calls intuition. One must dive back into the flux of the 'immédiatement donnée' if one wishes to know reality. What exactly this means can only be seen in the working out of the method in his three books.[7] (Perhaps the most brillant example of its success is his restatement of the case for free-will.) It is obvious that this is the exact antithesis of the Platonic metaphysics, where the changing flux is dismissed as appearances and reality is found in the stable concepts of the intellect.

'Bergson and Plato are the extreme terms of a philosophic evolution, of which Kant was a transition. The stable has become appearance, mobile has become reality.'

I can only state very shortly a few applications of the Bergsonian method. The first one was that of the distorting effect produced by the intellectualised idea of time as even-flowing. Zeno's Paradox is shown to be due to a confusion between conceptual and real time—'durée réel'.[8] More generally he analyses Laplace's boast, that the world could be completely stated in a series of differential equations. It is here perhaps that Bergson, in a reaction from his mathematical training, first took up his characteristic position. 'When a mathematician calculates the state of a system, at the end of time *t*, nothing need prevent him from supposing that between whiles the universe vanishes—it is only the *t*th moment that counts; that which flows throughout the interval—real time—plays no part in his calculations.'[9] We get here a conception of 'durée réel', which is his central discovery, round which the others are grouped. A time which exists and is not merely a fourth kind of space, a time in which there is continuous creation, in which Laplace's boast could never become true.

The dream of a 'mathématique universel', a survival of Platonism, is shattered. Starting from this conception of 'durée réel', he re-states the problem of determinism in a very seductive chapter, which always arouses my enthusiasm. In his last book[10] he applies his method to biology, giving a philosophy of evolution. It is impossible to give any idea of it here, except to say that it attacks both mechanism and finalism, and substitutes as the principle of life a kind of 'élan vital'.[11]

Searchers after Reality
I: Bax

[First published in *NA* 5/13 (29 July 1909), 265–6; reprinted in *FS* 3–6.]

When the clown at the circus puts his head through the paper disc, he appears framed in a ring of torn paper. This is the impression I have of Mr. Bax's position after reading the 'Roots of Reality'.[1] He has certainly put his head through a previously unpenetrated system, but he still remains surrounded by the ragged edges of the medium he has destroyed. His own original views appear surrounded with pieces of Kantian tissue-paper. There is no doubt that Bax has brought a really new idea into philosophy—the assertion of the ultimate reality of the alogical. But, alarmed at his own audacity, he seeks to make it perfectly respectable by giving it as a companion a curious mixture of all the German idealists. The frame in which he sets his new conception is antique and thoroughly orthodox, but it ill accords with the central picture.

He has made a brilliant and powerful attack from a new point of view on the Hegelian panlogism.[2] (Why does Mr. Bax pedantically employ the word pallogistic instead of the generally employed panlogistic?) This attack, in its lucidity and directness, is infinitely superior to the fumbling controversial method of Mr. Schiller and the pragmatists, but its significance only comes out when one sees it in its proper perspective in the general movement of European philosophy.

This modern metaphysical movement seems as strange to the layman as the preaching of the simple life would do to a savage. You must have been sophisticated and have sinned before you can experience the relief of repentance. You must first have been a Hegelian before you can get enthusiastic over the general anti-intellectualist movement in philosophy throughout Europe. Even Nietzsche admitted that perhaps it was better to have had the Wagnerian disease and to have recovered from it than to have merely been continuously healthy and unconscious. (The comedy of it is, however, that the anti-intellectualists are generally so lucid that a class of reader is drawn in which has not previously sinned with Hegel.) The disease in this case is intellectualism. The method of all systems of philosophy, when all the decorations and disguises are stripped off, ultimately resolves itself to this. One takes a little part of known reality and asserts dogmatically that it alone is the true analogy by which the cosmos is to be described. Good philosophy then consists in the choice of a good microcosm, just as surely as genius results from the avoidance of rashness and haste in selecting one's grandparents.

Intellectualism takes a bad analogy, logic and the geometric sciences, which are in essence identical, and asserts that the flux of phenomena which apparently contradicts this is not real, and can really be resolved into logical concepts. Chance is abolished, everything is reduced to law, so that omnipotent intelligence, able to seize the entire universe at a glance could construct from that its past and future. Bax, on the contrary, asserts that there is an alogical element which cannot be reduced to law.

The great antithesis before modern metaphysics is thus the old one between the flux of phenomena and the concepts by which we analyse it in thought. Which term of the antithesis is real? Here I distinguish four solutions. The Hegelian: that only the concept is real; positive significance only attaches to thought or relational elements as opposed to its alogical terms; the other side of the antithesis is argued away. The Bergsonian: that only the flux is real, the concepts being mere practical dodges. The pragmatist: that the concepts are only purposive instruments, but that purpose and will constitute the only reality. Then the Baxian: that both are real, and that the logical is like a serpent engaged in continually swallowing the endless meal of the flux, a task in which it can never succeed. 'Reality is the inseparable correlation of these two ultimate terms.'[3] There are thus two roots of reality.

Of these four solutions I am here concerned more particularly with the distinction between that of Bax and that of Bergson. There are two ways in which a man may be led to the denial of the possibility of including the alogical under the logical. If one emphasises the character of the flux as motion one sees that the static concepts can never represent it. So Bergson. If one emphasises the infinity of detail in the immediately given, its grittiness, its muddiness, and hence the impossibility of pulling it in the smooth, tidy, geometrical concepts, one arrives at Bax. This difference affects their view of the function of concepts in the flux. This is a rough analogy for Bergson's view. When I see in the changing shape of flame something which resembles a saw edge I may solely for the purposes of human communication call it that. But I have not by that altered the nature of the flame. So with concepts and universals of all kinds. We envisage the flux in certain static geometric shapes entirely for practical purposes, which have no ultimate reality at all. Proteus is god, and he cannot be seized in any formula. Bax, on the other hand, assumes that these forms which describe the flux have some ultimate reality. They do really contain and control the alogical as the hexagons in the comb contain the honey. He refuses, however, to go to the length of the intellectualists, who would say that in the last resort matter is abolished and absorbed in form. Bax's position is that there is always something left over, that when you dip the net of concepts and universals some of the reality always escapes through the meshes. He thus occupies a curious midway position which I think will in the end be found untenable.

Here we get to the actual frontier position of modern speculation. The intellectualists, the lay theologians, having been violently expelled from their temple and the final admission made that logical thought is by its nature incapable of containing the flux of reality, what remains? Are we to resign ourselves to ignorance of the nature of the cosmos, or is there some new method open to us?

Bergson says that there is—that of intuition. From a common origin life has divided in two directions; the 'élan vital', in its struggle towards the maximum of indeterminism, has employed two methods, the one instinct, the other intellect; one exemplified in animals, the other in man. (Intellect being understood here in a definite way as the capacity for making models of the flux, of reasoning in logic.) But round the central intellect in man there is a fringe, a penumbra of instinct. This instinct, or, as it is better to call it here, intuition, is the faculty that we must use in attempting to grasp the nature of reality. One must carefully guard here against a sentimental use of the word. Bergson gives it a precise technical sense. By intellect one can construct approximate models, by intuition one can identify oneself with the flux.

Here Bax stops and parts company with Bergson. Philosophy, he says, 'may not be inaptly defined as the last word of the logical'.[4] It is impossible for it to get beyond universals or abstractions. Both realise the unsatisfactory nature of the dry land of concepts on which philosophy has lived, and would not be content with it. Both set out and discovered the turbulent river of reality. Bergson jumped in and swam. Bax looked at it, then came back and merely recorded that the land was not all, that there was a river on which man could not walk, a reality that the logical reason will never grasp entirely. But he forgot that walking is not the only method of progression, and that the logical method of thought may not be the only way of understanding reality.

By many toilsome ways Bax, like Moses, leads us to the Promised Land; then, having privately surveyed it, informs us that, after all, it isn't really interesting, tells us to go back again, but always to bear in mind that there is such a place. That is, the intellect is still for him the only way of getting at Reality, though we are always to remember that by its very nature it can never reach it. What did he see in the promised land of the alogical which prevented him from wandering there? We can only surmise maliciously that somewhere in its pleasant valleys he saw a woman. Is not intuition too dangerous a process for an anti-feminist to suggest as the ultimate philosophic process?

Searchers after Reality
II: Haldane

[First published in *NA* 5/17 (19 Aug. 1909), 315–16; reprinted in *FS* 7–14.]

The Oriental despot is addressed by his followers as Most High, King of Kings, Son of Heaven, epithets having no accurate and precise meaning, but signifying a general state of admiration. If a western metaphysician had by some unhappy chance been enslaved among the circle of courtiers I feel sure that he would have given praise in the words, 'Oh, Ultimately Real'. Philosophers desire that their particular obsession shall be dignified with the name Reality as jealously as the hero of Maupassant's 'Decoré' desired the badge of the Legion d'honneur, and the desired end is often attained in just as surprising a way. Reality is merely the complimentary word that metaphysicians apply to what they particularly admire. At the present moment they go roughly into two classes, the admirers of Rest and of Motion, and strenuously and ingeniously they labour to identify their preference with Reality.

It is clear from his book that Mr. Haldane[1] admires order and organisation, and from this his metaphysic can be deduced. The flux of sensation by itself would be uninhabitable and uncomfortable. Reaction from its confusion may take two forms: the practical, which requires a mechanism to enable it to move easily in fixed paths through the flux and change, and the æsthetic which shrinks from any contact with chaos. The practical attitude, by the universals of thought, arranges the flux in some kind of order, as the police might arrange a crowd for the passage of a procession. The next step for the man who admires order is to pass from the practical to the æsthetic, to assert that what puts order into the confused flux of sensation alone is real, the flux itself being mere appearance. The mind that loves fixity can thus find rest. It can satisfy its æsthetic shrinking from the great unwashed flux by denying that it is real. This has proved an easy step for Mr. Haldane to take. The constant burden of his book is that Reality is a system; further, that it is an intellectual system, and the flux only has reality in so far as it fits into this system. One might caricature his position by saying that he believes in the ultimate reality of the police, or that a guide-book is superior to an actual visit, for in the former one has sensation systematised.

This is Mr. Haldane's particular trend in prejudice, but in philosophy the correct etiquette is to give excuses for the end we fix beforehand, and one must examine the exact method by which he justifies his assertion that Reality can be identified with Reason. His method and intent, like that of every other philosopher, are anthropomorphic, and narrowly so, for he wishes to prove not only that the cosmos is of the same nature as man, but of a particular faculty of man—the logical Reason. The task does not at first look promising; you are faced with a hard and fast objective world. How are you to explain this as being of the nature of mind, let alone of reason? The method adopted is an old familiar one. Like all idealists since Berkeley, he uses the formula 'esse is percipi',[2] as an acid wherewith to break up the apparent solidity of the objective world to a fluid form more suitable for digestion in a spiritual system. Once having reduced it to a flabby condition of this kind, he is in a better position to prove his second step, that it is moulded entirely by the laws of the intellect. There still remains the unfortunate particular, the alogical—the untameable tiger that arouses Mr. Bax's affection. How is it to be murdered that we may at last get a civilised and logical system into the cosmos? If, as Mr. Haldane does, you start off with a sacred conviction that only what is fixed is real, the procedure is quite simple. The immediate sensations of the moment are transient and have no abiding reality; they are different in different people. Reality must consist in the common system, the objective world, that which other people become aware of, when, and on the same ground as I do, in Mill's permanent possibilities of sensation. The next step consists in proving that this common system, this objective world, is entirely a construction of the intellect. The reason of the actuality of the world round me, the reason why I cannot alter it by my will, lies in the fact that my mind, like the mind of other people, is compelled to think the world according to a system of conceptions. Reality consists in an objective system, and that objective system consists of what we are obliged to think. The nature of the world is thus rational, 'Esse is intelligi.'[3] The universals of thought are the true foundations of the world. Thought creates things rather than things thought. The phenomenon of experience gets its fixity and definiteness from the universals of reflection. 'It is only in the intelligible notions which are embedded in sensation and which give them substance that these sensations have reality.'[4] I admit this in so far as it means that the flux is reduced to a practical order for personal life by the intellect, and made habitable, but I refuse to take the further step of saying that it is the only reality. When unhappy proximity forces me to survey

Edwardian architecture I am quite aware that what gives fixity to the extraordinary chaos of varied marble is the hidden steel girder, but I cannot console myself, as Mr. Haldane does, by saying that the steel alone is real and that the marble is a passing dream. I am prepared to admit that my mind is compelled to 'think' the world according to a system of concepts, but Mr. Haldane and the Hegelians here attribute some transcendental value to the word 'think'. It does not follow that because the logical faculty is compelled to think in that way that for other purposes other methods might be more valid. Thinking might be, and probably is, a method of distorting Reality.

Mr. Haldane, however, is most interesting regarded as a typical example of a certain philosophical manner. He is distinctly a 'counter' as distinguished from a 'visual' philosopher. I can best get at the meaning I intend by these epithets, by a digression on a certain difference of intention, between verse and prose. In prose as in algebra concrete things are embodied in signs or counters, which are moved about according to rules, without being visualised at all in the process. There are in prose certain type situations and arrangements of words, which move as automatically into certain other arrangements as do functions in algebra. One only changes the x's and y's back into physical things at the end of the process. Poetry, in one aspect at any rate, may be considered as an effort to avoid this characteristic of prose. It is not a counter language, but a visual concrete one. It is a compromise for a language of intuition which would hand over sensations bodily. It always endeavours to arrest you, and to make you continuously see a physical thing, to prevent you gliding through an abstract process. It chooses fresh epithets and fresh metaphors, not so much because they are new and we are tired of the old, but because the old cease to convey a physical thing and become abstract counters. Nowadays, when one says the hill is 'clothed' with trees, the word suggests no physical comparison. To get the original visual effect one would have to say 'ruffed', or use some new metaphor. A poet says the ship 'coursed the seas' to get a physical image, instead of the counter word 'sailed'. Visual meanings can only be transferred by the new bowl of metaphor: prose is an old pot that lets them leak out. Prose is in fact the museum where the dead images of verse are preserved. Images in verse are not mere decoration, but the very essence of an intuitive language. Verse is pedestrian, taking you over the ground prose—as a train delivers you at a destination.

One result of this difference is that both in prose and philosophy the 'derivative' man can manipulate the counters, without ever having been in actual contact with the reality of which he speaks; yet by the use of image the 'creative' man can always convey over the feeling that he has 'been there'. This partial distinction between verse and prose has an exact parallel between the 'visual' and the 'counter' philosopher. The visual and creative philosopher, like the saint in 'Kim', desires the hills, where he can meditate in concrete forms. His method of thinking is visual, and he uses words only secondarily for purposes of communication. He is like a poet delighted with the physical metaphors before him that press directly and actually to be employed as symbols of thought. Once these physical metaphors are embodied in smooth counterwords, the second rank, who have not seen the hills, take them for eternal verities, unaware of the earthy process by which they were born. Philosophy, then, instead of being a kind of institution, becomes a complicated game, the great rule being the 'principle of contradiction', in other words, 'no two counters must occupy the same square at the same time.' Thus, like the priests in the Tower of Manoi, Mr. Haldane sits, moving counters according to a certain ritual, and when all are on the central peg, Buddha will come again—perhaps. Conceive the body of metaphysical notions as a river; in the hills it springs from the earth, and can be seen to do so. But far down stream, on the mudflats where Haldane sits counting his beads with marvellous rapidity, the river seems to be eternal. Metaphysical ideas are treated as sacrosanct, and no one imagines they were born of humble metaphors, as the river was of earth.

The abstract philosopher has a great contempt for the visual one. Hence the steadfast refusal to recognise that Nietzsche made any contribution to metaphysics. Mr. Haldane constantly informs us that the region of philosophy is not a region of pictorial images, one must beware of similes as the devil. I picture him always standing impressively, holding up a warning finger, saying in an awed whisper, 'Hush, I hear a mere metaphor coming'; the supposition being that there is a mysterious high method of thinking by logic superior to the low common one of images. The counter philosopher, taking conceit unto himself, forgets that all his abstract words are merely codified dead metaphors. When we are all descended from monkeys—why put on side? As a matter of fact, the history of philosophy should be written as that of seven or eight great metaphors, and one might even say that the actual physical objects observed by men have altered the course of thought. For example, the mirror in the theory of perception, and the wheel in Eastern thought. One is rather apt in a reaction from Haldane's abhorrence of imagery to swing too much over to the other side. I guard myself against patronising abstraction too extensively, and recognise that the poor thing has after all a function in philosophy, though a secondary one. It is difficult to get the exact relation between the 'visual' and the 'counter' attitudes. One gets it best I suppose by thinking of them as creative and developing functions respectively. The root of metaphor and intuition must rise into the light of abstraction to complete itself, but it should not be allowed to run to seed there. There is no system of philosophy which did not originate in an act of intuition, or as I have previously put it, a perception of a physical analogy. Dialectic is necessary to develop the primary intuition, and to put it into concepts for the purposes of communication. Once having received the impulse from the act of intuition, the philosopher has to continue in the other plane of abstraction. But he must not go too far in this medium or he loses foot and must return to the primary act of intuition. Like Antæus, he must touch the earth for renewed strength. As in social life, it is dangerous to get too far away from barbarism. This new act of physical vision will destroy a good deal of the work done by the 'counter' manipulating of abstractions. For a recent example of this take the word 'concept' and the entirely new significance given to it by the pragmatists.

The legitimate function of logic only comes in the elaboration of the original 'visual' act. It adds point to it, as a large hat does to the calculated gestures of a woman's head, and as clothing does to flesh. But metaphysics could exist without it, and if I may be allowed to express a personal opinion, I think that what we require now is a race of naked philosophers, free from the inherited embellishments of logic.

Never moving on the physical plane where philosophy arises, but always in the abstract plane where it is finished and polished, Mr. Haldane has his reward in a perfectly extraordinary facility in moving his counter words. Who but he could have given in extempore lectures such a lucid exposition of Hegelianism? The only parallel I can think of here is that of the expert chess player who can mentally follow the game from the written notation. This faculty in moving on the plane of counter words is of course the secret of his versatility. He has the monotonous versatility of the soldier, who in many lands employs the same weapon. It is the very prose of philosophy. He moves his counters, and certainly gets them into new and interesting positions. All the time, however, we cannot believe in their validity, as we are conscious that he is treating as fixed entities things which are not so—which run into one another in inextricable blurs, and are not separate and distinct. He treats the world as if it were ultimately a mosaic, whereas in reality all the colours run into one another. For the purposes of communication we must label the places where one colour predominates, by that colour, but then it is an illegitimate manœuvre to take these names and juggle with them as if they were distinct and separate realities. I have one particular part of the book in mind, where for fifty pages he performs interesting movements with the four counters, Mind, Subject, Ultimate Reality and Aspect.

The word 'Aspect' is indeed a kind of queen and knight, and can move on the board in any direction. Whenever an absurdity of the Hegelian system obstructs the way, 'aspect' takes the poor pawn with miraculous ease.

The best way indeed to sum up Mr. Haldane is to say that he believes in the ultimate reality of language. He speaks with contempt of the 'thing in itself' as a notion which cannot be expressed in words. It comes to this: 'What cannot be expressed in intellectual forms does not exist.' What he can't say in a public speech isn't knowledge. It is not difficult to expose the origin of this heresy.

Men for the purposes of communication have joined themselves together by an abstract mechanism, a web of language, of universals and concepts. I picture this by thinking of a number of telegraph poles connected by a network of wires, the poles being concrete men, the wires being the abstract, thin concepts of the intellect, the forms in which we think and communicate. It is in the elaboration of this mechanism, and not in the change of the men it joins that all progress in knowledge has taken place. 'Science est une langage bien fait.' Here comes the great danger for philosophy. The success of the mechanism leads us on to think that it alone is real. The poles come to imagine themselves as built up on some subtle complication of wires. Accustomed to live and think externally in this mechanism of ours, and seeing its success in all the sciences, one comes to think it the only reality, and finally to explain the individual in terms of it. One's gaze being necessarily fixed in life on external communication of which logical thinking is a variety, one by an illegitimate analogy transfers it inward, and explains oneself in terms of what was in the beginning merely a tool.

This intellectual disease has attacked Mr. Haldane more strongly than any of the other Hegelians. The poor men who manufactured the concepts for communication are nothing. He even goes so far as to speak of the self as a mere bad metaphor in the same tone that one might speak of a bad egg.

Surely this is the greatest comedy in human history, that men should come to think themselves as made up of one of their own tools.

Searchers after Reality
III: Jules De Gaultier

[First published in *NA* 6/5 (2 Dec. 1909), 107–8; reprinted in *FS* 15–20.]

Jules De Gaultier's philosophy is a sign of the times. Taken together with that of Boutroux,[1] Bergson, Le Roy[2] and many others, it is a sign that the centre of interest in philosophy has shifted from Germany to France. The particular characteristic of this movement that first strikes one is the great success of lucidity it has brought. Wilde once asserted that he was the first philosopher to dress like a gentleman. But, unfortunately for this very desirable claim, he was no philosopher. These Frenchmen, on the contrary, while they write like gentlemen and not like pedants, at the same time write metaphysics of a very subtle and distinguished kind. Take De Gaultier for example. In some parts of his work, particularly in his account of what exactly is implied in an act of knowledge, he is treating the most intricate and giddiness-producing part of philosophy. He treats it in an extremely personal way, expressing often views of violent originality. Yet such matters, which a German would not be able even to approach without the creation of an entirely special jargon, he writes of in a charmingly lucid manner, with great literary distinction. This increased lucidity is, I think, more than a mere change of literary manner. It is rather the secondary characteristic of a more general change, that of their whole attitude towards philosophy. They always seem to me to treat it, either explicitly or implicitly, not as science but as an art. This in itself is a relief. Philosophy has released itself from the philosophical sciences.

At this point I want to make a long digression, to express some personal views, which at first sight may appear to have little to do with De Gaultier. I think that this digression, which will occupy the rest of the article, is justified for this reason—that there is a certain attitude of mind, a certain prejudice, which must be attacked before one can appreciate De Gaultier. I want to get this out of the way before giving any detailed account of his philosophy.

There are two aims that metaphysics conceivably might have. It might wish to be considered an art, a means of expressing certain attitudes to the cosmos, or it might be taken as a science, humbly groping after the truth.

If you take the second point of view then probably certain objections would rise up in your mind to De Gaultier's philosophy. The principal conception with which it works may seem so slight, that the extraordinary way in which he makes it account for the whole movement of the cosmos may seem too ingenious to be true. I want to attack the conception of philosophy which gives rise to this hesitation.

One finds it difficult to realise what a baleful fascination the word science has for some people. I never quite realised it until I came across a faded old copy of the once flourishing 'Westminster Review', whose gods were Mill and Spencer. In it I read a first review of Buckle's 'History of Civilization',[3] which gave me the same kind of sensation as one gets from turning up a stone and seeing the creeping things revealed. I don't mean to say that I feel superior, but simply that I was in the presence of an unexpected and quite alien world of things. The reviewer lamented that in the ordered uniform cosmos which science had revealed there had been up to now an impenetrable jungle, the field of human passions and activity. 'He rejoiced that at last with the appearance of Buckle's book this had been cleared up, and the whole world made trim and tidy. Law was universal.' You saw here what was repugnant to him, the idea of freedom and chance. The ideal was a certitude which should constrain us. This dominant ideal invaded philosophy.

It began to regard itself as a science, to consider itself a systematic structure, solidly built up, which should give us certain unquestionable results. As in the sciences the ultimate nature of the world would reveal itself to continuous and patient work, and not to bold speculation. Philosophy, tempted by science, fell and became respectable. It sold its freedom for a quite imaginary power of giving sure results. It was a solemn structure, in face of which light-heartedness was out of place, and individual idiosyncracy a sin. One felt uncomfortable in it. Nothing could be done by sudden insight and images; such things were mere folly, here was accumulated wisdom, here were no royal roads. The days of adventure were gone when we could set out to find new lands. Here was no place for the artist to impertinently express an attitude before the cosmos, but rather for the humble professor to work honestly in a corner.

To a certain extent this movement was correct. Logic, psychology, etc., look like, and as a matter of fact are sciences. The artist is here certainly out of place. But the danger was when they began to absorb philosophy itself, when it began to consider itself as merely a scientia scientium.

But with this modern movement, philosophy has at last shaken itself free from the philosophic sciences and established its right to an independent existence. In Bergson's 'Idée d'une Métaphysique'[4] one even finds it defined as the exact inverse method to that of science. The old conception of science prisoned us, restrained our vagaries, and made speculation seem childish. My gratitude to De Gaultier and these other critics of science is that they have rescued me from this nightmare and kept philosophy as an art. She has once more escaped the spirit that would make her a dull citizenness. Once more, without the expedient of turning herself into myrtle, Daphne has escaped the god's embraces, which promising love would but result in ungraceful fertility.

This is not a mere piece of reactionary or religious sentiment. We don't assert that a philosopher need not know the sciences, and that the simple man is in the best position to write metaphysics. It is not so; he must know them well.

But we assert that throughout the ages philosophy, like fighting and painting, has remained a purely personal activity. The only effect the advance of science has on the three activities is to elaborate and refine the weapons that they use. The man who uses a rifle uses it for the same purpose as a man who uses a bludgeon. The results of the sciences merely increase the number of colours with which philosophy paints. The possibilities of the rapier have been worked out till they have become a science, but the process of learning it does not convert the man himself into an automaton. There are not, and can never possibly be, any certain results in metaphysics as there are in science. It is an activity of a different kind, simply an elaborate means for the expression of quite personal and human emotions.

The ultimate point I want to get at here is that philosophy is an art and not a science. The attitude proper to science is this. By work and effort one may discover the truth by which in dealing with this matter one must guide oneself. Science constrains us; we have no freedom, we enter into it humbly to be told the truth. Now philosophy is nothing of this kind. We are free in philosophy. I grant it has all the appearance of a science. Its vocabulary and methods are those of the science, but the driving-power behind it is quite different; it merely uses the scientific terms for a purpose quite different: that of the artist. In it by work one can never discover the secret of the cosmos, one merely finds elaborate and complete ways of expressing one's personal attitude towards it.

From the outside it has all the appearance of a science. But this we might take as a piece of protective mimicry to ward off the multitude to preserve it in its seclusion as the rarest of the arts.

We have to a certain extent been taken in by the jargon, and taken it for an end in itself, a science; but at last we have won through, and found it to be but part of an art. It is a case something like the old Oriental mysteries; in the lower orders of priesthood all the ritual was taken literally. But when you had penetrated to the inner circle, through all the different kinds of magical formula and mysteries, the final secret turned out to be some perfectly plain human statement. So in philosophy, when one attains the central position, one finds no exact science, but simply an art, a means of ordinary human expression. With this little difference, however: that while the elaboration of ritual and the various mysteries of the Orientals were but means by which the priests controlled the ignorant multitude, in the case of philosophy the scientific terminology is the means by which we control ourselves, i.e., by which we completely express ourselves.

But I should be the first to attack the Philistine who thought he could dismiss this ritual terminology by saying that it corresponded to no reality. It is the finest and most delicately wrought language and means of expression of all the arts. Its elaborate technique enables it to get a leisurely effect of final statement where the other arts can only hint. It is the art of completion. The series of gradated words and definitions, the elaborate balancing and checking of meanings make it possible to isolate an emotion or idea from all accidental relations, so to study it completely. The jargon is a walled garden which enables conceptions to grow to their full expression, or to use a less sentimental metaphor, it is a kind of experimental tank, a laboratory where one can practise 'control' experiments on ideas. I give next week[5] an apt illustration of this isolating process in De Gaultier's own concept of Bovarysme,[6] which starting first as a fact of ordinary psychology, he finally fits in a metaphysical setting, in order to state it completely.

One must distinguish the means from the end. The means, the elaborate technique, is certainly a science. But the end, what the Compleate Philosopher practises, is certainly an art. He wishes to express some freely-chosen attitude towards the world. Conceive Plato considering a particular example of love, or a particular scene of beauty. These things in human life are transient. But to him, Stability is more noble than Change. His 'Theory of Ideas' is then the expression of this preference. He creates a system in which the ideas of love and beauty are eternal. The particular preference which De Gaultier's philosophy expresses I shall analyse later; roughly it is the exact antithesis of this, change is the only reality.

I anticipated the simple-minded question, 'Is it true?' and intended to make the question absurd. There can be no direct answer to that question

as there would be to 'Is the Eiffel Tower 1,000 ft. high?' One is ex-
trapolating the curve of truth outside its proper limits, applying it to fields
where it has no meaning. All philosophy is bound to be untrue, for it is
the art of representing the cosmos in words, which is just as much a
necessary distortion as the art of painting, which represents solidity in a
plane of two dimensions. 'He is a thinker—that is to say, he understands
how to make things seem simpler than they are.' One must judge De
Gaultier's philosophy as one judges a landscape. One must not ask is it
correct? but is it a good picture? The pleasure one takes must be that of
a connoisseur and not that of a surveyor. The principal criterion is then,
is it a consistent whole? In most of the pictures that philosophy gives us
there is a gap right down the middle of the canvas, in that they fail to
explain the very possibility of our knowledge. This gap does not exist in
De Gaultier; he presents a complete picture on a canvas that is whole. For
this reason I delight in him.

Notes on the Bologna Congress

[First published in *NA* 8/26 (27 Apr. 1911), 607–8; reprinted in
FS 21–7. The Fourth International Congress of Philosophy, held
in Bologna, Italy, 6–11 Apr. 1911, was attended by 500–600
philosophers from all over the world. For a more technical
account of the proceedings of the Congress, see Hulme's 'The
International Philosophical Congress at Bologna'.]

Bologna, April 7 [1911]

I

One may hold two very different views as to the value of congresses in
general. One of these views is always associated in my mind with a
simple-minded Scotch undergraduate I knew at Cambridge, whose constant topic of conversation at dinner in hall was the extraordinary progress
that would take place in science if only the leading people in mathematics
and physics could be got together in conference. If only Larmor,
Poincaré, J. J. Thomson, Kelvin, and the rest of them could be put
together in one room for a month, the exchange of views would solve the
problem. It was a real trouble to the poor fellow that the attempt had
never been made. I believe that at night, turning over on his pillow for
the last time before sleep overcame him, he was lost in amazed wonder
that the scandal of the ether's dubious position had been allowed to go
on, year by year, when such a simple thing would have finished the
matter once and for all.

To show that this congressomania is by no means confined to youth,
I can give another example of its ravages. At the last annual meeting of the
Aristotelian Society,[1] a member raised an objection to the *variety* of the
subjects proposed for discussion in the following year. Let the society take
some pressing subject like that of Neo-Realism and discuss it time after
time, until the truth had actually been discovered. I make no comment
on the fact that a 'pressing' subject can easily become 'oppressing'. What
concerns me here is the attitude represented by this request. I was
petrified when I first heard it, but after a time, as I looked at the stolid
countenance of the reformer, I began to see a kind of halo round him, a
coloured landscape of the inside of his mind. His attitude then became
less amazing for me. The vision, the sympathetic intuition I formed of his

mental make-up, his welt-anschauung was this: Somewhere at a great distance, Truth is hidden. She is always waiting to be discovered, and the reason that during the centuries she has not been found, lies in the perpetual anæmia of the human mind. We cannot keep in one direct path long enough to succeed—or perhaps we keep on dying too often—and so change the line of search. You have, then, a vision of the tragic history of metaphysical thought from Plato to the present time. At many crucial moments in that long and complicated search they were within a foot of Truth, trembling and shrinking in her hiding place, but always at this moment, this fatal anæmia, the desire for variety, turned the hunters off in a new and false direction. Now you see the masterpiece of organised strategy which would infallibly succeed where the ages had failed. Let the Aristotelian Society tie itself down beforehand to keep in one direction. I hasten to say that the society did not set off on this heroic adventure. So what would have happened must for ever remain a subject of pathetic speculation: one of those dreadful 'It might have beens' which torment the human mind. 'If only Shackleton had not eaten the Manchurian pony, and fallen ill, only 80 miles from the Pole.'

However, I have not quite lost hope. Some day a wealthy American lady may endow us, for the precise purpose of taking up the great adventure.

That is one attitude towards congresses. The other is, I think, best explained by a conversation I had with Bergson last July. I told him I was going to Bologna. 'I don't know', he said, 'whether these meetings actually do any good, but sometimes when you have been puzzled by a man's philosophy, when you have been a little uncertain as to his meaning, then the actual physical presence of the man makes it all clear. And sometimes, as William James used to say, one look at a man is enough to convince you that there you need trouble no further.' I went to Bologna in this frame of mind. I wondered how my views on certain people would be affected. I was curious to test the James theory. I wondered how it would work out.

* * *

I had not long to wait for the first conclusive test. On the way to Italy I stopped two days at Dieppe with Jules de Gaultier, about whom I have already written a little in this Review. It was a test under most favourable circumstances. Generally in discussing metaphysic one is, àpropos of the other man's point, immediately 'reminded' of something of one's own which one wants to drag out, and so one never passes outside the limits of one's first concept. But in this case fate made me a perfect listener, for while I understood him perfectly, I had not spoken French for so long that all my uprisings of interruption were stifled automatically before utterance. The result was that I was extremely impressed. Previously, while I enjoyed reading him, yet I always thought 'Bovarysme' to be a paradoxical though interesting position. While I admired the dialectic by which it was supported, I had not found it at all 'inevitable'. But since meeting him I have formed a much clearer and more definite conception of his philosophy.

This different view I now take of De Gaultier. I can only explain when I have first indicated my rather sceptical opinion of philosophy. Metaphysics for me is not a science but an art—the art of completely expressing certain attitudes which one may take up towards the cosmos. What attitude you do take up is not decided for you by metaphysics itself, but by other things. The number of such attitudes is, of course, necessarily limited—like the four points of the compass; the variety of metaphysic can only come in the different ways in which you can manage to indicate your preference for the North or South, as the case may be. But de Gaultier has convinced me that there is another attitude beyond the four traditional ones. It is not an attitude which many people can take up, but for those who take it De Gaultier has written the complete metaphysic. I cannot express how intensely I admire the logical consistency with which it is all worked out.

In so far as philosophers are still peripatetic and like to walk the road gesticulating, Bologna seems to be the ideal place for them to meet in.

Walking about its streets for the first time, this evening, I would go further and say that it is one of the few real towns still left on this earth. There is a great misconception as to what really constitutes a town. The usual idea is that city and country are a pair of opposites, and that the progress of events tends to spread the one and destroy the other. Nothing of the kind. The country is not the raw material out of which the town has been evolved. In the beginning was something I can vaguely call desert. Out of this matrix at one period of history civilisation had evolved two perfect correlatives of artificial and deliberate construction: the compact walled town, and the country. That was the ideal State. Now the period of decadence has set in, as you get it, for example, in South Kensington, is fully back to the state of desert again. Well, in so far as a street is to be a street, i.e., a place for strolling and talking in, and not a railway, Bologna seems to me to be the perfect town. It is all compact of little piazzas flanked by arcades, and never a broad straight street or an open vista in the whole place. You feel always, though you may never see it, the bracing feeling of a disciplinary wall keeping it up to the ideal pitch of town I require, and never allowing it to sprawl into desert. It is a quadrangle and cloister raised to the highest power, the only modern substitute for the groves of Academe.

*   *   *

I have now to chronicle what is perhaps the most important event that has yet happened to a philosopher. I was sitting in the hotel this morning, writing letters, and was vaguely conscious of the noise of bands in the distance, and various tones of shouting. Then after a time, troop after troop of soliders began to march past the window at which I was sitting. I began to be interested. Surely something important must be happening. I hurriedly left the hotel and rushed to the centre of the town. There were enormous crowds in the Piazza Vittoria Emanuelle. Great red banners hung from the brick Renaissance palaces which surround the square. Lining certain streets were troops with their red pistacchios flicked about by the wind, and behind them a mass of people ten deep, all in their characteristic toga cloaks, with one end thrown over the shoulder. When I say mass of people I ought to correct myself. It was not a crowd in the ordinary meaning of the term, but rather a garden city kind of crowd, for surrounding each man was the large space occupied by his cloak. The more I think of that crowd, the more I admire it. It had a peculiar kind of quality I had never seen before. It had achieved the impossible. It was a crowd without being a crowd. It was simply an aggregation of people who managed the extraordinary feat of coming together without becoming that very low class multicellular organism— the mob. If anyone could invent a kind of democracy which includes, as an essential feature, the possession of large and sweeping brown cloaks, then I will be a democrat. To find out what it was all about I bought a paper, 'L'Avveniri d'Italia'. With amazement, I saw in enormous letters across the front page, 'Filosofia'. All this was actually on account of philosophy! Really a world become so self-conscious as to care so much for the great question of the 'Why' is rapidly leaving the admirable plane of instincts and is nearing its end. This most important event really heralds the rapid approach of the final conflagration.

To descend, however, to detail, this was the welcome for the Duke of the Abruzzi, who had come from Rome to open the Congress on behalf of his cousin the King. I may as well say at once that I have not yet been introduced to him; so that any curiosity the reader of this article may feel about Miss Elkins will have to go unsatisfied.

At this moment circumstance forced on me a frightful dilemma. It was ten o'clock, the time of the official opening of the Congress. I ought at once to go to the 'Arch-Gymnasium' and hear the opening ceremony

and Professor Enriques' paper on 'Reality'.[2] But if I did this, I should miss
the street scene. I shouldn't hear the bands. I should not solve the
question whether the garden city crowd could also cheer with dignity. I
had to choose between the two, I could not do both. It was either the
street, or the Congress; truly a terrible dilemma for me, for I regard
processions as the highest form of art. I cannot resist even the lowest form
of them. [I must march even with the Salvation Army bands I meet
accidentally in Oxford Street on Sunday night, and here was a procession
among processions—and then the problem of the behaviour of the
crowd. The dilemma was a perplexing one.]

Inside, I knew from the programme that Professor Enriques would
speak of Reality. But alas! Reality for me is so old a lady, that no
information about her, however new, however surprising, could attain
the plane of interest legitimately described by the word gossip. Outside,
officers in wonderful sweeping blue capes were galloping past as the time
came for the procession to arrive. The inside seemed to suffer by comparison. My conduct was entirely my own concern, but if Pallas Athene,
or the indignant secretary of the Congress had taken it as a piece of lèse
majesté and called on me to justify it before a jury of my peers, I could
have done so. I would first have appealed to the school which considers
that an immediate sensation has reality, and that conceptual notions
diminish it. I could have taken the attitude of the æsthetes in the
exaltation of the sensation, and said, 'Mieux vaut un peu du pain bien
cuit, que tout Shakespeare.'[3] I could have gone further than that and
justified my preference for the particular aspect of sensation represented
by soldiers. In the first place, they would be certain to talk inside of
progress, while the only progress I can stand is the progress of princes and
troops, for they, though they move, make no pretence of moving
'upward'. They progress in the only way which does not violate the
classical ideal of the fixed and constant nature of man.

Then again, there would be much talk inside of the 'all' and the
'whole', and of the harmony of the concert of the cosmos, and I do not
believe in the existence of these things. I am a pluralist, and to see soldiers
for a pluralist should be a symbolic philosophic drama. There is no Unity,
no Truth, but forces which have different aims, and whose whole reality
consists in those differences. To the rationalist this is an absolutely
horrible position.

There is one Truth, one Good. It is for this reason that the conception
of nationality and everything connected with it appears so extraordinarily
irrational to the intellectual. He simply cannot conceive that these are not
one truth, but different truths which win or lose. But however symbolic
my remaining outside in the street might have been as an assertion of my

belief, yet the stage was hardly large enough, the limelight was lamentably absent. Time passed and here was I presenting this spectacle of indecision on the pavement. Finally inward ridicule decided the thing. To cross Europe with the sole purpose of attending a congress, and then to watch a procession instead, would be too much of a comic spectacle. To my lasting regret I went in. I missed a spectacle I shall never see again. I heard words I shall often hear again—I left the real world and entered that of Reality.

At least, I thought I had, but I was mistaken in thinking of myself as a reversed Faust. There was plenty of the world inside. I passed along long corridors, under many arches, and supporting each arch were several police, and soldiers of the heavy cavalry type, and firemen. I shall return to the subject of the enormous number of firemen which guarded us later. I finally reached the Salla di seduti generale.[4] My general impression is of a broad red line at the end, forming the drapery of the platform, and a regular garden of extraordinary hats; great numbers of pretty women— surely this cannot be the world of 'Reality'—I do hope they are not philosophers; and then, vaguely, some drums heard outside.

The International Philosophical Congress at Bologna

[This unsigned report by Hulme of the Fourth International Congress of Philosophy was published in *Nature*, 86 (18 May 1911), 399–400 (confirmed for me by David Davies, editor of *Nature*, in a letter dated 12 May 1977). For Hulme's description of the opening day celebrations, see 'Notes on the Bologna Congress'.]

The fourth International Congress, which met at Bologna under the presidency of Prof. Enriques, was formally opened on April 6 by the Duke of the Abruzzi. It has been by far the best attended of the series, the total number of members being more than five hundred, and has been most hospitably entertained by the committee and the various municipalities. The general tone of the debates was much more cordial than usual, and the congress was fortunate even in its conclusion, for the next day a general strike was declared in the town and province.

It is difficult to say what exactly we should expect from such gatherings. It is clear that they can never produce any definite result; but the contact of personalities does sometimes bring into clearer light the existence of general tendencies of thought which otherwise might not have been so definitely perceived. This congress did bring to light the existence of such a tendency, and this was the quite evident decline in the importance of 'system' in metaphysics. Philosophy does seem to be steering away from its traditional form. It is beginning to form a more fluent and a less rigid and systematic conception of truth. The working out of this tendency is connected with and was most clearly shown in the discussions of what really formed the main problem of the congress, the one it has spent the most time over—that of the relations between philosophy and science. This problem practically resolves itself into the question as to whether philosophy has any right to an independent existence, and it is perhaps one of the surest signs of the renaissance and vitality of the subject that it can discuss such a question with enthusiasm. This key-note of the congress was struck by Prof. Boutroux[1] in his opening speech. Charming though this was in manner, it was not remarkable for profundity of thought, and offered no more original solution than that science, quite legitimately for its purposes, considered the world impersonally, and that it was the business of philosophy to reintroduce for a complete synthesis the element which science left out.

The same subject formed the theme the following day of a paper by that picturesque personality, Fra Gemelli,[2] monk, biologist, and editor of the *Revista Neo-Scolastica*, which drew a reply from Prof. Hans Driesch,[3] in which he explained the scientific use of his conception of entelechy, as distinct from Aristotle's more metaphysical use. The same subject continued to be discussed each day, until the debate finally culminated in the lecture, that was awaited with the greatest curiosity, that which was given by Prof. Henri Bergson,[4] who is perhaps the most discussed and the most interesting philosopher in Europe at the present time. The main point he tried to establish in his *conférence* was that there were two different, and indeed inverse, ways of acquiring a knowledge of reality, the one that of scientific analysis, and another which he described as a kind of intuition, which should be the method of philosophy. Unfortunately, however, this is not the conception that philosophy has formed of itself. It has always attempted to use the same method as the science of its day; it has always attempted to do for the world in general what particular sciences have done for particular fields. It has conceived itself as the complete science, and therein lies the reason of its failure.

This is true historically; Greek philosophy is nothing but the extension into a different field of the method which prevailed in the science of the times, that of geometry. We get a similar phenomenon in modern philosophy. For the static geometrical concepts of the Greek, substitute the conception of scientific law, extend this to the general problem of reality as the Greeks did geometry, and you get the predominant types of modern philosophy. Always you get philosophy pursuing the same method as that of science, that of intellectual analysis, and having the same ideal, that of a complete science of existence. Now, said Bergson, philosophy, so long as it persists in following this method, is doomed to disappear, for it being obviously not wanted in the field of any particular and successful science, it must pursue its activities in the fields where science has not yet penetrated, *i.e.* in the field of the unknown; and this is not a very secure position for it, for as soon as science begins to penetrate the same field, and there is a contradiction between its conclusions and the conclusions of philosophy, it is philosophy that must give way, not science.

The only future of philosophy, then, lies in a recognition of the fact that it must pursue a different method entirely to that of science. It must give up the attempt to give a complete intellectual representation of the cosmos. There remains the allied question of the place of system in philosophy. Looking at the extraordinary complicated constructions of the great systematic philosophers, they certainly seem to have been animated by the conviction that they were creating a science of the real. But, said Bergson, that is only superficial appearance. If you study, say, Spinoza long enough, you will find that the whole elaborate system was merely the language by which he expressed one perfectly simple intuition, a thing which would be stated in one sentence if you yourself had been in a similar state and could at once recognise it. Here comes, then, the absurdity of explaining a philosopher by his sources—you only by that method catalogue the material by which he expressed himself. The important and central thing in a philosopher is a kind of intuition akin to that of the artist, and differing fundamentally from the kind of activity you get in science.

To get to the detailed work of the congress, particularly the work done in the various sections of logic, theory of science, esthetic, ethic, general philosophy, and psychology, one can only say that it was very abundant and very unequal, considerable so far as the magnitude of the subjects raised was concerned, and very little so far as actual results obtained go. This sterility was in great part due to the defective organisation of the congress and to the persistent keeping to the tradition of a free choice of subjects and free individual communication, with the result that there is never time to really discuss in a serious way the subjects raised. For this reason the most interesting work of the congress was done at the general meetings in the afternoon, and we refer here to the lectures which attracted the greatest attention.

The mathematician Henri Poincaré[5] examined the question which has been raised by Boutroux and certain other philosophers as to whether the laws of nature may change. In a world which evolves continually are the laws, *i.e.* the rules under which this evolution takes place, alone exempt from all variation? Such a conception could never be adopted by the man of science without denying even the possibility of science, but the philosopher has the right to pose the question. Imagine a world in which there was no difference of temperature. Certain laws would be discovered by the inhabitants, such as, for example, that water boils at a certain fixed pressure. Suppose, now, that in course of time this uniform temperature changed, all the laws would now change: water would boil at a different temperature, and so on. Now, however perfect might be the conductivity for heat of this planet, it would doubtless not be absolute, so that one day a physicist of genius might with his delicate instruments detect these imperceptible differences. A theory might then be erected that these differences of temperature had an effect on physical phenomena, and, finally, some bold speculator might affirm that the mean temperature of the world had varied in the past, and with it all physical laws. May there not be some physical entity as yet as entirely unknown to us as was temperature to the inhabitants of this imaginary world, which might vary and so create in the same way a change in all the laws?

Poincaré found something analogous to this, at any rate, in the ideas now being brought forward on the subject of mechanics, and which were later in the congress put forward by Prof. Langevin,[6] whose name is known in connection with work in radio-activity. It is now asserted that the laws of mechanics, once considered absolute, are not so. They must be changed, or at least enlarged. They are only approximately true for the velocities to which we are accustomed, and cease to be so for velocities comparable to that of light. One might say that, as a result of the constant dissipation of energy, the speed of bodies has much diminished, since their activity gets transformed into heat. Thus remounting back to the past, one would find an epoch when velocities comparable to that of light were not uncommon, and when, as a consequence, the classical laws of dynamics were not true. But if, on the other hand, we consider these laws as only approximate laws, and consider the laws of motion of molecules as the true laws, we can keep our faith in the immutability of laws in general. There is not, then, a sole law that we can enunciate with the certainty that it has always been true in the past. Nevertheless, there is nothing to hinder the man of science from keeping his faith in the principle of immutability, since no law can descend to the level of a secondary law without being replaced by another law more general and more comprehensive.

Prof. Durkheim,[7] the celebrated sociologist, examined the question of 'judgments of value' and social ideals. How do they arise? They cannot be accounted for on utilitarian principles, for they are often in direct conflict, not only with individual, but even with collective utility. They assert values which go beyond the practical. Must we, then, assume that the ideal is of a different nature from the world of fact. By no means. The ideal values are created in periods of great excitement, such as, for instance, the Renaissance and the French Revolution, when life for a time turns aside from the merely useful. Whilst the intenser life of such periods must of necessity soon die down, the judgments of value and the ideals they create survive into the periods of greater tranquillity, and it is from this that the apparent contradiction between the ideal and world of fact is born.

Prof. Ostwald,[8] the exponent of 'energetics', put forward a curious hypothesis in his paper 'La Volonté et sa base physique' on the connec-

tion between the second law of thermodynamics and the mental phenomena of will. He started from general considerations drawn from
Comte's and his own classification of the sciences. The notion of the
antecedent and more general sciences finds a regular and systematic
application in the subsequent and more special ones, while at the same
time these latter require, in addition, the use of new conceptions. There
is, for example, a mathematic and a geometry of chemistry, but not a
chemistry of mathematics or a biology of physics. He then examined in
this light the conception of energy. It appears for the first time in the
domain of the physical sciences, and for that reason, while it has no
application in the more general sciences of mathematics and logic, it
should play an auxiliary part in biology, psychology, and sociology. The
laws of the lower sciences cannot adequately explain the phenomena
dealt with by the higher, but they provide the framework inside which
the latter must work. How does this work out in detail? What meaning
have the laws of energy applied to mental life? Just this—that whatever
else mental life is, it has to work inside the limits of the second law of
thermodynamics. Each individual is occupied all its life with the task
of making circulate through its own body a part of the general course of
'free' energy on its way to energy of a lower intensity; and further, as only
part of this energy can be usefully employed, the rest being wasted in
heat, so whatever else mental life may be it must first be directed towards
getting as much out of this dissipation as possible. In the effort to increase
this percentage, to save energy, comes, in Ostwald's opinion, the whole
phenomena of the will. He does not pretend that the second law is an
adequate explanation of all mental process, but it is the conditioning
framework inside which all the rest must work. It is the dominating fact
of mental life. It is this which makes the tremendous importance of
the will. All human activity is devoted to get the most out of this limited
energy. (Incidentally, one may note the resemblance to Mach's[9] conception of science as a process of economy of thought.) It is this conception of the 'degradation of energy' which forms the basis of all
the processes in which Schopenhauer saw manifestations of the fundamental will.

The English element at the congress was very small, being responsible for only eleven papers out of a total of 200. Among these the
most important was Dr. Schiller's[10] paper on error, which provoked,
as any exposition of pragmatism always does at these meetings, a most
lively discussion. There was also a paper by E. S. Russell[11] on vitalism,
and an interesting little note by Miss Constance Jones[12] sketching out a
new law of thought, which attempted to lead logic out of the barrenness
of the law of identity, and which she enunciated in the phrase: 'Every

subject of predication is an identity (of denotation) in diversity (of intension).'

The next congress will be held in London in 1915, under the auspices of the University, and it is hoped that this will create a greater interest in these meetings than has heretofore been the case in this country.

Bax on Bergson

[First published in NA 9/14 (3 Aug. 1911), 328–31.]

Some four or five years ago, before 'Evolution Créatrice' appeared, and when I had only read 'Matière et Mémoire', being convinced that I had not quite grasped everything that Bergson had meant in that book, I started on a definite search for every criticism of any importance that had appeared on him. I thought I could ensure in this way that I should not, from a too hasty picking out of that one of Bergson's ideas which I had understood most easily from my own reading, jump to the conclusion that this was the central and essential part of Bergson. I thought that whatever kind of indigestion the reading of several hundred criticisms might produce in me, it would at any rate make certain that I should be brought in contact with all the other ideas which might possibly be regarded as the central one. I accumulated in this way a collection of some 200 articles and books. Ultimately the only actual use they proved to me was that I was able to hand them over to Mr. Pogson[1] for his bibliography. For the purpose for which I collected them they proved absolutely useless. For this reason. When I got to about the twentieth of them I began to notice a strange and curious phenomenon. Every critic explained Bergson in precisely the same phrases and the same metaphors, which were at the same time Bergson's own. No one ventured to go outside even the most trivial illustrations that Bergson himself used to elucidate his thesis. When I got to about the hundredth the thing became ludicrous. So regularly did the same phrases occur over and over again that they began to have quite a hypnotic effect on me. After a time I began to be suspicious. What was the reason for this peculiar phenomenon? It does not occur in the criticisms of other philosophers. People can talk about Kant without behaving like gramophones. It cannot be that the critics are behaving like the usual lazy reviewer, anxious to get the thing done with as little trouble as possible, for I am speaking of long and serious studies appearing in philosophical reviews. It gradually dawned upon me that they used Bergson's exact phrases and illustrations simply because they dare not use any other. If you are suddenly launched into a social event a little above those to which you are habituated, and your only guide is a book of etiquette, then you will take great care not to venture outside the phrases, the situations and the courses of action prescribed by that book. You feel morally certain that if you did you would be going wrong. Now I did not at first like to say that the critics were in this position. My sense of the fitness of things did not allow me even to think in my own mind that people who knew a great deal more about philosophy than I did had failed to grasp a thing which to me seemed as clear as daylight. But I am convinced now, after several years' rereading of the matter and after several conversations with Bergson himself, that it is so. I am perfectly certain that most of these critics (who are all naturally over a certain age) have their mental make-up so definitely crystallised round Kant and other philosophers, that they have not, curious though it may be, in the least grasped what it is exactly new that Bergson has brought into philosophy. My natural respect for my elders and betters prevented me from thinking that I understood what they did not. But I am now convinced that my suspicions were right. The reason that the critics cannot step outside the limits of Bergson's own phraseology is simply that they have not felt the thing which is at the centre of everything that he says. Being, however, intelligent people, they present a very good appearance of having done so by a careful observation and collection of the external features of his system. I do not mean to say that the result is a piece of fudge; they have honestly thought that they understand what he means, but the fact that they do not is most clearly shown by the nature of the attacks that they occasionally venture to make. They always miss fire because they are always attacks on the externals, they are always attacks on the vocabulary, on the definite conceptions which Bergson uses to express his meaning. They never seem to touch the meaning itself.

I derived at any rate one positive benefit from my plodding through all these criticisms. It enabled me to give a recipe for the writing of an article on Bergson. I will assume, for the sake of argument, that Bergson uses a hundred metaphors in any particular book. You pick out any ten that happen to strike you, or which you happen to remember, and you repeat them word for word with the alteration of a preposition here and there, and in the confused order in which they happen to come into your mind as you write. The result will always be interesting, and as it is very unlikely that any other critic will pick out the same ten metaphors, or at any rate that he will put them in the same order, it is very unlikely that your article will be uncomfortably similar to anybody else's. The cook can never appreciate what she herself has cooked, and so once having acquired a knowledge of this recipe I was unable after that to read any more articles on Bergson, and Mr. Bax's[2] is the first I have seen for a long time. I am sorry to say that my recipe has been the one followed in the making of this even. I should, however, differentiate it a little. I suppose there are three parts in the article. The phrases that come direct from Bergson, those that come from Bergson via Mr. Lindsay, and those provided by Mr. Bax himself. Of Mr. Lindsay I know nothing. I have not read his book, and I don't intend to. The kind of effort it represents is adequately suggested to me by an unforgettable sentence from his preface which was quoted in the publisher's puff. Mr. Lindsay, it appeared, had come to the conclusion that 'the brilliancy of Professor Bergson's style had perhaps prevented him being properly understood in England'. Mr. Lindsay then undertook what must have been a task very congenial to the heart of a Scotchman and an Oxford don, that of extracting the brilliancy. He really ought to go into an anthology.

I propose here only to examine Mr. Bax's contribution to the macédoine. I attack it with no eagerness. In the first place, as I have said before, I have a quite unnatural respect for my elders and betters. I have the further reason in this particular case that Mr. Bax has always been one of my admirations. I have always regarded the 'Roots of Reality'[3] as being one of the most important books on philosophy that has appeared in English since Bradley's 'Appearance and Reality'. But, really, this particular article has been a little too much for me. I object to its tone. It might be all right as a piece of journalism, but it seems to me to be emphatically not the way in which one philosopher should write about another. Heaven knows why I should be a censor of manners, but even the Strangers' Gallery may hiss at times. Take this for example: 'The reader may safely assume that where Professor Lindsay becomes less clear than usual the fault lies not in the exposition but in the original text of Bergson himself.' Now, this is a piece of downright fatuous complacency that I would not stand even if it were uttered by Plato himself. Especially exasperating is it in Mr. Bax's case, as one feels quite certain, from the kind of things he says about Bergson in this article, that his knowledge, such as it is, must have been derived, not from a reading of this philosopher's actual books and essays, but at second-hand from the excellent Mr. Lindsay. But the patronising tone of the whole article is calculated to give an entirely wrong idea of Bergson to anyone who hears of him for the first time from Mr. Bax's account. It is entirely misleading, and it is for that reason that I feel bound to protest.

I object particularly to his preface on the subject of fashion and his sneer about 'up-to-date' and the 'entente cordiale'. This is one of the favourite tricks of the controversialist who wishes to depreciate the value of his subject without giving any precise reasons. Without definitely stating it, the idea is subtly conveyed to the mind of the reader that the philosopher who can be described as fashionable must ipso facto be of very little importance. Now, Mr. Bax knows perfectly well that this is nothing but a trick, and it is not, perhaps, worth while discussing at length, but it so happens that it gives me an opportunity of making some remarks that I have wanted for some time to make on the subject of Bergson's popularity. It seems always to be the case that there are two definite stages in the reputation of a philosopher or of any writer. There is first a stage in which he is known to the few people who really care for and who are really able to understand subjects about which he writes. This is a kind of 'atomic' reputation. You can number the elements of which it is composed. This was the case with Bergson from about 1890 up to about six months after 'Evolution Créatrice' was written. Then suddenly, for no apparent reason, it seems a man's reputation spreads all over Europe. Articles appear in newspapers about him, the propagandists of the different sects utilise him for their own purposes, and, finally, last stage of all, he penetrates to the drawing-rooms, he is welcomed and read by the ladies who have ambitions salon-wise; and, finally, chatter makes his name stink in the nostrils of everyone who cares seriously for philosophy. This is what I call a 'flood' reputation as distinct from the 'atomic'. A man is never talked so much about, either before or after, as at this moment of his 'arrival'. This is the stage at which, by no fault and by no desire of his own, Bergson has arrived. Six months after the publication of 'Evolution Créatrice' comparatively few copies had been sold. This is as it should be. A book on pure philosophy has no business to sell in large numbers. Then suddenly the flood started and edition after edition began to come out. A few years ago his lectures at the Collège de France (not the Sorbonne, Mr. Bax; he has no connection at all with that) were attended by a few students, just the kind of people who ought to attend such lectures. Now it is impossible to get a seat without sitting through the hour before and listening to that intolerable bore, Leroy-Beaulieu,[4] and, further, when you do get a seat you are distracted by what an exasperated student recently described as the 'blasphemous scents' of fashionable women. Of course, a very small percentage of these people and of the people who read his books are in the least capable of understanding them. They are pieces of hard discipline in the way of thinking which no one who has not gone through the mill himself can possibly appreciate. In what, then, lies their attractiveness? It cannot all be put down to pure 'snobisme'. That would soon come to an end, and even at that there must be some further reason which causes his reputation in the first place. It lies in this, that while the real importance of Bergson lies in pure philosophy, lies in his method, lies in the category he works with, that of intensive manifolds, yet the conclusion to which the application of his method leads him, that of the dualism of soul and body, is precisely the conclusion which most people seek. It is nice for the timid to be assured on thoroughly respectable authority that there is a chance of immortality and that they have free will.

Now here comes the danger of all this, that while it is the conclusions which attract the mob, yet the very presence of this mob is apt to obliterate in the mind of the student of philosophy the extraordinary importance for him of what is, after all, the essential part of Bergson, the theory of intensive manifolds. This seems to me to be the error into which Mr. Bax has fallen. No doubt it is a temptation to attack a fashion, but Mr. Bax does not seem to me to have set about it in the right way. When one philosopher is writing about another, insinuations about fashion are out of place, and what one expects is a definite criticism of philosophical ideas entirely from the philosophical point of view. The other thing is rather cheap, and bad manners. It is especially ridiculous applied to Bergson, who provides an example of a concentrated attention to pure philosophy, which is extremely rare at the present time.

Of the part of the article which contains the actual exposition of Bergsonism such as it is, I will say nothing. It is made according to the recipe I gave earlier, and contains much the same selection of phrases as all the other articles I have talked about. What I am concerned about is the parts in which Mr. Bax attempts criticism. I am afraid they show a curious incomprehension of the actual new idea which Bergson has introduced into philosophy. He says himself that he cannot see in what lies the originality of the French thinker, and I should have guessed as much from the weird remarks he sometimes makes.

I cannot possibly cover the whole ground here, but I pick out four or five sentences for comment. In the first place, he fails to understand, as do most of Bergson's commentators, the point of the antithesis that is made between Space and Time. It is not, as generally supposed, the fundamental one in his system, but gets its whole point from a more clearly defined antithesis, that between intensive and extensive manifolds. Mr. Bax fails to understand the exact use of the word Space in Bergson.

For Bergson, ideal space may be a 'form of intuition', but his view differs from Kant's. For while he thinks that it is a habit of the mind, he at the same time thinks it reposes on a real quality of objects, that of 'extensiveness'. So that when he uses space as one term of antithesis, he is not thinking of space as it is, a synthesis of many divergent attributes, but only of that particular aspect of space in which the word can be used as a synonym for extensive manifolds. That space includes other things he would admit, but he is only concerned with it in this one aspect. This is the point which most accounts of Bergson miss. First in any exposition there should come an account of his method, of the categories with which he works, the purely theoretical contrast between intensive and extensive manifolds. This remains valid quite apart from the question as to whether such things as intensive manifolds exist. Only after this has been explained should come the application of the method to reality in the identification of these two terms with the space–time antithesis. That being so, Mr. Bax's remark about the non-spacial perception of notes simultaneously heard in a chord, a remark which he considers so pointed that he follows it up by an exclamation mark, shows such a ludicrous incomprehension of what Bergson really intends that one forgets for a minute one's annoyance and can only laugh.

Mr. Bax complains that he fails to find in Bergson any distinct pronouncement on the fundamental problem of the 'Theory of Knowledge'. Now, it seems to me that in the third chapter of 'Evolution Créatrice' and the first chapter of 'Matière et Mémoire' taken together, you have complete materials for such a theory. I ask myself what it is that Mr. Bax expects and that he finds wanting here, and I think I can supply an answer. He looks for, and naturally does not find, a 'Theory of Knowledge' in the Kantian sense of the word. What is so difficult for a man who has been brought up in one epoch of philosophy and lives on into the beginning of the next to understand is this, that not only are there new answers to old questions, but in many cases the old questions cease to have any interest and any meaning for the next generation. What is happening now, and what Mr. Bax cannot understand, is not that we are giving a new answer to the old questions, not that our fickle attention has passed on to new questions and left the old ones alone, but simply that the old questions which he takes so seriously have absolutely no meaning for us. I had occasion some years ago to compare Mr. Bax to a clown who puts his head through a hoop of paper at a circus;[5] he has brought a new idea into philosophy, but he still remains framed by the ragged edges of the system he has passed through. Those ragged edges are the Kantian phraseology and set of conceptions, inside which Mr. Bax was brought up. He is soaked in Kantianism and simply cannot understand that the resulting kind of questions he asks of nature are not 'inevitable'.

This seems to explain Mr. Bax's dissatisfaction. He belongs emphatically to the German idealist tradition. The highly-starched phraseology of the 'Roots of Reality' is enough to prove that. With any tradition in philosophy goes a certain attitude of mind, a conception of metaphysics as the answering of certain questions, and so when you come across a philosophy which does not even consider your questions, you are naturally annoyed. What is so difficult for anyone inside a 'tradition' of this kind to conceive, is that the questions may be as artificial as the answers. They are part of the 'tradition', part of the mechanism by which you orient yourself and move inside that tradition; they do not lie in the nature of the subject itself. It is, then, no defect in Bergson that he does not answer the questions Mr. Bax asks. When, then, Mr. Bax says, 'I find no theory of knowledge', 'his metaphysic is unbalanced'; what he really means is, 'I find no German idealist theory of knowledge'. Oh, these Germans, when shall we have finished with them! Though their 'idealist' tradition in philosophy will always be a memorable phenomenon, it is as dead, and has as little right to lay down canons of execution, as the Sienese tradition in painting.

I come now to Mr. Bax's remarks about the nature of individuality. Incidentally he says something here which, if I were malicious, I should say gave the key to his whole attitude. 'Here Bergson approaches the lines of an hypothesis originally put forward by the present writer some twenty years ago'. Here is the cloven hoof. The only appropriate exclamation I can think of here is 'At it again, Mr. Bax'. Mr. Bax has been for some time under the delusion that he anticipated Bergson, and in a letter to this review, two years ago, claimed priority.[6]

It is a double delusion. In the first place, as I carefully explained at the time in a letter in reply to Mr. Bax (NEW AGE, VOL. 5),[7] he did not anticipate Bergson. For 'Les Données Immédiates' was first published in '89, and was written about '85, that is six or seven years before Mr. Bax first put forward his conception. In the second place, there is in reality exceedingly little resemblance between Mr. Bax's philosophy and Monsieur Bergson's. It is true that they both deny that reality can be completely included under a system of laws, but so do more than half a dozen other philosophers, even in recent times, from Boutroux downwards. The thing which makes the real distinction and originality of Bergson, and which differentiates him from all the other philosophers of indeterminism, is something to which no analogy at all can be found in Mr. Bax's book.

What resemblance there is is purely superficial, and it is precisely at this point that Mr. Bax and a great many other people fail to understand Bergson. 'The unanalysable continuity' of the latter philosophy is not a mere limiting conception like the alogical of Mr. Bax, but has a positive internal structure. It is an intensive manifold. What precisely is meant by that I shall try to explain in later articles.

To return, however, to Mr. Bax's precise claim in this particular article. He thinks that Bergson, in his conception of the nature of the individual, is approximating to his (Mr. Bax's) own conception. Now, what, as a matter of fact, is the nature of this resemblance? Merely that one is the mathematical antithesis of the other! Mr. Bax's view, as I take it from his own description, is that gradually in the course of evolution a kind of consciousness will be developed which will supersede the ordinary individual consciousness in the same way as that superseded the separateness of the sentiency of its component organic cells. Bergson's view, far from approximating to this, exactly reverses the process. In the beginning and in reality you have always this general race consciousness, this élan vital which is split up into individuals by the nature of matter (the principle of matter being a principle of division and analysis), just as stones in a stream split it into separate eddies. This conception is, as I have said, the exact antithesis of Mr. Bax's.

Finally, says Mr. Bax, we can trace back most of his doctrines to nineteenth-century philosophic writers. Might I ask which ideas and from or to whom they can be traced? Mr. Bax very wisely avoids doing this; it is much easier to make a general statement. The only person who actually attempted this task was René Berthelot,[8] who attempted to analyse Bergson into a combination of two things—the English empirical method in psychology, and the romanticism of Schelling introduced into France by Ravaisson.[9] It is a singularly ineffective piece of genealogical research, and the best account of it was that given me by Bergson himself. Berthelot's father, he said, was a celebrated chemist, and we say that the son follows his parent's footsteps by trying to 'faire la chimie des idées'.[10]

Of course, there is a sense in which it can be said that Bergson's ideas can be traced to other people. It is perfectly true that no man can say anything absolutely new in any subject, least of all in metaphysics. The number of conceptions that the brain of man can form about the cosmos and its problems is necessarily as limited as the number of his organs and his limbs. In this sense it can be said that every idea of every philosopher always has a long ancestry. I could find Mr. Bax's alogical in St. Thomas Aquinas if I looked for it. It is this which makes it possible to say that the history of philosophy is the one subject where great knowledge is much more dangerous than a little knowledge. With a little knowledge each philosopher does appear to have a certain shape. One is under the impression that one does find in him a certain set of ideas one does not find in anyone else. Great knowledge reveals to us the fact that the same ideas can be found in nearly everyone. All the distinct conceptions one formerly had of separate philosophers begin to melt away into the common matrix, and finally one finds oneself in a state of confusion little different to a state of absolute ignorance.

But all this leaves the real question untouched. It is not in the ideas which philosophers use that their difference comes, but in the use they make of them, and the importance they attach to them. It is a question of emphasis. A man cannot invent an idea, but when he realises one so vividly that he rams it home by dialectic, reasoning, illustration, and metaphor until he makes it explain nearly the whole of experience; then that idea can legitimately be said to be the man's own. In odd corners of Hegel I have no doubt that I can find, either in the text or in foot-notes, every idea that has ever been employed in philosophy; but that does not make Hegel the complete philosopher. Now apply these considerations to Bergson. Take his conception of continuity. (In order to be fair I place myself here on Mr. Bax's own ground. I will suppress for the minute all the positive significance of Bergson's conception, and merely take it negatively as Mr. Bax does to mean something unanalysable.) It is quite true that Lotze[11] used this idea. But can Mr. Bax place his hand on his heart and honestly say that Lotze realised the full meaning of this conception or at all approached the extraordinary synthetic use that Bergson makes of it?

I commend to Mr. Bax's notice a recent story about another German idealist. Lord Haldane some little time ago gave an address to a set of young men who were preparing for the Scotch ministry,[12] in the course of which he told them in a pontifical manner, very like Mr. Bax's own, that the whole of Bergson could be found in Hegel. This was told to Professor Pringle Pattison,[13] and he is reported to have said, 'Haldane should speak the truth, even when he is talking to students of theology.'

Notes on Bergson

[First published in *NA* in five parts: 9/25 (19 Oct. 1911), 587–
8; 9/26 (26 Oct. 1911), 610–11; 10/4 (23 Nov. 1911), 79–82;
10/5 (30 Nov. 1911), 110–12; and 10/17 (22 Feb. 1912), 401–3.
The series was reprinted in *FS* 28–63. Note that parts III, IV,
and V were published after the material that constitutes the next
three chapters: 'Bergson Lecturing', 'Mr. Balfour, Bergson, and
Politics', and 'A Personal Impression of Bergson'. Keeping this
chronology in mind, the reader will see that Hulme's doubts
about Bergson occurred over a wider span of time than the
printing of all the 'Notes on Bergson' together might suggest.]

I

It seems to me that the best way to write about Bergson is to start some
distance off. I am the more inclined to this view as it happens to fit in
with my secret inclinations. The duty of a small person writing about a
big one is, I know, to give as plain an account of his subject as he can, and
keep himself out of it. But my anæmic mind shrinks from the kind of
concentrated perseverance involved in a straightforward 'compte rendu'.
The prospect of stolidly going through what has been already gone
through before fills me with depression. I realise quite clearly that this is
no superiority on my part, but is due simply to a certain lack of vitality.
I have, however, the excuse that at the present time, when all Bergson's
books have been translated, and when all the preliminary panegyric
necessary to make his name known has been more than successfully
accomplished, any straightforward account would be an entirely unnecessary performance. Those who want any such account cannot do better
than read the philosopher himself. No one can improve on the lucidity
of his own exposition, and any attempt to cut it short inevitably leaves out
all the point. Nor can I emulate the feats of those ingenious people during
the last few months, who, in most surprising places, ranging from sporting
papers upwards, have managed by the skilful choice and repetition of a
few magical phrases, such as 'Life overflows the intellect', to create the
illusion both in their own and their readers' minds that they have really
said something quite definite. I repeat, then, that I do not in these articles
intend to give any straightforward account of Bergson's system. I concern
myself with a much easier and to me much more amusing undertaking.

I intend giving simply a personal confession. At the time when I first read 'Les Données Immédiates'[1] it represented to me a great influence and a great excitement. All I am trying to do here is fix down exactly what that influence was, and why it was so exciting. My only justification for this kind of treatment is that it amuses me, and further that it does enable me to get the subject into some kind of perspective.

With this I can get back to the beginning of the article and explain what I meant by the first sentence in it. I said that the best way to explain Bergson was to start some distance off. What I meant was that you can only convey over a sense of his importance by first describing the state of things which existed before he arrived, and from which he relieved one. If the reading of 'Les Données Immédiates' was an influence and an excitement it could only have been so because it bore some relation to something which already existed in my own mind. If he made a tremendous difference to me I cannot explain what that difference was until I have explained the state of things before he arrived. If in my enthusiasm I pictured him as a kind of relieving force I cannot explain what the excitement was about until I have first explained the previously existing state of siege. But while my enthusiasm was due to the fact that reading Bergson put an end to an intolerable state, there was more in it than the feeling of mere relief. If that had been all there would not have been much justification for my describing my previous state of mind merely in order to say, 'This is what I was relieved from.' It was not simply a case of an intolerable state being changed into a pleasanter one; it was not merely that one state changed into its opposite. On the contrary, there was a certain resemblance between the initial and the final stages. There was a certain continuity between them. The first stage might even be considered as a very rough microcosm of part, at any rate, of the second. Certain elements present in one were present in the other. But these elements, which in the first state were tortured, vague, and confused, became in the second clear and definite. It is in this partial correspondence that I find my justification for describing the first state, and which at the same time was the cause of the extent of my enthusiasm. I felt the exhilaration that comes with the sudden change from a cramped and contracted to a free and expanded state of the same thing. It was an almost physical sense of exhilaration, a sudden expansion, a kind of mental explosion. It gave one the sense of giddiness that comes with a sudden lifting up to a great height. One saw clearly outlined in perspective the shape of things which before had only been felt in a muzzy kind of way. My enthusiasm was then a double one, and due to two separate causes. In the first place, there was a simple sentiment of relief. A solution was given to a problem which worried me. I had been released from a nightmare which had long troubled my mind. If I compare my nightmare to imprisonment in a small cell, then the door of that cell was for the first time thrown open. In the second place, the key with which this prison door was opened corresponded to the type of key which I had always imagined would open it. I had constructed for myself imperfect examples of keys of this type. I was shown the perfect and successful one which yet was on the lines I had vaguely imagined might be successful. There had been present in my mind in a very crude form something which did correspond to the solution actually given me by reading Bergson.

The sources of my enthusiasm were, then, the relief from the nightmare, and, in addition to this, the delight of seeing something done perfectly that I had wrestled with clumsily and unsuccessfully. I had the delight of escape, and I had the quite different delight of seeing an expert wield with the ease of Cinquevalli[2] an implement whose shape even I had only just been able to guess at.

I had the purely physical delight of freedom and at the same time the technical delight of seeing the facile and fertile use of an instrument I admired.

If now I am to keep to my announced intention of giving a merely personal account of my relations to Bergson's work and an explanation of exactly what it meant to me, I have, in order to give an adequate account of this enthusiasm, to give first the two elements in my previous state of mind which were responsible for and concerned in this enthusiasm. The enthusiasm I have explained was due to the sudden change in the state of clearness of two elements in my mind. Two things corresponded to what I found in Bergson. In the first place, I was concerned with the same nightmare, and, in the second place, I had a suspicion of his way out of it. Both these were changes from a state of dimness to one of clear light. A dark problem and a vaguely seen way of escape changed to a solved problem with the way out of it clearly defined. In order, then, to give an adequate account of my enthusiasm I must give an adequate account of this double change, and in order to give an adequate account of the change I must commence with a detailed description of these two elements before change of my preliminary state of mind. The first article will be about the nightmare I suffered from, and the second, which I call 'the chessboard', will be a description of the roughly-modelled key I had imagined might release me from the nightmare.

This I should have to do in order to explain to what exactly my enthusiasm was due. However, I have a better excuse than this for spending the space of two articles in giving an account of something that

Bergson did not say before passing on to what he did. I realise that some better excuse is needed for devoting two articles to something which has no more connection with Bergson than the fact that it gives the reason why I personally found him exciting. It would be rather a thin excuse by itself. Fortunately I can find a better one.

It seems to me to be worth while describing the nightmare, the locked door, in detail, because it enables me to give the state of things that Bergson was heaven-sent to relieve, and so enables me to convey over his immense importance and significance at the present moment. It enables me to show to what circumstances his importance is due. It gives me the age-old problem that he concerns himself with. In the second place, it seems to me to be worth while devoting a whole article to the crude form of escape which had dimly suggested itself to my own mind, as by that means I am enabled to get an easy line of approach to the most difficult part of Bergson and his method—this in the article on 'chessboards'. When I have got this out I have some kind of basis, some kind of leverage, with which I can get at the explanation of what he means by an intensive manifold.

II

Not exactly, however. I cannot leave it in that precise form, because it embodies a certain inaccuracy. That perhaps would not matter very much were it not that the form of the inaccuracy lays me open to a kind of accusation I particularly detest. I must, therefore, permit myself another digression before I can go straight forward. I have been incautious in the way I have stated things. I have made rather too frequent use of the word enthusiasm, and, worse even than that, I have hinted at the 'solution' of a world-old problem. This is where my danger comes in. These things are all signs.

I might be suspected of that particular form of youthful enthusiasm that imagines it has come across the secret of the world for the first time, the kind of enthusiasm that imagines Bergson supersedes all other philosophy.

This would be a most awful accusation. To me personally it would be the most offensive that could be uttered. For this reason, that it would identify me with a type of mentality which I regard with peculiar horror, and which has been particularly prominent in connection with appreciations and criticism of Bergson. It is a type which, while I dislike, I think at the same time that I thoroughly understand. It springs from a kind of mental debility which has left its mark in many other subjects besides philosophy. It is, in fact, one of the normal and common attributes of the human race.

Its external signs are quite easy to recognise. In philosophy you believe that you have got hold of something absolutely 'new'. You have found the secret of the universe. By the side of this all previous philosophy seems tedious groping. Paralled with this, in social matters, you have the belief that we are on the verge of an entirely 'new' state of society which will be quite 'different' from anything in the past. Something is going to happen. It may be Home Rule; it may be a social revolution; but at any rate, when it has happened things will be quite 'different'.

What is the psychology of this kind of belief? The first step towards a correct explanation of the phenomena is to recognise that your enthusiasm over your particular 'new' thing is not caused by the nature of the new thing itself, or only in a very minor degree. The new thing only provides accidentally, as it were, a nucleus round which an over-saturated solution of a certain kind of enthusiasm can crystallise.

One is led to this belief by observing the universality of the phenomena and the widely different subjects in which it is successively exhibited. If a man believes in the possibility of a new state of society, and at the same time thinks that Bergson has invented an entirely new philosophy, the objects of his enthusiasm have so little connection with each other that you are compelled to believe that the cause of it must lie in some disposition of his mind and not in the things themselves.

It is not so much then anything definite that Bergson says that moves them to enthusiasm as the fact that certain sentences perhaps give a pretext for this enthusiasm to empty itself in a flood. It is not because they have clearly seen in Bergson a completely new system that they are moved to talk in this ridiculous way as that they are in a constant state of wanting to talk like that, and he provides a convenient excuse. They are driven on to beliefs of this kind in all subjects by a certain appetite, a certain craving, which must be satisfied. What happens to satisfy it is quite a secondary matter. They seek, and will have, a certain kind of mental excitement; the desire is the governing factor, not the accidental thing it happens to fix itself on to. It is like falling in love at an early and inexperienced age. You may be under the delusion that it is the object that has so produced the state, but the more aged outside observer of the phenomena could tell you that it is more probably the state which produces the object.

What is behind all this? These are the external signs. What is the internal cause of it all? I should say that it was this.

The type is characterised by a certain malaise, a certain irritation of the mind, which seeks to relieve itself. A certain want of balance, which strives to put itself right, which manifests itself in an insatiable craving for a certain specific kind of excitement and exhilaration.

This malaise can be roughly described as a repugnance to and an irritation at the ordinary and the humdrum. We all suffer from this, but in this type the irritation is raised to a hysterical pitch which can almost be called a disease. It is so strong that it affects the balance of the mind. It can only keep its sanity by hugging to itself a balancing illusion. It must believe, in order that it may continue to exist, that there exists somewhere, or that there is about to come into existence, something emphatically *not* ordinary, something quite 'different' from humdrum experience.

This craving for something which can be thought of as 'different' might then almost be described as the instinctive effort of the organism to right itself. The truth would kill it; this over-belief is necessary in order that it may continue to go on living in comfort. It is like the instinctive action of a man stumbling who throws out his hands to restore his equilibrium. It is an unconscious process; it most generally takes the form of a belief that the future holds possibilities of the perfect which have been denied to the present and the past. This type of debility of mind finds sanity in the belief that it is on the verge of great happenings. It so finds restored equilibrium, but at what a cost! Compared with this fetish worship is an intellectual occupation. Belief of this kind is the most loathsome form of credulity. People in a state of unstable equilibrium support themselves at first sight in very odd ways. A tight-rope walker carries a long pole; Mr. Balfour,[3] we know, supports himself by holding on to the lapel of his frock coat. But as ludicrous spectacles both these altogether pale when compared with the romancist who prevents himself from falling by leaning on the 'future'.

*   *   *

It is at the back of all forms of romanticism. Translated into social beliefs, it is the begetter of all the Utopias. It is the source of all the idealist support of Revolution. By the use of this word you can indeed generally identify the type. You could get the most condensed expression of it by saying that it believes, and must believe, that something remarkable and revolutionary can happen. All demagogues have built on this fallibility of man. Persuade a people that they are about to do something dramatic, that they are about to make history, and they will proceed to follow you. To take a trivial instance of its workings: the appeal of the phrase about the 'rare and refreshing fruit' was not to material interests altogether. There was the much greater consolation involved in the idea that there could be such a thing as a rare and refreshing fruit. Well, just in the same way you persist in thinking that some day a rare and refreshing fruit will be discovered in philosophy. As you believe that a new social order vastly different from everything that had preceded it is about to arrive, so you want as a natural corollary to believe that there is also an absolutely new philosophy to fit in with this brand-new good time coming. It would pain you intensely to think that you had to have any old furniture in the new house. You read Bergson then not so much for any definite views he puts forward; indeed, you very rarely are enabled to give any coherent account of what he says, but simply because there you do get this craving satisfied.

This is the type which I regard with such peculiar horror, and from which I want to dissociate myself. And as the object of writing and of the making of theories is nothing more at bottom than the kind of thing aimed at by the Thirty-nine Articles, that is, the drawing of a peculiarly complicated but quite definite line which will mark you off finally and distinctly from the people you can't stand, I have thought it worth while to examine these people at length.

I want carefully to state that I do not belong to this type. When, therefore, I speak of a new solution to an old problem I do not at all attach the meaning to the phrase that this type would. I believe, on the contrary, that there is nothing absolutely new in either the problem or the solution of it which I am about to describe in Bergson. In substance the problem and its solution are the same in every generation. Every philosopher must deal with an old problem, and must escape from it by an equally world-old solution. It is impossible at this time of day to take up an absolutely new attitude towards the cosmos and its persistent problems. The conflicts of the constant attitudes recur in each generation, and the things we dispute about now are the same in substance as those which occupied the leisure of the theologians of the third and fourth centuries. It is as impossible to discover anything new about the ways of man in regard to the cosmos as it is to observe anything new about the ways of a kitten. The general conceptions we can form are as limited in number as the possible gestures of the dance, and as fixed in type as is the physiology of man himself. The philosopher who has not been antici- pated in this sense of the word does not exist, or, if he does, he breathes forth his wisdom in the ineffectual silence of solitary confinement.

But if that is so, what is the use of bothering about the matter at all? Why should you investigate even the relatively new? Just as one genera- tion after another is content to watch the eternally fixed and constant antics of kittens, so, one might urge, should one generation after another be content to watch the antics of the philosophers without sighing after anything new. There is this obvious objection: that while the antics of the kitten, like the art of the actor, die with it, the same is not true of philosophers.

It is necessary for the kittens of this generation to repeat the gestures of the past in order that we may see them at all, for the dead kittens who did the same things are gone beyond recall; but in philosophy the gestures of the dead are recorded in print. What justification is there for philosophy if it does nought but repeat the same old attitudes? This is a plausible but fallacious objection, and based on an illusion. The phrases of dead philosophers recorded in print are to most people as dead as dead kittens. In order that they may appear alive they must be said over again in the phraseology of the moment. This, then, is the only originality left to a philosopher—the invention of a new dialect in which to restate an old attitude.

This, then, is the sense that I might safely say that Bergson had presented a new solution to an old problem. I should restate the thing, to avoid any suspicion of romanticism, in this way: Bergson has provided in the dialect of the time the only possible way out of the nightmare.

When I said that in my article on the chessboard I should give the suspicion of this way out that was present in my own head, I mean rather that I must give the kind of embryo idea that was present in the minds of this generation ready to be developed. For a philosopher must be anticipated even in this more special way.

The thing that he has to say must already be present in a crude form to the minds of a considerable number of the men of his own generation for him to get a hearing. The ground must be prepared for him. What he says can have very little meaning or significance to the reader unless it hitches on to or resembles some similar idea already present in that reader's head. The egg must be there; all that the philosopher can do is to act as a broody hen. Or perhaps a more correct metaphor would be to say that out of the muddy stream of our own thoughts the philosopher dives in and dries on the bank into a definite and fixed shape the idea that in our own mind was but muddy, transient, and confused. This is in the sense in which every reader who derives anything from the philosopher must have anticipated him. Without you had already something which a little corresponded to what he has to say you would not be able to make very much of him. You anticipate him in this sense, that with several hundred other people in the same state of mind you form the confusion that the particular philosopher is heaven-sent to clear up.

There is nothing in all this derogatory to the originality of a philosopher. It is a grievous mistake to find the originality of a philosopher in his bare ideas. You cannot find the originality and peculiar qualities of an innovator merely in the ideas he brings forward. You wouldn't read him at all did you not find in him much the same ideas that were already present in your own head. There is nothing in having ideas. Anybody can have those much overrated articles of commerce. You or I out for a morning's walk may, if it be the first day of spring, or if we can hear a band in the distance, give birth to a crowd of ideas, each of which might serve as the starting point of a new system of philosophy. Each of them seems to hold the old-world process in its embrace. Probably this is not a matter of seeming only, probably each of them does, or has done so in reality, for the cosmos is by no means a prude in these matters. Surely the history of philosophy is there to prove that the cosmos, like the wife of Marcus Aurelius, has wandered very much. All the disputes come from the fact that the metaphysicians pitifully lacking not only in the physique, but also in the horse sense of the soldiers, are apt in their rapture to think that they are the only ones.

*   *   *

To return at length to the point, I am giving in the next article, the nightmare, the problem that I conceive Bergson to have finished off. This gives the pedestal he stands on the dark background which throws him into startling relief.

III

We have been treated during the last two weeks to a number of not very profound witticisms on the subject of Bergson.[4] It has been triumphantly demonstrated that all his conclusions are of extreme antiquity, and great play has been made, both in prose and verse, with 'the people who discovered for the first time that they had souls, being told that it was the latest thing from Paris'. In any case, this is a fairly mechanical form of wit, because it is the kind of attack which could have been predicted before-hand. The only effective kind of sneer is the one which only your enemy could have thought of, while these things, as a matter of fact, were anticipated in detail by me in the last of my Notes. I knew they would be sure to come and I defended myself in advance.

But my attitude towards the state of mind behind these attacks has become so complicated by the mixture of partial agreement and partial disagreement that I shall try to disentangle the thing out clearly.

I agree entirely with the point of view from which these jokes spring, but, at the same time, I do not see that they have any 'point'. Some jokes one can never appreciate because they spring from a general mental make-up which one dislikes. I don't appreciate jokes about stupid Conservative candidates, for example. But in this case I am on the same side as the people who make the jokes. Why, then, do they seem to be rather pointless?

Take first the sneer about the antiquity of Bergson's conclusions. I agree with the statement it makes. It is so true that it is merely a platitude. But if it is to have any point as an attack, behind it must lie the supposition that philosophers may, and, indeed, ought to, establish some absolutely new conclusion—if they are to be considered of any importance. This is the most vulgar of all superstitions. No new conclusions can ever be expected, for this reason, that when a philosopher arrives at his conclusions he steps right out of the field of philosophy and into that of common knowledge, where nothing new is, of course, possible. I don't mean by this that he has made a step which he ought not to have made; it is, on the contrary, a necessary and inevitable step, which is involved in the very nature of 'conclusions'. Every philosopher in his conclusions must pass out of his own special craft and discipline into the kind of knowledge which every man may and should have. He passes from the study to the market-place. I use market-place here something in the sense which is intended in the epitaph which I quote below. It is one which is fairly common, but I happened to see it myself first in a churchyard in Sussex. I put in the second verse just for the fun of the thing:—

> Life is a crowded town,
>   With many crooked streets.
> Death is a market place,
>   Where all men meets.
>
> If life were a thing
>   Which money could buy,
> The rich would live
>   And the poor would die.

By the 'conclusions' of a philosopher one means his views on the soul, on the relation of matter and mind and the rest of it. If, then, in the above epitaph I take the market-place not to be death itself, but 'thoughts and opinions about death', I get the position accurately enough. When the philosopher makes the inevitable step into this market-place, he steps into a region of absolute constancy. Here novelty of belief would be as ridiculous as novelty in the shape of one's body. In these matters, in this market-place, 'all men meets.' There can be no difference between the philosopher and the ordinary man, and no difference between the men of one generation and the men of another. There is a certain set of varied types of belief which recur constantly.

In this region there could not then be any new conclusion, and expectation of any such novelty could only spring from a confusion of mind.

But though I hold this opinion, yet at the same time I cannot see anything ridiculous in the people who have suddenly discovered that they have souls. I can explain the cause of my apparent inconsistency. To make the task more difficult in appearance I assert that not only do I accept the statement that there is no novelty as a truth, but I welcome it with considerable enthusiasm as the kind of truth that I like. My defence of the people who have 'discovered their souls' will be the more sincere from the fact that I personally sympathise with the attitude from which they have been laughed at. I find no attraction in the idea that things must be discovered, or even re-stated, in each generation. I would prefer that they were much more continuous with the same ideas in the past even than they are. There is tremendous consolation in the idea of fixity and sameness. If the various possible ideas about the soul at the present moment are represented by certain struggling factions in the market-place, then my own opinion in this flux and varying contests seems, if I confine myself to the present, to be a very thin and fragile thing. But if I find that a certain proportion of the men of every generation of recorded history have believed in it in substantially the same form that I myself hold it, then it gains a sudden thickness and solidity. I feel myself no longer afloat on a sea in which all the support I can get depends on my own activity in swimming, but joined on by a chain of hands to the shore. The difference it produces in the atmosphere of one's beliefs is like the difference which was produced in my outlook on London in the year when I discovered by actual walking that Oxford Street does actually go to Oxford and that Piccadilly is really the Bath road.

I need not be suspected, then, of the kind of excitement about Bergson which would be caused by the delusion that in him one was for the first time in the world's history, in the presence of the truth. That would have caused my instant flight in some other direction.

Though I do not, then, admit that there can be any real novelty in his 'conclusions', yet I can sympathise with the people who find their souls a novelty. I am prepared to defend these people as having instinctively seized an aspect of the truth which the traditionalists had neglected.

The traditionalist view, I take it, is this: To state the thing, I take one definite problem and state, in the terms of the market-place, a certain view of the soul which has always existed, and has always been represented by one of the factions. More than that, the objections to that view have also always existed and always been represented. What excuse is there, then, for the people who became suddenly excited at the discovery of their soul? It is not a new view of the soul that is put forward, and it has not overcome any special obstacles peculiar to this period. Why make this tremendous fuss then?

The answer to that I should put in this way: The opposing sides in this dispute, I supposed, represented by opposing factions in the market-place—always remembering, of course, that the market-place exists in you. These factions represent not only the various views it is possible to hold, but also the force with which these views press themselves on your mind. Beliefs are not only representations, they are also forces, and it is possible for one view to compel you to accept it in spite of your preference for another. Now, while it is impossible to create a new faction, it is possible to alter the weapons with which they are armed and so to decide which shall be predominant.

This is just what has happened in the matter of the beliefs about the soul. The growth of the mechanistic theory during the last two centuries has put a weapon of such a new and powerful nature into the hands of the materialist, that in spite of oneself one is compelled to submit. It is as if one side in the faction fight had suddenly armed themselves in steel breast-plates while the other went unprotected.

It is idle to deny this. It seems to me to be the most important fact which faces the philosopher. If one examines the psychology of belief one finds that brutal forces of this kind decide the matter just as they do more external matters. A candid examination of one's own mind shows one that the mechanistic theory has an irresistible hold over one (that is, if one has been educated in a certain way).

It isn't simply a question of what you would like to win. It is a matter simply of the recognition of forces. If you are candid with yourself you find, on examining your own state of mind, that you are forcibly, as it were, carried on to the materialist side.

It is from this frank recognition of forces that comes my excitement about Bergson. I find, for the first time, this force which carries me on willy-nilly to the materialist side, balanced by a force which is, as a matter of actual fact, apart from the question of what I want, able to meet on equal terms the first force. As the materialist side became for a time triumphant, because it became, to a certain extent, artificial by putting on heavy armour (this is how the effect of the mechanistic theory appears to me), so in Bergson, in the conception of time, I find that the other side, the scattered opposition to materialism, has taken on, for its part, a, to a certain extent, artificial form which is able to meet the other side on equal terms.

It could not be said, then, of me that I had 'discovered my soul'. But simply that for the first time the side that I favoured was able to meet fairly without any fudging the real force which was opposed to it. It would have been sheer silliness on my part to pretend that this force did not exist, for I knew very well that it did and affected me powerfully.

The attitude behind the sneer seems then to me to be childish, because it takes no account of real conditions. To ignore what one gets in Bergson seems to me to be as silly as to take no interest in Dreadnoughts because one is convinced that one Englishman is a match for fifty Germans. I could not be said to have suddenly discovered that I was an Englishman if I exhibited some delight in a naval victory, but merely that I had some sense of the real forces which move the things. There is, then, nothing comic in the attitude of the people who suddenly discovered their souls, but merely an admirable sense of reality, a sure instinct for the forces that really exist. They had the capacity to understand 'the Realpolitik' of 'belief'.

Summing it all up, then, there exists this constant struggle between the two attitudes we can assume about the soul. But during the last 150 years the balance between the two has been greatly disturbed. The materialist side has clothed itself in a certain armour which makes it irresistible, at least to people of a certain honesty of mind and a certain kind of education. In more concrete terms, what is all this?

*　　*　　*

The problem as it has always existed in the market-place, quite independently of its modern manifestations, can be stated quite simply: Is consciousness a mere local phenomenon appearing in certain places where there is a certain highly complex arrangement of matter and entirely at the mercy of the surrounding material circumstances? Or is it a permanent part of reality which only manifests itself under these circumstances, but which exists apart from them?

I put the difference between these two constant views in market-place terminology as a contrast between two different states of mind. I give these states merely as states that occur, without any suppositions as to whether the things we feel in them are true or delusive. They are illustrations by which the problem can be more easily stated. I give them entirely from the point of view of the novelist, then.

This, roughly, is the first state. Among the multifarious contents of a man's mind somewhere in the rubbish heap there is one mood which now and again comes to the top. In certain periods of mental excitement it seems quite clear to one that the active mind whose workings have just excited one, in the working out of a problem, say, or the seizure for the first time of a new idea, must exist independently of matter. When the mind is in full action in this way it seems inconceivable that it is not an independent and persisting entity. It seems ridiculous to think that it is less real than matter. One may get the same kind of sensation in a different way. Sometimes walking down an empty street at night one suddenly becomes conscious of oneself as a kind of eternal subject facing an eternal object. One gets a vague sentiment of being, as it were, balanced against the outside world and co-eternal with it.

Take, on the other hand, an absolutely different state of mind. To make the thing concrete, I will suppose that I am lying in bed ill, in some pain, and unable to get to sleep. This balance I have just talked about seems then upset. The two things that were balanced are no longer so, for all the weights have gone into the one pan. It is now only the material world that seems to be real and enduring. My own consciousness does not seem to me to be an enduring and solid thing at all. It seems as unsubstantial as the flame of a candle and as easily put out.

Now if either of these states occur alone there would be no need for philosophy. You would simply believe the evidence of the state you were in and which you happen to be in. But, unfortunately, for one's peace of mind these states do not occur alone. We pass continually, and sometimes rapidly, from one to the other. At one time one has a firm conviction of the reality and persistence of mind, and at another time one is equally convinced that it is as flimsy as a shadow. The memory of one mood persisting on into the other and forming thus a background of doubt to the firm assurance of the other, we are obliged to search out some system which will enable us to decide which is real and which is a delusion, to decide which is to be taken as a rock-like solidity and which is a temporary aberration of the mind due to the situation of the moment.

I do not, of course, put these two states forward as anything more than two sentiments which do exist and can be described. The question as to whether they correspond to anything real has to be decided in other ways. One can state the question at dispute a little more objectively, in order to bring to a focus the real point of difference which has to be decided. There exist, distributed in space, at this minute, so many centres of consciousness, just as there are so many electric lights in the streets outside. Is there any real resemblance between these two phenomena? Each light exists as the result of certain material conditions, and can be easily extinguished. It is possible for the whole of the lights to be put out. No one pretends that there is a kind of light-world independent of the real world and that light is immortal and endures. Is the same true of consciousness? To all appearances it seems as easy to extinguish a centre of consciousness as to extinguish a centre of light. Is, then, consciousness like light, a phenomenon occurring here and there as the result of certain local physical conditions, having no separate enduring existence? Or is each centre of consciousness, to continue my use of domestic metaphor, better compared to a water-tap, where if you turn off the tap you do not thereby annihilate water?

Is consciousness, then, a temporary phenomenon coming out in spots, or is it a permanent, continuous and enduring entity? The difference between these views is connected somehow with the idea of 'separation', and anything which increases your consciousness of your separation from other things increases your conviction that the electric-light view is the right one. Extreme cold, for example, increases your feeling of 'separation' from the world, and at the same time tends to convince you that consciousness is nothing but a mere local phenomenon. Personally, I can never walk down the narrow spiral stone staircases that you get in old castles and church towers without feeling what a frail thing consciousness is and how it is caught in the net of matter and is absolutely at its mercy.

On the other hand, we are told that if a man could go to the centre of his own mind and penetrate beneath the surface manifestations of consciousness he would feel himself joined on to a world of consciousness which is independent of matter; he would feel himself joined on to something which went beyond himself, and in no sense an isolated point at the mercy of local changes in matter. The retort to this, of course, would be that he was merely deluding himself.

This is the whole question in as crude a metaphor as I can get. There exist along Oxford Street various entirely separate red buildings known as Tube Stations. As far as outside appearances go, each has no physical connection with the other. Let the phenomenon of conscious life be represented by the ticket clerks at these stations. Suppose that for some mysterious reason they become extremely unpopular and a hostile crowd boards up one of the stations. The crowd represents the world of matter. Would the clerks as a result of this boarding up cease to exist? Obviously not, for they, on descending the lift, would find themselves in communication with an underground world which extended beyond themselves. Such is the position of consciousness from one point of view. The position from the opposite point of view would be represented by a number of men living at isolated points, who at the threat of danger dug down under the delusion that they would in that way reach down to an underground passage which did not, as a matter of fact, exist. There are the two views. Either the one or the other must be true. Either consciousness is joined on to something which passes beyond its local appearance in certain physical conditions, or it is not. That is the position as it has always existed. Though appearances, in the shape of death, seem to be in favour of the materialist view, yet the matter was always 'open'. One could take the opposite side without any flagrant absurdity.

The question in this stage is, then an open one. The balance of evidence is on the materialist side, but not sufficiently so to turn it into a nightmare. The arrival of the mechanistic view changes all this. It turns the open question into a closed one. It settles the thing definitely in favour of materialism. It is not merely that you may believe that this is the true view, but that you have to. The honest use of your reason leads you inevitably to that position.

IV

Before passing on to a description of this change, it is necessary to state briefly what the mechanistic conception of the world is. It can be given quickly by quotations. I begin with Spinoza: 'There is in Nature nothing contingent, but all things are determined by the necessities of the divine nature to exist and to operate in a definite way';[5] this from a recent book by Münsterberg: 'Science is to me not a mass of disconnected information, but the certainty that there is no change in the universe, no motion of an atom, and no sensation of a consciousness which does not come and go absolutely in accordance with natural laws; the certainty that nothing can exist outside the gigantic mechanism of causes and effects; necessity moves the stars in the sky and necessity moves the emotions in my mind';[6] or by Laplace's famous boast: 'An intellect which at a given instant knew all the forces with which Nature is animated and the respective situations of the beings that compose Nature—supposing that the said intellect were vast enough to subject these data to analysis— would embrace in the same formulæ the motions of the greatest bodies in the universe and those of the slightest atom; nothing would be uncertain for it, and the future, like the past, would be present to its eyes';[7] and Huxley's 'If the fundamental proposition of evolution is true—that the entire world, living and not living, is the result of the mutual interaction according to definite laws of the forces possessed by the molecules of which the primitive nebulosity of the universe was composed—it is no less certain that the existing world lay potentially in the cosmic vapour, and that a sufficient intellect could, from a knowledge of the properties of molecules of that vapour, have predicted, say, the state of the fauna of Great Britain in 1869 with as much certainty as one can say what will happen to the vapour of the breath on a cold winter's day.'[8]

There was a time when this was only a theory which you could adopt if you liked it. In that time it could hardly have been called a nightmare. If you did not like it you could refuse to believe it. But the situation in the last two hundred years has entirely changed. The result of the progress of the sciences has been to exhibit it not as hypothesis to which one might adhere if one wanted to, but as a solid fact which must be taken account of whether one likes it or not. It seems to me personally, at any rate, to be the one thing which overshadows everything else in any attempt to get a satisfactory view of the cosmos.

The arrival of this state of things could be pictured by thinking of a parallel phenomenon which the observer can watch in any public park. You start, say, with a square green plot of grass. Then it occurs to the authorities that there are people who want to cross diagonally from one corner to the opposite one. So two paths are cut along the two diagonals. Then a further difficulty presents itself to the ingenious official. People might want to cross hurriedly from the middle of one side to the middle of the opposite side. Paths are cut for them, and so on until the whole plot is converted from grass into concrete. This is a schematic representation of a process that can be observed each year in Hyde Park. This is what has happened to the cosmos. The pieces of green—that is, the areas of freedom—are constantly disappearing by a similar process. The whole world will, in the end, be all law—that is, all concrete. As Huxley put it: 'The progress of science . . . means the extension of the province of what we call matter and causation and the gradual banishment of what . . . we call spirit and spontaneity. The consciousness of this great truth weighs like a nightmare upon many of the best minds, the advancing tide of matter threatens to drown their souls, the tightening grasp of law impedes their freedom.'

The effect of this view of the world on the simple market-place beliefs about the soul is easily traced. It enormously strengthens the materialist side, for by making matter self-sufficing it makes consciousness a by-product and takes away from it all real action on things.

In the picture of the world as it existed before the arrival of the mechanistic theory you had a good deal of freedom in matter itself, and consciousness had this certificate, at least, to it—its independence and reality—that it was able to act directly on and to produce changes in this, the physical world. You might suspect its existence to be a precarious one; but, at any rate, it did exist temporarily, and could prove this existence by real action. But if you accept the mechanistic view of the world, not only does all freedom disappear from the material world, but also from the organic. The world is pictured as a mass of atoms and molecules, which are supposed to carry out unceasingly movements of every kind. The matter of which our bodies are composed is subject to the same laws as the matter outside. The motion of every atom of your brain is, then, subject to the same laws of motion as those which govern all matter. It is, then, completely mechanical and calculable. If, then, at any moment you knew the position of all the atoms of a human body, you could calculate with unfailing certainty the past, present, and future actions of the person to whom that body belonged. Consciousness, then, does nothing; it makes no difference; everything would go on just the same without it.

Before mechanism, consciousness occupied the position of a rather feeble king who still, by the favour of his troops, retained some power. The change produced by mechanism can be compared to the sudden discovery by the troops that they are self-sufficient and can manage things themselves. The monarchy then becomes a very flimsy thing. The effect of the change it produces may be got at also in this way. Suppose a number of figures arranged irregularly with a loose rope passing from one to the other. Let the figures represent consciousness and the rope inorganic matter. If you saw this from a distance you might think that the figures were real people and that the rope was to a certain extent subordinate to their purposes. But if as you watched you saw the rope suddenly tightened, and that as this happened the figures just hung loose on it, then you would recognise that they were merely dummies. Well, that is what happens to us as we gradually arrive at the mechanistic view. We suddenly see the matter under us, and which we to a certain extent felt that we rode, stiffen out to the rigidity of outside matter and move us independently of our own control. It is as if a living horse under us suddenly became a mechanical iron one which was self-acting. But, after all, I think the conception of the rope suddenly tightening gives the sensation best.

Before you can legitimately believe, then, in the existence of the soul, you have got to deal with this nightmare. This is the porch through which you must pass before you can arrive at any spiritual interpretation of the world. You can slip into such beliefs by getting in at side doors, but if you do you have not done the thing properly. There is nothing unusual in this phenomenon. In every age there has been such a porch. I have always been dissatisfied with the traditional division of the future life into heaven, hell, and purgatory. Or rather, I have always been dissatisfied with the conception of these states which makes them correspond as rewards to three divisions of merely ethical conduct. This has always seemed to me to be a singularly crude conception. If the reward is in any way to correspond to the tension and trouble which were necessary to attain it, then it is clear that the highest reward should not be given to a mere ethical perfection. Heaven should be reserved for a more trouble-some thing than that—not for those who pursued the good, but for those who had successfully wrestled with the grave doubts they had as to whether the good existed or as to whether the word had any real meaning. A struggle with fundamental unbelief of this kind is much more of a valley of darkness than any mere ethical struggle. It is a much more painful state and deserves a different reward. This kind of unbelief is not an unfortunate accident that comes to a few fidgety people. It is a necessary stage through which all the saints must and should pass, and is a sign of their superiority (1) to the placidly good who go to purgatory, where they are subjected to compulsory doubts before they can pass on, and (2) to the simply bad people who go to hell and stay there.

The saint, then, in every generation has to struggle with an obstacle which stands in the way of any idealist or religious interpretation of the universe. There is some tremendous tendency of things which you have to vanquish before you can legitimately retain your beliefs in any spiritual values. There are some things which you have to conquer before you have any right at all to any spiritual view of the world. If you leave them behind without meeting them fairly you are living on false pretences, or it would perhaps be more accurate to say you are living on credit. You are giving away things that do not in the least belong to you. You have no right to be in a certain position until you have passed to it through a certain struggle. If you have not successfully met this obstacle you are in the position of the philanthropist who has no money. You may have most high falutin' sentiments, but you have no 'effective demand', as the economists used to say. It seems that in beliefs about the cosmos there is the same brutal limiting condition. I may spend hours in talking about the soul in the most charming way, but if I have not first removed this obstacle I am then merely giving away something that does not belong to me: I am being merely futile. At the present time there is not the slightest doubt that this belief in mechanism constitutes the obstacle which the saint must surmount.

It is, fortunately, not necessary to labour the point very much that there is an essential incompatibility between the belief in mechanism and any religious attitude whatever towards the world. The incompatibility is so obvious and has been written about at such enormous length that it is certainly not worth while explaining in detail. It may, however, be worth while to indicate briefly two specimen ways of putting the matter. The beginning of any thought about these matters lies in the fact that we have certain preferences; we prefer good to evil, beauty to ugliness, etc. These preferences have of late years been indicated technically in philosophy by the word 'values'. Now it is the essence of any religious attitude towards the cosmos to believe (1) that these qualities are not merely valuable relatively to us, but are so absolutely, and lie in the nature of fundamental reality itself; (2) that the cosmos is so arranged that these things will be preserved and not perish. Höffding[9] has, indeed, defined religion as a 'belief' in the conservation of values, and the definition is as accurate as definitions of such indefinable things can be. It is more convenient for me to consider first the latter of these necessary beliefs. Can there by any 'conservation of values' if the world is to be considered as a mechanism? Obviously not, for the essence of mechanism is that it is self-acting and pays no attention at all to the things that we happen to attach value to. The conception of purpose is quite alien to it, for everything happens as the result of antecedent circumstance. It produced us and our values quite accidentally, and quite as accidentally it will snuff them all out again. Put more concretely in Mr. Balfour's often-quoted though still pleasing rhetoric:— 'Man's . . . very existence is an accident, his story a brief and transitory episode in the life of one of the planets—of the meanest of the planets. We sound the future and learn that, after a period long enough compared with the individual life, but short indeed compared with the divisions of time open to our investigation, the energies of our system will decay, the glory of the sun will be dimmed, and the earth, tideless and inert, will no longer tolerate the race which has for a moment disturbed its solitude. Man will go down into the pit and all his thoughts perish. The uneasy consciousness which in this obscure corner has for a brief space broken the contented silence of the universe will be at rest. Matter will know itself no longer. "Imperishable monuments" and "immortal deeds," death itself and love stronger than death will be as though they had never been. Nor will anything that is be better or be worse for all that the labour, genius, devotion, and suffering of man have striven through countless generations to effect.'

A world of this kind cannot concern itself with the 'conservation of values'. On the contrary, it seems doomed inevitably to destroy them all. In as far as we hold the mechanistic conception and are honest with ourselves we are bound to admit that the world will end either by cooling, or perhaps earlier by collision; but in either case 'accidentally', in the sense that this end will take no account of the things we value.

It will end 'accidentally', and not when it has fulfilled its purpose or any nonsense of that kind. This automatically knocks on the head any 'religion of progress' which attempts to reconcile one to materialism. I would judge any such so-called philosophy by its eschatology. Does it deal with this basic fact or does it attempt to fudge the thing? That it is a difficulty the ingenious authors of such half-baked concoctions evidently feel, for they will explain that by the time this end approaches man will have so 'evolved' that he will be able to escape the wrecked planet. Such pieces of childish nonsense are evidences of the truth that it is impossible, if mechanism be a true account of the world, for us to believe in any preservation of values. The world as presented by mechanistic theory is utterly alien and has from our point of view neither rhyme nor reason.

As to the second criterion. It is asserted that we cannot attach any real meaning to our judgments of value if we believe that they are merely personal and relative to man. They must correspond to something in the nature of fundamental reality itself. Is it, then, possible to believe in any values of this kind and at the same time that one holds the mechanistic view of the world? To examine this question I recall exactly what the mechanistic view is by a quotation:— 'Every occurrence in the universe is, then, ultimately only a change of position of indivisible particles of which each is completely determined in movement by the preceding movements of the whole system; even the life processes are only physical and chemical occurrences, and every chemical and physical change resolves itself ultimately and finally into mechanical movements of atoms.'

Now in such a world the word 'value' has clearly no meaning. There cannot be any good or bad in such a turmoil of atoms. There are arrangements which are simple and arrangements which are complex, but nothing gives the slightest warrant for the claim that the complex is better than the simple or the more lasting than the fugitive. If this view of the world is the true one, all the bottom drops out of our set of values. The very touch of such a conception freezes all the values and kills them. It remains as a perpetual menace. As long as it exists no idealist can live a quiet life, for he might at any moment be tripped up by the awful fact. It is a perpetual reminder that you are living in a fool's paradise. I am quite aware that this is a trouble only to a limited number of people—to those who have had a certain kind of education; but to them it is quite as annoying as was Banquo's ghost.

It is, perhaps, necessary to point out that at a certain stage this prospect does not appear to be a nightmare to us. At a certain stage of one's mental evolution the delight in finding that one can completely explain the world as one might solve a puzzle is so exciting that it quite puts in the shade the disadvantages of the conception from other points of view. It is not a nightmare to us—far from it. We delight in it. It is something like the feeling produced by a new toy or a steam-engine that 'works' to a boy. It exhilarates us to feel that we have got a neat key to the universe in our pockets, and this delight of acquisition obliterates the nightmarish effect it would naturally produce in a man. One delights in it so much that one resents any attempt to interfere with it or to show that it is not a fact but merely an hypothesis. I recall quite vividly the emotion I felt when I looked, in my school library, at Stallo's[10] quite harmless little book which makes fun of the conservation of energy. I positively detested the sight of the book on the shelves. I would have liked to have it removed from the library. My resentment was of exactly the same nature and due to the same causes as that with which an old lady, all of whose scanty income comes from land, might hear of a proposal for land nationalisation. My toy would have been taken away from me.

But this is only a temporary phenomenon. For the natural man this counteracting emotion would soon be removed and the mechanistic conception would once more become a nightmare. In the few cases in which it does not appear to be a nightmare it is because this kind of delight in the simplicity of a theory and the exhilaration and sense of power it produces have remained beyond the years of puberty to which it is appropriate, and still continue to veil to a man the real horror of his belief.

Those who have read the 'Arabian Nights', or failing that, have seen 'Sumûrun', will remember the story of the barber who, having swallowed a fish-bone, was taken for dead. How everybody, wishing to be free of the possible unpleasant consequences of having this corpse discovered in their own house, passed it on to someone else. The corpse always turned up at some inopportune moment. A man returning cheerful from a banquet found it on his staircase; a bridegroom found it in his bed, and so on. Well, it seems to me that you have an exact parallel here for the nightmare—of the conception of the world which considers that it is a vast mechanism. First Democritus put the fish-bone into the body of the cosmos, then Lucretius rammed it in; and ever since, after the banquet of an idealist philosphy or the delights of a romantist Weltanschauung we are confronted, when the lights are turned out and our powers of self-delusion with them, with this frightful and hope-killing apparition of the corpse of a 'dead world', of a cosmos which is nothing but a vast mechanism.

It is not to be escaped or passed on to your neighbour as long as it exists. No man can honestly hold any optimistic or cheerful view of the world. Of course, there are various ways of hiding it; you can cover it up with various cloths made out of words; you can agree to look at it 'sub species eternitas'.[11] But to the plain man none of these ways is successful. Whatever colour the corpse is painted it remains a corpse. You will remember that at the end of the story the barber was shaken and the fish-bone fell out, whereupon the corpse came back to life to the no small astonishment of the beholders. It seems to me that, as far as I am concerned, at any rate, the fish-bone has been taken out of the corpse of the cosmos; and it is to celebrate the accomplishment of this feat that I am about to execute a war-dance in these pages.

V

A correspondent in a number of this review some weeks ago pointed out that my parable of the barber and the fish-bone was only correct when properly interpreted.[12] It was necessary to notice that what happened was not that the barber's soul re-awoke on a new plane of existence, but that his *body* came to life again. This was precisely what I intended to convey; but as I may not have made my meaning sufficiently clear, I had better emphasise the point in more detail here. I can at the same time use this as a pretext for an examination of the general characteristics which any refutation of mechanism must possess if we are to find it completely satisfactory. I use the word 'satisfactory' with a definite intention. I carefully refrain from saying 'true'. I do not pretend to be discussing abstract philosophy here; I am only estimating things from a personal point of view. I want to find out what must be the characteristics of that refutation of mechanism which would, as a matter of actual fact, succeed in shifting the hold of mechanism over the emotions of a certain type of intelligence. If I am asked what kind of intelligence, I simply reply: the type of intelligence that *does* find mechanism a nightmare.

That answers, I think, the second point in the same correspondent's letter. He is surprised that anyone, even admitting the truth of mechanism, should find it a nightmare. I understand his point of view; I know that it is possible to look at the matter in that way. It is a possible position even for the man who at one time has felt mechanism to be a great difficulty. For some people, by a kind of slow and gradual change, and not by any definite and conscious process, the difficulty vanishes. Mechanism is never definitely dealt with and routed; it simply seems to lose its importance. In ten years' time you may find you have changed from a belief in materialism to the belief that ultimate reality is a republic of eternal souls, without knowing exactly how it has happened. There has been no definite rational act. It is like the dissolving pictures that one used to see in the pre-cinema age, where one scene melts away into the next and is not shifted to make room for its successor. In your view of the cosmos the things which at one time seemed the solid things melt away, and the flimsy, cloud-like entities gradually harden down till they become the solid bases on which the rest of our beliefs are supported. Whereas at one time you felt sure that matter was the only permanent thing; you now find that you are equally convinced, without any necessity for proof, of the permanent existence of individuals. In any argument you always rest on some base which is taken for granted, and you now find yourself in the position of taking the reality of individuality as such a base. It does not seem necessary to rest it on anything else. In this change mechanism has never actually been refuted; it has just gradually faded away into insignificance, and other things have come into the high lights. But it has not faded away altogether; it remains on the fringe of the mind. It is, however, no longer a difficulty, because all the emphasis and the accent are elsewhere. The best way to put it is to say that all the 'values' of the world landscape are altered. Mechanism is still in the picture, but it is no longer the high light, it no longer dominates everything else.

But here a curious situation arises. Pressed on the point, a man in this state would still have to admit that mechanism was a true account of things, yet it no longer seems to him to 'matter'; he is no longer disconcerted by the discrepancies between that and the rest of his beliefs. He has never refuted mechanism; time has simply packed the skeleton away. You bring it out of the cupboard and you find that it no longer has the power to startle. It is still the same skeleton, yet it no longer disconcerts. Why?

The process by which the mind manages not to be disconcerted forms a complicated and interesting piece of psychology. The mind executes a set of manœuvres which, on a different plane, is quite as complicated as the elaborate balancing of personal motives which took place on the lawn at Patterne Hall. I am myself incapable of giving anything more than a very crude outline of these manœuvres. To commence by a restatement of the preliminary position: the mechanistic theory, while never having been refuted, has gradually come to occupy a very subordinate place in the outlook of a certain type of intelligence. Occasionally, it may be under pressure from outside, or of its own inner buoyancy, it floats up to the surface of their minds; it no longer seems to be a nightmare? Why? The first step towards the solution of the problem is to recognise that the expression 'floats up to the surface of the mind' is not an accurate description of what does happen to these people. The idea 'the world may be a mere mechanism' does not, as a rule, float to the top, but only to a depth where it can just be vaguely perceived under the surface—a depth at which it is not a clearly-outlined idea, but rather a confused sentiment. In the kind of unconscious reasoning appropriate to this depth the man probably accommodates himself to the momentary chill produced fairly easily in the manner I am about to describe. It does not take the shape of a formulated argument; if it was, he would probably perceive its absurdity himself. It is rather an unformulated reaction to an unformulated doubt. The whole thing takes place on the plane of quality and feeling, rather than that of clear representation. I used the word 'chill' a minute ago. That is a more accurate description of the beginning of the process than the words 'perception of the consequences of mechanism' would be. Just below the surface of the stream of conscious life you have a vague apprehension of a quality, a sensation which has a disagreeable feeling tone and which contains within it the potency and the capacity for developing into an awkward and unpleasant idea—that of the truth of mechanism. At the depth in the stream of consciousness at which you first become aware of it, it is merely a closed-up parcel; but if you allowed it to come to the top it would pass from the state of feeling to that of representation, and would unpack itself into a clearly-perceived contradiction and fissure in your weltanschauung. But you do not generally allow it to do that. When its presence becomes felt merely as a chilling shadow thrown on the level of your clearly-focussed conscious life, you deal with it at once on the level at which you perceive it; you meet one sentiment by another. For that reason the arguments which I give here as those by which a man in this state deals with a revival of the mechanistic view in his own mind may seem too like caricature. It must be remembered that they do not represent the actual thoughts which pass through the mind. In fact, the thought-level is not involved at all. But the manœuvres I give here do represent what the closed parcel of sentiment would develop into were you so foolish as to actually unpack it into definite argument on the level of clear ideas.

The attitude of mind by which the revival of the mechanism nightmare is generally met consists mainly of the vague kind of idea that the matter has been dealt with and finished long ago. How or by whom is not clearly known. To persist in wanting it done in detail before our eyes is asking too much. There are some questions to which every person of intelligence is expected to know the answer because they are still live questions; but there are others to which no one need know the answer because they are finished with. It might reasonably be expected, for example, of every person interested in the matter, in the time of Copernicus, that they should know in detail the arguments by which the Ptolemaic astronomy was refuted. It is no longer necessary at the present moment to know the arguments in detail, for there is unanimous agreement that the refutation has been made. The people whose mental attitude I am describing are probably of the opinion that this is the case also with mechanism. Forty years ago, in that curiously remote barbaric Huxleyan period, it would have been necessary, if one disbelieved in mechanism, to be able to state definitely why one did so; but that is no longer necessary. Mechanism has been refuted years ago, and it is very démodé and provincial to be ignorant of the fact, to want to see it done again. A persistence in the demand for details would be out of place in the atmosphere in which you find yourself; you feel like a boor in a drawing-room, and you finally stop wanting even to ask questions. I am speaking here of myself as the outside questioner, though, of course, what I really am trying to get at is the state of doubt inside the other man himself. What does fortify these people in dealing with the doubt is really in the end nothing but just a kind of 'atmosphere' of this kind—an atmosphere which automatically overpowers certain objections and makes them seem silly. It seems to say: 'We don't do these things; we are past that stage.' In a certain famous play the nouveau riche tells everybody that he cleans his teeth every day now, the 'real gentleman' being supposed to clean his teeth three times a day without mentioning it. Something of the same kind is conveyed to you by the mental atmosphere of this type of people. It is not necessary to refute mechanism 'in public' or to talk about it. I must state here that I am not speaking of this state of mind with contempt; I have been perilously near it myself a good many times.

There is also a second type who, like the correspondent I am answering, find it difficult to believe that mechanism can be a nightmare, and who are impatient with the excessive importance attached to the problem. I heard Mr. Yeats lecturing on 'Psychical Research' in a drawing-room the other day. He started by stating that, in his opinion, the whole subject had been distorted by the extraordinary anxiety of most of the people who wrote about it to meet the scepticism of the kind of man they met at dinner. He seemed to imply that, if you put this pusillanimous belief in materialism on one side, you would advance much quicker. Your theories then, freed from the necessity of meeting certain objections, would be much simpler and much more likely to be true. This seems to me to be an exactly similar state of mind to that of the people who dream of the glorious new kind of poetry that would arise if inspiration could only be emancipated from the hampering restrictions of rhyme, metre, and form generally. Everybody can see the absurdity of sentiments of this kind applied to the arts. It is a platitude to say that form here is a liberating and not a restricting thing. But precisely the same statement can be made of theories about the soul. It is not by ignoring mechanism that you will arrive at anything worth having, but by struggling with it. I know this sentence has an uncomfortably ethical flavour, but I hasten to add that it is not intended; it is merely a plain statement of a universal law. The bird attained whatever grace its shape possesses not as a result of the mere desire for flight, but because it had to fly *in air against gravitation*. There are some happy people who can believe any theory they find interesting; others, as soon as they want to believe any theory, feel the full force of certain objections. They are in the position of a man who by jumping may leave the ground, but is at once dragged down again by his own weight. To all kinds of idealistic interpretations of the world there are certain objections of this kind. And just as the whole group of phenomena connected with falling bodies are summed up in the law of gravitation, so all the objections that have in the course of history been urged against the various idealisms seem to me to be summed up and focussed in the mechanistic theory. In it all the ragged doubts and objections seem suddenly to dovetail together and to close up, like certain kinds of box-lids, with a click. It is for that reason that I regard the problem of mechanism with a certain amount of actual enthusiasm. It is not merely an annoying obstacle, but it is the characteristic convention and form which the masters of the philosophic art have to conquer. It is only by dealing with it that any spiritual interpretation of the world can acquire validity, and what is quite as important, a decent shape. Anyone who ignores it will not only have attained his position illegitimately, but what is infinitely worse, he may be accused of being the 'Walt Whitman of the soul'.

So much for the people who, like the correspondent I have referred to, do not find mechanism a nightmare. I am concerned now with the tougher people who have realised the problem and have attempted to deal with it. For Bergson, of course, is not the only philosopher who has refuted mechanism. It is one of the favourite occupations of the tribe. You could if you liked write the whole history of philosophy, for the last two hundred years, at any rate, from that point of view. The question has been an obsession. One cannot read Coleridge, for example, without seeing what a very real worry it was to him. It seems necessary to mention some of these refutations, if only to be able to define the state of mind which finds them unsatisfactory. The account I give of them must be necessarily so short that it will resemble caricature.

The first and the simplest way of dealing with mechanism is to frankly accept it as a true account of the nature of the universe, but at the same time to hold that this fact makes no difference to ethical values. This is the view generally associated with Huxley's famous Romanes lecture. It has been stated quite recently by Mr. Bertrand Russell in an article which is called 'The Religion of a Plain Man', or something of that kind.[13] [It is some time since I read this, and I am rather vague about it. It has since been republished, but the book is always out of the London Library, and I have always felt sure that no new exposition of this ancient view could be worth six shillings. As far as I remember, however, it was very like Lange's[14] phrase: 'A noble man is not the least disturbed in his zeal for his ideals, though he be told, and tells himself, that his ideal world, with all its settings of a God, immortal hopes and eternal truths, is a mere imagination and no reality. These are all real for life just because they are psychic ideals.']

Consciousness generally, and ethical principles in particular, are supposed to be mere by-products of a world-process which produces them accidentally and which will in time inevitably destroy them. Yet we are to act as though these ethical principles had an absolute value. The world has no purpose; our ethical values do not, as a matter of fact, correspond to anything in the nature of ultimate reality, and yet we are to act as though they did. The fact that it all leads to nothing is supposed to give an added dignity to man's ethical endeavours. People who take this view can be called stoics in the literal meaning of the word. In my last 'note'

I called mechanism the 'porch' through which you had to pass to arrive at any legitimate spiritual interpretation of the world. These stoics really are 'porch' philosophers, for they sit contentedly on the steps and, pointing over their shoulders at the door, say: 'This is permanently closed; no one can ever get to the garden inside; but, bless you, we don't mind that—we *like* being outside—we keep on paying the entrance-money as a hobby.' I suppose I ought to qualify this a little and point out that I am expressing surprise, not at the fact that ethical conduct can be compatible with materialism, but at the absolute importance that such a view manages to give to such ethical values.

It is an attitude which has a long history, and which at every period has always satisfied a minority. There has always been a certain glamour attached to this form of 'resignation'. Owing, I suppose, to a certain coarseness in my nature, I have never been able to appreciate it. There has always seemed to me to be something ridiculous in the position, just for this reason: that it is a little 'too much'; it is a little pretentious; one instinctively feels that there is something wrong—something a little shoddy about it. One can understand that a man may feel himself compelled by facts to believe that mechanism is a true account of the universe—there is nothing objectionable in that. But it is mere perverse and inhuman romanticism to pretend that this gives added sanction and dignity to our ethical ideals. It violates common experience; it is a little inhuman, and has a certain element of posturing in it.

To assume this position—to believe that the purposelessness of the world gives an added and melancholy dignity to the position of man— may be an 'interesting' position to take up at a tea-party—you may then maintain it with vehemence and sincerity as a thesis; but it goes against all honest human instincts. I cannot admire it myself any more than I can ever admire the pale and unearthly high-mindedness of the agnostic who objects to people being good because they want to go to heaven. Shutting himself up in a corner he is condemning universal and legitimate instincts. The universal instinct has got hold of the truth. I cannot for the life of me see any particular reason for taking life seriously unless it is serious. I cannot see why mankind should be too big for its boots.

This way of dealing with mechanism can be legitimately called senti-mentalism, for it clouds over the real outlines of its own position. It shrinks from consistency and refuses to go 'to the end' of its belief. Its faith is anæmic. Real belief in the existence of a physical object means that one *acts* in accordance with its perceived shape. If I am convinced that the table is square, I do not try to cut off corners when I am walking past it as I should do if it were circular. So with materialism. To be a materialist should mean to act as a materialist. Consistent materialism is to a certain extent an attractive position. But this other thing—this combination of belief in mechanism and a belief in absolute values—is just irritating sloppiness. The sloppiness is betrayed by the rhetoric in which the position is stated. In the people who take this view you find that heightening of phraseology which always accompanies unconscious untruthfulness. Rhetoric is, I suppose, always unattractive, but it is never more loathsome than when it accomplishes this glazing over of material-ism. I say 'loathsome' because I think the epithet accurate. I find myself extremely surprised at the adjectives that jump into my mind when I read this kind of stuff. It must be that Nature takes her revenge on those perverted amongst us, to whom the phraseology of the robustious theatre seems unreal, by turning philosophy itself into a melodrama. At any rate, as I read these modern stoics I gain by an effort of sympathetic intuition an understanding of all those Adelphi phrases which before seen merely from the outside seemed so artificial. I understand now that occasions may arise when the natural expression of one's emotions can only be accomplished by the incoherent use of the words 'filth', 'sewerage', and the rest of it. My annoyance demands physical expression. I want to do something dramatic with the printed page. I find myself muttering: 'You think that, do you? You——!'

The second method of dealing with mechanism is a little more human.

Bergson Lecturing

[First published in *NA* 10/1 (2 Nov. 1911), 15–16; signed 'Thomas Gratton' (after Gratton Hall, Endon, Hulme's birthplace). Hulme is describing his experiences at one of the lectures which Bergson gave at University College, London, between 20 and 28 Oct. 1911.]

Of course, I know that the crisis I am about to describe depends on the things that preceded it. It wouldn't have been so serious if it were not for that. But everything seemed to lead up to it. My mind was too much prepared. I had been told, in the first place, that the lectures would be for advanced students only. Then when I applied for a ticket I received a note asking for *full* particulars of my qualifications. This increased my impression of the 'advanced' character of what I was going to hear. The approaches to the lectures seemed to be as well guarded as those to a harem. I thought I was in for something very esoteric indeed. I expected to find at the entrance to the hall a guard of the university eunuchs, and that my approach would be the signal for the officer's command, 'Present test papers!' I meditated getting in the night before through a window and hiding under the platform.

Well, here I am, I have got in; I won't say how I got in, but I am in—that's the main fact. I look round and find that my speculations about the harem have at least this basis of fact—that nine people out of ten present here are women, most of them with their heads lifted up in the kind of 'Eager Heart' attitude, which resembles nothing so much as the attitude of my kitten when gently waking up from sleep; it throws back its head and draws in, with an appearance of contemplation, a new smell from the higher air. The terrifying thought came into my head: If these are the elect, these the picked ones, *what were the rejected like?*

When I had finished these charitable reflections, and while engaged in the operation of leisurely survey, all unconscious of any danger, I was suddenly struck down by a most profound fit of depression. I went through a crisis which, from its suddenness and unpleasantness, I can only compare to the descriptions given by James of the preliminary state to the phenomena of religious conversion in the 'Varieties of Religious Experience'. I suddenly experienced a most remarkable fit of the profoundest and blackest scepticism—a scepticism that cut right down to the root of every belief that I had hitherto fancied I held as certain and fixed.

I proceed to describe it in detail. My description may be rather incoherent as the experience is too recent for it to be legitimately described as 'emotion remembered in tranquillity'. I begin as James would do with my state of mind before the crisis.

Being a Tory by disposition, I have a horror of change and a desire for a fixed and solid system of beliefs. Unfortunately, materialism—the only belief in the region of philosophy which seems to have any kind of fixity—is one that is repugnant to me. All the systems which profess to meet materialism seem to be vague and flimsy. This is a position I could not be satisfied with. I was left then in a position of indefiniteness that I could not permanently support. I must find salvation in fixity of some kind. I finally found what I wanted in Bergson. The beliefs I got there seemed to be of such a character that I could safely fix everything round them. There I determined to 'settle'. Every other belief crystallised round this.

I became a disciple in the full sense of the word. So much did he strike me, right in the centre of the mind, that I find it difficult to express my own individual ideas except through an atmosphere which has been formed in me by constant thinking over his phraseology and the set of conceptions in which his thought habitually works. His phraseology formed, indeed, the spectacles through which I have seen everything; but the spectacles were not external to me, fixed on my nose, removable at will, but were—if I may extend the metaphor illegitimately—fixed right in the centre of my mind, where I was not even aware myself of their existence. I was then a disciple in the full sense of the word; I had the greatest delight out of him that it is possible to get out of such a mild pursuit as philosophy.

Such, then, was the state of security and fixity I had attained to. If anything seemed certain then it was my belief that in Bergson I had found the final truth on certain matters. I was sure in my own mind that these were my fixed opinions, particularly as I had been at great pains to arrive at them.

If, now, this belief had been cut down by any great upheaval, by any catastrophic flood of argument, I should not have been plunged into any very profound scepticism. My belief in the reality of solidity would not have been disturbed, because my solid belief would only have been removed by an equal solidity in the way of force. But this did not occur. What did occur was something infinitely more disturbing. The whole edifice of my fixed beliefs, so laboriously constructed, was overturned by a trifle. I had no sooner sat down in this hall and felt the almost physical sensation produced by the presence all round me of several hundred people filled with exactly the same kind of attitude towards Bergson as my own, than I experienced a complete reversal of feeling. I was immediately repulsed by what before had attracted me. I was filled by a sentiment of most profound disgust and depression. My mind began at once, almost unconsciously, to feel that what these people thought about Bergson was entirely wrong. More than that, I passed on to the further belief that Bergson himself was wrong. The whole structure of beliefs so carefully constructed fell down like a house of cards. Something inside me determined, quite independently of my volition, that it would set about and prove that in Bergson was not the 'truth', but a bubble soon to be burst. What these people agreed on could not be right. It is not in the nature of truth to be grasped so easily or so enthusiastically. This was most profoundly depressing, not so much because it destroyed a particular set of fixed beliefs, but because it destroyed, so it seemed to me, the possibility of any 'fixed' belief whatever. If the mere accidental fact that several hundred people share your belief destroys it automatically, then obviously the phrase 'fixed belief' can never have the meaning we generally attribute to it. This feeling had cut down then to the roots of everything. You could never be sure of any belief. It leads to the most persistent, thorough-going scepticism. All 'solidity' in a belief seems not a real quality of that belief, but an accidental quality which gets attached to it by outside circumstance. It would be a temporary quality attaching to a belief at the time of one's first discovery of it, and which would pass with time and the spreading of the idea. Solidity would then be an illusion of a similar kind to that pursued by Don Juan. As a wise man I must, then, realise that I can never hope to attain in the future any 'solidity' of belief. It is necessarily only a temporary illusion attaching to the moment of arrival. Now this would be an intolerable opinion. It is too thorough-going a scepticism for mental equilibrium. My mind instinctively seeks some simpler explanation of my sudden revulsion of feeling. I must save myself by some comforting theory from such a scepticism.

There is first, of course, the obvious explanation that it arises from the half-baked feelings of superiority from which all of us suffer. We all react from what we are pleased to consider the mob. I knew a democrat who went to Hyde Park and was overcome with a feeling of repugnance to the crowd until a man standing by him talked of the 'great unwashed', when he immediately reacted back to the opposite position. But this simple kind of motive is not sufficient in this case, for the phenomenon would not have been altered, the reaction would not have been diminished, but rather increased if the 400 here present had been people of exactly the same kind of mentality as oneself. This would decidedly have increased the horror of the situation. One would have felt an even more imperative necessity to at once prove that Bergson was all wrong.

There is another obvious and simple reason for one's change of mind— that I was formerly in the position of a man who had a patent, and this patent had now run out. There was no longer any mild kind of distinction in knowing of someone of whom the rest were ignorant. This, of course, is one of the most deeply-rooted sentiments of the mind, and no one can escape from it altogether. Voltaire was only too anxious to talk about Shakespeare as long as he was the only man in France who had heard of him; but when some other poor creature came back from London and began to rhapsodise, the whole situation changed; Shakespeare was then 'the monster', etc.

But even when the effect of these two motives is debited, there is still something left over which must be accounted for. What is the reason of this extraordinary distaste we feel for sharing even our most cherished beliefs with a crowd. It seems as if we had a kind of physical repugnance to such polyandry—a kind of instinctive repugnance. This is not at all the kind of thing that ought to take place. We ought to be pleased at the spread of truth. As Mr. Chesterton somewhere says—and it shows how depressed I am when I descend to quotation from that particular source— 'A real religion is that in which any two solitary people might suddenly say the same thing at the same moment.'

My feelings at the present moment point decidedly in another direction. It seems as if ideas were only valuable in as far as they distinguish one from the people we dislike. The motive behind all writing and all invention of ideas would seem merely to be that of drawing a complicated line which shall definitely mark one off from the type of people one can't stand. The separation seems to be the important thing; the ideas are only means to that end. They serve as an elaborate kind of fence. The classic example of this kind of thing is, of course, the Thirty-nine Articles. I can never read that misunderstood work of genius without a thrill of admiration. I feel in it the genius of the race. It is the production of a type of mind which, in my present mood, I thoroughly understand. The truth of this view seems confirmed by the fact that where you have no enemy, there you have no precision of definition, for there you have no need of a fence. If one pursues the thing one will find that it can be exhibited as a fundamental law of thought, and not as a mere fallibility of human nature. One might assert that, as a matter of metaphysical truth, the feeling of repugnance was prior and more fundamental than any mere theory.

However, this is a most regrettable situation. I am being driven on to a kind of scepticism much more thorough than any of those from which I had fled in the first instance. Something must be done to avoid this kind of thing. Can I draw from it any lesson for future guidance? I think I can. The first thing is to recognise I have been exposed to this awful situation by the fact that 400 people have been allowed to come together to listen to a philosopher.

This is the source of all the evil. In doing this a fundamental law of human nature has been overlooked. The type of mind represented by my childish repugnance at this moment is not new. It has always existed, and it has always been provided for. The ancients knew what they were about. They never allowed these kinds of emotions to come to the surface. They prevented it by a most simple device, which it will be necessary for us to return to if we are to preserve ourselves from this most dangerous form of scepticism. They knew how foolhardy it was to violate the Cosmos's feelings of delicacy. Violate that delicacy by bringing 400 people to see her undressed, and she is sure to revenge herself by sowing these seeds of blighting scepticism. We must, then, re-establish the old distinction between the public and the esoteric doctrine. The difficulty of getting into this hall should have been comparable to the difficulty of getting into a harem, not only in appearance, but in fact.

By the time I had finished these futile reflections, various voluminous scarlet figures filed on to the platform, followed by a shrinking black speck which turned out to be Bergson. A person called Collins, the Vice-chancellor of the University I afterwards learned, then got up to introduce Bergson. His speech was a remarkable performance.

The attitude behind it appeared to be this: 'It is rather silly of so many of us to be prepared to listen seriously to lectures on a subject like metaphysics, and especially as expounded by this particular foreigner.' 'Metaphysics', he said, 'is, of course, like nothing so much as looking in a dark room for a black hat which wasn't there.' But then there are excuses for us. Mr. Balfour has thought it worth while to devote a whole article to Bergson. Then this university has always been renowned for its toleration. We are so broad-minded that we are prepared to welcome any race or type, however peculiar. In this particular case, of course, we had to do something, because we were invited over last year and entertained by the Collège de France, and we must be polite in return. The pronunciation of the last word in the title, 'Collège de France', was a great difficulty to the poor man. He said 'Collège de' with great boldness, but then there came a prolonged pause until finally he made the plunge with 'Frornce'. There was no necessity for him, as a matter of fact, to mention the word more than once; but it seemed to exercise a fatal fascination over him. As, when learning to ride a bicycle, one seems compelled by some demoniac force to turn automatically into every vehicle that passes us, so Collins had to return again and again to this fatal word. First it was

'Frornce', then it became 'Frarnce', then came other variations. Round and round it he flew, like a moth round a candle, until finally he finished one of the most vulgar and tactless exhibitions it has ever been my lot to witness with a perspiring plain-English 'Frannce'. Then at last Bergson got up.

Mr. Balfour, Bergson, and Politics

[First published in *NA* 10/2 (9 Nov. 1911), 38–40; signed 'T. E. H.']

It seems to be the function of certain men in the complicated mechanism of modern society to act as centres of publicity. If you can by some means or other hitch an idea in which you are interested on to them it vibrates to the four corners of the globe. They play the part in the world of advertisement that the central ganglions do in an organism.

Mr. Balfour is such a ganglion. Paris is only seven hours' journey from here, and there must have been quite a considerable number of people who for several years have known that Bergson was an important person, but it was necessary for Mr. Balfour to write an article, for him to become famous.[1] Really this article has had some remarkable effects. It has produced four columns about Bergson in the 'Evening Times', references in the 'Referee', and an article in the 'Saturday Review'.[2] This latter is an amateurish compilation of paragraphs from the two articles in the 'Hibbert', the only original remark in it being very original indeed. 'We all know', says the writer, 'the great wave of idealist revival that followed the publication of "Creative Evolution" some *ten* years ago.' There was also an article in the 'Nation',[3] but I refrain from reference to this remarkable production until later in my article.

What is to be said of Mr. Balfour's article itself? I find myself unable to deal with the actual criticisms it makes, for a reason which is explained in detail in the third of my 'Notes' on Bergson,[4] but which I can shortly anticipate here. The view I take of Bergson is that one finds in him three perfectly distinct parts. There is first the new 'method', the theory of intensive manifolds; there is secondly the result of the application of this method to the nightmare of universal mechanism, which constitutes the theory of duration; and finally there is what I might call his 'conclusions', his cosmology, his views on the soul, and the rest of it. Now in my opinion the first of these is by far the most important, and it is in these that his originality lies. But the conclusions are the part of Bergson which, while they are the easiest to explain and criticise, are also the most attractive to the ordinary man. The result of this is that all popular expositions of Bergson give an entirely wrong impression of the whole thing. For Bergson's conclusions, by the very nature of things, cannot differ very radically from those of other philosophers. After all, there cannot be more than a definite small number of theories about the soul; and in any case the whole reason why his conclusions are worth discussing at all is that they have been arrived at by this new method. Put forward merely as interesting theories, they would have no claim to be considered as anything more than preferences. If this is so, then no discussions of the conclusions without a preliminary discussion of the method on which they are based can be of much value.

But Mr. Balfour definitely states that in the limited space of his article it is impossible for him to give any systematic discussion of Bergson's system. This is why I find it impossible to make any serious criticism of his own remarks on Bergson's conclusions, for they are all admittedly made from a standpoint which, from my point of view, is inadmissible. What he does do is to criticise the conclusions as conclusions from the point of view solely of their attractiveness or satisfactoriness, quite apart from their claim to be considered as necessary conclusions drawn by the new method from empirical evidence.

Now while this is interesting and from one point of view quite legitimate, it would be quite absurd for me, holding the view I put forward in the previous paragraph, to attempt to meet it on the same ground. I can put my view of the matter perhaps more clearly by a metaphor. The state of my mind before I read Bergson, and while I was still obsessed with the idea that, after all, the truth about the world was that it was nothing but a vast mechanism, can be compared to the state of men imprisoned all their life inside a walled town from which they would fain escape. They have been told that outside the walls there are green fields and the rest of it, but they cannot legitimately believe in these things as long as the walls of the town remain unbroken.

Now suppose that a partial breach is made in the walls through which the inhabitants, though they cannot pass out, can yet see the particular fields which face the breach they have made. It would then be futile for a dissatisfied person to say, 'But I don't find these kind of green fields satisfactory; I would much have preferred to see the fields which we have pictured to exist behind the unbroken south wall.'

That would not be legitimate criticism. What you see depends entirely on the place in the walls which you have broken through. In this comparison the wall represents the mechanistic conception of the world. Obviously, the view of the world which we take after we have escaped from this mechanistic nightmare must depend on the nature of the criticism which has enabled us to escape. It is not simply that we escape, and that once free we are at liberty to choose that alternate view which seems to us to be most attractive. The theory with whose help we escape inevitably leads us on to a certain positive world-view which replaces the mechanistic one. The criticism and the conclusions, the method and the final world-view, then, hang together, and criticism of the second without examination of the first is not of much use.

But this is the line that Mr. Balfour takes, and so the whole thing seems rather in the air. One can put the position in this way: Both he and Bergson have found an escape from mechanism, the one by a consideration of the place of value in reality, and the other by the theory of intensive manifolds. To each method of escape there is a corresponding alternative to mechanism. What Mr. Balfour does is to take both methods of escape as equivalent in so far as they are both escapes, and then to proceed to a criticism of Bergson's conclusions without any consideration of the fact that he escaped in a particular way. I think that while this criticism is quite valid from his point of view, and fits in naturally with the kind of attack on naturalism, which was made in the 'Foundations of Belief',[5] it is not the kind of attack which could possibly be answered by anyone taking the view of Bergson I have outlined above. An attack for me could only be an attack if it attacked Bergson's initial method, but Mr. Balfour disclaims any such intention.

I said at the outset of this paper that I should deal later with the remarkable production that Mr. Balfour's essay had called forth from the 'Nation'. It is really annoyance at the smug and fatuous tone of this article which is making me write on the subject here. It reads like the lifeless production of the worst kind of dotard, the 'progressive' dotard. That peculiarly irritating form of Radical who irritates us, not because he is of a different opinion from oneself, but because, living, as a matter of fact, still in the 'seventies, he imagines that he is just 'the thing', that he is living in the forefront of time and can look on us with a kind of pity as benighted stragglers, left behind in the dark ages. This is irritating in any case, but it is doubly so in the case of the dotard, who should have lived that down. It becomes indecent.

I quote examples of this kind of fatuousness. The writer complains of a certain ambiguity in Bergson, which ambiguity 'can be twisted to sinister uses by philosophers like Balfour, who, having no firm philosophic attachment, are disposed to value theories just as they can be made use of for the purposes of Conservatism. . . . Balfour, even from his standpoint of orthodoxy or reaction, would have done better to have left alone this central thesis of Bergson.'

'Sinister' is delightful, but on the whole I prefer the sneer at 'no firm philosophic attachment'. This is a regular Tory sentiment. It is simply a translation into another sphere of the idea that the 'landless man' is a dangerous person, who must be regarded with suspicion. In any case, I should have thought that the less firmness there was about your philosophic attachments the more likely you were to arrive at truth. However, I have only dragged in this poor bemused creature from the 'Nation' because I get thereby a pretext for talking about Bergson's relation to political theory. A correspondent in this review a few weeks ago[6] informed us that 'Bergson stands for Democracy', and at the end of an article by Mr. Stephen Reynolds[7] there occurred the phrase, 'None of the critics of Bergson appear to have noticed that a complete theory of Democracy can be got out of him.'

Both these statements are untrue. Bergson no more stands for Democracy than he stands for paper-bag cookery. At the same time, the critics have got out of him a complete theory of Democracy. I advise Mr. Reynolds to look at Sorel's 'Réflexions sur la Violence', or to read the articles in 'La Mouvement Socialiste', which, during the first five or six years, have been written by Sorel, Bertheau, and the other members of the group.[8]

The fact is, of course, that while Bergson has in reality no connection with politics, the various sects can restate their positions in terms of his vocabulary, and thus manufacture new weapons for their own purposes. I do not propose to examine here the really interesting theory of democracy that can be got out of Bergson. I propose to deal with that in an article on Sorel. I am concerned here with the minor point, which is yet of some interest.

While the real influence of a philosopher must necessarily be very limited, he yet has a kind of spurious influence of a very widespread character. In his endeavour to state accurately his position a philosopher finds it necessary to create a certain special phraseology. The ordinary person reading his books retains only a vague feeling of excitement and the delusion that by repeating these phrases in an interjaculatory kind of way they are conveying over to the other person the kind of excitement that the reading of the book produced in them. It thus happens that all that survives as a rule of any system is a débris of phrases and catchwords which float down the floods of controversy for the next thirty years.

Something of the sort has already happened and is destined to happen still more here in regard to Bergson. One already meets people who, in arguments on all kinds of subjects, use phrases like 'le continu', 'élan vital', and 'la durée réelle'. Now this kind of thing has been going on for several years in France, and some interesting lessons for our own future may be drawn from it.

The particular thing I am interested in is the use of the phrase 'real time' in political controversy. The only two groups at the present time in

France which show any vivid interest in the theoretical basis of their position and which make an endeavour to find a thought-out consistent political philosophy are the Syndicalists and the brilliant set of Neo Royalist writers grouped around L'Action Française. I noticed early this year that one of the most interesting of the group, M. Pierre Lasserre, had made an attack on Bergson.

I was very much in sympathy with the anti-romanticism of his two books, 'La Morale de Nietzsche' and 'Le Romantisme français', and I wondered from what point of view exactly he was attacking Bergson. I was in agreement with both sides, and so I wondered whether there was any real inconsistency in my own position. When I was in Paris, then, last April I went to see Lasserre and talk to him about it. I reproduce here the substance of his criticism:—

'I have lectured on Bergson', he said, 'because I think that from the political point of view I represent he constitutes a real danger. Put very briefly, the attitude of L'Action Française is this: At the back of our position there is a certain intellectual discipline. We think that the only road to sanity in these matters is to take as a guide for theory and practice the natural and necessary relations of things. We believe, then, in the existence of laws which express what we know of the necessary and permanent characteristics of any social and political order, which laws can be drawn by induction from the experiences of history or by deduction from the elementary knowledge that any man may have of human nature and the exigencies of life in society. It is by the clear objective application of these laws and truths that we have shown the mischievousness of democracy and the necessity for the kind of polity which we recommend.

'It is on this ground that we have combated the sincere partisans of the French Revolution. They are inspired by a legitimate and necessary sentiment, that of the dignity and value of the individual and the right that he has to enjoy the institutions which will procure him the maximum of good.

'But when from this just postulate the democrats conclude that it is the individual who ought to govern and the will of the majority to decide the fate of institutions they misunderstand in the grossest fashion the necessary relations which hold between things and the law of facts. What is actually produced under the name of democracy is not this absolutely irrealisable government by the majority, but a régime which can be defined as an oscillation between two apparent contraries, the despotism of the State and general anarchy. These are the two conditions from which all the individuals suffer, with the exception of little groups and cliques who are able to exploit this régime for their own benefit.

'Our side', he said, 'can claim all the intellectual, if not the material victories. Nothing serious has been opposed to us by the "progressives". But recently there has been a change in their tactics. Formerly, if they attacked us, it was with the same weapons with which we attacked them. They have not contested our method, but solely our application of it. But now they wish to place us in the position of a barrister who has quite correctly interpreted certain articles of the code, but who is then told that the code in question is superseded. They have endeavoured to cut the ground from under us, so as to leave us suspended in mid-air, waving a now useless dialectic sword.

'To get down to more concrete terms, what is this code that they claim is superseded? Simply our assertion that there are such things as necessary laws governing societies, and more particularly that these laws can be discovered from past history. It is useless, they say, to search in the past for general truths which shall be applicable to the present, because there is no common measure between the political and social situations offered us by the past and those of the present.

'If we ask why, we are told that Bergson has now proved that *Time is real*—that is, that the present moment is a *unique* moment and can be paralleled by nothing in the past—"Time is real," so that there is no repetition. If we point out that history does or does not show us any prosperous, strong, and conquering nation, which was at the same time a democracy, they retort, history would not be history if it were not change itself and perpetual novelty.

'To our judgments on politics in the name of reason interpretating experience, the Bergsonians oppose to us what they call "Life"—life which is always creation and always incalculable.'

M. Lasserre then endeavoured to prove to me that Bergsonism was nothing but the last disguise of romanticism. If I thought this was true, I should be compelled to change my views considerably. I can find a compromise for myself, however, which I roughly indicate by saying that I think time is real for the individual, but not for the race. I shall try in a later article to work out the consequences of this. It means that one has to cut all the sentiments expressed at the ends of Bergson's chapters, but I believe that it preserves most of the essentials. I remember talking about it to M. Batault, who wrote one of the first articles that I read about Bergson,[9] and he assured me then that I was no Bergsonian. I asked Bergson himself and he said, 'M. Batault is, then, more of a Bergsonian than I am myself.'

A Personal Impression of Bergson

[First published in the *Westminster Gazette*, 18 Nov. 1911, p. 2, under the pseudonym T. K. White, 'K. White' being a play on 'Kibblewhite', the name of Hulme's friend Ethel Kibblewhite, who lived with her father, Thomas Figgis Curtis, and her two children at 67 Frith Street, Soho Square, London. Hulme seems to have used a spare room in the house for study and work, and also used the house for entertaining friends and acquaintances at teas and for literary and philosophical gatherings on Tuesday evenings.]

There have been stirring times lately for those peculiar people amongst us who take an interest in metaphysics. We have not been able to buy even a sporting evening paper without finding in it an account of a certain famous philosopher.[1] All of us in the craft have been shining with a certain amount of this reflected radiance. No less than five times recently wonderful young men have dashed up to my house in taxis, rung the bell furiously, and on being admitted have announced breathlessly: 'I am the representative of the *Daily*——. Can you give me Bergson's private address, as my paper wants to print a little talk with him.' In the course of its varied history philosophy has been many things, but never before has it attained the dignity of being 'news', and news which was so pressing that it had to be got out before a certain edition. One began to imagine that one would some day see the newsboys running along the street with the flaring placards 'The secret of the cosmos discovered: special interview'. The only other time that I remember philosophy being so prominent was last spring in Bologna, when the Philosophical Congress there was inaug-urated with an imposing military display.

Now, this is, of course, a very curious phenomenon and rather difficult to account for. For Bergson can't possibly mean anything to any very great number of people—no philosopher could. The idea, then, suggests itself to one that the elements in Bergson which give him this notoriety are certainly not those to which his real importance is due. A portrait has been manufactured which certainly has drawn immense popularity, which at the same time must be a tremendous distortion.

I imagine that this distortion, this imaginary portrait, has been fostered to a great extent by the character of the lectures which have been given at University College.[2] He seems to have felt the kind of audience he was going to get, and to have modified the character of his discourse considerably. Even the manner of his delivery seemed to me to be not at all characteristic.

To recapture the real man, I had to recall the image I had formed of him on former occasions. In particular I have a very vivid recollection of a lecture he gave at the Bologna Congress this year.[3] I was struck then by the extraordinary difference between the manner of his delivery and that of the Germans. I could describe it best by saying it was emphatically not fluent. It was not 'determined'. His eyes seemed always to be half-closed, and he gave you all the time the impression of a man describing with great difficulty the shape of something which he just saw. There was a curious pause and a gesture of the thumb and forefinger which looked as if he were pulling a fine thread out of a tangled mass. It carried over to one an extraordinary feeling of conviction. It appeared as if in the confused flux of things he was able by great attention to just see a certain curve, and that he was carefully choosing his words and picking out metaphors and illustrations in order to make sure he was conveying over to one just the exact shape of the curve he saw and no other. It is perhaps the most pleasing form of delivery possible, because in a subtle way it gives one continually the feeling that one is helping the lecturer to discover something.

The Germans presented a tremendous contrast to that. Their speech was emphatic, continuous, and fluent. They expressed not the attitude of a man who with difficulty sees a new shape, but on the contrary gave one the certain conviction that they saw nothing at all. There was no question of vision. Vision breeds dissatisfaction with ready-made phrases and an attempt to supplement the inadequacies of language by new metaphors. It was perfectly plain that no glimmering of the inadequacy of language had ever struck them. The concepts which they perpetually arranged in different orders, like a set of counters, were perfectly adequate to them for the representation of all the mysteries of thought.

Now it seems to me that in this quality of Bergson's speech, in the way in which he was contrasted with the other people I have described, you have the key to the whole of his philosophy. As I have said, I missed it a little in the University College lectures because there he only repeated in a popular form ideas which he had previously expressed. They are ideas which he has expressed so often that he has to a certain extent made them external to himself, and in dealing with them his manner loses that characteristic quality I have described and approximates to that of the Germans. For the ideas being externalised, he can deal with them as counters in the fluent and direct way. But I recaptured this quality at once when, after the lapse of some years, I was again privileged to talk with him privately. One always gets from his conversation that peculiar kind of instinctive feeling which an unexpected metaphor may give one in a great poet, that one is in the presence of something seen absolutely at first hand. He is never 'in' the language he is using. He is describing something actual, something seen, and is to that extent detached and above the words he is using. The academic metaphysician has often with a kind of half-sneer described Bergson as 'the artist' in philosophy. I heard the expression many times in Bologna. It is quite clear what they meant by the use of the word 'artist' here. They meant that by the help of his extraordinary command over the means of expression he was able to present as valid something which, seen coldly and rationally, is invalid. This is a fundamental misuse of the word 'artist'. It is a typical outsider's view of art, as something external added at the end of a process, a kind of decorative wall-paper. The process is as they conceive it, I suppose, that Bergson formed certain ideas and then turned his artistry on to them afterwards. This seems to me to show an absolute misconception of the process. An artist is one of those rare people who, seeing a definite thing, realise that the conventional means of expression, be they plastic or verbal, always let this definite thing leak through and do not convey it over. The artist is in the position of a man who sees for the first time a certain peculiar curve whose only means of drawing that curve is represented by a set of standard wooden curves such as architects use. It is not that by his artistry he polishes up or decorates the previously existing curves, but simply that he has to create a new curve in order to say anything at all.

It seems to me that this is the attitude of Bergson in everything that he has done. He has insisted always in dealing with any problem in an attempt to see it as it is, and to escape from the categories in which we most easily approach it. This leads one, of course, to the view that the real philosopher is as rare as a real artist, and right away from the view that metaphysics is a science which can be taught just as any other science can.

I asked Bergson what he thought of the tremendous réclame he had had in this country, and he seemed extremely amused, but at the same time rather regretted it. For this fictitious notoriety among people to whom what he says cannot possibly convey anything tends, human nature being what it is, to bring about a certain reaction among the philosophers themselves.

More than that, it leads to a wrong accentuation of the part of Bergson's work which is on the whole least important. Mr. Balfour's article,[4] said M. Bergson to me, 'asks many questions. I would answer them if I could but I cannot as yet. They are problems I am working at.

Some day I may see their answer but at present I don't.' In that phrase you have a spirit which is characteristic of the whole of M. Bergson's attitude, a spirit which has hitherto been much commoner in science than in philosophy.

I asked him if he intended to publish any new book. 'That is a thing which I never know', he said, 'in advance. I work always at five or six problems at the same time. If after some years these various lines of work converge then there is a book, if not then there is no book.' I was curious as to his method of work. Each book has taken almost ten years to write. Did he work at it in sections, writing and rewriting all that time, or what was his method? The actual writing of 'Evolution Créatrice', he said, 'was done in three months and at great speed, though of course I had been working at the ideas it contains for more than ten years, as even in the end of "Matière et Mémoire" you will find a reference to it. When I do write a new book it will probably be on æsthetics and ethics.'

The Philosophy of Intensive Manifolds

[This general essay on Bergson was originally given as a series of four lectures at the house of Mrs Franz Liebich in London, between 23 Nov. and 14 Dec. 1911. It was not published until *S*, when Herbert Read gave it the title 'The Philosophy of Intensive Manifolds' (letter from Read to C. K. Ogden, 16 Apr. 1923). The source of this text is *S* 173–214.]

If one wanted to give the broadest possible description of the aim that Bergson pursues in all his work one would have to say that it was an endeavour to prove that we arrive at a certain picture of the nature of reality, not because such is, as a matter of fact, the nature of things, but because a certain inveterate tendency of the mind distorts things in that direction. That is giving the broadest possible statement of it; the nature and importance of the effort becomes clearer when you state it in particular instead of general terms. The habit of mind which he thinks distorts instead of revealing is simply the ordinary use of the logical intellect. The theory to which we are led is that which considers the world as being in reality a vast machine. Huxley called it the nightmare of determinism—a nightmare most conveniently described by a quotation from a book of Münsterberg's:—

'Science is to me not a mass of disconnected information, but the certainty that there is no change in the universe, no motion of an atom, and no sensation of a consciousness which does not come and go absolutely in accordance with natural laws; the certainty that nothing can exist outside the gigantic mechanism of causes and effects; necessity moves the stars in the sky and necessity moves the emotions in my mind.'

The fact that Bergson does deal successfully with this nightmare seems to me to constitute his principal achievement. It forms the background which makes him appear so significant.

To repeat again, then, the general idea behind Bergson's work: It is an endeavour to prove that we seem inevitably to arrive at the mechanistic theory simply because the intellect, in dealing with a certain aspect of reality, distorts it in that direction. It can deal with matter but it is absolutely incapable of understanding life. In explaining vital phenomena it only distorts them, in exhibiting them as very complex mechanical phenomena. To obtain a complete picture of reality it is necessary to employ another faculty of the mind, which, after defining it, Bergson calls intuition. It is useless then to dream of one science of nature, for there must be two—one dealing with matter which will be built up by the intellect, and the other dealing with certain aspects of life which will employ intuition.

The idea that there are two methods of thinking, the rational or mechanical on the one hand, and on the other hand the vital and more instinctive, is of course an idea which has been familiar for a long time outside philosophy. It occurs, for example, in Burke's writings on social and political matters.

What Bergson has done is to analyse out accurately and exactly the nature of this difference, and it is precisely in this accurate analysis of the difference between the two contrasted ways of looking at things that you get the essence of his philosophy. It seems to me then to be absolutely useless in explaining him to give anything else but the precise and accurate statement of his conception of the difference. It is no use generalising it. It is no use saying that he thinks the logical intellect is unable to grasp the essence of life, and that reality flows through the meshes of the net set for it by reason. Such statements do represent what he says, but they represent it so loosely that the whole importance of what he is getting at slips through. If you are firmly convinced that the mechanistic theory is the true account of the world, you are not in the least likely to be shifted from your view by vague statements of that kind.

It is necessary then to show exactly in what way Bergson thinks that our ordinary methods of explanation distort reality. The process of explanation itself is generally quite an unconscious one. We explain things and it never strikes us to consider what it is we have done. We are as it were *inside* the process and we cannot observe it, but you may get a hint of its nature by observing its effects. In any explanation you start off with certain phenomena, and you transform them into something else and say: 'This is what really happens.' There is something about this second state that satisfies the demands of your intellect, which makes you say: 'This is perfectly clear.' You have in your mind a model of what is clear and comprehensible, and the process of explanation consists in expressing all the phenomena of nature in the terms of this model. I ought to say here that I am speaking not of ordinary explanation, but of explanation when it has gone to its greatest lengths, which is when it has worked itself out in any completed science like mechanics.

As an example of the kind of thing which the intellect does consider perfectly clear and comprehensible you can think of a lot of pieces on a draught board. When you are told where the pieces are, and what moves they make, then the mind is satisfied that it completely understands the phenomena. An omniscient intelligence could know no more about that board than you do. You find as a matter of fact that any science, as it tends towards perfection, tends to present reality as consisting of something exactly similar to this draught board. They all resolve the complex phenomena of nature into fixed separate elements changing only in position. They all adopt atomic theories, and the model of all the sciences is astronomy. In order to get a convenient nomenclature one calls all complex things which can be resolved into separate elements or atoms in this way 'extensive manifolds'.

It is suggested that this surprising unanimity in the results of the different sciences is not due to the nature of the phenomena they investigate, but rather to the nature of the instrument we use in explanation. We find atoms everywhere. We reduce everything to extensive manifolds. We always pursue the method of analysis simply because that is the only way in which the intellect can deal with things.

The question arises: Why is the intellect satisfied in this way? The answer to this is quite simple and can be got from the etymology of the words which indicate explanation. Explanation means *ex plane*, that is to say, the opening out of things on a plain surface. There is the phrase, *the chestnut explains its leaves, i.e.* unfolds them. Then the French word is expliquer (explico) to unfold. The process of explanation is always a process of unfolding. A tangled mass is unfolded flat so that you can see all its parts separated out, and any tangle which can be separated out in this way must be of course an extensive manifold.

It seems then that the intellect distorts reality (if it does distort it) because it persists in unfolding things out in space. It is not satisfied unless it can see every part. It wants to form a picture. It is possible then that there may be a method of knowledge which refrains from forming pictures. Put in Bergson's words in the preface to his first book,[1] which really contains in embryo the whole of everything he has ever done, 'We think in terms of space—the insurmountable difficulties presented by certain philosophic problems arise from the fact that we separate out in space, phenomena which do not occupy space.'

You might dimly suspect that there are other methods of knowledge besides that of analysis. I may have a perfect knowledge of a friend's face, *e.g.*, without being able to analyse it into parts. You may suspect that they are unanalysable. An expert can give a judgment on a picture, a judge on a complex case, without being able to give any reasons for their judgment, that is without being able to analyse out the element which was responsible for it. Anyone can add to this list indefinitely. In fact all of us are prepared to agree that at any rate such things as *apparent* intuitions exist. But if we have been sufficiently disciplined in science we refuse to admit that these are real intuitions or that there is any other method of knowledge which is different to the ordinary straightforward one. We say that the mind has unconsciously analysed and so arrived at its conclusions. We refuse to admit that things exist which can't be analysed. Life, we persist in thinking, appears to be unanalysable merely because it is so extremely complex. In the end we shall be able to analyse it. So with all these appearances of intuitive knowledge, they are really only complex examples of ordinary knowledge.

Now, as in the case of the intellect, it is necessary to make these things much more precise before it can be got at. I shall endeavour to show that intuition can be defined as the method of knowledge by which we seize an intensive manifold, a thing absolutely unseizable by the intellect.

Explanation is an endeavour to make things comprehensible. It is suggested that we have too narrow a standard of what is comprehensible and clear. Bergson is endeavouring to widen this standard, to make it more elastic, to provide an alternative model. It is because of the narrowness of our conception of what is clear that we are driven into so many difficulties. We feel convinced for quite other reasons that certain things exist which cannot be reduced to mechanical or spacial terms. As we have such a narrow standard of what is clear we can't fit them into any natural explanation, the result is that we have to give extremely unnatural explanations of them. We have to say that these things are Inconceivable and Inexpressible, both with capital I's. For example, as Free-will will not fit into the mechanical conception of things, and we are at the same time convinced that it exists, we have to find a place for it in a world of things in themselves. The result is that a certain condition of strain is set up. Bergson attempts to ease this strain and to let these things come back to the ordinary world by altering the standard of clear explanation. He endeavours to show that certain finite things, while quite incomprehensible by our ordinary standards, yet exist.

What exactly are these things? You will remember that the intellect which always thinks, as it were, in space, which always insists on having a clear diagram or picture, insists on analysing complex things into an aggregate of separate elements which we called extensive manifolds. In order that the intellect may be able to completely grasp reality, it is necessary that reality should be composed entirely in this way. Suppose, however, that there existed in nature certain finite things whose parts interpenetrated in such a manner that they could not be separated or analysed out. The intellect would then be unable to understand the nature of these things, for it persists in forming a diagram, and in a diagram each part is separated from every other part. It is difficult to give an idea of what one means by an interpenetration of parts which cannot be separated. One naturally supposes that what is meant here is an extraordinary inexplicable tangle which can't be unravelled. But that would not be at all what was intended for here one can't separate the parts because they are mixed in such an extraordinary complex way. In theory, at any rate, one could separate them out. One is to suppose rather an absolute interpenetration—a complex thing which yet cannot be said to have parts because the parts run into each other, forming a continuous whole, and whose parts cannot even be conceived as existing separately. It has differences, but these differences could not be numbered. It could not therefore be called a quantitative multiplicity, but a qualitative one. For the sake of convenience and the contrast with the other thing I prefer to call it an intensive manifold.

I don't suppose that I have succeeded in conveying a very clear idea of what an intensive manifold is, or would be, because by its very nature, one's intellect, as it were, wriggles away from the idea. One's ordinary intellectual imagination which persists in making spacial pictures of things naturally finds it inconceivable to imagine a thing which couldn't possibly exist in space.

One can illustrate the difficulty that one has in conceiving it by thinking of one epithet I have used to describe it, namely interpenetration.

You cannot even form a picture of the kind of interpenetration you mean. If you melt salt in water, after a time salt would be found in every particle of the water, and you might think then that here you had interpenetration. But no: your mind cannot support an idea of that kind. It sets to work and imagines that the molecules of salt fit in between the molecules of water. It so gets rid of the idea interpenetration and reduces everything to an extensive manifold. In this little instance it might be argued that there is no distortion. But if you suppose that there do exist in the world some instances of real interpenetration, then the intellect, working by analysis, would be incapable of understanding them.

All this is mere supposition. If such intensive manifolds exist, if there are cases of real interpenetration, then Bergson will have proved his point, namely, that the intellect cannot deal with the whole of reality, that there cannot be merely one science, and that completely to understand the nature of reality some other faculty of the mind, some second method of cognition, must be employed.

Two questions, then, have to be considered at this point:—

(1) Is there such a faculty as intuition, as distinct from the intellect, which enables one to know certain things without being able to analyse or to state them?

(2) Are there as a matter of fact existing in nature any such things as intensive manifolds?

This is the crucial point in Bergson's reasoning, the point at which it passes from mere supposition to fact.

It was suggested that the view of the world as a mechanism was due, not to the nature of reality itself, but to certain preferences of the intellect. That the intellect in fact distorts reality. It distorts it for this reason, that in explaining things it always insists on unfolding them into parts, or analysing them.

It was pointed out that if the intellect came across an intensive manifold—that is a finite thing—of such a nature that its parts interpenetrate and cannot be separated out, that it would endeavour in roundabout ways to replace them by complicated extensives, and so would distort reality.

But that remains pure theory, and no real step towards an attack on mechanism has been made until you have definitely proved the existence of such an intensive manifold.

If you can prove that even one of them exists then you have got the fulcrum with which you can begin to shift mechanism. You must find a concrete example; otherwise the thing remains entirely in the air.

The particular part of reality in which Bergson first attempted to prove the existence of interpenetration was that of our own mental life. This is the part of reality in which we may be supposed to get at the nature of things most intimately and which may give the key to the rest. This is the subject of Bergson's first book, *Time and Free-will.*

At first sight, mental life, like things in the physical world, does appear to be resolvable into separate elements. It does appear to form really an extensive manifold, and not an intensive one, as Bergson claims. You are able to describe what you feel, and no description is, of course, possible without analysis. I can say I feel annoyed, or that I was prompted to a certain action by a certain motive, or that I had such and such a sequence of ideas. You do appear to be able to form a picture of the mind then as composed of a succession of clearly outlined states following one another. If that were correct it could be dealt with by a science of exactly the same character as that constituted by the physical sciences. There is nothing here which the intellect cannot deal with; there is no necessity for any different way of knowing things.

But it is not difficult to see that such a description of the nature of the mind is a very superficial one. There are *no* clearly outlined and separated states; in fact there are no separate states of mind at all: each state fades away into and interpenetrates the next state. The whole thing being continuous, then consider any description such as 'He felt annoyed'. This is in no sense an accurate description of a man's actual state of mind. The feeling of 'annoyance' as it occurs to any one person is perfectly individual, and is coloured by his whole personality. Language, however, has to use, to describe this particular state of 'annoyance', the same word in every case, and is thus only able to fix the objective and impersonal aspect of the emotion. Every emotion is composed of a thousand different elements which dissolve into and permeate each other without any precise outline. In this lies the individuality of the emotion. As soon as you begin to analyse and to attempt to describe it in words you take away from it all the individuality which the emotion possesses as occurring in a certain person.

To describe accurately, then, any emotion—to give it accurately and not approximately—you would have to describe at the same time the whole personality in which it occurs, which is only another way of saying that mental life forms a whole which cannot be analysed into parts.

But the fact remains that superficially you can, as a matter of fact, analyse and describe the flow of mental life. How is this?

The fact that certain parts of the mind can be separated into elements is not due entirely to the nature of the intellect. The intellect, it is true, always insists on analysing things into elements, but it would not meet here with the success it does did it not correspond with something actual in the nature of the mind itself.

Bergson explains this by his theory of the two selves. Fundamentally, the mind is a flux of interpenetrating elements which cannot be analysed out. But on the surface this living self gets covered over with a crust of clean cut psychic states which are separated one from the other and which can be analysed and described. This crystallisation into separate states has come about mainly for the purposes of action and communication in social life. If each new idea gradually permeated the whole like a drop of water does a pool, then decision and action would be slow and ineffective. So for purposes of communication, you must be able to describe, and to do that you must have some stable crystallised-out states which you can talk about.

You thus have two different selves at two different levels. The superficial one which is the one usually perceived, and which comes into play at the ordinary level of daily life where each state can be separated out from each other state, and which so can be thoroughly understood by the ordinary intellect, and the more fundamental self which is only reached at certain moments of tension where all the states interpenetrate, and of which, it being an intensive manifold, no picture or description can be given.

For the purposes of a short exposition of Bergson it is inconvenient that it is so difficult to convey what he means by this fundamental self, because it is on the experiencing of this state that depends also what he means by an intuition. I said earlier that an intuition was the process of mind by which one obtained knowledge of an intensive manifold.

Obviously you can't understand, or be said to know in any way, an intensive manifold by means of the logical intellect because by the very nature of the thing you can't analyse it, and it is so indescribable. But although indescribable it is not unknowable, for Bergson supposes that in an intuition you have complete knowledge of these things. You have a complete and complex state of knowledge, of a complex thing, containing differences within it although these differences are not separable and can't be unfolded out. The simplest way of describing it would be to say that you had a complex feeling about the matter, were not 'feeling' such a dangerous word to use in this connection.

But all this has rather the appearance of a kind of abstract miracle and an elaborately built-up piece of abstraction which corresponds to no real process. You can only fill it in with the details that make it actual and real by the experiences drawn from the mental phenomena which Bergson calls the fundamental self.

In a moment of tension, when a man is moving on the level of the fundamental self, he will have a knowledge of what is happening in him which is of a fundamentally different character to the ordinary kind of knowledge. What that difference is can only be got at by crude metaphor. If you think of mental life as a flowing stream, then ordinary intellectual knowledge is like looking at that stream from the outside: you get a clear and perfectly describable picture. Imagine now that you are turned into a cross section of this flowing stream, that you have no sense of sight, that in fact your only sense is a sense of pressure. Then although you will have no clear picture or representation of the stream at all, you will in spite of that have a complete knowledge of it as a complex sense of the varying directions of the forces pressing on you. If you put yourself in this position with regard to your own inner life—and this is what Bergson means by an intuition—then you will realise that it is composed not of separate things but of interpenetrating tendencies. It is always a process which contains differences implicitly and not separated out. It is composed of a million different elements which at the same time are not elements at all, because they melt into one another with not the least tendency to be separated out from the other. Such a state can be directly experienced, and yet is a state which is absolutely inconceivable intellectually, simply because it can't be analysed.

But it is extremely important here to notice that there is nothing mysterious either about the state of mind or about the method of cognition by which you become aware of it. There is nothing infinite or ineffable about the fundamental self. It is a perfectly finite thing and at the same time there is nothing miraculous about one's intuition of it. And it is just at this point that a good deal of academic criticism of Bergson seems to me to go wrong. Because the process of intuition is by its nature an indescribable process, it seems to be assumed that it is not a part of normal experience. The critics then pass on to the statement that as, in Bergson's view, certain aspects of reality cannot be seized by the intellect but only by some mysterious faculty of the mind, that therefore his system is only a kind of subtly disguised agnosticism.

This seems to me to be an entirely wrong view. What Bergson means by an intuition is a perfectly normal and frequent phenomenon. It seems a curious thing to say, but in all probability any literary man or artist would understand—would grasp much more easily—what Bergson means by an intuition. It is a process with which they are perfectly familiar and which isn't in the least mysterious to them. Nearly all of them constantly exercise the faculty. 'Anyone who has attempted any literary composition, for example, knows that when the subject has been thoroughly studied and all the notes collected, it is necessary, before one begins the work of composition itself, to make sometimes a difficult effort to place oneself as it were at the heart of the subject.'[2] In this state of tension one receives an impulsion, a sense of direction, which, when it develops itself as it goes along, picks up and makes use of all the notes that have been made before. The point to notice here is that at the beginning of this act, at this moment of tension, all the separate parts which before and after were separated out, were gathered up together in this act of intuition. They didn't exist side by side in the mind as they would have done in any intellectual representation. In Coleridge's phrase, they were fused together in the central heat of the imagination.

In terms of this conception of the two layers of mental life, the superficial and the fundamental self, I can state very briefly Bergson's conception of Free-will. He thinks that on the level of the superficial self our actions are to a great extent quite determined and automatic. One clear cut psychic state influences the next, just as, mechanically, one body influences another in the physical way. In this state the real flux of our feelings isn't concerned at all. For example, when the alarum clock strikes in the morning, the impression does not as a rule disturb the whole consciousness like a stone falling into a pool of water, but merely stirs an idea solidified on the surface, the idea of getting up. The two ideas both solidified, as it were, on the top of the mind have in the end become tied up with one another, so that one follows the other without the deeper self being at all involved. The majority of our daily acts are performed in this way and it is greatly to one's advantage that such is the case.

But there are acts of a different kind to this when the outer crust gets broken by the inner self breaking through at a moment of tension and you get what may be called a free act. Such acts are of rare occurrence. It is only at moments of tension and crisis that we choose in defiance of what is generally called a motive. Thus understood our free acts are exceptional.

This theory of the difference between the two kinds of manifold, the intensive and the extensive, and the two kinds of knowledge by which they can be dealt with, intellect and intuition, constitutes only one half of Bergson's system. Parallel with this method, with this alteration of the tools with which we are to work, should go an account of the new theory of the nature of reality which the use of these new tools produces, which is involved in Bergson's conception of *Change and Time*.

To get at Bergson's conception of Change you have to remember his main point (that the intellect distorts things by insisting on one method of explanation) and turning to this particular question, try and find out whether one's difficulties are not due to some distortion of the real nature of Change produced in this way.

How does the intellect deal with Change? As we have seen it tries to make out that all bodies can be analysed out into separable elements, so that it has consequentially to reduce all change to a mere change in position of these particles. In fact it explains change by denying its existence.

One can get a picture of the type in terms of which the mind insists on conceiving change by thinking of the motion of billiard balls on an ideally smooth table where there is no friction. It would be impossible here to discover and conceive the existence of freedom. There is in fact no change at all. You can predict with certainty the position of the balls at any future moment, for you have a fixed number of elements moving under fixed laws.

But—and here comes one of the most important elements for the understanding of what Bergson is getting at—this is only a true account of change if you admit that everything can in reality be analysed into separate elements like the balls on the table. If it can, then the future must be determined; but we have just seen that mental life at the level of the fundamental self cannot. It is an interpenetrating whole: it is not composed of elements. It changes, but the way in which it changes will not fit into the kind of conception which the intellect forms of change.

If we suppose that free acts are possible we are landed: it follows that real novelty is possible; that things can happen which could not have been foreseen even by an infinite intelligence. It seems difficult to believe that not only is the future unknown to us, but that it is at the present moment undecided. We admit change relatively to our limited knowledge but we find it inconceivable that there is an element of absolute chance in the world. Our mind persists in thinking that if we only knew all the laws which govern things we could predict the future. If I picture my motion through time as being like motion along a country road, then I am quite prepared to admit that owing to my vision being limited by the size of the hedges I cannot see the course of the road ahead of me. But I am firmly convinced that the road ahead of me does exist all the time in a fixed direction, and that if I had absolute knowledge—if I could take a bird's-eye-view—I should be able to see it.

We find ourselves unable to rid ourselves of this idea. Freedom is inconceivable and this is the greatest argument as a matter of fact for determinism. The use of the word inconceivable suggests that here again you may have a difficulty caused solely by the intellect's persistence in explaining things in a certain fixed way.

The distortion that the intellect here produces is in our conception of the nature of change. It conceives change in such a way that the future seems always determined.

The inconceivability of an undetermined future does not in reality apply to it, for that inconceivability is only presented to the mind when it thinks of the changing phenomena as being composed of separated elements. It is possible to see then how, at this depth of mental life, where all the elements interpenetrate, and which so constitutes an intensive manifold, you may conceive the possibility of acts which could not have been predicted even by an absolute intelligence, and which were really creative acts.

With these two models of the kind of possible change one may more easily grasp what Bergson means by his doctrine of real time.

In the case where you have a number of elements merely changing in position, time is not really involved at all, for time makes no difference to them. They never alter; they never grow old. At the end of years they may return to the same position as that from which they started.

More than that, if you doubled the speed at which the change of positions took place it would make no difference at all to the system. Take any example of such a system, say the astronomical one. The planets following certain fixed laws follow certain fixed courses. It would make absolutely no difference to those courses if you supposed the speed doubled.

In the first kind of change, where you merely get a rearrangement of parts, time makes no difference at all. You can imagine the process twice as fast without any alteration being produced in the process. In any case nothing really new can be produced.

But in the case of the second kind of change—that which you get at a deeper level—this is by no means true. Time does make a difference. Here you have no mere rearrangement of parts, but a continuous and real change resulting in the production of absolutely new and unpredictable states. It is this kind of change that Bergson calls *real* duration, or real time.

One could get a gross kind of metaphor for the difference between these two kinds of time in this way: If you conceive a perfectly smooth machine working in air you could not double the speed without altering the resistence of the air. But if you had a perfectly smooth machine working in a vacuum then you could make the speed what you liked without any difficulty. Now if the air here is supposed to represent time, then you see that ordinary mechanism as conceived by the intellect does not exist in time at all, for time makes no difference to it.

But you cannot alter the speed of mental life in the same way. In the mechanical world, then, time might flow with infinite rapidity and the entire past, present and future be spread out all at once. But inside us it is very different. In us time is undeniable fact. If I want to mix a glass of sugar and water I have to wait willy-nilly until the sugar melts. This is *real time*; it coincides with my impatience, that is with a certain portion of my duration which I cannot contract as I like.

One could express the same idea in a different way, which brings out better the causes of it and the more important consequences of it. If a child has to fit together a jig-saw puzzle, it can learn to do it quicker and quicker. Theoretically indeed it requires no time to do it, because the result is already given. The picture is already created and the work of recomposing it can be supposed going faster and faster up to the point of being instantaneous. But to the artist who creates a picture, time is no longer an interval that can be lengthened or shortened. To contract it would be to modify the invention itself. The time taken up by the invention is one with the invention itself. It is the actual living progress of the thought, a kind of vital process like *ripening*.

Now here you get at the essence of the thing. *Real duration, real time* is an absolute thing which cannot be contracted or hastened because in it *real work* is being done, really new things are appearing.

In the world of mechanism, as you have seen, there is no real creation of new things, there is merely a rearrangement of fixed elements in various positions. They can't be said to exist in time, because nothing *new* happens, there is no *real time* because there is no *real change*. At a certain depth of mental life you experience real time because there is a real change; new things are produced and not a mere rearranging of old parts. Time then is creation. In real time you get real creation and so real freedom.

The importance of all this is that it is in terms of the nature of mental life that we hope to find the key to reality. If this turns out to be true, then you will form a conception of the world very different from the mechanistic one. One must think of it as duration, that is to say, continuous growth in creation. A becoming never the same, never repeating itself, but always producing novelty, continually ripening and creating. Corresponding to the two methods of explanation—that by intensives and that by extensives—you have then two conceptions of reality as existing in space and in duration.

It is important to see that the inability under which we suffer, of being unable to conceive the existence of a real change in which absolutely new and unpredictable things can happen, is entirely due to that fixed habit of the intellect which insists that we shall analyse things into elements, and insists on that because it will have a picture in spatial terms.

Real change does exist but we shall always find it inconceivable if we try to form a picture of what we mean. When we think in that way we shall always reduce real change to the kind of change that you get in any mechanical system.

This then is the point reached in the argument at the present minute—

I started off with Bergson's method. The first application of this to reality resulted in the conception of the self I have just outlined. You find that in this case the mechanistic theory does not hold, and that fundamentally mind is a free creative activity.

But so far you have not moved outside the limits of the individual mind. As far as that is concerned one may be said to have refuted mechanism. But the retort is still open that the whole thing is subjective. It may be a kind of self delusion. Outside you the world of matter might still be considered as a mechanism.

You now get the second passage to reality in a deeper application of the method. You have still got to prove that this state of flux—this feeling of a free activity which you feel in a certain state of tension—is not merely a subjective state of mind, but does give you real information about a reality which exists outside you.

The first involves the relation of the mind and the body, and to this Bergson devoted his second book *Matter and Memory*.

The novelty of his treatment of this question is that he attempts to deal with it not as a mere matter of speculation, but on a basis provided by an examination of a body of empirical observations. He asserts that the theory he puts forward is the right one because it is the only one which satisfactorily accounts for these facts.

The only body of facts which we actually know in connection with the relation of mind and body are those connected with aphasia, *i.e.* the various ways in which we lose our memory for words.

Bergson's own account of the phenomena is this: What exactly happens when I bring to consciousness the picture of something that I saw yesterday? We can understand it best by thinking of the process of becoming conscious or aware of the existence of an ordinary physical object.

I am not conscious of the existence of the table in the next room. Even if the table is brought into this room I shall not know that it exists until I have opened my eyes—that is until the table has managed to produce certain disturbances in the nerves which lead from my eyes to my brain. It is as if my brain were a keyboard and I only became conscious of the existence of things when they played on that keyboard.

Now apply this to the similar case of memory. Just as many things exist in the next room, of whose existence I am not conscious at this minute, so there exist trailed behind in me, as it were, a whole host of memories of my past of which I am at the present moment quite unconscious.

It is then as if all our memories existed quietly in a kind of next room where one was not conscious of their existence; but that now and then one emerged and became actual by playing on the keyboard of that special part of the brain with which it was concerned.

What, then, should we see if we were able to look into the brain and to see all the atoms in motion?

On the parallelist theory you would be able to tell everything that the person whose brain you were examining was thinking of.

If Bergson's account of the matter is the correct one, you would, when you looked into the brain, see only the parts of the whole thoughts of the man which had reached the stage when they were beginning to turn into, and to influence, action.

We should then know no more of what the man was thinking about than we should know about a play in a foreign tongue which we did not understand, from watching the movements of the actors.

That is, we should know only that part of his thoughts which involved action.

How much we shall learn from the movements of the actors will depend on the nature of the play—nearly everything if it is a pantomime, very little at all if it is a comedy. So with a man's brain. If he is pursuing a course of abstract reasoning we should be able to tell nothing at all from the state of his brain; but if, on the contrary, his mind was occupied with a distinct visual image, or was just preparing to act, we should know nearly everything.

This theory cannot be understood unless one has grasped his idea of the intensives.

You may persist in asking the question: Where are these past memories stored? The answer to that is that the whole of your past life is in the present. This inner stream which composes your inner self bears in it not the whole of your past in the form of completed pictures, but bears it in the form of potentiality. In this stream the elements are, as we have said, interpenetrated. All that happens in an act of recognition is that the interpenetrated parts get separated out.

The most familiar part of Bergson, which I can only state in a few sentences, comes in his account of evolution.

He holds that the only theory which will account for the fact of evolution is to suppose that it was produced by a kind of impulse which is something akin to the creative activity we find in our own mind, and which, inserted in matter, has gradually achieved the result which we now see.

This force or impulse is not a force in the ordinary sense of the term: it is not material at all. You cannot indeed give any representation of it at all for it is of the same nature as the kind of activity we find in ourselves, and which, being an intensive manifold, could not be understood by the intellect.

It is, I suppose, admitted as a fact that there has been such a thing as a real evolution in time. You get on the surface of the earth an amazing variety of different kinds of life from the simple to the very complex. It is generally believed that the very complex forms are descended and have evolved from the more simple ones.

That is the fact with which we start. What kind of explanation has been given of it?

There are two principal sets of theories about it which are known respectively as mechanism and finalism.

The first treats the whole of the phenomena of life and evolution as if they constituted merely an extraordinarily complicated kind of mechanism, and attempts to explain them in the same way as due to the action of the forces concerned. I have used the motion of billiard balls on an ideally smooth table as a convenient picture for any mechanistic system. I can use it again here. Suppose that you had a great number of balls on the table, all moving in various directions. Suppose that gradually, as a result solely of the forces exerted on them by their various collisions, they began to group themselves in large complex and fairly permanent arrangements. That represents the ordinary mechanistic conception of evolution. It represents exactly the kind of thing you get in Spencer, for example in his progress from homogeneity to heterogeneity. The important point about it is to see that the whole of the change has been produced solely as the result of the forces exerted upon the atoms. There is no plan or no desire to produce complexity.

. . . . In the finalistic conception life is supposed to be following a plan all laid down beforehand. It is supposed to be working towards some final end which is generally taken to be man.

Bergson's criticism of both these conceptions, mechanism and finalism, is that they both leave out duration altogether. Whether the complexity of life comes as the result of the working out of certain mechanical laws, or whether it is following a plan laid down for it, in both cases the future is fixed and could be known to an infinite intelligence. That is, they don't exist in real time at all—everything is *given*, there is no real creation. He asserts that the characteristic of all forms of life is that they emphatically exist in duration, *time* does make a difference to them. Time *bites* them and leaves the mark of his teeth on them. All living things grow old, whereas matter never does: it is always *constant* and always the *same*.

In life you do appear to get continuous evolution and creation. Bergson suggests then that the only theory which will fit the facts of evolution is to suppose that it is produced by a kind of *impulse* which is something akin to the creative activity we find in our own mind and which, inserted in matter, has, following out this creative activity, gradually achieved the result we see in evolution.

This impulse is not a force in the ordinary sense of the term; it is not material at all. You cannot, indeed, give any representation of it, for it is of the same nature as the kind of activity we feel in ourselves and which being an intensive manifold could not be understood by the intellect. You are to conceive the original élan or impulse of life to be of the same nature as our own inner self. That is, it is an intensive manifold which contained many differences potentially and interpenetrated.

What *matter* does is to separate out distinctly into separate elements the characteristics which in the original impulse were interpenetrated. Evolution then is not a process of organisation, of building up, but one of dissociation.

It is this which gives Bergson the basis for an empirical proof for the *existence of this élan*.

There are of course two proofs, the direct one which comes from the intuition we have in ourselves of the existence of such an activity. But it is also possible to give a more empirical proof. On Bergson's hypothesis, we have seen, evolution is a separating out of elements which interpenetrated in the original impulse. If then you get the same organs developed

on divergent lines of evolution, you have on Bergson's theory nothing to
be surprised at, for they both develop it from their common origin; but
on the mechanistic theory, the thing will appear rather surprising.

Take a definite case. On two quite separate lines of evolution, that
which includes the vertebrates and that which ends in the molluscs, you
get an eye produced. Moreover this eye is composed of almost the same
parts in both cases. Now on the mechanistic conception of evolution this
phenomena is very difficult to account for.

In the first place, the eye is composed of a multitude of anatomical
elements and tissues all of which are disposed with the greatest precision
and harmony to serve the function of vision. That this precise and
extremely complex arrangement of a vast multitude of parts, many of
which are of highly specialised construction, should have been achieved by the accumulation of happy accidents is a sufficiently incredible
supposition.

But another reason makes it more incredible still. An eye very similar
in construction to our own is independently evolved in some species of
mollusc. The mechanists are driven then to the supposition that the same
kind of happy accident has occurred independently in two branches of
the tree of life. It is as if two walkers starting from different points and
wandering at random should not only meet but should throughout their
walks have described two identical curves.

*Does Bergson's hypothesis enable us to give a better account of this phenom-
enon?* In the first place he would say that we approach the question of
explanation in the wrong way. The eye appears as an infinitely complicated structure. Any mechanical theory seeks to show how the infinite
multiplicity of the parts has been added bit by bit. The whole process then
becomes almost inconceivable. One cannot imagine however it has been
accomplished. Bergson says that this difficulty is as usual entirely due to
the intellect's persistence in analysing things. We persist in thinking that
the eye must have been *constructed* just as we construct a house by adding
piece to piece. Whereas if we could get at the act from inside we should
find that it was a simple indivisible process. The life impulse finding itself
opposed by matter makes an effort to overcome the obstacle and does this
in a simple unanalysable act which results in the visual apparatus.

But as long as we try to reconstruct the process intellectually, we shall
be landed in hopeless difficulty. The act of lifting my arm is a perfectly
simple one to me. But it becomes hopelessly complicated when one
attempts to analyse it out into all the molecular motions of the muscle of
which it is composed.

We have compared the process with which nature constructs an eye to
the simple act with which we raise the hand. To make it more accurate,

suppose that the hand meets with some resistance—that it has to pass through iron filings that are compressed and offer resistance to it. At a certain moment the hand will have exhausted its effort and at this moment the filings will be massed and arranged in a certain definite form. So with the evolution of the eye. The farther the hand goes the greater the complexity of the massed filings; and the farther the impulse in life has gone, the greater the complexity of the eye produced.

Now suppose that the hand and arm are *invisible*. Lookers-on would speculate as to the reason of the arrangement of the filings they see.

Some will account for the action of each filing by the action of the neighbouring filings. These are the *mechanists*. This is the kind of view you get in Spencer where the whole of evolution is supposed to follow from the various attractions of the atoms in the universe.

Others will prefer to think that a plan has presided over the details of these actions. These are the finalists.

But the truth is that there has been one indivisible act, that of the hand passing through the filings.

This is why you get similar eyes in divergent species, for the eye is not constructed by addition of parts, but springs from the same impulse present in every species, and springs from a common origin.

This enables one to see why it is that a similar kind of eye can be met with in two very widely removed animal species. If along both lines of evolution the progress towards vision has gone equally far, the visual organ will be the same in both cases, for the form of the organ merely expresses a measure in which the exercise of the function has been obtained.

It is easy then to see in what respect Bergson's view differs from the mechanistic one. That view of evolution considers that where you get a certain complex organism, owing to the action of natural forces you get a very complex organisation of matter; that there you get life and consciousness. Bergson's own view is the exact contrary of this. The complex organisation does not produce, but is produced by, life.

The characteristic of matter is necessity. The characteristic of the impulse which has produced life is, on the contrary, a free creative activity. The process of evolution can only be described as the gradual insertion of more and more freedom into matter. The original impulse of life builds up certain very complex explosive kinds of compounds which enable it to bring a certain indetermination into matter. In the amœba, then, you might say that the impulse had manufactured a small leak through which free activity could be inserted into the world, and the progress of evolution has been the gradual enlargement of this leak. But, on the other hand, it is necessary to differentiate this view from finalism.

On the surface it looks very like it. The gradual insertion of freedom into matter looks very like a plan laid down beforehand. But it is in reality quite different.

One can show in what exactly this difference consists, by showing the part that chance has played in evolution, and by explaining in what sense *Man* can be said to be the goal of the process.

As to the mechanism by which this has been accomplished. The brain of man looks very like the brain of some other animals. In what lies the difference? It is this: That in the animals any motor mechanisms in the brain which correspond to habits have no other function than the accomplishment of the movements necessitated by those habits. But in man these habits can have a second result, and so by holding other motor habits in check, can overcome automatism and set consciousness free. It is just the difference between a mechanism which engages the attention and a mechanism from which it can be diverted. Bergson illustrates this difference by the following metaphor. The primitive steam-engine required the presence of a person exclusively employed to turn on and turn off taps, either to let steam into the cylinder or to throw cold spray into it. A boy employed on this work and who had got very tired of it got the idea of tying the handles of the taps with cords to the beam of the engine. Then the machine opened and closed the taps itself. If you looked at the machine before and after this alteration without taking any notice of the boy, there would appear to be very little difference in structure. But if you look at the two boys, in the first case all his time was taken up by watching and in the second he was free to go and play as he chose. The difference between the brain of a man and the brain of an animal is probably of this kind.

You could describe the facts of evolution, then, by saying that it seems as if an immense current of consciousness had traversed matter, endeavouring to organise this matter so that it could introduce freedom into it.

But, in doing this, consciousness has itself been ensnared in certain directions. Matter has captured the consciousness which was organising it and entrapped it in its own automatism. In the vegetable kingdom, for example, automatism and unconsciousness have become the rule. In the animals consciousness has more success, but along the whole course of evolution, liberty is dogged by automatism, and is in the long run stifled by it. In man alone has it organised matter into any effective freedom. One can get at a picture of the course of evolution in this way: It is as if a current of consciousness flowed down into matter as into a tunnel, and, making efforts to advance on every side, digs galleries, most of which are stopped by a rock which is too hard, but which in one direction at least has broken through the rock and back into life again once more. This direction is the line of evolution resulting in man.

But if you accept this as a correct picture of the progress of evolution, the question naturally suggests itself to you: Why did this current of consciousness endeavour to assert itself in matter? What possible object could it have? Bergson suggests that an answer can be found to this question by considering the analogy of literary activity. You may start writing a poem in an endeavour to express a certain idea which is present in your mind in a very hazy shape. The effort to express that idea in verse, the struggle with language, forces the idea as it were back on itself and brings out the original idea in a clearer shape. Before it was only confused. The idea has grown and developed because of the obstacles it had to meet. It may be, then, that the function of matter in regard to consciousness is this: It is destined to bring to precision, in the form of distinct personalities, tendencies or potentialities which at first were mingled.

The passage through matter may give to a part of the current of consciousness a certain kind of coherence which enables it to survive as a permanent entity after its passage. And as it is only with man that consciousness has finally left the tunnel. Everywhere else it has remained in prison. And as every other species corresponds to the arrest of something which in man succeeds in overcoming resistance, so displaying itself in characters capable of remembering and of controlling their actions, we shall have no repugnance in admitting that in man, though perhaps in man alone, consciousness pursues its path beyond the bodily life.

The stage in the argument that has been reached at this point is this: You have proved that the inner self which you experience in a moment of tension is not produced by the brain and is to a great extent independent of it. At such moments of tension, then, you reach a reality which passes outside your physical self. But that is not a satisfactory conclusion to the argument, for it leaves the thing rather suspended in the air. The further question is suggested: What is this duration apart from you?

The principal object of Bergson's *Creative Evolution*, is to prove that this pure duration which we experience at the level of the deeper self is identical with the kind of current which runs through all life. In that way he rounds off his position. A certain dissatisfaction is left by the first book, *Time and Free-will*, because it is entirely subjective. It only concerns itself with the analysis of one's own mind. The second book, *Matter and Memory*, to a certain extent removes this, because it proves that in duration we have something independent of the body. A certain dissatisfaction is still left, and this is removed by *Creative Evolution*, which proves that this duration is identical with life.

In this latter book, then, he definitely sets his thought solidly on a fixed base. Once it is proved, nearly all the vagueness disappears from the terms which he uses. One has said vaguely that in an intuition you place yourself inside the object instead of surveying it from the outside. We are now able to give a definite meaning to that phrase. 'To place yourself inside the object' is no longer a merely metaphorical expression. In that state of mind in which you feel and experience duration, and which we have called intuition, you are actually inside that stream of impulse which constitutes life. The difference, too, between intellect and intuition, which before one had merely taken as given, as an ultimate fact which one couldn't explain, one is able to a certain extent to show how it originated. One is able to deduce the characteristics of the intellect from the fact that it is a faculty of mind designed to deal with material objects, and one is able in that way to show the relation between intuition and intellect.

The importance of *Creative Evolution* is of this kind: It does not add anything new to Bergson's thought. If one has understood the difference between intensive and extensive manifolds, you have grasped the whole of that. That was all present in an embryo form, at any rate, in the first book. You could thoroughly understand the actually original part of Bergson without ever having read *Creative Evolution*. But what it actually does do—and this is, of course, no small achievement—is to plant all his ideas solidly down on the earth and show them at work before you in a concrete form, in physical shape. If one were to a certain extent rather exhausted by abstractions, this brings a certain relief. More than that, it gives a certain stability and ballast to the system.

Bergson's Theory of Art

[Probably written in 1911 or 1912, and subtitled 'Notes for a Lecture'. First published posthumously in 1922 as 'The Note-Books of T. E. Hulme', ed. Herbert Read, in *NA* in three instalments: 30 (30 Mar.), 287–8; (6 Apr.), 301–2; and (13 Apr.), 310–12. Reprinted, with a few minor grammatical differences, in *S* 143–69. For a more detailed discussion of the probable date of composition, see K. E. Csengeri, 'The Chronology of T. E. Hulme's *Speculations*', *Papers of the Bibliographical Society of America*, 80 (First Quarter 1986), 105–9.]

1. The great difficulty in any talk about art lies in the extreme indefiniteness of the vocabulary you are obliged to employ. The concepts by which you endeavour to describe your attitude toward any work of art are so extraordinarily fluid. Words like creative, expressive, vital, rhythm, unity and personality are so vague that you can never be sure when you use them that you are conveying over at all the meaning you intended to. This is constantly realised unconsciously; in almost every decade a new catch word is invented which for a few years after its invention does convey, to a small set of people at any rate, a definite meaning, but even that very soon lapses into a fluid condition when it means anything and nothing.

This leads me to the point of view which I take about Bergson in relation to art. He has not created any new theory of art. That would be absurd. But what he does seem to me to have done is that by the acute analysis of certain mental processes he has enabled us to state more definitely and with less distortion the qualities which we feel in art.

2. The finished portrait is explained by the features of the model, by the nature of the artist, by the colours spread out of the palette; but even with the knowledge of what explains it, no one, not even the artist, could have foreseen exactly what the portrait would be. For to predict it would be to produce it before it was produced. Creation in art is not necessarily a mere synthesis of elements. In so far as we are geometricians we reject the unforeseeable. We might accept it assuredly in so far as we are artists, for art lives on creation and implies a belief in the spontaneity of nature. But disinterested art is a luxury like pure speculation. Our eye perceives the features of the living being merely as assembled, not as mutually

organised. The intention of life—a simple movement which runs through the lines and binds them together and gives them significance—escapes it. This intention is just what the artist tries to regain in placing himself back within the object by a kind of sympathy and breaking down by an effort of intuition the barrier that space puts between him and his model. It is true that this æsthetic intuition, like external perception, only attains the individual, but we can conceive an inquiry turned in the same direction as art which would take life in general for its object just as physical science, following to the end the direction pointed out by external perception, prolongs the individual facts into general laws.

3. In the state of mind produced in you by any work of art there must necessarily be a rather complicated mixture of the emotions. Among these is one which can properly be called an essentially æsthetic emotion. It could not occur alone, isolated; it may only constitute a small proportion of the total emotion produced; but it is, as far as any investigation in the nature of æsthetics is concerned, the important thing. In the total body of effect produced by music, nine-tenths may be an effect which, properly speaking, is independent of the essentially æsthetic emotion which we get from it. The same thing is most obviously true of painting. The total effect produced by any painting is most obviously a composite thing composed of a great many different kinds of emotions—the pleasure one gets from the subject, from the quality of the colour and the painting, and then the subsidiary pleasures one gets from recognition of the style, of a period or a particular painter. Mixed up with these is the one, sometimes small element of emotion, which is the veritable æsthetic one.

4. In order to be able to state the nature of the process which I think is involved in any art, I have had to use a certain kind of vocabulary, to postulate certain things. I have had to suppose a reality of infinite variability, and one that escapes all the stock perceptions, without being able to give any actual account of that reality. I have had to suppose that human perception gets crystallised out along certain lines, that it has certain fixed habits, certain fixed ways of seeing things, and is so unable to see things as they are.

Putting the thing generally—I have had to make all kinds of suppositions simply and solely for the purpose of being able to convey over and state the nature of the activity you get in art. Now the extraordinary importance of Bergson for any theory of art is that, starting with a different aim altogether, seeking merely to give an account of reality, he arrives at certain conclusions as being true, and these conclusions are the very things which we had to suppose in order to give an account of art.

The advantage of this is that it removes your account of art from the merely literary level, from the level at which it is a more or less successful attempt to describe what you feel about the matter, and enables you to state it as an account of actual reality.

5. The two parts of Bergson's general philosophical position which are important in the theory of æsthetic are (1) the conception of reality as a flux of interpenetrated elements unseizable by the intellect (this gives a more precise meaning to the word reality which has been employed so often in the previous pages, when art has been defined as a more direct communication of reality); and (2) his account of the part played in the development of the ordinary characteristics of the mind by its orientation towards action. This in its turn enables one to give a more coherent account of the reason for what previously has only been assumed, the fact that in ordinary perception, both of external objects and of our internal states, we never perceive things as they are, but only certain conventional types.

6. Man's primary need is not *knowledge* but *action*. The characteristic of the intellect itself Bergson deduces from this fact. The function of the intellect is so to present things not that we may most thoroughly understand them, but that we may successfully act on them. Everything in man is dominated by his necessity of action.

7. The creative activity of the artist is only necessary because of the limitations placed on internal and external perception by the necessities of action. If we could break through the veil which action interposes, if we could come into direct contact with sense and consciousness, art would be useless and unnecessary. Our eyes, aided by memory, would carve out in space and fix in time the most inimitable of pictures. In the centre of one's own mind, we should hear constantly a certain music. But as this is impossible, the function of the artist is to pierce through here and there, accidentally as it were, the veil placed between us and reality by the limitations of our perception engendered by action.

8. Philosophers are always giving definitions of art with which the artist, when he is not actively working but merely talking after dinner, is content to agree with, because it puts his function in some grandiose phraseology which he finds rather flattering. I remember hearing Mr. Rothenstein[1] in an after-dinner speech say that 'art was the *revelation of the infinite in the finite*'. I am very far from suggesting that he invented that phrase, but I quote it as showing that he evidently felt that it did convey something of the matter. And so it does in a way, but it is so hopelessly vague. It may convey the kind of excitement which art may produce in you, but it in no way fits the actual process that the artist goes through. It defines art in much the same way that saying that I was in Europe

would define my position in space. It includes art, but it gives you no specific description of it.

This kind of thing was not dangerous to the artists themselves, because being familiar with the specific thing intended they were able to discount all the rest. When the infinite in the finite was mentioned, they knew the quite specific and limited quality which was intended. The danger comes from the outsiders who, not knowing, not being familiar with the specific quality, take words like infinite in the much bigger sense than is really intended.

9. To describe the nature of the activity you get in art, the philosopher must always create some kind of special vocabulary. He has to make use of certain metaphysical conceptions in order to state the thing satisfactorily. The great advantage of Bergson's theory is that it states the thing most nakedly, with the least amount of metaphysical baggage. In essence, of course, his theory is exactly the same as Schopenhauer's. That is, they both want to convey over the same feeling about art. But Schopenhauer demands such a cumbrous machinery in order to get that feeling out. Art is the pure contemplation of the Idea in a moment of emancipation from the Will. To state a quite simple thing he has to invent two very extraordinary ones. In Bergson it is an actual contact with reality in a man who is emancipated from the ways of perception engendered by action, but the action is written with a small 'a', not a large one.

10. CREATION. The process of artistic creation would be better described as a process of discovery and disentanglement. To use the metaphor which one is by now so familiar with—the stream of the inner life, and the definite crystallised shapes on the surface—the big artist, the creative artist, the innovator, leaves the level where things are crystallised out into these definite shapes, and, diving down into the inner flux, comes back with a new shape which he endeavours to fix. He cannot be said to have created it, but to have discovered it, because when he has definitely expressed it we recognise it as true. Great painters are men in whom has originated a certain vision of things which has become or will become the vision of everybody. Once the painter has seen it, it becomes easy for all of us to see it. A mould has been made. But the creative activity came in the effort which was necessary to disentangle this particular type of vision from the general haze—the effort, that is, which is necessary to break moulds and to make new ones. For instance, the effect produced by Constable on the English and French Schools of landscape painting. Nobody before Constable saw things, or at any rate painted them, in that particular way. This makes it easier to see clearly what one means by an individual way of looking at things. It does not mean something which is peculiar to an individual, for in that case it would be

quite valueless. It means that a certain individual artist was able to break through the conventional ways of looking at things which veil reality from us at a certain point, was able to pick out one element which is really in all of us, but which before he had disentangled it, we were unable to perceive. It is as if the surface of our mind was a sea in a continual state of motion, that there were so many waves on it, their existence was so transient, and they interfered so much with each other, that one was unable to perceive them. The artist by making a fixed model of one of these transient waves enables you to isolate it out and to perceive it in yourself. In that sense art merely reveals, it never creates.

11. METAPHORS soon run their course and die. But it is necessary to remember that when they were first used by the poets who created them they were used for the purpose of conveying over a vividly felt actual sensation. Nothing could be more dead now than the conventional expressions of love poetry, the arrow which pierces the heart and the rest of it, but originally they were used as conveying over the reality of the sensation experienced.

12. If I say the hill is *clothed* with trees your mind simply runs past the word 'clothed', it is not pulled up in any way to visualise it. You have no distinct image of the trees covering the hill as garments clothe the body. But if the trees had made a distinct impression on you when you saw them, if you were vividly interested in the effect they produced, you would probably not rest satisfied until you had got hold of some metaphor which did pull up the reader and make him visualise the thing. If there was only a narrow line of trees circling the hill near the top, you might say that it was *ruffed* with trees. I do not put this forward as a happy metaphor: I am only trying to get at the feeling which prompts this kind of expression. You have continually to be searching out new metaphors of this kind because the visual effect of a metaphor so soon dies. Even this word *clothed* which I used was probably, the first time it was employed, an attempt on the part of a poet to convey over the vivid impression which the scene gave him. Every word in the language originates as a *live* metaphor, but gradually of course all visual meaning goes out of them and they become kind of counters. Prose is in fact the museum where the dead metaphors of the poets are preserved.

The thing that concerns me here is of course only the *feeling* which is conveyed over to you by the use of fresh metaphors. It is only where you get these fresh metaphors and epithets employed that you get this vivid conviction which constitutes the purely æsthetic emotion that can be got from imagery.

13. From time to time in a fit of absent-mindedness nature raises up minds which are more detached from life—a natural detachment, one

innate in the structure of sense or consciousness, which at once reveals itself by a virginal manner of seeing, hearing or thinking.

It is only by accident, and in one sense only, that nature produces someone whose perception is not riveted to practical purposes; hence the diversity of the arts. One applies himself to form, not as it is practically useful in relation to him, but as it is in itself, as it reveals the inner life of things.

In our minds—behind the commonplace conventional expression which conceals emotion—artists attain the original mood and induce us to make the same effort ourselves by rhythmical arrangements of words, which, thus organised and animated with a life of their own, tell us, or rather suggest, things that speech is not calculated to express.

14. '*Art should endeavour to show the universal in the particular.*' This is a phrase that constantly recurs. I remember great play was made with it in Mr. Binyon's little book on Chinese art.[2] You are supposed to show, shining through the accidental qualities of the individual, the characteristics of a universal type. Of course this is perfectly correct if you give the words the right meaning. It seems at first sight to be the exact contrary to the definition that we have arrived at ourselves, which was that art must be always individual and springs from dissatisfaction with the generalised expressions of ordinary perception and ordinary language. The confusion simply springs from the two uses of the word 'universal'. To use Croce's example. Don Quixote is a type, but a type of what? He is only a type of all the Don Quixotes. To use again my comparison of the curve, he is an accurately drawn representation of one of the individual curves that vary round the stock type which would be represented by the words loss of reality or love of glory. He is only universal in the sense that once having had that particular curve pointed out to you, you recognise it again.

15. From time to time by a happy accident men are born who either in one of their senses, or in their conscious life as a whole, are less dominated by the *necessities of action*. *Nature* has forgotten to attach their faculty for perception to their faculty for action. They do not perceive simply for the purposes of action: they perceive just for the sake of perceiving. It is necessary to point out here that this is taken in a profounder sense than the words are generally used. When one says that the mind is practical and that the artist is the person who is able to turn aside from action and to observe things as they are in a disinterested way, one should be careful to say that this does not refer to any conscious or controllable action. The words as they stand have almost a moral flavour. One might be understood as implying that one ought not to be so bound up in the practical. Of course the word *practical* is not used in this sense. It refers to something physiological and entirely beyond our control. This

orientation of the mind towards action is the theory which is supposed to account for the characteristics of mental life itself and is not a mere description of an avoidable and superficial habit of the individual mind.

When, therefore, you do get an artist, *i.e.*, a man who either in one of his senses or in his mind generally is emancipated from this orientation of the mind towards action and is able to see things as they are in themselves, you are dealing with a rarity—a kind of accident produced by Nature itself and impossible of manufacture.

The artist is the man, then, who on one side of his nature is born detached from the necessities of action. According as this detachment is inherent in one or other of the senses or is inherent in the consciousness, he is painter, musician, or sculptor. If this detachment were complete— if the mind saw freshly and directly in every one of its methods of perception—then you would get a kind of artist such as the world has not yet seen. He would perceive all things in their native purity: the forms, sounds and colours of the physical world as well as the subtlest movements of the inner life. But this, of course, could never take place. All that you get is a breaking through of the surface-covering provided for things by the necessities of action in *one direction* only, *i.e.*, in one *sense* only. Hence the diversity of the arts.

In one man it is the eye which is emancipated. He is able to see individual arrangements of line and colour which escape our standardised perceptions. And having perceived a hitherto unrecognised shape he is able gradually to insinuate it into our own perception. Others again retire within themselves. Beneath the conventional expression which hides the individual emotion they are able to see the original shape of it. They induce us to make the same effort ourselves and make us see what they see; by rhythmical arrangements of words they tell us, or rather suggest, things that speech is not calculated to express.

Others get at emotions which have nothing in common with language; certain rhythms of life at the centre of our minds. By setting free and emphasising this music they force it upon our attention: they compel us willy-nilly to fall in with it like passers-by who join in a dance.

In each art, then, the artist picks out of reality something which we, owing to a certain hardening of our perceptions, have been unable to see ourselves.

One might express the differences in the mechanism by which they do this most easily in terms of the metaphor by which we have previously expressed the difference between the two selves. Some arts proceed from the outside. They notice that the crystallised shapes on the top of the stream do not express the actual shapes on the waves. They endeavour to communicate the real shapes by adding detail. On the other hand, an art like music proceeds from *the inside* (as it were). By means of rhythm it breaks up the normal flow of our conscious life. It is as if by increasing the flow of the stream inside it broke through the surface crust and so made us realise the real nature of the outline of the inner elements of our conscious life. It does this by means of rhythm which acts something like the means used to bring about the state of hypnosis. The rhythm and measure suspend the normal flow of our sensations by causing our attention to swing to and fro between fixed points and so take hold of us with such force that even the faintest imitation of sadness produces a great effect on us. It increases our sensibility, in fact.

16. What is the nature of the properly 'æsthetic' emotion as distinct from the other emotions produced by art?

As I have said, I do not think that Bergson has invented any new theory on this subject, but has simply created a much better vocabulary. That being so, I think that the best way to approach this theory is to state first the kind of rough conception which one had elaborated for oneself, and then to show how it is all straightened up in his analysis. By approaching the theory gradually in this way one can get it more solidly fixed down.

Among all the varied qualities of good verse, and in the complex kind of motion which it can produce, there is one quality it must possess, which can be easily separated from the other qualities and which constitutes this distinctively æsthetic emotion for which we are searching.

This peculiarly *æsthetic* emotion here, as in other arts, is overlaid with all kinds of other emotions and is only perceived by people who really understand verse. To get at what it is quite definitely, I only consider it in as far as it bears on the choice of epithets and images. The same quality is exhibited in the other parts of verse, in the rhythm and metre, for example, but it so happens that it is most easily isolated in the case of epithets.

17. Could reality come into direct contact with sense and consciousness, art would be useless, or rather we should all be artists. All these things that the artist sees exist, yet we do not see them—yet why not?

Between nature and ourselves, even between ourselves and our own consciousness, there is a veil, a veil that is dense with the ordinary man, transparent for the artist and the poet. What made this veil?

ACTION. Life is action, it represents the acceptance of the utilitarian side of things in order to respond to them by appropriate actions. I look, I listen, I hear, I think I am seeing, I think I am hearing everything, and when I examine myself I think I am examining my own mind.

But I am not.

What I see and hear is simply a selection made by my senses to serve as a light for my conduct. My senses and my consciousness give me no more than a practical simplification of reality. In the usual perception I have of reality all the differences useless to man have been suppressed. My perception runs in certain moulds. Things have been classified with a view to the use I can make of them. It is this classification I perceive rather than the real shape of things. I hardly see an object, but merely notice what class it belongs to—what ticket I ought to apply to it.

18. Everybody is familiar with the fact that the ordinary man does not see things as they are, but only sees certain *fixed types*. To begin with, we see separate things with distinct outlines where as a matter of fact we know that what exists is merely a continuous gradation of colour. Then even in outline itself we are unable to perceive the individual. We have in our minds certain fixed conceptions about the shape of a leg. Mr. Walter Sickert is in the habit of telling his pupils that they are unable to draw any individual arm because they think of it as an arm; and because they think of it as an arm they think they know what it ought to be. If it were a piece of almond rock you could draw it, because you have no preconceived notions as to the way the almonds should come. As a rule, then, we never ever perceive the real shape and individuality of objects. We only see stock types. We tend to see not *the* table but only *a* table.

19. One can sum up the whole thing by a metaphor which must not, however, be taken too literally. Suppose that the various kinds of emotions and other things which one wants to represent are represented by various curved lines. There are in reality an infinite number of these curves all differing slightly from each other. But language does not and could not take account of all these curves. What it does do is to provide you with a certain number of standard types by which you can roughly indicate the different classes into which the curves fall. It is something like the wooden curves which architects employ—circles, ellipses, and so forth—by suitable combinations of which they can draw approximately any curve they want, but only approximately. So with ordinary language. Like the architect's curves it only enables us to describe approximately. Now the artist, I take it, is the person who in the first place is able to see an individual curve. This vision he has of the individuality of the curve breeds in him a dissatisfaction with the conventional means of expression which allow all its individualities to escape.

20. The artist has a double difficulty to overcome. He has in the first place to be a person who is emancipated from the very strong habits of the mind which make us see not individual things but stock types. His second difficulty comes when he tries to express the individual thing which he has seen. He finds then that not only has his mind habits, but that language, or whatever medium of expression he employs, also has its

fixed ways. It is only by a certain tension of mind that he is able to force the mechanism of expression out of the way in which it tends to go and into the way he wants. To vary slightly my metaphor of the curves. Suppose that in order to draw a certain individual curve which we perceive you are given a piece of bent steel spring which has a natural curvature of its own. To make that fit the curve you want you will have to press it to that curve along the whole of its length with all your fingers. If you are unable to keep up this pressure and at one end slacken the pressure, then at that end you will not get the curve you were trying to draw, but the rounded-off curve of the spring itself.

You can observe this actual process at work in all the different arts. You may suppose that in music, for example, a man trying to express and develop a certain theme in the individual form in which it appeared to him might, if he relaxed his grip over the thing, find that it had a tendency to slacken off into resemblances to already heard things. This comparison also illustrates what happens in the decay of any art. Original sincerity, which is often almost grotesque in its individuality, slackens off in the rounded curves of 'prettiness'.

21. The psychology of the process is something of this kind. You start off with some actual and vividly felt experience. It may be something seen or something felt. You find that when you have expressed this in straightforward language that you have not expressed it at all. You have only expressed it approximately. All the individuality of the emotion as you experienced it has been left out. The straightforward use of words always lets the individuality of things escape. Language, being a communal apparatus, only conveys over that part of the emotion which is common to all of us. If you are able to observe the actual individuality of the emotion you experience, you become dissatisfied with language. You persist in an endeavour to so state things that the meaning does not escape, but is definitely forced on the attention of the reader. To do this you are compelled to invent new metaphors and new epithets. It is here, of course, that the popular misunderstanding about originality comes in. It is usually understood by the outsider in the arts that originality is a desirable quality in itself. Nothing of the kind. It is only the defects of language that make originality necessary. It is because language will not carry over the exact thing you want to say, that you are compelled simply in order to be accurate to invent original ways of stating things.

22. The motive power behind any art is a certain freshness of experience which breeds dissatisfaction with the conventional ways of expression because they leave out the individual quality of this freshness. You are driven to new means of expression because you persist in an endeavour to get it out exactly as you felt it.

You could define art, then, as a passionate desire for accuracy, and the essentially æsthetic emotion as the excitement which is generated by direct communication. Ordinary language communicates nothing of the individuality and freshness of things. As far as that quality goes we live separated from each other. The excitement of art comes from this rare and unique communication.

23. Creation of imagery to force language to convey over this *freshness* of impression. The particular kind of art we are concerned with here, at any rate, can be defined as an attempt to convey over something which ordinary language and ordinary expression lets slip through. The emotion conveyed by an art in this case, then, is the exhilaration produced by the direct and unusual communication of this fresh impression. To take an example: What is the source of the kind of pleasure which is given to us by the stanza from Keats' 'Pot of Basil', which contains the line

'And she forgot the blue above the trees.'

I do not put forward the explanation I give here as being, as a matter of fact, the right one, for Keats might have had to put trees for the sake of the rhyme, but I suppose for the sake of illustration that he was free to put what he liked. Why then did he put 'blue above the trees' and not 'sky'? 'Sky' is just as attractive an expression. Simply for this reason, that he instinctively felt that the word 'sky' would not convey over the actual vividness and the actuality of the feeling he wanted to express. The choice of the right detail, the blue above the trees, forces that vividness on you and is the cause of the kind of thrill it gives you.

24. This particular argument is concerned only with a very small part of the effects which can be produced by poetry, but I have only used it as an illustration. I am not trying to explain poetry, but only to find out in a very narrow field of art, that of the use of imagery, what exactly the kind of emotion you call æsthetic consists of. The element in it which will be found in the rest of art is not the accidental fact that imagery conveys over an actually felt visual sensation, but the actual character of that communication, the fact that it hands you over the sensation as directly as possible, attempts to get it over bodily with all the qualities it possessed for you when you experienced it.

The feeling conveyed over to one is almost a kind of instinctive feeling. You get continuously from good imagery this conviction that the poet is constantly in presence of a vividly felt physical and visual scene.

25. You can perhaps trace this out a little more clearly in a wider art, that of prose description, the depicting of a character or emotion. You are not concerned here with handing over any visual scene, but in an attempt to get an emotion as near as possible as you feel it. You find that language

has the same defects as the metaphors we have just been talking about. It lets what you want to say escape. Each of us has his own way of feeling, liking and disliking. But language denotes these states by the same word in every case, so that it is only able to fix the objective and impersonal aspect of the emotions which we feel. Language, as in the first case, lets what you want to say slip through. In any writing which you recognise as good there is always an attempt to avoid this defect of language. There is an attempt by the adding of certain kinds of intimate detail to lift the emotion out of the impersonal and colourless level, and to give to it a little of the individuality which it really possesses.

26. Certain kinds of prose at any rate never attempt to give you any visual presentment of an object. To do so would be quite foreign to its purpose. It is endeavouring always not to give you any image, but to hurry you along to a conclusion. As in algebra certain concrete things are embodied in signs or counters which are moved about according to rule without being visualised at all in the process, so certain type situations and arrangements of words move automatically into certain other arrangements without any necessity at all to translate the words back into concrete imagery. In fact, any necessity to visualise the words you are using would be an impediment, it would delay the process of reasoning. When the words are merely counters they can be moved about much more rapidly.

Now any tendency towards counter language of this kind has to be carefully avoided by poetry. It always endeavours, on the contrary, to arrest you and to make you continuously see a physical thing.

27. Language, we have said, only expresses the kind of lowest common denominator of the emotions of one kind. It leaves out all the individuality of an emotion as it really exists and substitutes for it a kind of stock or type emotion. Now here comes the additional observation which I have to make here. As we not only express ourselves in words, but for the most part think also in them, it comes about that not only do we not express more than the impersonal element of an emotion, but that we do not, as a matter of fact, perceive more. The average person as distinct from the artist does not even *perceive* the individuality of their own emotions. Our faculties of perception are, as it were, crystallised out into certain moulds. Most of us, then, never see things as they are, but see only the stock types which are embodied in language.

This enables one to give a first rough definition of the artist. It is not sufficient to say that an artist is a person who is able to convey over the actual things he sees or the emotions he feels. It is necessary before that that he should be a person who is able to emancipate himself from the moulds which language and ordinary perception force on him and be able to see things freshly as they really are.

Though one may have some difficulty at first sight in seeing that one only perceives one's own emotions in stock types, yet the thing is much more easy to observe in the actual perception of external things with which you are concerned in painting.

28. POETRY. I exaggerate the place of imagery simply because I want to use it as an illustration.

In this case something is physically presented; the important thing is, of course, not the fact of the visual representation, but the communication over of the actual contact with reality.

It is because he realises the inadequacy of the usual that he is obliged to invent.

The gradual conclusion of the whole matter (and only as a conclusion) is that language puts things in a stereotyped form.

This is not the only kind of effect produced on one by verse but it is (if one extends the same quality to the other aspects of verse I have left out) the one essentially æsthetic emotion it produces on us. Readers of poetry may attach more importance to the other things, but this is the quality the poets recognise among each other. If one wants to fix it down then one can describe it as a 'kind of instinctive feeling which is conveyed over to one, that the poet is describing something which is actually present to him, which he realises visually at first hand'.

Is there anything corresponding to this in Painting?

29. The essential element in the pleasure given us by a work of art lies in the feeling given us by this rare accomplishment of *direct communication*. Mr. Berenson in his book on the Florentine painters expresses in a different vocabulary what is essentially the same feeling.[3] The part of the book I am thinking of is that where he explains the superiority of Giotto to Duccio. He picks out the essential quality of a painting as its *life-communicating* quality, as rendered by form and movement. Form in the figure arts gives us pleasure because it has extracted and presented to us the structural significance of objects more completely than we (unless we be also great artists) could have grasped them by ourselves. By emphasis the artist gives us an intimate realisation of an object. In ordinary life I realise a given object, say with the given intensity *two*. An artist realises this with the intensity of *four* and by his manner of emphasising it makes me realise it with the same intensity. This exhilarates me by communicating a sense of increased capacity. In that sense it may be said to be life-communicating. This emphasis can be conveyed in various ways: by form as in Giotto, and by movement expressed in line, as in Botticelli. This is

exactly what Bergson is getting at. But instead of saying that an artist makes you realise with intensity *four* what you previously realised with intensity *two*, he would say that he makes you realise something which you actually did not perceive before. When you come to the detailed application of this to art you find that they are both different ways of saying the same thing. They both agree in picking out this life-communicating quality as the essentially æsthetic one. And they both give the same analysis of the feat accomplished by the artist. The advantage of Bergson's account of the matter is that the expressions he uses are part of a definite conception of reality and not mere metaphors invented specially for the purpose of describing art. More than that he is able to explain why it is that the ordinary man does not perceive things at all *vividly* and can only be made to do so by the artist. Both these things are of very little advantage as far as actual art criticism is concerned, but they are distinct advantages to anyone who wants to place art definitely in relation to other human activities.

Political Theory

A Note on the Art of Political Conversion

[First published in the *Commentator* in three instalments: 2 (22 Feb. 1911), 234; (1 Mar. 1911), 250; and (8 Mar. 1911), 266–7. A sequel entitled 'The Art of Political Conversion' appeared in the *Commentator*, 2 (19 Apr. 1911), 357–8. The articles were signed 'Thomas Gratton'.]

Some day a wonderful book will be written on the art of persuasion, a new sophistic. One may suppose that psychology will ultimately become as complete a science as geometry and mechanics are now. It will be possible then to predict the effect of an argument on a man's mind as surely as one can now predict the eclipse of the moon. On the basis of this developed science will be built an infallible set of rules for converting a man to any opinion you like. The mechanism of mind will be as bare as that of a typewriter. You will press the right levers, and the result you want will follow inevitably. The lover will sigh no more, but will consult the manual and succeed—unless the lady be similarly armed. So dangerous will the art be that the knowledge of it must be confined to a special caste, like Plato's guards, disciplined and trained not to make any malicious use of their power. Or more probably the then prevailing form of government will seize it and make a monopoly of it as they now do of armed force, and use it for their perpetual preservation.

Pending the arrival of this political canvassers' millennium, one can sketch out the beginnings of the thing. Materials for the art already exist: Schopenhauer's 'Art of Controversy', Pascal's 'Pensées', the manuals which the credulous Protestant imagines that the Jesuits are brought up on, and, more recently, James' 'Will to Believe', and 'L'Arte di Persuadere' of the brilliant Italian pragmatist Pezzolini,[1] who would bring all philosophy to the service of such a sophistic.

All these are founded on a recognition of the basic fact of the absolute impotence of a mere idea to produce any change in belief. All conviction, and so necessarily conversion, is based on the motor and emotional aspects of mind. No intellectual conception has any moving force unless it be hinged on to an emotion or an instinct. In every man's mind there exist certain fixed instincts and prejudices, certain centres of emotion, tendencies to react to certain words. The expression 'centre' is not merely

metaphorical. In all probability there does exist a corresponding organisation of neurones in the brain. These are the parts of a man's mind which
lead to conviction expressed in action, ballotwise or otherwise. You have
got to get hold of these to produce any change. If you can't do this, then
the idea is 'dead', it has no motive power, the most logical presentation
will have no effect. There must be in any successful propaganda, then, an
element more important than good argument. A good case is the last, not
the first part of a successful conversion. In practice men have always
known this. Practice remains constant throughout the ages; it is not
reserved for any particular century to 'discover' anything new about
the ways of the human. With theory, however, it is very different. That
may be wrong continually, and may, at a definite moment, be put right.
In this case it certainly is so. For a long time reason was given a too
predominant place in psychology, and to it all other faculties were
subordinated. Gradually, during the last fifty years in philosophy, instinct
and emotion have asserted their rightful place, until at the present
time the reaction has gone so far that the intellect is regarded merely
as a subtle and useful servant of the will, and of man's generally irrational vital instincts. Bergson, Le Roy, Croce, Eucken,[2] Simmel,[3] are
all anti-intellectualists.

The particular effect of this change of view which concerns me here is
that of the difference it makes to the theory of politics. Formerly the
prevailing conception was something of this kind—you perfected the
mechanism of democracy until each man's carefully-thought-out opinion
had its effect. You then, on any particular measure, set out on a campaign
of careful argument. Each side stated their reasons to the best of their
ability, the elector heard both sides, and recorded his vote accordingly.
All this, of course, sounds very fantastical now in the light of what actually
does happen at a General Election. But the Bentham Mill School honestly
regarded it as a possible ideal. We all recognise this now as fantastical, but
what must be substituted for it as a true account of the psychology of the
matter? This kind of inquiry would have to go into two parts—an
account of the process by which the mass of the electors are converted,
and the quite different process in the minds of the intellectuals. The first
has been done very completely and amusingly by Gustave Le Bon in
'Psychology of the Crowd',[4] and in Graham Wallas's 'Human Nature in
Politics'.[5] They recognise quite clearly that the process of conversion here
is anything but intellectual.

They show the modern politician frankly and cynically recognising
this, setting out deliberately to hypnotise the elector, as the owners of
patent medicines hypnotise the buyers. They don't argue; they deliberately reiterate a short phrase, such as 'Pears' Soap' or 'Pea Food', until it

gets into the mind of the victim, by a process of suggestion definitely not intellectual. But no one has yet given any connected theory of the more interesting part of the subject—the conversion of the 'intellectual', of the leisured middle-class wobbler. Wallas himself somehow leaves you with a suspicion in your mind that he does still think that the 'intellectual' is in the position which Mill, in the age of naive belief in reason, imagined him to be—that of weighing arguments, and then calmly deciding a question on its merits. Now, nothing could be greater nonsense. No one can escape from the law of mental nature I have referred to. We are all subject to it. We may be under the delusion that we are deciding a question from purely rational motives, but we never are. Even the detached analyst of the phenomena is himself subject to the law. Conversion is always emotional and non-rational.

Now this does seem to me to be a point of practical importance if it helps us to convert this class. For though the type may not be numerous, it does have, in the end, a big influence in politics. Not very obviously or directly, for in no country do the intellectuals appear to lead less than in ours; but ultimately and by devious ways their views soak down and colour the whole mass. The first step is to recognise the fundamental identity of the two processes of conversion—that *en masse*, and that of the intellectuals; in this respect that mere logical presentment is of very little use. As the modern electioneer sets out on a cynical recognition of the fact to convert the mass, so he should just as directly try to capture the smaller class.

There must be two quite different methods of attack, for what attracts the one repels the other. Great words empty of sense, promises of Elysium a few years ahead, have been, and always must be, the means by which the mass can be stirred, but they leave the few very cold. In this case, sauce for the goose is not sauce for the gander, for the only resemblance is the fact of appetite. Now, here seems to me to be the weakness of the Unionists. They emphatically do not provide any sauce for the gander. They practise the other art well enough, the art which Graham Wallas analyses—that of manipulating the popular mind by advertisement and other means. But the smaller one they neglect, for no one can seriously think that Mr. Garvin[6] is fit food for the adult intelligence. I have in mind a particular minor variety of this class: the undergraduate who, arriving in London, joins the Fabian Society. Now there is nothing inevitable in this. He may imagine that an intellectual process landed him there. Nothing of the kind. The Fabian Society provides him with the kind of stuff to fit in with his complex prejudices, and the Conservatives do not. He is merely a Socialist *faute de mieux*. The emotions involved are fairly simple—an insatiable desire for 'theories', the vague idea to be 'advanced', and the rest of it. There is no reason in the nature of things why the other side should not cater for this. In France, *L'Action Française* has made it rather *bête démodée* to be a Socialist. The really latest and advanced thing is to be a Neo-Royalist. They serve their victim with the right kind of sauce. So successful has this been that Jaurès[7] recently warned his followers against the cleverness of the bourgeoise.

To get back, however, to the main position. I take the view for the time being that we are not concerned with truth, but with success. I am considering the problem that should present itself to the acute party *entrepreneur*—did such a mythical person exist—how can this particular type of people be converted? Here is the type; how can it be caught? They must be converted exactly as everyone else is—by hitching on your propaganda to one of their centres of prejudice and emotion. But the difficulty comes in the analysis and discovery of these centres. They must be there, but they are complex and elusive, and sometimes unknown even to the subject himself. Here is where the difference comes in between this and the other sophistic. The problem in the case of the labourer is not so much to find these centres as to get hold of them before the other man does and to stick to them. Some day, I surmise, all this analysis will be done for us in a neat little manual.

But meanwhile I can give data for the future compiler of such a book by analysing one of these typical complexes, which I found embedded in my own head and influencing my politics without my knowing it. I probed my mind and got rid of it as I might of a tumour, but the operation was a violent one.

It came about from watching my own change of mind on the subject of Colonial Preference. I was, I suppose, the typical wobbler, for while politically inclined to be a Protectionist, yet, as a pupil of Professor Marshall's, theory pulled me in the opposite direction. Now, amid the whirlwind of that campaign of argument, I noticed that two apparently disconnected and irrelevant things stuck in my head had a direct influence on my judgment, whilst the 'drums and tramplings' of a thousand statistics passed over me without leaving a trace. The one was a cartoon in *Punch*—Mr. Chamberlain landing at Dover and being passed quickly by the Customs officer: 'There is no bother here, sir; this is a free country.' The other was an argument most constantly used at the time, I imagine, by Sir Edward Grey,[8] and recently revived by a supposedly Conservative paper which does most of its thinking in its heels. 'To attempt', he said, 'to bind the Empire together by tariffs would be dangerously artificial thing; it would violently disturb its "natural growth." It was in opposition to the constant method which has made us a successful Colonial power.

Let other nations fail through trying to do things too directly.' This had a powerful effect on me, and I imagine must have had on a great many other people; for this reason: that whereas we all of us had a great many emotions and nerve-paths grouped round the idea of Empire, these were by this argument bound up with Free Trade. It seemed to bring Preference in conflict with a deeply seated and organised set of prejudices grouped round the word 'free' and 'natural', for the moving force of the cartoon and Grey's argument were the same. This may look like an intellectual decision, but it isn't. I could not, at the time, have formulated it as definitely as I do now. It was then just a kind of vague sentiment which, in the intervals of argument, pulled one in a certain way. This was so because, as I have maintained, conviction is in the end an emotional process. The arguments on each side were so numerous that each one inhibited the slight effect the other might have had, and in the resulting stalemate it was just odd little groups of emotions and prejudices, like the one indicated, that decided one.

Now this is only a prejudice—why should one have a definite distrust of any constructive scheme, and think that leaving it to nature was so much better and so much more in the English tradition? Looking at it from an *a priori* standpoint, it seems probable that a definite policy directed towards a certain end will gain that end. Examples are all around us to prove it—that of German unity in particular. There was no leaving it to nature there. Yet, in spite of its absurdity from a reasonable point of view, this idea of what is 'natural' and 'free' remained a fixed obsession. It was too deep-seated to be moved by any argument, and had all the characteristics of one of those complex prejudices which I said must be analysed as preliminary to the art of conversion. It has all kinds of ramifications, and affects opinion in many directions, on conscription, for example, and a score of other matters. This pernicious conception, however, has a rather amusing history. It can be traced back from its origin in the disputes of rival schools of mediæval physicians scholastically inclined. Berthelot[9] has analysed the influence of these medical doctrines on politics. It can be seen particularly well in Quesnay, at the same time a doctor and a economist, from whom Adam Smith borrowed the theory of free exchange. It can be followed through Adam Smith, Coleridge and Burke to the formation of the political theory of *laissez-faire* which dominated the nineteenth century. This theory of politics—and, of course, it is this which produced the personal prejudice which influenced me—may be considered as a kind of Hippocratic theory of political medicine whose principal precept in the treatment of the social 'body' is that on no account must the 'natural' remedial force of nature be interfered with.

Now, once I had got the theory out fairly and squarely before me, had seen its origin and history, its influence over me had gone. It was powerful before because I really didn't know that it existed. The thing that most interested me was how it got so firmly fixed in my mind-centre without my knowing it; and here comes really the only practical part of this paper. In my own case, the prejudice, I am certain, had been formed in this way—the histories I had been brought up on, while never stating this view as a theory, had yet so stated all events in our Colonial history as to convey it by suggestion. Always the English were shown as succeeding as by some vague natural genius for colonisation or something of that kind. Never by a consistent constructive effort. The people who did make definite plans, like the French under Colbert, and later the Germans, were always represented as failing. Now, this was the reason that the idea was so embedded in one. If it had been presented definitely as a theory, it would have been destroyed by argument. It became an instinct because it was suggested to one in this much more indirect and subtle way.

It took me years to get rid of the effects of this. For when an idea is put into your head in this indirect way, you are never conscious of its existence. It just silently colours all your views. Born with blue spectacles, you would think the world was blue, and never be conscious of the existence of the distorting glass. Ideas insinuated like this become in the end a kind of mental category; the naive person never recognises them as subjective, but thinks they lie in the facts themselves. Here, then, is my practical point. This kind of thing is dangerous. One is handicapped, as far as clear-thinking about politics goes, by being educated in Whig histories. It takes strenuous efforts to get rid of the pernicious notion implanted in one by Macaulay, say. My remedy would be this—prevention. I should adopt for secondary schools what was recently proposed as a solution of the religious difficulty in primary ones. Let there be so many hours set apart for history each week, and let each political party be allowed to send in their own historian. The first step towards this must be the writing of a definitely Tory history. The Whigs have too long had it their own way in this sphere. I can give a definite example of a recent successful accomplishment of this kind of thing in Charles Maurras' history of the French Monarchy, which is converting scores of young Republicans.[10]

After all, there is nothing ridiculous in the idea itself. It only appears so because it is a logical, definite application in a small scale of a process which is taken as a matter of course in greater ones. All national histories are partisan, and designed to give us a good conceit of ourselves. We recognise that even while we laugh at the American school-books and the Belgian accounts of the Waterloo campaign. But we are not familiar with the same process in small affairs inside the nation. But it is coming rapidly. I can mention Howell Evans' History of Wales, recommended recently by the Welsh Education Council, which ends up with a panegyric of the late Budget. Or take Mrs. Richard Green's History of Ireland, now being sold at half-price to all secondary schools of a Nationalist character. It is definitely written to convince the Irishman that his country was not civilised by the English conquest, but had itself, in earlier times, the most cultured civilisation in Europe. It is done by a careful selection and manipulation of old manuscripts. It goes flat against the known facts, for the poet Spenser described them as naked barbarians. But what does that matter? It fulfils its intention. Anyone who still has a lingering dislike of this frankly partisan type of history is under the influence of an opposite ideal. He would prefer an impartial record of facts. But this ideal standard by which he condemns the party history does not exist. True, there has been a school of scholars who definitely took it as their ideal—the modern Cambridge historians. But I remember the late Dr. Emil Reich telling me that the greatest triumph of his life took place in a room at Cambridge, when, after an argument on this very subject, he was able to take down from the book-shelves a well-known Jesuit history of the Elizabethan persecutions which contained nothing but facts, no biased comment or theory, but which, at the same time, produces an extreme anti-Protestant effect. According to his own account, this entirely si-lenced them.

No, the whole thing is impossible. No history can be a faithful mirror. If it were, it would be as long and as dull as life itself. It must be a selection, and, being a selection, must inevitably be biased. Personally, I don't regard this as a disagreeable necessity; I like the idea. After all, who would care an atom about the past were it not a reservoir of illustrations to back up his own social theories and prejudices? For purposes of political argument, I myself specialise on the history of the fourth century, for no casual opponent knows enough to contradict me. If I rashly illustrated them from the French Revolution, everyone can remember enough facts to back the opposite view.

The Art of Political Conversion

In a previous article[1] I discussed the problem of the young intellectual, or the person who imagines himself to be such. How was he to be converted? How was he to be seduced away from the arms of the Fabian Society? I explained at some length the peculiar type of motive which will move these people. It must be something rather abstract, something in the nature of a Utopia or an ideal. It is, then, quite ridiculous to attempt to meet them on a different plane entirely. They became Socialist as the result of a certain emotional process, and it is absolutely no use trying to convert them by means of hard facts, such as, for example, the type of argument that Mr. Harold Cox[2] or Mr. Loch[3] set out so lucidly. A controversy of this kind is like a game of draughts, which one person plays on the black squares and the other on the white. You simply don't meet each other. To be effective you have to meet one vague ideal by another vague ideal.

So I may as well definitely state at once that my arguments will only cover a very small part of the subject, that which is covered by the rather ridiculous word 'ideals'. The problem is to find something which shall come under this category on the Conservative side. I can imagine that people of the older generation can see here no problem at all. All that is necessary, they would think, is to speak the truth, to bring forward solid facts, and that should be sufficient. The answer to that is that experience simply shows that it isn't. This kind of argument only appeals to the converted. Take the vigorous and sound sense one gets in the editorials of this paper. Personally, I like and enjoy them; they state the truth as I see it. But then, you see, I am already converted. It so happens, however, that the days when I was a Socialist are not so far away that I have forgotten the kind of emotion which moved me then. And I can see that these articles, though full of sense, wouldn't have had the slightest effect on me then. We might statically regard them as admirable, but they have no dynamic power to draw us over to the position they represent. A woman of fifty and a girl of sixteen may both have the same excellent qualities, but there is never any hesitation as to which draws you. Now, nearly all Conservative editorials, from the young intellectuals' point of view, are like the woman of fifty—she may have most excellent things to say, but, unfortunately, you never hear them. Seen in a ballroom, an inward dynamic force steers you in other directions.

Without any metaphor there is a quality distinct from sense which has a certain magnetic effect. It is question of dialect. Take an extreme case to get my point clear. I won't take newspaper editorials, they are, perhaps, too obviously addressed *ad populem*. I will take a book which definitely attempts to appeal to the intellectual from the Conservative point of view—Mr. Lilly's 'Idola Fori', just recently published.[4] Now, in reading this book as in reading editorials, I feel that it is perfectly sound, that it contains the exact truth, and that it exactly represents my own position. But, at the same time, I have enough detachment left to tell me that it has no propaganda qualities. It is never likely to make the undergraduate enthusiastic. It is sense, but it is not 'catching'.

The reason, I take it, is this, that each generation has to think out the fundamentals of political theory for itself. That when this process has been got through, the result gets embodied in certain phrases, certain catch-words, which embody for a particular generation a definite theoretical standpoint which underlies them. They act as call-boys to the theory in fact. Mention the catch-word in an article or leader and the whole worked-out theory behind them is at once summoned up in your mind. But here comes in the dreadful part of the business—that the catch-words of one generation have absolutely no effect on the next. Take a phrase like 'the rights of property'. After it has been bandied about in political controversy for some fifty years it becomes absolutely of no effect and loses all meaning. After a time one's constitution gets hardened to such phrases, and they never even get inside us to produce any effect at all. It is something analogous to what happens in the case of disease. Bring a microbe of measles or some other simple disease in contact with an Australian aborigine and it kills him. But in Europe so many generations have had this disease that at last we have become hardened to it, and it is not, as a rule, fatal. Another instance: the West Coast native has become hardened to malaria, which for the European is a fresh disease and so, fatal. This is just what happens with political catch-words. Like the microbe, after a time they work themselves out, and a *Daily Telegraph* leader is no more fatal to a Socialist than a bad cold is to a European.

I am firmly convinced that just at the present moment Conservative thought has come to an important crisis. The old set of catch-words in which its philosophy embodied itself are now absolutely worked out. They now appeal only to the older generation, to the new they appear to be mere dead nothings. The average young Socialist, listening, say, to Sir Frederick Banbury,[5] is not irritated because he is hearing an expression of a view different to his own, but simply because he is listening to a set of phrases which for him are as absolutely devoid of meaning as an eighteenth century sermon. He thinks there is nothing there, he thinks there is no such thing as a rational Conservative position. He can understand that a rich man can oppose Socialism, but he simply cannot understand that there is any intellectual objection to it. This I know to be a fact, as I have talked to dozens of them. They simply cannot conceive any rational opposition. They always suspect that there is some interested motive behind your opposition. Incidentally I may note that this will be an element of weakness, for the man who underrates his enemy may easily be beaten.

What concerns me here now is, however, the cause of this. I repeat that is just a question of the death of a set of political catch-words. The Socialist is mistaken in thinking that Banbury is saying nothing, that there is nothing real behind the phrases, 'rights of property', 'for king and country'. On the contrary, there is, and it is exactly what I or any other young Conservative holds. But I should never dream of expressing myself by those phrases, because to the younger generation they don't carry any conviction. When I hear them used from the platform I always feel slightly uncomfortable, although I agree with the attitude from which they spring.

The phrases feel dead in exactly the same way as clichés in bad poetry do. It is only by a certain unexpectedness of phrasing that a certain feeling of conviction is carried over, and you feel that the man was actually describing something real, that he had seen something at first hand. In verse one chooses fresh epithets and fresh metaphors, not so much because they are new and we are tired of the old as because the old cease to convey over the actual vivid meaning that we intend. Nowadays, when one says that the hill is clothed with trees, the word suggests no physical comparison. One doesn't have a picture as the man who first used the word did, of a definite realisation of the metaphor. There is no vivid analogy in your mind of the hill being actually clothed as a woman might be. To get the original visual effect one would have to say 'ruffed' with trees, or use some other new metaphor. The point is, that any metaphor or image in time becomes conventionalised, and so ceases to convey any real concrete meaning. The result of this is that you must have freshness and unexpectedness in any art, not because there is anything desirable in freshness *per se*, but because, owing to this law which I have just sketched out—that of the inevitable decay of metaphors—it is only by means of freshness that one can be convincing. This makes my position clear in regard to the dead phrases by which Conservatism expresses itself. I don't object to them because they are old. It isn't simply that I want something new simply because it is new, but because I realise most intensely, both from my own personal experience and from conversation with the type of intellectual I have been discussing, that these phrases now carry no conviction. They must be restated in order to appear real at all.

The theory of the thing is this, then. The political theory behind Conservatism remains the same in every generation, but to remain living and to have any effect it must clothe itself in a different set of catch-words in each generation. Here is our crisis. Our old set of catch-words is dead, and a new one has not yet been worked out. That and nothing else is the cause of the landslides amongst the intellectuals to the Socialist side. The most pressing need of Conservatism is a set of writers who will make our faith living by giving it a fresh expression. It seems to me that an excellent example of this process of restating an old dialect is to be found in the group of people in France who call themselves L'Action Française. If any party in the world seemed dead intellectually, it was the French Conservative party in the nineties. Radicalism seemed to have definitely conquered. There was hardly a Conservative student to be found. (I know this is an exaggeration, but I mean student of the particular type I am discussing.) Now, in ten years the situation has been entirely changed. I should say that outside the ranks of those who expect later to get a job in the immense bureaucracy, there is hardly to be found a genuine 'jeune republicaine'. All the young men tend to belong, on the one hand, to the Neo-Royalists, or, on the other, to the Syndicalistes. These latter must not be confused with the kind of Parliamentary Socialist that we are accustomed to over here. They have as great a hatred of these people as they have of Liberals.

Of course, this doesn't show very much outwardly. The Liberals still seem to be overwhelmingly in power. Their deputies are returned automatically at each election. But I maintain that this is simply a case of the form remaining while the vital spirit has departed. In another generation the form itself will disappear. While the mass remains Liberal, the minority, that formally created Liberalism by its enthusiasm, has now revolted from it, and where this active minority tends now, the rest will be in time. The solid body of Liberalism is beginning to crumble.

I can give two small instances to confirm this. One is a speech by Jaurès, which so acute an observer as M. Paul Adam thinks will become historic, as marking a turning-point in political tendencies. It was made some years ago to a gathering of Socialists, and in it he solemnly warned them against the cleverness of the middle classes. The meaning of this was that he had become aware that the dogmas on which the appeal of Socialism to the intellectual is based, the stock of ideas which they had never argued about, which both sides had taken for granted, were themselves being attacked, that democracy itself was no longer considered sacred. The ground was moving under their feet. He saw quite clearly that this was a much more dangerous thing than any mere attack on details. Formerly, when a man.had doubts about the actual working out of Socialism, doubts born of the experience which seems to show that it leads to bankruptcy, he could be reassured by the emotion which comes from an irrational and almost religious belief. But when the dogmas of this belief were themselves attacked, then you were getting into a really dangerous position.

The other small fact is that the Liberals themselves are so alarmed at the progress of reactionary ideas that they have, within the last few weeks, instituted a definite propaganda, a system of lectures and conferences designed to re-capture the students.

On Progress and Democracy

[First published in two instalments in the *Commentator*: 3 (2 Aug. 1911), 165–6, and (9 Aug. 1911), 179–80. Signed 'Thomas Grattan' [*sic*].]

Certainly one of the most familiar things in politics is and always has been the extraordinary difficulty which an intelligent man finds when he tries to conceive how it can come about that another intelligent man can hold a diametrically opposite opinion to his own. This is particularly true in regard to vital issues, and at times of crisis. Then a man sees so clearly that a certain step will be ruinous to his country, that he finds it almost impossible to understand the mentality of those who regard it as beneficial—that is, presupposing that the other man is disinterested and honestly comes by his opinion. That the people who are concerned with it, that the people who are gaining popularity by it, that the people who are 'making their careers' in carrying it out, and that the masses who hope to gain something by acts of spoliation should welcome it, that he can understand. But what is beyond all comprehensibility is that people in the same position as himself, reasoning from apparently the same data, come to an entirely opposite conclusion. The particular event which gives rise to these general reflections is, of course, the proposed plunge into unrestrained Single-Chamber Government. The particular type of mentality one finds it almost impossible to understand is that of the middle-class intellectual, who welcomes this change, or at least sees nothing to fear in it.

One finds no difficulty at all in understanding why the Socialists and the Radicals are in favour of it. The Socialist can obviously feel no misgiving at the prospect of government by his own class, uncontrolled by any other class, and the way entirely open for the kind of sensation he wants. The case of the middle-class Radical is perhaps slightly different. In the long run he will certainly bitterly regret the abolition of the Peers. But he may be pardoned for not realising this at the moment, because the immediate benefits to him are so great. The delights of disestablishment are so dazzling that they quite obliterate the possible, though perhaps distant, 40 per cent income-tax.

The enthusiasm of these two types, then, is perfectly understandable, but what of the third type—the middle-class intellectual? He is, as a rule, quite indifferent to the measures which seem so exciting to the Nonconformists, and which satisfy their social resentment. On the other hand, his case is quite different to that of the Socialist—he at first sight appears to have everything to lose. His enthusiasm, or at least his equanimity, seems puzzling. One can put the case in the form of a parable. If you are at the back of a crowd watching a procession, and can see nothing, you are obviously only too willing to take part in any rush designed to break up the line. Disorder has no terrors for you, because no position that you can bring about will be worse than the one you are in, and the chances are that you may manage to get to the front. That is the position of the Socialist, and from his point of view it is a perfectly rational one. But what does pass all comprehension is that the people in the front rows should see without any regret the police removed, and should even believe that something good will come out of it.

There certainly do exist people of this kind, people of the type, say, of Lord Haldane. That he himself personally should believe in democracy is quite understandable, because he himself is taking part in the leading of it. Leaving aside all pecuniary motives, it is always nearly impossible for a man who is in a movement, who is organising it, who is in the centre of it, to believe that it can do any harm. What is rather surprising is that there are thousands of people in the country of Lord Haldane's type, the middle-class intellectual, who are quite detached from any active participation in politics, who have everything to lose from the advent of unrestrained democracy, and who yet blindly believe in it as they would in a religion.

The reasons why one would expect them to fear a democracy are quite definite. Historically, it has always been a failure, for it has never succeeded in maintaining for any length of time a healthy social order. I do not mean by order the mere prevention of rioting or anything of that kind. I am using the word in a different sense. The State or nation can only be in a healthy condition when it submits itself to a kind of discipline. There must be a hierarchy, a subordination of the parts, just as there must be in any other organisation. A pure democracy ends all this, for discipline can only be kept up when the centre of authority is to a certain extent independent of the people governed. When there is no such independence of authority, when the rulers only continue in power during the pleasure of the ruled, then they must continually shrink from right action for fear of unpopularity. There is no discipline in any army in which the officers are elected by their own men. The record of the first two years of the American Civil War is enough to prove that. The wielders of authority must have a tenure which, while it may depend partially, must not depend entirely upon their popularity with the governed. The lamentable state of affairs which results when it does so depend has been the direct cause of the ruin of every experiment in pure democracy in the past. (You can see signs of the beginning of such a state in the present time in France, in the vacillations of M. Monis' Cabinet in the matter of the railwaymen dismissed during the last strike, and the acts of sabotage which continually recur without punishment, though the authors of them must be well known to the Government.)

I should say here, in a parenthesis, that when I say democracy I mean a pure democracy. Very few examples of such a state exist at the present time, for the very good reason that the makers of Constitutions, recognising its fatuousness, have taken care that the form of government they are creating, while it shall have the appearance of and be called a democracy, shall in reality be held in check by all kinds of restraints. The Constitution of the United States is the most prominent example of this—its Senate is the strongest Second Chamber in existence.

But we in England are not going in for democracy of this kind. We are going in for the pure and unrestrained type, the type which always has and always will end in national bankruptcy. You would expect, then, that most men able to take a detached view of things, seeing the drift there is already towards this state, would hold on with all the tenacity they could to what checks and restraints have been bequeathed to us from the past. However irrational and unsatisfactory these checks might be (as from one point of view the hereditary principle might appear to the intellectual), they should stick to them with tenacity, because, once you are in the flux of a pure democracy, it is then almost impossible, except by the exercise of military force, such as you get in the case of Napoleon, to re-establish once more in the heart of this flux any independent and restraining authority.

That is how you would expect the intellectual, looking at things from a rational point of view, to behave. But instead of this you find the threatened demolition of the last actual restraint left, the 'throwing of everything into the melting-pot', hailed with delight and enthusiasm by these very people whom you would expect to see the folly of it, and will in the end suffer most from it. Now this is a very curious phenomena, and seems to me to be worth looking into. It cannot merely be a case of 'those whom the gods wish to destroy they first make mad'. There must be something more; there must be some kind of rational motive.

What interests me is that question of what it is at the back of their minds that makes them act in this way. Here you have a proposal to do away with all the traditional restraints, the hierarchy, that makes social life possible and healthy. And here you have people with enough intelligence to see what nonsense the ordinary abuse of the Peers is, and enough knowledge to know how experiments in uncontrolled democracy have always ended, yet passionately believing in it. You have people who will admit the cogency of all arguments in favour of restraint, yet in some entirely irrational way saying at the end of it all, 'Yet I think it will be all right; I believe in democracy.' And that finishes it. No mere rational argument is of any avail against convictions of that kind.

What is at the bottom of this religious conviction? It is a perfectly simple thing. It is a belief in inevitable 'Progress', the belief that the forces of things are themselves making for good, and that so good will come even when things are left to themselves. Here it seems to me that you get the fundamental difference between the Conservative standpoint and the democratic. The Conservative does not believe in progress, of this kind at any rate. He believes that man is constant, and that the number and types of the possible forms of society are also constant. And, further, that history shows that the only types which are healthy and enduring are those in which there is an independent authority, in which the rulers are to a certain extent independent of the ruled, and that the only way in which to preserve a good social order is to take definite steps towards it by preserving the restraining framework inside which such order is alone possible.

The Radical, I take it, is the exact opposite of this. A good state of society, I take him to believe, cannot depend on what he would be pleased to call the artificial aid of restraints. It lies in the nature of things in themselves, and is a natural growth. There is a mysterious thing called Progress which is making for good. It is this comforting belief which enables the middle-class intellectual to look on with equanimity while all the restraints which formerly made good government possible are being tumbled over. 'Though it looks foolhardy,' he will say, 'yet it will turn out all right, because the natural force of progress embodied in democracy will make it so.'

The question then arises, is there any such thing as a constant progress in mankind? This becomes the rock on which all argument with this type of people must be based.

Before a man can make up his mind as to which of these two attitudes is the right one, two preliminary questions will first have to be decided. (1) Is it historically true that all unrestrained democracies have come to grief? (2) Is there anything in the facts, as far as they are known in regard to the past, which bears out the supposition that civilisation has continuously progressed from early savages up to its culmination in us?

As to the first question, it does not seem to be that this is in reality an independent question. It really depends on the second. When it is pointed out to the Radical that all previous democracies have come to grief—the Athenians in the antique world and the Tuscan Republics just before the Renaissance—he can always answer by saying that these were not democracies in the modern sense. He refuses to believe that the world recurs in any way, or is constant; he refuses to believe that there is any real resemblance between the little Tuscan Republics and the great modern ones. He believes that the present moment is a new moment, in the sense that we have a situation now which has never happened before. That being so, he can set on one side the melancholy fate of all previous democracies, and can then quite honestly believe that the modern one will bring the millennium, in spite of all previous experience to the contrary. But his belief that the present state is a new one, differing absolutely from all the rest of the world's history, involves necessarily, you see, the belief in progress which I have put down in the second question, so that I want to discuss that now, as it is obviously the more fundamental of the two.

Now, to consider the second question. In so far as a conception of progress is not merely a kind of religion, and can be based on facts, it will have to be stated in this way, that the progress and civilisation of humanity have been slowly and steadily increasing from the earliest known times up to the present day; that the present day is the highest point yet reached, and so that, judging from the past, we may predict that it will increase from now, as it has increased up till now. Now, does this correspond to anything in the facts? I will take as my authority an examination of this question the little book called 'Revolutions of Civilisation', which has just been published by the celebrated Egyptologist, Dr. Flinders Petrie.

He deliberately sets before himself this very problem, has civilisation been a continuous and uninterrupted growth? Is the shallow optimism that most people who use the word 'progress' exhibit justified by facts? To both of these questions Dr. Petrie gives an emphatic negative. These kinds of problems have always troubled mankind, and the solutions to them are as inaccurate as they are varied; nor could any better results be expected from the very insufficient acquaintance with the past. But at the present time, as Dr. Petrie points out, the problem can be approached in a very different way, and we can, for the first time, attempt to give a scientific instead of a merely emotional answer. The archæological researches of the last fifty years, and the new methods of exact scientific inquiry, have put us in a very different position with regard to this problem. What is the answer that this new knowledge gives? 'Can we then extract a meaning from all the ceaseless turmoil and striving and success and failure of these thousands of years? Can we see any regular structure behind it all?'[1] Dr. Petrie thinks that we can, and we can formulate it in a general law, which is this, that civilisation is not a constantly increasing, but a recurrent phenomena. It has its periods of splendid growth and of inevitable decay. Formerly there could have been but one example which would lead us to suppose that such a law existed, that of the great classical civilisation which finished in the barbarism of the middle ages, and that is hardly sufficient basis for the proof of such a tremendous generalisation. But the excavations which have taken place both in Egypt and in Crete enable us to trace the rise, growth, and decay of fourteen civilisations of equal length with the classical one, eight of them in Egypt and six of them in Crete and Europe. Each of these civilisations exhibits precisely similar characteristics. In each of them the arts pass from archaic simplicity through the perfection of the best period to their final decay. There is an exact parallel in the late Cretan civilisation to the difference between the perfection of Phidias and the degeneracy of the late Roman sculpture. Dr. Petrie illustrates this inevitable decay by examples drawn from the arts of all the other civilisations. The result of his inquiry is, then, that civilisation is a recurrent phenomena, and not an ever-sweeping onward movement. He is able to trace the common causes for the rise and fall of each period. The necessary foundation, he asserts, of any new period of civilisation, so far as government is concerned, is strong personal rule. The next stage is an oligarchy in which the unity of the country is maintained by law instead of by autocracy. Then comes the transformation to a democracy, and with it the gradual end of things. 'When democracy has obtained full power the majority without capital necessarily eat up the capital of the minority, and the civilisation steadily decays until the inferior population is swept away to make room for a fitter people. The consumption of all the sources of the Roman Empire from the second century, when democracy was dominant, until the Gothic kingdoms arose on its ruin, is the best-known example in detail.'[2]

What is the application of this to politics? Obviously, it sweeps right away that naïve belief in inevitable progress which enables the intellectual to welcome with enthusiasm the sweeping away of all the checks on an uncontrolled democracy, a phenomena which otherwise his reason would compel him to detest. But, on the other hand, it is not a fatalist view. One must not say that because all civilisations are doomed to inevitable decay that it is no use troubling, for there is as much difference between a healthy and an unhealthy civilisation, as much to care for and strive for, as there is between a man worn out by middle life and one who is vigorous and useful to a green old age. The rational position to take up is this: History shows that it is only by the action of certain checks that a democratic State can continue to exist in a healthy condition. One should do all one can to preserve those restraints that providentially still exist.

Theory and Practice

[First published in two instalments in the *Commentator*, 3 (8 Nov. 1911), 388, and (15 Nov. 1911), 404–5. Signed 'Thomas Gratton'.]

There are certain catchwords which, while they embody truth, at the same time kill it. They kill it in this fashion, that so familiar are they, so easy is it for the most thoughtless fools to trot them out, like the old market woman does her proverbs, that it becomes impossible for the reasonable man to believe that they can have any meaning at all. The particular catchword that I am thinking of here is the antithesis of theory and practice as applied to Socialism. Some years after reading Mengers'[1] big book on the juridical aspect of Socialism, I tried, with the enthusiasm of youth, to explain some of the ideas in it to a typical suburban dweller who was travelling up to his business in an early morning train. After listening to me for some time with an amused and tolerant attention, he suddenly leaned over his *Daily Telegraph* and said, 'My dear fellow, these things may be all right in theory, but they would be very different in practice.' The fatuous complacency with which this remark was uttered, and the unction with which he pronounced the word 'theory', drove me to a pitch of frenzy in which I would willingly have destroyed him instantly with a blow from the heavy book which had started the discussion, and which lay ready on my knees.

As a matter of actual fact, the remark contains a great piece of wisdom, the greatest that can be uttered on this particular subject. Why, then, did it seem to me to be so fatuous? Why does it always appear so meaningless and silly to the propagandist Socialist, who hears it on an average at least a dozen times in each conversation he has? Simply for the reason I gave above—that any fool can say it. It is a catchword; that is to say, it springs from no personal observation, it is not the result of any actual process of thought inside the mind of the man who utters it, but is a dead, ready-made thing, passed on like a worn-out coin.

This is the secret of the irritating effect of the use of such phrases in argument. We feel it to be a piece of bad manners to oppose to a theory that at any rate is living to us, and has been arrived at by a perhaps mistaken but at any rate vital process, a purely mechanical extinguisher of this kind.

The pity of it is that, as a rule, we do not rest here. We pass on from mere irritation to a more definite conclusion, because on all occasions on which we have met it, it has been used without any thought at all. We gradually slide into a position in which we imagine that it is not true. Because the phrase is used by fools, we make the quite illogical deduction that it corresponds to nothing real at all. There is a certain psychological law which says that we are only conscious of differences and of change. A thing does not arrive at consciousness because it is real, but because it is just beginning, just ending, or, at any rate, changing. A thing which comes into our consciousness and then remains the same gradually fades out of consciousness. We are not conscious then of sensations, but only of changes in sensation. If in the house I live in there is a sound of constantly dripping water, I am not, as a rule, conscious of the noise at all, but only of its cessation or recommencement. A similar rule holds good in the realm of argument and conviction. You did not hear the dripping water because, after a time, your brain made allowances for the drips, it knew when they were coming, and it, as it were, ticked them off, and said, 'This need not be attended to'; so in the same way in regard to this argument about theory and practice, you hear it so often that you in the end, by an almost unconscious process, tick it off as meaning nothing. I say unconscious, because, as a rule, the process is quite unconscious. You come to imagine gradually that the phrase means nothing, and to think that you have refuted it, when as a matter of fact, you have never really considered it seriously once.

The problem for us is, then, I take it, to find some way of restating the old commonplace that will force it on the Socialist as a real and vital objection. It is a real thing, and there must be some way of stating it that will convey over to one's opponent the conviction that one is describing a personally observed idea, and not merely passing on a mechanical set of catchwords and clichés. To take an example from literature of what I mean here by this instinctive conviction that one is in presence of a vital idea, Leigh Hunt was once reading out to young Keats a part of Spenser's 'Faery Queene'. When he came to the phrase about 'sea shouldering whales', Keats jumped up in a state of wild enthusiasm about the epithet 'sea shouldering'. Why? It doesn't seem very interesting at first sight. Simply for this reason, that the choice of an epithet like this at once communicated in a kind of direct instinctive way to Keats the feeling that Spenser was not merely decorating his story with the conventional adornments in the way of animals that the age approved of, was not merely using one of the catchwords of the poets, but that he had in his mind a distinct visual sensation, a real personal vision of the thing he was describing, and this resulted in the choice of the unusual epithet in order to convey this feeling over directly. In a similar situation, then, if Spenser had wished to communicate the reality that lies behind the conventional antithesis of 'theory and practice', what would he have had to do? In what way must one put it if one is to convey over the feeling that it does really stand for something in our minds? Taking the dripping water phenomena as a guide, obviously there must first of all be a change in expression before the minds of one's opponents are to become conscious of it at all.

The next principle that should guide us is the one that can be drawn from that example of Spenser. It is that one must describe the idea with such choice of detail that the Socialist will recognise you are describing a concrete and actually realised phenomenon.

I proceed, therefore, to an attempt to deal in this way with the old cliché about 'theory and practice'. I can first get at it in a rather obvious and bald way, which still puts a certain amount of life into it. The argument depends on the fact, which I suppose no one will deny, that the percentage of intelligent people, or of people disinterestedly concerned with the right working of the State, is at present, and likely to remain for some considerable time, very small.

That being granted, I can now attempt the translation into detail of the cliché about theory and practice that I undertook earlier in the article. Socialism, we can take it, is now a matter of theory. What does that mean? Simply that it is in the hands of those alone who can appreciate theory—that is, of the relatively more intelligent portion of the community, and perhaps to a certain extent of the more altruistic. The result of this is that it is in the best position that it will ever be in. Read the 'Soul of Man under Socialism',[2] listen to Shaw or Webb lecturing to the Fabian Society, or, finally, read the 'Utopia' of Morris, or Wells's propaganda book, 'New Worlds for Old', and it is difficult to avoid being carried away. This is, then, what I should substitute for the theory part of the old antithesis. Socialism in theory means Socialism in the hands of a select and superior part of the community. It could hardly fail to be attractive.

Now for the other term of the cliché. What does Socialism 'in practice' mean when we attempt to state the phrase in a more concrete fashion? To put the case conclusively, I make first a very large assumption, which is in favour of the side against which I am arguing. I will assume that these theoreticians would in practice endeavour to carry out in a capable and honest way the high-minded sentiments to which they so frequently give expression. Would this insure that Socialism in practice meant the same thing as Socialism in theory? Certainly not. The answer to that depends on another question. Are we to expect that if Socialism succeeds it will remain in the hands of the relatively superior people who now control it? Certainly not. Being an élite, they would in a democracy be a minority. The day that Socialism becomes triumphant will be the last day in which people of the type of Wells or Shaw will be of any importance in it. It will be run by exactly the same type of politician which now flourishes in town councils. The passage from theory to practice is then simply the passage from the capable few to the many who have very different qualities.

With that change will disappear all the attraction that Socialism now has for the 'idealist'. He, if one can judge him by his writings, is probably attracted to Socialism because it seems to him to be so much more intelligent than the sordid chaos of the present state of things. This type of mind, disgusted with the corruption of present-day politics, turns with relief to the life suggested by books, like those I have just mentioned. It forgets that the realisation of Socialism means nothing less than participation in it by the majority—that is, by the very people who now 'run' the politics which so much disgust them. The kind of sordidness, veniality, and corruption that now disgusts the idealist in the present régime, and which make him fly to Socialism as expounded by Wells, Shaw, Webb, etc., as an escape, would be the distinguishing characteristic of that doctrine itself on the day of its success, for on that day the movement must pass inevitably out of the hands of the idealist élite which gave it birth, and into the hands of exactly the same venial majority who are responsible for all the characteristics of the existing state which he dislikes so much.

The phrase 'from theory to practice' is then no mere cliché, but expresses an extremely important and actual change in concrete reality.

There would be nothing abnormal, extraordinary, or out of the common in the change. It has been the normal evolution of all new conceptions of society. To illustrate it by the greatest example of all, that of Christianity in the first few centuries. You have first of all only the small band of the sincere enthusiasts. It was in the hands of an élite. Then comes the conversion of Constantine. Christianity has now 'arrived', has now triumphed even officially. There enters into it the people who do not belong to the élite. You get, in fact, exactly the same kind of phenomena that we shall get under the triumph of Socialism. With what result? The whole character of Christianity was changed, and it was possible for even a believer like Eusebius to write about 'the unspeakable hypocrisy and dissimulation of the so-called Christians'.[3]

One could then enunciate it as a general law that the first state of any movement is always the best, for at that time it is in the hands of the best people. First Peter, then the Borgias—first Proudhon, then the swindling councillors and the job hunters.

All this depends on the assumption with which I commenced, that the percentage of capable and disinterested people in any society is always the same and is always small. Once that is granted, it follows almost mathematically that the triumph of democracy, that is to say the actual participation in power of the majority, must always lead to a lamentable state of affairs.

Faced with a syllogistic argument of this kind, the democrat can only escape by denying the major premise. He can slip out of the conclusion by denying that the percentage of the disinterested is always constant.

'It is true', he would say, 'that in the present state of society the people capable of taking a disinterested view of their position and of politics is extremely small, and that if this were always so, then Socialism in practice would be an extremely sordid business. But I deny that this is a permanent state of things. I believe that the fact that the majority are what they are is due to the conditions in which they live. Alter these and the percentage will rise enormously.' To give the words actually urged upon me by a prominent member of the Fabian Society committee: 'I believe that it will be possible by developing a kind of education that has never before been tried, the education of "the imagination", to raise the majority to the level of the minority.' I then asked what it was he meant here by the imagination. He replied, and I give his answer purely as a human document, a guide to the type of mentality that guides the Fabian Society: 'I mean here by imagination the faculty of mind which can appreciate emotionally human progress.' This is, of course, sheer, downright nonsense, and means nothing at all. But, though it means nothing, it is the kind of irrational belief on which Socialist romanticism has to base itself.

The basic fact which all theories of government have to take account of is a law which directly contradicts this sentiment—the indisputable fact that percentages of men of different kinds of capacity remains the same in every generation. It is a physical law that cannot be got round by education or any other method. Variations of intellect follow just the same invariable law as variations in the length of limbs in the animal species. As De Vries puts it, 'The same variations in the same proportion recur in each generation inside the limits of any particular species.' It is then no good planning out any state of society whose successful working would depend on the assumption that the percentage of intelligent and disinterested people can be indefinitely increased.

The objection of the man in the train which so annoyed me was then founded on a perfectly right instinct. He knew by instinct what I have only been able to arrive at by a process of reasoning, that the passage from theory to practice being merely the passage from a few who are capable of conceiving a high ideal to the many who cannot must always bring disillusionment.

In my next article I shall examine a second method of revitalising this old 'cliché'.

A Tory Philosophy

[First published in the *Commentator* in five instalments: 4 (3 Apr. 1912), 294–5; (10 Apr. 1912), 310; (1 May 1912), 362; (8 May 1912), 380; and (15 May 1912), 388–9. Signed 'Thomas Grattan' [*sic*]. Reprinted in A. R. Jones, *The Life and Opinions of T. E. Hulme* (London and Boston, 1960). The typescript, which is the source of this version, is at the University of Keele Library.]

I.—THE TWO TEMPERAMENTS

It is my aim to explain in this article why I believe in original sin, why I can't stand romanticism, and why I am a certain kind of Tory. In regard to this last I ought to say exactly on what kind of level I am discussing the thing. I am not concerned with any facts or worked-out theories about it, but only with certain sentiments. In any piece of political argument use is made of certain catchwords and phrases, which stand for certain emotions to the believer. They provide the basis which the argument takes for granted; and though they may only appear in the peroration, yet they really provide the emotional background behind everything.

It is instructive in this connection to note the method by which the Boxers in the last Chinese rebellion made converts to their side. A messenger was sent to some remote inland village. Arrived there, he gathered round him all the inhabitants, and taught them to repeat after him certain phrases, which were called 'words of power'. He kept them repeating these phrases the whole of the evening until they had worked themselves up into a state of frenzy and excitement, which was sufficiently great to give them courage to dash out and kill the people they could not stand. Political parties in this country make use of similar 'words of power'.

Generally, these phrases are only 'alive' to one side. To the other they appear to be mere empty clichés. What I am trying to do in this article is to set out the kind of emotion which vivifies for me certain expressions which to you, if you are progressives, appear to be shrivelled up and empty, meaning nothing; and at the same time to pick out the sentiments on your side which appear to me to be loathsome and disgusting.

I think that I am justified in spending time over these sentiments, because they are the really important and deciding factors. Your theories in this subject are in the last resort merely the expression of your prejudices. To illustrate this by an analogy: if you wanted to investigate the cause of the peculiar route taken by a certain railway, it would be useless to go into the general principles which should govern the laying down of such railways. It would be a waste of time to seek for the cause, as it were, inside the subject itself. What you would have to do would be to find out what particular landlord refused to have railways on his property at any price, and what others consented—at a price. The shape of the railway would then, to a great extent, depend on the varying prejudices through which it had to pass. This, then, is the point of view I adopt in this paper. It can be put more academically in Renan's phrase, 'Philosophies and theories of politics are nothing in the last resort, when they are analysed out, but the affirmation of a temperament'; or in Nietzsche's more theatrical manner, 'Philosophy is autobiography.'

I am simply trying, then, to pick out certain contrasts in temperament. It might be urged that this is not a very hopeful attitude for anyone to take who wants to 'convince' anybody. If one's theories in politics and in these other matters are simply the expression of one's fundamental prejudices, it would seem perfectly hopeless to argue with anyone about such things. But argument may have, however, one result. It is quite possible, under the influence of a certain environment, that a man may adopt a theory which is not at all the expression of his own prejudices; his own prejudices may even be hidden from him. By picking out these prejudices and showing that they have a natural expression in a completely worked-out attitude in all kinds of subjects, it is quite possible to convert a man.

You are in reality setting out to convert someone under the most promising circumstances. You do not propose to convert him, but only, to attempt to aid him, to change himself. You attempt solely to remove a certain veil which hides the man's own real position from himself. The influence of the present environment is so strong, its mere power of suggestion is so powerful, that a man may find himself advocating, with a certain enthusiasm, opinions which are in reality the exact contrary of those to which his own character would naturally take him. In more detail the method to be adopted in the removal of this veil is this. The type we are considering differs from other types in that a consistently worked-out theory has a strong attraction for it. It only finds at the present moment such a theoretical development on one side in politics. It does not suspect that the same consistency can be found on the other side. If you can present it with the developed theory of this other side, it will then be in the most favourable position for suddenly discovering its own inner sentiments. Previously its attraction for theories was such that, not finding one on this side, it was unable even to perceive its own

prejudices. When you have led a man to perceive his own inside preferences in this way it is possible that you will produce not only a difference
in his political view, but a series of reversals of judgment on a great variety
of activities, for the detailed judgments in those other subjects being in
reality only the manifestations of his prejudices, a change in prejudice will
change the judgments everywhere.

I am trying to maintain, then, that behind the opposed attitudes, and
one can take up a great many different subjects, from politics to art, lie
two contrasted sets of prejudices and sentiments, two different points of
view as to the nature of man, which I am calling the romantic and the
classical.

It might be objected that I have no business to use words which have
by now such an extraordinarily vague meaning. I justify myself in the first
place by pointing out that it so happens that Lasserre, Maurras, etc., the
people who have done most work on this particular aspect of political
theory, have happened, as a matter of fact, to employ these two words,
and it seems convenient for me to follow them, as I shall later on have
frequent occasion to refer to them and to quote them. I could justify
myself in the second place in this way. It seems to me that in the history
of such words there are three stages. In the first and earliest stage a word
has a definite and precise meaning. You are certainly justified in using it,
then. After this there comes a period when the word has about a dozen
meanings. At this stage it is dangerous, and should be left alone. But,
finally, you get to the stage when it had three hundred meanings. It has
then once again become useful and innocuous, for no one will have any
preconceived notion of what it means, and will attentively wait to see
exactly the shade of meaning, and the sense, which you yourself intend
to give it. Their minds are in the receptive state; they are prepared to
receive once again an accurate impression from a word. Now the words
'classic' and 'romantic' have, after their long history from their first use by
Goethe, at last reached this stage; and as I am prepared to give precise and
accurate definitions, I think that I am justified in using them.

I want to give first a kind of Euclidean demonstration of the difference
between these two attitudes. It will sound rather artificial, but I want
simply to show the connection between the sets of adjectives one uses to
describe the difference when it becomes more concrete. It is a kind of
criticism of categories; it is not meant at this state to refer to anything real.

The 'classical' point of view I take to be this. Man is by his very nature
essentially limited and incapable of anything extraordinary. He is incapable of attaining any kind of perfection, because, either by nature, as the
result of original sin, or the result of evolution, he encloses within him
certain antinomies. There is a war of instincts inside him, and it is part of

his permanent characteristics that this must always be so. The future condition of man, then, will always be one of struggle and limitation. The best results can only be got out of man as the result of a certain discipline which introduces order into this internal anarchy. That is what Aristotle meant by saying that only a god or a beast could live outside the State. Nothing is bad in itself except disorder; all that is put in order in a hierarchy is good. Moreover, man being by nature constant, the kind of discipline which will get the best out of him, and which is necessary for him, remains much the same in every generation. The classical attitude, then, has a great respect for the past and for tradition, not from sentimental, but on purely rational grounds. It does not expect anything radically new, and does not believe in any real progress.

In art this spirit shows itself in the belief that there are certain rules which one must obey, which do not in themselves give us the capacity for producing anything, but in which the experience of several generations of artists has traced the limits outside which one can produce nothing solid or excellent. The idea of a personal inspiration jumping all complete from nature, capable of creating, by a kind of divine act, the whole organism of adaptable means of expression, is ridiculous to it. 'The root of classicism is this, that if the rules are of no value without genius, yet there is in them more of genius than there is in any great genius himself.'

I do not at this stage put this forward as anything more than a kind of game. I do not ask you to admit that it is a true account of anything. I merely say that, supposing it is true, it does join up together in some kind of logical sequence all the epithets that one naturally uses in expressing a certain attitude, such as 'order', 'discipline', 'tradition', and the rest of it.

Most people have been in the habit of associating these kinds of views with Nietzsche. It is true that they do occur in him, but he made them so frightfully vulgar that no classic would acknowledge them. In him you have the spectacle of a romantic seizing on the classic point of view because it attracted him purely as a theory, and who, being a romantic, in taking up this theory, passed his slimy fingers over every detail of it. Everything loses its value. The same idea of the necessary hierarchy of classes, with their varying capacities and duties, gets turned into the romantic nonsense of the two kinds of morality, the slave and the master morality, and every other element of the classic position gets transmuted in a similar way into something ridiculous.

The 'romantic' point of view is the exact opposite of this. It does not think that man is by nature bad, turned into something good by a certain order and discipline, but that, on the contrary, man is something rather wonderful, and that so far he has been prevented from exhibiting any wonderful qualities by these very restrictions of order and discipline that the classic praised. You get the most famous expression of it, of course, in Rousseau. I quote from one of his letters: 'The fundamental principle of all morality is that man is a being naturally loving justice. In *Emile* I have endeavoured to show how vice and error, foreign to the natural constitution of man, have been introduced from outside, and have insensibly altered him.'

When one has this conception of the infinite possibilities of man thus imprisoned, one is carried on to the conception that anything that increases man's freedom will be to his benefit. This attitude shows a certain impatience of tradition, for it thinks that tradition is only a hampering restriction which prevents the greater possibilities of man appearing. It gets a certain amount of generous emotion out of its destructive work. It has faith and ardour and awakes great hopes. In freeing mankind from tradition and discipline it imagines that it is preparing a new age. One can see most clearly its contrast with the classical point of view in literature. The romantic imagines everything is accomplished by the breaking of rules. The romantics of 1830 thought that they had, by freeing themselves from rules and traditions, attained liberty— that is to say, absolute spontaneity in artistic creation.

While the classic thinks that certain effects are got in certain fixed ways, the romantic persists in trying to get them in an absolutely new way. He is so compelled to search for interest in novelty, and in the pursuit of extraordinary subjects, of the exotic. It is in this way one can see how the definition of romantic I have given enables one by a process of deduction to pass from it to the more usual and derivative uses of the word. Take the matter to which it was first applied. The romantic movement in poetry started with the cult of Ossian and the old ballads, i.e., something exotic and strange to the eighteenth-century people. In them they found a different, a supernatural, and heightened conception of man, and it was that which makes any movement properly a romantic one.

In however many ways these two points of view differ, you can always in the end trace it back to this quite simple difference in their conception of the nature of man.

In order to avoid one misunderstanding in the use of the word classic, certain historical remarks should be made. What Taine called the classical spirit of the early eighteenth century was not classical, because it used the word 'reason' in a romantic way. Diderot and the encyclopaedists generally were romantics, in my sense of the word, because, like the modern political romantic, they despised tradition and thought that man in 'reason' possessed a kind of divine faculty which would enable him to alter his own nature into something better than had yet ever existed.

There is always at the back of any romanticism a certain characteristic sentiment, a certain kind of exhilaration. In fact, I should define a romantic as a person who was in a certain disordered state of mental health in which he can only remain sane by taking repeated doses of this kind of emotion. It is the kind of exhilaration you get from a sudden sense of release from weight, the sense of lightness and exhilaration you would get from rarer air. It is a necessity of your existence that you should go on believing that something wonderful and extraordinary can and is about to happen to man.

Just as in looking at the shading of a line drawing there is a certain distance at which the lines vanish and look like a wash, so in reading certain books there may come a point, if you are in this state, at which the definite contours of the ideas you are following melt away into this kind of exhilaration I have just been talking about. It betrays itself in certain clichés, 'breaking down barriers', freedom, emancipation, and the rest of it; but, above all, it betrays itself in the epithet NEW. One must believe that there is a NEW art, a NEW religion, even a NEW age.

To make the thing as concrete and as local as possible, however, I will quote a couple of sentences which seem to me to give you the whole secret of the psychology of romanticism: 'The spirit of man will go on its way with songs, and the burden of its most triumphant song will always be, "My soul is escaped like a bird out of the net of the fowler. The snare is broken, and we are delivered."' That's what the romantic is, somebody who is always just about to escape from something. Always 'escaping', that is it!

The important thing, for the purposes of getting at the exact emotion excited by romanticism, is to recognise that it isn't that it wants to escape from anything in particular, but just that it shall ESCAPE.

I am trying to define this emotion exactly, because it is only by doing so that I can avoid misunderstanding in getting at what I consider to be romanticism in politics. I have said that it is associated with the idea of progress, but the word progress can mean two quite different things. It can in the first case mean the metaphysical notion of automatic progress, the kind of thing you get in Hegel and Fourier. In that sense it is, of course, easily recognised as romanticism; but it is quite possible for anyone to retort that this has no necessary connection with what is generally known as the progressive side in politics. All that we believe they might say is that a certain progress can be achieved if we bring it about by definite effort. We don't believe that it is automatic. The answer to this is that, as a matter of actual fact, the real thing that does supply the enthusiasm which brings about certain changes, the emotion that you can actually observe at work, is the religious belief in absolute and inevitable progress. That, and not the more limited belief, is what you find in the propaganda of the side. I quote a typical example of the kind of thing I mean from Dr. Clifford's address on New Year's Eve: 'The soul of the world aspires and yearns for the highest and the best.'

Having now defined this difference of temperament, I shall endeavour in the next article to show the exact difference that the change from one to the other would probably make in one's political views.

II.—PROGRAMME

At the end of my last article I had roughly outlined the difference between the two temperaments that I considered were at the root of the pairs of contrasted attitudes and parties which one finds in a series of subjects ranging from politics to art. Let me recall for a moment my object in doing this, and the exact nature of the aim that I am pursuing in these articles. I am dealing with the question of 'conviction', and, more precisely, with that of 'conversion'. All that any argument can do, I urged, was to develop the consequences of some first position, which itself rests on nothing further, but which is an arbitrarily assumed basis. A dispute, then, between two persons, in which the reasoning is correct and logical, would always end in a definite result one way or the other; one of the parties to the dispute would find that he had been in the wrong. We know, as a matter of fact, that disputes do not have this logical conclusion; it is very seldom that any effect is produced by reasoning at all. What is the reason of this? Simply this, that the parties to the dispute start from different premises, the premises being the things which they take for granted as requiring no proof. If you started from the same premises and committed no errors of logic, you would infallibly finish by agreeing. The only employment for reasoning in these matters seems, then, to be in the extremely small field provided by those people who have mistakenly drawn the wrong conclusion from the same premises as you yourself start from. The number of people that you could convert from this cause is extremely small, and it is from not recognising this that most political polemic is so barren of result. Logical reasoning is simply a means of passing from a certain premise to certain conclusions. It has in itself no motive power at all. It is quite impotent to deal with those first premises. It is a kind of building art; it tells you how to construct a house on a given piece of ground, but it will not choose the ground where you build. That is decided by things outside its scope altogether. This enables me to fix the kind of purpose I have in mind in these articles. I am simply conducting an investigation of these 'premises'. Every man has inside himself a kind of rock on which he builds. I am concerned entirely with these rocks. I do believe that it is possible by getting down to the root of the matter in this way to conduct an attempt at political 'conversion', which shall not be entirely barren, but only in this way can it be done. I concluded the article which set out what I thought were the two contrasted temperaments and sets of prejudices on which political belief is ultimately based by saying that I would then endeavour to trace out the detailed consequences which would be produced in your beliefs as the result of the discovery that you did in reality start from a different base, and that your most fundamental prejudice was in reality different from what you had supposed it to be. (It would more accurately describe the process to say that you, for the first time, made the effort necessary to discover that you had such a basis, and then found that the development of that basis led you to the opposite side from that which you had formerly supposed yourself to be on.) What, then, would be the detailed consequences of a change from the romantic to the classical point of view? Following the natural slope down from your new starting-point, to what actual difference of opinion are you led? What different sets of catchwords do you respond to in political discussion? What phrases become alive to you, and what others which formerly moved you now turn into dead clichés?

I shall endeavour to answer this question by dealing in each article with that particular aspect of, and deduction from, the general contrast between the two attitudes which is embodied in each of the following pairs of contrasted epithets.

(1) 'Constancy and Progress'.—A history of the idea of progress, from the time of Turgot and Condorcet, through Saint Simon, down to its present use by the Socialists, tracking its pernicious and disastrous influence on political thought and action.

(2) 'Order, Authority, and Liberty'.—A discussion of the principles (as distinct from opportunist dodges) which ought to govern the action of the State during strike disturbances, etc.

(3) 'Equality and Hierarchy'.—A discussion of the Tory view of education, and an attack on the present disastrous democratic conception of it (together with an account of the French Syndicalist, Georges Sorel, who, strangely enough, takes the Tory view).

(4) 'Nationalism and Universalism'.—An attack on universalism, not on the ground that nationalities do, as a matter of regrettable though actual fact, still exist, but because it is desirable even on abstract grounds that they should.

Of this list two things can be said. All the contrasts in it can be shown to follow logically from the fundamental difference of attitude I started with. Also that the working out of the details does provide a set of Tory principles which are consistent with each other, and from which consistent judgments can be passed on the various matters which form the actual subject matter of modern political thinking. It is this kind of theoretical basis of conviction which is lacking to the average Conservative—at any rate, to the average Conservative leader. In his actions he opposes the progressives in that he wants to turn them out and obtain office for himself, but in his ideals he seems indistinguishable from them. He talks in many cases exactly as if he were a Socialist. He does so because he is not in reality a Tory at all. He has not the firm conviction which springs from a thought-out attitude, which enables one to judge matters of detail from the standpoint provided by certain principles.

We have been beaten, to a certain extent, because our enemies' theories have conquered us. We have played with those to our own undoing. Not until we are hardened again by conviction of the sort I have been talking about are we likely to do any good. In accepting the theories of the other side, we are merely repeating a well-known historical phenomenon. The Revolution in France came about, not so much because the forces in its favour had great strength, as because the forces which should have resisted were half-hearted in their resistance. They themselves had been conquered, intellectually, at any rate, by the theories of the revolutionary side. It was because the classes who were enthusiastic about Rousseau had not enough grip of reality to see that they were accepting ideas which would ultimately make for their own undoing that the Revolution was so successful. (Incidentally, one may note as typical of the curious ways in which these theories had penetrated the ruling classes, that the 'return to Nature', which was so popular in the form of shepherdesses' parties at the Court, and exemplified in the pictures of the time, was merely Rousseauism—that is, the ideals which made against authority and for liberty—in another form.)

However, for the proper working out of my argument I must for the moment leave the detailed exposition of these principles. It is necessary if one is to be effective, so far as conversion goes, to get at, first of all, as accurately as possible, the exact contours of the prejudice from which one starts. So for the present let us leave this worked-out plan, to consider the sentiment which is at the root of the differences exhibited in that plan.

I stated that difference of prejudice is a difference in the conception one forms of the nature of man. Is it constant, or is man capable of development and progress into something much less limited and more perfect than at present? The Tory side, I asserted, depends on the conviction that the nature of man is absolutely fixed and unalterable, and that any scheme of social regeneration which presupposes that he can alter is doomed to bring about nothing but disaster. This conception of the constancy of man, which he may arrive at by way of induction from history, or by introspection and inner observation, which reveals what is and must be the characteristics of man's nature, is the basis of his whole belief. But the question may then be put, and must be answered before anything else can be done, 'What exactly do you mean by the constant nature of man? He appears, superficially at any rate, to change in every generation. In what sense do you conceive him to be constant?'

After that comes the further problem, which is really getting at the root of the matter as far as my argument is concerned: What is it which makes a man contemplate the idea of a constant world with such repugnance, so that he insists, in spite of all evidence, in believing that progress is continuous, and that man may and does change? At this stage I shall be getting at the sentiment which is at the root of all the evil.

To start with the first question. We must make the idea of constancy a little more precise. What is meant is not that man does not change at all, but that it is impossible that he should change in the remarkable way which would justify that particular kind of emotion I defined as 'romantic', the emotion of 'escaping'. I could get a crude kind of picture of the way I consider man is constant in this kind of way. Various instincts seem to me to be mixed up in him, as valuable metal might be in an ore. But the metaphor is inaccurate, because you can extract the ore. If you suppose an ore of such a kind of sticky nature that the whole thing held together and so was of fixed and unalterable composition, then you would get an accurate picture of what one intends. You are firmly convinced that nothing extraordinary in the way of change or improvement could happen to man, simply for this reason, that he is by nature made of this fixed composition. It is this kind of assurance of his nature that makes you impatient of the kind of enthusiasm that the romantic is always getting up about the 'future of man', and which makes it seem vulgar. I suppose it is all summed up in the profound truth that no man can be a hero to his valet. The modern romantic tends to put his heroes in the future, for, by the nature of things, no man can valet that.

Of course, man is capable of a certain kind of progress. He builds up sciences and civilisation, but the progress is here rather one of accumulation than of alteration in capacity. There is no necessary difference in mental capacity between a man driving a steam engine and a man driving a wooden plough, and progress in thought is exactly of the same kind; and though man has developed more complex mental conceptions and ways of dealing with things, the capacity which uses them remains the same. It is necessary in considering this question to make this division

between intellectual 'capacity' and its 'content'—the number of conceptions which it can use. If you compare the intellect to a sponge, it is easy
to see that the sponge can be empty or full of water, without its 'capacity'
being altered. From the moment that the human species has been constituted, its intellectual possibilities were fixed at the same time. At the
beginning of its career the white race was capable of genius in the same
proportion as it is now, and the average intellectual capacity of a tribe in
the Stone Age was probably exactly the same as any modern village at the
present time.

This constancy is, of course, only true as far as capacity goes. As far as
the content of the mind goes, the number of conceptions it can manipulate or is familiar with, there certainly is progress.

The important point to notice here is, so far as the point I am now
trying to make is concerned, that this doesn't matter. In order that you
shall be able to get the kind of emotion, either in politics associated with
the kind of religious enthusiasm about progress, or that which in literature
you call Romanticism, it is necessary that you should believe that man
can change in a very different way to this. It is necessary to believe in a
change of capacity.

I am, of course, only treating the question of intellectual constancy as
an analogy for the case of moral constancy. Just the same holds good of
that set of qualities, instincts, and prejudices which go to make up man's
constitution as a member of society and a political unit. Any plan which
supposes that his ethical standard can be raised, or that he can contain a
less percentage of egoism, is building on sand.

The question might, by opponents, be forced out of the plane of
sentiment and on to that of fact. They would triumphantly assert that man
had evolved from the brute, and that there was no reason to suppose that
the evolution had finished. There is no reason, they might say, why we
should not suppose that selfishness will be gradually eliminated and a new
kind of man, better fitted to live in the Socialist Utopia, be evolved. This
is, of course, mere supposition; but the objection can be met on its own
ground. It rests on an antiquated theory of evolution. There is hardly I
suppose, one biologist left in Europe who could be described as an
orthodox Darwinian. If you are a Darwinian, you suppose that each step
in evolution has come gradually, by an accumulation of favourable small
variations. If that were true, then it would be possible to conceive that
man himself might, by the accumulation of such variations, gradually
change into something better. But the theory of evolution which is now
gradually accepted is that of De Vries. His Mutation theory gives quite a
different account of the origin of species. It supposes that each new
species came into existence in one big variation, as a kind of 'sport', and,

that once constituted, a species remains absolutely constant. There would then be no hope at all of progress for man. Each race of man once having come into existence, is created with a certain mental and moral capacity, which is fixed from the moment of its creation, and never changes or increases.

There is another feature of De Vries' theory which might be noticed here, as it will be important later in considering the question of equality and hierarchy. 'Not only', he says, 'is the average level of each species absolutely constant, but the percentage of slight variations in different directions also remains constant.'

To pass from these biological suppositions to the consideration of the sentiment which prompts a man to escape from the acceptance of constancy at all costs. What is this hidden prejudice which insists that a man shall believe in progress? Here we are getting at the irreducible prejudice from which everything else springs.

This sentiment, then, putting it in the most abstract way possible, is this: the modern mind (if the expression may be permitted) is unable to support with equanimity the idea of an absolutely constant world, and any account of romanticism comes to nothing, in the end, but an examination of the various ways in which the mind wriggles away from constancy. To prove that this shrinking from the idea of constancy does exist, I give three quotations.

I may say that I quote from these people, not because I consider them of the slightest importance, but simply because other people seem to, that is, they represent a very widespread state of mind.

The first thing I have in mind is the opening chapter of Wells' 'Modern Utopia'. It commences, as far as I remember, by satirising all previous Utopias, for this reason, that when they had attained their perfect state, they expected it to go on for ever in the same constant state of perfection, one generation following another, until the gods were sick of it. Any Utopia which would satisfy him would not have to be constant. You can see the man perfectly appalled at the idea of a constant state of society. At any rate, a constant state of society could not possibly be fitted in in his mind with any ideal. His own Utopia would have to be dynamic. It is a very curious thing, the number of people who are obsessed by the word dynamic.[1] Everything must be dynamic, even publishers' advertisements. Nobody knows exactly what it means, but that doesn't matter; it is your only epithet. There are other words of this kind. There was once a lady, the terror of my life, who used to take me aside in drawing-rooms, and whisper, 'Don't you think everything is vibration?' And now there is a whole set of people who live on the word 'rhythm'. They have a paper. If you look at rhythm in the dictionary, you find it means regular repetition. That doesn't seem particularly exciting in itself, but, in spite of that, everything must be rhythm, and so it will be, I suppose, for the next five years. It's all part of one phenomenon. There must be one word in the language spelt in capital letters. For a long time, and still for sane people, the word was God. Then one became bored with the letter 'G', and went on to 'R', and for a hundred years it was Reason, and now all the best people take off their hats and lower their voices when they speak of Life. The Deities' wanderings about the alphabet would make an interesting Odyssey.

However, to get back to the point. When you meet people who have got 'dynamic' on the brain in this way, you simply know that they are suffering from this modern disease, the horror of constancy.

I will take a more definite expression of the same feeling. In the *Hibbert Journal* a good many years ago Mr. Lowes Dickinson[2] published a paper on what he considered were the three necessary conditions for an optimist. It was necessary that the world should be progressing in a certain direction, that we personally should be able to help that purpose, and, finally, that we should be able to go on helping that purpose, that we should be in some way immortal. The childlike simplicity of this is almost pathetic. It is like a toy steam engine.

I just quote this, because it seems to me to show this same modern nervousness and horror of the idea of constancy. You must believe in progress if your mind is to maintain its equilibrium.

My third example, which is rather different, is from Mr. Benn's book on 'Greek Philosophy'.[3] He is describing Aristotle's views, and, by his manner of doing so, conveys an impression of the extraordinary way in which they surprised him.

'He did not, like the Ionian physiologists, anticipate in outline our theories of evolution. He held that the cosmos had always been, by the strictest necessity, arranged in the same manner; the starry revolutions never changing, the four elements preserving a constant balance, the earth always solid, land and water always distributed according to their present proportions, living species transmitting the same unalterable type through an infinite series of generations, the human race enjoying an eternal duration, but from time to time losing all its conquests in some great physical catastrophe, and obliged to begin over again with the depressing consciousness that nothing could be devised that had not been thought of an infinite number of times already, and the existing distinctions between men and women grounded on the everlasting necessities of nature. He did not hope, like Plato, for the regeneration of the race by enlightened thought.'[4]

I am not concerned at all with the truth of this conception of the world. I am only concerned with its effects on Mr. Benn's emotions. It is obvious that, like Mr. Dickinson and Mr. Wells, he couldn't stand the idea of a world of this kind. It appeared to him a kind of nightmare. In fact, he gets quite rhetorical and abusive about it. He comments: 'It seemed as if philosophy, abdicating her high function and obstructing the powers which she had first opened, were now content to systematise the forces of prejudice, blindness, immobility, and despair.'[5]

This quotation brings to the sharpest focus the difference between the two attitudes. It is easy to see here that it is this repugnance to the idea of fixity which is at the bottom of a great many political ideals. But if you once face this repugnance in its nakedest form, you will find that it vanishes. Why should the idea of a constant, continuous, and endless progress be any more rational or satisfactory than the idea of constancy? Either the progress attains its end (when it is finished with), or it never attains its end, and then it is still more irrational; for progress towards an end which constantly recedes cannot be said to be a satisfactory view of the world-process. If you can only release yourself from this obsession by the words 'dynamic' and 'change', you will find that there is nothing absurd or repugnant in the notion of a constant world, in which there is no progress. But here the question verges on a philosophical one, which is outside the scope of this paper, and which I have treated elsewhere in book form.[6]

It is quite as easy and natural for emotion and enthusiasm to crystallise round the idea of a constant world as round the idea of progress. An extraordinary solidarity is given to one's beliefs. There is great consolation in the idea that the same struggles have taken place in each generation, and that men have always thought as we think now. It gives to religion a great stability, for it exhibits it as a permanent part of man's nature, and the nature of man being constant, it places these beliefs beyond all change. All the pleasure that one takes in old literature comes from the fact that it gives us this strange emotion of solidarity, to find that our ancestors were of like nature with ourselves.

This concludes the abstract part of my argument. I have tried to show that an opposite sentiment to the one which provides the motive force of romanticism is possible. I have now to show the detailed consequences to which this leads in the shape of the four antitheses which I gave in a previous issue.[7]

Translator's Preface to Georges Sorel's Reflections on Violence

[The preface reproduced here is from the 1916 London edition of Hulme's translation of Georges Sorel's *Réflexions sur la violence*, published by George Allen & Unwin. A slightly different version was published in *NA* 17/24 (14 Oct. 1915), 569–70. The American edition, published in New York in 1914 by B. W. Huebsch, did not have a preface. The footnotes in the text are Hulme's.]

> . . . que si par impossible, la nature avait fait de l'homme un animal exclusivement industrieux et sociable, et point guerrier, il serait tombé, dès le premier jour, au niveau des bêtes dont l'association forme toute la destinée; il aurait perdu, avec l'orgueil de son héroïsme, sa faculté révolutionnaire, la plus merveilleuse de toutes, et la plus féconde. Vivant en communauté pure, notre civilisation serait une étable. . . . Philanthrope, vous parlez d'abolir la guerre, prenez garde de dégrader le genre humain. . . . *Proudhon.*[1]

Nearly all the criticism of Sorel's work goes wrong, not so much in details as in its complete inability to understand its main motive; the sympathetic accounts being as irritating and as wide of the mark as the others.

What exactly is the nature of this general miscomprehension? In a movement like Socialism we can conveniently separate out two distinct elements, the working-class movement itself and the system of ideas which goes with it (though the word is ugly, it will be convenient to follow Sorel and call a system of ideas an *ideology*). If we call one (I) and the other (W), (I + W) will be the whole movement. The ideology is, as a matter of fact, *democracy*.[a] Now the enormous difficulty in Sorel comes in this—that he not only denies the essential connection between these two elements, but even asserts that the ideology will be fatal to the

---

[a] *Democracy*—the word is not used here either (1) as a general name for the working-class movement or (2) to indicate the true doctrine that all men are equal. It is not used then in its widest sense as indicating opposition to all aristocratic, oligarchic or class government, but in a narrower sense, to recall which I have always put the word in italics. Liberal might have been a better word, were it not that Socialists, while proclaiming their difference from liberalism in policy, at the same time adopt the whole liberal *ideology*; and though they do not acknowledge it to be liberal, they will recognise it under the label *democratic*.

movement. The regeneration of society will never be brought by the pacifist *progressives*.

They may be pardoned then if they find this strange. This combination of doctrines which they would probably call reactionary, with revolutionary syndicalism, is certainly very disconcerting to liberal Socialists. It is difficult for them to understand a revolutionary who is anti-democratic, an absolutist in ethics, rejecting all rationalism and relativism, who values the mystical element in religion 'which will never disappear', speaks contemptuously of modernism and *progress*, and uses a concept like *honour* with no sense of unreality.[b]

As a rule such sentiments, when the *democrat* meets with them, are conveniently dismissed as springing from a disguised attempt to defend the interests of wealth. But this obviously will not fit the case of Sorel. There is then some danger of a foreign body lodging itself inside the system of democratic thought. The latter deals with this irritant very much as one would expect. It calls to its aid the righteous indignation which every *real progressive* must feel at the slightest suspicion of anything *reactionary*. Instead of considering the details of the actual thesis, the *progressive* prefers to discredit it by an imagined origin. Sorel's attitude is thus attributed to mysticism, to neo-royalism, or to some confused and sentimental reaction against Reason. This summary dismissal is accompanied by a distinct feeling of relief. 'You see there is nothing in it. It is only our old adversaries in a new disguise.' The people who make this kind of criticism are clearly incapable of understanding the main thesis of the book. The misunderstanding will be very stubborn. How can it be removed?

The first step is to note more exactly the feelings of the simple-minded democrat towards this thesis. His behaviour may indicate the source of his repugnance, and give some hints as to its removal. What he mostly feels, I suppose, is a kind of exasperation. He cannot take the *anti-democratic* view seriously. He feels just as if some one had denied one of the laws of thought, or asserted that two and two are five. In his natural state, of course, he never thinks of the movement as composed of two elements (I + W). It is one undivided whole for him. When, however, the denial of the connection between I and W forces the separate existence of (I) on his notice, he at once thinks of it, not as one possible *ideology* amongst

---

[b] An *ideology* naturally includes a system of sentiments. In this respect the book is even more confusing to the democrat than in that of ideas. The divergence in sentiments is most striking, however, in what Sorel says about the feelings of envy and retaliation as the basis of liberal *democracy*. A careful analysis of this sentiment and its historical connection with democracy can be found in Max Scheler's *Über Ressentiment u. Werttheorie*.

others, but as an *inevitable* way of thinking, which must necessarily accompany (W) as it accompanies everything.

It is this notion of the *necessary*, the inevitable character of the *democratic* system of ideas, which is here the stumbling-block. It is this which makes him think Sorel's *anti-democratic* position and views *unnatural* or perverse. He has not yet thought of *democracy* as a system at all, but only as a natural and inevitable equipment of the emancipated and instructed man. The ideas which underlie it appear to him to have the *necessary* character of categories. In reality they are, of course, nothing of the kind. They depend on certain fundamental attitudes of the mind, on unexpressed major premises. If he could be made conscious of these premises, the character of inevitability would have been removed. The explanation of how these major premises get into the position of *pseudo-categories* goes a long way towards removing a man from their influence. They are unperceived because they have become so much part of the mind and lie so far back that we are never really conscious of them as ideas at all. We do not see them, but see other things *through* them, and consequently take what we see for the outlines of things themselves. Blue spectacles making a blue world can be pointed out, but not these pseudo-categories which lie, as it were, 'behind the eye'.

All effective propaganda depends then on getting these ideas away from their position 'behind the eye' and putting them facing one as *objects* which we can then consciously accept or reject. This is extremely difficult. Fortunately, however, all ideologies are of gradual growth, and that rare type of historical intelligence which investigates and analyses their origins can help us considerably. Just as a knowledge of the colours extended and separated in the spectrum enables us to distinguish the feebler colours confused together in shadows, so this type of history, by exhibiting certain ideas in a concreter form, existing as it were as objects in time, enables us to distinguish the same ideas, existing in us 'behind the eye' and to bring them to the surface of the mind. Their hidden influence on our opinions then at once disappears, for they have lost their status as categories. This is a violent operation, and the mind is never quite the same afterwards. It has lost a certain virginity. But there are so many of these systems in which we unwittingly 'live and move and have our being' that the process really forms the major part of the education of the adult. Moreover the historical method by exhibiting the intimate connection between such conceptions—that of *Progress* for example—and certain economical conditions at the time of their invention in the eighteenth century, does more than anything else to loosen their hold over the mind. It is this method which Sorel has so successfully applied in *Les Illusions du progrès*[2] to the particular democratic ideology, with which we are here concerned.

This *democratic* ideology[c] is about two centuries old. Its history can be clearly followed, and its logical connection with a parallel movement in literature. It is an essential element in the romantic movement; it forms an organic body of middle-class thought dating from the eighteenth century, and has consequently no necessary connection whatever with the working-class or revolutionary movement. Liberal Socialism is still living on the remains of middle-class thought of the last century; and when vulgar thought of to-day is pacifist, rationalist, and hedonist, and in being so believes itself to be expressing the inevitable convictions of the instructed and emancipated man, it has all the pathos of marionettes in a play, dead things gesticulating as though they were alive. Our younger novelists, like those Roman fountains in which water pours from the mouth of a human mask, gush as though spontaneously from the depths of their own being, a muddy romanticism that has in reality come through a very long pipe.

Democratic romanticism is then a body of doctrine with a recognisable and determinate history. What is the central attitude from which it springs, and which gives it continued life? What is the unexpressed major premiss here?

Putting the matter with the artificial simplicity of a diagram for the sake of clearness, we might say that romanticism and classical pessimism differ in their antithetical conception of the nature of man. For the one, man is by nature good, and for the other, by nature bad.

All Romanticism springs from Rousseau,[d] and the key to it can be found even in the first sentence of the Social Contract—'Man is born free, and he finds himself everywhere in chains.' In other words, man is by nature something wonderful, of unlimited powers, and if hitherto he has not appeared so, it is because of external obstacles and fetters, which it should be the main business of social politics to remove.

What is at the root of the contrasted system of ideas you find in Sorel, the classical, pessimistic, or, as its opponents would have it, the reactionary ideology? This system springs from the exactly contrary conception of

[c] The opposed ideology in Sorel can most conveniently be described by thinking of the qualities of seventeenth as contrasted with eighteenth century literature in France, the difference, for example, between Corneille and Diderot. Sorel often speaks of Cornelian virtue. But the antithesis of Classical and Romantic is not enough to make the *Classical* comprehensible to a *Romantic*; it is necessary to get down to the two fundamental attitudes from which the difference really springs.

[d] For a history of the romantic movement in French Literature from this point of view, see Pierre Lasserre's excellent *Le Romantisme français*.

man; the conviction that man is by nature bad or limited,[e] and can consequently only accomplish anything of value by disciplines, ethical, heroic, or political. In other words, it believes in Original Sin. We may define Romantics, then, as all who do not believe in the Fall of Man. It is this opposition which in reality lies at the root of most of the other divisions in social and political thought.[f]

From the pessimistic conception of man comes naturally the view that the transformation of society is an heroic task requiring heroic qualities . . . virtues which are not likely to flourish on the soil of a rational and sceptical ethic. This regeneration can, on the contrary, only be brought about and only be maintained by actions springing from an ethic which from the narrow rationalist standpoint is irrational, being not *relative*, but absolute.[g] The transformation of society is not likely to be achieved as a

[e] This is by no means identical with materialism; rather it is characteristic of the religious attitude—cf. Pascal's *Pensées*. Romanticism confuses both human and divine things by not clearly separating them. The main thing with which it can be reproached is that it blurs the clear outlines of human relations—whether in political thought or in the treatment of sex in literature—by introducing into them the Perfection that properly belongs only to the non-human.

[f] Not only here but in philosophy itself; this can be made clear by a parallel. The change of sensibility which has enabled us to appreciate Egyptian, Indian, Byzantine, Polynesian, and Negro work as *art* and not as archæology or ethnology, has a double effect. While it demonstrates that what were taken for the necessary principles of æsthetics are merely a psychology of Classical and modern European art, it at the same time suddenly forces us to see the essential unity of this art. In spite of its apparent variety, European art in reality forms a coherent body of work resting on certain presuppositions, of which we become conscious for the first time when we see them denied by other periods of art (cf. the work of Riegl on Byzantine art). One might say that in the same way, an understanding of the religious philosophy which subordinates man (regarded as a part of nature) to certain absolute values—in other words, a realisation of the sense of this dogma—forces us to see that there is a much greater family resemblance between all philosophy since the Renaissance than is ever recognised. The philosophy rests, in reality, on the same presuppositions as the art, and forms a coherent system with it. It seems as if no sooner had Copernicus shown that man was not the centre of the universe, then the philosophers commenced for the first time to prove that he was. You get expressed explicitly, for the first time (in Pico della Mirandola for example), this idea of the sufficiency of natural man, and it has generally been assumed by all philosophers since. It may be expressed in very different languages and with very different degrees of profundity, but even Hegel and Condorcet are one, from this point of view. Humanism thus really contains the germs of the disease that was bound to come to its full evil development in Romanticism.

It is promising to note signs of the break-up of this period in art, and there are some slight indications of a corresponding anti-humanistic movement in thought and ethics. (G. E. Moore, Duguit,[3] Husserl and 'Phænomenologie'.)

[g] *Virtue.*—Without too much exaggeration it might be said that the objective and absolute view of ethics to which Sorel adheres has at the present moment more chance of being understood. There has always been something rather unreal about ethics. In a library one's hand glided over books on that subject instinctively. That is, perhaps, because the only ethical questions that came before parasitical literary men were those of sex, in which (may I be forgiven, being here no disciple of Sorel) there seems very little but expediency,

result of peaceful and intelligent *readjustment* on the part of literary men and politicians. But on the optimistic and romantic view this is quite possible. For the optimistic conception of man leads naturally to the characteristic democratic doctrine of inevitable *Progress*.

An understanding of the classical side of this antithesis entirely removes the strangeness of Sorel's position. But though this tendency can be seen, even in his earlier work (the first book on Socrates[4] maintaining that Socrates represents the decadence in Athens, having introduced expediency and calculation into ethics)—yet his final disillusionment with *democracy* came only after the bitter experience of political events which followed the Dreyfus case. A good part of the book consequently is concerned with people who are to us somewhat obscure. But it should be remembered that these obscure figures all have their counterparts here, and that the drama they figure in is a universal one.

The belief that pacifist democracy will lead to no regeneration of society, but rather to its decadence, and the reaction against romanticism in literature, are naturally common to many different schools. This is the secret, for example, of the sympathy between Sorel and the group of writers connected with *L'Action française*, which is so eagerly fastened on by those anxious to discredit him. His *ideology* resembles theirs. Where he differs is in the application he finds for it. He expects a return of the classical spirit through the struggle of the classes.[h] This is the part of his thesis that is concerned with facts, and it would be impertinent on my part to offer any commentary on it. I have been only concerned with certain misapprehensions about the purely theoretical part of the argument.[i] One may note here, however, how he makes the two interact. Given the classical attitude, he tries to prove that its present manifestation may be hoped for in working-class violence, and at the same time the complementary notion that only under the influence of the classical ideal will the movement succeed in regenerating society.

---

nothing that a man could honestly feel objective. But many sensualists lately have had to make an ethical decision for the first time, and uncomfortably recognise that as there is one objective thing at least in ethics, so there may be many more.

[h] It is this which differentiates Sorel's from other attacks on the democratic *ideology*. Some of these are merely dilettante, having little sense of reality, while others are really vicious, in that they play with the idea of inequality. No theory that is not fully moved by the conception of justice asserting the equality of men, and which cannot offer something to all men, deserves or is likely to have any future.

[i] In doing this I have laid a disproportionate emphasis on one aspect of Sorel. I have not endeavoured, however, to give any general account of his work here, but only to remove the most probable cause of misunderstanding. Otherwise, I should have liked to have noted his relations to Marx, Proudhon, and to Vico, and also to have said something of his conception of history, of which Croce has written in the preface to the Italian translation.

Sorel is one of the most remarkable writers of the time, certainly the most remarkable socialist since Marx; and his influence is likely to increase, for, in spite of the apparently undisturbed supremacy of rationalist hedonism in popular thought, the *absolute* view of ethics which underlies his polemic, is gradually being re-established. A similar combination of the classical ideal with socialism is to be found, it is true, in Proudhon, but Sorel comes at a happier moment. The *ideology* attacked by Proudhon has now reached a fuller development, and its real consequences can be more easily perceived. There are many who begin to be disillusioned with liberal and pacifist *democracy*, while shrinking from the opposed *ideology* on account of its reactionary associations. To these people Sorel, a revolutionary in economics, but classical in ethics, may prove an emancipator.

*Art
Criticism*

Mr. Epstein and the Critics

[First published in *NA* 14/8 (25 Dec. 1913), 251–3; reprinted in *FS* 103–12. The avant-garde sculptor Jacob Epstein (1880–1959) was exhibiting work at the Twenty-One Gallery in London. Hulme continued to champion Epstein's work throughout his life, and was supposedly writing a book about the sculptor at the time of his death in 1917. Hulme's folder of photographs for the book is at the Brynmor Jones Library, University of Hull. Of Hulme's defence of his work, Epstein later said: 'Although written seventeen years ago this article is remarkably fresh and with the substitution of a name here and there might apply to the discussions that I have to face after all my exhibitions. . . . I always remember it as the sanest article written about me' (Arnold L. Haskell, *The Sculptor Speaks: Jacob Epstein to Arnold L. Haskell* (London, 1931), 151).]

I begin with an apology. All through this article I write about Mr. Epstein's work in a way which I recognise to be wrong, in that it is what an artist would call literary. The appreciation of a work of art must be plastic or nothing. But I defend myself in this way, that I am not so much writing directly about Mr. Epstein's work, as engaged in the more negative and quite justifiable business of attempting to protect the spectator from certain prejudices which are in themselves literary. This is an article then not so much on Epstein as on his critics. When I see the critics attempting to corrupt the mind of the spectator and trying to hinder their appreciation of a great artist, I feel an indignation which must be my excuse for these clumsy, hurriedly-written and unrevised notes.

An attack on critics could not have a better subject matter than the Press notices on Mr. Epstein's show. They exhibit a range and variety of fatuousness seldom equalled. It is not necessary to spend any time over notices which, like that of 'C.B.' in the 'Athenæum',[1] are merely spiteful, or that in the 'Illustrated London News',[2] which compared him unfavourably with the Exhibition of Humorous Artists. I propose rather to deal with those which, in appearance at any rate, profess to deal seriously with his work.

Take first the merely nervous. Their method is continually to refer to Mr. Epstein as a great artist and at the same time to deplore everything he does. It reminds one of the old philosophical disputes about substance.

Would anything remain of a 'thing' if all its qualities were taken away? What is the metaphysical nature of an artist's excellence that seems to manifest itself in no particular thing he does? The truth is, of course, that they dare not say what they really think. The particular kind of gift which enables a man to be an art critic is not the possession of an instinct which tells them what pictures are good or bad, but of a different kind of instinct which leads them to recognise the people who do know. This is, of course, in itself a comparatively rare instinct. Once they have obtained a 'direction' in this way, their own literary capacity enables them to expand it to any desired length. You can, however, always tell this from a certain emptiness in their rhetoric (cf. Arthur Symons' article on Rodin). There is no one to give them a 'direction' about Mr. Epstein's drawings, and they are at a loss. They seek refuge in praise of the 'Romilly John', which has been universally admitted to be one of the finest bronzes since the Renaissance. It shows how incapable the critics are of judging even Mr. Epstein's earlier work, that one critic has been found to couple this superb head with Mr. John's thin and unconvincing painting of a child, at present exhibited in the New English Art Club.[3]

I come now to the most frequent and the most reasonable criticism: that directed against the 'Carvings in Flenite'. It is generally stated in a rather confused way, but I think that it can be analysed out into two separate prejudices. The first is that an artist has no business to use formulæ taken from another civilisation. The second is that, even if the formula the artist uses is the natural means of expressing certain of his emotions, yet these emotions must be unnatural in him, a modern Western. I shall attempt to show that the first objection really has its root in the second, and that this second prejudice is one which runs through almost every activity at the present time. These 'Carvings in Flenite', we are told, are 'deliberate imitations of Easter Island carvings'. This seems to me to depend on a misconception of the nature of formulæ. Man remaining constant, there are certain broad ways in which certain emotions must, and will always naturally be expressed, and these we must call formulæ. They constitute a constant and permanent alphabet. The thing to notice is that the use of these broad formulæ has nothing to do with the possession of or lack of individuality in the artist. That comes out in the way the formulæ are used. If I or the King of the Zulus want to walk, we both put one leg before the other; that is the universal formula, but there the resemblance ends. To take another illustration, which I don't want to put forward as literally true, but which I only use for purposes of illustration. A certain kind of *nostalgie* and attenuated melancholy is expressed in Watteau by a formula of tall trees and minute people, and a certain use of colour (I am also aware that he got this feeling, in the Gilles, for example, by a quite other formula, but I repeat I am only giving a sort of hypothetical illustration). It would be quite possible at the present day for a painter, wishing to express the same kind of emotion, to use the same broad formula quite naturally and without any imitation of Watteau. The point is, that given the same emotion, the same broad formula comes naturally to the hands of any people in any century. I may say that I have not, as a matter of fact, any great admiration for the particular painters who use this particular formula, but I am trying to give an illustration of a formula which the critics who attack Mr. Epstein would not have attacked. To be legitimate, of course, the formula used must be a natural expression of the feeling you are getting at and not a mere imitation of an exotic or a romantic past. The form follows the need in each case. It may quite easily be the same need divided by many civilisations.

I think that in this way we can force these people back on to the real root of their objection, the second prejudice I mentioned, the feeling that it is unnatural for a modern to have the kind of emotion which these formulæ naturally express. In getting at this, one is getting at something that is really fundamental in modern life. I do think that there is a certain general state of mind which has lasted from the Renaissance till now, with what is, in reality, very little variation. It is impossible to characterise it here, but it is perhaps enough to say that, taking at first the form of the 'humanities', it has in its degeneracy taken the form of a belief in 'Progress' and the rest of it. It was in its way a fairly consistent system, but is probably at the present moment breaking up. In this state of break-up, I think that it is quite natural for individuals here and there to hold a philosophy and to be moved by emotions which would have been unnatural in the period itself. To illustrate big things by small ones I feel, myself, a repugnance towards the *Weltanschauung* (as distinct from the technical part) of all philosophy since the Renaissance. In comparison with what I can vaguely call the religious attitude, it seems to me to be trivial. I am moved by Byzantine mosaic, not because it is quaint or exotic, but because it expresses an attitude I agree with. But the fate of the people who hold these views is to be found incomprehensible by the 'progressives' and to be labelled reactionary; that is, while we arrive at such a Weltanschauung quite naturally, we are thought to be imitating the past.

I have wandered into this by-path merely to find therein an illustration which will help us to understand the repugnance of the critic to the 'Carvings in Flenite'. It is, says the critic, 'rude savagery, flouting respectable tradition-vague memories of dark ages as distant from modern feeling as the loves of the Martians'. Modern feeling be damned! As if it was not the business of every honest man at the present moment to clean the world of these sloppy dregs of the Renaissance. This carving, by an extreme abstraction, by the selection of certain lines, gives an effect of tragic greatness. The important point about this is that the tragedy is of an order more intense than any conception of tragedy which could fit easily into the modern progressive conception of life. This, I think, is the real root of the objection to these statues, that they express emotions which are, as a matter of fact, entirely alien and unnatural to the critic. But that is a very different thing from their being unnatural to the artist. My justification of these statues would be then (1) that an alien formula is justifiable when it is the necessary expression of a certain attitude; and (2) that in the peculiar conditions in which we find ourselves, which are really the breaking up of an era, it has again become quite possible for people here and there to have the attitude expressed by these formulæ.

I have dealt with these in rather a literary way, because I think that in this case it is necessary to get semi-literary prejudices out of the way, before the carvings can be seen as they should be seen, i.e., plastically.

To turn now to the drawings which have been even more misunderstood by the critics than the carvings. I only want to make a few necessary notes about these, as I am dealing with them at greater length in an essay elsewhere. I need say very little about the magnificent drawing reproduced in this paper,[4] for it stands slightly apart from the others and seems to have been found intelligible even by the critics. I might, perhaps, say something about the representative element in it—a man is working a Rock Drill mounted on a tripod, the lines of which, in the drawing, continue the lines of his legs. The two lines converging on the centre of the design are indications of a rocky landscape. It is the other drawings which seem to have caused the most bewildered criticism; they have been called prosaic representations of anatomical details, 'medical drawings', and so on. It is perfectly obvious that they are not that. What prevents them being understood as expressions of ideas is quite a simple matter. People will admire the 'Rock Drill', because they have no preconceived notion as to how the thing expressed by it should be expressed. But with the other drawings concerned with birth the case is different. Take for example the drawing called 'Creation', a baby seen inside many folds. I might very roughly say that this was a non-sentimental restatement of an idea which, presented sentimentally and in the traditional manner, they would admire—an idea something akin to the 'Christmas crib' idea. If a traditional symbol had been used they would have been quite prepared to admire it. They cannot understand that the genius and sincerity of an artist lies in extracting afresh, from outside reality, a new means of expression. It seems curious that the people who in poetry abominate clichés and know that Nature, as it were, presses in on the poet to be used as metaphor, cannot understand the same thing when it occurs plastically. They seem unable to understand that an artist who has something to say will continually 'extract' from reality new methods of expression, and that these being personally felt will inevitably lack prettiness and will differ from traditional clichés. It must also be pointed out that the critics have probably themselves not been accustomed to think about generation, and so naturally find the drawings not understandable. I come now to the stupidest criticism of all, that of Mr. Ludovici.[5] It would probably occur to anyone who read Mr. Ludovici's article that he was a charlatan, but I think it worth while confirming this impression by further evidence. His activities are not confined to art. I remember coming across his name some years ago as the author of a very comical little book on Nietzsche, which was sent me for review.[6]

I shall devote some space to him here then, not because I consider him of the slightest importance, but because I consider it a duty, a very pleasant duty and one very much neglected in this country, to expose charlatans when one sees them. Apart from this general ground, the book on Nietzsche is worth considering, for it displays the same type of mind at work as in the article on art.

What, very briefly then, is the particular type of charlatan revealed in this book on Nietzsche. It gave one the impression of a little Cockney intellect which would have been more suitably employed indexing or in a lawyer's office, drawn by a curious kind of vanity into a region the realities of which must for ever remain incomprehensible to him. Mr. Ludovici, writing on Nietzsche, might be compared to a child of four in a theatre watching a tragedy based on adultery. The child would observe certain external phenomena, but as to the real structure of the tragedy, its real moving forces, it would naturally be rather hazy. You picture then a spruce little mind that has crept into the complicated rafters of philosophy—you imagine him perplexed, confused—you would be quite wrong, the apperceptive system acts like a stencil, it blots out all the complexity which forms the reality of the subject, so that he is simply unaware of its existence. He sees only what is akin to his mind's manner of working, as dogs out for a walk only scent other dogs, and as a Red Indian in a great town for the first time sees only the horses. While thus in reality remaining entirely outside the subject, he can manage to produce a shoddy imitation which may pass here in England, where there is no organised criticism by experts, but which in other countries, less happily democratic in these matters, would at once have been characterised as a piece of fudge. I have only drawn attention to this in order to

indicate the particular type of charlatan we have to deal with, so that you
may know what to expect when you come to consider him as an art
critic. I want to insist on the fact that you must expect to find a man
dealing with a subject which is in reality alien to him, ignorant of the
aims of the actors in that subject and yet maintaining an appearance
of adequate treatment with the help of a few tags.

That a man should write stupid and childish things about Nietzsche
does not perhaps matter very much; after all, we can read him for
ourselves. But when a little bantam of this kind has the impertinence to
refer to Mr. Epstein as a 'minor personality—of no interest to him', then
the matter becomes so disgusting that it has to be dealt with. The most
appropriate means of dealing with him would be a little personal violence. By that method one removes a nuisance without drawing more
attention to it than its insignificance deserves. But the unworthy sentiment of pity for the weak, which, in spite of Nietzsche, still moves us,
prevents us dealing drastically, with this rather light-weight superman. To
deal definitely then with his criticism. He dismissed Mr. Epstein with the
general principle 'Great art can only appear when the artist is animated by
the spirit of some great order or scheme of life.' I agree with this.
Experience confirms it. We find that the more serious kind of art that one
likes sprang out of organic societies like the Indian, Egyptian, and Byzantine. The modern obviously imposes too great a strain on an artist, the
double burden of not only expressing something, but of finding something in himself to be expressed. The more organic society effects an
economy in this. Moreover, you might go so far as to say that the
imposition of definite forms does not confine the artist but rather has the
effect of intensifying the individuality of his work (of Egyptian portraits).
I agree then with his general principle: we all agree. It is one of those
obvious platitudes which all educated people take for granted, in conversation and in print. It seems almost too comic for belief, but I begin to
suspect from Mr. Ludovici's continued use of the word 'I' in connection
with this principle, that he is under the extraordinary hallucination that
the principle is a personal discovery of his own. Really, Mr. Ludo, you
mustn't teach your grandmother to suck eggs in this way. That you
should have read of these truths in a book and have seen that they were
true is so much to the good. It is a fact of great interest to your father and
mother, it shows that you are growing up; but I can assure you it is a
matter of no public interest.

Admitting then, as I do, that the principle is true, I fail to see how it
enables Mr. Ludovici to dismiss Mr. Epstein in the way he does, on a
priori grounds. The same general principle would enable us to dismiss
every artist since the Renaissance. Take two very definite examples.

Michelangelo and Blake, neither of whom expressed any general 'scheme of life' imposed on them by society, but 'exalted the individual angle of vision of minor personalities'.

The whole thing is entirely beside the point. The business of an art critic is not to repeat tags, but to apply them to individual works of art. But of course that is precisely what a charlatan of the kind I have just described cannot do. It is quite possible for him in each gallery he goes to, to find some opportunity of repeating his tags, but when (as he was in his book on Nietzsche) he is entirely outside the subject, when he is really unaware of the nature of the thing which artists are trying to do, when he gets no real fun out of the pictures themselves, then, when he is pinned down before one actual picture and not allowed to wriggle away, he must either be dumb or make an ass of himself. It is quite easy to learn to repeat tags about 'balance', but put the man before one picture and make him follow with his finger, the lines which constitute that 'balance' and he can only shuffle and bring out more tags.

Now apply this test to Mr. Ludovici. We have seen him dismiss Mr. Epstein with a tag. When he makes individual judgments about individual pictures in The New English Art Club, what kind of judgments are they? We start off with Mr. John. Here he thinks he may be fairly safe; here is a reputation ten years old which has at last reached him. But, alas! we are not dealing with Mr. John as a painter, but with one painting by Mr. John. Mr. Ludovici falls. He picks out for extravagant praise Mr. John's cartoon 'The Flute of Pan', a thing universally admitted to be the worst thing John has ever exhibited, a macédoine of Botticelli–Mantegna drapery, Rossetti faces, rocky backgrounds from Leonardo, and a ridiculous girl on the right pretending to be dancing in order that she may show a Botticelli leg and foot, on the left a sort of crapulous Michelangelo and the little Peter Pan boy so much admired by Mr. Ludovici, the whole messy, smudged and in parts badly drawn, the design itself so clumsy that the right third of the picture is left so empty that one feels a girder should be run up from the corner to prop up the rest, which seems in imminent danger of toppling over. The whole thing expresses, with the impotence of old age, the kind of dream appropriate to puberty. It lacks precisely that quality of virility which Mr. Ludovici finds in it, and is admired by precisely those 'spinsterly', sloppy and romantic people whom, he imagines, dislike it. It is the result of no personal creative idea, but is entirely a derivative conglomeration of already existing pretty ideas. I emphasise this point because your critic insists so much on a picture being the expression of a definite 'scheme of life'. I am not dealing with this picture as Mr. Ludovici did with Mr. Epstein, contemptuously, but pointing out that it marks a degeneration, temporary perhaps, of a great talent.

Of the other pictures that he praises, it is only necessary to mention Von Glehn's No. 2,[7] which is merely a bad fake, and Mr. D. G. Well's hackneyed Victorian cliché,[8] and Mr. Steer's 'Sunset',[9] which expresses nothing but a romantic nostalgia. Are these the feeble derivative things the 'creators of new values' admire?

That a critic of this calibre should attempt to patronise Mr. Epstein is disgusting. I make this very hurried protest in the hope that I may induce those people who have perhaps been prejudiced by ignorant and biased criticism to go and judge for themselves.

Modern Art
I: The Grafton Group

[First published in NA 14/11 (15 Jan. 1914), 341–2; reprinted in FS 113–18.]

I am attempting in this series of articles to define the characteristics of a new constructive geometric art which seems to me to be emerging at the present moment. In a later series, to be called the 'Break up of the Renaissance', I shall attempt to show the relation between this art and a certain general changed outlook.

I am afraid that my use of the word 'new' here will arouse a certain prejudice in the minds of the kind of people that I am anxious to convince. I may say then that I use the word with no enthusiasm. I want to convince those people who regard the feeble romanticism which is always wriggling and vibrating to the stimulus of the word 'new', with a certain amount of disgust, that the art which they incline to condemn as decadent is in reality the new order for which they are looking. It seems to me to be the genuine expression of abhorrence of slop and romanticism which has quite mistakenly sought refuge in the conception of a classical revival. By temperament I should adopt the classical attitude myself. My assertion then that a 'new' art is being formed is not due to any desire on my part to perceive something 'new', but is forced on me almost against my inclination by an honest observation of the facts themselves.

In attempting thus to define the characteristics of a new movement a certain clearance of the ground is necessary. A certain work of dissociation and analysis is required, in connection with what is vaguely thought of as 'modern' in art. A writer on art may perform a useful function in pointing out that what is generally thought of as one living movement consists really of many parts, some of which are as a matter of fact quite dead. The words, 'modern', 'Post-Impressionist' and 'Cubist' are used as synonyms, not only in the more simple form of instinctive reaction to an unpleasing phenomena, but also in a more positive way, the psychology of which seems to me to be rather interesting. The Post-Impressionist or Cubist appearances, at first perceived chaotically as 'queer' and rejected as such, became after a mysterious act of conversion, a signal for exhilarated acceptance, irrespective of the quality of the painting itself. They give every picture, good or bad, which possesses them, a sort of cachet. But although this complex of qualities passes from the stage in which it is repulsive to that in which it is attractive, yet for most people it remains unanalysed. It must be pointed out that what has been grouped together as one, really contains within itself several diverse and even contradictory tendencies. One might separate the modern movement into three parts, to be roughly indicated as Post-Impressionism, analytical Cubism and a new constructive geometrical art. The first of these, and to a certain extent the second, seem to me to be necessary but entirely transitional stages leading up to the third, which is the only one containing possibilities of development.

This show at the Alpine Club provides a convenient illustration of these points.[1] Mr. Fry[2] organised the first Post-Impressionist exhibition in London and was thought to have established a corner in the movement. He probably regards himself, and is certainly regarded by many others, as the representative of the new direction in art. The earlier shows of the Grafton group were sufficiently comprehensive and varied to make this opinion seem plausible. . . . There was a mixture of a sort of æsthetic archaism and a more vigorous cubism which corresponded very well to the loose use of the words 'modern art' which I have just mentioned, and helped to maintain the illusion that the whole formed in reality one movement. But the departure of Mr. Wyndham Lewis, Mr. Etchells,[3] Mr. Nevinson[4] and several others has left concentrated in a purer form all the worked-out and dead elements in the movement. It has become increasingly obvious that Mr. Fry and his group are nothing but a kind of backwater, and it seems to me to be here worth while pointing out the character of this backwater. As you enter the room you almost know what to expect, from the effect of the general colour. It consists almost uniformly of pallid chalky blues, yellows and strawberry colours, with a strong family resemblance between all the pictures; in every case a kind of anæmic effect showing no personal or constructive use of colour. The subjects also are significant. One may recognise the whole familiar bag of tricks—the usual Cézanne landscapes, the still lifes, the Eves in their gardens, and the botched Byzantine. As the Frenchmen exhibited here have really no connection with the Grafton group, I will omit them and confine myself to the English painters. In Mr. Fry's landscape you can see his inability to follow a method to its proper conclusion. The colour is always rather sentimental and pretty. He thus accomplishes the extraordinary feat of adapting the austere Cézanne into something quite fitted for chocolate boxes. It is too tedious to go on mentioning mediocre stuff, so

I should like to point out the two things which are worth seeing, No. 29, a very interesting pattern by Mr. Roberts,[5] and M. Gaudier-Brzeska's sculpture.[6]

However, I find it more interesting to escape from this show for a minute, by discussing a general subject which is to a certain extent suggested by it—the exact place of archaism in the new movement. I want to maintain (i) that a certain archaism was a natural stage in the preparation of a new method of expression, and (ii) that the persistence of a feeble imitation of archaism, such as one gets in this show, is an absolutely unnecessary survival when this stage has been passed through.

In the first place then, how does it come about that a movement towards a new method of expression should contain so many archaic elements? How can a movement whose essence is the exact opposite of romanticism and nostalgie, which is striving towards a hard and definite structure in art, take the form of archaism? How can a sensibility so opposed to that which generally finds satisfaction in the archaic, make such use of it? What happens, I take it, is something of this kind: a certain change of direction takes place which begins negatively with a feeling of dissatisfaction with and reaction against existing art. But the new tendency, admitting that it exists, cannot at once find its own appropriate expression. But although the artist feels that he must have done with contemporary means of expression, yet a new and more fitting method is not easily created. Expression is by no means a natural thing. It is an unnatural, artificial, and, as it were, external thing which a man has to install himself in before he can manipulate it. The way from intention to expression does not come naturally as it were from in outwards. It in no way resembles the birth of Minerva. A gap between the intention and its actual expression in material exists, which cannot be bridged directly. A man has first to obtain a foothold in this, so to speak, alien and external world of material expression, at a point near to the one he is making for. He has to utilise some already existing method of expression, and work from that to the one that expresses his own personal conception more accurately and naturally. At the present moment this leads to archaism because the particular change of direction in the new movement is a striving towards a certain intensity which is already expressed in archaic form. This perhaps supplements what I said about the archaism of Mr. Epstein's 'carvings in flenite'.[7] It perhaps enables me to state more clearly the relation between those works and the more recent work represented by the drawings. You get a breaking away from contemporary methods of expression, a new direction, an intenser perception of things striving towards expression. And as this intensity is fundamentally the same kind of intensity as that expressed in certain archaic arts, it quite naturally and legitimately finds a foothold in these archaic yet permanent formulæ. But as this intensity is at the same time no romantic revival, but part of a real change of sensibility occurring now in the modern mind, and is coloured by a particular and original quality due to this fact, it quite as naturally develops from the original formula one which is for it, a purer and more accurate medium of expression. [That the great change in outlook is coming about naturally at the present moment, I shall attempt to demonstrate later by a consideration which has nothing whatever to do with art. I shall then be able to explain what I meant by the 'dregs of the Renaissance'.]

To return then to the discussion from which I started. A certain archaism it seems is at the beginning a help to an artist. Although it may afterwards be repudiated, it is an assistance in the construction of a new method of expression. Most of the artists who prepared the new movement passed through this stage. Picasso, for example, used many forms taken from archaic art, and other examples will occur to everyone. It might be objected that a direct line of development could be traced through Cézanne showing no archaic influence. But I think it would be true to say of Cézanne, even in much of his later work, that he seeks expression through forms that are to a certain extent archaic. So much then for the function of archaism. Apply this to what you find in the Grafton group. If it were only a matter of serious experimentation in archaic forms, after the necessity for that experimentation had passed by, the thing would be regrettable but not a matter for any violent condemnation. But you do not find anything of that kind, but merely a cultured and anæmic imitation of it. What in the original was a sincere effort towards a certain kind of intensity, becomes in its English dress a mere utilisation of the archaic in the spirit of the æsthetic. It is used as a plaything to a certain quaintness. In Mr. Duncan Grant's 'Adam and Eve',[8] for example, elements taken out of the extremely intense and serious Byzantine art are used in an entirely meaningless and pointless way. There is no solidity about any of the things; all of them are quite flimsy. One delightful review of the show described Mr. Fry's landscapes as having 'the fascination of reality seen through a cultured mind'. The word 'cultured' here explains a good deal. I feel about the whole show a typically Cambridge sort of atmosphere. I have a very vivid impression of what I mean here by Cambridge, as I have recently had the opportunity of observing the phenomenon at close quarters. I know the kind of dons who buy these pictures, the character of the dilettante appreciation they feel for them. It is so interesting and clever of the artist to use the archaic in this paradoxical way, so amusing to make Adam stand on his head, and the donkey's ear continue into the hills—gentle little Cambridge jokes.

It is all amusing enough in its way, a sort of æsthetic playing about. It can best be described in fact as a new disguise of æstheticism. It is not a new art, there is nothing new and creative about it. At first appearance the pictures seem to have no resemblance to pre-Raphaelitism. But when the spectator has overcome his first mild shock and is familiarised with them, he will perceive the fundamental likeness. Their 'queerness', such as it is, is not the same serious queerness of the pre-Raphaelites, it is perhaps only quaint and playful; but essentially the same English æsthetic is behind both, and essentially the same cultured reminiscent pleasure is given to the spectator. This being the basic constituent of both arts, just as the one ultimately declined into Liberty's, so there is no reason why the other should not find its grave in some emporium which will provide the wives of young and advanced dons with suitable house decoration.

What is living and important in new art must be looked for elsewhere.

Modern Art and Its Philosophy

[Delivered as a lecture to the Quest Society of London on 22 Jan. 1914, with the title 'The New Art and Its Philosophy' (letter from Herbert Read to C. K. Ogden, 16 Apr. 1923). The essay was not published until 1924, when Read included it in *S* 75–109, which is the source of this version. The footnote is Hulme's.]

I

My title is perhaps misleading, in that it lays emphasis on modern art itself, rather than on its philosophy. Only the last half of what I am going to say deals with the art itself; the first part is devoted to entirely general considerations, which seem to me to be necessary to its proper understanding. I know that this may appear an unnecessary and rather fantastic superstructure. An artist might feel that I was merely bringing in all kinds of vague literary considerations, which have very little to do with the art itself. New movements in art are generally accompanied by muddle-headed but enthusiastic attempts to connect them with quite unconnected movements in philosophy, which appear to the journalist's mind to be coloured by the same quality of excitement. There are people, for example, who try to connect cubism with Plato. The artist, recognising these interpretations as the mere confused sentimentality that they are, may yet accept them good-humouredly, in as far as they lend some kind of support to a new movement.

But it seems to me that there is another way of dealing with an art from a general point of view which follows the contours of the thing itself a little more closely. It may be justified in that it attempts to deal, not so much with the art itself, as with the language in which the artist or critic attempts to explain that art. The critic in explaining a new direction often falsifies it by his use of a vocabulary derived from the old position. The thought or vocabulary of one's period is an extraordinarily difficult thing to break away from. While an artist may have emancipated himself from his own period as far as his art is concerned, while a spectator may have emancipated himself by looking at the art of other periods in museums, yet the mental, or more accurately speaking, the linguistic emancipations of the two, may not have gone forward parallel with the artistic one.

Quite definitely what I mean is this: I think that the new art differs not in degree, but in kind, from the art we are accustomed to, and that there is a danger that the understanding of the new may be hindered by a way of looking on art which is only appropriate to the art that has preceded it. The general considerations I put forward are of this kind. This new art is geometrical in character, while the art we are accustomed to is vital[a] and organic. It so happens that there have been many other geometric arts in the past. I think that a consideration of these arts may help one to understand what is coming, and to avoid the falsification I have spoken of. I may also by this method be enabled to remove certain prejudices which stand in the way of appreciation of this art.

My remarks are likely to appear confused, as my argument, such as it is, is composed of three or four parts, only one of which I have space enough to develop in detail. I can perhaps give them more shape, by laying down to begin with certain theses which I assert to be true, but do not attempt to prove here:—

(1) There are two kinds of art, geometrical and vital, absolutely distinct in kind from one another. These two arts are not modifications of one and the same art but pursue different aims and are created for the satisfaction of different necessities of the mind.

(2) Each of these arts springs from and corresponds to a certain general attitude towards the world. You get long periods of time in which only one of these arts with its corresponding mental attitudes prevails. The vital art of Greece and the Renaissance corresponded to a certain attitude of mind and the geometrical has always gone with a different general attitude, of greater intensity than this.

And (3)—this is really the point I am making for—that the re-emergence of geometrical art may be the precursor of the re-emergence of the corresponding attitude towards the world, and so, of the break up of the Renaissance humanistic attitude. The fact that this change comes first in art, before it comes in thought, is easily understandable for this reason. So thoroughly are we soaked in the spirit of the period we live in,

---

[a] I might add a note here on my use of the word vital. This word instead of having the specific meaning it should have, has come to have the meaning of living in the sense of strong and creative as opposed to weak and imitative. In fact the difference between vital and non-vital has simply come to be the difference between good and bad. It need perhaps hardly be pointed out that my use of the word vital in this lecture has nothing whatever to do with this sense of the word. Vital and mechanical or geometrical arts may both be vital or non-vital in the current use of the word. A man might conceivably say that the geometrical Byzantine art displayed a certain lack of vitality in this sense. I might dispute that; but even if I did not I think that my use of the word vital, defined as I have defined it, is permissible.

so strong is its influence over us, that we can only escape from it in an unexpected way, as it were, a side direction like art.

I am emphasising then, the absolute character of the difference between these two arts, not only because it is important for the understanding of the new art itself, but because it enables me to maintain much wider theses.

That is the logical order in which I present my convictions. I did not naturally arrive at them in that order. I came to believe first of all, for reasons quite unconnected with art, that the Renaissance attitude was coming to an end, and was then confirmed in that by the emergence of this art. I commenced by a change in philosophy and illustrated this by a change in art rather than vice versa. A thesis like my last one is so sweeping that it sounds a little empty. It would be quite ludicrous for me to attempt to state such a position in the space of the half page I intend to devote to it, but perhaps I can make it sound more plausible by saying how I came personally to believe it. You will have to excuse my putting it in autobiographical shape, for, after all, the break-up of a general attitude if it ever occurs will be a collection of autobiographies. First of all comes the conviction that in spite of its apparent extraordinary variety, European philosophy since the Renaissance does form a unity. You can separate philosophy into two parts, the technical and scientific part, that which more properly would be called metaphysics, and another part in which the machinery elaborated in the first is used to express the philosopher's attitude towards the world, what may be called his conclusions. These emerge in the last chapter of the book. In the first chapters the philosopher may be compared to a man in armour; he intimidates you, as a kind of impersonal machine. In the last chapter you perceive him naked, as perfectly human. Every philosopher says the world is other than it seems to be; in the last chapter he tells you what he thinks it is. As he has taken the trouble to prove it, you may assume that he regards the final picture of the world he gives as satisfactory.

Now here is my point. In a certain sense, all philosophy since the Renaissance is satisfied with a certain conception of the relation of man to the world. Now what is this conception? You get the first hint of it in the beginnings of the Renaissance itself, in a person like Pico Della Mirandola, for example. You get the hint of an idea there of something, which finally culminates in a doctrine which is the opposite of the doctrine of original sin: the belief that man as a part of nature was after all something satisfactory. The change which Copernicus is supposed to have brought about is the exact contrary of the fact. Before Copernicus, man was not the centre of the world; after Copernicus he was. You get a change from a certain profundity and intensity to that flat and insipid optimism which, passing through its first stage of decay in Rousseau, has finally culminated in the state of slush in which we have the misfortune to live. If you want a proof of the radical difference between these two attitudes, you have only to look at the books which are written now on Indian religion and philosophy. There is a sheer anæmic inability to understand the stark uncompromising bleakness of this religious attitude.

It may seem paradoxical in view of the extraordinary emphasis laid on life by philosophy at the present day, to assert that this Renaissance attitude is coming to an end. But I think that this efflorescence is its last effort.

About the time that I arrived at this kind of conviction I saw Byzantine mosaics for the first time.[1] This led me a step further towards the conviction I have expressed in this thesis. I had got myself away from the contemporary view, and (as I shall illustrate later in the case of art, the first attempt to formulate a different attitude being always a return to archaism) I was inclined to hold a view not very different from that of that period. At that time, then, I was impressed by these mosaics, not as by something exotic, but as expressing quite directly an attitude I agreed with. Owing to this accident, I was able to see a geometrical art, as it were from the inside. I then saw how essential and necessary a geometrical character is in endeavouring to express a certain intensity.

Finally I recognised this geometrical character re-emerging in modern art. I am thinking particularly of certain pieces of sculpture I saw some years ago, of Mr Epstein's.

I had here then, very crudely, all the elements of the position that I put before in my three theses. At that time, in an essay by Paul Ernst on Byzantine art, I came across a reference to the work of Riegl[2] and Worringer. In the latter particularly I found an extraordinarily clear statement, founded on an extensive knowledge of the history of art, of a view very like the one I had tried to formulate. This last year I heard him lecture and had some conversation with him at the Berlin Congress of Æsthetics. What follows is practically an abstract of Worringer's views.

II

You have these two different kinds of art. You have first the art which is natural to you, Greek art and modern art since the Renaissance. In these arts the lines are soft and vital. You have other arts like Egyptian, Indian and Byzantine, where everything tends to be angular, where curves tend to be hard and geometrical, where the representation of the human body, for example, is often entirely non-vital, and distorted to fit into stiff lines and cubical shapes of various kinds.

What is the cause of the extraordinary difference between these geometrical arts and the arts we are accustomed to admire? Why do they show none of the qualities which we are accustomed to find in art?

We may at once put on one side the idea that the difference between archaic and later art is due to a difference of capacity, the idea that geometrical shapes are used because the artist had not the technical ability necessary for carving the more natural representation of the body. The characteristics of archaic art are not due to incapacity. In Egypt, at the time when the monumental sculpture showed a stylification as great as any we find in archaic art, the domestic art of the period exhibited a most astonishing realism. In pure technical ability in mastery of raw material, the Egyptians have never been surpassed. It is quite obvious that what they did was intentional.

We are forced back on the idea, then, that geometrical art differs from our own because the creators of that art had in view an object entirely different from that of the creators of more naturalistic art. The idea that an art is a satisfaction of some specific mental need, and so, that in looking at a work of art of this type it is necessary not only to think of the object itself, but of the desire it is intended to satisfy, is one which it is very difficult for us to realise for the following reason. The subjective side of an art is never forced on our notice, because it so happens that the arts with which we are familiar, the classical and our own, have the same subjective element. It never occurs to us therefore that classical art is the satisfaction of one among other possible desires, since we always think that this art is the satisfaction of *the* desire which must inevitably be behind all art. We thus erect the classical and our own conception of art into an absolute and look on all art before the classical as imperfect strivings towards it, and all after as decadence from it.

It is necessary to realise that all art is created to satisfy a particular desire—that when this desire is satisfied, you call the work beautiful; but that if the work is intended to satisfy a desire and mental need different from your own, it will necessarily appear to you to be grotesque and meaningless. We naturally do not call these geometrical arts beautiful because beauty for us is the satisfaction of a certain need, and that need is one which archaic art never set out to satisfy. What from our standpoint appears as the greatest distortion must have been, for the people who produced it, the highest beauty and the fulfilment of some desire.

Consider the difference between these two kinds, then, from this point of view.

Take first the art which is most natural to us. What tendency is behind this, what need is it designed to satisfy?

This art as contrasted with geometrical art can be broadly described as naturalism or realism—using these words in their widest sense and entirely excluding the mere imitation of nature. The source of the pleasure felt by the spectator before the products of art of this kind is a feeling of increased vitality, a process which German writers on æsthetics call empathy (Einfühlung). This process is perhaps a little too complicated for me to describe it shortly here, but putting the matter in general terms, we can say that any work of art we find beautiful is an objectification of our own pleasure in activity, and our own vitality. The worth of a line or form consists in the value of the life which it contains for us. Putting the matter more simply we may say that in this art there is always a feeling of liking for, and pleasure in, the forms and movements to be found in nature. It is obvious therefore that this art can only occur in a people whose relation to outside nature is such that it admits of this feeling of pleasure in its contemplation.

Turn now to geometrical art. It most obviously exhibits no delight in nature and no striving after vitality. Its forms are always what can be described as stiff and lifeless. The dead form of a pyramid and the suppression of life in a Byzantine mosaic show that behind these arts there must have been an impulse, the direct opposite of that which finds satisfaction in the naturalism of Greek and Renaissance art.

This is what Worringer calls the *tendency to abstraction*.

What is the nature of this tendency? What is the condition of mind of the people whose art is governed by it?

It can be described most generally as a feeling of separation in the face of outside nature.

While a naturalistic art is the result of a happy pantheistic relation between man and the outside world, the tendency to abstraction, on the contrary, occurs in races whose attitude to the outside world is the exact contrary of this. This feeling of separation naturally takes different forms at different levels of culture.

Take first, the case of more primitive people. They live in a world whose lack of order and seeming arbitrariness must inspire them with a certain fear. One may perhaps get a better description of what must be their state of mind by comparing it to the fear which makes certain people unable to cross open spaces. The fear I mean here is mental, however, not physical. They are dominated by what Worringer calls a kind of spiritual 'space-shyness' in face of the varied confusion and arbitrariness of existence. In art this state of mind results in a desire to create a certain abstract geometrical shape, which, being durable and permanent shall be a refuge from the flux and impermanence of outside nature. The need which art satisfies here, is not the delight in the forms of nature, which is a characteristic of all vital arts, but the exact contrary. In the reproduction of natural objects there is an attempt to purify them of their characteristically living qualities in order to make them necessary and immovable. The changing is translated into something fixed and necessary. This leads to rigid lines and dead crystalline forms, for pure geometrical regularity gives a certain pleasure to men troubled by the obscurity of outside appearance. The geometrical line is something absolutely distinct from the messiness, the confusion, and the accidental details of existing things.

It must be pointed out that this condition of fear is in no sense a necessary presupposition of the tendency to abstraction. The necessary presupposition is the idea of disharmony or separation between man and nature. In peoples like the Indian or the Byzantine this feeling of separation takes quite another form.

To sum up this view of art then: it cannot be understood by itself, but must be taken as one element in a general process of adjustment between man and the outside world. The character of that relation determines the character of the art. If there is a difference of 'potential' between man and the outside world, if they are at different levels, so that the relation between them is, as it were, a steep inclined plane, then the adjustment between them in art takes the form of a tendency to abstraction. If on the contrary there is no disharmony between man and the outside world, if they are both on the same level, on which man feels himself one with nature and not separate from it, then you get a naturalistic art.

The art of a people, then, will run parallel to its philosophy and general world outlook. It is a register of the nature of the opposition between man and the world. Each race is in consequence of its situation and character inclined to one of these two tendencies, and its art would give you a key to its psychology.

It is easy to trace these parallel changes. I have spoken of that feeling of space-shyness which produced the tendency to abstraction in primitive art. This tendency would have been impossible in the case of a people like the Greeks at the time when they had finally got free from the oriental elements of their origins and had not fallen afresh to oriental tendencies. In such a people you get a feeling of confidence in face of the world which expresses itself in religion in a certain anthropomorphism. The feeling of disharmony with the world had been destroyed by certain favourable conditions and by increased knowledge (Rationalism). You can speak here, then, of a classical religious period as you speak of a classical art period. Both are only different manifestations of the same classical conception which Goethe defined as that in which man 'feels himself one with nature and consequently looks upon the outside world not as something strange, but as something which he recognises as answering to his own feelings'.

In the case of the orientals the feeling of separation from the world could not be dispelled by knowledge. Their sense of the unfathomable existence was greater than that of the Greeks. A satisfaction with appearances is limited to Europe. It is only there that the superhuman abstract idea of the divine has been expressed by banal representation. No knowledge could damp down the Indian inborn fear of the world, since it stands, not as in the case of primitive man before knowledge, but above it. Their art consequently remained geometrical.

It is in the light of this tendency to abstraction that I wish to deal with modern art. Before doing that, however, I want to make the tendency clearer by giving some concrete examples of its working in sculpture.

In the endeavour to get away from the flux of existence, there is an endeavour to create in contrast, an absolutely enclosed material individuality. Abstraction is more difficult in the round than in the flat. With three dimensions we get the relativism and obscurity of appearance. A piece of sculpture in the round seems quite as lost in its context as does the natural object itself. There is consequently stronger stylification used in the round than is necessary in the relief. In archaic Greek sculpture, for example, the arms are bound close to the body, any division of the surface is as far as possible avoided and unavoidable divisions and articulations are given in no detail. The first gods were always pure abstractions without any resemblance to life. Any weakening of these abstract forms and approximation to reality would have let in change and life and so would have done what it was desired to avoid—it would have taken the thing out of eternity and put it into time. In monumental art, the abstract and inorganic is always used to make the organic seem durable and eternal. The first rule of monumental art must be a strong inclosure of cubical forms. It is ridiculous to suppose that the masons who carved the face of an archaic figure did not possess the capacity to separate the arms or legs from the body. The fact that they did so later in classical Greek art was not due to a progress in technical ability. The Greeks left behind the intensity of these cubical forms and replaced the abstract by the organic simply because, as their attitude to the world changed, they had different intentions. Having attained a kind of optimistic rationalism they no longer felt any desire for abstraction. They did not create gods like these earlier ones because they no longer possessed any religious intensity.

When we turn to Egyptian art, we find that in the endeavour to escape from anything that might suggest the relative and impermanent there is always the same tendency to make all the surfaces as flat as possible. In the sitting figures the legs and the body form a cubical mass out of which only the shoulders and head appear as necessary individualisation. The treatment of drapery and hair is only another example of this desire to make what is most obviously flexible and impermanent look fixed.

III

I come now to the application of the distinction thus elaborately constructed between geometrical and vital art to what is going on at the present moment.

If the argument I have followed is correct, I stand committed to two statements:—

(1) ... that a new geometrical art is emerging which may be considered as different in kind from the art which preceded it, it being much more akin to the geometrical arts of the past, and

(2) ... that this change from a vital to a geometrical art is the product of and will be accompanied by a certain change of sensibility, a certain change of general attitude, and that this new attitude will differ in kind from the humanism which has prevailed from the Renaissance to now, and will have certain analogies to the attitude of which geometrical art was the expression in the past.

Naturally both of these sweeping statements run a good deal ahead of the facts and of my ability to prove them. I must here, therefore, make the same qualification and warning about both of the statements. Though both the new Weltanschauung and the new geometrical art will have certain analogies with corresponding periods in the past, yet it is not for a moment to be supposed that there is anything more than an analogy here. The new geometrical art will probably in the end not in the least resemble archaic art, nor will the new attitude to the world be very much like the Byzantine, for example. As to what actually they both will culminate in, it would obviously be ludicrous for me to attempt to say. It would be more ludicrous to attempt to do this in the case of the general attitude, than it would in the case of the art itself. For one of my points at the beginning of this paper was that one's mind is so soaked in the thought and language of the period, that one can only perceive the break-up of that period in a region like art which is—when one's mind is focussed on thought itself—a kind of side activity.

One can only make certain guesses at the new attitude by the use of analogy. Take two other attitudes of the past which went with geometrical art: say primitive and Byzantine. There is a certain likeness and a certain unlikeness in relation to man and the outside world. The primitive springs from what we have called a kind of mental space-shyness, which is really an attitude of fear before the world; the Byzantine from what may be called, inaccurately, a kind of contempt for the world. Though these two attitudes differ very much, yet there is a common element in the idea of separation as opposed to the more intimate feeling towards the world in classical and renaissance thought. In comparison with the flat and insipid optimism of the belief in progress, the new attitude may be in a certain sense inhuman, pessimistic. Yet its pessimism will not be world-rejecting in the sense in which the Byzantine was.

But one is on much surer ground in dealing with the art itself. On what grounds does one base this belief that a new geometrical art is appearing? There is first the more negative proof provided by a change of taste.

You get an extraordinary interest in similar arts in the past, in Indian sculpture, in Byzantine art, in archaic art generally, and this interest is not as before a merely archæological one. The things are liked directly, almost as they were liked by the people who made them, as being direct expressions of an attitude which you want to find expressed. I do not think for a moment that this is conscious. I think that under the influence of a false conception of the nature of art, that most people, even when they feel it, falsify their real appreciation by the vocabulary they use— naïve, fresh, charm of the exotic, and so on.

A second and more positive proof is to be found in the actual creation of a new modern geometrical art.

You get at the present moment in Europe a most extraordinary confusion in art, a complete breaking away from tradition. So confusing is it that most people lump it altogether as one movement and are unaware that it is in fact composed of a great many distinct and even contradictory elements, being a complex movement of parts that are merely reactionary, parts that are dead, and with one part only containing the possibility of development. When I speak of a new complex geo-metrical art then, I am not thinking of the whole movement. I am speaking of one element which seems to be gradually hardening out, and separating itself from the others. I don't want anyone to suppose, for example, that I am speaking of futurism which is, in its logical form, the exact opposite of the art I am describing, being the deification of the flux, the last efflorescence of impressionism. I also exclude a great many things which—as I shall attempt to show later were perhaps necessary prelimi-naries to this art, but which have now been passed by—most of the work in fact which is included under the term post-impressionism—Gauguin, Maillol, Brancusi.

If space allowed I could explain why I also exclude certain elements of cubism, what I might call analytical cubism—the theories about interpenetration which you get in Metzinger[3] for example.

IV

Before dealing actually with this work I ought to qualify what I have said a little. I have put the matter in a rather too ponderous way by talking about the new general attitude. That is perhaps dealing with the matter on the wrong plane. It would have been quite possible for this change to come about without the artists themselves being conscious of this change of general attitude towards the world at all. When I say 'conscious' I mean conscious in this formulated and literary fashion. The change of attitude would have taken place, but it might only have manifested itself in a certain change of sensibility in the artist, and in so far as he expresses himself in words, in a certain change of vocabulary. The change of attitude betrays itself by changes in the epithets that a man uses, perhaps disjointedly, to express his admiration for the work he admires. Most of us cannot state our position, and we use adjectives which in themselves do not explain what we mean, but which, for a group for a certain time, by a kind of tacit convention become the 'porters' or 'bearers' of the complex new attitude which we all recognise that we have in company, but which we cannot describe or analyse. At the present time you get this change shown in the value given to certain adjectives. Instead of epithets like graceful, beautiful, etc., you get epithets like austere, mechanical, clear cut, and bare, used to express admiration.

Putting on one side all this talk of a 'new attitude' of which the artist in some cases may not be conscious at all, what is the nature of the new sensibility which betrays itself in this change of epithets? Putting it at its lowest terms, namely that a man was unconscious of any change of aim, but only felt that he preferred certain shapes, certain forms, etc., and that his work was moulded by that change of sensibility, what is the nature of that change of sensibility at the present moment? Expressed generally, there seems to be a desire for austerity and bareness, a striving towards structure and away from the messiness and confusion of nature and natural things. Take a concrete matter like the use of line and surface. In all art since the Renaissance, the lines used are what may be called vital lines. In any curve there is a certain empirical variation which makes the curve not mechanical. The lines are obviously drawn by a hand and not by a machine. You get Ruskin saying that no artist could draw a straight line. As far as sensibility goes you get a kind of shrinking from anything that has the appearance of being mechanical. An artist, suppose, has to draw a part of a piece of machinery, where a certain curve is produced by the intersection of a plane and a cylinder. It lies in the purpose of the engine and it is obviously the intention of the engineer that the line shall be a perfect and mechanical curve. The artists in drawing the two surfaces and their intersection would shrink from reproducing this mechanical accuracy, would instinctively pick out all the accidental scratches which make the curve empirical and destroy its geometrical and mechanical character. In the new art on the contrary there is no shrinking of that kind whatever. There is rather a desire to avoid those lines and surfaces which look pleasing and organic, and to use lines which are clean, clear-cut and mechanical. You will find artists expressing admiration for engineer's drawings, where the lines are clean, the curves all geometrical, and the colour, laid on to show the shape of a cylinder for example, gradated absolutely mechanically. You will find a sculptor disliking the pleasing kind of patina that comes in time on an old bronze and expressing admiration for the hard clean surface of a piston rod. If we take this to be in fact the new sensibility, and regard it as the culmination of the process of breaking-up and transformation in art, that has been proceeding since the impressionists, it seems to me that the history of the last twenty years becomes more intelligible. It suddenly enables one to look at the matter in a new light.

Put the matter in an a priori way. Admitting the premiss that a new direction is gradually defining itself, what would you expect to happen? As a help to this reconstruction, recall what was said about the relation between the various geometrical arts of the past at the beginning of the last part of my paper, to the effect that there are always certain common elements, but also that each period has its own specific qualities. This new art, towards which things were working, was bound, then, to have certain elements in common with past geometric archaic arts, but at the same time as an art springing up to-day, it would necessarily exhibit certain original and peculiar qualities due to that fact. Consider then the beginning of the movement. No man at the beginning of a movement of this kind can have any clear conception of its final culmination—that would be to anticipate the result of a process of creation. Of which of the two elements of the new geometric art—that which it has in common with similar arts in the past, or that which is specific and peculiar to it—is an artist most likely to be conscious at the beginning of a movement? Most obviously of those elements which are also to be found in the past. Here then you get the explanation of the fact which may have puzzled some people, that a new and modern art, something which was to culminate in a use of structural organisation akin to machinery, should have begun by what seemed like a romantic return to barbarous and primitive art, apparently inspired by a kind of nostalgia for the past.

Another cause reinforcing the tendency to the archaic is the difficulty of at once finding an appropriate method of expression. Though the artist feels that he must have done with the contemporary means of expression, yet a new and more fitting method is not easily created. The way from intention to expression does not come naturally, as it were from in outwards. A man has first to obtain a foothold in this, so to speak, alien and external world of material expression, at a point near the one he is making for. He has to utilise some already existing methods of expression and work from them to the one that expresses his own personal conception more accurately and naturally. What happened then was this—a certain change of direction took place, beginning negatively with a feeling of dissatisfaction with, and reaction against, existing art. You get a breaking away from contemporary methods of expression, a new direction, an intenser perception of things striving towards expression, and as this intensity was fundamentally the same kind of intensity as that expressed in certain archaic arts, it quite naturally and legitimately found a foothold in these archaic yet permanent formulæ. A certain archaicism then, just as it is at the beginning helpful to an artist though he may afterwards repudiate it, is an almost necessary stage in the preparation of a new movement.

This seems to me to be the best way of describing and understanding the movement that has had the label of Post-impressionism affixed to it in England. Though perhaps the individual artists of that time would never have gone further than they did, yet looking at them from this general point of view, it is best to regard them as the preliminary and temporary stage of experimentation in the preparation of a suitable method of expression for a new and intenser sensibility. It is not necessary to do more than mention an obvious example such as Gauguin.

The case of Cézanne is more important for it is out of him that the second stage of the movement that I have called analytical Cubism has developed. It is also interesting since it is only lately that it has been recognised how fundamentally Cézanne differed from his contemporaries, the impressionists. It was against their fluidity that he reacted. He wanted, so he said, to make of impressionism something solid and durable like old art.

Before commenting on this, I must recall again the distinction I have used between naturalism and abstraction. I want to point out that even in a period of natural and vital art a certain shadow of the tendency to abstraction still remains in the shape of formal composition. Some kinds of composition are attempts to make the organic look rigid and durable.

In most landscapes, of course, the composition is rhythmical and not formal in this extreme sense, and so it is not an expression of a tendency to abstraction. With this in mind, look at one of Cézanne's latest pictures, 'Women Bathing', where all the lines are ranged in a pyramidal shape, and the women are distorted to fit this shape. You will, if you are accustomed to look for pleasing rhythmical composition in a picture, be repelled rather than attracted by this pyramidal composition. The form is so strongly accentuated, so geometric in character, that it almost lifts the painting out of the sphere of 'vital' art into that of abstract art. It is much more akin to the composition you find in the Byzantine mosaic (of the empress Theodora) in Ravenna, than it is to anything which can be found in the art of the Renaissance.

If you deny the existence of a 'tendency to abstraction' at all in art, you will naturally deny the apparent appearance of it in Cézanne. You will say that the simplifications of planes (out of which of course cubism grew), is not due to any 'tendency to abstraction', but is the result of an effort to give a more solid kind of reality in the object. You will assert that when Cézanne said that the forms of nature could be reduced to the cone, the cylinder, and the sphere, that he meant something quite different from the obvious meaning of his words. This misconception of Cézanne results from the fact that you have refused to see the obvious truth, that there is in him a hint of that 'tendency to abstraction' that is found in certain arts of the past. The difference between the use of planes in Cézanne and in the cubists themselves, is not that between a simplification based on observation of nature and a mere playing about with formulæ. Both simplifications are based on the research into nature, but their value to the artist does not lie in their origin, but in the use that is made of them.

That is, I think, how one ought to look on these painters, quite apart from the qualities they show as painters belonging to the past vital period of painting. They are interesting to us as showing the first gradual emergence in a state of experimentation, of this new geometrical art which will be created by a tendency to abstraction. I should, properly speaking, now attempt to define the characteristics of the new art as they emerge from this experimental stage, but that is difficult for me to do as the thing itself is still to a large extent experimental. I cannot say what artists will make of this method; the construction of this is their business, not mine. That is the fun of the thing. I await myself the development of that art with the greatest impatience. My feeling about the matter is this. I look at most cubist pictures with a certain feeling of depression. They are from a certain point of view, confused. If I may be allowed to go against my own principles for a minute, and to describe abstract things in a metaphor borrowed from organic life, I should say they look rather like embryos. I think they will soon open out and grow distinct. I picture what is about to happen in this way. A man whose form is, as it were, dimly discerned in hay, stands up, shakes the hay off him, and proceeds to walk, *i.e.* he proceeds to do something. Dropping the metaphor then, cubism ceases to be analytical, and is transformed into a constructive geometrical art. The elements and the method patiently worked out by analysis begin to be used. If you want a concrete example of the difference I mean, compare the work illustrated in Metzinger's book on cubism, with that of Mr Epstein and Mr Lewis. This difference seems to me to be important for this reason. There are many who, when the matter has been explained to them, can understand what the early cubists are trying to do. They follow the sort of analysis they have made, but they cannot for the life of them see how it can go on, or how it can develop into a new art. And I believe that this is in reality the source of the baffled feeling of most people when confronted by such art.

V

In conclusion, I might hazard some conjectures as to the probable nature of the specific and peculiar quality which will differentiate this new geometrical art from its predecessors. As far as one can see, the new 'tendency towards abstraction' will culminate, not so much in the simple geometrical forms found in archaic art, but in the more complicated ones associated in our minds with the idea of machinery. In this association with machinery will probably be found the specific differentiating quality of the new art. It is difficult to define properly at the present moment what this relation to machinery will be. It has nothing whatever to do with the superficial notion that one must beautify machinery. It is not a question of dealing with machinery in the spirit, and with the methods of existing art, but of the creation of a new art having an organisation, and governed by principles, which are at present exemplified unintentionally, as it were, in machinery. It is hardly necessary to repeat at this stage of the argument, that it will not aim at the satisfaction of that particular mental need, which in a vital art results in the production of what is called beauty. It is aiming at the satisfaction of a different mental need altogether. When Mr Roger Fry, therefore, talks as he did lately, of 'machinery being as beautiful as a rose' he demonstrates what is already obvious from his work, that he has no conception whatever of this new art, and is in fact a mere verbose sentimentalist.

This association of art and machinery suggests all kinds of problems. What will be the relation to the artist and the engineer? At present the artist is merely receptive in regard to machinery. He passively admires, for example, the superb steel structures which form the skeletons of modern buildings, and whose gradual envelopment in a parasitic covering of stone is one of the daily tragedies to be witnessed in London streets. Will the artist always remain passive, or will he take a more active part? The working out of the relation between art and machinery can be observed at present in many curious ways. Besides the interest in machinery itself, you get the attempt to create in art, structures whose organisation, such as it is, is very like that of machinery. Most of Picasso's paintings, for instance, whatever they may be labelled, are at bottom studies of a special kind of machinery.

But here an apparently quite legitimate objection might be raised. The desire to create something mechanical in this sense might be admitted as understandable, but the question would still be asked, 'Why make use of the human body in this art, why make that look like a machine?' Those who are accustomed to a vital art, the basis of whose appreciation of art is what I have called empathy, and who consequently derive pleasure from the reproduction of the actual details of life, are repulsed by an art in which something which is intended to be a body, leaves out all these details and qualities they expect.

Take for example one of Mr Wyndham Lewis's pictures. It is obvious that the artist's only interest in the human body was in a few abstract mechanical relations perceived in it, the arm as a lever and so on. The interest in living flesh as such, in all that detail that makes it vital, which is pleasing, and which we like to see reproduced, is entirely absent.

But if the division that I have insisted on in this paper—the division between the two different tendencies producing two different kinds of art—is valid, then this objection falls to the ground. What you get in Mr Lewis's pictures is what you always get inside any geometrical art. All art of this character turns the organic into something not organic, it tries to translate the changing and limited, into something unlimited and necessary. The matter is quite simple. However strong the desire for abstraction, it cannot be satisfied with the reproduction of merely inorganic forms. A perfect cube looks stable in comparison with the flux of appearance, but one might be pardoned if one felt no particular interest in the eternity of a cube; but if you can put man into some geometrical shape which lifts him out of the transience of the organic, then the matter is different. In pursuing such an aim you inevitably, of course, sacrifice the pleasure that comes from reproduction of the natural.

Another good example to take, would be Mr Epstein's latest work, the drawings for sculpture in the first room of his exhibition. The subjects of all of them are connected with birth. They are objected to because they are treated in what the critics are pleased to term a cubistic manner. But this seems to me a most interesting example of what I have just been talking about. The tendency to abstraction, the desire to turn the organic into something hard and durable, is here at work, not on something simple, such as you get in the more archaic work, but on something much more complicated. It is, however, the same tendency at work in both. Abstraction is much greater in the second case, because generation, which is the very essence of all the qualities which we have here called organic, has been turned into something as hard and durable as a geo-metrical figure itself.

The word machinery here suggests to me a point which requires a short discussion. You admit here this change of sensibility. You find the artists seeking out and using forms and surfaces which artists of our immediate past have always shrunk from. What is the cause of this change of sensibility? Any one who has agreed with the historical part of this paper will probably agree that this change of sensibility follows from a certain change in intention in art, the tendency towards abstraction instead of towards empathy. But another explanation may be given which, while it has an appearance of making the thing reasonable, seems to me to be fallacious. It may be said that an artist is using mechanical lines because he lives in an environment of machinery. In a landscape you would use softer and more organic lines. This seems to me to be using the materialist explanation of the origin of an art which has been generally rejected. Take the analogous case of the influence of raw material on art. The nature of material is never without a certain influence. If they had not been able to use granite, the Egyptians would probably not have carved in the way they did. But then the material did not produce the style. If Egypt had been inhabited by people of Greek race, the fact that the material was granite, would not have made them produce anything like Egyptian sculpture. The technical qualities of a material can thus never create a style. A feeling for form of a certain kind must always be the source of an art. All that can be said of the forms suggested by the technical qualities of the material is that they must not contradict this intended form. They can only be used when the inclination and taste to which they are appropriate already exist. So, though steel is not the material of the new art, but only its environment, we can, it seems to me, legitimately speak of it exercising the kind of influence that the use of granite did on Egyptian art, no more and no less.

The point I want to emphasise is that the use of mechanical lines in the new art is in no sense merely a reflection of mechanical environment. It is a result of a change of sensibility which is, I think, the result of a change of attitude which will become increasingly obvious.

Finally I think that this association with the idea of machinery takes away any kind of dilettante character from the movement and makes it seem more solid and more inevitable.

It seems to me beyond doubt that this, whether you like it or not, is the character of the art that is coming. I speak of it myself with enthusiasm, not only because I appreciate it for itself, but because I believe it to be the precursor of a much wider change in philosophy and general outlook on the world.

Modern Art
II: A Preface Note and Neo-Realism

[First published in *NA* 14/15 (12 Feb. 1914), 467–9; reprinted in *FS* 119–28.]

As in these articles I intend to skip about from one part of my argument to another, as occasion demands, I might perhaps give them a greater appearance of shape by laying down as a preliminary three theses that I want to maintain.

1. There are two kinds of art, geometrical or abstract, and vital and realistic art, which differ absolutely in kind from the other. They are not modifications of one and the same art, but pursue different aims and are created to satisfy a different desire of the mind.

2. Each of these arts springs from, and corresponds to, a certain general attitude towards the world. You get long periods of time in which only one of these arts and its corresponding mental attitude prevails. The naturalistic art of Greece and the Renaissance corresponded to a certain rational humanistic attitude towards the universe, and the geometrical has always gone with a different attitude of greater intensity than this.

3. The re-emergence of geometrical art at the present day may be the precursor of the re-emergence of the corresponding general attitude towards the world, and so of the final break-up of the Renaissance.

This is the logical order in which I state the position. Needless to say, I did not arrive at it in that way. I shall try to make a sweeping generalisation like the last a little less empty by putting the matter in an autobiographical form. I start with the conviction that the Renaissance attitude is breaking up and then illustrate it by the change in art, and not vice versa. First came the reaction against the Renaissance philosophy, and the adoption of the attitude which I said went with the geometrical art.

Just at this time I saw Byzantine mosaic for the first time. I was then impressed by these mosaics, not as something exotic or 'charming', but as expressing quite directly an attitude which I to a certain extent agreed with. The important thing about this for me was that I was then, owing to this accidental agreement, able to see a geometrical art, as it were, from the inside. This altered my whole view of such arts. I realised for the first time that their geometrical character is essential to the expression of the intensity they are aiming at. It seemed clear that they differed absolutely from the vital arts because they were pursuing a different intention, and that what we, expecting other qualities from art, look on as dead and lifeless, were the necessary means of expression for this other intention.

Finally I recognised this geometrical re-emerging in modern art. I had here then very crudely all the elements of the position that I stated in my three theses. At that time, in an essay by Paul Ernst on religious art, I came across a reference to the work of Riegl and Worringer. In the latter particularly I found an extraordinarily clear statement founded on an extensive knowledge of the history of art, of a view very like the one I had tried to formulate. I heard him lecture last year and had an opportunity of talking with him at the Berlin Æsthetic Congress. I varied to a certain extent from my original position under the influence of his vocabulary, and that influence will be seen in some, at any rate, of the articles.

* * *

To turn now to Mr. Ginner's defence of Neo-Realism.[1] His article having somewhat the character of a painter's apologia, inevitably raises points over the whole range of the subject. I confine myself therefore to the main argument, which, put shortly, is that (1) All good art is realistic. Academism is the result of the adoption by weak painters of the creative artist's personal method of interpreting nature, and the consequent creation of formulæ, without contact with nature. (2) The new movement in art is merely an academic movement of the kind, springing from the conversion of Cézanne's mannerisms into formulæ. (3) The only remedy is a return to realism. Only a realistic method can keep art creative and vital.

These statements are based on such an extraordinarily confused and complicated mass of assumptions that I cannot give any proper refutation. I shall just try to show exactly what assumptions are made, and to indicate in a series of notes and assertions an opposite view of art to Mr. Ginner's. I can only give body to these assertions and prove them much later in the series.

Taking first his condemnation of the new movement as academic, being based on the use of formulæ. My reply to this is that the new movement does not use *formulæ*, but *abstractions*, quite a different thing. Both are 'unlike nature', but while the one is unlike, owing to a lack of vitality in the art, resulting in dead conventions, the other is unlike, of deliberate intent, and is very far from being dead. Mr. Ginner's misconception of the whole movement is due to his failure to make this distinction, a failure ultimately arising from the assumption that art must be realistic. He fails to recognise the existence of the abstract geometric art referred to in my prefatory note.

If you will excuse the pedantry of it, I think I can make the matter clearer by using a diagram:

$$R \ldots\ldots\ldots p_{(r)} \ldots\ldots\ldots a_{(r)} \ldots\ldots\ldots A$$

I take (R) to represent reality. As one goes from left to right one gets further and further from reality. The first step away being $p_{(r)}$, that is the artist's interpretation of nature. The next step $a_{(r)}$ being an art using abstractions (a), with a certain representative element $_{(r)}$. The element (a) owes its significance to, and is dependent on the other end (A) of this kind of spectrum—a certain 'tendency to abstraction'. I assert that these are two arts, the one focussed round (R), which is moved by a delight in natural forms, and the other springing from the other end, making use of abstractions as a method of expression. I am conscious that this is the weak point of my argument, for I cannot give body to this conception of the 'expressive use of abstraction' till later on in the series.

Looking at the matter from this point of view, what is the source of Mr. Ginner's fallacy? He admits that $p_{(r)}$ is the personal interpretation of reality, but as he would deny the possibility of an abstract art altogether, any further step away from reality must appear to him as decay, and the only way he can explain the (a) in $a_{(r)}$ is to look on it as a degeneration of (p) in $p_{(r)}$. An abstraction to him then can only mean the decay of mannerism in formulæ which comes about when the artist has lost contact with nature, and there is no personal first-hand observation. When, therefore, Mr. Ginner says the adoption of formulæ leads to the decay of an art, it is obvious that this must be true if by art you mean realistic art. Inside such art, whose raison d'être is its connection with nature, the use of formulæ, i.e., a lack of personal, creative and sincere observation, must inevitably lead to decay. But here comes the root of the whole fallacy. Realistic art is not the only kind of art. If everything hangs on the (R) side of my diagram then the (a) in $a_{(r)}$ must seem a decayed form of (p) in $p_{(r)}$. But in this other abstract art the (a) in $a_{(r)}$ gets its whole meaning and significance from its dependence on the other end of the scale A, i.e., from its use by a creative artist as a method of expression. Looked at from this point of view, the position of *abstraction* is quite a different one. The *abstractions* used in this other art will not bring about a decadence, they are an essential part of its method. Their almost geometrical and non-vital characters is not the result of weakness and lack of vitality in the art. They are not dead conventions, but the product of a creative process just as active as that in any realist art. To give a concrete example of the difference between formula and abstraction. Late Greek art decays into formulæ. But the art before the classical made deliberate use of certain abstractions differing in kind from the formulæ used in the decadence. They were used with intention, to get a certain kind of intensity. The truth of this view is conveniently illustrated by the history of Greek ornament, where abstract and geometrical forms precede natural forms instead of following them.

To these abstractions, the hard things Mr. Ginner says about formulæ have no application.

We shall never get any clear argument on this subject, then, until you agree to distinguish these two different uses of the word formula. (1) Conventional dead mannerism. (2) Abstraction, equally unlike nature, but used in a creative art as a method of expression.

The first effort of the realists then to give an account of abstraction comes to grief. Abstractions are not formulæ. In their effort to make the matter seem as reasonable as possible the realists have a second way of conceiving the nature of abstractions which is equally misleading. They admit the existence of *decorative* abstractions. When they have managed to give partial praise to the new movement in this way, they then pass on to condemn it. They assert that the repetition of empty decorative forms must soon come to an end, that pure pattern does not contain within itself the possibility of development of a complete art. But their modified approval and their condemnation are alike erroneous. This second mis-conception of abstractions as being decorative formulæ, is as mistaken as the first conception of them as being conventionalised mannerisms. Like the first, it springs from a refusal to recognise the existence of an art based on the creative use of abstraction, an art focussed on the right hand side (A) of my diagram. As long as that is denied, then abstractions must inevitably be either conventionalised mannerisms or decorative. They are neither.

Now to apply the first distinction between *formulæ* and *abstraction* to Mr. Ginner's argument about the new movement in art. This art un-doubtedly uses abstraction. Are these abstractions *formulæ* in his sense of the word or not? If they are, then his argument is valid and we are in presence of a new academic movement.

I deny, however, that the abstractions to be found in the new art are dead formulæ. For the moment, I do not intend to offer any proof of this assertion, as far as Cubist art itself is concerned. I intend to deal rather with the precursor of the movement, that is Cézanne himself. The point at issue here then is narrowed down to this. The Cubists claim that the beginnings of an abstract art can be found in Cézanne. Mr. Ginner, on the contrary, asserts that Cézanne was a pure realist. It is to be noticed that even if he proved his case, he would not have attacked the new art itself, but only its claimed descent from Cézanne.

One must be careful not to treat Cézanne as if he actually were a Cubist; he obviously is not. One must not read the whole of the later movement into him. But there are in his paintings elements which quite naturally develop into Cubism later. You get, as contrasted with the Impressionists, a certain simplification of places, an emphasis on three-dimensional form, giving to some of his landscapes what might be called a Cubist appearance. It is true that this simplification and abstraction, this seeing of things in simple forms, as a rule only extends to details. It might be said that simplifications are, as it were, 'accepted' passively, and are not deliberately built up into a definite organisation and structure.

The first thing to be noticed is that even supposing that Cézanne's intentions were entirely realistic, he initiated a break-up of realism and provided the material for an abstract art. Picasso came along and took over these elements isolated by Cézanne, and organised them. If the simplifications in Cézanne had passed beyond details and become more comprehensive, they would probably of themselves have forced him to build up definite structures.

But not only are the elements of an abstract art present in Cézanne, I should say also that there was an embryo of the creative activity which was later to organise these elements.

I put again the opposed view to this. I have already said that the simplification of planes is based on that actually suggested by nature. The realist intention, it might be said, is directed towards weight and three-dimensional form, rather than towards light, yet it still remains realist. This is quite a conceivable view. It is quite possible that a realist of this kind might prepare the material of an abstract art automatically. The abstractions might be produced accidentally, with no attempt to use them creatively as means of expression.

It seems to me, however, that there are many reasons against the supposition that this was the case with Cézanne. In looking for any traces of this abstract organising tendency, one must remember that Cézanne was extraordinarily hampered by the realism of his period; in some ways he might be said to have carried out the complete impressionist programme. Yet showing through this you do get traces of an opposed tendency. I should base this assertion on two grounds:

(1) Though the simplification of planes may appear passive and prosaic, entirely dictated by a desire to reproduce a certain solidity, and from one point of view almost fumbling, yet at the same time one may say that in this treatment of detail, there is an energy at work which, though perhaps

unconscious, is none the less an energy which is working towards abstraction and towards a feeling for structure. If one thinks of the details, rather than of the picture as a whole, one need not even say this energy is unconscious. In this respect Cézanne does seem to have been fairly conscious, and to have recognised what he was after better than the contemporary opinion which looked upon him as an impressionist. I should say that expressions like 'everything is spherical or cylindrical', and all the forms of nature 'peuvent se ramener au cône, au cylindre et à la sphère',[2] yet show the working of a creative invention, which had to that extent turned away from realism and showed a tendency towards abstraction. (It is obvious that these words were not used in the sense in which a Cubist might use them; they apply to details rather than to wholes. Yet a denial of the wider application does not, as many people seem to suppose, justify the idea that they were meant in the sense in which a Cubist might understand them.) These sentences seem to me to destroy the whole of Mr. Ginner's argument, unless, of course, you go a step further than those who explain Cézanne's painting as the result of astigmatism and incompetence, and assert that the poor man could not even use his mother tongue. The simplification of planes itself, then, does seem to show a tendency to abstraction which is working itself free. (2) But the fact that this simplification is not entirely realistic and does come from a certain feeling after structure, seems to me to be demonstrated in a more positive way by pictures like the well-known 'Bathing Women'. Here you get a use of distortion and an emphasis on form which is constructive. The pyramidal shape, moreover, cannot be compared to decoration, or to the composition found in the old masters. The shape is so hard, so geometrical in character, that it almost lifts the picture out of the realistic art which has lasted from the Renaissance to now, and into the sphere of geometric art. It is in reality much nearer to the kind of geometrical organisations employed in the new art.

That is a theoretical statement of the errors Mr. Ginner makes. I think it might be worth while to go behind these errors themselves, to explain the prejudices which are responsible for their survival.

As a key to his psychology, take the sentence which he most frequently repeats. 'It is only this intimate relation between the artist and the object which can produce original and great works. Away from nature, we fall into unoriginal and monotonous formulæ.' In repeating this he probably has at the back of his mind two quite different ideas, (1) the idea that it is the business of the artist to represent and interpret nature, and (2) the assumption that even if it is not his duty to represent nature that he must do so *practically*, for away from nature the artist's invention at once decays. He apparently thinks of an artist using abstractions as of a child playing with a box of tricks. The number of interesting combinations must soon be exhausted.

The first error springs from a kind of Rousseauism which is probably much too deeply imbedded in Mr. Ginner's mind for me to be able to eradicate. I merely meet it by the contrary assertion that I do not think it is the artist's only business to reproduce and interpret Nature, 'source of all good', but that it is possible that the artist may be creative. This distinction is obscured in Mr. Ginner's mind by the highly coloured and almost ethical language in which he puts it. We are exhorted to stick to Mother Nature. Artists who attempt to do something other than this are accused of 'shrinking from life'. This state of mind can be most clearly seen in the use of the word simplification. There is a confusion here between the *validity* and *origin* of simplification. The validity of simplification is held to depend on its origin. If the simplification, such as that for example you get in Cézanne's treatment of trees, is derived from Nature and comes about as the result of an aim which is itself directed back to Nature, then it is held to be valid. I, on the other hand, should assert that the validity of the simplification lay in itself and in the use made of it and had nothing whatever to do with its descent, on its occupying a place in Nature's 'Burke'.

Take now the second prejudice—the idea that whatever he may do theoretically, at any rate practically, the artist must keep in continual contact with Nature—'The individual relying on his imagination and his formula finds himself very limited, in comparison with the infinite variety of life. Brain ceases to act as it ceases to search out expression of Nature, its only true and healthy source.'[3]

You see here again the ethical view of the matter—the idea of retribution. Get further and further away from dear old Mother Nature and see what happens to you: you fall into dead formulæ.

My answer to this argument is: that while I admit it to be to a certain extent true, I deny the conclusion Mr. Ginner draws from it.

I admit that the artist cannot work without contact with, and continual research into nature, but one must make a distinction between this and the conclusion drawn from it that the work of art itself must be an interpretation of nature. The artist obviously cannot spin things out of his head, he cannot work from imagination in that sense. The whole thing springs from misconception of the nature of artistic imagination. Two statements are confused: (1) that the source of imagination must be nature, and (2) the consequence illegitimately drawn from this, that the resulting work must be realistic, and based on natural forms. One can give an analogy in ordinary thought. The reasoning activity is quite different in character from any succession of images drawn from the senses, but yet thought itself would be impossible without this sensual stimulus.

There must be just as much contact with nature in an abstract art as in a realistic one; without that stimulus the artist could produce nothing. In Picasso, for example, there is much greater research into nature, as far as the relation of planes is concerned, than in any realist painting; he has isolated and emphasised relations previously not emphasised. All art may be said to be realism, then, in that it extracts from nature facts which have not been observed before. But in as far as the artist is creative, he is not bound down by the accidental relations of the elements actually found in nature, but extracts, distorts, and utilises them as a means of expression, and not as a means of interpreting nature.

It is true, then, that an artist can only keep his work alive by research into nature, but that does not prove that realism is the only legitimate form of art.

Both realism and abstraction, then, can only be *engendered* out of nature, but while the first's only idea of living seems to be that of hanging on to its progenitor, the second cuts its umbilical cord.

Modern Art
III: The London Group

[First published in *NA* 14/21 (26 Mar. 1914), 661–2; reprinted in *FS* 129–34.]

This group has been formed by the amalgamation of the Camden Town Group and the Cubists.[1] It thus claims to represent all the forward movements in English painting at the present moment. Judging from its first exhibition, it is probably destined, since the decline of the New English, to play a very important role in the next few years. Of the most realist section of the society I shall not say much here, as I intend to write about it at greater length later. Mr. Spencer Gore's 'The Wood',[2] and Mr. Harold Gilman's 'Eating House'[3] show in very different ways the same intimate research into problems of colour. Mr. Charles Ginner's 'La Balayeuse'[4] is the best picture of his that I have seen as yet. His peculiar method is here extraordinarily successful in conveying the sordid feeling of the subject. Mr. Bevan[5] exhibits a characteristic and interesting painting of horses. Although at the moment I am more in sympathy with the other section of the society, yet I am bound to say that the work of the painters I have just mentioned is better than that one finds at the New English,[6] and infinitely better than the faked stuff produced by Mr. Roger Fry and his friends. It is possible to point out, however, in looking at this kind of painting, the dissatisfaction which inclines one towards Cubism. These pictures are filled by contours which, when one is moved by the dissatisfaction I am speaking of, one can only describe as meaningless. They are full of detail which is entirely accidental in character, and only justified by the fact that these accidents did actually occur in the particular piece of nature which was being painted. One feels a repugnance to such accidents—and desires painting where nothing is accidental, where all the contours are closely knit together into definite structural shapes.

The Cubist section is particularly interesting, as it shows very clearly the unsettled state of the new movement. Though it has finally got clear away from its Post-Impressionistic beginnings, it cannot be said to have reached any final form. Two different tendencies can be distinguished. The main movement is that which, arising out of Cubism, is destined to create a new geometric and monumental art, making use of mechanical forms. It is possible, I think, to give an account of this movement, which will exhibit it as an understandable and coherent whole, closely allied to the general tendency of the period, and thus containing possibilities of development.

But this has now generated a second movement based simply on the idea that abstract form, i.e., form without any representative content, can be an adequate means of expression. In this, instead of hard, structural work like Picasso's you get the much more scattered use of abstractions of artists like Kandinsky. It seems, judging by its development up to now, to be only a more or less amusing by-product of the first. Lacking the controlling sensibility, the feeling for mechanical structure, which makes use of abstractions a necessity, it seems rather dilettante. It so happens, however, that all explanations of the new movement as yet given, have been explanations of this second tendency only. In this way the real importance of the main tendency has been veiled. It has seemed rather in the air, rather causeless. The driving force behind it remained hidden.

What is really behind the main movement, what makes it important is the re-emergence of a sensibility akin to that behind geometrical arts of the past. At first, at its rather fumbling search for an appropriate means of expression, it naturally went back to these past arts. You thus got a period in which the work produced had a certain resemblance to Archaic, Byzantine and African art. But this state has already been left behind. The new sensibility is finding for itself a direct and modern means of expression, having very little resemblance to these past geometric arts. It is characterised, not by the simple geometric forms found in archaic art, but by the more complicated ones associated in our minds with machinery. Minor effects of this change of sensibility are very obvious in the pictures here. They do not shrink from forms which it is usual to describe as unrhythmical, and great use is made of shapes taken from machinery. The beauty of banal forms like teapot-handles, knuckledusters, saws, etc., seems to have been perceived for the first time. A whole picture is sometimes dominated by a composition based on hard mechanical shapes in a way which previous art would have shrunk from. It is not the emphasis on form which is the distinguishing characteristic of the new movement, then, but the emphasis on this particular kind of form.

But it is easy to see how this main movement, with its necessary use of abstraction of a particular kind for a particular purpose, has engendered on the side of it a minor movement which uses abstractions for their own sake in a much more scattered way. I do not think this minor movement is destined to survive. I look upon it rather as a kind of romantic heresy, which will, however, have a certain educative influence. It will lead to the discovery of conceptions of form, which will be extremely useful in the construction of the new geometrical art. But temporarily, at any rate, most of the painters in this exhibition seem to be very much influenced by an enthusiasm for this idea. One has here, then, a good opportunity for examining this heresy. Theoretically it is quite plausible. It seems quite conceivable that the directions of the forms in a picture, the subordination of the parts to the whole, the arresting of one form by the other, the relation of veiled to exposed shapes, might make up an understandable kind of music without the picture containing any representative element whatever. How does it work out in practice? Take Mr. Wyndham Lewis's large canvases, which at first look like mere arbitrary arrangements of bright colours and abstract forms. Judged from this point of view, what can be said about them? They fail, in that they do not produce as a whole, the kind of coherent effect which, according to the theory, they ought to produce. The forms are not controlled enough. In the 'Eisteddfod', for example, long tranquil planes of colour sweeping up from the left encounter a realistically painted piece of ironwork, which, being very large in proportion to the planes, dwarfs any effect they might have produced. The second picture, 'Christopher Columbus', is hard and gay, contains many admirable inventions, but is best regarded as a field where certain qualities are displayed, rather than as a complete work of art. In Mr. Lewis's work, there are always certain qualities of dash and decision, but it has the defects of these qualities. His sense of form seems to me to be sequent rather than integral, by which I mean that one form probably springs out of the preceding one as he works, instead of being conceived as part of a whole. His imagination being quick and never fumbling, very interesting relations are generated in this way, but the whole sometimes lacks cohesion and unity. The qualities of Mr. Lewis's work are seen to better advantage in his quite remarkable drawing, 'The Enemy of the Stars'. Equally abstract is Mr. Wadsworth's work.[7] In the most successful, 'Scherzo', a number of lively ascending forms are balanced by broad planes at the top. The painter whose work shows the greatest advance is Mr. C. F. Hamilton.[8] His 'Two Figures' shows a great sense of construction, and is one of the best paintings in this section. Mr. F. Etchells' drawings are admirably firm and hard in character; but it would obviously be premature to form any sure judgment about this artist's work at a time when he almost seems to be holding himself back, in a search for a new method of expression. His fine 'Drawing of a Head' shows this state of hesitation and experiment very clearly. Mr. Nevinson is much less abstract than the others. His best picture is 'The Chauffeur',[9] which is very solid and develops an interesting contrast between round and angular shapes. I admire the ability of Mr. Gaudier-Brzeska's sculpture; the tendencies it displays are sound though the abstractions used do not seem to me to be always thoroughly thought out.

In all the painters I have mentioned so far abstract form has been used as the bearer of general emotions, but the real fanatics of form reject even this abstract use as savouring of literature and sentiment. Representation has already been excluded. They want to exclude even the general emotions conveyed by abstract form, and to confine us to the appreciation of form in itself *tout pur*. Some such intention must be behind the largest picture in the show, Mr. Bomberg's 'In the Hold'.[10] Stated in more detail, the theory on which it is based seems to be this. In looking at a picture one never sees it as a whole, one's eye travels over it. In doing so, we continually find certain expectations fulfilled—a boot is followed by a leg, and even when there is no representation at all, certain abstract forms are naturally continued by other forms. Apparently this fulfilled expectation is an added non-æsthetic emotion, and must be excluded by those who wish to take an absolutely 'pure' pleasure in form itself. Mr. Bomberg therefore cuts his picture up into sixty-four squares, and as each square is independent of its neighbours, the 'fulfilled expectation' I spoke of above is excluded, and whatever pleasure we take must be in the arrangement of shapes inside each square. The picture appears to have started off as a drawing of an actual subject, but that apparently was only because a purely mental invention of form would have inevitably produced those 'sequences' it was desired to avoid. The representation of the outside scene generates, in its passage through a square, an entirely accidental and 'unexpected' shape. The square I might call K.Kt.6, for example, makes an interesting pattern. That the picture as a whole is entirely empty is, I suppose, on the theory I have just put forward, no defect. All the general emotions produced by form have been excluded and we are reduced to a purely intellectual interest in shape. This particular picture, then, is certainly the reductio ad absurdum of this heresy about form. I see no development along such lines, though such work may be an excellent discipline. I look forward, however, to Mr. Bomberg's future work with interest; he is undoubtedly an artist of remarkable ability. For the present, I prefer his drawings. 'The Acrobats' breaks away from the sculptural treatment of his recent work and seems to me to be admirable.

Most of the work I have been talking about is experimental and is interesting because it is on the way to something else. Perhaps the only really satisfying and complete work in this section is that of Mr. Epstein. He possesses that peculiar energy which distinguishes the creative from the merely intelligent artist, and is certainly the greatest sculptor of this generation; I have seen no work in Paris or Berlin which I can so

unreservedly admire. At the present moment he has arrived at an interesting point in his development. Starting from a very efficient realism, he
passed through a more or less archaic period; he seems now to have left
that behind and, as far as one can judge from the drawings for sculpture
he exhibits, to have arrived at an entirely personal and modern method of
expression. The 'Carving in Flenite' comes at the end of the second
period. Technically, it is admirable. The design is in no sense empty, but
gives a most impressive and complete expression of a certain blind, tragic
aspect of its subject—something akin perhaps to what Plato meant by the
vegetable soul. The archaic elements it contains are in no sense imitative.
What has been taken from African or Polynesian work is the inevitable
and permanent way of getting a certain effect. The only quite new work
Mr. Epstein exhibits, the 'Bird Pluming Itself' is in comparison with this
profound work, quite light in character, but the few simple abstractions
out of which it is built are used with great skill and discretion.

Contemporary Drawings

[Hulme, as editor of this series, published five drawings in all. They appeared in the *NA* bi-weekly, from 19 Mar. to 30 Apr. 1914, as follows:
  (1) *A Dancer*, by Henri Gaudier-Brzeska (19 Mar.)
  (2) *Chinnereth*, by David Bomberg (2 Apr.)
  (3) *Study*, by William Roberts (16 Apr.)
  (4) *The Chauffeur*, by C. R. W. Nevinson (30 Apr.)
  (5) *The Farmyard*, by Edward Wadsworth (30 Apr.)]

(2 APRIL 1914)

This series will include drawings by David Bomberg, Jacob Epstein, F. Etchells, Gaudier-Brzeska, C. F. Hamilton, P. Wyndham Lewis, C. R. W. Nevinson, Roberts, and E. Wadsworth. Most of them are members of the London Group, which is now holding an exhibition in the Goupil Gallery. Some of the drawings are Cubist, some are not. Perhaps the only quality they possess in common is that they are all abstract in character. The series includes everyone in England who is doing interesting work of this character. In view of the amount of capable work continually being produced it is difficult to realise that the only part of this which is important, that which is preparing the art of the next generation, may be the work of a relatively quite small group of artists. I claim, however, that this series includes all those artists in England at the present moment who are working in the direction which alone contains possibilities of development.

Appended to each drawing will be a short note for the benefit of those who are baffled by the abstract character of the work. For this the editor, and not the artist, is alone responsible. You have before you a movement about which there is no crystallised opinion, and consequently have the fun of making your own judgments about the work. You will have, moreover, the advantage of comparing these drawings with the not very exhilarating work of the more traditional school—with those, shall I say, in the series Mr. Sickert[1] is editing?

Mr. David Bomberg's drawing[2] contains four upright figures in various attitudes. If you ask why the legs look like cylinders and are not realistically treated, the answer I should give would be this—the pleasure you are intended to take in such a drawing is a pleasure not in representation, but in the relations between certain abstract forms. Take, for example, the figure on the left of the drawing; consider particularly the line which runs up one leg, across the hips and down the other leg. If you take any interest in that form, just as a form, then you will see quite easily that it could not have been given with the same force and directness in a more realistic drawing. The accidental details of representation would have veiled or, better, 'damped down' this directness.

CONTEMPORARY DRAWINGS—NO. 3
(16 APRIL 1914)

This drawing[3] contains four figures. I could point out the position of these figures in more detail, but I think such detailed indication misleading. No artist can create abstract form spontaneously; it is always generated, or, at least, suggested by the consideration of some outside concrete shapes. But such shapes are only interesting if you want to explain the psychology of the process of composition in the artist's mind. The interest of the drawing itself depends on the forms it contains. The fact that such forms were suggested by human figures is of no importance.

CONTEMPORARY DRAWINGS
(30 APRIL 1914)

Mr. Wadsworth's drawing[4] this week suffers somewhat by reproduction, as in the original it is coloured; the light background being yellow and grey, and the dark parts a very dark blue. The lighter parts of the drawing represent three farm buildings grouped round a pool. The space they enclose is concave to the spectator, the middle building being farther back than the two side ones. The darker parts represent the trunks and foliage of a tree standing on a slight mound.

It is interesting to compare this with the previous drawings in this series for it represents a much earlier stage in the process of abstraction. By considering this halfway stage, one can perhaps make this kind of art more comprehensible.

A school of painting is often interested in and emphasises one aspect of nature to the exclusion of others; but, though a painting may only pick out one of the hundred elements of which a natural scene consists, yet enough trace of the other ninety-nine remains in the picture for one to be able to recognise it as a representation. In impressionism, though the chief emphasis is on light and colour, yet the other elements—shape, outline, solidity, etc.—though not emphasised, do appear to an extent sufficient to make the picture a recognisable representation. (Though the first time the simple man sees an impressionist picture he finds it an incoherent chaos, he is as unable to synthesise its elements into a whole as he is those of a Cubist picture.) But a Cubist picture is in slightly different position to an impressionist one, for this reason: Like the impressionist picture, it emphasises one aspect out of many possible ones. But the nature of the element emphasised here—the relations between planes—is such, that emphasis on these relations disintegrates the thing as representation. In a drawing like Mr. Wadsworth's this process has not gone far. It is a drawing made before an actual landscape, in which the planes which interested the artist are given in the objects in which they occurred. But it is easy to see how this emphasis on the relation between planes inevitably developed into later cubism, where the planes are given without any representation of the objects which suggested them.

Mr. C. R. W. Nevinson's 'Chauffeur'[5] is the study for the picture he exhibited in the London Group. I need not add much to what I said when I criticised it in my notice of that exhibition, except that the elongation of the right side of the face is an attempt to show the distortion produced by light.

Modern Art
IV: Mr. David Bomberg's Show

[First published in *NA* 15/10 (9 July 1914), 230–2; reprinted in
FS 135–44. William Lipke claims in *David Bomberg: A Critical
Study of his Life and Work* (London, 1967) that 'it is to Hulme that
Bomberg owes much of his reputation in that [pre-World War
I] period'.]

Mr. Bomberg stands somewhat apart from the other English Cubists. I
noticed that in signing a collective protest, published a few weeks ago, he
added in a footnote that he had nothing whatever to do with the Rebel
Art Centre[1]—very wisely, in my opinion, for his work is certainly much
more individual and less derivative than the work of the members of that
group. The tendency to abstraction does seem in his case to have been a
logical development of tendencies which were always present even in his
earlier drawings, and not merely the result of a feverish hurry to copy the
latest thing from Paris. The fact that his work shows these individual
qualities justifies much more than is generally the case a one-man show,
and separate consideration. But while I have great admiration for some of
Mr. Bomberg's work, that does not make it any easier for me to write an
article about it. An article about one man's pictures is not a thing I should
ever do naturally. The only absolutely honest and direct and straightforward word expression of what I think as I go round such an exhibition
would be a monotonous repetition of the words 'This is good or fairly
good. How much does that cost?' for I would certainly rather buy a
picture than write about it. It seems a much more appropriate gesture.
Any more rotund or fluent expression than these short sentences must,
however admirable, be artificial. Only the expert art critic can prolong
the gesture of admiration artificially by cliché—that, of course, is his
métier. I wish I could do it myself. The fact that naturally one's expression is inadequate, springs entirely from a certain physical difference of
pace. What you feel before a picture is long, slow, seems important. The
rattle of sounds which expresses it is quick, short and unimpressive. The
body as a tool of expression is obviously a failure, it is too light weight.
Your sentence over, you feel that you have finished too soon; you feel
uncomfortable and want to prolong the gesture. Hence is born the whole

system of cliché; a system enabling you to 'last out' the feeling; hence also we might even say to the whole mechanism of literary expression. It all exists to cover the body's inefficiency. If only our arms were so heavy that an appreciative sweep lasted ten minutes we should be saved from literature. Opera, of course, can 'last out' by raising the sentence into *aria*. The American has his drawl, and consequently has no literature—not needing any. But I haven't these expedients; nor as an outsider in this business have I the necessary cliché at my command. I can only then write an article on one man's pictures by using the only form of incense natural to me; I can get up an argument about them—which I therefore proceed to do.

Mr. Bomberg starts off by stating in the preface to his catalogue that his object in all his painting is the construction of 'pure form', and that he appeals constantly to a sense of form. We might all admit that this is true as a description of pure fact, at any rate. All the paintings are of the character he describes. They do appeal to very little else but a sense of form. Take, for example, one of the best of the drawings (No. 6) 'Ju Jitsu'. What strikes you first as excellent is the contrast between the bareness of certain parts as contrasted with the complex and intricate liveliness of others. Wherever it was felt to be necessary, representation has been sacrificed. The body line of one figure, which would be in reality hidden behind another figure in the foreground, is clearly shown. The realist would here urge that if that line was necessary in order to get a certain arrangement of form, it should have been continued by a line on the front figure, so that representation should not have been sacrificed. I will deal later with the validity of this kind of objection; I only mention the point here to show that the intention of the artist is clearly what he announces it to be. It is still clearer in the remarkable drawing, 'Zin' (No. 26), which contains hardly any representative element at all. In the upper part, which strikes me as best, there are no recognisable forms at all, but only an arrangement of abstract lines outlining no object. It is very difficult to state why one considers a drawing of this kind good when one hasn't it before one. Perhaps the best way of describing it would be to say that it looks like a peculiarly interesting kind of scaffolding. It is obvious, therefore, that the only interest in it must be an interest in form. I should probably find it difficult to say what I found interesting in it if I had the drawing here before me and could show it you. Its interest depends on qualities peculiarly indescribable in words. Indescribable not for any mysterious reason, but because forms are of their nature rather indescribable, and even difficult, to point out. They depend, for example, very often on a three dimensional relation between planes which is very difficult to get at. The artist in front of a picture endeavouring to explain it, by inexpressive motions of his hands, has often been laughed at; but laughed at, I think, for a wrong reason. It is supposed that he waves his hands, makes strange gestures with his thumbs, peculiar twists with his wrists, because he lacks the power of expressing himself in words; because he is a painter, in fact, and not a literary man. This I believe to be a mistaken view of the phenomenon. He is not using his hands through poverty of words, through lack of the ability to express himself in the proper manner. He is trying to describe the qualities of the picture in the only way they can be described. But he is a figure for laughter because he is employing a miserably inadequate tool. It is impossible to suppose that those ancient prehensile implements, our hands, could ever be turned to this new use—a description of the subtleties and intricacies of form. It cannot be done, and surely the designer of the universe never intended that it should be done. I think of designing a little brass instrument which shall adequately perform the function which the hands now so inefficiently perform. An arrangement of revolving graduated spheres will enable you to indicate at once all the complicated twists and relations of form that you perceive in a picture. This invention would have two advantages. It would do away with the art critic. On each picture would be an indication as to how you must graduate your instrument, in order to grasp the relations of forms the artist was after; this would do away with any necessity for the confused and stuttering metaphors by which the critic endeavours to express the inexpressible; one painful scene the less in this world of trouble. Moreover, it would please the conservatives in these matters, for the manufacture of my instrument would soon fall into the hands of a trust, who, whenever a new generation began to experiment with a new kind of form unprovided for by the instrument, would see that the Press unanimously denounced it.

To return, however, to Mr. Bomberg's exhibition. Those who are curious as to the genesis of abstract form, as to the way in which it is actually constructed in the artist's mind, should find Nos. 23, 11, 1, which probably represent three stages in the development of the same idea, interesting. The first step towards the understanding of this process of genesis is to recognise that the mind cannot *create* form, it can only *edit* it. In this, as in other very different matters, existing here in this world, bound to this body, we have little spontaneity. Asked to fill a space with a *new* abstract design, and told at the same time to empty his mind of all recollection of the external world, an artist would produce nothing but a few arbitrary and uninteresting repetitions. The first suggestion must always come from some existing outside shape. This sets the mind going. Consider now the three things I mentioned above. No. 23 is the first drawing. The artist probably got the lines of his main design from some accidental material arrangement. The suggestions of form this contained were then probably continued and developed by thinking of them as parts of human figures. (This use of doll-like human figures is a characteristic of Mr. Bomberg's work, as those who saw his drawings in THE NEW AGE will remember.) In the final stage, these figures are so abstract that they are not recognisable as such. In all this process what suggestions of real objects occur, are only as a means of getting the mind going, as fertiliser of the design. In themselves they are of no importance, the controlling interest all the time being the selection and production of abstract form. The first of these three works, No. 23, I do not think successful, taken by itself. One notes it as interesting, but it produces no definite effect. The two paintings developed from it, however, are much more interesting; No. 1, 'The Mud Bath', being one of the best things Mr. Bomberg has done; the colour in it being much more vigorous than in the earlier study, No. 11 of the drawings, which, while being abstract, at the same time contains recognisable representative elements. No. 5, reading from Torak, seems to me to be the best. The abstract shapes here do reinforce a quite human and even dramatic effect, at the same time being interesting in themselves merely as a construction of shapes. They would probably be even more interesting carried out as three dimensional shapes in wood or something of that kind. Another extremely good drawing of an almost sculptural quality is 'Chinnereth', about which, however, I need say nothing, as it has already been reproduced in this paper.[2]

So far I have only been concerned to show that on the assumption that an interest in pure form is a sufficient basis in itself Mr. Bomberg's work is, as a matter of fact, good work. It may be worth while here to examine that assumption. Is pure form alone a sufficient basis for interest in art? The best answer is, of course, that certain people find it enough. They find that they are moved by, and interested in, the suggestions of abstract form they see about them, and do feel themselves prompted either to then organise these suggestions, or to look for them in art. When a man simply says: 'I do feel interested in abstract form, as another might in atmosphere and landscape', no objection can be made to his statement. But there is an erroneous way of transforming the statement into a theory, which makes it impossible for the layman to understand the motives of abstract art. For this reason I want to contradict it. The theory is that we contemplate *form* for its own sake—that it produces a particular emotion different from the ordinary everyday emotions—a specific *æsthetic* emotion. If this were a true account of the matter, it would be incomprehensible to the layman. 'Pictures with some dramatic or human interest I like, . . . but this damned stylistic bunkum. . . .' And he would be right.

If form has no dramatic or human interest, then it is obviously stupid for a human to be interested in it.

But the theory is erroneous. There is no such thing as a specific *æsthetic* emotion, a peculiar kind of emotion produced by *form* alone, only of interest to æsthetes. I think it could be shown that the emotions produced by abstract form, are the ordinary everyday human emotions—they are produced in a different way, that is all.

What happens, then, is not

$$S_{(f)} \dots\dots\dots\dots\dots F$$

where S is the spectator, F the outside form, and (f) the specific form emotion, but much more this—

$$S_{(de)} \dots\dots\dots\dots\dots F_{(if)}$$

where (de) stands for quite ordinary *dramatic human emotions*, which occur in daily life, and not only in the contemplation of works of art. I do not say that in looking at pure form we are *conscious* of this emotion they produce. We are not fully conscious of it, but *project* it outside ourselves into the outside form F, and may only be conscious of it as (if) '*interesting form*'. But the (if) only exists because of the (de).

After all, this possibility of living our own emotions *into* outside shapes and colours is the basic fact on which the whole of plastic art rests. People admit it in the case of atmosphere, colour, and landscape, but they will not admit it in the case of abstract form. Very possibly the number of people who can thus be affected by form is much more limited, but the phenomena is the same. There is nothing mysterious in this process by which *form* becomes the *porter* or *carrier* of internal emotions. It admits of a simple, psychological explanation which I need not give here, however; all that concerns us for the moment is the *fact*. Bare abstract form can be dramatic; the mere shape of a tree as tragic has a long explicit history. As a rule, of course, much milder emotions of tension, balance, contrast, etc., are called up. But it remains possible to say all one wants about arrangements of pure form without ever once using the word beauty and employing always the vocabulary with which one would speak of a man's character, commonplace . . . vigorous . . . empty, etc.

It must be insisted that there is nothing esoteric or mysterious about this interest in abstract forms. Once he has awakened to it, once it has been emphasised and indicated to him by art, then just as in the case of colour perception and impression the layman will derive great pleasure from it, not only as it is presented to him organised in Cubism, but as he perceives it for himself in outside nature. He will feel, for example, probably for the first time, an interest in the extraordinary variety of the abstract forms suggested by bare trees in winter (an interest, I must repeat, which is really an interest in himself as these forms, by an obscure psychological process, become for him the bearers of certain emotions) or in the morning, he may contemplate with interest the shapes into which his shirt thrown over a chair has fallen.

Here comes a common objection. Admitting the existence of this special interest in form, it is asked, why cannot these forms, instead of being abstracted, be given *in* the objects in which they actually occurred, i.e., *in* a realistic setting? If an artist looking out of a high window on the street beneath is interested in the fish-like interweaving of the motor traffic, why cannot that interweaving be given in a representation of the motor? Why attempt to give the interweaving alone? Why attempt to give the soul without the body—an impossible feat? Why could not Mr. Bomberg have given the shape-design of his 'Men and Lads' or his 'Acrobats', embodied *in* a more realistic representation? For two reasons: First that the only element of the real scene which interests the artist is the abstract element; the others are for that interest irrelevant, and, if reproduced, would only damp down the vigour of the naked form itself. And secondly, the fact that the abstract element did occur as a matter of fact in external nature mixed up with other things is of no importance. The forms are either interesting in themselves, or not. They derive no justification from their natural occurrence. The only importance of nature in this connection is that it does suggest forms, which the artist can develop; the mind here, as elsewhere, having very little natural spontaneity.

The use of form is then constructive. The same may be said of Mr. Bomberg's use of colour. The relations of colours used are not *right* because they are the kind of sets of colour that do, as a matter of fact, actually occur in nature. In some of his earlier work, however, this is the case. (No. 23) 'The Song of Songs', a very beautiful work, is an example of this older use of colour. The combination of greys, dead black and gold strikes one as distinguished, but at the same time the pleasure it gives may be partly the pleasures of association; it is the kind of colour that might occur in nature at times of the day which have a certain emotional accompaniment. In the 'Mud Bath', on the contrary, the colour is used in an entirely constructive way, and in no sense derivative from nature. Here I might deal with a quite reasonable objection which is frequently brought against this kind of art. I went round Mr. Bomberg's show with a very intelligent painter of an older school. 'Although I find these abstract drawings extremely interesting,' he said, 'yet if I were buying I should get this'—pointing out No. 32, I think. 'I feel abstract work would become tiring when one continually saw it in a room.' Though this sounds plausible, yet I don't think that it would as a matter of fact turn out to be the case. Personally, I think I should find drawings in which your imagination was continually focussed in one direction by a subject more fatiguing. The proportions of a room or the shape of a good window, though they exercise a definite effect on one, do not become tiresome. And the pleasure to be got from good abstract art is of the same kind, though infinitely more elaborate, as the pleasure you get from these other fixed elements of a room.

To turn now to Mr. Bomberg's earlier work. Here I have a convenient opportunity of dealing with an entirely fallacious argument which I am now thoroughly tired of reading. The baffled art critic, being entirely at sea in dealing with quite abstract work, and feeling himself unable to pass any secure judgment on it, turns to the artist's earlier and more conventional work, and says, 'This earlier work which I *can* understand is commonplace, I can therefore legitimately infer that this abstract work which I cannot understand is also entirely commonplace.' Now this argument, although attractively simple, is a *non sequitur*. Suppose that the qualities of a good naturalistic drawing are A B C . . . . F where F is a sense of form. In any particular case (F) might be good, but the man's attention and interest might be so concentrated on (F) that A B C were comparatively uninteresting, so that on the whole the drawing might be pronounced commonplace. But when you came to the man's abstract work which entirely depended on his sense of form, his work might be far from commonplace. I see, however, that one critic has already applied this faulty criterion to Mr. Bomberg's earlier work. 'This earlier work', he says, 'shows energy without patience . . . is very ordinary student's work . . . he has never had the patience to master form,' and so on. These judgments I consider to be entirely unjust. Bearing in mind what I said in the last paragraph, I find it decidedly *not* commonplace, because all of it shows emphasis on, and understanding of, that quality which, while it may only be one element in the excellence of a naturalistic drawing, is yet the whole of a more abstract one—a sense of form. That seems to have been always excellent. He has all the time, and apparently quite spontaneously, and without imitation, been more interested in form than anything else. Take No. 46, a bedroom picture, for example. I mention it because it shows the transitional period very clearly—the bed and room quite in the Sickert tradition, quite realistic and with Sickert's ideas about paint, but the figure of the girl in it treated quite differently, very much simplified, getting on to abstraction, and looking consequently very unreal in the midst of the other very solid realistic things. All the early drawings show a preoccupation with form—the heads, though, less than the figure studies. In all of them, there is an insistency on shapes running through. You can see this most clearly in the figure study in the first room. Done realistically the lines of the deltoids in the two arms, and the line of the chest, would form three broken parts of one line. As he has done it, the three are joined to make one line running through. I am quite aware, of course, that this sort of thing has always been one element in good drawing, but I do think you find it emphasised here in a way which makes his later development very understandable. No. 32 is good, and gets a certain monumental effect.

That his work shows the impatience the critic regrets is only to be expected. People with any guts in them do not have catholic tastes. If they realise in a personal and vivid way the importance of *one* element, if they feel that they have anything fresh to say about that, they are naturally impatient with the other elements. Why, if you are only interested in form, should you be asked—once you have got down the elements of that form adequately—to add to it the alien elements which would make it into a solid realistic representation? The watercolour 'Rehoboam' (No. 21) admirably expresses the idea it is based on. Why should it be carried any further? Why not stop with the idea which started it—why artificially prolong it into something not present on that initial idea?

To sum up, then—in my notice of the London Group I said that I thought Mr. Bomberg was an artist of remarkable ability. This show certainly confirms that impression. It also adds something. It convinces me that his work has always been personal and independent—much more independent than that of most Cubists—and never reminiscent. If I am to qualify this, I should add that as yet his use of form satisfies a too purely sensuous or intellectual interest. It is not often used to intensify a more general emotion. I do not feel, then, the same absolute certainty about his work that I do about Epstein's. In Mr. Epstein's work the abstractions have been got at gradually, and always intensify, as abstractions, the general feeling of the whole work. But then Mr. Epstein is in a class by himself. I think that in this merely intellectual use of abstraction Mr. Bomberg is achieving exactly what he sets out to achieve. But at the same time it is quite legitimate for me to point out why I prefer another use of abstraction. In any case, I think he will develop remarkably, and he is probably by this kind of work acquiring an intimate knowledge of form, which he will utilise in a different way later.

War
Writings

Diary from the Trenches

['Diary from the Trenches' is the name Samuel Hynes gave to a series of letters which Hulme wrote to his family from the front between Dec. 1914 and Apr. 1915; they were first published in *FS* (Minneapolis, 1955), 147–69. The text reproduced here is that of *FS*, its source being, according to Mr Hynes, a transcript of the original letters made by a family member. The footnotes are Hynes's, from *FS*.]

Dec. 30th, 1914

We left Southampton about 4 p.m., after marching down the principal street, all out of step, and all the girls waving from the windows. (On the way down on Sunday, people waved to us from the back windows; all the troops go down that line so they have formed a habit.)

We had a very smooth crossing, 700 of us in a tramp steamer which was fitted out to carry cattle or horses. We slept in the stalls, hurriedly whitewashed to make them clean, with notice painted over our heads 'This is for urine only not for dung'. It sounds dreadful but it's really all right.

We were accompanied all the way by two English destroyers, as escort, got to the port I said we should come to about 4 a.m., but did not leave till about 9. As we entered the harbour, some French soldiers, drilling on the quayside in white trousers looking from the distance exactly like penguins, called out 'Air we downhearted'. We marched then, with all our equipment up a fearful hill about 4 miles to what is called a Rest Camp, a fearful place, deep in mud, where we have to sleep in tents which makes me very depressed. I hope we shan't stay here long. All my clothes are wet through with sweat.

I am writing this in a little café, by the camp. Crammed full of Tommies of all sorts, where we are eating tremendously. We are all dreading the night for we are 12 in one tent & it looks like rain. The town seems absolutely empty but for the soldiers in red trousers, of all ages.

I thoroughly enjoy all the events, like being seen off at the dock, except that there were only about 10 people to cheer us as the ship left the side, but its all very amusing—and the girls at the windows.

We are in one of a series of similar Rest Camps on the top of a hill.

Send the first part of this letter to my Aunt.[1] Ask her to send me a large pair of chauffeurs gloves, line with felt. (Any socks must be long in the leg). Also a piece of soap & a night light each week.

Jan. 5th, Sunday. Rest Camp
We are leaving here to-day. A wire came at midnight that we were to be ready. I shan't be sorry to leave this mud. You must imagine a large space of clayey earth, no grass, like an undeveloped building plot, all pulped up into mud and covered with tents with large trenches round them. We get up at 5:30 & march down to the docks, as a rule without breakfast. Here we do——[a] work in an enormous shed. Here is the base for the army & here is all the food. The shed is $\frac{5}{8}$ of a mile long & 79 yrds wide. On one side are the ships coming in and on the other a luggage train of—— covered in vans and the same length as the shed. Each truck is marked with chalk with the amount of stuff that has to go in. So many boxes of corned beef, pepper, salt, bran, hay, oats etc. We work in gangs and have to fill so many trucks from the piles inside the shed. The train goes off in 4 parts each night, to feed the whole army. The shed inside is quite nice, as it's quite new, all light iron work and has of course immense distances in it, men and horses at the end of long avenues, between the mountains of boxes looking quite tiny. There are two cafés inside the limit of the camp (otherwise we have no leave) & we go and talk to the Tommies there. There are all people from all kinds of regiments, some wounded, some lost etc., a kind of sorting camp. We spent one evening with some Belfast Tommies, men about 35, who had rejoined, very simple people with faces like pieces of wood, who told us fearful stories of this sort. Some Ghurkas were left in charge of German prisoners. In the morning all the Germans were found with their heads off. Asked for an explanation, they opened their haversacks, each of which had a German head in it & said, 'Souvenir Sahib'. All this in the most wonderful accent you ever heard.—Three men have been sent back with pneumonia already & I'm not surprised. In the enormous shed we worked in, were batches of English prisoners, people sent back from the front for various reasons, a sergeant 5 years for cowardice, another 15 years for looting. At one end of the shed was an enormous cage, in which all the rum was kept. This was to keep it from being stolen by the A.S.C. men, who are really London dockers enlisted for the war. It was really impressive to see all the piles of food, all done up into cases a convenient size for men to handle.

[a] Spaces in the text of the diary indicate similar gaps in the Hulme family manuscript, which is a transcript of the original letters made by a member of the family. The gaps apparently represent words which could not be deciphered from Hulme's extremely difficult handwriting, though some may also be due to military censorship.

It makes the word 'base' & 'lines of communication' seem much more real to have seen it. It was all guarded by English Territorials who slept in a little enclosure made of packing cases in the middle. All the men doing clerks work live in little houses made of packing cases put together. They say that when the Germans were 12 miles off some months ago they had to shift the whole contents in a day.

Monday. I was called off suddenly at this part of the letter, as we were told we must fall in to leave at once for Rouen. We left about 12, marched 7 miles to the station got here about 8 & then they left us in a railway siding till this morning. We did not know where we were going—it's rather amusing travelling in this way. It was a fearful night however. I woke with a pain behind my right back & could hardly walk. However after going about 200 yds it passed off. We marched off in the morning about 7 miles to an enormous camp up here, through acres of mud, but finally to quite a dry new camp, where we are again under canvas, but much more comfortable. I've got a bad headache so can't write much—am writing this in the Y.M.C.A. shed, there are dozens of them about the camps. I expect we shall be off to-morrow, or in a few days, to the trenches. We have had our fur coats issued to us—I have a kind of goat or wolf skin, look like a bear, great long fur stretching out all over from me. I haven't had my clothes off since I left Southampton. I have chucked my extra pair of boots away, as I couldn't stand the weight. With these heavy packs we perspire like anything on the march, though we go very slowly, very different to marching in England. This camp is on a kind of plateau on the hills outside Rouen & is enormous.

Tuesday, Jan. 12th
We did not have such a long journey as I expected. We left about 4 p.m. and arrived here at the frontier (& the front) about 10 this morning. We travelled up in wagons between 30 & 40 in closed horse or cattle trucks. They are fitted up inside with rough seats down the centre. We marched down to the station, to a kind of railway siding where the cattle train was waiting for us. They kept us standing about for $\frac{3}{4}$ hour, so that we should be thoroughly uncomfortable and then we had to scramble in, everyone of course fighting for the corners. As it got dark people dug their clasp knives into the sides of the truck and fastened their candles to them, so the whole place looked dark and mysterious eventually, with little groups playing cards under the candles. Trucks as you know are fastened with a kind of iron sliding door. It was fearfully uncomfortable. The rain made the floor a pool of black mud, & the few of us who could get down to sleep there had to do it in the mud with continually feet fighting all the night.

As we got near here, we saw on the flat kind of horizon lines of cavalry on horseback, exercising their horses I suppose. When we got here we were marched up into a kind of greenhouse for grapes. It's a very large one and there are about 300 or 350 of us sleeping in it. It's a steel thing, looking like a small Olympia. We have strict instructions not to hang anything on the vines. Just now when everyone is writing letters or getting to bed, it looks like the opening of one of the scenes of the 'Miracle'.

I have just been outside the greenhouse now 7:30 p.m. You can hear all the heavy guns going off. It's like the sound of summer thunder a long way off. We are only about 8 miles from the firing line here and from the part of the trenches, we shall probably march to to-morrow. To continue, every now & then on the horizon, you see a flash, its a kind of illuminating shell used to light up things so that the artillery can fire at anything they see moving. If you listen carefully you can hear from time to time, quick firing by the men's rifles in the trenches. The men are standing watching it by——fire outside, as if it were a fireworks exhibition. We have just met some men I used to know in the 1st Battalion. They are very gloomy about the trenches. An officer and two men have just been killed by snipers. We shall either move up to the trenches to-morrow, or else in 6 days time when the rotation comes round again. We have not rejoined the regiment who are in billets 3 miles nearer the fighting line. There's no doubt about us actually being at the front at last.

Wednesday, Jan. 13th
We left the place I last wrote from on Wednesday. It was pouring with rain and we had to march about 6 miles altogether I should think. It sounds very little but when you have all your equipment and very heavy packs it becomes very tiresome. We were told before we set out that we should, in a few miles, be inside the area of shell fire. The roads are simply fearful with mud and you keep meeting supply motors and carts which push you to the side of the road in the mud. All you can think of on the march, is various ways of shifting the weight of your pack from one shoulder to another, every now and then you rest and you bend down something like this[b] in order to save the weight of your pack on the shoulders. You look reflectively at your feet & the patterns of the mud as you do this, & that will be the predominant impression I shall carry away from this war. The first thing that looked at all characteristic of war (in the old Boer War scene) was when we were overtaken by a transport wagon

[b] Here Hulme has inserted a sketch of a man with a pack on his back, bent at the waist and leaning on his rifle.

taking food, guarded by men on horseback with rifles slung across their shoulders. These we met at the corner of a road where we seemed to have lost our way. Our feet of course were all wet through. About midday we passed through a village, where a lot of our H.A.C. men were resting & people recognised each other. They kept us standing here 20 min. without letting us take our packs off, every man swearing. Finally about a mile further on, after the man on horseback who was supposed to be guiding us, had cantered up to various farmhouses, one about 100 yards off the main road was pointed out to us as the one where we were to eat. There was a big barn there, where we could shelter from the rain. We waded across a field & through a farmyard with mud above our ankles, only to be turned back by a staff officer who said we had made a mistake. This was the last straw—some of us wandered off by ourselves and found a little cowshed where we took off our packs at last and ate bully beef. When we got a $\frac{1}{4}$ mile from the village we were making for, we had to stop and wait till dusk, as it is rather exposed to shell fire. We heard fearfully unpleasant noises of guns going off, but they were our own batteries just behind us. After dusk we got in the village where our men were. About half the houses have one side or a roof missing, as this place has often been bombarded and there are great holes at the side of the road made by Jack Johnson shells.[2] All the houses in this place are empty, a few of the whole and shelled houses being used as a billet for our men. We could see some of them asleep & some washing as we came in. There is a very incongruous bandstand in the centre, surrounded by barbed wire entanglement ready to be moved to the trenches.

We were marched up to some large schools where we were billeted. In the evening I went round to see some of the people I used to know in the 1st Battalion. All looked very different, their faces & clothes a sort of pale mud colour, all very tired of it and anxious to get back.

Thursday, Jan. 14th
We had to mend the holes in the road made by the shells, great holes that are very dangerous at night.

Friday, Jan. 15th
We had to dig a deep trench to clear away the water from a lot of dug outs (holes made as a protection from shell fire). All the time we were doing this the Germans were dropping shells onto a hill above us. One fell about 70 yds away, by the bandstand. You hear a noise like a train high up in the air appearing to go very slowly, then you see a thick cloud of black smoke going up where they have burst, then you hear the bang, then after that the whistling noise seems to end.

Nobody is in the least frightened because they are all being aimed at a point a few hundred yards away, where they think an English battery is. Everybody stopped digging when they heard the first whistling noise in order to run to a place where they could see them burst. How we should behave if they started shelling us I don't know. This village has several times been bombarded & probably will be again, only the Germans don't know we are here. In order that they shan't find it out, no fires are allowed at night, all candles must be kept on the floor and window spaces blocked up. A regiment near here neglected this and got a shell in the middle of their place, killing about 10 men.

Friday, Jan. 15th
They have not amalgamated us yet with the 1st Battalion, so we did not go into the trenches with them. I wanted to see what the trenches were like, so I volunteered to go as one of a party which was going up to the trenches at night, to take up large bundles of wood to put at the bottom of them for the men to stand on. These parties go up almost every night. They are fairly safe, though it so happened that the party that went the night before had one man killed. But they go night after night and nothing happens. There were about 100 of us. We wore our overcoats & carried rifles. We were formed up about 5 o'clock when it was dark, told to load our rifles & then we filed past a barn where each man drew a long bundle of faggots about 8 ft long. We then went off in single file, down a long road lined with poplars, nearly all the way. The Germans kept firing off rockets & star shells. These latter hang in the air for a few minutes & light up the whole road. We were told that whenever one of these went off we were to stand still & bend our heads down so that the white of our faces could not be seen. After a time we began to hear bullets whizzing over our heads all fairly high. All that worries anyone is the uncomfortableness of the faggots. Also I had not put the sling of my rifle on properly & was wondering all the while whether it would not slip off my shoulder on to the ground & draw attention to me personally & my clumsiness. After about a mile along the road, we turned off along the fields & made for the trenches. Here the uncomfortable part started. It seemed to be absolutely all mud. Its bad enough walking over uneven ground in the dark at any time when you don't know whether your foot is landing on earth or nothing the next step. Every now & then you fell over & got up to your knees in the mud. As the trenches here are rather this shape——you got bullets flying over your head from the German trenches in all directions. Nobody worries about these however, all you can think of is the mud. What makes it infinitely worse is that, every now & then you lose sight of the man in front of you. The line ahead of you

runs over a rather more dangerous part & you must keep up at all costs, though it's all in the dark & you are floundering about all the time. You simply must keep up, because if you once lost the man in front, you wouldn't know what on earth to do, you might even walk up to the German lines. We finally had to cross a series of great ditches of mud & deposit the faggots under the shelter of some rising ground about 40 yds behind the trenches. Its fairly quiet up in the trenches, & all we heard was an average of about 20 a minute & as we were a short distance behind the trenches they were flying over our heads all the time. The only thing that makes you feel nervous is when the star shells go off & you stand out revealed quite clearly as in daylight. You have then the most wonderful feeling as if you were suddenly naked in the street and didn't like it. It isn't that really but the impression it makes on you, as if you were walking across a flat heath or common at night & along a long line in front of you the lights were shooting off all the time silhouetting all the trees & bushes. It's really like a kind of nightmare, in which you are in the middle of an enormous saucer of mud with explosions & shots going off all round the edge, a sort of fringe of palm trees made of fireworks all round it. One thing I forgot to mention, when you do lose the man in front of you, if you crouch down low in the mud you can see the profile of the men in front of you, but with these faggots in a sort of frieze—like the procession in Scheherezade, or rather very unlike it. It took me the *whole* of the next morning to scrape the mud off my clothes, it was all over my coat up to my waist.

Saturday, Jan. 16th

At 7 o'clock on Saturday we had to parade in the road outside the school where we lived, to march back in the dark, some 3 or 4 miles to a place further back from the firing line, out of range of shell fire, for 4 days rest. After that we shall go back for 4 days in the firing line again & so on. It was an awful confusion as we marched out in the dark, as the other regiments to take our place, were entering the place & we got mixed up in the road with another regiment also leaving for the night. We seemed to be about 3 different regiments abreast going different ways. We marched in single file all the way, it was pitch dark. When we got to the next town we were told off to different cottages where we were billeted. There are 36 in the room I'm in. Here in the time during the 4 days rest, I'm spending all my time with my old section & am really quite comfortable. They have been here for weeks & know the ropes. They have things sent them out from England, have made friends with a Flemish cobbler & we all 12 of us, sit in their back room all day, cooking our meals ourselves on the stove that all the villages have here. You must feed well these days of rest in order to keep well in the trenches. Here is where we find a little money useful. We can buy ourselves eggs etc. & all kinds of things. The bully beef gives everyone bad dysentery. In the afternoon we go up a hill where we can see for miles our own & beyond the German lines, the flash from an English gun, & then later see, it seems miles away, the white smoke of the shell bursting. Then you see all over the landscape the white puffs from which German shells are bursting over our trenches. We can see a town about——miles away that was bombarded. I can't go into details about anything or the letter would be torn up.

To-morrow, Wednesday we go back to the trenches for 4 days. It so happens however that the next 4 days, all No. 2's officers are away on leave, so to my annoyance my company will not go to the trenches this time, but will act as reserve, but we shall probably go up to the trenches to carry up things.

Jan. 27th

I have had a very uncomfortable time this week. As I told you last week after 4 days rest we go down to a place near the trenches. We marched off there last Wednesday, late in the day so as to get there after dark, or we might be shelled on our arrival. We never know whether we shall get a good or a bad billet when we arrive there, it's always different. We were led into the chapel attached to a school and our section managed to get a corner by the altar. It looks very curious to see a lot of troops billeted in a place like this, rifles resting on the altar, & hanging over statues of the saints, men sleeping on the altar steps. (You had better leave this part out in sending it to Stanbrook).^c It was rather cold as all the windows were smashed & we have no blankets now. We lit a brazier, i.e. an old bucket with holes knocked in it, burning charcoal & coke. We had nothing to do the first night, as it was some other company's turn in the trenches. Next morning one of the men went out & dug up some vegetables from a deserted garden & made a kind of stew without meat. We get no cooked meat in the 4 days. The next night we went up to a kind of circular reserve trench. You go up a long file, as I described in my last letter. We were challenged at the entrance & then entered a narrow passage going down to the level of the trenches. I don't think I've been so exasperated for years as I was in taking up my position in this trench. It wasn't an ordinary one but was roofed over most of the way, leaving passage about 4 ft: absolutely impossible for me to walk through. I had to crawl along on my hands & knees, through the mud in pitch darkness & every now & then seemed to get stuck altogether. You feel shut in and

---

^c A convent near Worcester where two of Hulme's aunts were nuns.

hopeless. I wished I was about 4 ft. This war isn't for tall men. I got in a part too narrow and too low to stand or sit & had to sit sideways on a sack of coke to keep out of the water. We had to stay there from about 7 p.m. till just before dawn next morning, a most miserable experience. You can't sleep & you sit as it were at the bottom of a drain with nothing to look at but the top of the ditch slowly freezing. It's unutterably boring. The next night was better, because I carried up a box to sit on & a sack of coke to burn in a brazier. But one brazier in a narrow trench among 12 men only warms about 3. All through this night, we had to dig a new passage in shifts. That in a way did look picturesque at midnight—a very clear starry night. This mound all full of passages like a mole hill & 3 or 4 figures silhouetted on top of it using pick or shovel. The bullets kept whistling over it all the time, but as it's just over the crest of a hill most of them are high, though every now & then one comes on your level & it is rather uncomfortable when you are taking your turn at sentry. The second night it froze hard, & it was much easier walking back over the mud.

In reality there is nothing picturesque about it. It's the most miserable existence you can conceive of. I feel utterly depressed at the idea of having to do this for 48 hours every 4 days. It's simply hopeless. The boredom & discomfort of it, exasperate you to the breaking point.

It's curious to think of the ground between the trenches, a bank which is practically never seen by anyone in the daylight, as it is only safe to move through it at dark. It's full of dead things, dead animals here & there, dead unburied animals, skeletons of horses destroyed by shell fire. It's curious to think of it later on in the war, when it will again be seen in the daylight. We had to do this for every night for 12 hours. Next week we shall be in the firing line, in two periods of 24 hours each. On our way down we generally meet someone being brought up wounded or killed to cheer us up.

Feb. 10th

The last day of the last 4 days rest here was like summer. We had breakfast outside the cobbler's cottage and in the afternoon went up to the Inn on the hill and they all drank wine outside. A regular who was up there said 'Who says there's a war now' & it certainly did seem absolutely remote from it, though we could see here and there the——of heavy artillery firing at the Germans. The same evening we marched straight from here up to the trenches. We went to the firing line again. But this time it was not a new properly constructed trench like the last one I told you of but an——average trench. We had to spend the night in the open air as there were very few dugouts. There was a German rifle trained on a fixed part

of the trench just where we were. It's very irritating to hear a bullet time
after time hit the same spot on the parapet. About lunch time this rifle
continually hitting the same place, spattered dirt from the parapet over
my bread and butter. It gets very irritating after a time & everybody
shouts out 'Oh stop it'. It showed however that it was a dangerous corner
and the next day another company of our regiment took our place in this
trench, a man in exactly the place where our section was, getting curious
at the repetition of a shot in the same spot, got up to look with his field
glasses. He stayed up a second too long and got shot through the head
dead. Field glasses are rather a temptation, they make you stay up too
long. Towards the end of our——the same day, the Germans started to
shell our trench. It was a dangerous trench for shelling because it was very
wide so gave no protection to the back. Our N.C.O. told us to shift to
a narrower part of the trench. I got separated from the others in a narrow
communication trench behind with one other man. We had seen shells
bursting fairly near us before and at first did not take it very seriously. But
it soon turned out to be very different. The shells started dropping right
on the trench itself. As soon as you had seen someone hurt, you began to
look at shelling in a very different way. We shared this trench with the X
regiment. About 10 yds away from where I was a man of this regiment
had his arm and $\frac{3}{4}$ of his head blown off a frightful mess, his brains all over
the place, some on the back of that man who stands behind me in the
photograph. The worst of shelling is, the regulars say, that you don't get
used to it, but get more & more alarmed at it every time. At any rate the
regulars in our trenches behaved in rather a strange way. One man threw
himself down on the bottom of the trench, shaking all over & crying.
Another started to weep. It lasted for nearly $1\frac{1}{2}$ hrs and at the end of it
parts of the trenches were all blown to pieces. It's not the idea of being
killed that's alarming, but the idea of being hit by a jagged piece of steel.
You hear the whistle of the shell coming, you crouch down as low as you
can and just wait. It doesn't burst merely with a bang, it has a kind of
crash with a snap in it, like the crack of a very large whip. They seemed
to burst just over your head, you seem to anticipate it killing you in the
back, it hits just near you and you get hit on the back with clods of earth
& (in my case) spent bits of shell & shrapnel bullets fall all round you. I
picked up one bullet almost sizzling in the mud just by my toe. What
irritates you is the continuation of the shelling. You seem to feel that
20 min. is normal, is enough—but when it goes on for over an hour, you
get more & more exasperated, feel as if it were 'unfair'. Our men were as
it happened very lucky, only three were hurt slightly & none killed. They
all said it was the worst experience they have had since they were out
here. I'm not in the least anxious myself to repeat it, nor is anyone else

I think. It was very curious from where I was; looking out and over the back of the trench, it looked absolutely peaceful. Just over the edge of the trench was a field of turnips or something of that kind with their leaves waving about in a busy kind of way, exactly as they might do in a back garden. About 12 miles away over the plain you could see the towers & church spires of an old town very famous in this war. By a kind of accident or trick, everything was rather gloomy, except this town which appeared absolutely white in the sun and immobile as if it would always be like that, and was out of time and space altogether. You've got to amuse yourself in the intervals of shelling and romanticising the situation is as good a way as any other. Looking at the scene the waving vegetables, the white town & all the rest of it, it looks quite timeless in a Buddhistic kind of way and you feel quite resigned if you are going to be killed to leave it just like that. When it ceased and we all got back to our places everybody was full of it. We went back that night to a new billet in a barn, so near the line that we weren't allowed to have light at all, but spread our bread & butter in the dark, or by the intermittent light of electric torches pointed down. The next night we went up to new trenches altogether. This time we weren't in the firing line, but in a line of dug-outs, or supports.

These dug-outs were about 2 ft deep, so you can imagine how comfortable I was. They put me in one by myself. It felt just like being in your grave, lying flat just beneath the surface of the ground & covered up. And there I had to be for 24 hours unable to get out until it was dark next night for we could be seen from the German lines.—We were relieved very late and altogether were out 30 hours instead of 24. We had a couple of men wounded on the road up, so we went back by a safer way across the fields. A man I know quite well had a bullet entered one side of his nose & came out near his ear. They have sent him back to England & say he will remain.

I'm getting more used to this kind of life and as long as I don't get hurt or it doesn't rain too much, don't mind it at all.

Feb. 20th

We went down to the trenches on a Saturday. We form up at dark in the one street of the town here. There is generally a lot to be done on the last day as we have to clean up all our billets ready for the other brigade marching up after their 4 days at the trenches. While we are formed up there in the street waiting, some of the other regiments of our brigade who go to the trenches at the same time as we do are sure to march past. A regiment on the march here is a very curious sight. In spite of the fact that they have to clean themselves and their clothes in their 4 days of rest, they all look a general pale, washed out, dusty muddy colour. The officers march on foot generally at the head of their platoons, looking very little different to their men, except that they generally carry a roughly trimmed piece of wood, about as long as a shepherds crook, as a walking stick. They find these useful in the muddy paths up to the actual trenches. Very few are in any kind of step and they slouch along generally two deep, for only the centre of the road is really passable. The exception to the slouching is an occasional section when the two front men play a mouth organ or bones, when they march well to-gether. Their packs look a good deal lighter than ours, they don't get so many parcels. At intervals come the officers horses, generally unmounted (they ride them however at the end of 4 days when they are coming *back* from the trenches & are more tired). At the end come the mules carrying extra ammunition, the transport & finally the field kitchens, usually boiling something & stuffed up with odd bits of wood ready for fuel & the cooks leaning on them as they walk behind. This time we did not go straight up to the trenches but into 'close billet' for the night. This is a large barn. It's comfortable except that it's well within range & if only the Germans one day find out we are here, they will drop a shell on us, and then we should most of us be done for. On the morning of the next day we had all suddenly to get ready & come downstairs, because shells were falling uncomfortably near. We always have a guard outside to report aeroplanes & the nearness of shells for this purpose. None of us are ever allowed out in the daytime. How near it is to the trenches may be judged from the fact that this time one of our sentries was shot dead by a stray bullet. The next night we went up to the trenches. I think I told you in my last letter that we are now holding a different part of the line, a mile of so N of our old trenches, worse trenches and a worse path up to them. Last time we went up to them by a road but we had one man wounded (there are too many stray bullets passing over it) so we went up by a new way over the fields. Suddenly when we were going up a fearfully muddy field by the side of a wood in a long line & single file, a shell whizzed over us & burst a few yards behind the last man. I happened to be looking backward when it burst. Being night it was very bright & looked more like a firework than anything else. We at once got the order to lie flat in the mud on our faces and although it isn't pleasant to be flat on your face in pure mud, yet the presence of the shells makes us do it without any reluctance. I didn't see much after that, for I had my head down flat, but they put about 20 shells over us, rather smallish shells they must have been which seemed to go whizz-bang—very quickly. They fell all along the line of the 50 men, but all a little wide. We got bits of earth flung over us but nothing more. They all thought their last hour had come for to be caught & shelled in the open like that is the most dangerous thing that can happen to you. You have no protection like you have in a trench. It was soon over however & then we got up and continued our walk to the trenches, most of us expecting suddenly to hear the same explosion again. We had to cross several shell & Jack Johnson holes full of water bridged by a single plank & in the dark most of us fell in once before we got there. We got to miserable trenches where we were not allowed to have a brazier and we sat there absolutely wet through up to the pips for 24 hours. That's the worst of getting wet here, it isn't like after a day's shooting when you can get home & change. The next night when we got back, an attack from the Germans was expected. We had to sleep in our boots etc all night & couldn't take anything off. That made 48 hours thoroughly wet through. The extraordinary thing is that it doesn't hurt you. It hasn't hurt us at any rate, though when the regiment last spent 3 days in the trenches before Xmas they lost 250 men & 11 officers through sickness. It makes you very depressed however & weakens you—it gave me diarrhoea. This last 6 days have been unusual for all kinds of things have been happening to the N of us of which we hear rumours. We are told over night that further up the line certain trenches are to be retaken & next day we hear they have been taken. I expect you have read all about it in the papers & of course as it is only a few miles from us, it affects us. We have to be ready for a counter attack. That first night we were up we could tell that something was up. It was a pitch black night, one of those nights that exasperate you because you are afraid of losing the man in front of you. All the heavy guns on both sides were firing, never a minute without a report and you could see the flashes from the muzzles all round the horizon. In the trench that day (it couldn't properly be called a trench, just a ditch with sandbags on the top) we sat all day and watched shells burst in the field behind us. Fortunately never nearer than 20 yards. In the next trench, a different company of our regiment in, they killed one man & wounded 15 that afternoon. The most annoying part of being in the trenches is the waiting for the 'relief'. You get ready long before it comes. Sometimes it comes hours after you expect it. You listen & think you hear voices & feet. At last it's coming. Then it turns out that you were mistaken. Finally a German star shell reveals them to you half-way across the field. They are all standing immobile in the middle of the field bent down. It is curious how this continuous shelling and the apprehension of it has altered some men. They keep very quiet all day long & hardly say anything. This day in the trenches I should think 50 or 60 dropped in the one field, making holes all over it like a sort of smallpox. It is these holes filled with water which make walking up the roads at night so annoying. The 4 days when we came back we were told we shouldn't be relieved for some days. However we were relieved after 6 days and marched back very late to our rest town, everyone fearfully exhausted. I have written much too long a letter. I want to post it at once so that it won't be delayed like the others were. I can't tell you much, but as a result of the recent fighting there are all kinds of changes. We are now in a different brigade etc.

[NOTE BY CENSOR. Please inform sender next letter of this length will not be passed. H. P. G. M——]

March 2nd
The first time up we went back again into the trenches where we were shelled. This is a bad trench in which you just have to sit out in the open all night. It froze hard and all the rifles were white in the morning. The next time it was our turn to have a rest, but they gave us (the platoon about 40 men) a fatigue up to the trenches, carrying up hurdles and barbed wire. Except for the danger from stray bullets, this is compared to going into the trenches, a pleasure trip. You are very light carrying only a rifle. It was a bright moonlight night, and the way up to the trenches is a straight narrow road. There were far too many men to carry the stuff and 4 of us carried one hurdle ragging each other all the way up, suggesting that the fat man should sit on top of it and we would carry him up. Half way up we met the stretcher bearers, carrying down one of our men who had been killed during the day. They hurry along quite in a different way when they are carrying a dead and not a wounded man. I think they break step and hurry along like lamplighters to avoid getting caught by a stray bullet themselves. It's curious how the mere fact that in a certain direction there really are the German lines, seems to alter the feeling of a landscape. You unconsciously orient things in reference to it. In peacetime, each direction on the road is as it were indifferent, it all goes on ad infinitum. But now you know that certain roads lead as it were, up to an abyss.

When we came back from this fatigue it so happened it was very quiet no bullets about at all, and we strolled back exactly as though we were walking home late from a party on a moonlight night. These fatigues are not always so lucky. Last week the tennis player Kenneth Powell was killed carrying up corrugated iron. (It seems curious the way people realize things. I heard a man say 'It does seem a waste. Kenneth Powell carrying up corrugated iron.' You see he was interested in games.) This is a curious life—in that there is nothing certain or fixed. You never come back to the same billets. You can never leave anything. You have no place that belongs to you. You really are as nomadic as an animal. You never depend on any routine. You may be there 4 or 6 or 10 days. You

may come back to a different place altogether. The only fixed thing seems
to be the letters you get from home. It's very difficult to describe
anything to you, to at all make you realize what it is *actually* like. Not that
it is above the common place, & too difficult to describe, for that reason
it isn't. But just actually in its own peculiar way. If I describe a tiring day
in the trenches to you & the weary march back at night to the farm, in
the dark, you go wrong at once, because when I use the word farmhouse,
you must have some fixed idea in your head of a farmhouse, which isn't
at all the——of the one we——in.

We have not gone back to the trenches to-day as we generally do, the
4 days rest being up, but are to stay up here an extra 2 days. I suppose it
will mean that when we do go to the trenches it will be for 6 days, so it's
not as pleasing as it might otherwise have been. So that we shouldn't
enjoy the extra rest too much, they had us out in the middle of a field to
do company drill—we were all drawn up to hear an announcement—we
all expected something dramatic, but it was only to say that Gen. Smith
Dorrien[3] was very pleased with us, or something equally uninteresting,
finishing up by saying that they hoped we should continue to uphold our
reputation 'till the end of the campaign'. This fell very flat as all everyone
hopes is that we shall get back as soon as possible. I am afraid we are in
for it. We may get a fortnight's rest but there's no chance of us getting
back at all. It still continues wonderful weather & the country looks
absolutely different. One can see now how it will look in the Spring. I
don't suppose any of us ever waited for the Spring with so much interest.
One does notice physical things here tremendously. You reckon up when
it will be full moon, it means a very uncomfortable clear walk up to the
trenches. To-day it's frosty, but a hard wind, everything is very clear and
bright. Along the crest of a hill I have just seen a lot of Indians, leading
donkeys & mules, leaning forward to meet the wind, & silhouetted on the
sky line, looking just like the conventional illustrations of the East. You
have no idea what a difference the hard weather makes.

Must stop here.

March 21st, Sunday
I think I told you that for the first nine days we were continually in a kind
of reserve trench. The second morning there we saw what so far I think
has been the most complete war scene yet. I mean the most conventional,
shut off, the most like war in a theatre as it were. Just below us about 300
yards away was a large farm with its buildings (on a position very like that
of Gratton (on a hill, below another hill) looking at it from Dunwood[4]
but about half the distance away). To make the thing comprehensible I
must explain that after 24 hours in the trenches, troops go back for the

next 24 hours to what are called 'close billets' i.e. places where they are still under shell fire & so where they must remain invisible all the time. It is the business of the artillery on both sides to shell likely 'close billets', sometimes getting the information as to which farms & villages are close billets from spies. Most of the farms round about have been destroyed only the walls standing & another man said early in the morning that it was curious that this farm was entirely untouched looking very peaceful (& as I say exactly like Gratton about the same size). In the middle of the morning we suddenly heard a shell whistling over which burst just over the roof. Then a second, whose smoke was all red showing that it had hit the roof, the red tiles broken up into dust mixing with the smoke. Three or four more shells & then we saw two pigs rushing out of the courtyard. We thought the place was empty & that the Germans were wasting their shells. Then we saw one figure going across a field on the other side of the farm but we couldn't tell whether a soldier or perhaps a Belgian civilian. The shelling went on dropping all over the roof till one caught fire. Then we caught sight of about 30 bent figures creeping along the road along the ridge from the farm. To make you realize the actual scene, there was a hedge on this side of the road & an avenue of trees. There were more shells & finally the whole of one roof burning. More & more groups of men creeping along the road (at this distance we could only see a kind of bent silhouette). This went on till I should think several hundreds more had left (they were probably all asleep resting after the trenches). Then there was a fearful row of ammunition popping off sounding exactly like continuous rifle fire in the trenches. Then another building caught fire (in which I suppose those wounded by the shells had been put). One man came out of an open door & ran across a field & behind a haystack after a minute another followed, then there were about ten there, when the Germans dropped a few shells over it. Then along the road men began to come back & fetch out the wounded from the burning barn. As they came back along the road very slowly helping the men along they were spotted & got German rifle fire at them. The place went on burning for nearly two days. The whole scene being extremely depressing. Enormous red flames, exactly like a poster of war & destruction & then miserable looking black figures & probably very tired people crawling out. What happened later in the week I can't tell you about for it would probably be crossed out by the censor. I was on sentry one night & saw a whole regiment passing up in single file to take up their position for an attack. One man was shot about 20 yds from me. I saw in the dark, the line stop & people cluster round him, the line pass on & then finally stretcher bearers carry him off. I saw his equipment——in the place where he had fallen. I had myself too one night up there the unpleasant job of carrying down one of our men who had been shot dead through the heart. This is a very unpleasant job when you have to go in pitch darkness a way you don't know very well over mud & ditches. I'm glad it wasn't a man I knew but it's very queer as you carry him down shoulder high, his face is very near your own. One day after an attack I saw a man come staggering across a field as if he were drunk, holding his head, finally falling down just outside our barbed wire entanglement. It turned out to be a Tommy who had been blown right out of our trenches by our own artillery. All that day there had been a terrific bombardment, English shells whistling over our heads every second.

Must stop now.

If you don't hear from me again, you will know I have gone to the trenches again for 4 or 6 days.

April 19th 1915[5]

We left the filthy barn we are billeted in about seven o'clock, marched down a side road over a hill about three miles to a smashed up village just behind the new trenches we were going to. We were marched up to a chateau all blown to pieces. When we got there we had to wait about 2 hours outside while they tried to find places for us inside. That's how they do things in the army. They never seem to think 5 minutes before they do a thing. Eventually some of us were stowed in a dug-out just deep enough for us to crawl through, just like a rabbit hole and told we were to stay there for 48 hours a perfect nightmare for people of my size. Eventually they came and after looking round had found us a room in a house in a village that had a roof on it. The room had no windows and was filled with layers of straw which we daren't move for fear of what might be underneath. However it was very comfortable after the dug-out. Here we stayed for 48 hours, the second night being out from 10 till 2 carrying barbed wire up to the trenches. This was a hideous affair. When we got there nobody knew where they were to go and so we stopped there for 30 minutes behind the firing trench while they found out, a very uncomfortable time. One bullet hit the trestles the fat man was carrying and a piece of the wood flew up his arm. It's the kind of fooling unnecessary business which makes one so fed up. After 48 hours we went up to the trenches. A wretched night continually soaking and through a blunder the——fully equipped as we were carrying up boxes about 1000 rounds of ammunition over ditches and soaked fields. I dont know how some of the men ever got up. We got into an open trench about 1:30 having started at 10, so you may tell what sort of a job it was, to go along 2 miles. There were no shelters and it poured continually for several hours. Fortunately the next 36 hours it was finer and then we marched back about 10 p.m. to a rest barn. After going about a couple of miles we stopped at some cross roads for nearly an hour and a half absolutely tired out. It's the kind of thing——you more than anything. You try to sleep on the side of the road but it's too cold. And now for our rest here. Every night we have had to march back to the trenches about 4 miles and dig. The night before last we were out from 8 p.m. till 4 in the morning. We have only had a proper night's rest in the last three weeks. This isn't a proper diary I have just told you in a hurry what we have been doing. I'll write a proper account in the trenches directly. I've no time here, as ——to sleep all day. We are back again to the trenches to-night for four days continuously. We shall be glad when we do get our rest, this three weeks is all for some special reason when that is over I hope we shall go back to the old system. This is a curious thing, we move as you know always at night and troops going always in the same direction make definite paths. One of our snipers walking about in the daylight discovered that one of these paths that we walk over led right over the chest of a dead peasant (Belgian).

War Notes

[These commentaries on the First World War were written in 1915–16 while Hulme was at home, recuperating from wounds he had received in battle in Apr. 1915. They were published in *NA* in seventeen instalments: 18/2 (11 Nov. 1915), 29–30; 18/3 (18 Nov. 1915), 53–5; 18/4 (25 Nov. 1915), 77; 18/5 (2 Dec. 1915), 101–2; 18/6 (9 Dec. 1915), 125–6; 18/7 (16 Dec. 1915), 149–51; 18/8 (23 Dec. 1915), 173–4; 18/9 (30 Dec. 1915), 197–9; 18/10 (6 Jan. 1916), 222–3; 18/11 (13 Jan. 1916), 246–7; 18/12 (20 Jan. 1916), 269–70; 18/13 (27 Jan. 1916), 293–4; 18/14 (3 Feb. 1916), 317–18; 18/15 (10 Feb. 1916), 341–2; 18/16 (17 Feb. 1916), 365–6; 18/17 (24 Feb. 1916), 389–91; and 18/18 (2 Mar. 1916), 413–14. They were signed 'North Staffs.'. Abbreviated versions of the Notes for 20, 27 Jan., 3, 10, 17, 24 Feb., and 2 Mar. 1916 were published in the *Cambridge Magazine* two days later each week with new titles. C. K. Ogden recalled, in a letter to Samuel Hynes in 1953, that he had asked Hulme to contribute to the *Cambridge Magazine*: 'I told him I could only take what space might allow, so he could also print in *The New Age* if he wanted to—the same or more. This I think he did, as there was no overlap with the *New Age* circulation, and Orage had plenty of space for anything Hulme might write' (letter dated 16 Dec. 1953, courtesy of Mr Hynes).

The versions reproduced here are the more complete *New Age* versions. Any differences between the two versions are given in the end-notes.]

[11 November 1915]

The first remark of a foreigner visiting England to-day or of a soldier back from the front is that England does not yet realise that we are at war. Even allowing for our habitual taciturnity, usually intensified during critical periods, the remark is not only true, but it is considerably within the truth. Much less than the war itself are its issues realised; and since these, and not the event, are of the first importance, our failure to grasp the significance of the war may easily prove more disastrous than our failure to believe that a war is actually in progress. The inability of the mass of Englishmen to appreciate the issues of the war arises from a number of mental predispositions, some of them native to the English character, and others resulting from recent conditions and prevalent doctrines. Among the former is the reluctance of the national mind to dwell upon the subject of war at all. We are by nature one of the kindest people that ever lived, good-natured, sentimental and fundamentally amiable; and the contemplation of war, particularly in its realistic aspects, is naturally disagreeable to us. But this pleasing characteristic has unfortunately been flattered into something like a national vice by doctrines associated mainly with the Liberal school of opinion. Some of them are as follows.

There is, to begin with, the Liberal assumption, practically never challenged, that things are fixed more or less as they are, and cannot radically change. The map of Europe, for example, is commonly conceived of as having somehow become what it is, never greatly to change again. A petty political transformation, such as the republicanisation of Portugal, may occur here, or a party dispute in Russia may establish a Duma there; but in the distribution of the main units of Europe no change can be expected. From this reasoning, it will be seen, no event can be regarded as of really great importance; for why should we concern ourselves deeply when the outcome of every event is predestined to be comparatively small? An Armageddon may be upon us in the opinion of isolated thinkers and rhetorical journalists; but an Armageddon, in fact, threatening any fundamental transformation of European civilisation, is ex hypothesi impossible. To this it can only be replied that the hypothesis is not only wrong in fact, but it is likely to prove fatal when it becomes a doctrine. Far from being fixed in its now familiar features, both as regards distribution of political power and prevalence of a particular type of culture, Europe, it is the simple truth to say, is in a continual flux of which the present war is a highly critical intensification. The common phrase about things being in the melting-pot is neither hyperbole nor cliché when applied to the present war. It is, on the other hand, an exact metaphor. Literally every boundary in Europe, of political, social, intellectual and cultural importance, is at this moment in dispute, not of argument alone, but of force; and as the war subsides, so will these boundaries be left where it places them, to determine the *form* of Europe during the coming period of peace.

An illustration from the trenches may illuminate the matter. From the point of view of the uninstructed observer, the line of trenchworks extending from the Channel to the Alps appears to have several of the characteristics of fixity. Mutually hostile forces meet at the line and there, too, each party attempts to nibble at the other; but the main conformation of the line may be said to be relatively fixed; and such a fixed line, variously drawn, marked out Europe before the war. But we know very well that not only was the trench-line determined at every inch by local circumstances over which men *had* control, but it is also the will of both parties, and, we hope, the destiny of the Allies, to change the position of the line completely. Similarly our Liberal friends may be reminded that the lines now making a map of Europe are the result in every instance of local circumstances governable by men; and as they were determined by men they can be changed by men. Europe, in short, is a creation, not a blind evolutionary product; and nothing connected with its mental features is any more fixed than the present relations, as expressed in the trench-lines, between the Allies and the enemy.

Another prevalent Liberal assumption, hostile to a proper appreciation of the significance of the war, is that progress is both inevitable and of necessity in one direction. That change, like the girl in the play, may of itself or by the intention of those who bring it about, take the wrong turning seems never to enter the heads of some of our most popular doctrinaires. All that is not Liberal in Europe or elsewhere is in their opinion not even fundamentally anti-Liberal or other-than-Liberal,—it is merely an arrested development of an evolution which in any case must needs be Liberal in the end, or a reaction against, but still upon the line of, Liberalism. This, I need not say after stating it, is not only an error, but a particularly insular error. In the first place, evolution in our sense of the word—that is, evolution towards democracy—is not only not inevitable, but it is the most precarious, difficult and exigent task political man has ever conceived. And, in the second place, far from it being the predestined path of every nation and race, only one or two nations have attempted to pursue it, while the rest deliberately and even, we might say, intelligently, pursue another path altogether as if *that* were progress, and are thus sincerely hostile to our own.

To take the instance that ought to be best known to us by now—that of Germany—how impossible it still appears for English Liberal opinion (Conservatives have, of course, no opinions) to eradicate from its mind the assumption that Germany is Liberal at heart. Nothing can be more contrary to the fact. Knowing Germany as I do from residence there as well as from history, past and present, I affirm that the mind of Germany is neither Liberal nor even Liberalising, that is, disposed to become Liberal. Of the two orders of German intelligence—the first-rate and the second-rate—both, it is true, are split upon the subject of democracy; but into parties of which in the first the anti-democratic party is intellectually the more able, and in the second more numerous. Set beside the names of the first-rate minds in Germany who support the present Government and the theories upon which it is based, the names of its opponents of the same rank; it will be found that the former outweigh the latter. Similarly, if the numbers of the second-rate minds in Germany (the professional educated classes) who accept the State theory and practice are compared with the minds of the same order that challenge it, the result is equally menacing to democracy. It may be replied that the progress in numbers and influence of the German Social Democrats is opposed to my statement. But while admitting it partially, no great value attaches to it. The Social Democrats are without power, and they are, in private at least, without hope. English Liberals may entertain the belief that the German bureaucracy will collapse if it is defeated; nay, even, as I have heard said, find its leaders at the end of the war swinging upon lamp-posts. But German Social Democracy believes nothing of the kind. The parallel between the present German and the pre-revolutionary French Government is fictitious, and no hopes built upon it have any foundation. The Government of Louis was inefficient, unpopular, and, what is more, did not believe in itself. The German Government is, on the other hand, efficient, popular and self-confident. No hope of revolution from internal causes can therefore be anticipated. For the time being Germany is not only not Liberal, but it is actively bureaucratic and anti-Liberal, and appears likely to remain so. The only hope—and that is faint—for the victory of Social Democracy in Germany is the victory of the Allies.

Wolf, wolf, has been cried so many times in this country that, on the one hand, we have lost the sensation and almost the very notion of national peril, and, on the other hand, we have presumed upon our historic security to leave our future security to chance. In the matter of peril, for example, it is doubtful whether more than one in a thousand of our intelligent population has had his mind once crossed during the war by the thought that perhaps England is really in danger. And even fewer, I imagine, have once asked what are likely to be the consequences to the English of England's defeat. All we mean by democracy will certainly take a second place in our daily lives if the Central Powers have their way. It cannot be otherwise. Democracy and bureaucracy are obviously incompatible principles; both cannot be dominant at the same time; they are the professional and the human ideals which are always in antagonism. For German bureaucracy to succeed is to ensure the failure of English democracy, and with it of all the secondary variations dependent upon it. One of these, paradoxical as it may seem, is the freedom from the necessity to be pre-occupied by a narrow politic. Think of the psychology of the Poles, and, in another way, of the Irish. Both are, in the particular sense we are discussing, more than merely defeated nations; they are nations which their conquerors cannot assimilate, and which, equally, cannot assimilate themselves with their conquerors. With what result? Their politic is born of resentment, bred on conspiracy, and brought up in an atmosphere of whispered gossip. Everything must be subordinated to the Catilinarian in nations such as these. Free thought, free speech, free culture, all these are resented among a conquered but unconvinced people as diversions of energy from the one occupation of recovering their independence. It is to this state that the victory of Germany, though it stopped short of an actual conquest, would bring us in England. And I leave it to be reckoned what further losses would result from it.

* * *

It will be seen, I hope, that in the discussion of the war at this stage the question of causes is comparatively unimportant. Subsequently, when history comes to be written, and when, if happily it be so, the peril is past, the causes, immediate and remote, may be examined, and judgment may be passed upon them. But it is with consequences that our first concern should be at this moment. Let it be supposed, if you please, that we got into the war by the worst of all possible means; that no crime was left uncommitted by our diplomacy and our politic to bring it about—the fact still remains that the consequences of defeat are such as nobody in England can face with his eyes open. Pacifists, Little-Englanders, Social revolutionaries, pedants—all alike are equally involved in the results of the war. Not one can afford to be indifferent to it. At the same time, not one can afford to wish anything less than the victory of the Allies. In a national melting such as the present, everybody is concerned primarily, not with the question of how we got into it, but how we are to get out of it. All other questions are secondary if not irrelevant.

That Germany has a theory is well known; but what her theory is our publicists have taken less trouble than the publicists of any other nation to discover. That it is, as I have said, not only the contrary but the *challenging* contrary of the democratic theory on which England stands is certain. Moreover, it is singularly complete after its fashion, and is aimed against England at every point. In a recent work on the war,[1] for example, Max Scheler, an exceedingly intelligent German, undertakes to prove that the English doctrine of the European Balance of Power is purely selfish and not even incidentally of benefit to Europe; and he contrasts it, from this ethical and cultural standpoint, with the doctrine now being exercised by Germany. England, he says, has a selfish interest in the maintenance of division on the Continent, for the simple reason that her sea-supremacy might be endangered by a united Europe. Moreover, the ideas for which England stands are not of a sufficiently elevated character to warrant

Europe in submission. They are, says Scheler, democratic and hence capitalist. Hence, again, in the *German* conception of progress, they are reactionary. To argue against this criticism of England's policy is easy. We can say, for example, that the doctrine of the Balance of Power is one of the most disinterested policies ever pursued by a nation. Compare it with its precise opposite, the Monroe doctrine of the United States. The Monroe doctrine declares Hands off the American continent to every Power but America. The English doctrine of the European Balance of Power declares, on the contrary, England's own Hands off. No one, I think, of any importance has ever accused England of desiring to possess another square inch of European soil. Again, it is manifestly absurd to deny that incidentally, if not directly, our maintenance of the Balance of Power has been of advantage to Europe, if nationality, democracy, and liberty have any value. The policy of maintaining the integrity of small European nations may, it is true, be conceived as a means of preserving our own integrity; but incidentally it is good for the small nations as well. They, at least, will not deny the benefit Europe has received at the hands of England. Once again, what is the alternative Germany offers to Europe for our English doctrine of the Balance of Power? Is it a European Commonwealth of nations, a new Hellas, such as, indeed, is the hope of our English policy? On the contrary, it is a European Empire, a Macedonian military empire, in which Germany would play the same part that Prussia plays to-day in Germany itself. Bad as the consequences for Europe from our Balance of Power may be, the consequences from the German hegemony would be far worse. No politics is ideal; but in a world of real politics, the German is hateful to all but Germans. But, as I said, to argue is easy. To-day it is a matter of force. What is being settled in the present war is the political, intellectual, and ethical configuration of Europe for the coming century. All who can see an inch in front of their nose must realise it. The future is being created now.

As a further evidence that English opinion has not yet grasped the significance of the war, its personalities in our Press may be cited. Strictly speaking, a war of the present character ought, except for history, to be anonymous. The effective combatants are much more powers than men; they are certainly much greater than the personalities of any of the figures on either side. Yet see with what eagerness opinion seizes upon the Kaiser or Miss Cavell[2] to reduce the image of the war to their mind's capacity; as if the power of thought upon impersonal causes were lost among us. Neither the Kaiser, being human, can stand effectively for the diabolonianism of the German theory; nor can Miss Cavell, however brave, stand effectively for the virtue of the Allied cause. Personalities, if they are allowed to become symbolic and to absorb the attention of the mind, disguise by diminution the magnitude of the super-personal issues at stake. Abstract terms would better express the combatants; only the abstract terms must be understood.

[18 November 1915]

Much the most depressing episode of the war so far has been the conduct of the Allies towards Serbia. Everybody must now be able, with the information already published, to conclude for himself that our governing motives cannot have been political or diplomatic, since with these as our guide nothing but simple despair is possible. The determining cause must needs therefore have been military; and it is with the hope of elucidating the mystery or, at least, of lending the squalid story an appearance of intelligibility, that the following notes are written.

From a superficial point of view it may appear that our efforts in the early stages of the war were confined to stopping the on-rush of the enemy as best we could. The existence of a plan seems to be doubted; and in any event it is commonly supposed that every pre-arranged plan, even if such existed, must have been swept by the board. The facts, however, are otherwise. Not only was there a plan in the mind of our Generals in the early stages of the war, but it is demonstrable that fairly consistent attempts were made to carry it out. The defence of Antwerp and the landing of Rawlinson's cavalry[3] and the 7th Division at Zeebrugge, for example, so far from being isolated phenomena designed at sudden notice to intercept the German advance, were actually co-ordinated parts of a plan that had for its objective the formation of a line from Antwerp to Ypres. And when, again, this plan failed, another was instantly substituted for it, of which the unsuccessful attack of the 7th Division along the Menin road (where, by way, our wounded were found with their throats cut) was an integral part. The question is thus not why or even whether our General Staff had a plan or a series of plans; but what the main plan has been, and why each successive application failed. The reply is as follows.

There is not the smallest doubt that in every case the numbers of the enemy actually available against us in any given engagement have been grossly *under-estimated*. In the first place, we did not realise that the existence of reserves whose sole function shall be to wait upon events is no longer a part of German strategy. German strategy, on the contrary, aims always at putting as many men as possible into the front line. And, in the second place, our estimate of the effective casualties among the

German army has always been too high. From this double cause it will be seen that our calculations of the German strength have been hopelessly wrong. Always we were assuming that only a proportion of their army would be actually available, and that their casualties were as heavy as we hoped, when, in fact, practically the whole of their army was at the front ready to engage, and their casualties were comparatively few. This misconception of our relative strengths was in itself the source of many of our reverses; but an even greater fallacy than an arithmetical existed.

The Germans quickly realised that the discovered possibilities of Defence enabled them, even with the handicap of inferior numbers, to apply and extend their characteristic strategical doctrine of outflanking. This was combined with the advantages of Position. In the matter of Defence, it is well known that if not 'in yon straight path a thousand may well be stopped by three', at any rate a defending force need not exceed a third of an attacking force in order to maintain its position. Suppose, for example, that two opposing armies are equal in number—say, a couple of million each. The army that chooses to assume the defensive can manage this part of the battle with as few as 800,000 men. The rest are thus available for a flanking movement. Now note that from the opening of the war this combination of a comparatively small containing defensive fixed force with a comparatively large attacking and mobile force has characterised the German plan uniformly. And not only has this been seen in the restricted front in Flanders, but on the largest scale of the war the same out-flanking movements have been carried out. When, for instance, the Flanders front was contained and no further out-flanking was possible there, the Germans turned to the Russian front, and with their free force proceeded to attempt to out-flank the Allies in Russia. And when, once more, the Russian front was contained, a fresh out-flanking movement was begun in the attack upon the Serbian section of the Allied line. The aim, it will be seen, was in every case the same: to lengthen the line on every arc of the total front; and to employ every possible man on it.

But if they had been wise, the Allies would have taken this leaf out of the German book very early in the war. For it is clear that, provided both sides had adopted the same tactics, the relative advantages would have been reduced mainly to one of numbers. If, by lengthening, and thereby thinning, the line, the Germans were able to obtain an advantage, how much greater an advantage the Allies would have obtained by the use of the same means in view of their superior collective numbers! What is more, the advantage would not have stopped with numbers. Anybody can see for himself that, for the time being at any rate, not only is the front fixed, and fixed at the discretion of the Germans (who alone have deliberately extended it), but, as it is, the whole set of operations known as manœuvring are rendered impossible. There is only stone-walling. Our extension of the front, on the other hand, to make finally a single line *as long as possible* round about Germany, would have brought manœuvring once more into play by substituting everywhere a thin flexible line for a heavy fixed line. In view both of our superior numbers and of the need we had to avoid exclusively fixed lines, we ought, therefore, early in the war, to have played the game as Germany played it, and to lengthen our front (thereby compelling her to lengthen hers at *our* discretion) until Germany's line became too thin to be a defence. M. Briand,[4] I understand, as long ago as last November, came to the same conclusion. While the Allies were doing their best to minimise the length of front, and the Germans were doing their best to maximise it, M. Briand conceived the plan above described of out-doing the Germans in the matter of front, and of anticipating and surpassing their possible maximum. The Russians being then in Galicia—that is, in occupation of a longer line than they occupy to-day—M. Briand suggested that the Allies should dispatch troops to Serbia and invade Hungary at the same time. The operation might have been described at the time as a wanton diversion of strength; and no doubt, many silly people would have opposed it. In fact, they did, and successfully. But in view of the present situation, in view of the example set by Germany, and in view, finally, of the certainty that in the end such a plan must be adopted, M. Briand was, in my opinion, absolutely right.

In those days, I believe, M. Briand was opposed by M. Delcassé[5] among others; and unfortunately M. Delcassé was powerful enough to influence the Allied plan of campaign in his own direction. To him, therefore, in the instrumental sense, we owe it not only that Serbia was left to her present fate, but that the strategy of the Allies has been everywhere inadequate. What were his reasons? To begin with, it must be said that they were popular. We know how, even at this stage, a certain section of public opinion, here and in France, is disposed to resent the dispatch of Allied troops to Serbia on the ground that the enemy occupies Flanders and a part of France. All too true; but the reply can be made that the enemy must be fought where he is weakest, and by the best means that circumstances dictate. If it should happen that Germany's weakest spot were in Galicia, and the proper means of attacking her were the invasion of Hungary, military science would dictate this course, though in the meanwhile German troops should be in Paris. Again, M. Delcassé's reasons (I take him only as an example—he had many supporters even in our own Cabinet) were romantic and sentimental. It appears even to-day that a strong prejudice exists in favour of ending the war in Flanders. Mr. Buchan[6] has just repeated this fallacy almost in the same words as it was first enunciated: 'we shall free Serbia in Flanders.' But this is again to ignore the real facts of the situation in favour of a sentiment. There is a priori no more reason for supposing that Flanders must necessarily be the scene of the decisive battle than for supposing that the spot may be in Gallipoli, in Serbia, or on the Russian front. The war is not local or confined to France and Belgium: it is a European war, and the front, and possibly the decisive front, is at any mile of the whole circle surrounding the German army.

Finally, it must be said that whatever the grounds of M. Delcassé's theory, they have been practically disposed of by the actual facts. For the undeniable fact which ought to have been grasped after the first Ypres battle is this: that concentrated trench warfare is of necessity indecisive. I know very well that explanations and excuses are offered and accepted for the failure of every one of our grand attempts to break the German line. It is argued that if only this commander had come up to time or that battery had been more effective, the result would have been different. It is always a mistake or an accident that has brought about our failure. But, on the contrary, I maintain that mistakes and accidents have little or nothing to do with the result, which is inherent in the very nature of the strategy employed. The mind that attributes to accident what is susceptible of calculation deludes itself and imagines what is not. Trench warfare, I repeat, conducted as it is being conducted at present, is not only a prolongation of the war, it is a prolongation to infinity. There is and can be no military conclusion to it.

If this is doubted, I invite my readers to examine the case of the Russian army. The successful retreat of the Russian army has been the cause of rejoicing among us; but, in my judgment, and as a military augury, it should fill us with dismay. Or, if not us, at least those of us who pin our faith to breaking the German front in Flanders. For what does Russia's success signify but that a thick line cannot be broken? Everything from the standpoint of the Delcasséists was in favour of Germany in the attack upon the Russians. The Russian army was in retreat and in confusion; it scarce had time to dig a trench before it was compelled to march again; and yet—the Russian line was never broken. But if not under these circumstances, how can we hope to break the German line in Flanders? Or, again, how can we even hope to break the German line when the

German army is in retreat? The Russian retreat is, we may hope, a rehearsal of the performance destined to be made by the Germans from France and Belgium. And its success—upon which, as I say, we are congratulating our Ally—is at the same time a warning to us of the success Germany in like case may certainly expect.

To penetrate, however, still deeper the reasons for the failure of the Allies, we must discuss the second principle I have enumerated as constituting the strength of the German strategy—the principle of Position. In Defence, as we have seen, the Germans were the first to realise that three men can be held by one. On the principle of Position they have likewise been the first to realise that one man in the right position is equal to at least three in the wrong. This accounts for the obvious fact that everywhere, upon every front they have occupied, the first step of the Germans has been to secure the most favourable positions for their trenches. The French, on the other hand, whose strategy has naturally dominated the conduct of the Western Allies, were not only slow to realise the importance of position, but they required, first, an experience of a threatened disaster, and, even then, the intervention of a civilian (M. Thomas[7]) to teach them its value. It is now permissible to publish the fact that after the battle of the Aisne,[8] our French Allies found themselves not only short of shells, but actually without them. Nor is it indiscreet to say that at the same moment the Army, despite its experience, was wholly opposed to the use of heavy guns on the ground that these entailed the adoption of positional warfare. M. Thomas, the Socialist Minister, had to override the judgment of the military. Now, the reason of the inability of the French command to realise the nature of the war was that the French had hitherto been accustomed to mobile and not stationary warfare. Their genius (or, let us say, their tradition) was for rapid and dashing advances, surprise attacks, forced marches and the like. They did not easily accustom themselves to a strategy that required them to seize a position and hold it. The Germans thus had the advantage in three ways. They had the initiative in the invention of the method of trench warfare (for it is known that German mortars were prepared for early use in the war); their initiative enabled them to occupy the strongest positions before the Allies knew what their intention was; and they could count on the reluctance of the French to abandon their traditional mobility theory. I have read many pre-war French books on strategy, but nowhere do I remember seeing either the German theory discussed or any system but the mobile system advocated. It was thus only to be expected that the military commanders so trained would find it wellnigh impossible to re-arrange and revolutionise their ideas as soon as they were on active service.

Let me now review the course of the argument, the design of which, as I began by saying, is to offer a coherent, if not the actual, explanation of our lamentable failure in Serbia. I maintain that the proper course was that indicated a year ago by M. Briand—the extension of the Allied front *faster and farther* than the Germans extended theirs. This would have involved the dispatch of troops to Serbia, the invasion of Hungary, and the reinforcement, if this were needed, of the Russian lines in Galicia and Poland. It would, at the same time that it secured us the advantage of the German principle of Defence, also have secured us the advantage of the principle of Position. Instead of having reluctantly to extend our front to meet the German flanking movements, the book would have been on the other leg; theirs would have been the reluctance. And instead of having to see our superior numbers discounted by the superior *position* taken by the enemy, our numbers would have been multiplied by the positions occupied at our own discretion. The reason for our failure is the slowness of the military mind to adapt itself, saturated with prejudice, to new conditions; and this reason has been supplemented in the present instance by the sentimental wish of a section of opinion to beat the Germans, not where they can be most easily beaten, namely, at the weakest point on the longest front, but in Flanders, where they are strongest. Meanwhile Serbia pays for our mistakes.

[25 November 1915]

Now that an Allied War Council has been formed, we may hope that the direction of the war will be considered as a whole. Hitherto, it is obvious, each of the Allies has gone his own road with as little collusion with the group as possible; and the effect has been what might have been expected: Germany has had as a free gift the advantages of a divided enemy which Napoleon had to scheme to obtain. Particularly ought the new super-Command to take into immediate account the general strategy, now that, for the first time in history, strategy on the grand scale is rendered both possible and necessary. I referred briefly to this subject last week. In the Hegelian dialectic it is well known that thesis and antithesis are supposed to be resolved by a third operation into a synthesis, and that this triple process is regarded as one of the laws of thought. Similarly, I would lay it down that in the sequence of practice, following thought, the same succession of phenomena can be observed. In the case of strategy, for example, the first phase, and one that has occupied the stage of war for centuries, is the strategy of Mobility. Everything turns in this 'thesis' upon the rapidity with which units can be directed, dispersed or concentrated; and the skill of the commander is demonstrated by his success in Manœuvring. The present war, however, has definitely superseded this particular form of strategy by substituting Positional for Mobile strategy; in other words by opposing antithesis to thesis. Finally the war will take a form which, like the synthesis of the Hegelian dialectic, will combine the two methods by including them both. This is the strategy which, for want of a better word, I have called the Mobile-Positional; and it consists in holding positions by means of trenches, machine guns, and artillery with as few men as possible, while employing the rest as a mobile force engaged in perpetually compelling the enemy to extend his lines. The final outcome would be, in the present instance, two vast concentric circles, the Allies without and the Central Powers within; and these lines being flexible, Manœuvring would be once more possible, though in a form somewhat different from the old plan. Under the new circumstances, the object of Manœuvring would be the discovery of the weakest segments of the enemy's circle and the rapid concentration of force against them with the intention of breaking his line. I need scarcely say that once broken such a line would be most difficult to mend.

I pass on to the vexed subject of Conscription. Thought upon the matter has no immediate concern for me; and I must examine Señor de Maeztu's case[9] more at leisure. In the meanwhile it is, in my judgment, a matter for sentiment as well, and as follows: On the one hand, it is almost unthinkable that, under any circumstances whatever, we English should consent to the intrusion of the police into our houses for the purpose of carrying off one of the family to kill and to risk being killed. It is all very well to say that other nations submit to it; the feel of it is not in our blood. Even the most patriotic of us experience a chill when a newspaper office is forcibly entered and a paper is suppressed—how much more should we resent the forcible entry of our houses? On the other hand, sentiment is no less against allowing ourselves to be defended by volunteers when all the while capable men remain is safety at home. The gilt does come off the gingerbread of liberty a little at the reflection that in order to preserve the freedom of the individuals who stay at home the volunteers must labour twice as hard to defend this same freedom. As it is, it is well known that wounded men, after partial recovery, nerve-stricken men before recovery, and men utterly unfit in many ways for prolonged exertion, must be hurried back to the lines to fill the places left vacant by those who do not choose to volunteer. For it must be remembered that our voluntary army is voluntary only at the outset. Once over the chalk-line that separates the civilian from the soldier, freedom has gone completely; the voluntary soldier is as much under the orders of his superiors as if he were a conscript.

Not only, then, does the soldier undertake the duties common to the whole class of eligibles; but, by reason of the fact that the rest do not perform their share, *his* share is made much harder. He suffers twice that they may escape suffering once; he is necessarily harshly used, over-worked and over-strained, simply in order to preserve their fine feelings of freedom. As a sentiment alone, I contend that the sense of outraged justice in this is equal to the sentiment, on the other side, of outraged liberty. One is undoubtedly anti-conscription; the other is as undoubtedly pro-conscription for those who do not offer themselves of their own accord. I will not attempt to solve the antinomy; each must solve it for himself. Another aspect may here be considered. A soldier who finds himself in the trenches for the first time and experiences the almost mortal depression that sooner or later falls upon him, is disposed to reflect at the first attack, that, after all, he is there voluntarily. As, therefore, he has made his bed, so he must be content to lie upon it; there is nobody else to blame. This, however, proves to be a piece of false psychology; for, in fact, there is no solace in it. On the contrary, I am inclined now to think that a more solacing reflection is the thought that one had no choice in the matter, but that it was inevitable. Against a calamity that could have been avoided, we may conceivably chafe; but against a calamity that is forced upon us we can perhaps bear up more cheerfully. That, at any rate, is the common experience. The bearing of this, it will be seen, upon the question of Conscription is direct. Would compulsion, in fact, induce in conscripts a greater sense of despair, when the ordeal came, than the voluntary system? I do not think it would, but on the contrary. Talking of depression, by the way, an argument against the employment of very young soldiers is this: they have never had the experience of profound depression, and consequently do not know, when it first seizes them, that it will pass off. They are thus inclined to give utter way to it. An older man can say to his heart: 'Courage, thou hast endured greater trials than this; the worst also passes.'

The authorities are certainly to blame for not making up their minds sooner either definitely for or definitely against Conscription. It appears that they are more afraid of the word that of the thing; for it is notorious that, in all but the metaphysical sense, compulsion has been freely employed. Under the veil of the voluntary system, moreover, a good deal of downright trickery has taken place such as ought to be resented by a truthful people. Even bad faith is not below the dignity required to maintain the voluntary fiction. For example, in the household canvass initiated twelve months ago men were told that if they would signify their willingness to serve when called upon, they could safely go about their occupation in the meanwhile, and possibly for months. As a matter of fact, every man was called up within three weeks. Another example of duplicity is taking place at this moment. Married men are being asked to register on the assurance that single men will be called upon first. Yes, but how many single men, and who is to decide upon the proportion to be left in industry? My belief is that every married man who registers will find himself called up in a very short time, whether single men *generally* have enlisted or not. We shall see. The point is that such tricks are thought to be necessary to the maintenance of the appearance of the voluntary system.

[2 December 1915]

At the outset of the war the Germans affirmed that our insurmountable difficulty would be the getting of new officers for our new armies. Strange to say, however, our so far insurmountable difficulty has been not this, but the very reverse, namely, the getting rid of our old officers. I do not speak now of the regimental officers, the old regulars, who are soldiers by instinct, and, without exception, the best in the world: but of the Generals and Staff officers. Of these I would say, brutally, that if the Expeditionary Force was designed as a shield, intended to be broken while serving as a shield for new armies in process of formation, it is a pity that it could not be entirely composed of Staff officers and of battalions of generals over a certain age. Of these two different handicaps under which we suffer I propose to consider this week that of the Staff. There can be no doubt whatever that, in the bulk, our Staff work has been execrable, and that we owe to its badness the loss of thousands of lives as well as the prolongation of the war. At Neuve Chapelle,[10] at Loos,[11] and at Suvla Bay[12] (where a Staff College Professor was in command), by the common consent of everybody who took part in these engagements, our Staff work was not only bad, it was not far short of a scandal. This is so generally known that one need not go very much into detail about it, but we may consider for a little what happened at Loos. The principal business of a Staff is, of course, to prepare alternative plans, the choice between which is left to the General. A Staff officer is supposed to know so much about the difficulties of each of the plans he has prepared that he is quite unable to make any decision himself. That direct act has to be made by the General. Apart from this pre-battle work, the principal practical work which the Staff has to accomplish in this war is the organisation of the roads, etc., behind the battle front in such a way that roads are not blocked, that reserves are in positions from where they can be rapidly brought up when required, and that the men can be properly fed after they have advanced. It is in this work that the Germans excel even the French. The bringing up of the reserves on the second day at Neuve Chapelle, for example, was wonderfully managed. This results, as I shall point out later, from the fact that such work in the German army is a specialised career. An officer who specialises in this kind of work devotes himself to that, and to nothing else, almost from the commencement of his life in the army. Now how was this sort of work managed for us at Loos? What happened there is now known almost to everybody. The Germans, having full knowledge of the coming French attack in Champagne,[13] withdrew all their reserves from other parts of the front to meet this coming attack. The result was, of course, that the French were definitely held up at the second line of trenches, and the attack failed to get through. A consequence of this concentration of the German reserves was that, once we had broken through the first lines at Loos, we had practically no troops whatever in front of us. Some regiments actually got into Lens itself, while farther north another division got through for miles. Why were these early successes not maintained? Simply on account of atrociously bad Staff work. When the French made an advance, the ground immediately behind the advance is placed under the control of certain regiments who act as police. I received a letter the other day from a French cavalry officer who had fulfilled this function in Champagne. At Loos, as the result of inadequate arrangements of this type, all the roads were blocked up with traffic of various kinds. The men who had made the first advance were without food, many of them for a couple of days. The arrangements for bringing up reserves went wrong. As for the division farther north which had advanced so far, although there were several bodies of troops which could have been sent up to support them, the authorities chose, of all people, to send a body of Kitchener's[14] New Armies who had just arrived from England, who immediately after detraining marched for a day and a half practically without stopping, and who were sent up without any additional rations. The result was, of course, that they gave way and the ground gained had to be abandoned. This is one instance among many of the fatuous policy of sending entirely new troops into action, of which Suvla Bay is another example. It is not that new troops are less courageous than old. It is simply that experience has not established in their minds a kind of scale or barometer of what is and what is not bad shelling. I do not wish here to exaggerate the consequences of this atrociously bad Staff work. I do not think that we should have accomplished that almost mythical 'breaking through' that so many seem to dream of. But we should, at any rate, have gained a very important stretch of country.

How does it come about that our regimental officers are so good and our Staff so bad? Partly, of course, the old tradition, that the Staff is a place of ease. In the second place, the fact that the very qualities which make our regimental officers so good tend to produce the kind of milieu from which a good Staff could not arise spontaneously. But are not these things true of every country and of every army? How does it come about that both France and Germany have good Staffs?

Many different reasons could be given for this. The most obvious method is, of course, to point out in detail the methods by which the Staff officers are selected—the extraordinary esprit de corps in a regiment which makes it very difficult for the best men to leave a regiment—the local interests of a regiment interfering with the general interests of the army; then the fact that sufficient distinction is not made between the Administrative and General Staff, which in reality, of course, ought to be entirely different services; the fact that connection with the regiment still has to be kept, a man doing four years on the Staff and then four years back in the regiment again; while a German Staff officer specialises almost as soon as he leaves the military academy, and has nothing to do with regimental life.

One might go on pointing out in detail these differences in system which result in efficient or inefficient Staff officers. But that is not going far enough down to the root of the matter. You get a good system in Germany, a worse system here, as a secondary result of a more fundamental difference which I want to point out. The difference is this, that in the case of France and Germany there is an outside pressure which maintains almost automatically a good internal organisation, and that this outside pressure is lacking in the case of England. France and Germany have all the time a problem to face, which ensures the existence of an excellence in the Staff which could never have arisen or had continued existence spontaneously without this pressure. Of its own nature no army tends towards intelligence. The popular view in every country of the army as stupid is not entirely justified, but it is a crude expression of something which has a certain basis of fact, which I have already stated but which I may as well repeat—that the kind of qualities which make excellence in a regimental officer do not produce an environment in which the more civilian and more detached intelligence of the Staff officer is likely to flourish. This natural tendency, as I said, is overcome in France and Germany by the existence of the very serious problem which they both have to face. Both the German and French Staffs have had the advantage during the last forty or fifty years of having their main military problem defined for them by the circumstances of the case. The military problem of Germany was the defeat of France or of France and Russia combined, or, very doubtfully, of France and Russia with England as a naval partner.

The French military problem was war with Germany. These defined objectives gave to their respective Staffs not only a particular problem to which a solution must be found, but the necessity for a criterion of efficiency in the selection and promotion of Staff-officers. The English Staff, on the other hand, have had no such well-defined objective. War might turn out to be with South Africa, or in India, in Egypt, or anywhere on the globe. The Continent certainly was among the contingent places for the operations of our General Staff; but never as an inevitability, still less as an only inevitability. There did not exist in England that pressing necessity which, as it were, insists on the efficiency of the Staff system, when the consequences of inefficiency are so appallingly obvious. The Navy, it should be added, was never tempted to the same fate, for, like the Continental Armies, it, too, had a particular problem, that of clearing the sea of enemy vessels; and all its organisation was designed to this end. Moreover, the Navy has during the last ten years become more and more efficient as its problem became more and more evident. Only the Army lacked its problem, and dearly we have paid for it.

But this special condition of the Army in this country is likely to endure. We are never likely to have the same pressing problem to face that the Continental Powers have. As the outside pressure will probably always be lacking, is our Staff system doomed always, then, to remain inefficient? Cannot some special way be devised for meeting the special situation of this country? I think it can, and in some spirit of satire I offer it here. Let the army be divided into two parts, a military and a civilian part, or 'regimental' and 'Staff'. The regimental part of our Army is excellent. I have no sympathy whatever with democratic attacks on the Army whose main motive is, in reality, social resentment—the desire of one class to get its own back on another and more privileged one. So much do I admire our regimental system that I would allow every colonel to do in practice what he now only dreams of—that is, never to allow a good man to leave his regiment. I think the regiment should be the whole Army as we know it. Staff work and, in certain cases, higher command should be entrusted to a new civil service, modelled somewhat on the lines of the Indian Civil Service. There should be no uniforms for these superior officers; they should all wear top-hats. They should have no titles and none of those special privileges attached to the soldier as a man doomed to sacrifice. Such a civil service would, I think, spontaneously generate in itself a kind of atmosphere and the kind of organisation which make for efficiency along its own narrow lines.

[9 December 1915]

I want this week in these Notes to repeat and emphasise certain simple facts which are so simple that they can be called platitudes. I repeat them here, however, because my object in these notes is the purely practical one of convincing someone of the importance of this war.

There has been a meeting to protest against Conscription this week. The question discussed was not so much 'what are the reasons which justify a man being *compelled* to serve in this war' as 'what reasons are there why a man should *voluntarily* offer to fight'. If the question were asked me, I should answer, not being the least afraid of rhetoric, when it is a true rhetoric: 'Because we are fighting to preserve the liberties of Europe; which are in fact in danger, and can only be preserved by fighting.'

The question as to whether this is true or not is entirely a matter for investigation into actual facts. I shall later on attempt to answer the question carefully. But in the notes this week I do not propose to offer an ounce of evidence on the matter. When the pacifist rejects this contention about liberty, he is moved, as a rule, by certain instinctive, almost a priori reasons, *which precede any examination of the question of fact*. I feel that I am justified myself in examining the nature of these instinctive reasons, and in leaving the question of fact in abeyance. That such actually is the procedure of the pacifists is shown by the fact that all the arguments they have used so far have been stock arguments, which one could have predicted long before this war actually came about. Every historical fact is to a certain extent a novelty, and an objective examination of that fact by the pacifists would have produced arguments which could not have been predicted beforehand, which would have had a certain freshness.

Most of these instinctive reasons are merely particular instances of a certain general phenomenon. The world of men can be divided into two fundamental types—Crude People and the Superior People. They stand to each other in a relation which the new logic would call *transitive*. While the attention of the Crude is focussed on things, the attention of the Superior is focussed on the Crude. The Crude People are perhaps then superior, in that their eyes are fixed, however crudely, on *events*. On the occurrence of any event they at once offer their *Crude* opinions upon it. The Superior People on the other hand are so eager to demonstrate at once, that they are clever enough to perceive the crudeness of these opinions, that they entirely forget to look at the events themselves. Before the war extremely Crude Colonels in club armchairs and the editor of the 'National Review' expressed very crude opinions on the German danger. This crudity so set the nerves of the Superior People on edge that, in their eagerness to demonstrate this, they entirely forgot to look at Germany itself. They probably in the end convinced themselves that the Germans were merely inventions of the Crude People. When the war actually came the same comedy continued. The Crude People began to explain their conception of the fundamental cause of the war, of the fundamental difference between the English and the German character, and, being very crude, the antithesis came out to be something like the difference between white and black. The Superior People have been so eager to demonstrate that they are not taken in by this extremely simple reasoning that they have entirely forgotten to look at the actual facts.

To such people one can only make this kind of personal appeal: 'I quite agree with you that the contrast between the justness of the Allies' cause and that of Germany is not so simple as it is painted by Crude People. But pray do not get so excited about this fact as to omit to notice, or even to deny, that the difference really exists. It is true that this country is not pure white. We live in a grey world; but people who refuse to call Germany black because they know this country to be grey had better renounce action altogether, for it is certain that if such principles had always prevailed nothing would ever have been accomplished in history. The dispute is between a grey and a very much blacker grey. It should be your business to look at the actual facts themselves in this spirit. Look at the actual complex facts themselves and not at them through an apparatus of ready-made pacifist clichés. Forget for a moment that you are sharp enough to point out that the spectacle of a pot calling a kettle black is a comic one, and look to see if this is in reality the nature of the conflict we are engaged in. After all the truth is important.' This continual attempt of the Superior People to distinguish themselves from the Crude is, after all, a very human and understandable phenomenon. It is quite possible to understand a man so passionately engaged in this occupation that like the lover or the chess player he counts 'the world well lost'. But in this case it is his duty to pull himself together. The man who continues to be more interested in his own superiority than in this war is a contemptible creature.

The instinctive reasons for which I said the pacifist would reject the assertion about liberty without troubling to examine it as a fact requiring investigation, are all of the type of this question: 'But how can this irrational thing be so?' . . . to which the correct answer should always be 'it just is so.'

Take the first example: 'It is comic to suppose that we are fighting for the liberties of Europe, for we can see from their newspapers that the Germans say exactly the same thing about themselves.' This is very modern. It might legitimately be urged against the idea that God took sides in the conflict, for that is a subject on which completely objective evidence is difficult to obtain. It is entirely irrelevant when we are dealing with an essentially human thing like liberty. Here the facts are easily perceptible, and can be investigated in an entirely objective manner. The question as to whether the liberties of Europe would be increased or decreased by a German victory is a question of simple deduction from ascertainable facts and has nothing to do with a balancing of 'claims'. If I am to believe certain German writers, this pacifist objection is typical of the reverse side of the English virtue of 'toleration', being the belief that truth itself in some way or other depends on a consensus of opinion. Only those things which all men agree on can be true—which is rubbish. If the whole German nation really believes that it is fighting for liberty then the whole German nation is wrong. At any rate the question as to whether it is right or wrong depends on an examination of facts; an examination which the pacifist as a rule never troubles to give. He can dismiss the matter for a priori reasons.

Another example of the 'How can it possibly be so' argument is: 'How can the aims of a nation of intelligent, kindly and cultured people like the Germans in any way menace the liberties of Europe? The idea is in itself absurd and crude.' The answer is quite simple: 'It may be absurd, but it *just is so*.'

In arguments about the causes of the war, one should be careful to keep closely to this way of putting it. The annoying thing about the war to many people at the commencement was that all the stupid people had been right and the intelligent people wrong. The club colonels and the 'Express' had more sense than the intellectuals. This is perhaps because intellectuals have always considerable difficulty in grasping the fact that stupid things like war really do happen. They can perhaps only under-stand easily phenomena capable of a rational interpretation. A secondary result of this is, that those intellectuals who have been enlightened by the event, proceed to falsify the real nature of the dispute by over-rationalis-ing it. This is an error to be avoided. It is necessary to realise that we are fighting against a danger which is in the proper use of the word an *accident*, something which might not have been, but just is. In dealing with the causes of this war there is no necessity to drag in Froissart.[15] We are not concerned with some eternal principle of the German nature which makes them eternally different from us and dangerous to us. We have to deal with quite ordinary people, who, as the result of a *certain* history and under the influence of *certain* ideas, form part of a mechanism that, directed by *certain* hands, is at this given moment of time, capable of doing permanent injury to the liberties of Europe. We have to do with that entirely empirical phenomenon, a 'Power', and quite apart from what is a priori likely or what is *reasonable*, we have to recognise this fact as a fact and act accordingly, just as we should get out of the way of a train.

I see that the president of the 'no conscription' meeting of last week was Mr. Clifford Allen,[16] a specimen of that miserable type the fussy undergraduate, who neglects work for the Workers, and leaves the river to address mass meetings of the girl-hands of the neighbouring jam factory, they being the nearest available specimens of the People. After an academic career of an entirely undistinguished kind—Mr. Allen obtained, if I remember rightly, a very second-class degree—these people often take up 'the profession of *thinking* for the proletariat'.

At this meeting I see that conscription was denounced as a 'violation of individuality'. That, of course, is quite beyond me. When it is described as 'unjust', a language is used which I can follow. I sincerely hope that conscription will not prove necessary; I have all our traditional feelings against it. It would be undoubtedly a tragedy in this country, where a man is entirely unprepared for it, that he should be suddenly in the middle of his life sent out to his death for a cause about which he has probably never before concerned himself. It is certainly sad, but is it unjust? It can only be unjust if man has an inalienable right to a happy and undisturbed life. If only the pacifists who talk in this way possessed the profound sense of their nonconformist ancestors, who recognised that this life was a 'vale of tears'. The cause is a just one. Certain of your liberties are really at stake. Liberty is an *achievement*, not an inevitable constituent of the world. In being asked to fight for liberty then, you are not being asked to fight for the law of gravitation. It does not become you to sulk about the matter.

If ever conscription does become necessary, the authorities have nothing to fear from the 'no-conscription fellowship'. They may be dealt with in a very simple way. In the voluntary recruiting effort all kinds of special battalions were formed. We have the 'Clerks', the 'Bantams', and the 'Pals' battalions. All that is necessary here is to put all the pacifists together. Call them the 'No Conscription' Battalion, 55th Royal Fusiliers. Let them talk on parade, and instead of regimental concerts, let Prof. Pigou[17] address them repeatedly. I would not send them into the trenches, for their overweening vanity, leading them to look at their own cessation of existence as not only a personal but a world catastrophe, would be an undue handicap to the courageous facing of death. But keep them in rest-billets and let them, under the Yellow Flag, sweep the roads and fill up latrines for their betters.

[16 December 1915]

It is the general opinion that two of our greatest handicaps in this war have been the atrociously bad Staff work and the age of our commanding officers. I propose to deal this week with this latter handicap. The best method seems to me to get at it rather indirectly.

In this war, so far, it has seemed as if all the new ideas and all the initiative and inventiveness had been on the side of the Germans. At the best all we have done is to follow in the new directions opened up by them after the lapse of a greater or less amount of time. Sometimes we have not even managed to follow. Now, it is not obvious why this should be so. That the Germans should have sprung many surprises upon us at the beginning was to be expected, for they had been preparing seriously for this war for years; the preparation of such things had been a profitable career for intellect, and the same was in no way true of England. But I am not thinking so much here of these surprises prepared carefully in peace time; I am thinking rather of the things that could not have been foreseen, and which have been elaborated during the course of the war itself. In these matters we ought to have been on an equality with the Germans. But, even here, we have always been imitators.

What is the reason for this? It will not do to explain this by saying that the Germans are naturally a more ingenious people than we are. The facts of the history of industrial inventions prove the contrary.

The facts, at any rate, are sufficiently obvious, and, in this respect, the war has been a process of education for the simple Englishman. Everything seems to conspire to produce the impression on his mind that in these things we must be naturally inferior to our enemies. It is the only conclusion which seems possible for him to draw from the data presented.

Take the case of the simple subaltern going out to the front for the first time—at the end of last year shall we say—with his head full of the ideas of Germany presented to him by his daily newspaper. The first sight of the actual front[18] will be at night; for troops, except in very rare cases, do not march inside the two-mile area behind the trenches in daylight. They might be 'spotted' and get shelled. The first actual sign of war that he will see will be right along a very long horizon (for the front is for the most part very flat)—a constant succession of rising and falling rockets and 'star' shells. He will see this long before he gets to a distance when he can hear occasional bursts of musketry firing. The officer who described this to me said he thought this the most depressing sight he had ever seen, particularly when it was in the drizzling rain. The path of a rocket is itself as pure form very expressive of melancholy. It rises only to fall hopelessly again, a constant state of 'coming down like a stick'. When a rocket goes off on a fine night at a fair, the excitement of the light, and the upward rush, to some extent weakens the depressing effect of the actual curve described. But when it is in drizzling rain this is eliminated, and we get to the depressing effect of the curve in all its purity. No greater expression of hopeless futility can be imagined than this long line of vainly labouring rockets.

The purpose of this continual succession of rockets and star shells is to provide an illumination which would enable a night attack to be immediately discovered, and perhaps enable them to spot the 'reliefs' coming up to a trench, when they might catch them with the machine guns. Our simple Englishman will naturally assume, then, that half of these rockets are sent up by the English, and half by the Germans. As he notes the many different types, he will speculate as to which is the English type and which the German. Sad to say, however, when he actually gets to our trenches he will discover that all the rockets, without exception, are German; that not one is English. When for a few minutes there is a stoppage, the people in the English trenches may get nervous, and someone may fire off from a brass pistol a kind of penny squib, vastly different from the soaring lights of the enemy. It will probably sputter out uselessly halfway between our trenches and theirs. The event is such a rare occurrence that a sporting section may raise an ironical cheer. It is certain that at the commencement of trench warfare the Germans themselves cheered when they saw our pathetic efforts. The simple subaltern will discover that this is a fair sample of many other things. Let us suppose that he went to the trenches last November. He would find that while the Germans were continually lobbing over shells from trench mortars there was not a single mortar on our side in the whole brigade he was in. He would be told that the 'knife-rest' arrangements of barbed wire which can be placed in front of the trench so much more expeditiously than the old fixed-post arrangement, is an idea copied from the Germans. He would find that the Germans never fire over the top of the trench, thus exposing themselves, but through elaborate loopholes on the level of the ground, thus very difficult to detect, and that they make great use of trained rifles (all of which things we, at that time, had never thought of).

One could give a dozen similar instances, all of which go to confirm the explanation which will probably be given him very early after his arrival by another simple subaltern who has been out a little longer than him: 'You'll soon drop newspaper notions about the Germans. You soon learn to respect them out here. They are a damned sight cleverer than we are in these things,' etc.

If by 'we' is understood simple subalterns on both sides then the statement is untrue. The corresponding subaltern in the German lines opposite at that moment is by no means cleverer or more ingenious than the subaltern who is expressing admiration for his cleverness.

The mechanism of which the subaltern forms a part certainly exhibits greater signs of ability. Why? In the first place, I suppose, because a great institution like the Germany army offers a career in times of peace for men of ability, and ours does not. You cannot expect an army suddenly to improvise brains.

But that does not account for everything. Why is it that the smaller ingenious ideas for which this kind of warfare offers so many applications seem to spring from the other side? That is not due to a difference of ability. There is the same proportion of ingenious people everywhere, I suppose. Officers here and there are, to my knowledge, continually bringing forward little 'ideas'. I knew a pioneer officer who invented a very ingenious loophole for a trained rifle. We certainly 'produce' these ideas, but there it ends. The pioneer officer showed it to his colonel, but nothing more came of it. If anything is wrong, then, it must be in the system which makes no use of such ideas.

I think the cause a very simple one. A new idea is of no use unless it is taken up by a commanding officer (a brigadier or a divisional general) and *forced* upon all the officers under his command, the majority of whom will, of course, not be ingenious, or fond of change. Such changes require *decision* and energy, as well as adaptability. But these are exactly the qualities which you can only expect from the young. And practically all our generals are old men. There is something inherent in the profession of war which makes older men as a rule inefficient. In action they are unable to take rapid decisions. In the quieter periods of the kind of war I am discussing they are disinclined to take an interest in any new method, any new 'dodge', or if they do go so far as to approve of it, they lack the energy which can at once *enforce* it thoroughly and completely on every officer under their command. They may get a 'dodge' tried once; they are unable to make other people who take no interest in it carry it out not once but regularly as an unquestioned part of routine. I am thinking here not of the occasional genius of war, but of the ordinary commanders, who are no more likely to be remarkable men than is the ordinary general practitioner. Now, while the average age of Napoleon's brigadiers was about thirty, the average age of ours is, I should say, between fifty and sixty.

I think it can be put down to a great extent to the age of our generals that (1) what little inventions are made by our officers are never spread systematically; (2) that we are so slow even in imitating the Germans.

To prove that we are slow, I can give an example. It became clear nearly a year ago that in this war musketry was of very little importance; and that the principal weapon of infantry in the attack should be the hand-thrown bomb. But musketry was a great tradition in our Army. We prided ourselves upon our excellence in musketry, and this type of training was regarded as forming the basis of a soldier's general training. It stood for much more than mere excellence in shooting. The result of this is that it has taken us the best part of a year to realise the change in the conditions of the attack, to realise the decreased importance of musketry, and its replacement by bombing. At any rate, it has taken us all this time to draw the full consequences of an appreciation of this fact, consequences which the Germans drew long ago. From letters found on captured officers it has been found that quite early in the year bomb-throwing formed the principal element at the sport meetings which the Germans often get up to amuse the soldiers in reserve behind the lines. We have realised this now, and on Salisbury Plain and all the other similar centres the men in training are taken out to actual trenches in the Plain, and exercised in attacks by bombing both by night and day. But about a couple of months ago, while an adequate supply of bombs for a division should have been about a hundred thousand, the number actually allowed was about *five* thousand. To turn to artillery. It was the tradition of this arm that guns should never be abandoned. Saving the guns was the first duty of the would-be V.C., and scores of lives have been sacrificed to this. How does it work out in this war of positions? It has often happened when French and English batteries have been in neighbouring positions, and have been 'found' by the opposing artillery, the French artillerymen have retired some distance from the guns, and waited till the shelling had ceased, while the English remained with the guns and got badly cut up. Of course, if a battery is in action, the men must serve the guns at all costs, but this is an incident in a comparatively quiet time, when the battery has been 'found' by accident as it were. Then, why are not field guns more often brought right up to the firing line to support an attack? Of course, they run a great risk of being smashed up, but the risk must be taken. It has been done locally, I believe, in the attacks in the summer at Festubert,[19] but it ought to be done regularly.

At the beginning of the war brigadiers had to be found for the new armies. In the majority of cases the actual people chosen were 'dug-outs', i.e., men who had left the army for many years. What might have been done and ought to have been done is quite obvious. In every brigade of regulars there may be perhaps at a given moment between ten and sixteen captains. At least four of these are quite fit to command a battalion, probably to command a brigade even. In the situation that we are in they are wasted when they remain in their regiments. And if brigade commanders had been appointed in this way, they might have been of an age in which energetic action is possible. I know of one stretch of trenches not far from Ypres which was in charge of a Territorial company of Engineers under the command of a 'dug-out'. For three months this company practically did nothing. No reserve trenches were built, and finally when about the time of Neuve Chapelle the Germans attacked here and got through our front line, they found nothing in front of them. Warned by this, a new company of Engineers was put in charge and had thousands of soldiers on fatigue under their charge every night for months constructing line after line of reserve trenches and redoubts, all work which ought to have been done long ago. Yet while this old fool was in command I know of a neighbouring company of sappers which had at least three regular officers, each of more than ten years' service, all young men, all knowing their work well.

We seem to make no attempt to economise what good men we have, or to make any use of them. This economy is extremely important. It is a curious fact that none of the officers captured at Loos was above the rank of lieutenant. This is because the Germans do not allow officers of higher rank to go in the first line trenches.

But this is only a partial reason. We have old generals and bad generals, as a secondary consequence of a more fundamental cause.

It is a mistake to suppose that the change from peace to war brings about any radical change in the spirit of an army any more than legal marriage can profoundly alter human nature. We had, in a certain sense, an *amateur* army before the war, and it tends to remain amateur *during* the war. Under new conditions it tries to preserve its old values and to move in its old way.

Only one thing would bring about the appointment of young generals, and insist on necessary change, and that is *ruthlessness*. The ruthlessness, for example, with which Joffre[20] sent all the generals who failed to Limoges. It is only this kind of spirit which can make an essentially stupid thing like an army efficient.

This is the one thing I admire in the Jacobin spirit—the mercilessness with which it turns on generals who have been failures. It is not required in the ordinary paths of life, but it wants a very dry wind indeed to take the limpness out of an army.

This, of course, is precisely the spirit which in this country we are not likely to display. We hesitate to hurt a man's feelings by dismissing him. Delcassé had to go after the scandal of the Balkans; who has gone here?

Is this a permanent part of our national character? By no means, no more permanent than our toleration. We flatter ourselves that toleration, as it certainly exists here to a greater extent than in other countries, is due to some special virtue in our national character. This is bunkum. It merely springs from our exceptional security and wealth. Millionaires can be 'tolerant' about losses of half-a-crown. That is our virtue of 'tolerance'.

So far from this being a 'natural' virtue of ours, I do not think it will last to the end of this war. When once we lose our ridiculous sense of security and realise our actual position in the war it will disappear rapidly. If we lose the war, our pacifists may expect surprises from a 'tolerant' country.

[23 December 1915]

Is it possible to produce any effect on a pacifist by argument? Probably not; but the attempt has to be made. It is evidently more important to convert them than to insult them; though the latter will always remain a pleasant and a necessary duty. At any rate, I want to consider again some arguments bearing on the assertion that we are 'fighting for liberty'. When later I come to deal with actual facts, I will use more precise statements, but for my purpose here the rhetorical phrase will do well enough. The arguments I use might appeal only to those people who, if they thought the statement *true*, would act upon it.

In dealing with this statement about liberty, I believe that the attempt to prove the statement to the pacifist, by the enumeration of facts, will be useless. This is an essential element in an attempt to produce conviction, but, unsupported by other methods, it will always fail, for the facts are so extremely complicated that though they may unmistakenly point to one conclusion, it will always be possible for the pacifist to produce *enough* facts on the other side to justify him, in scepticism at any rate. A man's desire will always lead him to the facts he wishes to find.

Perhaps this is too crude an explanation of what happens. It would not be true to say that the pacifist first perceives certain awkward facts and then more or less deliberately suppresses them. The matter is more complicated. Everything happens as if the apparatus of *perception* itself was in some way falsified, so that the pacifist did not even *perceive* these awkward facts.

Before any examination of facts, then, it is necessary to deal with this falsification of the *perceptual* system. It is this necessity which makes me more and more convinced that the only propaganda which has the slightest chance of success is one which is, in a certain sense, entirely *abstract*. A method which instead of dealing at once with facts, begins by an investigation into quite abstract ideas, which seem at first irrelevant, but which are, in reality, the source of the diversity of concrete opinion.

Turn back to the concrete statement from which we started, 'we are fighting for liberty.' I should be inclined to assert that any detailed argument about a statement of that kind would be entirely wasted, unless you had first of all dealt with a certain *reluctance* on the part of the pacifist to examine the facts at all. It is an emotion which can be quite clearly described. He feels it unnecessary to examine the facts, because of a certain inherent absurdity implicit in them. He can dismiss the statement, not on *a priori* reason, but from what might almost be called on *a priori* feeling. This type of pacifist finds it impossible to seriously entertain the notion that big *fundamental* things like the development of liberty can really be in any way dependent on a small, trivial, *material* and stupid thing like a gun-mechanism. I shall repeat the word gun, meaning by it always all those small, detailed, technical things on which the result of wars, and, consequently, the fate of liberty does depend. The detail might be of any kind, geographical, for example, the possession of a strait. The point is that it must be a *detail*. The pacifist feels that big *fundamental* human movements can only be hindered by big *fundamental obstacles*. He refuses to believe that a *reasonable* thing can depend on an *unreasonable* one. His imagination at once draws back from this conception.

I do not think that it is an entire exaggeration to explain many things, in a certain type of liberal opinion about the *conduct* of the war, as due to this same cause. There is behind many acts, the unexpressed, probably unconscious, belief that our greater *resources* alone will win the war. Consequently a certain lack of interest in the immediate mobilisation of these resources into *detailed* things at particular places. Again, the disinclination to see the dependency of big results on small mechanisms.

This *reluctance* is no myth, imagined by me as a plausible explanation. It really exists and is an important element in a certain kind of pacifism.

What, then, is the source of this *Reluctance*?

This is where the justification of what I said about an *abstract method* comes in. The only hope of removing this *reluctance* is, I think, the employment of the kind of abstract method I want to suggest here.

On what facts is the existence of such a method based? One can get at it best indirectly by considering the devious route by which the *abstract* ideas of the philosophers do in the end reach the crowd. In the first place the abstract ideas of the pure philosophers pass into a wider sphere in the thought of the political philosophers and literary men. These latter are read by journalists who themselves write under the influence of these ideas. This process goes on till the relatively least educated read broadsheets, papers, tales, and hear speeches, which, while never once mentioning these ideas explicitly, yet contain them implicitly, being at the bottom based on them. A clear example of the first part of this process can be found in the seventeenth century, where you get a popular political philosophy built up under the influence of three main currents of *abstract* ideas: (1) The systematisation of the Stoic tradition through the work of the Dutch philogists; (2) The transference of the mechanical philosophy of Galileo into the explanation of mental life; and (3) The foundation by Grotius of a natural system of Rights and Law. This process, of course, takes considerable time before it penetrates to the lowest layer and thus accounts in some way for the existence of different systems of manners at different levels. I remember reading this observation of a French writer some ten years ago: 'At the present moment it is only the tinker who kills his unfaithful wife, the other classes do not. Why? Because the latter are now under the influence of the modern sceptical conceptions of these matters, while the romantic movement has only just penetrated down to the tinker.' Leaving the truth of this out of the question, it does, at any rate, serve to illustrate a process which in the development of political thought is a very real phenomena.

It is possible here to establish some sort of rough parallel to Von Baer's law in embryology,[21] which asserts that the development of the embryo *repeats* the history of the species. I believe that the opinions and clear beliefs, of which we are fully *conscious*, often really depend on a number of *abstract* ideas which lie so much at the centre of our minds that we are often unconscious of their existence. If you picture the mind in this way like the section of a tree, as a number of concentric rings, you will find that in passing from the central *abstract* ideas to the outside concrete political beliefs (such as the one I am considering in this note), you are, as a matter of fact, *repeating* in yourself the historical movement by which these abstract ideas gradually penetrated into and transformed social and political thought. If we can make a man conscious of the central ideas, from which his convictions spring, it is possible, at any rate, that by exposing them we may free him from their influence. He may, when fully conscious of them, reject them. This is the *abstract* method of propaganda. To put the matter once more, concretely. The pacifist often finds it almost *irrational* and unnatural to believe that a fundamental thing like liberty can depend on a *trivial* material thing. An appeal to facts would not shake this belief, for it is grounded in the way he *perceives* facts. The only way to shake it is to exhibit the *abstract* idea, which is really the source of this reluctance.

What is the *abstract* conception from which the *reluctance* of this type of pacifist to understand the dependence of liberty on accident depends? Very roughly it may be described as a false conception of the relation between values and existence. Values, as such, are absolute, but they have no force in themselves tending to bring about their realisation. The decay in the belief in absolute values, in an absolute ethic, was followed by a curious change. When values were no longer absolute in the true sense, they became absolute in another. You get developed more particularly in the eighteenth century the conception of *inevitable* progress. Values are then *grounded in existence*. They are permanent, not in the sense in which values are properly absolute, but as *natural* forces. There is something in Nature itself which *ensures* progress and which will consequently ensure the development of liberty.

From this comes the difficulty of the pacifist we are dealing with. It is from this *abstract* idea, that his tendency to think that a great thing like liberty cannot be helped or hindered by small things like armaments comes.

The consequences of the correct abstract conception of value are clear. If the pacifist adopted this view he would see that while the truth of certain values—of the desirability of liberty, for example—is *absolute* and unaffected by changes in this world, yet the *existence* of institutions which embody these values is *entirely at the mercy of change* and chance. He might then be in a position to recognise that the future of liberty *does depend on guns*.

This reluctance to recognise the dependence of *liberty* on *force*, is by no means a necessary characteristic of democracy. There is no essential connection between pacifism and democracy. This reluctance was not found, for example, in seventeenth century England, when Milton spoke of the nation that had 'been valourous enough to win liberty *in the field*'. Nobody then had any ideas of *inevitable* Progress or of Liberty realising itself. They had a thoroughly realistic conception of the means by which it could be achieved. It is worth while noting that in the disputes after the victory it was the army that was always the more democratic, while the lawyers were conservative; that army which said of itself: 'We are not a mercenary army, but called forth to the defence of our just rights and liberties.'

The pacifists should cure themselves of the habit of thinking that pacifism is another name for democracy. They should rid themselves also of the habit of putting down any opposition to pacifism, to an admiration for *Prussianism*. This parrot cry is trotted out delightedly by people who have as much acquaintance with what Prussia really is as they have with the other side of the moon. I am opposed to *pacifism* as a *democrat*, but I beg leave to point out that democracy is a little older than the tabernacles in which these people imbibed it. If I could correct their tenets by Ireton's[22] belief that 'men are born corrupt and will remain so', I should prefer to call myself a *Leveller*; for not only did they think '*liberty* a right inherent in every man . . . meaning by liberty . . . definite participation in whatever political arrangements the community finds it desirable to make', but they were prepared themselves to fight for this right.

This was seventeenth-century democracy, the source of all modern democracy. It had a certain virility and had not then fallen into the sentimental decadence of *humanitarianism*. The truth is, that there are two ideas of democracy. The pacifist founded on *sympathy* and the other founded on the conception of *Justice*, leading to the assertion of equality. To the latter conception, I must subscribe whether I desire to or not, as I must to an *ethical* conception. The inferiority of democracy founded on sympathy depends, however, also on a practical question. It seems demonstrable to me that the kind of ethic it fosters will never develop the force which is likely to radically transform society. That is only probable in movements which, like the democracy of the seventeenth century in England, or the Socialism of Proudhon, are founded on the idea of Justice. It is only too likely that the ideology which produces pacifism in external affairs will also produce *social pacifism*. It will [be a] broadened and extended form of *liberal* corruption.

[30 December 1915]

Most of us who read both pacifist and warlike literature experience a strange vacillation. When we read the pacifists we begin to understand the reactionaries, and when we read the reactionary exaltation of the heroic virtues, we begin to look for the first time with sympathy on the flat rationalism which takes individual comfort to be the principal aim of existence. After examining pacifist democracy at close quarters we begin to play with the notion that the anti-democratic theory of the State may be true, but further acquaintance with this again drives us back to the flattest individualism.

In the end, however, the war puts an end to this vacillation. In a way, which I shall roughly describe below, war brings precision and definiteness to our political ideas, and so does us some slight service. While nothing but disgust can be felt at the undisguised satisfaction of certain writers, who believe that the war has put an end to ideas they dislike, I see no reason why we should not draw this small consolation from the tragedy. It is a consolation, since the increased precision in our conception of democracy will not be without its influence in the future.

In our natural state, most of us tend to have a very confused idea of the relations between the abstract conceptions which underlie our political views. We get rid of this confusion, only so far as is necessary, to enable us to pursue certain practical ends. We are models of precision in those parts of political theory which enable us to outline clear boundaries separating us from the people to whom we are opposed. When that object has once been attained, the residuum of the theory is left confused; for the mind is economical of its energy, and only clears up and analyses ideas in as far as they are necessary for action.

This can be made clearer by the use of symbols. Suppose that I realise very clearly that the doctrine (D) is false, and object very strongly to the people who hold it as true. Let A. O. R. T., etc., be opinions, each of which if true, would be a reason for considering (D) false. We shall clear up the confusion of our ideas to this extent: that we shall clearly separate (D) from A. O. R. T., etc. . . . . But that is the extent of the confusion we shall clear up, for that is the extent to which action requires an analysis.

It is only when we object to certain views that the necessity for clearness arises. We wish to differentiate ourselves from these things. But when this has once been accomplished, the mind has no further stimulus, and tends to evade the effort necessary to introduce further precision in our thought. It is sufficient then to have rejected (D); and as the mind only analyses where the desire to differentiate exists, we may have (A. O. R. T.) left confused and *undifferentiated*. We know that each is a reason for rejecting (D), and we tend to think that in some way they are all *one* reason. The state of the mind then will be

(D) . . . . (A. O. R. T., etc.).

As long as we only talk about these things, the confusion is not likely to be discovered.

Two things may lead to further analysis. In the first place, the effort to explain in *writing* why you reject D. Unaccountable difficulties will arise in settling the right order for the exposition. What you write will come out indifferently as O. A. O. T. R., A. O. R. A. T. A. R. etc. You gradually realise that your confusion in *writing* springs from a confusion in *thought*, and that you reject (D) not for *one*, but for *several* distinct reasons.

There is another more potent method, in which the confusion may be further cleared up. The opinion (O) may be embodied in a movement which you dislike and consider wrong. Another desire for differentiation then springs up, that between

(O) and (A. O. R. T.)

You then begin to analyse (A. O. R. T.) in order to get rid of the (O). So that consequently, the cynic might observe that if you only disliked enough people, your ideas would in the end be quite clear. But I say this without any touch of scepticism. Your desire to differentiate yourself from some movement, does not *create* the new analysis in your ideas, it only provides you with the energy necessary to *discover* the hidden but real differences.

What do the symbols represent in this case. (D) is liberal, hedonist, pacifist democracy; (A) is the absolute conception of ethics; (O) is the 'organic' view of the State. I dislike (D). I approve, therefore, of the attack on relativist, utilitarian ethics to be found in Proudhon, and also, be it added, in many reactionary writers. I tend also to believe in the 'organic' theory of the State, since that also is diametrically opposed to (D). And there the matter rests, and I confuse O and A together, tending to think they are somehow *one* or *necessarily* connected. And thus from a perfectly legitimate rejection of *utilitarian democracy*. I might incline towards an anti-democratic position. I certainly have been interested in the theories of this kind to be found in Taine, Barrès,[23] and in Maurras. It so happens, however, that the (O) is the characteristic German theory of the State. When circumstances force me to consider very attentively the consequences of this 'organic' theory, I may then realise that its connection with (A), the absolute view of ethics, is no *necessary* one; and consequently be driven to realise that the right theory of society is to be found in Proudhon, and *not* in the *reactionaries*. In this way I believe that this war has greatly, to their own surprise, converted many men to democracy.

[An instance, perhaps a wrong one, of the working of this tendency, may be pointed out in France. Charles Maurras, who has endeavoured for years in 'L'Action Française', to combat German romanticism and to create an ideology which should be truly national and French, has lately been accused of introducing, in the endeavour to combat anarchic individualism, the German conception of the organic State.]

I shall attempt to give a clearer notion of what this German conception is, by giving an account of two representative German books on the war. I ought to say more definitely in what sense I use the word *representative* here. There are two kinds of war apologists. While we claim that we are 'fighting for liberty', for 'democratic' ideas, etc., there are a number of Germans who claim that they also are fighting for the same ideas. But they are certainly in a minority, and the prevailing type of apology pursues an entirely different method. When we assert that we are fighting for democracy, for 'Western ideas', it replies: 'Yes, and that is exactly what we Germans are fighting against.' This type of apology is the one it is best to consider; for not only does it correspond most closely with the facts, but it also leads to a form of discussion which is much more to the point. Our greatest objection to the Germans is not so much to the fact that they are brutally aggressive *without justification*, but just precisely to the things which they do consider *justify* them.

As examples of this type of apologist, I take Werner Sombart[24] and Max Scheler. Of Max Scheler, who is by far the more important of the two, I will say nothing at present, as the detailed consideration I shall give later to the German political theory will consist of a careful examination of his book on the war. In the short space left me in these notes, I intend to deal only with the more cosmic presentment of the similar ideas in Sombart's 'Helden und Händler'.

It should be noted that I have picked out two men who are, in different ways, important. It would serve no purpose to pick out any of the innumerable books on the war, written by asses, who are of course as numerous in Germany as in this country. To give a very approximate idea

of their position, I might compare one of them to the philosopher G. E.
Moore, and the other to Professor Pigou. But no comparison of this type
is of much use, as it is difficult to convince the ordinary Englishman of the
influence exerted by the *professors* in Germany. That, of course, was one
of the difficulties people experienced in warning this country of the
danger before the war. It was no use translating such books. The instinctive reply would be: 'What does it matter what a *professor* says?' I agree,
but it *does* matter in Germany. People are sometimes surprised at the blind
admiration so often expressed in scholastic circles here for German work.
The reason is quite simple. Schoolmasters instinctively feel that a land in
which the schoolmaster enjoys such respect, and such a high status, must
indeed be a wonderful country.

It should be noticed that both are what would be described as liberal-
minded men. Werner Sombart is perhaps best known here by his history
of Socialism. While he himself could not be described as a Socialist, he is
certainly no reactionary. He is a professor of economics, and while he
may not be the profoundest, he is certainly one of the most entertaining
writers on that subject. He supports original views on the origins of
capitalism with an astonishing knowledge of out-of-the-way facts. I
believe that his last book of this type, a history of the development of the
bourgeois, has just been translated into English. I heard him lecture some
years ago in Berlin.[25]

The thesis of Sombart's book is, of course, that this war is a war
between two conflicting *ideals*. He evidently regards the conflict with us
as the most important part of the struggle, and speaks always of the
contrasting ideals of Germany and England. 'Western European ideals' he
takes to be in origin 'English' ideals. What are these two contrasted ideals?
I will condense what he says of the English spirit as much as possible; you
may find it platitudinous. The essence of the English character is pure
commercialism; everything follows from that. By quoting a letter from a
stray Venetian merchant, he demonstrates that this has always been so,
even in the fifteenth century, and a testimony from a Venetian on this
subject is decisive. The result of this is that we have produced nothing in
art, literature or philosophy of any importance. We have a purely *commercial* view of the State as an artificial mechanism designed to further the
interests of the individual. That English philosophy is merely the carrying
of commercial categories into the subject, is proved from old Herbert
Spencer. 'Spencer, whom I cite most frequently as representing what is
most *characteristic in the English mind*.' 'Whenever an English writer shows
any signs of profundity he is always an Irishman . . . e.g., Ruskin, Oscar
Wilde . . . and Bernhard Shaw.' (One may note here as the most obvious
sign of the poverty of mind of the modern Germans, that it was they

alone who have created a reputation as a serious poet for a shallow journalist like Wilde, who enjoyed a reputation as a wit amongst extremely stupid people.) I have met them. 'As for poets, only a couple of Irishmen'—you wait with curiosity for their names. You may be surprised; they are 'Lord Byron and Shelley'. This, you see, is the *thorough*, the *gründlich*[26] German professor.

'In Art, nothing but the sugariness of Gainsborough and Reynolds.' This is surprising. No German professor can be expected to have a personal appreciation of art, but in as far as they refrain from illustrating theories of æsthetics by the inevitable Raphael, and are *modern*, they read Maier-Graefe, and there Sombart might have found Constable hailed as the 'father of all modern art'. Obviously in the plastic arts, we have nothing that can be compared with the production of the French. But in Germany, *since Dürer there has been absolutely nothing of any importance whatever.*

We are in a bad way generally; commercialism has had such influence over us 'that every class in England stands far below the corresponding class in Germany. As typical of this we have only to notice the profound difference between the mentality of a man like Grey[27] and that of Bethmann-Hollweg.'[28] My reply to this is, that the mentality of both these people is so exceedingly commonplace that it hardly seems possible to point out any difference between them.

The truth is, of course, that commercialism is nothing specifically English, but is a general phenomena, not destined, we may hope, to last for ever. If at the time when its influence over thought was at its height the most able writers were English, rather than German, that is nothing very much to be ashamed of. The same spirit in Germany manifested itself in an imitation of the English.

We turn now to the German spirit. 'The essence of this is duty, and the spirit of heroism. Naturally, therefore, there can be no resemblance between German patriotism and the natural pride of the Englishman, which is only that of the commercial man in being a partner in the largest business in the world. The difference is seen when it comes to sacrifices . . . There is a great drum-beating for recruits in England now. But no one answers the call from a spirit of sacrifice. Those who answer the call do so only because they think they *are doing good business for themselves*'!

What concerns me here, however, is what he says about the German theory of the State. 'The richness of the German spirit is shown by the fact that it is this, until recent times almost *State-less* people had produced a conception of the State of a profundity that has never been equalled since the time of Plato . . . Even in the people like Wolf and Kant, who seem to have adopted the mechanical English theory, a profound difference can be noted . . . What is the essence of this German conception? It is that of the *objective-organic* view of the State. . . . The State is a living organism, but a meta-biological, spiritual organism. . . . in which the individual forms a part.' 'As contrasted with the classical conception of the State in Greece, in which the individual disappeared, . . . it is the characteristic of the German conception of the State that it has known how to *reconcile* German individualism with the omnipotence of the State.' This leads to the German idealism about war. 'War will always appear senseless to the business man, who can think of nothing higher than the happiness of the individual.' (Yes, we can, but thank God it isn't the State.)

'But we know that there is a higher life . . . the life of the State . . . the single life is destined to be sacrificed itself to this higher . . . War is holy,' etc.

'With the exception of Kant in his old age, you will find no pacifist writing in any representative German. . . .'

As to militarism: 'It is stupid for foreigners to represent our militarism as the product of a war-loving officer class . . . as a decay from the tradition of our poets and thinkers. Potsdam and Weimar are one on this point. . . . Everything that foreigners have said about our militarism is further proof of the impossibility of a foreigner ever attaining to an understanding of a German . . . They all wish to free us from militarism . . . But militarism is not merely an institution . . . it is the German spirit itself . . . Potsdam and Weimar in highest union . . . Faust and Zarathustra and Beethoven in a rifle-pit. . . . Everything, including industry, is rightly subordinated to it. . . . The high valuation of military virtues in Germany, courage and *obedience.* . . . these are the *true virtues of the free man.* . . . Discipline . . . within and without.'

As to war. 'It follows from this conception of the State that it must continually measure itself with other States . . . It has always a tendency towards *growth.* . . . This *lebendiger Wachstum*[29] of the organic State is quite different from the dead, purely commercially grounded tendency to expansion, which dominates mechanical States like England . . . So war is an unavoidable accompaniment of all State life that is really living . . . The justification of war lies in the natural conditions of all living things.'

And so on.

One of the greatest benefits of our 'commercial' spirit is that any Englishman would at once feel this conception of the State and its consequences to be rubbish. Amid many foolish recruiting appeals, I do not remember one which asked us to die 'for the State'. I never met a soldier who ever thought of this war as anything but a stupidity . . . a necessary stupidity, but still a stupidity . . . (So much so that he is even reconciled to the necessary stupidity of generals.) And this I think is the greatest justification of our attitude that I know.

There are subjects in which Realism is perhaps the true doctrine, but the greatest gift the Heavens ever allotted to this country was our endowment of an all-prevailing *Nominalism*. It will always save us from belief in the bastard phenomena of the 'organic' State. We have never taken kindly to Bosanquet's.[30] There are some absolute things above the individual, but the State is not one of them.

It is better, I think, to leave detailed discussion of this to the time when I can examine the more serious work of Scheler. It may not be inappropriate, however, at this festive season, to conclude with a few more extracts from Sombart's book on general subjects.

'The commercial people cannot understand war. The most disgusting example of this is the praise given to the Captain of the "Emden", for *sportsmanlike* conduct. On another occasion, some imprisoned Englishmen offered to shake hands with our soldiers like footballers after a match, and were astonished when they got what they deserved, kicks on a certain part of the body.' 'We must get rid of this poison of sport in our midst. We must cultivate only those games which prepare us for war, . . . women must be broad-hipped that they may bear healthy soldiers . . . Away with Tennis, Football, and *Krikett!*'

'The war may kill international relationship in science, but that does not matter. We Germans, in spiritual culture need no one . . . No people on earth can give us anything of value in Science, Technology, Art or Literature, that we could not do without. . . . Reflect on the inexhaustible richness of the German essence that includes everything in itself . . . We understand all foreign peoples, but none can understand us. . . . We recognise as far below us all "Western European ideas" . . . We may nevertheless occasionally take pleasure in the production of other cultures, always excepting the English, who produce no cultured values at all, and unlike the Latins, Scandinavians, Celts, and Slavs, have nothing to give us.

'So must we Germans (like the Greeks) go through the world to-day with proud, elevated heads, in the certain conviction that we are God's people. As the German bird, the Eagle, soars high above all other animals, so must the German feel to all the other peoples whom he sees at infinite depths below him.'

In this breathless silence one can almost hear the rustling of the 'von' as it drops from the princely heavens on our energetic author.

'But do not be afraid . . . we do not want to bite pieces out of
you . . . Quite rightly we shall always be *bad colonists* . . . We have no
desire to accumulate possessions . . . We leave that to the English. *But*
when it is necessary to extend our land possession to find room for our
increasing population, we shall take what is *necessary for this purpose.* We
shall set our Foot on places which strategically are necessary for the
preservation of our *untouchable* strength. . . . We shall take as bases for our
Fleet, Malta, Suez, and *Dover* . . .

'We do not want to expand. We have something more to do. We have
to keep the German soul pure, . . . for Germany is the last dam against the
filthy stream of commercialism.'

Now was any of us ever as this man is?

[6 January 1916]

In answer to a request for an explanation of the delay in the publication
of the Dardanelles report,[31] Mr. Tennant[32] said that as Sir Ian Hamilton[33]
was a writer of distinction, he was probably taking some time to polish up
his phrases.

Mr. Tennant explained that the name of the general responsible for the
failure of the Suvla Bay landing could not be given, as the publication of
the name would be too punitive. In answer to a further question, as to
whether this general still retained any command, Mr. Tennant said that a
general could only be removed from the Army as the result of a court
martial, and that, of course, could only follow on some *really disgraceful act.*

If we take all the circumstances into consideration, it would be no
exaggeration, I think, to look upon the incident recorded above as one of
the most disgraceful of the whole war. The bad taste of the first reply is
a small matter; what is important is the revelation of an attitude which is
only too clearly that of our rulers generally. From that point of view
nothing could be more depressing.

The news that, after all, we are to have compulsion, comes not very
long after this incident. The two things may profitably be discussed
together; for they are not merely events closely related in time, but there
is a real connection between them. In the forms distributed by the
canvassers under the Derby scheme,[34] men if not willing to enlist were
invited to state their reasons. In a town in the North with which I am
acquainted, among many foolish answers, there was this very sensible
one. 'When I see some signs that a real attempt is being made to end the
disgraceful mismanagement of the war, both on the part of civilians and
of the generals, I shall be prepared to enlist. At present I have no
inclination to join such a rotten concern.' I want in these Notes to offer
some justification of this.

None of the men, who will now be compelled to serve, have ever been brought up to contemplate the possibility of this compulsion. It is, undoubtedly, tragic, that such men should in the middle of their lives be suddenly by force taken from their occupations, perhaps to their deaths. It is certainly very painful to think of. But there are certain conditions in which the whole business becomes to some extent less painful, and men's minds more easy about it. The psychology involved is worth examining; it depends, I think, on the notion of *inevitability*. Everyone on active service is bound at one time or other to get extremely depressed. I used to think that in such moments the state of mind of the volunteer would be better than that of the conscript; he would not have to bear the additional depression of knowing that he had been forced, unjustly, in this situation. But this, I now see, is bad psychology. Probably nine-tenths of the depression a man feels not only in this particular instance, but in ordinary life also, is due to the thought that it might not have been, that had he pursued a different course it would not have happened. If an unpleasant situation is seen to be *inevitable* it still remains unpleasant, but the element which exasperated it into a *worrying* depression has been removed. It might be argued, then, that in some ways the state of mind of the conscript may be better than that of the volunteer. It is for reasons of this kind that the *embusqué*[35] is hunted out. It is not because the numbers then obtained are important, but because of the effect on those already serving. The *inevitability* is made more absolute. It is then a kind of mental hygiene.

Take, now, a more specific instance of the same phenomena. Consider what happened in any one of the numerous, small, and often unrecorded, minor attacks we made early last year. Everyone knows beforehand that the attack is to be made. The men stumble up in the night to the shallow special trenches which are dug in preparation for an attack. They lie cramped up there till dawn, when the attack is to take place. At dawn, however, it is perhaps misty, the artillery cannot 'prepare' the attack, and it is postponed till the afternoon. When it finally comes off, the men amble up hill three-quarters of the distance to the German trenches, by which time most of them are shot down. Probably most of the officers will have been killed. Consider the state of mind of the officers before they get over the parapet to lead the attack. The prospect is not a cheerful one. But if you postulate that the attack has been ordered by an infinitely wise commander for a definite, clearly seen purpose, then a man might go cheerfully to such an attack even knowing that it would bowl him out. For the business would then have seemed necessary and *inevitable*. The greatest cause of depression would then be absent. If, however, he imagines that some of the bungling asses who direct our operations had merely ordered this attack because they felt *something* must be done, and this was the only idea that occurred to them—looking at the map of the line of trenches, they said, 'There's a *kink* here. Let us order it to be straightened out'—then his depression is likely to be very much greater.

I give this as a parallel for what is on a much bigger scale the position of the man who is to be 'fetched' at this moment. He can make this perfectly legitimate objection. This war so far, he might say, has been carried on by incompetent Ministers and incompetent generals. Moreover, enormous illegitimate profits have been made by certain capitalists, whose names are well known to the Government. *But in spite of this, since the beginning of this war, no member of the ruling classes has been punished.* No names are given; that 'would be too punitive'; and in spite of terrific blunders, the same people still direct affairs. Well and good, if you prefer to be governed in this way, let it continue. But you have no right to use my life as further material to feed your incompetence. In the case of the free citizen who is compelled to serve, there should be an *implied contract*. He has not the right to expect that everything will go well. But when he surrenders his liberty, he has the right to expect that what he then suffers, if it is the result of incompetence and stupidity, will always be followed by the drastic punishment of those responsible. It is not a matter of punishment according to ordinary standards, but there ought to be a much greater severity to balance the sacrifice of his liberty made by the citizen. Above all things, it is necessary that he shall feel that this implied *contract* has been loyally carried out. It is necessary that he shall have this feeling of *inevitability* about the sacrifice he is called upon to make. Otherwise, he might object. 'I am forced against my will into a position in which I may lose my life, yet the name of the man responsible for the failure at Suvla Bay cannot be given, for it might *hurt his feelings*. But if *things are so serious that I must be forced to fight, then they are also so serious that incompetence should be punished by disgrace.*'

The incompetence, and the fact that no one has been punished, are patent to everyone. Take the subject of the first quotation at the head of these Notes. It is well known that the general in command at the Dardanelles made repeated demands for reinforcements which were never sent till months after they were asked for, and then always in inadequate numbers. The people, whoever they were, who were responsible for this, ought to have been removed from office. Instead of that, we get the report delayed, and the delay excused by insolent remarks like the one quoted. Much worse than this is, of course, the Servian business. The consequences of this criminal stupidity are by no means finished with. Yet no one has to leave on account of it. In France, whose interest in the question is infinitely less than ours, it has led to the fall of Delcassé. The reason for our policy, then, whether it was the result of a too great reliance on Russia or not, does not matter; the *implied contract* should lead to the disgrace of the Minister responsible. Yet, greatest farce of all, even his opponents 'chivalrously' defend Grey when he is attacked. And, now, apparently, the same tragic policy of indecision is being repeated over the East African expedition.[36] It is the same with our generals. The commander at Suvla Bay still remains in the army, for 'he will only be dismissed after he has done something *really disgraceful*'. But what will be more disgraceful in time of war than failure? It does not matter in the least that a general pockets the silver spoons from the mess table; if we had a really successful general, we could well afford to let him swindle us out of half a million in stores; he would be cheap at the price.

The loyal carrying out of the *implied contract* with the citizen soldier demands a ruthless and drastic punishment for all these failures. But this objection will be made. If every failure is followed by removal, we should soon have neither generals nor Ministers.

We need not trouble to ask anxiously in the case of Ministers: 'But who shall we put in their place?' We have got past the stage of thinking that no one could replace the politicians. The objection has greater plausibility in the case of the generals. It does seem here as if this were a very technical profession, in which only a few people, after long training, had qualified. But this is fallacious. Talent in military leadership is a peculiarly hidden quality; there are probably few outward signs by which it can be detected in time of peace, and it might be possessed by a head waiter.

The only way to discover it is by a continual process of trial and error. Such a method is *hard* on generals of long service. But things are not to be judged in this way, 'what is *fair* to a general or not'. Increased severity is called for in the *first* place by the military situation, by the necessity of winning. But much more is it called for by the necessity of keeping loyally the *implied contract* with the citizen soldier.

The motives behind this refusal to punish are diverse. While some of them are interested motives, the most powerful of all, one, I think, shared by almost everyone in this country, is the feeling of toleration, the sentiment of good taste, which prevents us telling the truth in public about public characters. This hypocrisy is really a kind of moral blight over the country, and the German writers who describe it are certainly right in this one point. It is no use our calling it toleration, and thinking that it is a special virtue of this country. It is not a virtue, nor has it always been characteristic. It is merely a secondary by-product of Victorian security. In the times before this period of security we were as drastic in punishment, and as coarse in polemic, as any nation in Europe. The French were surprised by the way we hung admirals, and even Casanova was shocked by the license of our Press. We may as well rid at once of the idea that toleration and good taste are peculiarly English characteristics. Our security has gone, and these will soon disappear with it.

At present, however, we are in an unfortunate position, as we combine the disadvantage of actual insecurity with a complacent ignorance of the fact, and a method of thinking appropriate only to security.

I intend to deal at greater length later with this extraordinary inability to realise how entirely our security has disappeared. It is to be seen not only more positively in our conduct of the war, but also indirectly in writings of the pacifists. Behind most of the categories in terms of which they think lies the assumed *postulate* of security. In proposing terms of peace, they always behave like the sons of rich people, entirely ignorant of how money is made, and who propose to *give away* money which they have not even got to spend.

I shall begin to admit that this fatuous sense of security has at last disappeared, when, one morning, I see Lord Haldane[37] swinging from a lamp-post—whether justly or unjustly is immaterial. I shall then begin to think two things: (1) that we are at last developing the kind of spirit which will make the army efficient and win the war, and (2) that we have at last earned the right to *compel* men to sacrifice their lives.

[13 January 1916]

Recruits must still be found, even if they have to be drawn from very unlikely sources. I propose, therefore, to induce some literary men to enlist by the most suitable means I can think of—a series of articles addressed to them individually. I have not at present consulted Lord Derby about my scheme, but I hope eventually to gain his approval.

In the course of the present article, I shall probably be rather personal in my remarks. I gather from some letters which followed an earlier article of mine, that certain pacifist readers object to this method of controversy when it is used by other than pacifists. I propose, therefore, to state my views about the ethics of polemics. I think Mr. Bell[38] is a wretched creature, and I propose to say so. The toleration and good taste which we can well afford in times of security make such statements then unnecessary; but, at the present moment, they are needed. It is only after a series of controversies carried in this spirit that we shall rid ourselves of certain false and dangerous opinions.

The general principle that guides our use of personal detail in such controversy should be that it is only legitimate to use such detail when it is a matter which has been made public by the person concerned. I refer to Mr. Bell as a rich man; I think that justified, not only because of the internal evidence provided by his book on Art,[39] but because Roger Fry at a public banquet in his presence addressed him as the Mæcenas[40] of the modern Art movement, or something equally silly. Then, I ask, Why does he not enlist? That, in normal cases, is a purely private matter. But Mr. Bell has himself made the matter public. He has not been content to remain comfortably a civilian, but has issued a pamphlet to prove that in so doing he is superior to his betters who have enlisted. This is too much. Nobody minds people running away with other people's wives. We are all human. But we do object to people who say they did it from a sense of duty.

Finally, when I refer to Mr. Bell as a contemptible ass, I ought to say that I know nothing of him personally, but I base my assertion on the very full and adequate evidence provided by his own writings.

As very few who read these 'Notes' will ever have heard of this somewhat obscure individual, I had better say something about him at once. He is a particularly foolish specimen of the æsthete, and has written a book on Art. I propose to justify what I say of it by a more careful examination later. For the purpose of the discussion in these 'Notes', all that is relevant is the admiration he expresses for people who sacrifice material comfort for certain abstract values. 'In Paris, I have seen young painters penniless, half-fed, unwarmed, their women and children in no better case, work-ing all day in feverish ecstasy at unsaleable pictures, and, quite possibly, they would have killed or wounded anyone who suggested a compromise with the market . . . they stole newspapers and boot-blacking that they might continue to serve their masterful passion. They were superbly religious.' (Exactly, but why the blacking? Did they draw with it on the newspapers or what? I thought we had finished with this silly middle class romantic conception of the life of the artist.) It is only necessary to remember later that for Mr. Clive Bell there are things for which physical existence may legitimately be sacrificed, 'the austere and thrilling raptures of those who have climbed the cold, white peaks of art'.

He is not afraid of giving himself testimonials. 'If other writers on æsthetics failed, it was because they lacked that very rare but absolutely necessary combination of an exquisite sensibility with the power of robust thinking.' Has Mr. Bell failed? Oh no. His claim to have provided a new and original theory is continually insisted on: 'I believe in my theory; it makes history more comprehensible.' He continually gives himself the airs of a Columbus who has opened up a new continent. Now, putting these ridiculous claims on one side, what kind of theory has he actually produced? This is easily answered. A certain amount of money makes people mobile. They can get hold of the new movement in other countries, some years before the journalist. This knowledge gives predominance at dinner parties and drawing-rooms. But gradually this advantage goes, and you get the pathetic horror of this type of amateur—when they find that the fact that they were the *first to know* is being forgotten. Then the advantage must be placed on record, be crystallised, as it were, in a book. That such is the origin of this book is fairly obvious from the introduction. Mr. Bell is best known as a pup of Mr. Roger Fry. This seems to rankle. It will hardly be believed that this 'epoch-making new æsthetic' descends to such small beer as this. 'I met Fry in a railway carriage plying between Cambridge and London. . . . Fry had recently become acquainted with the modern French masters. . . . Cézanne, Gauguin, Matisse . . . *I enjoyed the value of a long acquaintance.*' Who cares what commercial traveller first introduced these masters to our notice!

Like every amateur magnum opus it contains his opinions not only on Art but on every subject. To illustrate the banality to which an 'exquisite sensibility' and 'robust thinking' can descend, I may quote some of his utterances on Religion. 'Religion, as I understand it, is an expression of the emotional significance of the universe. . . . *I should not be surprised* to find that Art was an expression of the same thing. Christianity by a deplorable mischance has been unwilling to abandon dogmas . . . that are utterly irrelevant to its essence.' 'Religion . . . an affair of emotional conviction should have nothing to do with intellectual beliefs', should, I suppose, take the form actually suggested later of 'dancing and shouting in some significant formal way'. Here, for a moment, we may leave the profound reflections of this male Mrs. Humphry Ward.[41]

Turn now to the pamphlet, 'Peace at Once'. As the author never says anything original, he may usefully serve us as a fair sample of the type of pacifism we have to deal with.

We need say nothing of his more positive arguments, founded on facts, for he merely repeats all the clichés of the school. Everything is there, from the 'decline in the height of Frenchmen during the Napoleonic era' to our old friend 'the colonial expansion which Germany's growing population demands'.

The argument based on facts, however, is entirely subsidiary here to a main argument which is independent of any fact. 'You are prepared to suffer the evils of war, that certain greater evils may be avoided. I deny that many of these evils would accompany peace. But even granting all you urge, admitting that all these evils would come about, I deny even then that war is worth while.' 'Even if the German armies were to conquer England and make it a province of the German empire . . . immediate peace would be best.' The emphasis is always on the price that must be paid. What then is this dreadful price we have to pay which makes conquest a lesser evil?

It consists always in a morbid emphasis on death. 'Would the average Englishman rather *kill and die* than see his children . . . , etc.,' '. . . the question which everyone who is not afraid of the truth should ask himself. . . . Is the ordinary man . . . willing to give and *take death* . . . and break the heart of the world rather than live under a foreign government . . . ? Must men really . . . *die* for an abstraction?'

There is continual emphasis on what men lose by death. 'Men do not love by abstraction, Professor, not of such stuff as Life' (our old friend Life again). 'There goes a lad of two-and-twenty . . . Life is all before him . . . The rain and fair weather and a sense of being alive in a world which is full of pleasant places and jolly days . . . That is the life of the common man, and you send him to the trenches.' Whatever difference the war may make, 'it can hardly be the difference between life and death'. This is the only reality. . . . There are pages of such sickly, faked stuff. This disgusting whining—with its canting affectation of simplicity that makes one squirm, requires further comment. For what in the end does it imply? Remember the argument. Even with England a German possession death is so terrible that we ought to submit. It comes to this, then: that for the emancipated man death is too great a price to pay for anything. Life and comfort are the ultimate goods—and if we sacrifice them to any 'abstraction' it is only because we are deceived by words. It was not so in the case of the Paris painters who stole blacking—but that was for Art—not for empty words like Honour. The ideology from which this all springs can be most shortly described as one that finds no place whatever for the heroic. For heroism means risk of death, and death means leaving 'the wind and the rain, the daisies, the buttercups, the butterfly, the cowslip, fair women, the sun, the moon, the stars . . .'. I call such an attitude rotten, because, leaving consequences out of the question, it is in itself, objectively, rotten and false. But the consequence of the prevalence of such an ideology may be pointed out. The entire decay of the heroic would certainly make wars impossible, but it would make revolution also impossible. That workmen should think only of their immediate comfort is an excellent doctrine for the Mæcenas of the Cubists, who have never, he says, 'been able to believe in the political genius of the masses'. It is this which the pacifist Proudhon saw more clearly. 'Philanthrope vous parlez d'abolir la guerre, prenez garde de dégrader le genre humain.'[42]

His whole argument comes back always to this rhetorical question, 'What cause can be great enough to make a man sacrifice his life?' I can best answer him by explaining what causes may be small enough. The argument (it seems very like the reasoning of a paralytic funk) seems to be, men must be so afraid of death that only the most cogent reasons— reasons that war could never provide—should ever make men face it cheerfully. But normal men are not made like that. A man may take the risk for quite trivial reasons.

One may make the difference clearer by an analogy. If I am very short of money, then I shall only buy things when there are urgent reasons for doing so. But if I have plenty of money the position is altered, I may buy things for the most trivial reasons. If we establish a distinction between the 'real' and the 'releasing' causes of an action—then we may say that when I buy some trivial object I do not really require the 'real' cause is my super-abundant money, the object bought is merely the 'releasing' cause, the excuse. This is a parallel for the position of men in regard to the risk of death. Mr. Clive Bell is baffled by the fact that men spend their lives freely; the only way he can explain it is by supposing them to be very simple, and easily taken in by empty phrases, 'honour', and the like. But the normal man takes much more the attitude of the man with plenty of money to spend. He takes the risk for a hundred different reasons—even for adventure, to 'see the world'. I don't say that men are always capable of this—far from it; but at a crisis they are. Now, these trivial reasons are only the 'releasing' cause. It is not so much that an overwhelming cause like national necessity overcomes an overwhelming fear of death. It is rather that 'national necessity' lets go a cause already existing in the man; and may in a special way be even welcomed. What corresponds here to the super-abundant money; what is the 'real cause' here? The occasional people who do formulate their reasons would probably say that it was the desire 'to prove to themselves that they were not the sort of men who didn't—a kind of personal test'. The aspect of adventure, of carelessness about the matter, springs from the sentiment men may have that 'in the centre of their being is a feeling of security and certainty which cannot be affected by, and makes them even indifferent to, what happens on the more superficial layers'. I am not for a moment pretending that any man ever constantly had this feeling—we are much too sensible for that. But most men at a given moment may feel this carelessness. If you say that this is too metaphysical, I disagree with you. All men may be metaphysical in their actions. On this point all men are equal. Whether it is explicit or implicit makes little difference.

The difference between the two attitudes can be illustrated by a story of Mr. Bell's. He tells of a 'shopman from my quarter' whom he bumped into one night. We have the Life stunt again. 'He enjoyed picture-palaces and music-halls, his tobacco and a poached egg at an A.B.C. . . . He had his friends, too. . . . Who knows? Some day he must have fallen in love. . . . He had life and youth and health . . . He was lighting a cigarette, that was how I came to run into him. . . . I apologised; he shouted a jolly "good night" and hurried after . . . two rather pretty girls. . . .' 'He was shot through the head at Ypres. For what universal good . . . did that man die?' I may here interject that the atmosphere of 'superiority' in which this is related should be enough to sicken any decent man; it makes one want to kick the pompous ass. Quite obviously there is less regret at the youth's death than complacent satisfaction at his own sensibility to the pathos of the event. 'What did you do, father, in the war?' 'I bumped into a man who was killed and wrote an article about it.' Such is the story. The impression it is intended to make on you is clear—the simple youth and the kindly, wise philosopher. Poor simple fellow—he was young to die—and all because he was not as clever as our author.

We may now consider a more practical question. These have all been negative arguments. Can we give any positive reasons why Mr. Clive Bell should enlist? I can give two here. First, the argument derived from opportunity. Various views may be held as to the duties of the rich, but all would agree in this—that the comfortably off should be the first to go in war. That, at any rate, they owe society in return for the comparatively good time they have. You do not compound for this obligation by writing a pamphlet telling the poor what to think. It is a widespread but entirely mistaken idea to suppose that you amend for the advantages of wealth by asserting verbally that you are a Socialist.

The second argument, though it has less appearance of reason, is, perhaps, more effective. You think the war a tragic mistake brought about by certain illusions about 'national honour', etc. . . . Yet, under the influence of this illusion, people whose lives have been infinitely less comfortable than your own have gone out to their deaths. Under-paid clerks, with nothing behind them but lives that have always been cramped, have, mistakenly perhaps, thought they had to face this tragic duty and faced it. The lives they lead in the trenches is a wretched one. Though a man of a more leisured class, like yourself, may think it would be wrong to join, yet if, under such circumstances, he did not feel that he must, he would be a despicable creature. 'Who am I, that others should lead this wretched life while I escape?' There is a certain generosity of mind which makes such a feeling unsupportable to most men. It was probably a reason of this kind that made the sculptor Gaudier-Brzeska go back to France. It is sickening to think that a man like this who showed promise of becoming a considerable artist should be killed, while this wretched artistic pimp still survives.

Why does he remain? We recall his admiration for the painters who sacrificed everything for 'the austere and thrilling rapture of those who have climbed the cold white peaks of art'. Is it only in art that these higher values exist to which comfort must be sacrificed? Or is it because in art other people do it for you, and here you have to do it for yourself?

There are no 'cold white peaks' here; there is nothing, alas, but cold feet.

[20 January 1916][43]

We cannot win this war unless we obtain more reinforcements for the Army than those which the Derby Scheme (without compulsion) provides. I regard this not as an opinion but as a fact.

That being so, two views on the subject of compulsion are possible. Either you admit regretfully that compulsion is necessary, or you say that you look upon conscription as so great an evil that no threatened danger, however great, can make it justifiable; you then proceed to make immediate peace. It is this latter position that I want to discuss in these 'Notes'.

Before this clear issue can be discussed, however, certain attempts on the part of the pacifists to confuse the question must be considered. There is nothing very complicated about these attempts, they are merely lies. I used the word lies quite objectively; the statements made by these people are entirely false. That is quite a different thing, of course, from saying that the authors of them are liars. I don't think most of them are. They are merely unable to distinguish between what they, for quite idealistic reasons, desire, and what is, in fact, true.

When last June[44] I began to read the 'Nation' again, I was extremely surprised to discover—what otherwise I might not have noticed—that we were doing exceedingly well everywhere. More than that, our future prospects were even better. No further attacks on the part of Germany, either in Serbia or elsewhere, were to be looked for, as her reserves were completely exhausted. In my innocence, I was much cheered up, until I gathered that this was simply an extremely elaborate method of *implying* that we had no need of conscription here. Unfortunately, this particular method is no longer possible. It is only too obvious that we have this year been beaten in almost every theatre of the war. A temporary refuge was then found in the invention of mythical figures about the size of our army. The 'New Statesman' told us that four million men had enlisted. When it was found that the figures were under two million, this method also came to an end.

I think some of these people show wonderful powers in the way of self-delusion. I recall a conversation I had with the editor of an anti-conscriptionist paper. He asked me, very impressively, 'Do you know how many English troops alone there are in Gallipoli? . . . over 300,000.' Yet Hamilton's report[45] makes it clear that we never had more than 100,000 there at any time. But still the method continues, until one really does begin to suspect that they are liars. The quibbling over the Derby figures[46] is very little short of downright lying. Even supposing that the 600,000 single men were entirely composed of the halt, the maimed, and the blind, it still remains true that, without compulsion, you cannot take any of the attested married men. What is contemptible about the whole business is that they do not in reality believe in what they say, and when the facts prove that most of the 600,000 are available, not a single one of them will acknowledge his mistake. One hasn't patience to go into detail over the matter; it is merely silly, and there's an end of it.

There can be no possible doubt about the fact that the men really are wanted. Don't run away with the idea that the 30,000 a week is an artificial figure invented for the purpose. There is no bunkum about that. You can work out the matter for yourself, when you have been told that the rate of wastage of an infantry battalion is 18 per cent per month. Perhaps a more personal way of putting it might be more convincing. I remember last June hearing an officer make an appeal for recruits in a theatre. He dealt entirely in generalities about the necessity for more men taken from the newspapers. If, instead, he had spoken of his own regiment, and the wastage it had to meet, he might have had more success. I know, personally, of one regiment that went for the first time into the trenches near Loire early in November, 1914, about 800 strong, and by the beginning of January, 1915, was down to 400. During this time it had taken part in no action, but was merely doing ordinary trench work; 300,000 recruits will not carry us on for ten weeks.

We are then forced back to the question of principle—that conscription is so great an evil that nothing can make it justifiable. I get to this with some relief, as this is the real root of the opposition; the pretext that the facts show conscription is not necessary, being merely a faked disguise for this real objection.

Before we get to it, however, there is one other objection not based on principle, 'whether necessary or not, they say, conscription in this country is impossible; in *fact*, the miners will strike, etc. . .'.

Now, in the first place it must be recognised that there is a very strong body of opinion even inside the unions in favour of compulsion for single men. You may deprecate the trick by which it has been created, but do not ignore the fact that this body of opinion really does exist. And this public opinion is founded on the most solid basis—that of self-interest. About a month ago I found that preparations had been made in many large towns to organise associations of married men to resist the Government if the pledge were not kept.

Turn now to this threatened strike. Two preliminary cautions should be observed: Don't mistake what you want to happen for what is likely to happen. Be under no illusion about fact. Then put on one side for the moment all questions of justice and injustice. Don't mistake what you, perhaps rightly, think *ought* to happen for what will happen. Don't pass from the fact that you think economic strikes are always right to the false conclusion that this particular political strike is likely to succeed.

I don't believe myself that there will be any strike, but if there is, nobody need worry about it. For what will happen? Human nature being what it is, the only strikes that can either last, or succeed, are those directed to specific ends, within the power of the employees to bring about. But this strike would fulfill no condition of that kind. The miners themselves are not to be conscripted. The fact that they strike will not prevent the other men attesting or being made to attest. They will simply be striking in the air. The affair would soon become tedious, then ridiculous—then collapse. No strikes which were merely 'demonstrations' of this kind have ever succeeded. The only example to the contrary is the first general strike in Belgium on the suffrage question; and that succeeded merely because the Government wanted it to; they were only too pleased to be able to overawe the more reactionary element in their own party. When it was repeated, some years later, and this time the Government were opposed, it failed.

What, on the other hand, ought to be done, is to obtain a guarantee from the Government that they will repeal the whole of the 'Defence of the Realm' Acts[47] on the day the war ends.

So we get back to the question of 'principle'. 'We admit', the polite pacifist might say, 'that you are fighting for the principle of liberty.' But it is no good fighting for the principle of liberty in external affairs, and denying it at home. In opposing conscription we also are 'fighting for liberty'.

As long as it is put in that way, of course, the opposition can never be resolved. A 'principle' has an absolute, infinite character, it is not a quantity and, consequently, cannot be measured. When two principles oppose each other then nothing can be settled.

But it is inaccurate to say that we are fighting for the 'principle' of liberty. If liberty is a value it exists as a principle out of time and change. No one can fight for a principle. It is better, then, to say that we are fighting for the *'fact* of liberty'. The anti-conscriptionists can say that they are fighting for the *fact* of liberty here at home. Now facts can be measured and compared. It then becomes possible to argue as to whether the amount of liberty we lose by temporary compulsion is not infinitesimal in comparison with the loss of liberty which would follow a defeat.

The difficulty about a comparison of this kind is that neither side can understand how the phrase 'loss of liberty' has any meaning when used by their opponents. When the pacifist speaks of the 'loss of liberty' involved in conscription, or in the alteration of trade union rules, his opponents do quite sincerely think that he is using empty phrases to disguise sordid motives. They are really unable to imagine what meaning he attaches to the words under such conditions. In the same way the pacifist never really at heart thinks that our 'liberty' would be in any way endangered by the loss of this war.

Perhaps, then, I may get a pacifist favourably inclined to admit that I do mean something when I say we are fighting for liberty, when I admit that there is considerable danger to liberty at home in the process. I do fully recognise how much of our liberties we do surrender under the various 'Defence of the Realm' Acts, and the really considerable danger that we shall not recover all of them at the end of the war. The middle classes, as a whole, are inclined to be impatient of such talk when it is concerned with Trade Unions' privileges. The reality of the danger may be brought home to them by the trivial example of the freedom we alone, among European nations, enjoyed from the irksome necessity of registration, of filling up forms at hotels, etc. Once lost, this trivial liberty may be difficult to regain, for there are many of the *good* who would like to see us all registered.

What is our reply to this?

We assert that the danger to liberty involved in this Act, and in the use of compulsion, is infinitesimal in comparison with the loss of liberty that would follow our defeat. The controversies which these things create are like disputes as to relative position *inside* a structure which may at any time be *overturned* by external causes. But this is entirely ineffective as an argument, for it depends on an assumption to which the other side do not agree. We assume that defeat would involve a very real curtailment of our liberty. It is evident from everything they do and say that the pacifists do not believe there is any such danger. Though they make perfunctory reference to it, they do not at heart believe in it. They take no real interest in the matter, their enthusiasm is directed to other ends. Loss of liberty in this connection is to them an empty phrase, and they treat it with the same impatience that the middle classes treat the same phrase when it is applied to Trade Union troubles under the Munitions Act.[48] Our first business, then, should be with this incapacity to realise the consequences of defeat. Until that has been dealt with, the argument about the 'overturning structure' will remain meaningless.

These people have, at any rate, no vivid realisation of the consequences of defeat. They receive statements based on such assumptions with a polite incredulity. I understand this incredulity well enough. It is exactly the spirit in which before the war they received statements about the danger of Germany's aggressiveness. They knew better; such irrational things did not exist. Well—they have had one surprise. Mr. Bertrand Russell's pamphlet says: 'To all liberal-minded and humane men this war has come as a *shock* . . . shattering hopes.' You are preparing for yourselves an even more hope-shattering shock, when you think lightly of the danger to liberty in an inconclusive peace.

*   *   *

This scepticism about the consequence of defeat springs from two sources.

(1) The fatuous belief that liberty cannot at any rate be permanently endangered, for 'Germany herself will *inevitably* develop towards democracy'.

(2) The inability to see that Europe will be really altered in structure by this war. The facile and false analogy with wars like the Crimean or the Franco-Prussian, which, while they increased the power of one nation, or diminished that of another, yet still left Europe a society of independent nations. *There is no analogy between this war and the other wars.* A German victory means an end of Europe as a new Hellas, a society of nations. It means a Europe under German leadership. The pacifists cannot see this, for, curiously enough, while they *repudiate the balance of power as a doctrine of policy, they do so because they unconsciously assume that the balance of power will take care of itself, being grounded on the nature of things.* Being assumed,

like democracy, to be of the nature of the law of gravitation, it would be absurd to fight for it.

I realise the source of your incredulity. 'You may make out a case for the danger to liberty—but it lacks reality. Europe has had many wars—many spoke of them as a danger to liberty—but always things were much the same after.'

But this time they won't be. Forget easy analogies and examine carefully the obvious facts.

You are slowly realising the nature of that irrational thing, Force. Force does settle things, does create facts, which you have henceforth to deal with. The situation round the Dardanelles has probably now crystallised. Russia will not get through to the Mediterranean, and we shall be unable always to prevent Germany's access to Asia. Another situation created by force is being prepared for us nearer home. Europe is in flux; it will settle after the war into a physical structure which will probably endure for a century.

The most accurate metaphor for the new structure that will follow the victory of Germany is that of the emergence of a mountain in a plane. You are not to think that such an emergence leaves surrounding countries unaffected. It produces the same effect on them as putting a parcel under the tablecloth would do—all of them have to live on an inclined plane.

As evidence of the existence of the intention of Germany really to alter the framework of Europe in this way, I may conveniently quote a few sentences from a recent book on the war by Max Scheler.[49] Scheler is not a sensational journalist, or a military writer like Bernhardi,[50] but one of the most intelligent of the younger German philosophers, and one who, moreover, belongs to the school that is beginning to have the greater influence on this generation of students.

After a long preliminary discussion on the real nature of 'international' and 'cosmopolitan' the main object of the war is stated to be the destruction of the balance of power; and the creation for the first time of a solidarist Continental Europe under *German military leadership*. . . . 'Then we shall see the creation of a new Mediterranean culture grounded on the *military power* of Germany.'

To attain this end Russia must be finally driven out of Europe, and France completely crushed.

What is the position of England then?

He attacks the Germans, who are surprised and shocked at our entry into the war. 'It was inevitable that England should come in. Her whole existence as an Empire was threatened by the building of the German fleet.' He reproves those who, 'with an imitation of English cant', have pretended that the fleet was built for defensive purposes.

'The only possible aim in the building of the German fleet was directed against England.' 'Our first object always must be the destruction of the English naval supremacy, for this stands between us and the fair division of the earth. If this object is not attained now further struggles must and will follow.'

[27 January 1916][51]

After a course of reading in pacifist pamphlets, I have attempted to group together the arguments most frequently used into a kind of order. Many different arguments really derive their force from the same unconscious assumptions, and the mere demonstration of that connection, even when no detailed account of the arguments is given, may be useful.

Controversy may assume two forms—you may give specific reasons for your own views, or you may endeavour to explain the psychology of your opponents. The second method is only valid in conjunction with the first. It is perfectly legitimate when it accompanies definite reasoning about the facts, but not otherwise.

First, then, for reasons based on facts—stated very shortly. I think the writer who said the war was the most important European event since the French Revolution and probably since the Reformation, was right in this point, though he has been wrong in almost everything else. You probably reject such a statement as exaggeration, because you are very much aware of the sordid motives and the petty, unimaginative people who brought it about. You prefer to look at it as a small event on a very large scale. In doing so you exhibit a certain romanticism about the past, an ignorance of the way in which really great events have been brought about. But even taking the war at your estimation, the statement quoted still remains true. You admit that it is on a very large scale—It is the mere material consequences that will follow the war as a material *fact*, that create its importance. Perhaps it is better to speak of the *conditional* importance of the war. It would be comparable to the Reformation if the Germans won; if they don't it is not an important event in the same sense. Why would it then be so important? Because a German victory means an end of Europe as we know it, as a comity of nations. If you ask, further, why that is important, the answer is in the enormous reactions inside the beaten nations that would follow this enormous change in their external situation. When a box is turned over on to another base, the arrangement of the loose things inside alters with it. In our own case, our liberties have to a great extent depended on our security, and our security would now have disappeared. We should all be obliged to become conspirators. Our energies, instead of going in useful directions, would all be directed to the overthrow of this tyranny, for the world would not support a German hegemony for ever, whatever the Germans may think. The man who put social politics before this object would be suspect. One may make this more convincing by a trivial *ad hominem* argument for progressives. You know the extent to which the opposition to your policies before the war depended, on the concern (natural, or stimulated by scares) which was felt about questions of defence. After a defeat that opposition would be a hundred times increased.

Only arguments of this type—i.e., about actual facts depending on a realisation of the nature of force, have any real relevance. War is a fact of a particular kind, nothing would be easier, you might think, than to look straight at the fact and draw deductions from it. Unfortunately it is very difficult for a certain type of mind to look directly at this type of fact. And here the method of controversy which consists in giving the psychology of your opponents finds legitimate scope. There are certain habits of thought, which make a realisation of the actual nature of Force, very difficult. This applies not only to the opponents of the war, but to its supporters. Take the case of writers like Mr. Wells. You remember the old story of the man who was taken ill suddenly. The strange doctor who was called in exhibited a certain hesitation. 'I'm not exactly a doctor,' he said, 'in fact, I'm a vet. I don't know what's the matter with you, but I can give you something that will bring on blind staggers, and I can cure that all right.' Now Mr. Wells had never taken the possibility of an Anglo-German war seriously—he was pacifist by profession. It was not exactly his subject then, and last August may have found him somewhat baffled as to what to say. So he gave it blind staggers; he turned it into a 'war to end war', and there you are. Such writers, in dealing with a matter like war, alien to their ordinary habits of thought, are liable to pass from a fatuous optimism to a fatuous pessimism, equally distant from the real facts of the situation.

What are the most common of such habits of mind, which lie behind the pacifist's inability to see the consequences of defeat?

A.—Of all these habits of thought, perhaps, the one that has the most unfortunate influence is the belief in *inevitable* progress. If the world is making for 'good', then 'good' can never be in serious danger. This leads to a disinclination to see how big fundamental things like liberty can in any way depend on trivial material things like guns. There is no realisation of the fact that the world *may* take a wrong turning. In a pacifist lecture by Mr. Bertrand Russell I read 'the only things worth fighting for are things of the spirit, but these things are not subject to force.'[52] Make the matter more concrete by taking liberty as an instance as a 'thing of the spirit'. The things not subject to force may be, then, one of two things: (1) The *principle* of liberty or (2) the *fact* of liberty. If the first, the statement is self-evident and entirely unimportant. A *principle* . . . the ethical principle, e.g., that 'liberty is good', is true timelessly and eternally. It cannot be affected by force, any more than the truth that two and two make four. But he cannot have meant this trivial statement; he must mean, then, the 'good' which follows from the *fact* of liberty. But in that case the statement could only be true, if you suppose some tendency at the heart of things which is all the time 'making for an increase of the *facts* of liberty',—in other words, you must believe in *inevitable* Progress. But we know from other sources that Mr. Russell believes nothing of the kind. What does he mean, then?

Consider now two specific examples of the way in which this habit of thought distorts the pacifist perception of the facts:

(1) Even admitting that the facts as put forward by you are true; even admitting that our defeat will be followed by a German hegemony, we refuse to see in this any permanent danger to liberty. To do so would be to 'assume that Germany lacks the power of *development*. . . . her *natural* line of development towards a tolerant liberalism'. There is a richness of fallacy in this quotation, which makes choice somewhat embarrassing. For our purposes here, of course, the important word is *natural*. It is natural to *progress*; Nature herself tends of her own accord to progress, etc. This is complicated, however, by a further assumption, an example of what the Germans call the characteristic English view of mistaking *Umwelt* for *Welt*,[53] in other words, of mistaking the conditions of our own particular environment for universally valid laws. Even if the Germans must *naturally* develop, how can we assume that they will develop towards a tolerant liberalism? Is that also part of the essential nature of the cosmos? Free trade and all. . . . Anyone who has known Germany at all intimately during recent years knows that facts go to prove the contrary. The most intelligent of the younger men, those having the greatest influence on students, seem to be constructing a theory of society very far removed indeed from the liberal. I suppose that I have during the last four years read a great deal more German than I have English, and the statement I make is an entirely honest deduction from the knowledge I have acquired.

(2) There is a second type of pacifist, who admits that if the consequences of defeat were the hegemony of Germany and the end of Europe as a collection of independent States—that the case for war would have been proved. But he does not admit that such will be the consequences

of defeat; he does not seem able to perceive this obvious fact. Why? For exactly the same reason as that given in the first case. Liberty is a 'good'; so, also, is the existence of Europe as a comity of independent nations. He finds it ridiculous to fight for liberty, for there can never be any real danger to liberty. The world is inevitably developing towards liberty, and liberty is thus *natural*, and grounded on the nature of things. In exactly the same way he assumes that the comity of nations is also *natural*, and cannot be disturbed by the artificial activities of man. The matter is complicated here by (1) a habit of interpreting war by entirely *personal* categories and (2) a misuse of facile historical metaphor. . . . (1) They tend to look on war as of the same nature, and probably as caused by the same childish motives, as the struggles of a number of boys in a room. Some may get more damaged than others, but the *framework* of the struggle is not changed—in the end, as at the beginning, you have a number of boys in a room. Moreover, it is a mistake to punish one boy too much, as he may then turn nasty, and be a nuisance in the future. 'Germany would regard defeat not as evidence of guilt . . . and would resolve to be better prepared next time.' Here the real nature of the situation is entirely ignored, and an interpretation—in terms of the categories appropriate only to the description of personal conduct—is substituted for it. There is no realisation of the *particular* facts of force involved, no realisation of the *actual* danger which victory avoids and—such being the nature of the forces concerned—probably avoids for good. (2) 'Beaten nations develop into the strongest. It was her defeat by Napoleon that created Prussia as a military power.' Generalisation depends, I suppose, on the possibility of repetition. The amount of possible repetition in history is very small and consequently historical generalisations are necessarily very thin; but I think I hardly remember anything quite so thin as this. If I put this phrase out of my head, and look at the concrete situation at the time of the battle of Jena, and the concrete situation now, I should probably fail to discover any common elements whatever. We need no such fantastic guidance from history. What is needed is merely an objective examination of the sufficiently complicated situation we have before us *to-day*. It will not be very difficult, then, to perceive that this time it is not merely that individual combatants, will get more or less damaged with every possibility of recovery, but that the room in which they fight, the framework, itself will be permanently changed.

B.—There is a type of pacifist argument which seems to depend on reasonableness, on toleration; in reality it leads to a certain scepticism about the nature of truth. It is used by people who seemed so obsessed by the fact that there are two sides to every question, that they in the end get into a kind of anæmic state in which they are incapable of grasping the fact that one side may be right and the other wrong. They match every claim we make by a corresponding claim by the Germans. They seem to look on truth merely as a universal agreement of opinion. The reply to this method is to point out that truth has nothing to do with opinion. Those things are true which correspond to fact, and not merely those which are not opposed by any considerable body of opinion. The question is here also complicated by the desire to show oneself superior. By matching every crude English claim by a corresponding German one, a man shows that he himself is not taken in by crudity. The reply to this method is always to point to the facts. 'The Germans believe they are fighting a war of defence against aggression.' 'They are mistaken.' 'They say they are fighting for liberty.' 'They are not.' 'They say that English *marinism* is as oppressive as German militarism.' 'It isn't.'

A variant of the method is to attempt to discredit our present claims by the production of similar claims made by us in the past. 'You have in the past made many unjust wars which at the time you claimed to be just.' That is so, but this time it *so happens* that we are fighting a just war.

'You have always had a bogey. Formerly it was Russia that was the danger.'

This is quite irrelevant. We may have been right in fearing Russia then, or wrong. All that is relevant is: 'Does an examination of contemporary facts show that we are right in fearing Germany now?'

C.—Arguments that spring from a confusion between origin and validity. The question as to whether the statement 'two and two make four' is true or not has nothing whatever to do with the psychology of the process by which different people come to *believe* it to be true. The states of mind of Mr. Whitehead,[54] the mathematician, and the morning milkman when they reflect on this statement probably differ very widely, but the statement is the same in both cases.

(1) I intend later to examine this fallacy, as exhibited by Mr. Russell, of all people, in some recent lectures.[55] Instead of examining certain arguments about war, he merely gave a psychology of the process by which people came to believe them.

(2) A more familiar example of the same fallacy is to be observed in a certain repugnance, which is probably the pacifist's greatest obstacle to an objective examination of the facts. The pacifist is entirely unable to dissociate the validity of the anti-German case from its previous history. It has generally in the past been associated with the party which stands for the defence of privilege, and he still tends to think that the German army is an invention of the Conservatives. He thinks these things cannot be true because the 'Daily Mail' said them. But it is necessary to distinguish

clearly between causes and their prophets. Truth is still truth, even if it comes from the gutter. If a man makes a statement about a gold mine in Alaska, or something equally unverifiable, then it may be excellent policy on your part to investigate his psychology and motives rather than the statement itself. But if a man makes a statement about arithmetic, or about the verifiable facts of the European situation, then an account of his motives in making the statement is entirely irrelevant. It only becomes relevant *after* you have shown by actual objective reasoning that the statement itself is false.

The effect of this fallacy is again complicated by the consequences of the desire to be superior. What stupid people believe cannot be true. Then there is the protective covering against certain arguments provided by laughter. It is agreed that certain views are 'fearfully crude', and worthy of ridicule. This protects you from any necessity to examine the validity of these statements. Any appeal to arguments habitually employed by the other side, to conceptions like 'honour', for example, always provoked giggling. And that the fact that at meetings you all learned to giggle in unison, that all of you could 'see through' these crudities, spread a delightful, warm, satisfactory feeling of a brotherhood in intellectual superiority throughout the room. . . .

But the stupid people were right.

D.—These on the whole have been the more negative sources of the pacifist disinclination to examine the facts of the actual situation. I have left to the end the more positive side of pacifism, of which these other reasons are probably only secondary consequences. This is a certain general attitude towards life, which I find expressed in various ways in the 'report on a conference on Pacifist Philosophy of Life,' lately published. I find indications of this general attitude in all the papers, from the more comic expression in the writer who says 'the task of pacifism . . . is the task of producing the perfect man . . . liberation from the shackles which have restrained the highest possibilities of humanity', to the less ingenious lecture by Mr. Bertrand Russell, which I intend to examine in detail next week.

[3 February 1916][56]

> Ce qui est certain, c'est que pour en finir avec
> la guerre, il faut d'abord l'avoir comprise. . . .[57]
> —Proudhon.

At this period of the war a constant preoccupation with the pacifists may seem somewhat pointless; most of the things at issue have now been decided by fact. But this is much more than a controversy about the war.

A polemic has been started which will continue long after the conclusion of peace.

The pacifists themselves clearly recognise this, and we have an abundance of prophets hastening to tell us of the *Liberal* principles on which society must be re-organised after the war. There is a certain shamelessness in the eagerness they exhibit, for a year and a-half ago, most of them proved to be very false prophets indeed. Mr. Bertrand Russell's pamphlet, for example, commences: 'To all liberal-minded men the war has come as a shock . . . shattering hopes,' and he now confesses he had never imagined that the real nature of humanity was anything like what it now appears. You might then suppose that this overwhelming surprise would have taught these people a certain modesty. It might occur to them, you think, that people who have committed such a fatal error in their perception of events were not, perhaps, the best guides for the future. Moreover, since what a man perceives is to a great extent dependent on the categories in terms of which his mind habitually thinks, you might have expected that their colossal error of judgment might have made them overhaul their categories. There is no necessary reason why the war should make a pacifist change his principles, but they might exhibit some traces at least of the influence of such an event. But they seem entirely untouched and unchastened. Mr. Russell is giving lectures on 'Some Principles of Social Reconstruction', and I read in last week's 'Nation', 'We think that in the coming re-organisation of a society—which will be based on a different order from the existing one, an order in which *women will have a part consonant. . . .*' Need we continue? It is not only the Bourbons apparently who can 'learn nothing and forget nothing'. I admit that the new order of society will be different from the old; the old was breaking up before, the war did not cause the decay, it merely announced the fact on a hoarding.

I was able the other day to attend one of the series of lectures by Mr. Bertrand Russell I have already referred to. Now, Mr. Russell seems to be the only man of any real distinction amongst the English pacifists; he has a European reputation as a writer on logic and the philosophy of mathematics. Unfortunately, however, it is not always 'philosophy' that speaks whenever a philosopher opens his mouth; and a man may exhibit great originality in his own subject, and extreme commonplaceness about other subjects. Anyone who expected the ingenuity displayed in the Lowell lecture,[58] to be applied to the discussion of political principles, must have been painfully surprised at the series of platitudes to which he was treated. Instead of analysis there was nothing but an entirely uncritical acceptance of all the *Liberal* principles. As was once said of Condorcet: 'Il semble que, sitôt sortie du domaine des mathématiques, sa pensée sort en proie à une sorte d'éblouissement favourée par le peu de nourriture de ces notions, sur le contenu, de la nature humaine.'[59]

Mr. Russell started by an admission that he had been entirely surprised by the war. He was, therefore, anxious to arrive at an understanding of how this strange irrational thing became possible. What made people acquiesce in it?

This is an excellent beginning, but, unfortunately, however, the method of inquiry adopted is the reverse of excellent. Instead of considering the reasons put forward by the people who support the war, he prefers to give the psychology of the process by which they come to believe in these reasons.

He drew a preliminary distinction between 'desire' and impulse. Sometimes our actions are reasonable. . . . i.e., we 'desire' certain things and take the necessary steps to acquire them. The 'reasons' we give are here the 'true' reasons for our action. But more often the springs of action are unconscious. We act on impulse, and give reasons afterwards. But such 'reasons' are merely the homage instinct pays to intelligence. We may come to believe that these reasons were the cause of our action, but such is not the case. The true cause is the 'blind' impulse.

Any endeavour to understand the causes which make war possible should then be founded on an analysis of such impulses.

There is no doubt that this provides a happy method of controversy for general use by pacifists. They thus avoid the necessity for any tedious examination of the actual arguments used by their opponent, by depriving their arguments at one stroke of all validity. All the reasons are secondary, the blind impulse is the real cause. You thus get a delightfully simple picture of the true nature of the controversy. On the one hand, the bellicose, moved in reality by the 'impulses of aggression and resistance to aggression', fondly imagining, however, that they are acting under the influence of reason, and, on the other hand, the wise and tolerant pacifists, seeing things by the light of their disinterested intelligence. But this method assumes the whole point at issue. If someone says that two and two make five, then *after* it is seen that this is wrong, it becomes legitimate to describe the psychology of the process by which a man came to believe it. But it must first of all be obvious that the statement is absurd. It is calmly assumed here that all the reasons given by those who support the war are so absurd and irrational that we need only attend to the *real* cause, the *hidden* impulse.

The worst, then, that can be said about this method, however, is that it defeats its own avowed object. As long as you regard all the reasons put forward by your opponents as unreal, as merely the result of the 'homage paid by instinct to intelligence', you are not likely to obtain any very complete understanding of the nature and causes of war. For is blind impulse the only possible explanation of those who acquiesce in war? Is there not another possible alternative? If I examine my own state of mind about the matter, it is certainly true that such impulses do play a considerable part in it. But my attitude as a whole is *not* determined by such impulses, although it may be reinforced by them. The reasons I give are the *real* causes of my action. A method of controversy which seeks to explain away my reasons by dragging in the subconscious, seems to me to be largely insolent. What is at the root of this insufferable complacency—which is so satisfied that its own ideals are the *inevitable* ideals of man—that opposition appears almost pathological, and is regarded with tolerant pity?

Mostly, I expect, because the difference is not so much one of opinion as of fundamental ways of thinking, or categories. There are two ways in which I may differ from a pacifist who asserts that A is bad because it leads to B. (1) I may deny that in fact A does lead to B; or (2) I may deny that B itself is bad. It is a difference of the latter kind that we have to deal with, in controversies about the war: a difference, then, ultimately about the things we consider 'good'. I think B is good, you think it bad. But I do not mean that this is the last word to be said on the matter. I do not take the relatively sceptical view of ethics which would here leave us in an impasse. I do not disagree, then, with Mr. Russell in his conception of ethical values as *objective*. But I do disagree most profoundly as to the scale or order in which particular 'values' should be placed. Some are higher than others. The argument I should use about the war, then, would differ from those employed by the pacifists, principally because I regard other 'values' as superior to that which they usually appeal to as the highest.

What, in more detail, is the nature of the 'value' on which *their* arguments are based?

In Mr. Russell's lectures, the establishment of the future 'principles of social reconstruction' seems always based on an appeal to the values first made prominent by Rousseau, and the romantic movement. The words 'personality' and 'natural growth' seem enough to settle everything. Most evils are exhibited as the result of 'thwarted growth'. Enmity, for example, is the result of a 'thwarted joy of life'. This attitude finds a more ingenuous expression in another writer in the volume of pacifist essays to which Mr. Russell also contributes. 'Bound up in the universe awaiting liberation is an infinity of fine and splendid entities.' He inclines to find the fundamental creed of pacifism in 'the wonderfully beautiful words of Wilde. . . . It will be a marvellous thing . . . the true personality of man. It will grow naturally as a tree grows.' I agree; this is the kind of attitude on which pacifism is based; and it is precisely because we object to this kind of rubbish that we oppose it. This faded Rousseauism is based on an entirely false conception of the nature of man, and of the true hierarchy of values; the hierarchy is not objective, but is merely the result of an uncritical acceptance of the romantic tradition.

It is not possible here to go into any detail about the history of these values. It is sufficient to point out that there is nothing *inevitable* about them. They form part of one *ideology* amongst other possible ones. Above all, it is necessary to notice that there is no *necessary* connection between this ideology and the democratic movement. As a rule the two things are never even thought of as separate. Arguments are based alternatively on the one and on the other, as if you thought that you were merely using different names for the same thing. It is this innocence—the source of so much of pacifist complacency—that must be destroyed. Your ideals may be right or wrong; but they are not to be identified with democracy. It is quite possible for a democrat to deny all the ideals on which Mr. Russell's principles are based. Certainly Sorel and Proudhon, both much better examples of the real as distinct from the dilettante democrat, could feel nothing but disgust for every sentiment Mr. Russell appeals to.

This appeal might then be addressed to the pacifist: Put out of your mind the illusion that those who differ from you must do so for one of the following reasons: (1) A more sordid one—a disguised attempt to defend the interests of wealth. (2) The more ideal case—reasons invented afterwards to account for actions which were really the result of blind impulse.

Your reasons are opposed by other 'reasons', which may *also* be disinterested, ethical, and *not* emotional.

It is important that you should realise this, for the polemic will continue after the war. The principles on which society will be re-organised may not be those you so confidently urge. The polemic is not one between *reason* and *impulse*. It is a polemic between two systems of value. You may win in this struggle if you clearly recognise the true character of the things at issue. Do not, however, falsely simplify matters by assuming that it is a struggle between the assailants and defenders of privilege. It is not Democracy against Privilege, but, rather,

One ideology + Democracy . . .
against
Another ideology + Democracy.

The character of the second ideology is such that it does not attach the same positive value to the abolition of minor privileges that the first does. Nor does it make the same appeal to *ressentiment*. But I am now convinced that the abolition of such privileges is a necessary political measure, in order that the clear character of this opposition may not be disguised.

[10 February 1916][60]

Reasons which are sufficient to make us reject 'pacifist philosophy' are not sufficient to make us accept this *particular* war. The fact, for example, that a high value should be attached to military heroism, has nothing to do with the justification of a particular event in which such heroism may be displayed. This is an absolutely different question.

There are, moreover, at this moment, a class of pacifists who do not accept a 'pacifist philosophy', and whose reasons for objecting to this war are based on the nature and causes of *this* war itself. I was talking recently to a pacifist of this type, and what he said threw a good deal of light—for me, personally, at any rate—on the nature of a certain opposition to the war. He had no objection to killing; and conveyed the impression that he was quite prepared to fight himself in some more 'ideal' type of struggle—one with some positive and definite aim—in a war, for example, which would bring about the final disappearance of capitalism. But he was not prepared to fight in *this* war, which in as far as it was not an entirely unnecessary stupidity, was concerned with interests very far removed from any which had any real importance for the individual citizen, and more definitely the individual workman.

I admit that this attitude, if we *agree to certain tacit assumptions*, does seem justified. As the attitude is very real and fairly widespread it is perhaps worth while examining the nature of these assumptions. Though it may not be very conscious or formulated, I think it demonstrable that there is floating before the mind of the man who makes this objection, a certain false conception of the character of human activities. What makes the objection possible and gives force to it, is the conception of Progress. By that I do not mean merely the hope that capitalism will ultimately disappear. It is rather, that progress is looked upon as *inevitable* in this sense—that the evils in the world are due to definite oppressions, and whenever any particular shackle has been removed, the evil it was responsible for has disappeared for ever; for human nature is, on the whole, good, and a harmonious society is thus possible. As long as you hold this conception of the nature of history, you are bound, I think, to find nothing in *this war* which makes it worth while. But this is a false conception: the evil in the world is not merely due to the existence of oppression. It is part of the nature of things; and just as man is not naturally good and has only achieved anything as the result of certain disciplines, so the 'good' here does not preserve itself, but is also preserved by *discipline* also. This may seem too simple to be worth emphasising, but I think this way of treating the objection justified, for it really does spring from this quite *abstract* matter, this false conception of the nature of evil in the world. It is only under the influence of this false conception that you demand an ideal war where great sacrifices are for great ends.

So it comes about that we are unable to name any great *positive* 'good' for which we can be said to be fighting. But it is not necessary that we should; there is no harmony in the nature of things, so that from time to time great and useless sacrifices become necessary, merely that whatever precarious 'good' the world has achieved may just be preserved. These sacrifices are as negative, barren, and as *necessary* as the work of those who repair sea-walls. In this war, then, we are fighting for no great *liberation* of mankind, for no great jump upward, but are merely accomplishing a work, which, if the nature of things was ultimately 'good', would be useless, but which in this actual 'vale of tears' becomes from time to time necessary, merely in order that bad may not get worse.

This method of stating the question avoids the subterfuges to which those who hold the optimistic conception of man are driven—of inventing imaginary positive 'goods' which the war is to bring about—'to end war' and the rest.

But if this argument is to have any effect, it must be possible to give a clear account of the definite evils which would follow our defeat.

We are fighting to avoid (1) a German Europe, (2) the inevitable reactions which would follow this inside the beaten countries.

The consequences of such a defeat seem so perfectly clear and definite to us, that we think that if we could only for once actually *focus* the attention of a pacifist on them, we should convince him. But we are mistaken; to perceive things is not enough; it is necessary to attach *weight* to the things perceived. It is not sufficient that you shall merely *perceive* a possible German hegemony; it is necessary that you shall have a vivid realisation of what it means. It is like the distinction which writers on religion are accustomed to make, between *assent* to some proposition, and real *faith*—leading to action. There are many pacifists who will assent to what you say about German hegemony—they agree verbally, but the things they remain interested in, the questions which excite them, show that they do not attach importance to the facts you point out. The facts seem so clear to you that this behaviour is exasperating, even baffling. It is as if you pointed out to an old lady at a garden party, that there was an escaped lion about twenty yards off—and she were to reply, 'Oh, yes,' and then quietly take another cucumber sandwich.

But it won't do to ignore these consequences of defeat. If you are sitting in a room carrying on a discussion with another man, on some very abstract subject, and suddenly you notice that the floor is beginning to tilt up, then you have to pay attention to the fact. In comparison with the abstract discussion it interrupts, it may be a low, material fact, but it has to be dealt with. This is exactly the position many pacifists are in. German hegemony, in the effects it would produce, can be compared exactly to the tilting up of the ground. We should all (including the neutrals) be living on an inclined plane, and the whole of our life would be artificially altered in consequence; whether we thought it reasonable or not—it would limit our liberties, and would, for example, greatly alter the conditions under which the struggle between capital and labour is carried on. But these people talk vaguely of a hundred irrelevant things.

What stands in the way? Why cannot they realise the importance of the fact? In our innocence, we are unaware that most people are, as it were, physically incapable of *seeing* facts, which would necessitate a change in their opinion, or in some other way, humiliate them. Trying to indicate the consequences of German hegemony to this type of pacifist is like trying to show a cat its reflection in a mirror. It isn't interested, its mind is full of other interests—it smells, for example, Mr. Blatchford.[61]

In approaching this subject (the consequences of German hegemony) I feel at once the presence of certain difficulties. The people one wishes to convince seem instinctively inclined to *discount* what one says in advance. Before going into any detail, then, it is best to deal with the reasons which prevent due weight being attached to these things.

(1) They seemed disinclined to consider reasons drawn from the consequences of German hegemony because they think that reasons we give are not the real causes of our actions. We are in favour of the war because we are moved by certain impulses of national pride and aggressiveness, and we then desire to *find* good reasons to justify our attitude. This scepticism has a good deal of force because it does describe accurately the position of many people. Many people are moved not only by the impulses mentioned above, but by a certain instinct which makes men want life at a higher pitch and intensity (the instinct which makes a man seek the excitement to be got from gambling)—and they imagine that war will provide them with this. Under these circumstances we might deceive ourselves; we should tend to think the issues at stake were much more important than we shall think them in peace time. There is, then,

something unreal about the justification we give for the war, because our action is really not dependent on the reasons we give.

But, without any undue concern about the matter, I feel convinced that I am, personally, at any rate, free from such influences. I do not say that I was not moved by such impulses at the beginning of the war; but I am writing now at a period when any such bellicose impulses in us, any exuberance in this direction, have been cured by experience; I don't think I have an ounce of bellicosity left. I probably have quite as intense a *desire* for peace as any pacifist. I am fully aware of the wretched life led by those in the trenches—practically a condition of slavery—and would like to see it ended at once. It is true that if I read in a German paper some vainglorious boasting over our coming defeat, I should at once feel a very strong revival of these impulses of aggressiveness and pride, and a desire to humiliate at all costs the people who have written these things. But putting such moments out of court, I can honestly say that my convictions about the consequences of defeat, whether right or wrong, are founded on observation, and not on *impulses*. The reasons I give are in no sense special pleading. I think they are true, but wish they were not.

(2) There is another way in which such reasons may be misleading. People who can read foreign newspapers, and who take an interest in foreign policy, tend to acquire certain special interests, which they often mistake for the real interests of their country. They tend to look on these things as a kind of drama, and wish their own country to play a distinguished part. If I know the whole history of a certain disputed part of Africa, if I am fully aware of the secret designs of some other country, I have a great longing then to see my own country intervene at all costs. I then attach an undue importance to the matter, for my special interest in the subject is out of all proportion to the country's real interest. It is like the passion which may be aroused by a game of chess. The pacifist who wishes to think of all these problems in terms of individual welfare rather than national glory, tends to treat all reasoning of this kind with a smiling and tolerant disdain—'funny little German professors who write about weltpolitik . . . these dreams of writers on foreign politics are not very real when compared with the actual interests of the workman.'

The answer I make is the same as in the first case. I am fully aware of the influence of these things on one's opinion, and I think that I am able to discount their effect on my own mind. The fears I have about German hegemony have nothing whatever to do with the concern of the man interested in foreign policy. The things at issue are realities which will affect very strongly the life of the ordinary citizen.

(3) This last objection has proved more effective than either of the other two. The usual presentment of the consequences of German hegemony as it might be given, for example, by the 'Morning Post', is soaked with false reasons, which make it seem entirely unreal to you. It is based on assumptions—Imperialist and others—which you do not share. But many false reasons can be given for true things. The two should be carefully distinguished here. I share most of your assumptions. I have no disguised reactionary motives. I am not in favour of the war, because I think all wars favour reaction. I am, on the contrary, inclined to think that this war will hasten the disappearance of the rich. I think it possible to state the reasons based on the probable reactions that would follow German hegemony, in a way that should be convincing to the democrat. I shall endeavour to do this in next week's 'Notes'.

[17 February 1916][62]

Most of the arguments used by the pacifists in their repudiation of the balance of power as a doctrine of policy really rest on the tacit assumption that this balance will take care of itself, being grounded on the nature of things. In describing the evil consequences of the policy, they forget that the alternative is not simply the same world, minus those evils; there would be the much greater evils that would follow the destruction of the balance of power.

The only alternative at the present moment to the Balance of Power is a German hegemony in Europe. The only legitimate discussion of this doctrine, then, is one which tries to estimate the relative greatness of (1) the evils which accompany the attempt to maintain the balance of power—the present war, for example; and (2) the evils which would accompany a 'united Europe under German military leadership'. (I quote this sentence from a book on the war by a well-known German philosopher.[63])

In stating the matter in this way, however, I am perhaps assuming too much. The following types of pacifists would not accept this as a true account of the things at issue.

(1) Those who deny that the Balance of Power is the only alternative to the hegemony of one Power. They have visions of something better: (a) No Powers at all, (b) a harmony of Powers.
(2) Those who deny, or fail to realise, the *possibility* of such a hegemony as a result of our defeat in this war.
(3) Those who refuse to believe that a German hegemony would be necessarily evil.
(4) Those who are sceptical as to the possibility of preventing such a hegemony by war. These *fatalists* speak of the growth of Germany

as *natural*. We cannot stop it by artificial means. They even imply that it is almost sinful on our part to attempt to interfere with a *natural* force.

(5) Those who admit that a German hegemony is possible; but assert that the evils of war, and the possible evils of hegemony, belong to entirely different classes or grades of evil, as different, say, as tons and ounces. The evils of war are so great that everything else . . . honour, independence, nationality, etc. . . . becomes trivial in comparison with them. People who hold these views are quite naturally led to discuss, as Mr. Russell did in a recent lecture, whether German hegemony might not be welcomed as the best means of preserving peace in Europe—a Pax Germanicum.

Two things may be said about this attitude: (a) Accepting for the moment the system of ethical values from which the belief springs—I admit that the evils of war are certainly more immediate; in comparison with them, the evils of subjection and loss of independence seem somewhat trivial. But, it is quite arguable that, in the long run, the evils that would follow the inevitable refusal to accept the hegemony as permanent would bring about evils of the same scale as those of the war—the ounces would become tons. (b) I deny that this system of ethical values is the true one. There are values which are more important than *life*.

But while the enumeration of the actual evils of war does not, as such pacifists believe, serve to *decide* the matter, it does serve as a useful standard by which the reasons we give may be tested. Many of the reasons given by us enthusiastically as a justification for this war, suddenly appear astonishingly thin when we ask ourselves the question: 'Do I really think this so important that I am willing to accept the fact that I and half my friends may be killed to prevent it?' It acts as an excellent dissolvent on any undue preoccupation with the 'beautiful dream of Bagdad'.

I want here to consider the *second* type of pacifist indicated above. How does it come about that they cannot believe in the *possibility* of a German hegemony? Why do they tend to think that the evils of such a hegemony are merely the inventions of hysterical journalists; and if not imaginary, at least, enormously exaggerated? In using such arguments one *feels* that they carry no weight with these people. The facts seem clear, how is it that they are not perceived? What are these facts?

Many things in Europe which we have been accustomed to regard as fixed are now temporarily in a state of flux. When the war ends the new state in which it leaves things will probably continue, fixed and permanent, for another half century. Now it is possible that the new state of

Europe produced by the war may be a permanent German hegemony, with the enormous reaction which would follow this *inside* the beaten countries. The immense importance of the war lies in the fact that in a short space of time, when the world is, as it were, plastic, things are decided, which no effort afterwards may be able to shift. All our future efforts will take place in a framework settled by the war.

One may illustrate this by a metaphor taken from the war itself. The line of trenches on the Western front has now remained practically unaltered for over a year. The position and shape of this line are the brute facts on which all calculations as to future military action have to be based. The apparently accidental details of its shape have to be taken into account, like the similarly accidental and irregular lines of some great natural obstacle, such as a range of mountains. They form the fixed data of the problem which has to be solved. But though now it seems fixed, there was a short period in which it was plastic; and all the accidental details of an outline which seems irregular as the course of a river are due to known causes operating inside that short period. The salient at one point, the concavity at another are perhaps due to the results of the events of an afternoon, when a general under-estimated the number of men required at one particular point, and over-estimated the number required at another. This provides an accurate parallel for the relation of this war to the future of Europe. The relation between the three months of mobility and the year of stalemate is the same as that between the state of flux in which Europe now is and the fixed outlines it would determine for the next fifty years.

If I assert that the moon to-night is green, and ask you to put yourself to some trouble in order to come outside to look at it, I may meet with two difficulties. In the first place, you may refuse, because you say that you know I have some interest in making this false statement; that craving always the excitement of new sensation, I am naturally credulous, or that my past history makes all my statements worthy of suspicion.

There is, however, a different type of difficulty which has its origin in the character of the *facts* indicated. All the arguments used are based on facts, ultimately connected with *Force*. Now, these people have certain habits of mind, are accustomed to think in certain ways which makes it exceedingly difficult for them to perceive the real nature of such facts. If you look for the moon with a microscope, you are not likely to find it. If you persist in thinking of mental processes in terms of the categories appropriate only to matter, you are not likely to see these processes as they really are.

Now, there is no obscurity about the facts in this question; the *possibility* of hegemony is sufficiently clear. But the pacifists persist in thinking of this fact (of Force) under the influence of certain habits of mind, which make them apt to undervalue and distort it.

What are the 'habits of mind' which prevent the pacifists realising this? How does it come about that they tend to disregard any description of the consequences of German hegemony? Probably for this reason—they discount all these arguments, because they are *not* really convinced that things are in a flux. They do not really believe in the possibility of any fundamental change in Europe. As they do not at heart believe that the effects of Force can be so irrevocable, or that such profound changes can take place, they cannot attach serious importance to any argument which postulates such a change.

At bottom, I think, their attitude is the result of the fact that they, perhaps, unconsciously, tend to think of all events of the 20th century in Europe as taking place within the framework impressed on our minds by the history of the nineteenth. This history, in a sense, hypnotises one, and makes the possibility of radical change very difficult to conceive. With many reservations it is, on the whole, true to say that in the history of the wars of the past century and a half the protagonists remain much the same, England, France, Prussia, Austria and Russia. While the power of each of them has varied, none has ever established a permanent hegemony, or been able to destroy the others; Europe has always remained divided into independent States. The result of this is that we tend to think of these nations—the elements of this history—as the permanent and indestructible elements of all future history; the games may be different, but they will always be played with the same pieces.[64]

[24 February 1916][65]

In 'Press-Cuttings' this week will be found a letter by Mr. Bertrand Russell which contains a reply to some remarks I made about his lectures in these 'Notes'. The first and last paragraphs are based on a misunderstanding. I was not responsible for the sub-title given to my article, and the 'final exhortation' which he mentions did not refer to him but to other pacifists who were his fellow contributors in the volume of essays on a 'Pacifist Philosophy'.

The part of the letter, however, which is concerned with the criticism I did make, shows that he has entirely failed to grasp the real nature of this particular attack on pacifism. It is then perhaps worth while again trying to make the matter clear.

He complains that my criticism shows such profound misunderstanding of his lecture that I must have been reading the 'Daily Express'. Might not this somewhat faded form of retort have been left to the lesser lights of pacifism? Its only point is the implication that I am a somewhat stupid and *crude* person. But even if I were, what has that to do with the matter? All that is relevant is the correctness or falsity of the arguments I put forward. The psychology which lies behind his favourite retort of the minor pacifist is perhaps amusing. The most characteristic thing about them is that they are all of them, people who mistake the fact that they hold certain opinions for that entirely different thing—intellectual *superiority*. They thus form a little orthodoxy of superior people, and they tend to look on all attacks not as due to real objections springing from intellectual difference, but as the crude gesture of the 'outsider'. The use they make of the 'Express' reminds me of a scene in one of Peacock's novels, in which an abstract discussion about God is recorded. A man was stationed behind a curtain with instructions to shout 'The Church is in Danger' whenever the argument seemed to be going against the defender of religion. In this case, it is only necessary to shout 'You read the "Express"', and the necessity for a serious consideration of the objection is avoided. By thus convincing themselves that all opposition is due to crudity they may be confirmed in their belief that theirs is the only possible belief of the emancipated man; but in thus disguising the real nature of the opposition they have to face, they are preparing for themselves unpleasant surprises, not only about war, but as to the future course of democracy.

I greatly resent the accusation that I have entirely failed to understand the lecture. In the first place, Mr. Russell is a very lucid writer, and, in the second place, he would, I suppose, be the first to admit that the main contention of his lecture was not exactly novel. It expressed a view of the springs of human action which I first saw worked out in any detail in MacDougall's 'Social Psychology'.[66] [In listening to the lecture, I recalled with some amusement a meeting in Mr. Lowes Dickinson's rooms in Cambridge a few years before the war, when one very well-known pacifist made this extraordinary remark: 'The unfortunate thing is that people like MacDougall, who have worked in Germany, persist in thinking that there is every probability of a war.']

In what way exactly have I misrepresented him? He complains that I falsely suppose that he looks on the dispute as one between *Impulse* and *Reason*, '"North Staffs" . . . begins by suggesting that I regard the bellicose as moved by *impulse* and the pacifists as moved by *reason*. . . . My whole lecture, on the contrary, was concerned to represent *both* sides as moved by impulse.' Now, I entirely agree with the last sentence, but I fail to see that it in any way proves that my version of the lecture misrepresents it; it only does this if a certain assumption is made. The matter at issue can perhaps be made evident in this way. Two distinct questions should be separated, a *theoretical* and a *practical*: (1) Is war always evil? and (2) assuming that it is, how can it best be avoided? Mr. Russell always tacitly assumes the first question as settled, and deals only with the second and *practical* matter; the emphasis laid on *Impulse* is then quite legitimate. If you have already made up your mind that war is always wrong, then it becomes necessary to search out some other purpose which will counter the effect of the impulses that make for war. 'If Impulse is necessary to vigorous action, then it is necessary not to weaken impulse, but to direct it to life and growth, not to death and decay, etc. . . .'

I admit all this; and if I had said (in reference to this *practical* problem) that the pacifists wished to meet *Impulse* by *Reason*, I admit that I should have misrepresented Mr. Russell. But I was not thinking of this *practical* question. When I spoke of the differences between the pacifists and their opponents, I was thinking of the theoretical question, of the dispute about the ethics of war, Is war ever justified? In a controversy about this theoretical question a reference to impulse is irrelevant. Reasons on one side should be opposed by *reasons* on the other. But the pacifists do not discuss the matter in this way. They seem so entirely unable to imagine that war may be justified by definite reasons, that they seek its only possible explanation in impulse. They themselves, however, reject war not on impulse, but for clear definite *Reasons*. Mr. Russell himself gives many detailed Reasons why we should regard war as always evil; while he regards all *justification* of war, as springing entirely from hidden *Impulses*. Now, in speaking of the dispute between the pacifists and their opponents, it is clear that we mean this *theoretical* dispute; for until this has been settled, the *practical* question is of very secondary importance. In saying, then, that the pacifists tend to regard the dispute as one between Reason and Impulse, I do not in the least misrepresent Mr. Russell, but, on the contrary, give an accurate description of the way in which he treats the question.

My complaint is, then, that in dealing with theoretical questions Mr. Russell gives many *Reasons* why wars are evil, and only deals with the *Impulses* that made men think them justifiable. He never seems to admit that any real Reasons exist on this side. He ought, on the contrary, to have dealt with the *Reasons* on both sides. He now claims, in this letter, that he has in various other pamphlets dealt with such Reasons. He refers me to ' "Justice in War-Time", where he will find that I have set forth the detailed discussion which I *presupposed* in this lecture'. I may say at once that I have bought this pamphlet and find very little indeed of this 'detailed discussion'. What I do find is repetition after repetition of an account of the nature of the instincts, which he supposes to be the real causes of our justification of war.

When I say that all discussion of such impulses is irrelevant, until the Reasons which we say justify war have been dealt with—what kind of Reason do I intend? There are two types of such *Reasons*: (1) those dealing with facts; (2) those concerned with ethics. The first to *prove* that this war was necessary, the second to prove that the pacifists' assertion that war is essentially evil is not correct.

(1) Reasons based on the *facts* of the European situation which show that this war was unnecessary. The only discussion of the kind I can find in this pamphlet is the somewhat vaguely treated suggestion that we are responsible for the German militarism because we tried to hinder in every possible way the efforts of Germany to found a Colonial Empire of a size proportionate to her power. This seems to me a very inadequate account of our motives in the war. We are fighting to prevent the establishment, not of a *Colonial* empire, but of a *European* hegemony, an aim which justifies any sacrifices. I have already dealt with this earlier; all I need say here is this: that in demonstrating the possibility of such a hegemony it is not necessary to say much about the German Government itself—all governments and bureaucracies of that type desire hegemony—that we may take as axiomatic. It is only necessary to show the existence of a public opinion which is willing to make enormous sacrifices for this purpose. To do this I shall quote, not as Mr. Russell does in his pamphlet, 'Professor Rudolf Eucken, a world-famous leader of religious thought' (but a philosopher for whom in reality he must have the greatest contempt), but a philosopher of the school in Germany which has many resemblances to that to which Mr. Russell belongs—a follower of Husserl.

(2) *Ethical* reasons: In the case of the type of Reasons just mentioned (those based on facts) there is some slight justification for his claim that the discussion he presupposed in his lecture had been given in his pamphlets. But there is no justification for the claim in the case of *ethical* reasons. There is no serious attempt to meet the ethical considerations, which are said to justify wars. He consistently refuses to admit that any such reasons can possibly exist. When I assert that the fundamental difference in this controversy about the war is an ethical one, he replies: 'No doubt this is true *on the surface*. But ethical differences usually spring from differences of *impulse*. Whole philosophies . . . spring up in this way; they are the embodiment of a kind of thought which is subservient to

impulse, which aims at providing a *quasi-rational ground for the indulgence of impulse.*' You see, no ethical discussion is then needed. I, poor man, imagine I am moved by ethical reasons; but Mr. Russell knows better; in reality I only want to provide myself with sham reasons for the indulgence of certain evil impulses. But this kind of discussion leads nowhere. I can retort that the ethical reasons which lead pacifists to condemn war are also quasi-rational grounds for the indulgence of certain impulses.

It is not very clear, however, what Mr. Russell really intends here. Does he mean merely that my ethics is quasi-rational, while pacifist ethics is *objective*; in other words, is he still thinking of the dispute as one between Reason and Impulse? Apparently not, for he continues: 'The difference of opinion will *seem* to be ethical . . . its real basis is a difference of impulse. . . . No genuine agreement will be reached . . . so long as the differences of impulse persist.' But even this is ambiguous. It may merely be meant as a *psychology* of the matter; in that case it might be accepted as correct. It might be true to say that we were led to different ethical valuations because we were moved by different impulses . . . But this, even if true, has no bearing whatever on this discussion. If it were universally agreed that war was always ethically unjustifiable, then the psychology of how some few abnormal people came to have opposed ethical views might be relevant. But this is not the situation. The opposition which pacifism has to face (on this plane of ethical discussion) comes from people who sincerely believe their own ethical valuations to be objective; they think, moreover, that the humanitarian ethics on which pacifism is based, is not objective, but the product of certain historical conditions which can be easily traced.

If what Mr. Russell says here is to have any point, then (as a reply to my assertion that the difference is ultimately an ethical one), he must mean something more than this. When he says that systems of ethics are only quasi-rational grounds for the indulgence of impulse, he must be giving more than a psychology of their origin. He must mean that all systems of ethics are, in their nature, *nothing more than this*. None of them have any objective validity, they are all merely an expression of impulse. If there is nothing objective about ethics then, all purely ethical discussion is futile, 'no genuine agreement will be reached so long as the difference of impulse persists'. All ethical valuations are, then, a matter of taste. This certainly provides a relevant answer to what I said about an ethical difference. But does Mr. Russell really accept this complete ethical scepticism? When he says that my ethics are merely an attempt to give a quasi-rational ground for the indulgence of certain instincts, and I retort that the same is true of his ethics, must the matter rest there? As he is debarred from saying that pacifist impulses are *better* than the low atavistic instinct behind the opposed ethic, all he can say is that he *prefers* pacifist instincts.

All this is very surprising, and seems to show that Mr. Russell has completely changed his views on this matter. In his 'Philosophical Essays' he rejects 'the widespread ethical scepticism which is based upon observations of mere differences in regard to ethical questions. . . . If X says A is good, and Y says A is bad, one of them *must be mistaken.*'[67] I do not say that the quotations Mr. Russell gives from his lecture are sufficient in themselves to prove that he has completely changed his conception of ethics, but it is clear that it is only on the basis of such scepticism, that his statement that the difference between the pacifists and their opponents is only *superficially* an ethical one, can be justified.

But if he has changed his views, I think that this was only to be expected. In any system of ethics may be distinguished (1) the nature of the conception of 'value' or 'good' on which it is based; and (2) the scale or hierarchy of ethical valuation it establishes. Without going into the matter here, we may assume that there is a certain connection between these two things. The predominant ethic of the last two centuries, the humanitarian, rationalist or utilitarian, did not look on *values* as absolute. It could only conceive of certain things as 'good' or having value, in their relation to *Life*; they lead naturally then to pacifist ethic: Herbert Spencer's pacifism was a perfectly logical development from his conception of ethics. I think it demonstrable that the objective ethic which regards values as absolute and not relative to life, which thus looks on certain *values*, as higher than life, should logically lead to a hierarchy of values, somewhat different from that established by utilitarianism. It is evident, however, from what Mr. Russell has said in his other lectures, about education, etc., and from the character of his rhetoric and his *perorations*, that his views on the subject are the result of an entirely commonplace and uncritical acceptance of the *liberal* ideology that has prevailed since the eighteenth century. Now such a combination of a rejected utilitarianism (using the word not very precisely) with an almost complete acceptance of the utilitarian scale of values, seems to be essentially *unstable*. It seems to me that the realisation that ethical values are *objective* and not relative to life is in the long run bound to lead to either (1) the ending of the unstable state described above, by the abandonment of this objective view of ethics. If you keep, as Mr. Russell does, the pacifist hedonist scale of values, you are bound to end, as he seems to have done, by a return to a relativist view of ethics; or (2) I believe that the objective conception of ethics, properly realised, leads in the end to a way of looking at things, and to a scale of values differing fundamentally from that of rationalism. It leads, in particular, not only to a different attitude towards war, but to a different conception of democracy—to that, for example, which is suggested by Proudhon and Sorel.

I find, here, that I have no space left to complete my answer to Mr. Russell. I shall try next week (1) To examine in detail the instincts which he alleges to be the real cause of wars; and to show (a) that they are not the real causes of the war—which is about real and not imaginary interests; (b) to show that he entirely misunderstands the *instincts* he condemns as *atavistic*.

(2) A more positive aim: to show in detail the nature of the ethics, and the scale of values which lie behind (a) the justification of this war; (b) the different conception of democracy, suggested by Sorel, the development of which, after the war, will probably surprise the pacifists as much as the war itself did.[68]

[2 March 1916][69]

The discussion last week was left at this point:—In reply to Mr. Russell's assumption that the opposition to pacifism springs from certain *impulses*, and that even where reasons are given they are only quasi-rational grounds for the indulgence of these impulses, I attempted to show that these reasons are *not* quasi-rational, and that the difference is not only superficially but fundamentally an ethical one. When Mr. Russell condemns war for reasons based on the unquestioned acceptance of a rationalist, utilitarian ethic, I reply by *denying* the validity of this ethic. This ethic, so unquestionably accepted, that it seems not merely an ethic but Ethics itself, is entirely subjective and false, the product of a certain historical tradition.

My object in this note is to make the real character of this difference evident and obvious. It is necessary to put the matter as bleakly and barely as possible that no pacifist may be unaware that the ethical difference really exists. They are able, as a rule, to ignore its existence, because it is mixed up and confused in the very complicated mass of possible arguments about war on very different planes. If the possible arguments about war refer to (a, b, c, etc.), then, as a rule, a reason about (a) draws a reply relevant only to (b). As this second reason seems to the man who urges it sufficient to settle the whole matter, he fails to notice that it may not settle (a). This is very evident in the proceedings of the Tribunals—which have provided the only example in our time of public disputation about abstract questions of ethics. They make very painful reading for anyone who realises how entirely unexpected for most men here must be the fate which they have suddenly to face (the whole thing is so obviously a sham that if I were a pacifist I should certainly refuse to appear at all); but if we can forget this for a moment, the proceedings are interesting as illustrating how entirely unaccustomed most of us are to thinking about ethics. Lacking tradition they are at present somewhat crude and formless; but if such public disputations were to continue, I suppose a ritual would be evolved which would make chairmen realise that abstract questions of right and wrong are not to be settled by investigations into psychology. It would become impossible to substitute for an ethical discussion, a psychological investigation into the state of mind of the applicant when faced by certain hypothetical outrages on his mother. I suppose they might justify themselves by saying that their business had nothing to do with abstract ethics, but was psychological—they had not to ascertain whether certain views were right, but whether the applicant really held them. It seems quite evident, however, that they think they settle the second question by dealing with the first; by proving such views absurd, they prove that the applicant cannot possibly hold them. But what you would do to protect your mother is a matter of *impulse*, and probably independent of what you thought you ought to do.

If the real character of this ethical difference about war is to be clearly seen, it must then be disentangled from the other differences about the same subject, with which it is generally confused. In particular—it must be realised that the discussion in this note has nothing whatever to do with:

(1) A justification of *this* war. I might as well say at once that the discussion here is in reference to this merely a side issue. All I urge here against Mr. Russell's ethical premises might be entirely true, and yet, at the same time, this war might be the most colossal stupidity in our history. It gives no positive justifications for this war, but only combats certain ethical condemnation of it.

(2) In a sense, the validity of certain pacifist arguments is untouched by this discussion. Granted the premises, a rationalist ethic, you may be led inevitably to a condemnation of war. This justification, at any rate, can be given for pacifist propaganda—that many more people who are not now pacifists would be so if they were consistent in their beliefs. But, fortunately, their *blind* impulses lead them to better conclusions. What Mr. Russell said about *impulse* is, then, correct here, but only in so far as it applies to these people. It has no application to those who deny the premises from where the pacifist reasons start—the rationalist, humanitarian ethic.

The position, then, is this: I do not deny that your reasoning against war is accurate, if your premises are accepted; but I deny that your premises are sound. In this discussion, then, I am very far from giving any panegyric of war in general—that is a stupidity we may leave to the Germans; but I want to show that the *ideology*, the ethic, on which your condemnation of force rests, is not only false in itself, but leads you to such a distorted and ridiculous misconception of the real nature of war, that your propaganda is bound to be ineffective.

The question of this *ideology* and *ethic* which leads to pacifism, is extremely important; for it involves much more than a discussion about the war. The views expressed in Mr. Russell's other lectures, on marriage, maternity etc., are sufficient to show how this rationalist, humanitarian ethic leads to false views of the nature of human relations. It is, moreover, generally, but quite erroneously, identified with democracy. I think it demonstrable that as long as the ethic prevails, no radical regeneration of society is likely to come about.

What, then, are the two opposed ethics? Very roughly:

(1) Rationalist, humanitarian; the fundamental values are *Life* and *Personality*, and everything has reference to that. It is almost universally, but, I suppose, not essentially, connected with the optimistic conception of human nature, and consequently with a belief in Progress. Mr. Russell talks of 'ever widening horizons . . . shining vision of future . . . life and hope and joy'. It first became widespread in the eighteenth century, and must be sharply distinguished from Christian ethics, with which it is often identified. I propose later to illustrate the absolute difference between the two by an analysis of Christian and humanitarian 'love'. As life is its fundamental value, it leads naturally to pacifism, and tends to regard conceptions like Honour, etc., as empty words, which cannot deceive the *emancipated*.

(2) The more heroic or tragic system of ethical values.—Values are not relative only to life, but are objective and absolute, and many of them are *above* life. This ethic is not, therefore, bound to condemn all sacrifice of life. In a sense it may by called *irrational*, if we give the word *rational* the narrow meaning given it by the first ethic, i.e., those values are rational which can be reasonably based on *life*. It is generally associated with a more pessimistic conception of man, and has no belief in Progress.

If the pacifists could only recognise the existence of this radical ethical difference, discussion would become much clearer; they might then recognise that if we differ from them, it is not because we are not intelligent or disinterested enough to follow their arguments.

The difficulty, however, about this, is that the rationalist ethic appears so *natural* and *inevitable* to them, they find it impossible to imagine that the other ethic can have any reality at all. They offer, instead, explanations of the ways in which men falsely come to believe in the empty words, which this ethic asserts to be values. Mr. Russell talks of 'the quasi-rational grounds for the indulgence of impulse . . . the blindness of inherited instinct and the sinister influence of anti-social interests . . . the lust for blood'. It is, then, first of all necessary to show the reality of the 'heroic' ethic.

The principal feature about this ethic is the 'irrationality' of certain values (i.e., the assertion that certain actions, though good, may involve sacrifice of life; a sacrifice which it may be impossible to *rationalise*, by showing that it furthers life in other ways). We can conveniently call this *Heroism*, using the word in the widest possible sense. Now for this ethic this particular hierarchy among values is as *objective*, and absolute, as independent of the subjective feelings of particular men, as the laws of arithmetic. The rationalist will admit that men do feel these values as superior to the more rational values; but he explains the inner necessity men may feel about the matter, e.g., calling it an atavism—a survival from the 'early stages, when a disposition to ferocity . . . was a biological advantage . . . now no longer economically advantageous, to invent imaginary reasons for the exercise of this instinct' (Russell). Such an explanation of the heroic values is on a level with Bain's explanation of maternal affection.[70] It seems to me quite untrue. In a moment, when a man, after much weighing of motives, suddenly brushing calculations on one side . . . sees clearly that this is an absolute value, and must be accepted as absolute, above calculation . . . and superior to values based on *life* and *personality* . . . then, I think it wrong to say that he has been moved by some underlying atavistic impulse which has suddenly come to the surface. On the contrary, I should say that he was understanding the nature of ethics for the first time. He is discovering the facts of ethics, as objective as the facts of geometry, by the only adequate method of apprehension. Even drums, then, may not blind a man's eyes by rousing forgotten animal instincts, but rather enable him to see the real nature of an ethical value by breaking up the habits which hinder his perception of such facts in a calmer rational life.

I shall try to show later that this question of the nature of Heroism (taken in this wide sense) is the key to the whole question of the nature of ethics.

Although it was quite impossible that they should understand it fully, yet the rationalists seem in some curious way to have felt that this was the case. They seem to have known *instinctively* that this conception of heroism was the central *nerve* of the ethic they opposed; and have consequently always tried to disintegrate it by ridicule. The author of 'Arms and the Man' thus reminds one of the wasps described by Fabre,[71] who sting their prey in the central ganglia in order to paralyse it, thus acting as if they were both expert entomologists and expert surgeons, while, in reality, they can have no conscious knowledge of what they are doing.

I believe this to have been vaguely felt also, by many who instinctively rejected the rationalist utilitarian ethic, without being able to state clearly the real nature of the true ethic. Many of these people might have been called reactionary. There is no necessary connection of ideas here. How does it come about that we so often find it? For this reason probably: when we almost instinctively reject any idea, say (A), without clearly knowing why, and (m, n, o . . .) are *each* reasons, which, *if true*, would prove that (A) was false, then we tend to think that (m, n, o . . .) are themselves true. This is a very natural process; now reactionary principles would involve a rejection of this rationalist ethic, and this is the explanation, I think, of the motives of many intellectual reactionaries. The work of certain writers has lately made it much more possible to think clearly about ethics, and it is now possible to completely *dissociate* the reactionary spirit, and the rejection of a rationalist humanitarian ethic.

There are two senses in which the Heroic values are the key to a proper understanding of ethics.

(a) It is most probably only through a realisation of these values that the sceptic about ethics comes to see what there is that is *objective* and *absolute* in the subject.

(b) Any system of ethics establishes a hierarchy of values, the lower terms of which are founded upon the higher. In this sense it may be said that most of the commoner virtues *presuppose* and rest upon the heroic values; just as these rest (not as a matter of individual psychology, but essentially) on the values given in religion.

(a) It must be very difficult for the writers on ethics (who seem to be more happily endowed than most of us) to realise how excessively difficult it is for the ordinary modern to realise that there is any *real* subject 'Ethics' which can be at all compared with 'Logic' or even with 'Æsthetic'. It seems almost impossible for us to look on it as anything objective, everything seems to us arbitrary and human, and we should at a certain age no more think of reading a book on ethics than we should reading one on manners or astrology. There may even seem something ridiculous about the word 'Virtue'. Why is this? It was not always so. The Greeks, the early Romans, and the men of the Middle Ages spoke of Virtue, as they might of Beauty, as something attractive and full of charm.

To a certain extent, I suppose, because we are under the influence of a sceptical reaction against the pathetic apostrophes addressed to Virtue by the men of the eighteenth century; but much more, I think, on account of its narrow connection in our minds with sex; for this is almost the only ethical question the undergraduate, for example, is likely to come across—for he does not want to kill, or to steal either, when he can have credit. And in the matter of sexual ethic, for the most part, the question, as presented to him, contains not real ethical conceptions at all, but only taboo, expediency, custom, and good form; consequently, if he is honest with himself he cannot take ethics as a serious science. As he is intelligent to perceive that the only part of ethics he comes across has (as presented to him) nothing objective, or 'binding', he tends to think that the whole subject must be of like nature. At an age when, like the novelist George Moore, he may long 'to see Elizabeth Hawkins naked', he cannot honestly read his namesake's 'Principia Ethica'; with a prosperous life this may continue, until the necessity perhaps arrives one day of making a decision in the region of one of the heroic values. Then having felt for the first time something binding, something objective, which he felt himself, to his own surprise and against his inclination, bound to follow, he may suddenly realise for the first time, that there is such a thing as Ethics. For the first time the real nature of an ethical value is revealed to him. From that he may gradually proceed to realise that other virtues are really virtues, and not mere expediency or subject for ridicule. I am not describing any mere process of moral conversion or awakening in a man, who having always known the virtues, suddenly decides to practise them; but rather the psychology of the process by which many sceptics of the kind have suddenly realised that there was such a thing as ethics.

(b) More important, however, than this is a more speculative assertion about the heroic values; a statement this time, not about the psychology of the process by which we come to *understand ethics*, but about ethics itself.

I think it is possible to range the ethical values in a certain order or hierarchy; and this order, though it is concerned with 'feelings', is yet absolute, *not relative* to human life, and in certain respects a priori—a 'logique du coeur' (those 'feelings' which form part of the subject of ethics can only be studied as they occur in man, just as in the case of mathematical reasoning, yet there is nothing specifically human about them). In this hierarchy the 'lower' are founded on, and are dependent on, the 'higher' values. I think that a careful examination into many values more specifically concerned with life (*fidelity*, for example) as we feel these in ourselves will show that they owe their meaning almost, and certainly their truth, to the 'higher' 'heroic values' which are more absolute and quite independent of life. Virtues, like 'fidelity' draw their meaning and *sustenance*, as it were, from these 'heroic values'. While humanitarian ethic attaches ultimate value to *Life* and *Personality*, true ethic can only value Life as a 'bearer' of certain higher values, which themselves are quite independent of any relation to life.

Mature
Philosophy

A Notebook

[First published in *NA* in seven instalments: 18/5 (2 Dec. 1915), 112–13; 18/6 (9 Dec. 1915), 137–8; 18/7 (16 Dec. 1915), 158–60; 18/8 (23 Dec. 1915), 186–8; 18/10 (6 Jan. 1916), 234–5; 18/13 (27 Jan. 1916), 305–7; and 18/15 (10 Feb. 1916), 353–4. They were signed 'T. E. H.' An abridged version of the piece was published by Herbert Read as 'Humanism and the Religious Attitude' in *S* 3–71. This is the original and complete version of the piece.]

RISK AND ETHICS. Behind the Liberal pacifists' incapacity to understand the importance of war lies probably this fundamental error. Certain historical accidents—security being the first—have made it difficult for them to grasp the nature of *Risk*; not of the incidental kind, but of Risk as an ultimate thing; they cannot take *certain entirely relative things for absolute*.

This explains two things: more proximately their incapacity to realise the consequences of defeat, and further back the source of the whole *ideology* from which this incapacity springs.

First, the proximate effect: They hypostatise their school atlases, and fail to realise that others do not regard Europe as fixed like arithmetic, but wish to change it; not temporarily and minutely, but permanently and on the large scale, justifying themselves by talk of *dynamic* as opposed to *static* justice. Moreover, regarding democracy, and all the other things for which they care, as grounded in the nature of things, they cannot understand that these can be seriously threatened by an arbitrary irrational cause like war. Their inane confidence rises above details, for they never realise that the best things are *constructions*, full of risk and not *inevitable*.

As for the *ideology*: It is based as a rule on a relativist utilitarian ethics. Why? Because taking relative things for absolute, it has no need of the real absolute. In the shadow of these mountains which are not really mountains, it lives securely and comfortably, finding a sufficient support in a sceptical rationalism. Individuals in a condition of danger, when these pseudo-absolutes melt away into a flux, require once more a real absolute, to enable them to live. While this may be admitted as a fact, it may be explained away by saying: 'This occasional and abnormal state requires a temporary but unreal consolation, as men when ill require medicine. It is natural that the sailor should be superstitious, that each ship in Pierre Loti's "Icelanders"[1] should carry a Madonna. In a state of flux rafts are required, but not on dry land.' Or they might give as a parallel Pascal's advice to the sceptic on the remedy for unbelief: 'There are people who know the way . . . follow the way by which they began . . . by acting as if they believed . . . taking the holy water, having masses said . . . this will make you believe and *deaden your acuteness*.'[2] But this is always misrepresented. It is *not pragmatism*, you are not to deaden your *natural acuteness*, but the false and artificial acuteness of an artificial condition. Living in a sceptical atmosphere, you are in an unnatural attitude which prevents you seeing objective truth. Taking the holy water, the attempt to assume another artificial attitude, will at least break up the first state, and, making your mind a *tabula rasa*, will enable you to see the truth as it is objectively, independent entirely, of your attitudes.

The same is true of security and ethics. It is not by way of *privation* that danger makes us believe in absolute ethics, but that danger *liberates*—by making us see the relativity of the things we took to be fixed.

THE EXIT. I put forward the contents of this note not as true but as a passage from a false to a true opinion. I at one time thought that the pragmatists, relativists, and humanists were right, and that all the 'ideal' sciences, logic, mathematics, ethics, etc., could all have meaning and validity only, in reference to the human mind; that the laws of thought were the ways in which the human mind *had* to think, that ethics was the way in which men must behave if they were to live together, etc. Moreover, since man is the result of a long evolution in which accident must have played a considerable part, there is nothing *inevitable* about these actual characteristics of the human mind. If the path of evolution had been different, the categories which govern our thinking would have been different.

I could now give any of the accepted refutations of the falsity of this position; in the matter of logic, for example, those in the first volume of Husserl's 'Logische Untersuchungen'.[3] But as I said at the beginning, that is not my object in this note. I am only concerned here with a very much smaller matter, the means by which I did actually grope my way out of this error. I began to put the matter to myself in this way—The human mind is not merely the mind of man, it is *mind* itself, as it must always be; not human mind but 'it'. Take the kind of example a relativist might give: life on a supposed planet of which chlorine formed the surrounding atmosphere. If life could exist under such conditions it would obviously be very different from life as we know it, but if it managed to produce the highest type, the mental characteristics of this type would exactly resemble those of men, for they would be the inevitable characteristics of all *mind*. Many would admit this in a matter like arithmetic. They would probably admit that if the chlorine men thought arithmetically they would think that 'two and two were four', but I think it would also be true of almost every other side of the mind. It would be true of their ethics and even of their affections. There are certain statements about the difference, for example, between such apparently human and relative things as 'love' and 'sympathy' which would also be absolutely true of the affections of the imaginary men.

To turn back again for a moment to the picture of the 'lines' of evolution leading up to man; lines which might have had many different shapes. If you drop lead pellets down a funnel, the paths of each of the pellets will be different, but they all finish up in the same place, the tube to which the funnel narrows; for that is the only *exit*. In the same way one can say that whatever the lines of evolution that lead up to man might have been, the result would always have been the same, for *man is the only exit from the animal world.*

These very crude conceptions, constitute, at any rate, a first step away from subjectivism, though they still remain tainted with it. The fact asserted is true, but the explanation given 'for it is not human mind but mind itself' is false, having exactly the subjectivism of the Kantian philosophy.

MAN AS A FALLEN ANGEL. That philosopher was called the 'melancholy' who taught that all things are in a flux; and certainly nothing is so depressing as incapacity to arrive at a fixed opinion. 'If only', a philosopher might say, 'I could for once feel in my own subject, the absolute conviction that accompanies my belief that Free Trade principles are rubbish. The further away from the centre the subject lies, the solider my conviction seems; and I intensely dislike having a hard circumference and a fluid hub.' If one wishes to luxuriate in this feeling, to heighten it artificially, one cannot do better than read through the back numbers of a philosophical review. I remember one occasion, when failing to find an article I was looking for, and depressed by the museum dome, I let myself drift aimlessly through the controversies of three years. When the last ounce of solidity seemed thus to melt away in the universal deliquescence, the thing became a horror, and I had to rescue myself. I drew up a list of antitheses, of perpetual subjects of dispute, on each of which I had convictions, based on a *brutal* act of assertion, which no argument could touch. These were solid rock, whatever might be the extent of the flux elsewhere.

*   *   *

The first of these assertions was: 'There is an absolute difference between men and animals. It is impossible to completely explain the nature of man, as a complex development out of the animal world.'

This is perhaps best understood when it is taken as the crucial instance of a number of parallel assertions of a similar type; assertions which depend on the answer to this question: 'Can all the phenomena we are accustomed to call "higher" be explained as *complexes* of "lower" elements?' For the empirical philosophy this is so, and in every subject it tends to pursue the same kind of explanation. All 'height' for it, then, is of the type of the pyramid, a more or less elaborate *construction* of 'lower' elements. For another philosophy, however, the 'higher' phenomena contain an *irreducible* element. As an example, I give the following sentence which I happen to have read to-day in Max Scheler's 'Phänomenologie der Sympathiegefühle':[4] 'One must entirely exclude all attempts to reduce love and hate to simpler facts or to any complex of such facts.' The difference may be illustrated by a grotesque example. Some years ago, the Reichstag passed a vote of censure on Bethmann-Hollweg, who took no notice of it whatever. This prompted a cartoon in which the Chancellor was represented with both his feet cut neatly off, but still upright, and smiling, being supported by the Kaiser's hand stretched from a cloud. Is there anything like this in reality? or is the world with which philosophy deals entirely governed by the parliamentary system? (Perhaps the fact that this system, and the empirical philosophy, grew up at the same time has some significance.) For the present, I content myself here with re-asserting that the contrast between men and animals is the typical example of all these other antitheses. They all stand together.

* * *

I called the assertion I am discussing, a brutal assertion; in doing so, I was thinking of two things—of the kind of conviction that attaches to the assertion, and of the manner in which the assertion should be made in face of all 'idealist' humbug.

First, as to the conviction—in comparison with the variable opinion which we come to by argument, it seems to belong to another level of certitude altogether. Psychologically, perhaps, for this reason. A man's beliefs are made up of two strata, his opinions and what we call his prejudices, so that his whole attitude can be labelled (O + P). Now, the only men it is possible to convert are those in which the (O) is not consonant with the (P). This disaccord is possible because most men are ignorant of the more central (P), and mistake their accidental opinions for their unchangeable prejudices. By a difficult, but not impossible operation, a man's own fundamental prejudices may be laid bare. If he finds the opinions which he falsely took to be final, are not in accord with these prejudices, he may change them. Now to this conviction about the nature of man, no shadow of doubt is attached. It consequently seems to seek out the phenomena which superficially throw the greatest doubt on it, and so place it in the greatest danger. It seeks out these things, precisely because the assertion of the absolute difference between men and animals in the events which seem most to obliterate that difference, manifests most definitely its own uncompromising nature. Take the two phenomena often chosen to illustrate the animal nature of man—War and Sex. War is essentially human, and the pacifists falsify its nature when they attempt to reduce it to a development of animals' struggles for food. And just because man is man, and not an animal, there is, in spite of many common elements, a profound and radical difference between the sexual unions of mankind and of animals.

Secondly, as to the manner in which the assertion should be made in face of 'idealist' humbug. 'Idealism' in philosophy, is to a large extent, merely a specious substitute for religion. Being neither religious nor materialist, it depends on an endeavour to combine incompatible things under cover of a conveniently obscure terminology, thus giving an unreal consolation to men. It is a bastard phenomena, and it is time it was got rid of, and the only way to get rid of it, is to face its plausible rhetoric, by the brutal question, 'Is man an extra-natural phenomena or not? Does he differ absolutely from the animal world or not?'

A METHOD.—One of the main achievements of the nineteenth century was the elaboration and universal application of the principle of *continuity*. The destruction of this conception is, on the contrary, a pressing necessity of the present.

Originally urged only by the few, it has spread—implicit in the popular conception of evolution—till it has attained the status of a category. We now absorb it unconsciously from an environment already completely soaked in it; so that we regard it not as a principle in the light of which certain regions of fact can be conveniently ordered, but as an inevitable constituent of reality itself. When any fact seems to contradict this principle, we are inclined to deny that the fact really exists. We constantly tend to think that the discontinuities in nature are only *apparent*, and that a fuller investigation would reveal the underlying continuity. This shrinking from a *gap* or jump in nature has developed to a degree which paralyses any objective perception, and prejudices our seeing things as they really are. For an objective view of reality we must make use both of the categories of continuity and discontinuity. Our principal concern then at the present moment should be the re-establishment of the temper or disposition of mind which can look at a *gap* or chasm without shuddering.

I am not concerned in these notes, however, with gaps in nature, in the narrow sense of the word. I am thinking rather of general theories about the nature of reality. One of the results of the temper of mind I have just discussed is that any general theories of this kind which assert the existence of absolute gaps between one region of reality and another, are at once almost instinctively felt to be inadmissible. Now the method of criticism I wish to employ here is based on the fact that most of the errors in certain subjects spring from an almost instinctive attempt on our part to gloze over and disguise a particular *discontinuity* in the nature of reality. It was then necessary first of all to deal with the source of this instinctive behaviour, by pointing out the arbitrary character of the principle of continuity.

*   *   *

What is this Method? It is only possible here to describe it quite abstractly, leaving the details till later. Certain regions of reality differ not relatively but absolutely. There exists between them a real discontinuity. As the mind looks on discontinuity with horror it has attempted to exhibit these opposed things, as differing only in degree, as if there is in reality a continuous scale leading from one to the other. From this springs a whole mass of confused thinking in religion and ethics. If we first of all form a clear conception of the nature of a discontinuity, of a chasm, and form in ourselves the temper of mind which can support this opposition without irritation, we shall then have in our hands an instrument which may shatter all this confused thinking, and enable us to form accurate ideas on these subjects. In this way a flood of light may be thrown on old controversies.

A necessary preliminary to this however must be some account of the nature of the particular absolute discontinuity, that I want to use.

In order to simplify matters, it may be useful here to give the exposition a kind of geometrical character. Let us assume that reality is divided into three regions separated from one another by absolute divisions, by real discontinuities. (1) The inorganic world, of mathematical and physical science, (2) the organic world, dealt with by biology, psychology and history, and (3) the world of ethical and religious values. Imagine these three regions as the three zones marked out on a flat surface by two concentric circles. The outer zone is the world of physics, the inner that of religion and ethics, the intermediate one that of life. The outer and inner regions have certain characteristics in common. They have both an *absolute* character, and knowledge about them can legitimately be called absolute knowledge. The intermediate region of life is, on the other hand, essentially relative; it is dealt with by *loose* sciences like biology, psychology and history. A muddy mixed zone then lies between the two absolutes. To make the image a more faithful representation one would have to imagine the extreme zones partaking of the perfection of geometrical figures, while the middle zone was covered with some confused muddy substance.

*   *   *

I am afraid I shall have to abandon this model, for to make it represent faithfully what I want, I shall have to add a further complication. There must be an *absolute* division between each of the three regions, a kind of *chasm*. There must be no continuous leading gradually from one to the other. It is these *discontinuities* that I want to discuss here.

A convenient way of realising the nature of these divisions is to consider the movement away from materialism, at the end of the nineteenth century. In the middle period of the century, the predominant popular view entirely ignored the division between the inner and outer zones, and tended to treat them as one. There was no separating chasm and the two were muddled together. Vital phenomena were only extremely complicated forms of mechanical change (cf. Spencer's Biology and the entirely mechanical view involved in the definition of life as adaptation to environment). Then you get the movement represented in very different ways by Nietzsche, Dilthey, and Bergson, which clearly recognised the chasm between the two worlds of life and matter. Vital events are not completely *determined* and mechanical. It will always be impossible to completely describe them in terms of the laws of physics. This was not merely a local reaction against a local false doctrine. It contained an original element. This movement made the immense step forward involved in treating life, almost for the first time, as a unity, as something positive, a kind of stream overflowing, or at any rate not entirely enclosed, in the boundaries of the physical and spatial world. 'In Dein Auge schaute ich O Leben,'[5] etc.

So far so good. But the same movement that recognises the existence of the first absolute chasm (between the physical and the vital), proceeds to ignore the second, that between the biology, and the ethical, religious values. Having made this immense step away from materialism, it believes itself adequately equipped for a statement of all the *ideal* values. It does not distinguish different levels of the non-material. All that is non-material, must it thinks be *vital*. The momentum of its escape from mechanism carries it on to the attempt to restate the whole of religion in terms of vitalism. This is ridiculous. Biology is not theology, nor can God be defined in terms of 'life' or 'progress'. Modernism entirely misunderstands the nature of religion. But the last twenty years has produced masses of writing on this basis, and in as far as thought to-day is not materialistic, it tends to be exclusively of this kind.

It is easy to understand why the absolute division between the inorganic and the organic is so much more easily recognised than the second division. For the first falls easily into line with humanism, while the second breaks the whole Renascence tradition.

It is necessary, however, that this second *absolute* difference should also be understood. It is necessary to realise that there is an absolute, and not a relative, difference between humanism (which we can take to be the highest expression of the vital), and the religious spirit. The *divine* is not *life* at its intensest. It contains in a way an almost *anti-vital* element; quite different of course from the non-vital character of the outside physical region. The questions of Original Sin, of chastity, of the motives behind Buddhism, etc., all part of the very essence of the religious spirit, are quite incomprehensible for humanism. The difference is seen perhaps most obviously in art. At the Renascence, there were many pictures with religious subjects, but no religious art in the proper sense of the word. All the emotions expressed are perfectly human ones. Those who choose to think that religious emotion is only the highest form of the emotions that fall inside the humanist ideology, may call this religious art, but they will be wrong. When the intensity of the religious attitude finds proper expression in art, then you get a very different result. Such expression springs not from a delight in life but from a feeling for certain absolute values, which are entirely independent of vital things. The disgust with the trivial and accidental characteristics of living shapes, the searching after an austerity, a monumental stability and permanence, a perfection and rigidity, which vital things can never have, leads to the use of forms which can almost be called *geometrical*. (Cf. Byzantine, Egyptian and early Greek art.) If we think of physical science as represented by geometry, then instead of saying that the modern progress away from materialism has been from physics through vitalism to the absolute values of religion, we might say that it is from *geometry through life and back to geometry*. It certainly seems as if the extreme regions had resemblances not shared by the middle region. This is because they are both, in different ways, absolute.

We can repeat this in a more summary form. Two sets of errors spring from the attempt to treat different regions of reality as if they were alike. (1) The attempt to introduce the *absolute* of mathematical physics into the essentially relative middle zone of life leads to the *mechanistic* view of the world. (2) The attempt to explain the *absolute* of religious and ethical values in terms of the categories appropriate to the essentially relative and non-absolute vital zone, leads to the entire misunderstanding of these values, and to the creation of a series of mixed or bastard phenomena, which will be the subject of these notes. Cf. Romanticism in literature, Relativism in ethics, Idealism in philosophy, and Modernism in religion.

To say that these bastard phenomena are the result of the shrinking from discontinuity would be an entirely inadequate account of the matter. They spring from a more positive cause, the inability of the prevailing ideology to understand the nature of this absolute. But they are certainly shaped by this instinctive effort to dig away at the edges of the precipice, which really separates two regions of reality, until it is transformed into a slope leading gradually from one to the other.

Romanticism for example confuses both human and divine things, by not clearly separating them. The main thing with which it can be reproached is that it blurs the clear outlines of human relations—whether in political thought or in the literary treatment of sex, by introducing in them, the *Perfection* that properly belongs to the non-human.

The *method* I wish to pursue then is this. In dealing with these confused phenomena, to hold the real nature of the *absolute discontinuity* between vital and religious things constantly before the mind; and thus to clearly separate those things, which are in reality separate. I believe this to be a very fertile method, and that it is possible by using it, not only to destroy all these bastard phenomena, but also to recover the real significance of many things which it seems absolutely impossible for the 'modern' mind to understand.

A CRITIQUE OF SATISFACTION: In a previous Note, I made this assertion, 'In spite of its extreme diversity, all philosophy since the Renascence is at bottom the *same* philosophy. The family resemblance is much greater than is generally supposed. The obvious diversity is only that of the various species of the same genus.' It is very difficult to see this when one is *inside* this philosophy; but if one looks at it from the standpoint of another philosophy it at once becomes obvious. A parallel may make this clearer. The change of sensibility which has enabled us to regard Egyptian, Polynesian and Negro work, as *art* and not as archæology has had a double effect. It has made us realise that what we took to be the necessary principles of æsthetic, constitute in reality only a psychology of Renascence and Classical Art. At the same time, it has made us realise the essential *unity* of these latter arts. For we see that they both rest on certain common pre-suppositions, of which we only become conscious when we see them *denied* by other arts. (Cf. the work of Riegl on Byzantine art.) In the same way an understanding of the religious philosophy which preceded the Renascence makes the essential unity of all philosophy since seem at once obvious. It all rests on the same conception of the nature of man, and exhibits the same inability to realise the meaning of the dogma of Original Sin. Our difficulty now, of course, is that we are really incapable of understanding how any other view but the humanistic, could be seriously held by intelligent and emancipated men. To get over this difficulty I intend in later Notes, to say a good deal about those compara-tively unknown philosophers at the beginning of the Renascence, who are exceptionally interesting from this point of view, because they exhibit clearly the transition from one ideology to the other. They at least were capable of understanding that an intelligent man might not be a humanist.

*   *   *

But we can leave this on one side. In order to explain this family likeness between all philosophers since the Renascence, it is not necessary to state *specifically*, what the likeness consists in. The fact can perhaps be made comprehensible by the *manner* of its occurrence; by stating the aspect or *department* of philosophy in which the resemblance occurs, without stat-ing in detail what it is.

Philosophy is a surprising subject to the layman. It has all the appear-ance of an impersonal and exact science. It makes use of a terminology as abstruse as that of mathematics, and its method is so technical that he cannot follow it; yet he can see for himself that it is not a science, or it would have the same solid growth as the other sciences. It ought surely to have arrived by now at results valid for everyone. But the scandal in philosophy of the contrast between apparently *impersonal*, scientific method, and its results—which are often so *personal*, that no one but their author accepts them—is obvious to everyone.

This scandal is so evident, that certain philosophers have endeavoured to end it, by *acknowledging* it. They say that the subject should renounce its claim to be a science, and should acknowledge itself to be, what it clearly is, a *weltanschauung*, or expression of an attitude towards the world. The personal element in it would then be legitimate.

This I now believe to be a false solution.

What is the right solution? To recognise that actual Philosophy is not a pure but a *mixed* subject. It results from a confusion between two subjects which stand in no essential or necessary relation to each other, though they may be combined together for a certain practical end. One of these subjects is a science, the other not. The scientific element in philosophy is a difficult investigation into the relations between certain very abstract categories. Though the subject matter is abstract, the method employed should be as purely scientific and impersonal as that of mathematics.

Mixed up with this is the function which philosophy has assumed of acting as a pale *substitute* for religion. It is concerned here with matters like the nature and destiny of man, his place in the universe, etc., all matters which would, as treated, fit very well into a personal *Weltanschauung*. Here the word 'standpoint' may legitimately be used, though it is quite illegitimate in the scientific part of philosophy.

The two elements are mixed after this fashion. The machinery elaborated by the first element in philosophy is used to further the aims of the second. Put very crudely these aims make it first of all necessary that the world should be shown to be in *reality* very different from what it *appears* to be. It must be moulded 'nearer to the heart's desire'. By the aid of his technical equipment—the result of the first element—the philosopher is able to disintegrate the solid structure of the world as it appears to common sense. In the last chapter in his 'conclusions' he presents us with his reconstructed world; with the world as it is *in reality*. Consider the nature of this second feature for a moment. The philosopher undertakes to show that the world is other than it appears to me; and as he takes the trouble to prove this, we should expect to find, that consciously or unconsciously, the *final* picture he presents, will to some degree or other *satisfy* him.

*   *   *

It is in these final pictures that it was true to say that there was a family resemblance between all philosophers since the Renascence. Though the pictures are as different as can be, yet curiously enough they are all *satisfactory* for approximately the same reasons. The *final* pictures they present of man's relation to the world all conform to the same probably unconscious *standards* or *canons* of what is *satisfying*. It would be more accurate to say that it is the similarity of these *canons* that constitutes the unity of modern philosophy. If we think, then, of philosophy as divided into a *scientific*, and a more *personal* part, we may say that the various systems agree where they might have been expected to differ—and disagree where they ought to have been impersonal; they vary where no variation should have been possible—in the scientific part.

It should be noticed that these canons of *satisfaction* are quite unconscious. The philosophers share a view of what would be a *satisfying* destiny for man, which they take over from the Renascence. They are all satisfied with certain conceptions of the relation of man to the world. These *conclusions* are never questioned in this respect. Their truth may be questioned, but never their *satisfactoriness*. This ought to be questioned. This is what I mean by a *critique of satisfaction*. When Croce, for example, finishes up with the final world picture of the 'legitimate' *mystery of infinite progress and the infinite perfectibility of man*—I at once want to point out that not only is this not true, but what is even more important, if true such a shallow conception would be quite unworthy of the emotion he feels towards it.

These *canons of satisfaction*, which are the results of an entirely uncritical humanism, should be subject to a *critique*. This is a special subject, having no connection with philosophy. I hope to be able to show that it is a real and complicated subject inside the limits of which detailed investigation is possible, by the aid of a refined and subtle analysis.

This is a very rough account of the matter. To make it convincing, it is first of all necessary to examine in more detail, the nature of the alleged confusion in actual philosophy. In pointing out that the scientific part of the subject was actually used to serve very human ends, I did not want to imply any scepticism as to the possibility of a really scientific philosophy. I do not mean what Nietzsche meant when he said, 'Do not speculate as to whether what a philosopher says is true, but ask how he came to think it true.' This form of scepticism I hold to be just fashionable rubbish. Pure philosophy ought to be, and may be, entirely objective and scientific.

*   *   *

The best account I know of the sense in which Philosophy may be a science is that given by Husserl in *Logos*, 1911— 'Philosophie als strenge Wissenschaft'.[6] One definition would be that of philosophy as the science of *what is possible* as contrasted with the *science of what is*—something similar to what Meinong means by *Gegenstandstheorie*.[7] I have no space here to explain what is meant by these definitions. All that it is necessary to keep in mind here is that Philosophy may be a patient investigation into entities, which although they are abstract, may yet be investigated by methods as objective as those of physical science. There are then two distinct subjects.

(P.) Pure Philosophy.

(H.) This should be the critique of satisfaction; but instead it is, as a matter of fact, an entirely uncritical acceptance of Humanist views of man's nature, and destiny.

These two ought to be clearly separated. What you actually do get in philosophy, is a presentment of these humanist ideas, with a tremendous and overwhelming appearance of being *impersonal objective* science. You get something perfectly human and arbitrary cloaked in a scientific vocabulary. Instead of H or L, you get L(h) where the (h) is the really important factor. H moves in the stiff armour of L. Something quite *human* but with quite *inhumanly* sharpened weapons.

I remember being completely overawed by the vocabulary and scientific method of the various philosophers of the Marburg School, and in particular by Hermann Cohen's 'Logik der reinen Erkenntniss'.[8] But one day, hearing Cohen lecture on religion, where his views are, as is well known, entirely sectarian, I realised very easily that the overwhelming and elaborate method only served to express a perfectly simple and fallible human attitude.

This was very exhilarating and enlightening. One could at last stand free, disentangled from the influence of their paralysing and elaborate method. For what was true of their work in religion was also true elsewhere. It becomes possible to see a good deal of Cohen's work as the rigid, scientific expression of an attitude that is neither rigid nor scientific, but sometimes romantic, and always humanist. One can illustrate the effect of such work on the mind by this parallel. A man might be clothed in armour so complicated and elaborate, that to an inhabitant of another planet who had never seen armour before, he might seem like some entirely impersonal and omnipotent mechanical force. But if he saw the armour running after a lady or eating tarts in the pantry, he would realise at once, that it was not a godlike or mechanical force, but an ordinary human being extraordinarily armed. In the pantry, the essence of the phenomena is *arms, and not the man.*

When you have recovered from the precision and refinement of the *method* in such philosophers, you will be able to recognise the frequent vulgarity of their *conclusions*. It is possible to combine extreme subtlety in the one, with exceeding commonplaceness in the other.

If you ask what corresponds to the pantry which betrayed the man in armour, I should answer that it was the *last* chapters of the philosophers in which they express their conception of the world as it really is, and so incidentally expose the things with which they are satisfied. How magnificently they may have been clad before, they come out naked here!

*   *   *

This emancipation is however only a secondary matter. What I wish to emphasise here is the corrective, the *complexity* of this supposed '*Critique of Satisfaction*'. By the complexity of this subject, I mean amongst other things, the many possible different ideals, or *canons of satisfaction*. It is difficult to make the people I am attacking realise this, because they always assume automatically, that all *ideals* must be *one* ideal, and that everything that is not sceptical materialism, must be some form of *humanism*. One of the causes of this assumption can be easily dealt with. The difficulty is exactly parallel to the difficulty the scientific materialists

of the last century used to experience, in realising that metaphysics was a
real region of knowledge.

One can put the parallel clearly.

(1) The *Naturalists* refused to recognise metaphysical knowledge
because

(2) They themselves were under the influence of an *unconscious
metaphysic* which consisted in

(3) Taking physical science as the only possible *type* of real knowledge.

The parallel is:

(1) The *Humanists* would refuse to recognise the existence of a subject,
like the critique of satisfaction because

(2) They themselves are under the influence of an *unconscious critique* of
this kind which consists in

(3) Taking the satisfaction and consolation which can be obtained
from humanist idealism, and its view of man, as the only possible
type of satisfaction.

This removes an *a priori* objection to the subject. What then finally is
the nature of the subject?

*   *   *

I feel grave doubts about this last Note. I have no space to give any
account that will be full enough to be *comprehensible*, and yet I don't like
to leave the argument of the article hanging in mid-air.

What actually would be the subject matter of a *Critique of Satisfaction*?

Very roughly, the *Sphere of Religion*. But to say this at once calls up a
different conception, than the one I am driving at.

It is on the whole correct to say that while Ethics is concerned with
certain absolute values, and has nothing to do with questions of *existence*,
that Religion fills in this gap by its assertion of what Höffding[9] calls the
characteristic axiom of religion: the '*conservation of* values'. It gives us the
assurance that values are in some way permanent.

This is in a sense correct, in that it gives us so to speak the *boundaries*
of the subject. But it is entirely empty. To get at the motive forces one
would have to start in an entirely different way. I should say that the
starting point for the religious attitude was always the kind of discussion
you find in *Pascal, fragment* 139 (*Brunschvig edition*); and that is exactly what
I mean by a *Critique of Satisfaction*. You get exactly similar discussion in
the Buddhist books (entirely misunderstood of course by their translators
and editors). My point is that this is a *separate* subject. It is *not* philosophy,
nor is it *psychology*. Always the subject is the '*Vanity of desire*' but it is *not*
desire merely as a psychological entity. And it is this special region of

knowledge, marked out from all other spheres of knowledge, and absolutely and entirely *misunderstood* by the moderns, that I have baptised for the purpose of this Note only with the somewhat grotesque title of the *Critique of Satisfaction*.

In attempting, in my notes of last week, to state the whole sequence of an argument, I left parts of it rather obscure. I want to remedy this here, by treating these parts in more detail. The subject of the Notes was the mixed nature of Philosophy, and the necessity of analysing it with *Scientific* philosophy and *weltanschauung*. What I have to say here bears upon (1) a more detailed account of the *existence* of these two elements; and (2) a discussion of the consequences of this separation.

* * *

(1) A *weltanschauung* is by no means necessarily connected with a philosophy. The effort to find some 'interpretation of life', to solve what it feels to be the riddle of existence, is obviously a permanent characteristic of the human mind. It may find expression not only in philosophy, however, but in literature; where in a relatively formless way attempts may be made to deal with the relation of man to the world, and with all those questions, the answers to which used to be designated as *Wisdom*.

But though it can thus exist quite independently of philosophy, yet a *weltanschauung*, a particular view of the relation of man to existence, always tends to lose its independent status for this reason—the people who are under its influence want to *fix* it, to make it seem not so much a particular *attitude* as a *necessary* fact. They then endeavour, by expressing it in the elaborately worked out categories of a metaphysic, to give it a universal validity. Philosophy in this way provides a conceptual clothing for the interpretation of life current in any particular period. But the interpretation of life should always be distinguished from the refined organisation of concepts by which it has been expressed.

This process can be illustrated more concretely by taking a definite period. Consider the most obvious example of the emergence of a new *weltanschauung*—the Renascence. You get at that time the appearance of a new attitude which can be most broadly described as an attitude of acceptance to life, as opposed to an attitude of renunciation. As a consequence of this, there emerges a new interest in man and his relationship to his environment. With this goes an increasing interest in character and *personality* for its own sake, which makes *autobiographies* such as that of Cellini possible for the first time. An autobiography for its own sake would have been inconceivable before.

[Though these are platitudes, yet their real significance is entirely missed by people who do not see this change as a change from one *possible* attitude to another, but as a kind of discovery, like that of gravitation. They thus fail to realise the possibility of a change in the contrary direction, and also to understand the real nature of such *attitudes*.]

When this new *attitude* became firmly established, men sought to make it seem *objective* and *necessary* by giving it a philosophical setting, exactly as in the case of the religious attitude which had preceded it. This was a need actually felt by many men of the Renascence. One has only to read of the reception given to the philosophers who attempted to ground the new attitude on a theory of the nature of things . . . of the travels of *Bruno*,[10] and the recorded eagerness of the men to whom he talked at a banquet in Westminster.

To make this clear, I shall later on attempt to describe the working out of the process in the sixteenth and seventeenth centuries. It is interesting to see how the conceptual expression of the new attitude was affected by the influence of the physics of Galileo, and the revived knowledge of Stoicism, to name only two things. It becomes possible to see the whole period as very much more of a unity than it appears superficially, when the existence of the new *attitude* as the driving force behind very diverse phenomena has once been realised. This is, of course, a process which is repeated whenever the general 'interpretation of life' changes. At the *end* of such periods you get a constant phenomenon, the unsystematic philosopher. When the *weltanschauung*, the interpretation of life, changes, the values expressed by the elaborate and subtle conceptual form of a developed philosophy no longer fit the changed conditions. You then get philosophers of the type of Marcus Aurelius, who express the new attitude in a more personal, literary, and unsystematic way. Perhaps Marcus Aurelius is not a good example of this type, for behind his unsystematic expression lay a certain remnant of the Stoic principles. A more perfect example of the type is Montaigne, coming after the decay of the scholastic system. There are people at the present day who look for a philosophy of this character, who desire an 'interpretation of life' without the elaborate conceptual system of the older philosophy. 'Their eyes are directed with great earnestness on the Riddle of Life, but they despair of solving it by a universally valid metaphysic.' The fact that philosophy has always contained this element of *weltanschauung* can be illustrated by some examples of the use of the word. *Justin*[11] called Christianity a philosophy, for he claimed that it had solved all the riddles with which philosophy had busied itself. Minucius Felix[12] spoke of philosophy as perfected in Christianity . . . eternal truths about God, human responsibility and immortality, which are grounded on Reason, and can be proved through it. . . . For Porphyrios[13] the motive and end of philosophy was the salvation of the soul . . . and even Böhme[14] called his own life-work, a holy philosophy.

Such has been, in fact, the relation between *weltanschauung* and Pure Philosophy. What *ought* to be the character of this relation?

* * *

(2) As typical of the demand for a truly scientific philosophy, we can take the article by Edmund Husserl I cited last week,[15] and in England various lectures and essays of Bertrand Russell. These two writers have most clearly insisted on the necessity for an absolute separation between *Pure* Philosophy and *Weltanschauung*.

RUSSELL: 'It is from science rather than from religion and ethics that philosophy ought to draw its inspiration.' He cites Spinoza as a philosopher whose value lies almost entirely in the second element. 'We do not go to him for any metaphysical theory as to the nature of the world. What is valuable in him is the indication of a new way of feeling towards the world.' His conclusion is 'the adoption of the scientific method in philosophy compels us to abandon the hope of solving the more ambitious and humanly interesting problems of traditional philosophy.'[16]

HUSSERL: 'Es treten also scharf auseinander: Weltanschauungs philosophie und wissenschaftliche Philosophie als zwei in gewisser Weise auf einander bezogene aber nicht zu *vermengende* Ideen. . . .'[17] The first is *not* the imperfect anticipation of the second. . . . Any combination or *compromise* between these two subjects must be rejected. . . . *Weltanschauung* philosophy must give up all pretence to be scientific.

While I entirely agree with what they say as to the possibility of a purely *scientific* philosophy and the necessity for a clear separation between that and a *weltanschauung*, yet for the purpose of my argument in this Notebook I must lay emphasis on a different aspect of this separation. They insist on a clear separation, because they wish to free the scientific element in philosophy from bad influence of the other. They want the *weltanschauung* separated from philosophy because they think it has often injuriously affected the scientific part of the subject. I, on the contrary, want it separated because I think it also forms part of a *separate* subject, which has in reality no connection with philosophy.

My interest, then, is a different one, and I examine what they have to say on the separation from a different point of view. I find that while what they say is satisfactory in its description of the nature of a purely scientific philosophy, it is extremely unsatisfactory in what it has to say about the nature of a *weltanschauung*. After the remarkably clear exposition of the scientific element, one expects but does not find a similarly clear explanation of the other element.

What Mr. Russell has to say on the subject in 'A Free Man's Worship' is so extremely commonplace, and is expressed in such a painful piece of false and sickly rhetoric, that I have not patience to deal with it here.

HUSSERL, though he is better than this, is not very satisfactory. 'A *weltanschauung* should be the highest possible exaltation of the life and culture of the period. The word "Wisdom" taken in its widest sense comes to mean the most perfect possible development of the idea of Humanity. Personality is to be developed, to the greatest intensity in a many-sided activity—the result will be a *philosopher* in the original sense of the word . . . while science is impersonal, . . . a *weltanschauung* can only spring from the highest possible development of personality.'

The emphasis laid on the word *personality* at once shows us that instead of the complicated subject it really is, *weltanschauung* philosophy is for Husserl, as it is for most moderns, merely an uncritical humanism.

* * *

How does it come about that the writers who show such subtlety in the scientific part of the subject, exhibit when they come to the subjects, which I propose to deal with by a Critique of Satisfaction, such entirely uncritical and naïve crudity; what is the reason for this commonplace, unquestioning acceptance of humanist ideas?

In general perhaps for some reason of this kind. The ordinary citizen reasons correctly, without necessarily being aware that the cogency of a chain of reasoning depends on the fact that it approximates to certain standards or *canons* of implication. The philosophers, in their *conclusions*, in the region of *weltanschauung* are exactly in the position of the citizen in regard to logic. They are moved by certain unconscious *canons* of satisfaction. But while this was legitimate in the case of logic, it is not legitimate here, for the *canons* of satisfaction are not inevitable norms, like those of logic. The humanist *canons* are, I think, demonstrably false. But it is difficult to make these people realise that the canons are *false*, for they do not yet recognise that they exist. Now we only become conscious of such hidden presuppositions when they are *denied*; just as we become conscious of the existence of air, when we breathe something that is not air. It is possible to destroy this *naïveté* about the subject, by an historical investigation of the varied ideals of a *satisfactory* position of man that have as a matter of fact been held. I shall deal with this matter later. For the moment, I want to try to get at the *critique of satisfaction*, by the *direct method*.

*   *   *

My notes here will necessarily be rather disjointed; but I only intend to suggest the kind of subject matter to be dealt with by such a Critique.

This subject matter was, I asserted in my last Notes, that of religion; but in a very radical sense. Most explanations of the religious attitude deal with the *consequences* of that attitude rather than with the attitude itself; they are concerned more than they ought to be with the statements about the ultimate nature of things, which it, as it were, projects out from itself. The only fertile method is to start at the real root of the subject, with reflections on the nature of the 'satisfying'. You then get at a unique subject, with a special structure; of such a nature, that the reasonings it employs have real cogency and real effect on action.

You get thus to the actual source of religion. Moreover, it might be pointed out here, that the difficulty about religion at the present day, is not so much the difficulty of believing the statements it makes about the nature of the world, as the difficulty of understanding *how if true* these statements can be satisfactory. (Cf. Original Sin.)

Put very crudely, the question from which everything here springs is then 'what is finally *satisfying?*'

For the purpose of this discussion, I assume the truth of the statement I made in an earlier note: 'The whole subject has been confused, by the failure to recognise the *gap* between the regions of vital and human things, and that of the *absolute* values of ethics and religion. We introduce into human things the *Perfection* that properly belongs only to the divine, and thus confuse both human and divine things by not clearly separating them.' To illustrate the position, imagine a man situated at a point in a plane, from which roads radiate in various directions. Let this be the plane of actual existence. We place *Perfection* where it should not be—on this human plane. As we are painfully aware that nothing *actual* can be *perfect*, we imagine the perfection to be not where we are, but some distance along one of the roads. This is the essence of all Romanticism. Most frequently, in literature, at any rate, we imagine an impossible *perfection* along the road of sex; but anyone can name the other roads for himself. The abolition of some discipline and restriction would enable us, we imagine, to progress along one of these roads. The fundamental error is that of placing Perfection in *humanity*, thus giving rise to that bastard thing Personality, and all the bunkum that follows from it.

For the moment, however, I am not concerned with the errors introduced into *human* things by this confusion of regions which should be separated, but with the falsification of the *divine*.

If we continue to look with satisfaction along these roads, we shall always be unable to understand the religious attitude. The necessary preliminary *preparation* for such an understanding is a realisation that satisfaction is to be found along none of these roads.

I am not thinking here of actual experience, but of an *understanding* of religious experience. It is only when the 'conclusions' of the philosophers are seen to be even if true, *unsatisfactory*, that a beginning has been made towards an understanding of religion.

This realisation, that there is nothing wonderful in man, will not lead necessarily to this. It is only the necessary preparation. By itself, it leads only to a rejection of Romanticism, and the adoption of the classical attitude. But to those who have a certain conception of Perfection, a further step is taken.

The effect of this necessary *preparation* is to force the mind back on the centre, by the closing of all the roads *on* the plane. No 'meaning' can be given to the existing world, such as philosophers are accustomed to give in their last chapters. To each conclusion one asks, 'In what way is that *satisfying*?' The mind is forced back along every line in the plane, back on the centre. What is the result? To continue the rather comic metaphor, we may say the result is that which follows the snake eating its own tail, an *infinite* straight line *perpendicular* to the plane.

In other words, you get the religious attitude; where things are separated which ought to be separated, and Perfection is not illegitimately introduced on the plane of human things.

It is the closing of all the roads, this realisation of the *tragic* significance of life, which makes it legitimate to call all other attitudes shallow. Such a realisation has formed the basis of all the great religions, and is most conveniently remembered by the symbol of the *wheel*. This symbol of the futility of existence is absolutely lost to the modern world, nor can it be recovered without great difficulty.

One modern method of disguising the issue should be noticed. In November 1829, a tragic date for those who see with regret the establishment of a lasting and devasting stupidity, Goethe—in answer to Eckermann's remark that human thought and action seemed to repeat itself, going round in a circle,—said: '*No, it is not a circle, it is a spiral.*' You disguise the wheel by tilting it up a bit; it then becomes 'Progress', which is the modern substitute for religion.

I ought here to point out that these crude conceptions are designed only to *suggest* the subject-matter, which properly developed has no connection with philosophy. And just as exceeding refinement and subtlety in pure philosophy may, we have seen, have been combined with exceeding commonplaceness in the subject, so the reverse of this is also true. It may and has happened that a cobbler may on this subject exhibit a refined sensibility, and yet be incapable of thought in philosophy at all.

This crude discussion about the wheel must sound entirely unreal to the humanist. The direct method of approval will not do for propaganda purposes. Fortunately a more indirect method is open to us. We can make a preliminary attempt to shake the humanist *naïveté* by the historical method.

HISTORY.—The greater part of these Notes will be taken up by an analysis of the history of ideas at the *Renascence*. A proper understanding of the Renascence seems to me to be the most pressing necessity of thought at the present moment. It would be quite impossible to discuss the subjects of these Notes, without continual use of the historical method. I entirely agree then with Savigny that 'history is the only true way to attain a knowledge of our own condition'. When I say I agree with Savigny's phrase, I am however attributing an entirely different meaning to the words. As actually used in 1815, they were an incident in the dispute as to the nature of the ideal sciences—economics, law, ethics, etc. Are they capable of a theoretical foundation like geometry, or are the principles they involve merely expressions of the conditions at a given moment in history? While the eighteenth century had attempted to change legal institutions in accordance with the Rights of Man deduced from theoretical principles, Savigny was opposing to these the entirely historical foundation of jurisprudence. This historical scepticism has now been vanquished in every subject. I approve of this victory; in what sense then do I think Savigny's words true?

I think that history is necessary in order to *emancipate* the individual from the influence of certain *pseudo-categories*. We are all of us under the influence of a number of abstract ideas, of which we are as a matter of fact unconscious. We do not see them, but see other things *through* them. In order that the kind of discussion about 'satisfaction' which I want, could be carried on, it is first of all necessary to rob certain ideas of their status of categories. This is a difficult operation. Fortunately, however, all such 'attitudes' and ideologies have a gradual growth. The rare type of historical intelligence which investigates their origins can help us considerably. Just as a knowledge of the colours extended and separated in the spectrum enables us to distinguish the feebler colours confused together in shadows, so a knowledge of these ideas, as it were *objectified*, and *extended* in history enables us to perceive them hidden in our own minds. Once they have been brought to the surface of the mind, they lose their *inevitable* character. They are no longer categories. We have lost our *naïveté*. Provided that we have a great enough length of history at our disposal, we then thus always vaccinate ourselves against the possibility of harbouring false categories. For in a couple of thousand years the confused human mind works itself out clearly into all the separate attitudes it is possible for it to assume. Humanity ought then always to carry with it a library of a thousand years as a balancing pole.

The application of this to the present subject is this: It is possible by examining the history of the Renascence, to destroy in the mind of the humanist, the conviction that his own attitude is the *inevitable* attitude of the emancipated and instructed man.

We may not be able to convince him that the religious attitude is the right one, but we can at least destroy the *naïveté* of his canons of *satisfaction*.

NEO-REALISM.—Having lived at Cambridge at various times during the last ten years,[18] I have naturally always known that the only philosophical movement of any importance in England is that which is derived from the writings of Mr. G. E. Moore. I now find these writings extremely lucid and persuasive, yet for years was entirely unable to understand in what lay their value. It was not so much that I did not agree with what was said, as that I was entirely unable to see how any meaning could be attached to some of its main contentions. I give examples of these contentions later on.

A few years ago I came across similar views differently expressed in the work of Husserl and his followers. I then began for the first time, if not to agree with these views, at least to understand how they came to be held. It is not that the Germans are better or more lucid than Mr. Moore—that is very far from being the case. The reason is entirely personal; but it seems to me worth while explaining, for my difficulties are at least the *typical* difficulties of the dilettante. It would be no exaggeration, I think, to assert that all English amateurs in philosophy are, as it were, *racially* empiric and nominalist; there is their hereditary endowment. And so long as their interest in the subject is a dilettante one they are unlikely to find much meaning in philosophers who are intellectualist and *realist*. For the reading of the dilettante in philosophy, though it may be extensive and enthusiastic, always proceeds along easy slopes. As he only reads what he finds interesting, the only arguments he is likely to come into close contact with—or, at any rate, into that extremely close contact which is necessary for the understanding of disputed points in this subject—will be those which approximate to his own position. If his own mental make-up at a given moment be A, his only chance of understanding an opposed position B will be in the case when the detailed exposition of B as b_1, b_2, b_3, a, contains one element (a) which he can lay hold of. This is the only way in which he will ever obtain a foothold. From that he may gradually proceed to understand the rest. But without that he would never exhibit the concentration of mind necessary to grasp the meaning of an argument which he rejects. There is, you perceive, nothing very admirable about this type of mind. In the end it probably gets everywhere, though as it always shrinks from precipices, and proceeds along easy slopes, through a hundred gradations of a_1, a_2, a_3, before it gets from A to B—it will always require an unlimited time. As its interests change, it may read many different parts of the same book, at long intervals, until finally as the result of many enthusiasms, it has read the whole. This blind following of interest along long and intricate paths may indirectly approximate to the results which concentration achieves directly. At any rate, I prefer people who feel a *resistance* to opinion. Except for the gifted few, this may be the best method to pursue in philosophy up to forty. It might be argued that a concentrated direct study of such matters should be postponed to this time, when a man really has prejudices to be moulded. There is, perhaps, more chance of getting *shape* out of stone than out of undergraduate plasticine. That this is a fair analysis of that very wide-spread phenomenon 'Superficial thinking', we can verify by examining our own procedure in these matters. It, at any rate, enables me to explain my own difficulties. When, with entirely empirical and nominalist pre-judices, I read Moore and Russell, there was no foothold for me; they dealt with logic and ethics, and holding, as I did, entirely relativist views about both, I naturally found nothing familiar from which I might have started to understand the rest. The Germans I mentioned were useful in this way; they made the intellectualist, non-empirical method comprehensible to me, by enlarging its scope—applying it not only to logic and ethics, but to things which at the time did interest me. This provided me with the required foothold. When I had seen in these further subjects the possibility of the *rationalist, non-empirical* method, I began to see that it was this method which formed the basis of the writing on logic and ethics which I had before found incomprehensible.

This will be then the order of my argument here. I give certain views of the Realists, which I at one time found incomprehensible. When I began to see for the first time the possibility of a non-empirical type of knowledge, the incomprehensibility of these views disappeared. In this Note I am, however, not concerned with their realism, but with the attitude (the assumption of this type of knowledge) from which the realism and its attendant difficulties spring.

In this kind of knowledge, the same type of non-empirical reasoning is possible as in geometry; and its subject-matter stands in much the same relation to the concepts we generally, but falsely, call mental, that geometry does to physical matter. When the only admitted kind of knowledge is empirical, the only type of explanation considered legitimately is that which reduces all the 'higher' concepts to combinations of more elementary ones. It is for this reason that I deal here with a subject that does not seem to have much relation to the general argument of this Notebook. For this false conception of the nature of 'explanation' prejudices the understanding of the 'critique of satisfaction'. It is first of all necessary before entering on this subject to destroy prejudices springing from empiricism, which tend to make us think certain concepts unreal.

* * *

The first difficulty was that Moore's only book was about Ethics. To anyone taking a thoroughly sceptical and relativist view of this subject, the whole discussion would quite wrongly appear almost entirely verbal. The only solution to this difficulty is the gradual realisation of the fact that there are objective things in Ethics, and this seems to me the only solution. I do not think any argument on the matter would have any effect unless a man had by some change in himself come to see that ethics was a real subject.

* * *

The principal difficulty, however, is the importance the Neo-Realists seem to attach to *language*. Mr. Russell says, 'That all sound philosophy should begin with an analysis of propositions is a truth too evident perhaps to demand a proof.' 'The question whether all propositions are reducible to the subject predicate form is one of fundamental importance to all philosophy.'

'Even amongst philosophers, we may say, broadly, that only those universals which are named by adjectives or substantives have been much or often recognised, while those named by verbs and propositions have been usually overlooked. . . . This omission has had a very great effect upon philosophy, it is hardly too much to say, that most metaphysics, since Spinoza, has been largely determined by it.'

Mr. G. E. Moore in an article on the 'Nature of Judgment'. 'It seems necessary, then, to regard the world as formed of concepts . . . which cannot be regarded as abstractions either for things or ideas . . . since both alike can, if anything be true of them, be comprised of nothing but concepts . . . an existent is seen to be nothing but a concept or complex of concepts standing in a unique relation to the concept of existence.'[19]

Such assertions must seem meaningless to the nominalist and empiricist. The whole thing seems to him to be a new kind of scholasticism. He cannot understand how the study of such an apparently relative and trivial thing as the nature of propositions, the study of the accidental characteristics of human speech should be an indispensable preliminary to philosophy.

The first step towards making the matter intelligible is to note the use of the word *human*. A proposition in the sense used in the above quotation is not something relative to the *human*. 'A proposition . . . does not itself contain words . . . it contains the entities indicated by words.' One recalls Bolzano's 'Sentences in themselves.'[20] Logic, then, does *not* deal with the laws of human thought but with these quite *objective* sentences. In this way the anthropomorphism which underlies certain views of logic is got rid of. Similarly, ethics can be exhibited as an objective science, and is also purified from anthropomorphism.

All these subjects are thus placed on an entirely objective basis, and do not in the least depend on the human mind. The entities which form the subject-matter of these sciences are neither physical nor mental, they 'subsist'. They are dealt with by an investigation that is *not* empirical. Statements can be made about them whose truth does not depend on experience. When the empirical prejudice has been got rid of, it becomes possible to think of certain 'higher' concepts, that of the good, of love, etc., as, at the same time, *simple*, and not necessarily to be analysed into more *elementary* (generally sensual) elements.

To make this intelligible, two things must be further discussed: (1) the possibility of this non-empirical knowledge; (2) what is meant by saying that these entities are neither physical nor mental, but *subsist*?

A PROGRAMME.—It has been suggested that I might make these rambling notes a good deal more intelligible if I gave first a kind of programme, a general summary of the conclusions I imagine myself able to establish.

*   *   *

The main argument of these notes is of an *abstract* character; it is concerned with certain ideas which lie so much in the centre of our minds, that we quite falsely regard them as having the nature of categories. More particularly, I am concerned with two opposed conceptions of the nature of man, which in reality lie at the root of our more concrete beliefs—the Religious and the Humanist.

It would perhaps have been better to have avoided the word religious, as that to the 'emancipated' man at once suggests something exotic, or

mystical, or some sentimental reaction. I am not, however, concerned so
much with religion, as with the attitude, the 'way of thinking', the
categories, from which a religion springs, and which often survive it.
While this attitude tends to find expression in myth, it is independent
of myth; it is, however, much more intimately connected with dogma.
For the purposes of this discussion, the bare minimum without any
expression in religion is sufficient, the abstract categories alone. I want to
emphasise that this attitude is a possible one for the 'emancipated' and
'reasonable' man at this moment. I use the word religious, because as in
the past the attitude has been the source of most religions, the word
remains convenient.

A.—The Religious attitude: (1) Its first postulate is the impossibility,
I discussed earlier, of expressing the absolute values of religion and
ethics in terms of the essentially relative categories of life . . . Ethical values are *not* relative to human desires and feelings, but absolute
and objective . . . Religion supplements this . . . by its conception of
Perfection.

(2) In the light of these absolute values, man himself is judged to be
essentially limited and imperfect. He is endowed with Original Sin.
While he can occasionally accomplish acts which partake of perfection,
he can never himself *be* perfect. Certain secondary results in regard to
ordinary human action in society follow from this. As man is essentially
bad, he can only accomplish anything of value by discipline—ethical and
political. Order is thus not merely negative, but creative and liberating.
Institutions are necessary.

B.—The Humanist attitude: When a sense of the reality of these
absolute values is lacking, you get a refusal to believe any longer in the
radical imperfection of either Man or Nature. This develops logically into
the belief that life is the source and measure of all values, and that man is
fundamentally good. Instead, then, of

Man (radically imperfect) . . . apprehending . . . Perfection,

you get the second term (now entirely misunderstood) illegitimately
introduced inside the first. This leads to a complete change in all values.
The problem of evil disappears, the conception of sin loses all meaning.
Man may be that bastard thing, 'a harmonious character'. Under ideal
conditions, everything of value will spring spontaneously from free 'personalities'. If nothing good seems to appear spontaneously now, that is
because of external restrictions and obstacles. Our political ideal should
be the removal of everything that checks the 'spontaneous growth of
personality'. Progress is thus possible, and order is a merely negative
conception.

*   *   *

The errors which follow from this confusion of things which ought to be kept separate are of two kinds. The true nature both of the human and the divine is falsified.

(1) The error in human things; the confusion blurs the clear outlines of human relations by introducing into them the Perfection that properly belongs to the non-human. It thus creates the bastard conception of *Personality*. In literature it leads to romanticism . . . but I deal with the nature of these errors later.

(2) The confusion created in the absolute values of religion and ethics is even greater. It distorts the real nature of ethical values by deriving them out of essentially subjective things, like human desires and feelings; and all attempts to 'explain' religion, on a humanist basis, whether it be Christianity, or an alien religion like Buddhism, must always be futile. As a minor example of this, take the question of immortality. It seems paradoxical at first sight, that the Middle Ages, which lacked entirely the conception of personality, had a real belief in immortality; while thought since the Renascence, which has been dominated by the belief in personality, has not had the same conviction. You might have expected that it would be the people who thought they really had something worth preserving who would have thought they were immortal, but the contrary is the case. Moreover, those thinkers since the Renascence who have believed in immortality and who have attempted to give explanation of it, have, in my opinion, gone wrong, because they have dealt with it in terms of the category of individuality. The problem can only be profitably dealt with by being entirely re-stated. This is just one instance of the way in which thought about these things in terms of categories appropriate only to human and vital things distort them.

THE TWO PERIODS.—The importance of this difference between the two conceptions of the nature of man becomes much more evident when it is given an historical setting. When this somewhat abstract antithesis is seen to be at the root of the difference between two historical periods, it begins to seem much more solid; in this way one gives it body.

The first of these historical periods is that of the Middle Ages in Europe—from Augustine, say, to the Renascence; the second from the Renascence to now. The ideology of the first period is religious; of the second, humanist. The difference between them is fundamentally nothing but the difference between these two conceptions of man.

Everyone would assent to the statement that on the whole the first period believed in the dogma of original sin, and the second did not. But this is not enough. It is necessary to realise the immense importance of this difference in belief, to realise that in reality almost everything else springs from it. In order to understand a period it is necessary not so much to be acquainted with its more defined opinions as with the doctrines which are thought of not as doctrines, but as FACTS. (The moderns, for example, do not look for their belief in *Progress* as an opinion, but merely as a recognition of fact.) There are certain doctrines which for a particular period seem not doctrines, but inevitable categories of the human mind. Men do not look on them merely as correct opinion, for they have become so much a part of the mind, and lie so far back, that they are never really conscious of them at all. They do not see them, but other things *through* them. It is these abstract ideas at the centre, the things which they take for granted, which characterise a period. There are in each period certain doctrines, a denial of which is looked on by the men of that period just as we might look on the assertion that two and two make five. It is these abstract things at the centre, these *doctrines* felt as *facts*, which are the source of all the other more material characteristics of a period. For the Middle Ages these 'facts' were the belief in the subordination of man to certain absolute values, the radical imperfection of man, the doctrine of original sin. Everyone would assent to the assertion that these beliefs were held by the men of the Middle Ages. But that is not enough. It is necessary to realise that *these beliefs were the centre of their whole civilisation, and that even the character of their economic life was regulated by them*—in particular by the kind of ethics which springs from the acceptance of sin as a fact. It is only lately that the importance of the relation has been recognised, and a good deal of interesting work has been carried out on these lines in investigating the connection between the ideology of St. Thomas Aquinas and the economic life of his time.

Turn now to the second period. This does not seem to form a coherent period like the first. But it is possible to show, I think, that all thought since the Renascence, in spite of its apparent variety, in reality forms one coherent whole. It all rests on the same presuppositions which were denied by the previous period. It all rests on the same conception of the nature of man, and all exhibits the same complete inability to realise the meaning of the dogma of Original Sin. In this period not only has its philosophy, its literature, and ethics been based on this new conception of man as fundamentally good, as sufficient, as the measure of things, but a good case can even be made out for regarding many of its characteristic economic features as springing entirely from this central abstract conception.

Not only that, but I believe that the real source of the immense change at the Renascence should be sought not so much in some material cause, but in the gradual change of attitude about this seemingly abstract matter. Men's categories changed; the things they took for granted changed. Everything followed from that.

There are economists now who believe that this period has been capitalist because it *desired*, it had the will, to be so. An essential preliminary to the growth of capitalism for them is, then, the growth of the capitalist 'spirit'. Other ages have not been industrial, not because they lacked the capacity, the scientific intelligence, but because on the whole they did not *desire* to be industrial, because they lacked this particular 'spirit'. We may note that Max Weber, one of the most remarkable economists of this school, sees in 'the spontaneous change in religious experience (at the Renascence), and the corresponding new ethical ideals by which life was regulated—one of the strongest roots of the capitalist spirit'.

The thoroughness with which these two conceptions of man penetrate the life of their respective periods can be illustrated by the difference between their arts. What is the difference between modern art since the Renascence, and Byzantine mosaic, which we may take as most typical of the other period? Renascence art we may call a 'vital' art in that it depends on pleasure in the reproduction of human and natural forms. Byzantine art is the exact contrary of this. There is nothing vital in it; the emotion you get from it is not a pleasure in the reproduction of natural or human life. The disgust with the trivial and accidental characteristics of living shapes, the searching after an austerity, a *perfection* and rigidity which vital things can never have, leads here to the use of forms which can almost be called geometrical. Man is subordinate to certain absolute values: there is no delight in the human form, leading to its *natural* reproduction; it is always distorted to fit into the more abstract forms which convey an intense religious emotion.

These two arts thus correspond exactly to the thought of their respective periods. Byzantine art to the ideology which looks on man and all existing things as imperfect and sinful in comparison with certain abstract values and *perfections*. The other art corresponds to the humanist ideology, which looks on man and life as good, and which is thus in a relation of harmony with existence. Take Goethe as typical of the period. 'Human nature knows itself one with the world, and consequently feels the outer world not as something foreign to it, but recognises it as the answering counterpart to the sensations of its own inner world.'

Such a humanism in all its varying forms of pantheism, rationalism and idealism, really constitutes a complete anthropomorphisation of the world, and leads naturally to art which is founded on the pleasure to be derived from vital forms.

THE END OF HUMANISM.—Now it should be noted that the coherent attitude and art of these two periods have occurred many times before in history. The Renascence period corresponds very nearly both in its conception of man and in its art to the classical. The Byzantine art corresponds to many other geometric arts in the past, to Egyptian and Indian, for example, both, also, civilisations with a similar religious, non-humanistic conception of man. In the same way, then, it may be possible that the humanist period we live in, may also come to an end, to be followed by a revival of the anti-humanist attitude. In saying this I do not in the least wish to imply any mechanical view of history as an inevitable alternation of such periods; I am so far from such scepticism about the matter, that I regard difference between the two attitudes as simply the difference between true and false. The great obstacle which prevents people seeing the possibility of such a change is the apparently *necessary* character of the humanist conception. But the same situation formerly existed in æsthetics. One result of the fact that both classical and modern art, springing from a similar attitude to the world, is that we tend to look on these arts, as *Art* itself; the art of other periods we have regarded as archæology or ethnology. We neglected Byzantine art, for example, just as we neglected scholastic philosophy . . . May it not, then, be significant that it is only just lately that we have begun to understand these other arts . . . May not the change of sensibility, in a region like æsthetics, a by-path in which we are, as it were, off our guard, be some indication that the *humanist tradition is breaking up*—for individuals here and there, at any rate.

*   *   *

When I say that it may be breaking up for individuals, I ought to correct a little this picture of the two contrasted periods. While such periods are on the whole coherent, they are never absolutely so. You always get people who really belong to the other period. At the beginning of a period you have the people who continue the tradition of the preceding period, and at the end those who prepare the change to that which follows. At the beginning of the Christian period you have many of the Fathers continuing the classical conception of man. At the same time as St. Augustine, you get Pelagius, who has many resemblances to Rousseau, and might easily be applauded at a meeting of *progressives*. It is, as a rule, on such people that the man like Pico,[21] who come at the end of a period, and prepare the change to the next, base themselves.

There is a similar overlapping of the religious period into the humanist one. It was this overlapping which was in reality responsible for the virtues which we often find in the earlier humanists, and which disappeared so completely when humanity attained its full development in romanticism. Compare, for example, the early Protestants and the Puritans with the sloppy thought of their descendants to-day.

Moreover, you may get, at any stage in the history of such a period, isolated individuals, whose whole attitude and ideology really belong to the opposed period. The greatest example of such an individual is, of course, Pascal. Everything that I shall say later in these notes is to be regarded merely as a prolegomena to the reading of Pascal, as an attempt to remove the difficulties of comprehension engendered in us by the humanism of our period.

*   *   *

When I say that I think that humanism is breaking up, and that a new period is commencing, I should like to guard against exaggeration by two reservations.

(1) I do not in the least imagine that humanism is breaking up merely to make place for a new mediævalism. The only thing the new period will have in common with mediævalism will be the subordination of man to certain absolute values. The analogy of art may again help us here. Both Byzantine and Egyptian art spring from an attitude towards life which made it impossible to use the accidental shapes of living things as symbols of the divine. Both consequently are geometrical in character; but with this very general quality the resemblance ends. Compare a Byzantine relief of the best period with the design on a Greek vase, and an Egyptian relief. The abstract geometrical character of the Byzantine relief makes it much nearer to the Egyptian than to the Greek work; yet a certain elegance in the line-ornament shows that it has developed out of the Greek. If the Greek had never existed it could not have the character it has. In the same way, a new anti-humanist ideology could not be a mere revival of mediævalism. The humanist period has developed an honesty in science and a certain conception of freedom of thought and action which will remain.

(2) I do not imagine that men themselves will change in any way. Men differ very little in every period. It is only our categories that change. Whatever we may think of sin, we shall always be sensual. Men of different sorts exist in constant proportion in different generations. But different circumstances, different prevailing ideologies, bring different types to the top. Exactly the same type existed in the Middle Ages as now. This constancy of man thus provides perhaps the greatest hope of the possibility of a radical transformation of society.

THE RENASCENCE.—For an understanding of the way in which everything really depends on these abstract conceptions of the nature of man a study of the Renascence is important.

The best-known work on the Renascence, while valuable historically, seems to me to miss the whole point, for this reason: It describes the emergence of the new attitude towards life, of the new conception of man, as it might describe the gradual discovery of the conception of gravitation—that is, as the gradual emergence of something which once established would remain always, the period before being characterised thus as a *privation* of the new thing. The whole point of the thing is missed if we do not recognise that the new attitude towards man at the Renascence was thus just an *attitude*, one attitude amongst other possible ones, deliberately chosen. It is better to describe it as a heresy, a mistaken adoption of false conceptions.

*   *   *

In an account of the Renascence three things should be noticed:

(1) The changed conception itself, the putting of the Perfection into man, man no longer endowed with original sin, but by nature good. In Machiavelli you get the conception of human nature as a natural power, as living energy. Mankind is not by nature bad, but subject to passions. The absolute standards in comparison with which man was sinful disappear, and life itself, is *accepted* as the measure of all values. You get Lorenzo Valla (1407) in his *De Voluptate*, daring to assert for the first time that pleasure was the highest good.[22] A secondary consequence of this acceptance of life is the development of the conception of personality. The stages in this emphasis on the individual from Petrarch (1304) to Montaigne can be easily followed. Michelet writes, 'To the discovery of the outward world the Renascence added a still greater achievement by bringing to light the full, the whole nature of man.' This is ridiculous. The proper way to put the matter is to say that the decay into a false conception of values did in this way bring certain compensations with it.

(2) So with the establishment of the new conception of man as good, with the conception of personality comes an increased interest in the actual characteristics of man. This is at first merely manifested directly in literature. You get autobiographies for the first time—those of Cellini and Cardano,[23] for example. It leads later, however, to more direct study of man's emotions and character, of what we should call psychology. You get works like Vives,[24] *De Anima*, and Telesio, *De Rerum Natura*.[25]

(3) This new study of man, this new psychology, or anthropology, has considerable influence on the philosophers who provided a conceptual clothing for the new attitude, and worked out its consequences in ethics and politics . . . on Descartes, Hobbes, and Spinoza, for example.

This process is worth while following in considerable detail for the following reason: It is necessary to emphasise how very coherent in thought such periods are, everything being in them really dependent on certain instinctive ways of judging, which, for the period, have the status of *natural* categories of the mind. The moderns, whether philosophers or reformers, make constant appeals to certain ideals, which they assume everybody will admit as natural and inevitable for the emancipated man. What these are you may discover from peroration of speeches—even from scrap books. 'To thine own true self, etc . . . Over the portal of the new world, *Be Thyself* shall be written . . . Culture is not satisfied till we all come to a perfect man . . . the free growth of personality'—and so on. We think these things not because they are inevitable ways of thinking, but because we absorb them unconsciously from the humanist tradition which moulds the actual apparatus of our thought. They can all be traced back to the Stoics, Epicureans, and Pantheists of the Renascence. The detailed exposition of the process by which this attitude was gradually embodied in the conceptional apparatus we inherit may do more than anything else to convince us how very far it is from being an inevitable attitude.

PARTIAL REACTIONS.—It is important to distinguish two stages inside the modern period—*humanism* properly so called, and *romanticism*. The new conception of man as fundamentally good manifests itself at first in a more heroic form. In art, Donatello, Michael Angelo, or Marlowe might stand for this period. I do not deny that humanism of this kind has a certain attraction. But it deserves no admiration, for it bears in itself the seed which is bound inevitably later to develop into sentimental, utilitarian romanticism. Such humanism could have no permanence; however heroic at the start, it was bound sooner or later to end in Rousseau. There is the parallel development in art. Just as humanism leads to Rousseau so Michael Angelo leads to Greuze.[26]

There are people who, disgusted with romanticism, wish for us to go back to the classical period, or who, like Nietzsche, wish us to admire the Renascence. But such partial reactions will always fail, for they are only half measures—it is no good returning to humanism, for that will itself degenerate into romanticism.

*　　*　　*

This is one type of an *inadequate reaction* against humanism. There are at the present many indications of other *partial* reactions. In philosophy and ethics, for example, the work of Moore and Husserl, which is often attacked as a kind of scholasticism. A complete reaction from the subjectivism and relativism of humanist ethics should contain two elements: (1) the establishment of the *objective* character of ethical values, (2) a satisfactory ethic not only looks on values as *objective*, but establishes an order or *hierarchy* among such values, which it also regards as absolute and objective.

Now while the school of Moore and Husserl break the humanist tradition in the first matter, they seem to continue it quite uncritically in the second. In as far, then, as they free ethical values from the anthropomorphism involved in their dependence on human desires and feeling, they have created the machinery of an anti-humanist reaction which will proceed much further than they ever intended.

THE RELIGIOUS ATTITUDE.—In discussing the religious as contrasted with the humanist attitude, in my last notes, I said, 'While it tends to find expression in myth it is independent of myth; it is, however, much more intimately connected with dogma.' I want to make this clearer by a more detailed account of what I mean by 'an attitude' in this context.

* * *

The main purpose of these notes is a practical one. I want to show that certain generally held 'principles' are false. But the only method of controversy in any such fundamental matter of dispute is an 'abstract' one; a method which deals with the abstract conceptions on which opinions really rest.

You think A is true; I ask why. You reply, that it follows from B. But why is B true, because it follows from C, and so on. You get finally to some very abstract attitude (h) which you assume to be self-evidently true. This is the central conception from which more detailed opinion about political principles, for example, proceeds. Now if your opponent reasons correctly, and you are unable to show that he has falsely deduced A from B, then you are driven to the abstract plane of (h), for it is here that the difference between you really has its root. And it is only on this abstract plane that a discussion on any fundamental divergence of opinion can usefully be carried on.

* * *

Any attempt to change (h), however, should be prefaced by some account of the nature of such abstract attitudes, and the process by which we come to adopt them.

It is possible to trace, in every man's mind, then, trains leading in various directions, from his detailed ethical and political opinions, back to a few of these central attitudes.

A . . . . B . . . . c . . . . g . . . . . . (h)

Instead, of the first concrete statement 'A is true', we might have 'A is good'; in which case (h) would be an ultimate *value*; the process, however, is the same. Another metaphor, by which we may describe the place of (h) in our thought, is to compare it to the axes, to which we refer the position of a moving point, or the framework, on which A and B are based. This is, perhaps, a better description, for the framework, inside which we live, is something *we take for granted*; and in ordinary life we are very seldom conscious of (h). We are only led up to it by this dialectical questioning, described above. All our 'principles' are based on some unconscious 'framework' of this kind. As a rule, then, we are quite unconscious of (h), we are only conscious of the detailed principles A and B, derived from it. Now while we probably acquire the opinions A and B consciously, the same is not true of (h). How do we come to hold it, then? For we did not produce it ourselves, but derived it ready made from society. It came to be an essential part of our mind without our being conscious of it, because it was already implicit, in all the more detailed opinions, A and B, society forced upon us. It was thus embedded in the actual matter of our thought, and as natural to us as the air; in fact, it *is* the air that all these more concrete beliefs breathe. We thus have forced upon us, unconsciously, the whole apparatus of categories, in terms of which all our thinking must be done. The result of (h) having in this way the character of a category, is that it makes us see (A) not as an opinion, but as a fact. We never see (h) for we see all things *through* (h).

In this way these abstract categories, of course, *limit* our thinking; our thought is compelled to move inside certain limits. We find, then, in people whose mental apparatus is based on (h) while ours is not, a certain obstinacy of intellect, a radical opposition, and incapacity to see things which, to us, are simple.

Now the limitation imposed on our thinking by such categories is sometimes quite legitimate. Some categories are objective. We cannot think of things outside of space and time, and it is quite right that we are subject to this limitation.

But (h) often belongs to the large class of pseudo-categories—categories which are not objective, and it is these that I wish to deal with here. They are exceedingly important, for the difference between the mentality of one great period of history and another really depends on the different pseudo-categories of this kind, which were imposed on every individual of the period, and in terms of which his thinking was consequently done. It is not difficult to find examples of this.

(1) A Brazilian Indian told a missionary that he was a red parrot. The missionary endeavoured to give some explanation of this statement. You mean, he said, that when you die you will *become* a red parrot, or that you

are in some way related to this bird. The Indian rejected both these plausible attempts to explain away a perfectly simple fact, and repeated quite *coldly* that he *was* a red parrot. There would seem to be an impasse here then; the missionary was *baffled* in the same way as the humanist is, by the conception of sin. The explanation given by Lévy Bruhl, who quotes the story, is that the Indian, has *imposed* on him by his group a conception of the nature of an object, which differs radically from ours. For him an object can be something else without at the same time ceasing to be itself. The accuracy of this explanation need not detain us. The point is that it serves as an illustration of the way in which minds dominated by *different* pseudo-categories, may have a very *different* perception of fact.

(2) Greek. It has been recently argued that the only way to understand early Greek philosophy is to realise that it continued on the plane of speculation the categories, the ways of thinking that had earlier created Greek religion, . . . the conception of *Moira*,[27] to which even the gods submitted, . . . etc. The difference between the religious attitude and myth is here quite clear.

The more intimate connection with dogmas I referred to, depends on the fact that dogma is often a fairly intellectual way of expressing these fundamental categories—the dogma of Original Sin, for example. At the Renascence, in spite of opinion to the contrary, the philosophy did *not* express the categories, the ways of thinking which had earlier been expressed in the Christian religion; it reversed them.

* * *

It is these categories, these abstract conceptions, which all the individuals of a period have in common, which really serve best to characterise the period. For most of the characteristics of such a period, not only in thought, but in ethics, and through ethics in economics, really depend on these central abstract attitudes. But while people will readily acknowledge that this is true of the Greeks, or of Brazilian Indians, they have considerable difficulty in realising that it is also true of the modern humanist period from the Renascence to now. The way in which we instinctively judge things we take to be the inevitable way of judging things. The pseudo-categories of the humanist attitude are thought to be on the same footing as the objective categories of space and time. It is thought to be impossible for an emancipated man to think sincerely in the categories of the religious attitude.

The reason for this is to be found in the fact noticed earlier in the 'Note' that we are, as a rule, unconscious of the very abstract conceptions which underlie our more concrete opinions. What Ferrier[28] says of real categories, 'Categories may be operative when their existence is not consciously recognised. First principles of every kind have their influence, and, indeed, operate largely and profoundly long before they come to the surface of human thought, and are articulately expounded,' is true also of these pseudo-categories. We are only conscious of A, B, . . and very seldom of (h). We do not see that, but other things *through it*; and, consequently, take what we see for facts, and not for what they are— opinions based on a particular abstract valuation. This is certainly true of the *progressive* ideology founded on the conception of man as fundamentally good.

*   *   *

It is this unconsciousness of these central abstract conceptions, leading us to suppose that the judgments of value founded on them are *natural* and *inevitable*, which makes it so difficult for anyone in the humanist tradition to look at the religious attitude as anything but a sentimental survival.

But I want to emphasise as clearly as I can, that I attach very little value indeed to the *sentiments* attaching to the religious attitude. I hold, quite coldly and intellectually as it were, that the way of thinking about the world and man, the conception of sin, and the categories which ultimately make up the religious attitude, are the *true* categories and the *right* way of thinking.

I might incidentally note here, that the way in which I have explained the action of the central abstract attitudes and ways of thinking, and the use of the word *pseudo*-categories, might suggest that I hold relativist views about their validity. But I don't. I hold the religious conception of ultimate values to be right, the humanist wrong. From the nature of things, these categories are not inevitable, like the categories of time and space, but are *equally objective*. In speaking of religion, it is to this level of abstraction that I wish to refer. I have none of the feelings of *nostalgie*, the reverence for tradition, the desire to recapture the sentiment of Fra Angelico, which seems to animate most modern defenders of religion. All that seems to me to be bosh. What is important, is what nobody seems to realise—the dogmas like that of Original Sin, which are the closest expression of the categories of the religious attitude. That man is in no sense perfect, but a wretched creature, who can yet apprehend perfection. It is not, then, that I put up with the dogma for the sake of the sentiment, but that I may possibly swallow the sentiment for the sake of the dogma. Very few since the Renascence have really understood the dogma, certainly very few inside the Churches of recent years. If they appear occasionally even fanatical about the very word of the dogma, that is only a secondary result of belief really grounded on sentiment. Certainly no humanist could understand the dogma. They all chatter about matters which are in comparison with this, quite secondary notions—God, Freedom, and Immortality.

*   *   *

The important thing about all this—which I hope to make clearer when I come to deal with its effect on literature[29]—is that this attitude is not merely a *constrasted* attitude, which I am interested in, as it were, for purpose of *symmetry* in historical exposition, but a real attitude, perfectly possible for us to-day. To see this is a kind of conversion. It radically alters our physical perception almost; so that the world takes on an entirely different aspect.

NOTES

Poetry

1. The version reproduced here is from *Ripostes*. The only difference between it and the *NA* version is that in *NA* there is a semicolon instead of a comma at the end of l. 5. The version in the Poets' Club anthology also has the semicolon; but there is no dash at the end of l. 1, and there is a comma at the end of l. 3.

2. Hulme sent F. S. Flint an early draft of this poem on 7 Sept. 1909: written on the back of a postcard from Exmouth, with Hulme's own crossings-out and emendations, the draft reads:

> Mana Aboda whose bent form
> The sky in arched circle is
>   s ever mourning
> Seem~~ed weeping~~ for a grief unknown,
>   cry
> Yet on a day, I heard her ~~whisper~~
> 'Damn the roses and the singer's poets
> Josephs all, not tall enough to *try*.'

The poem was accompanied by a hastily drawn sketch of a bent-over form supposed to represent the goddess of the poem. The revised version was first published as part of the 'Complete Poetical Works', and the *NA* and *Ripostes* versions are identical.

3. It is not clear when Hulme wrote this poem. It was first published in the 'Complete Poetical Works'. The versions in *NA* and *Ripostes* are identical, except that in *NA*, 'mid night' is written as one word.

4. The punctuation of the 1909 version differs slightly from the two 1912 versions: there is no comma at the end of l. 1, after 'Oh' in l. 5, or at the end of l. 6. The most important difference, though, is that l. 2 in the 1909 version reads: 'And in the flash of gold heels on the pavement grey' ('pavement grey' probably echoing Yeats's 'Lake Isle of Innisfree'). In the 1912 *NA* version the line was changed to: 'In the flash of gold heels on the pavement hard'. In a letter to Michael Roberts in 1938, Ezra Pound drew attention to the change from 'pavement grey' to 'pavement hard', clearly implying that he, Pound, had had something to do with it. When the poem finally appeared in *Ripostes* later in 1912, it had taken on a still more 'modern' look: 'In the flash of gold heels on the hard pavement'.

5. The only difference between the *Ripostes* and *NA* versions is that in *NA*, the first words of ll. 4 and 5 are not capitalized. In the 1909 version l. 3 reads: 'Till suddenly beauty like a scented cloth'.

6. First published in Jan. 1909 in *For Christmas MDCCCCVIII*, but not included in the 'Complete Poetical Works'. The version published in 1938 by Michael Roberts differs from the 1909 version in several ways: 'Earth seducing' in l. 1 is written as 'earth-seducing'; 'coquettes' replaces 'reigns' in l. 2; 'passer by' in l. 5 is hyphenated; the comma at the end of l. 9 is omitted; and 'heaven's jocund maid' in l. 10 appears as 'heaven's wanton'. In addition, in

Roberts, the poem is divided into three stanzas of 3, 4, and 7 lines respectively. There are, it should be noted, several versions of this poem in Hulme's notebooks now at the University of Keele Library. I have used the 1909 version, since it was the only one published during Hulme's lifetime.

7. Date of composition unknown; first published by Michael Roberts in appendix to *T. E. Hulme* (1938). In the course of three broadcasts on the BBC in July 1959, Ezra Pound, in an interview with D. G. Bridson, discussed how he came across Hulme's poem:

> I came on six lines of Hulme's the other day—no importance unless you think that it is important that a guy who has left only a few pages of poetry should have a style so unmistakable that you come on it and know that it's Hulme's.

8. Not published until included in appendix to Roberts's *T. E. Hulme*; date of composition unknown.

Cinders

1. Included as a note in fourth instalment of 'The Notebooks of T. E. Hulme'; in *S*, Read printed it as 'Preface' to the whole collection.
2. Jules de Gaultier (1858–1942), French philosopher. In 1909 Hulme saw him, together with Bergson, as part of the movement away from the construction of systems in metaphysics, and he devoted the third of his 'Searchers after Reality' articles to him. (This reference to de Gaultier was omitted in *S*.)
3. Aphra was to be the central figure of this work.

Notes on Language and Style

1. Hulme illustrates this with a sketch of an inverted U-shaped curve intersected by a straight horizontal line (the line of meaning).
2. Probably a reference to Hulme's notebook later published as 'Cinders'.
3. William Samuel Lilly, late Victorian and early twentieth-century British man of letters who wrote on literature and various social issues. Hulme discusses one of his books in 'The Art of Political Conversion'.
4. Material or matter (as used by Aristotle).
5. Hulme illustrates this with a series of five sketches in which mind, which is pictured as a sort of bubble growing out of the clay, gradually separates itself from the clay. In the last drawing, 'pure mind' is represented as a balloon or cloud floating above the flat, clay earth.
6. Concepts.
7. Hulme illustrates this with two drawings: one, a circular squiggle with half a dozen lines radiating out from it; and the other, a rectangle.
8. Hulme has a sketch of a small circle rolling inside another.

A Lecture on Modern Poetry

1. Henry Simpson, Scottish banker who founded the Poets' Club and was president from 1907 to 1930.

2. William Ernest Henley (1849–1903), late nineteenth-century British poet, editor, and critic, whose poetry included some impressionistic free verse.

3. Probably Catulle Mendès (1842–1909), Parnassian poet and man of letters.

4. Sully-Prudhomme, pseudonym of René François Armand Prudhomme (1839–1907), French poet and essayist, who went through a Parnassian phase as a poet.

5. Gustave Kahn (1859–1936), French poet who set out the principles of *vers libre* in his 'étude sur le vers libre', in *Premiers Poèmes* (Paris, 1897). In the paragraph on p. 50 which begins 'It must be admitted', Hulme is in large part paraphrasing Kahn.

6. Poem.

7. Jean-Marie Guyau (1854–88), French philosopher and writer on aesthetics. Hulme is here paraphrasing Guyau's *Les Problèmes de l'esthétique contemporaine* (Paris, 1884), 176. In the paragraph that follows, Hulme is paraphrasing Guyau's *L'Art au point de vue sociologique* (Paris, 1889), 86. It should be noted, however, that Hulme did not merely construct a mosaic from the works of writers like Guyau; rather, he put the borrowed materials into his own context, which was different from that of any of his sources. For a full discussion of Hulme's borrowings from Guyau, see K. E. Csengeri, 'T. E. Hulme's Borrowings from the French', *Comparative Literature*, 34/1 (Winter 1982), 16–27.

8. Sir William Watson (1858–1935), English poet who gained a certain reputation with *Wordsworth's Grave and Other Poems* (London, 1890) and *Lachrymae musarum* (London, 1892), but whose subsequent volumes were derivative and verbose.

9. Matter, as opposed to mind.

[Review of Tancrède de Visan's] *L'Attitude du lyrisme contemporain*

1. Hulme's introduction to modern French poetry seems to have been André Beaunier's *La Poésie nouvelle* (Paris, 1902). In addition to Émile Verhaeren, Henri de Régnier, Paul Fort, Maurice Maeterlinck, and Francis Vielé-Griffin, Beaunier discusses Rimbaud, Laforgue, Gustave Kahn, Jean Moréas, Stuart Merrill, Francis Jammes, and Max Elskamp—all of whom, he claimed, helped to bring new life and vigour into French poetry between 1885 and 1900.

2. Émile Littré (1801–81), French philosopher and linguist, who was a follower of Comte and at one time heir apparent to the movement; author of *Dictionnaire de la langue française* (Paris, 1863–77).

Romanticism and Classicism

1. Charles Maurras (1868–1952) and Pierre Lasserre (1867–1930) were leading members of the French reactionary political movement *L'Action française*. What Hulme liked about them was their opposition to 'romanticism'. In the spring of 1911, during the height of his interest in Bergson, Hulme met literary critic Pierre Lasserre, who endeavoured to prove to him that Bergson 'was nothing but the last disguise of romanticism' (for Hulme's account of the meeting, see 'Mr. Balfour, Bergson, and Politics'). Their meeting was a factor in Hulme's eventual rejection of Bergson.

2. Hugo de Vries (1848–1935), Dutch botanist.
3. A heresy which denied the transmission of original sin.
4. George M. Robertson, physician. His paper 'Reflex Speech' was read at a meeting of the Medico-Psychologist Association in Edinburgh on 10 Nov. 1887, and was printed in the *Journal of Mental Science*, Apr. 1888. Bergson refers to the work in *Matière et mémoire* (Paris, 1896).
5. From the 'screech-owl' passage in *The Duchess of Malfi*, IV. ii, usually given as 'groan' not 'moan'.
6. A line in 'Delight in Disorder'.

German Chronicle

1. At 68 Regent Street, not far from Piccadilly Circus; a popular meeting-place for writers and painters in pre-First World War London.
2. The date-line of 'The Old Vicarage, Grantchester' is '(Café des Westens, Berlin, May 1912)'.
3. 'Things the Germans Lack' is a chapter title in *Twilight of the Idols* (*Die Götzen-Dämmerung*, Leipzig, 1889).
4. Michael Georg Conrad (1846–1927), German critic, novelist, and editor; a pioneer theorist of German naturalism and a defender of Zola's work.
5. Heinrich Hart (1855–1906) and Julius Hart (1859–1930), leading theorists and critics in German naturalism.
6. 'To get free from Naturalism'.
7. Detlev von Liliencron, the name under which the German lyric poet Friedrich, Freiherr von Liliencron (1844–1909) published.
8. Richard Dehmel (1863–1920), German poet, representative of the transition from naturalism to classic restraint.
9. Max Dauthendey (1867–1918), German poet and novelist; an impressionistic and exotic writer.
10. A cultural review (1892–1919) founded by Stefan George, together with Hugo von Hofmannsthal, Paul Gerardy, and Karl August Klein; important in the literary history of the period.
11. Alfred Mombert (1872–1942), German poet not belonging to any particular school.
12. Peter Hille (1854–1904), German arch-bohemian poet, novelist, and playwright.
13. Otto Julius Bierbaum (1865–1910), German poet, novelist, critic, and bibliophile. In 1892 he published a book on Liliencron, and in 1895 founded the art magazine *Pan*.
14. Gustave Falke (1853–1916), German music teacher turned poet.
15. Arno Holz (1863–1929), German poet, literary theorist, and dramatist; contributed to German naturalism, but later published modernistic poetry.
16. Carl Spitteler (1845–1924), Swiss poet and novelist; remembered primarily for his epic *Olympischer Frühling* (4 vols., 1900–6).
17. Richard von Schaukal (1874–1942), Austrian poet, novelist, and essayist. Best known for his lyric poetry, his work is seen as illustrating the virtues of neat craftsmanship and restrained elegance.
18. Herbert Eulenberg (1876–1949), best known for his plays with sensational action directed against conventional society.
19. Paul Ernst (1866–1933), German playwright, prose-writer, and critic; a principal champion of neo-classicism.

20. Probably Samuel Lublinski (1868–1910), German critic who began as a dramatist and championed the move towards neo-classicism.
21. A radical artistic periodical published and edited by Herwarth Walden (pseudonym of Georg Levin) from 1910 to 1932 which supported expressionism in literature and painting.
22. *Die Aktion*, a political and (until 1918) literary journal published from 1911 to 1932, which was, along with *Der Sturm*, the leading journal of the German expressionist movement; contributors included Max Brod, Else Lasker-Schüler, and Franz Werfel.
23. Kurt Hiller (1885–1946). Ten of his poems were included in the anthology.
24. A series of volumes of verse planned by Rupert Brooke, Harold Monro, and Edward Marsh, five volumes of which appeared between 1912 and 1922. The poetry tended to be of a pastoral nature, and the term came later to have a pejorative sense. Included in the first volume were Brooke, W. H. Davies, Masefield, D. H. Lawrence, and Walter de la Mare.
25. Snobbery, or snootiness.
26. In addition to the poets Hulme discusses, S. Friedlaender, Ferdinand Hardekopf, Ludwig Rubiner, and Paul Zech were also included in the anthology.
27. Ernst Blass (1890–1939), a bank clerk turned journalist who wrote expressionistic poetry. Twelve of his poems were included in *Der Kondor*.
28. In this poem, Hulme has substituted 'ss' for 'ß' in *Weiss* (l. 4) and *grosse* (l. 8).
29. Else Lasker-Schüler (1869–1945), wife of Herwarth Walden, who was at the centre of the expressionist circle in Berlin. Ten of her poems were included in *Der Kondor*.
30. Hulme has substituted 'ss' for 'ß' in *Füsse* (l. 5), *Süsser* (l. 7), and *küsst* (l. 8).
31. Georg Heym (1887–1912), sometimes called 'the German Rimbaud' because of his obvious imitation of the French poet.
32. Contemporary English poet whose *Poems and Songs (Second Series)* was reviewed by Ezra Pound in *Poetry*, Oct. 1913.
33. In this poem entitled 'Berlin', Hulme has substituted 'ss' for the 'ß' used in *Der Kondor* in *russig* (l. 4), *Russ* (l. 7), and *liessen* (l. 12). Nine more of his poems are included in the anthology.
34. Hulme is quoting the first 2 lines of this 8-line poem. Ten of Drey's poems were included in *Der Kondor*.
35. René Schickele (1883–1940). Five of his poems were included in *Der Kondor*.
36. Hulme has substituted 'ss' for 'ß' in *stösst* (l. 3).
37. Franz Werfel (1890–1945). Although better known today for his prose fiction, ten of his poems were included in the anthology.
38. Alfred Lichtenstein (1889–1914), an early expressionist poet who died in the First World War, but whose poetry was not included in *Der Kondor*.
39. Max Brod (1884–1968), later to become world-famous as editor and biographer of his close friend Kafka. Five of his poems were included in *Der Kondor*.
40. René Schickele's *Weiß und Rot* (1910).
41. Herbert Grossberger. Three of his poems were included in *Der Kondor*.
42. Arthur Kronfeld. Five of his poems were included in *Der Kondor*.
43. Hulme did not in fact publish another chronicle. Not long after he returned to England from Germany in late 1913, he began to write about modern art.

The New Philosophy

1. What James says in full is: 'The struggle was vain; I found myself in an *impasse*. . . . I have now to confess (and this will probably re-animate your interest) that I should not now be emancipated, not now subordinate logic with so very light a heart, or throw it out of the deeper regions of philosophy to take its rightful and respectable place in the world of simple human practice, if I had not been influenced by a comparatively young and very original french writer, Professor Henri Bergson. Reading his works is what has made me bold' (*A Pluralistic Universe*, 208, 214).

2. Ibid. 265.

3. 'Gradual development', or 'becoming'.

4. 'Knowledge and becoming exclude one another.'

5. 'The immediately given'.

6. 'To philosophize is to invert the habitual direction of the work of thought' (Bergson, 'Introduction à la métaphysique', *Revue de métaphysique et de morale* (Jan. 1903), trans. Hulme as *An Introduction to Metaphysics* (London, 1913), 59).

7. Bergson, *Essai sur les données immédiates de la conscience* (Paris, 1889); *Matière et mémoire* (Paris, 1896); and *L'Évolution créatrice* (Paris, 1907).

8. 'Real duration'.

9. Bergson, *L'Évolution créatrice* (Paris, 1907), 23, trans. in James, *A Pluralistic Universe*, 236.

10. *L'Évolution créatrice*.

11. 'The vital or life-giving impulse'; the force hypothesized by Bergson as a source of causation and evolution in nature, independent of physical or chemical action.

Searchers after Reality—I: Bax

1. Ernest Belfort Bax (1854–1926), British philosopher and author of *The Roots of Reality* (London, 1907).

2. A term coined by J. E. Erdmann to describe the philosophy of Hegel as one which holds that only the rational is truly real. Bax preferred the term 'pallogism', claiming that the word 'panlogism' was 'less elegant' (see *Roots*, 26 n. 1).

3. In *Roots*, 148 n. 1, Bax writes:

It should perhaps once more be premised here that reality, *as opposed to abstraction*, is always identical with concreteness, that is, it implies a synthesis. It involves at least two elements. The synthesis cannot be reduced to less than the union of matter and form, of potentiality and actuality; or to that of the cardinal antithetics, namely, the alogical and the logical, which to me seem more comprehensive than either of the two former pairs. Reality, then, viewed in this connection, means nothing but the inseparable correlation of at least two ultimate terms as factors. We can distinguish those two elements in reflection, but they cannot be presented in consciousness as separate. Each is *by itself* an abstraction.

4. Ibid. 176.

Searchers after Reality—II: Haldane

1. Richard Burdon Haldane (1856–1928), British statesman who published several volumes on philosophy. His Gifford Lectures at St Andrews (1902–4) became the 2-vol. *Pathway to Reality* (London, 1903, 1904), which Hulme is here discussing.
2. *Esse est percipi*, meaning 'to be is to be perceived', is often taken to be an epitome of the metaphysics of Berkeley.
3. *Esse est intelligi*, meaning 'to be is to be understood'.
4. Haldane, *Pathway to Reality*, i. 58.

Searchers after Reality—III: Jules De Gaultier

1. Émile Boutroux (1845–1921), French philosopher of science.
2. Édouard Le Roy (1870–1954), French philosopher of science, ethics, and religion, whose thought was deeply indebted to Bergson.
3. In *Westminster and Foreign Quarterly Review*, NS 12 (1 Oct. 1857), 375–99.
4. Probably a reference to Bergson's *Introduction à la métaphysique*.
5. Although Hulme did not publish another full-length article on de Gaultier, he discussed him again in 'Notes on the Bologna Congress'.
6. A term derived from Flaubert's character Emma Bovary, used by Jules de Gaultier in his book *Bovarysme* (1892) to describe the process by which man invents reality.

Notes on the Bologna Congress

1. Formed in 1880, the Aristotelian Society of London met monthly from Nov. to June to hear papers and discuss various issues in philosophy. Hulme was admitted as a member on 6 June 1910. Other members at the time included G. E. Moore, Bertrand Russell, Henri Bergson, F. H. Bradley, William James, and R. B. Haldane; Samuel Alexander was president, and H. Wildon Carr honorary secretary. Carr attended the Congress as official representative of the Society; his report was published in *Proceedings of the Aristotelian Society*, 11 (1910–11), 223–6.
2. Federigo, Enriques (1871–1949), Italian mathematician and president of the Philosophical Society of Italy, 1905–13. His paper was entitled 'Il problema della realtà'.
3. 'A little dry bread is better than all of Shakespeare.'
4. Meeting room of the general session (of the Congress).

The International Philosophical Congress at Bologna

1. Émile Boutroux, whose paper was entitled 'Du rapport de la philosophie aux sciences'.
2. Edoardo Agostino (1878–1959), Italian psychologist. His paper was entitled 'Scienza e filosofia'.
3. Hans Adolf Eduard Driesch (1867–1941), the German biologist who is, after Bergson, the best-known twentieth-century vitalist.
4. Bergson's talk, entitled 'L'Intuition philosophique', was later published in *Revue de métaphysique et de morale* (Nov. 1911), 809–27.

5. His paper was entitled 'L'Évolution des lois'.

6. Paul Langevin (1872–1946), a leading practitioner and expositor of modern mathematical physics in France. His paper was entitled 'L'Évolution de l'espace et du temps'.

7. Émile Durkheim (1858–1917), French sociologist and philosopher. His paper was entitled 'Les Jugements de valeur et les jugements de réalité'.

8. Friedrich Wilhelm Ostwald (1853–1932), German chemist and recipient of the Nobel Prize for chemistry in 1909.

9. Ernst Mach (1838–1916), Austrian physicist and philosopher who is sometimes said to have initiated the systematic study of philosophy of science.

10. F. C. S. Schiller (1864–1937), the English pragmatist. His paper was reprinted in *Proceedings of the Aristotelian Society*, 11 (1910–11), 144–65.

11. Edward Stuart Russell (1857–1954), biologist. In a letter to his friend C. K. Ogden, editor of the *Cambridge Magazine*, early in 1912, Hulme mentioned lunching with Russell, and suggested the possibility of Russell's writing something on vitalism for Ogden (who was interested in the subject at the time). Russell contributed an article on vitalism to the *Cambridge Magazine* of 27 Apr. 1912.

12. E. E. Constance Jones of Girton College, Cambridge. Her paper, entitled 'A New Law of Thought', was reprinted in *Proceedings of the Aristotelian Society*, 11 (1910–11), 166–86. In Feb. 1912 she invited Hulme to Cambridge to deliver a lecture on Bergson at Girton College.

Bax on Bergson

1. F. L. Pogson published the authorized English translation of Bergson's *Essai sur les données immédiates de la conscience* as *Time and Free Will: An Essay on the Immediate Data of Consciousness* (London, 1910). Hulme's bibliography of books and articles by and about Bergson was appended to it.

2. E. Belfort Bax's essay-review of A. D. Lindsay's *The Philosophy of Bergson* (London, 1911) was published as 'Bergson', *NA* 9/12 (20 July 1911), 280.

3. For Hulme's essay-review of Bax's *Roots of Reality*, see 'Searchers after Reality—I: Bax'.

4. Paul Leroy-Beaulieu (1843–1916), French economist who became professor of political economy at the Collège de France in 1880.

5. See opening of 'Searchers after Reality—I: Bax'.

6. Bax's letter, 'Bergson and Bax', *NA* 5/10 (8 July 1909), 226.

7. Hulme's reply was published as 'Bergson and Bax', *NA* 5/12 (22 July 1909), 259.

8. His father, Pierre Eugène Marcellin (1827–1907), was a pioneer in modern organic chemistry. René Berthelot published *Évolutionisme et platonisme* (Paris, 1908).

9. Jean Gaspard Félix Ravaisson-Mollien (1813–1900), French spiritualist philosopher and art historian.

10. 'To make a chemistry of ideas' (corrected from Hulme's original 'faire la chimique des idées').

11. Rudolf Hermann Lotze (1817–81), German philosopher who thought that metaphysics must be founded on science and that all philosophical systems must remain open and undogmatic.

12. Reference to Haldane's Gifford Lectures, published as *The Pathway to Reality* and reviewed by Hulme in his second 'Searchers after Reality' article.
13. Andrew Seth Pringle-Pattison (1856–1931), Scottish philosopher.

Notes on Bergson

1. Bergson, *Essai sur les données immédiates de la conscience*.
2. Paul Cinquevalli (b. Poland 1859, d. UK 1918), probably the greatest juggler of the music-halls at the turn of the century.
3. The Right Hon. Arthur James Balfour, M. P. (1848–1930), British statesman and philosopher. His article on Bergson, entitled 'Creative Evolution and Philosophic Doubt', was published in the *Hibbert Journal*, 10 (Oct. 1911), 1–23.
4. A good many articles on Bergson appeared during Oct. and Nov. 1911, following Balfour's *Hibbert Journal* essay and the visit by Bergson himself to the University of London in late October. In the following paragraphs Hulme probably had particularly in mind the letters by Horace C. Simmons which appeared in *NA* for 2 and 16 Nov. 1911; he answered them more specifically in letters published in *NA* on 9 and 23 Nov. 1911.
5. Spinoza, *Ethics*, Part I: 'Of God', proposition 29.
6. Hugo Münsterberg (1863–1916), German-born psychologist who was invited by William James to Harvard, where he became professor of psychology and director of the Psychology Laboratories.
7. Laplace, 'Introduction à la théorie analytique des probabilités', in *Œuvres complètes* (Paris, 1886), vol. 7, p. vi; quoted in Bergson, *L'Évolution créatrice* (1907; Paris, 1989), 38.
8. Quoted in Bergson, *L'Évolution créatrice*, 38–9.
9. Harald Höffding (1843–1931), philosopher and professor at the University of Copenhagen. He claims that 'the conservation of value is *the characteristic axiom of religion*' several times in his *Religionsfilosofi* (Copenhagen, 1901), trans. B. E. Meyer as *Philosophy of Religion* (New York, 1906).
10. Johann Bernhard Stallo (1823–1900), German-born philosopher of science whose *Concepts and Theories of Modern Physics* (New York, 1881) questioned some of the assumptions of Newtonian physics.
11. From the point of view of eternity.
12. Letter by M. B. Oxon, *NA* 10/7 (14 Dec. 1911), 167.
13. Hulme is probably referring to Russell's 'A Free Man's Worship', first published in 1903 and since then reprinted many times.
14. Friedrich Albert Lange (1828–75), German philosopher and sociologist, important for his refutation of materialism and for establishing a tradition of neo-Kantian philosophy at the University of Marburg.

Mr. Balfour, Bergson, and Politics

1. A. J. Balfour's 'Creative Evolution and Philosophic Doubt', *Hibbert Journal*, Oct. 1911, pp. 1–23.
2. 'Mr. Balfour and M. Bergson', *Saturday Review*, 112 (7 Oct. 1911), 450–1.
3. 'Mr. Balfour as Philosopher', *Nation* (London), 14 Oct. 1911, pp. 85–6.
4. See *NA* 10/4 (23 Nov. 1911), 79–82; pp. 133–40 above.
5. By the Right Hon. Arthur James Balfour (New York and London, 1895).
6. Leighton J. Warnock, 'Pragmatism' [letter], *NA* 9/24 (12 Oct. 1911), 574–5.

7. Stephen Reynolds, 'An Introduction to "Seems So"', *NA* 9/23 (5 Oct. 1911), 541–3.

8. *La Mouvement socialiste* (1899–1914) was a French journal, which became a leading publication for the syndicalists after 1904. Sorel's *Réflexions sur la violence* was originally published here, as a series of articles in the first six months of 1906.

9. Hulme included George Batault's 'La Philosophie de M. Bergson', *Mercure de France*, 16 Mar. 1908, pp. 193–211, in his bibliography of works about Bergson that was appended to F. L. Pogson's translation of Bergson's *Time and Free Will* (London, 1910).

A Personal Impression of Bergson

1. Bergson.

2. Bergson's series of lectures at University College, London, on 20, 21, 27, and 28 Oct. 1911. For Hulme's account of his experiences at one of these lectures, see 'Bergson Lecturing'.

3. Fourth International Congress of Philosophy held in Bologna, 6–11 Apr. 1911. For Hulme's accounts of the Congress, see 'Notes on the Bologna Congress' and 'The International Philosophical Congress at Bologna'.

4. Hulme discusses Balfour's 'Creative Evolution and Philosophic Doubt' in 'Mr. Balfour, Bergson, and Politics'.

The Philosophy of Intensive Manifolds

1. *Essai sur les données immédiates de la conscience*, trans. into English as *Time and Free Will*. The Author's Preface (in translation) begins:

We necessarily express ourselves by means of words and we usually think in terms of space. That is to say, language requires us to establish between our ideas the same sharp and precise distinctions, the same discontinuity, as between material objects. This assimilation of thought to things is useful in practical life and necessary in most of the sciences. But it may be asked whether the insurmountable difficulties presented by certain philosophical problems do not arise from our placing side by side in space phenomena which to not occupy space.

2. Bergson, *An Introduction to Metaphysics*, trans. T. E. Hulme (London, 1913), 76.

Bergson's Theory of Art

1. Sir William Rothenstein (1872–1945), British painter, draughtsman, writer, and teacher, who later became principal of the Royal College, London.

2. Laurence Binyon, *The Flight of the Dragon; An Essay in the Theory and Practice of Art in China and Japan, Based on Original Sources* (London, 1911).

3. Bernhard Berenson, *The Florentine Painters of the Renaissance, with an Index to*

their Works (London, 1896). Hulme is paraphrasing Berenson in his explanation of how art can double the intensity with which we realise a given object, thereby giving us pleasure.

A Note on the Art of Political Conversion

1. G. Pezzolini also wrote on Bergson, and Hulme included two of his works in the bibliography that was appended to Pogson's translation of Bergson's *Time and Free Will*. In a letter dated 27 Nov. 1911 to his friend C. K. Ogden, Hulme also refers to Pezzolini's work on Georges Sorel, in whom Hulme was then becoming interested.
2. Rudolf Christoph Eucken (1846–1926), German philosopher, who saw life as organized into 'systems'.
3. Georg Simmel (1858–1918), German philosopher and sociologist, who conceived of life as a process ('more-life').
4. Gustave Le Bon, *La Psychologie des foules* (Paris, 1895). The English translation, which has gone through several printings since 1896, is entitled *The Crowd*.
5. (London, 1909).
6. James Louis Garvin (1868–1947), editor of *Outlook* (1905–6), *Pall Mall Gazette* (1912–15), and the *Observer* (1908–42); he made the *Observer* a political force.
7. Jean Jaurès (1859–1914), French pacifist and leader of the Socialist party, who was opposed to the more violent tactics proposed by syndicalism.
8. Sir Edward Grey of Fallodon, viscount (1862–1933), British statesman, Liberal leader in the House of Lords, and Foreign Minister (1905–16).
9. Pierre Eugène Marcellin Berthelot (1827–1907), French chemist and statesman.
10. Probably Charles Maurras, *Enquête sur la Monarchie* (Paris, 1909).

The Art of Political Conversion

1. 'A Note on the Art of Political Conversion'.
2. Harold Cox (1859–1936), economist and journalist, Liberal member of Parliament (1906–9), editor of *Edinburgh Review* (1912–29). He collaborated with Sidney Webb in *Eight Hours Day* (1891), though he later opposed Socialism and wrote *Economic Liberty* (1920).
3. Sir Charles Stewart Loch (1849–1923), social worker. As secretary to the Council of Charity Organisation Society (1875–1914), he made the Society's influence felt in social legislation.
4. W. S. Lilly, *Idola Fori* (London, 1911) discussed such current political topics as popular government, the 'social question', the Indian question, and the Irish question.
5. Sir Frederick Banbury (1850–1936), Conservative member of Parliament for Peckham division (1892–1906) and City of London (1906–24), authority on finance and an uncompromising champion of the old order.

On Progress and Democracy

1. W. M. Flinders Petrie, *Revolutions of Civilisation* (1911; New York and London, 1922), 2.
2. Ibid. 124.

Theory and Practice

1. Probably the economic theorist Carl Menger (1840–1921).
2. By Oscar Wilde (London, 1904).
3. Probably the Bishop of Caesarea (*c.*260–*c.*339), called Father of Church History.

A Tory Philosophy

1. This sentence is not in Hulme's typescript, though it was added to the published version of the essay in the *Commentator*.
2. Goldsworthy Lowes Dickinson (1862–1932), English humanist and philosophical writer; lecturer in political science at Cambridge, 1896–1920.
3. A[lfred] W[illiam] Benn, *The Greek Philosophers* (London, 1882).
4. A slightly edited version of ibid. 320–1.
5. Ibid. 321; a continuation of the passage above, except that Benn capitalized the word 'Philosophy' and has 'paths' instead of 'powers'.
6. Hulme takes up the subject of progress in the preface to his translation of Georges Sorel's *Reflections on Violence*. But while he may in 1912 have already been working on the translation, the book, complete with his preface, was not published until 1916.
7. Hulme did not publish any further articles on this subject.

Translator's Preface to Georges Sorel's *Reflections on Violence*

1. '. . . if by mistake, nature had made man an animal exclusively industrious and sociable, and not warlike, he would have fallen, on the first day, to the level of animals, the association to which forms all destiny; he would have lost, with the pride of his heroism, his revolutionary faculty, the most marvelous of all and the most fruitful. Living in a Rousseauesque type of society, our civilization would be a pig-sty. Philanthropist, you speak of abolishing war, take care of degrading the human being.'
2. Georges Sorel, *Les Illusions du progrès* (Paris, 1908).
3. Léon Duguit (1859–1928), French jurist and political theorist.
4. Georges Sorel, *Le Procès de Socrate* (Paris, 1889).

Mr. Epstein and the Critics

1. *Athenaeum*, no. 4493 (6 Dec. 1913), 665.
2. 'Art Notes', by E.M., *Illustrated London News*, 13 Dec. 1913.
3. Artists' society founded in London in 1886, whose members included Walter Sickert, Augustus John, and Philip Wilson Steer.
4. Epstein's drawing *Rock Drill*, published on p. 256 (of *NA* 14/8 (25 Dec. 1913)), was meant to accompany Hulme's article.
5. Anthony M. Ludovici's review of current London art shows, including that of Epstein's works, appeared in *NA* 14/7 (18 Dec. 1913), 213–15. Hulme's attack on Ludovici led to a controversy in *NA* through the early months of 1914.
6. *Nietzsche and Art* (London, 1911).
7. *From a Gondola*.

8. *The Masquerades.*
9. Philip Wilson Steer (1860–1942), a founding member of the New English Art Club. Glehn, Well, and Steer were all part of the New English Exhibition.

Modern Art I: The Grafton Group

1. Hulme is reviewing an exhibition of the Grafton group, one of the coteries of pre-First World War artists in London. It was formed from two other groups, the Friday Club (whose chief figures were Roger Fry, Vanessa Bell, and Duncan Grant) and the Camden Town group (which included Walter Sickert, Harold Gilman, Charles Ginner, and Wyndham Lewis). In the autumn of 1913, Lewis and some of the other avant-garde artists broke away from the Grafton group and formed a new coterie, which by 1914 was called the London group.
2. Roger Fry (1866–1934), English artist who organized the first major Post-Impressionist Exhibition in London in 1910. His second Post-Impressionist Exhibition in 1912 included an English section, with paintings by Fry, Spencer Gore, Duncan Grant, Edward Wadsworth, and Wyndham Lewis, all of whom belonged, for a time in 1913, to the Grafton group. Fry noticed Hulme's article, and sent it to his friend Duncan Grant, with a note: 'The Lewis group have got hold of the *New Age* critic and he's written an amazing thing which I send to you; please sent it back' (*Letters of Roger Fry*, ed. Denys Sutton (New York, 1972), ii. 378).
3. Frederick Etchells (1886–1973), English painter, architect, and designer. He contributed to the Second Post-Expressionist Exhibition in 1912, and also participated in the London Vorticist Exhibition in 1915.
4. Christopher Richard Wynne Nevinson (1889–1946). Although his later work was more conventional, he was a leading exponent of futurism in painting during this time. Hulme included one of Nevinson's drawings in his 'Contemporary Drawings' series.
5. William Roberts (1895–1980), English painter. He became a member of the Vorticist movement. Hulme included one of Roberts's drawings in his 'Contemporary Drawings' series.
6. French sculptor, Henri Gaudier (1891–1915), who added his Polish mistress's name to his own to become Henri Gaudier-Brzeska. He and Jacob Epstein were the most stylistically advanced sculptors in pre-First World War London. Hulme included his drawing *A Dancer* in his 'Contemporary Drawings' series.
7. See 'Mr. Epstein and the Critics'.
8. Duncan Grant (1885–1978), English painter, designer, and decorator. He contributed to the Second Post-Impressionist Exhibition in 1912, and exhibited at the New English Art Club and also with the London group.

Modern Art and Its Philosophy

1. Hulme and the other participants at the 1911 International Philosophical Congress at Bologna were taken as guests of the Italian government to Ravenna and the old Roman port of Classe, where they visited such monu-

ments as the church of San Vitale and the mausoleum of Galla Placidia, both famous for their mosaics and stonework. Hulme mentions the mosaics of Ravenna later in the lecture.

2. Alois Riegl (1858–1905), Austrian art historian and professor of history of art, remembered mainly as originator of the concept of *Kunstwollen* ('will to form'). He claimed that every work of art was produced to satisfy some innate desire, and that stylistic differences were due to different mental demands rather than to differences in materials or techniques.

3. Jean Metzinger (1883–1956), French painter and writer on art. He is remembered mainly as the co-author with Albert Gleizes (1881–1953) of *Du cubisme* (1912), generally regarded as the most important exposition of the theoretical principles of the cubist aesthetic.

Modern Art—II: A Preface Note and Neo-Realism

1. Contemporary painter Charles Ginner (1879–1952) published an article entitled 'Neo-Realism', *NA* 14/9 (1 Jan. 1914), 271–2.

2. 'Can be reduced to a cone, a cylinder and a sphere'; quoted also by Ginner (Ibid. 271).

3. Ibid. 272, 271.

Modern Art—III: The London Group

1. See 'Modern Art—I: The Grafton Group', n. 1.

2. Spencer Gore (1878–1914), English painter. He was the first president of the Camden Town group in 1911, exhibited in the Second Post-Impressionist Exhibition in 1912, and became a member of the London group in 1913.

3. Harold Gilman (1876–1919), English painter. He was a member of Sickert's circle, a founder of the Camden Town group, and the first president of the London group.

4. See 'Modern Art—II: A Preface Note and Neo-Realism'.

5. Robert Bevan (1865–1925), English painter and a founding member of the Camden Town group and the London group.

6. See 'Modern Art—I: The Grafton Group'.

7. Edward Wadsworth (1881–1949), English painter and graphic artist. He worked for a short time with Roger Fry at the Omega Workshops, and was then associated with Wyndham Lewis and the Vorticist group. Hulme included one of Wadsworth's drawings in his 'Contemporary Drawing' series.

8. Cuthbert Hamilton (1884–1959), English painter. He exhibited in the Second Post-Impressionist Exhibition, became a member of the London group in 1913, and was associated with Wyndham Lewis and the Vorticists.

9. Hulme included Nevinson's study of this work in his 'Contemporary Drawings' series.

10. David Bomberg (1890–1957), English painter and founding member of the London group. Hulme devoted the fourth of his 'Modern Art' series to his work.

Contemporary Drawings

1. Walter Sickert edited a series of 'Modern Drawings' by the Camden Town group in *NA* from Jan. to June 1914.

2. *Chinnereth.*
3. William Roberts's *Study.*
4. *The Farmyard.*
5. For Hulme's comments on Nevinson's painting, see 'Modern Art—III: The London Group'.

Modern Art—IV: Mr. David Bomberg's Show

1. Short-lived centre in London, organized in 1914 by Wyndham Lewis and fellow artist and friend Kate Lechmere. Although intended as a centre for lectures, plays, exhibitions, and afternoon and evening meetings between artists, it closed within a few months of opening when Lewis turned his energies to Vorticism and *Blast.*
2. In *NA* for 2 Apr. 1914, as part of Hulme's 'Contemporary Drawings' series.

Diary from the Trenches

1. Alice Pattinson, who took a special interest in Hulme, and even helped to support him when he was in London.
2. Jack Johnson was a famous Black pugilist of the time.
3. Sir Horace Lockwood Smith-Dorrien (1858–1930), British general who commanded various forces during the First World War.
4. Dunwood Hall, in Staffordshire, where Hulme's grandparents lived; not far from Gratton Hall, Hulme's birthplace.
5. I am not sure of the accuracy of this date. Hulme was, according to army records, wounded on 14 Apr. 1915, sent home, and admitted to St Mark's College Hospital, Chelsea, on 19 Apr. He did not return to active service until he was granted a commission in the Royal Marines Artillery in Mar. 1916.

War Notes

1. At the outbreak of the First World War, the German social philosopher Max Scheler became an ardent nationalist, and wrote *Der Genius des Krieges und der deutsche Krieg* (Leipzig, 1915).
2. Edith Louisa Cavell (1865–1915), British nurse; first matron of Berkendael Medical Institute, Brussels, 1907, which was subsequently organized as a Red Cross hospital in 1914. She was arrested by the Germans on 5 Aug. 1915, and pleaded guilty to charges of sheltering their enemies. She was court-martialled and shot on 11 Oct. 1915, after saying, 'Let there be no bitterness.'
3. British military man Sir Henry Seymour Rawlinson (1864–1925) was sent to Belgium early in Oct. 1914 to take command of two divisions being landed at Zeebrugge and Ostend for the relief of Antwerp. He arrived too late, however, and the city fell to the Germans on 10 Oct. He later led the IV Corps at the battle of Neuve Chapelle in Mar. 1915, and for the remainder of that year guided it at Aubers Ridge, Festubert, and Loos. (See n. 19 re Festubert and n. 11 re Loos.) Rawlinson commanded several other divisions during the war, and was promoted to general in Jan. 1917.
4. Aristide Briand (1862–1932), French statesman, Premier, and Foreign Minister. He was an early and violent critic of France's concentration of men and energies on the Western front. In Jan. 1915 he and Premier Viviani urged

General Joffre (see n. 20 re Joffre) to implement a Balkan offensive; and in Oct. he succeeded Viviani as Premier, and assumed the post of Foreign Minister.

5. Théophile Delcassé (1857–1923), French statesman. His career as Foreign Minister during the early years of the First World War was controversial. In Oct. 1915 he stood alone in the cabinet against landing a large French expeditionary force in Salonika; he resigned on 12 Oct. 1915, after which Briand replaced Viviani, and committed France to a Balkan front.

6. Possibly John Buchan, first Baron Tweedsmuir (1873–1940), journalist, author, and later governor-general of Canada, who became a major in the Intelligence Corps in 1916.

7. Albert Thomas (1878–1932), French statesman; a Socialist.

8. The first battle of Aisne was the Allied attack on the German positions from 13 to 28 Sept. 1914. The British and French forces were under Field Marshall Joseph Joffre.

9. There was a good deal of debate during the First World War over conscription. The Spanish political theorist, Ramiro de Maeztu, who published a series of articles about the war in *NA* at the time, knew Hulme and mixed in his circle. In *Authority, Liberty and Function in the Light of War* (London and New York, 1916), de Maeztu acknowledged his debt to Hulme for the idea 'of the political and social transcendency of the doctrine of original sin' (p. 5).

10. Scene of unsuccessful British attack, 10–13 Mar. 1915. This failure contributed to a public outcry in England about the shortage of shells on the Western front.

11. French village, a suburb of Lens, where between 25 Sept. and 8 Oct. 1915, the British and French took the offensive against Germany; but little ground was gained, and the British suffered great losses.

12. Part of the unsuccessful British Balkan campaign in 1915.

13. Scene of French offensives in Sept. 1914.

14. Horatio Herbert Kitchener, 1st earl (1850–1916), British general. As field marshal and War Minister, he helped organize the British army in 1914.

15. Jean Froissart (1337–1410), French chronicler; his history of 1325–1400 was among the first published books.

16. Afterwards Lord Allen of Hurtwood; at the time, chairman of the No Conscription Fellowship. He was imprisoned as a conscientious objector three times.

17. Arthur Cecil Pigou (1877–1959), professor of political economy at Cambridge 1908–43. Though best known for his contributions to the theory of economic welfare, he was active in social causes, and protested against conscription in the First World War.

18. See 'Diary from the Trenches' for Hulme's own experiences at the front.

19. French village which was the scene of an unsuccessful British offensive against the Germans, 9–24 May 1915.

20. Joseph Jacques Césaire Joffre (1852–1931), field marshal of France; commander-in-chief, 1914; with supreme command of all French armies, 1915.

21. Karl Ernst von Baer (1792–1876), Russian biologist, noted for his research in embryology.

22. Henry Ireton (1611–51), English parliamentary general and regicide; Cromwell's son-in-law; a prime mover in Pride's Purge.

23. Maurice Barrès (1862–1923), French writer and publicist.

24. Werner Sombart (1863–1941), German economist and social theorist, professor of economics in Berlin 1906–31.

25. It is not clear when Hulme heard him lecture, but it was probably during one of his two sojourns in Germany, in 1912 or 1913.

26. 'Profound'.

27. Lord Grey of Fallodon, Edward, viscount.

28. Theobald von Bethmann-Hollweg (1856–1921), German statesman; Imperial Chancellor, 1909–17.

29. 'Living growth'.

30. Bernard Bosanquet (1848–1923), English philosopher, who had an 'organic' theory of the state and thought that there was a correlation between the individual and social worlds such that for every element in one there was a corresponding element in the other.

31. Report regarding the unsuccessful British military expedition in the Dardanelles in 1915.

32. Unidentified, but probably a British government or military spokesman or politician; possibly Harold John Tennant, Liberal MP.

33. Sir Ian Hamilton (1853–1947), British general who commanded the Mediterranean Expeditionary Force in the Dardanelles in 1915. His account of the operation was later published in his *Gallipoli Diary* (2 vols.; London and New York, 1920).

34. Named after Lord Derby (Edward George Villiers Stanley), director of recruiting in 1915–16. He favoured voluntary service, and proposed a system whereby all eligible single men between the ages of 18 and 41 be enrolled for possible enlistment. The scheme had failed by Dec. 1915, as only one-half of the eligible two million single men ever bothered to register. On 5 Jan. 1916 Prime Minister Herbert Asquith agreed to enact the first Military Service Act, calling up single men under the age of 41. The full Conscription Act was not passed until Mar. 1918.

35. Shirker.

36. Fought between a small German/African force and a very large Allied force, 4 Aug. 1914–25 Nov. 1918.

37. Richard Burdon, Secretary of State for War, 1905–12, and Lord Chancellor, 1912–15; he left office in 1915.

38. Clive Bell (1881–1964), English critic and aesthetician.

39. Clive Bell, *Art* (London, 1914). All the quotations in the section that follows are from this book.

40. Gaius Mæcenas (*c*.78–3 BC), Roman statesman and patron of artists and writers. Bell is sometimes seen, with Roger Fry, as largely responsible for propagating in Great Britain an appreciation of Post-Impressionist painters, especially Cézanne.

41. Popular English novelist (1891–192c).

42. 'Philanthropist, you speak of abolishing war, take care of degrading the human being.'

43. An edited version of this instalment (beginning with the sentence 'When the pacifist' in para. 16) was published in the *Cambridge Magazine* of 22 Jan. with the subtitle 'On "Liberty"'.

44. In April 1915, while serving in the trenches, Hulme was wounded, and sent home to hospital. He did not return to active service until Mar. 1916, when

he was granted a commission as temporary second lieutenant in the Royal Marines Artillery.

45. Sir Ian Hamilton's Dardanelles report.
46. Lord Derby's figures regarding the recruiting of men.
47. Series of parliamentary acts passed during 1914–15 to enable Britain's government to make regulations 'for public safety and defence' during the war. The first of these acts was passed in Aug. 1914, and successive acts broadened the scope of the regulations.
48. The Munitions of War Act (1915) was a 'Treasury agreement' negotiated between the government and the trade unions, relaxing trade practices and accepting compulsory arbitration.
49. Max Scheler, *Der Genius des Krieges und der deutsche Krieg* (Leipzig, 1915).
50. Friedrich von Bernhardi (1849–1930), German general and military writer. His *Germany and the Next War* (Stuttgart, 1912) was translated into English by Allen H. Powles (London and New York, 1914).
51. A condensed version of this instalment was published in the *Cambridge Magazine* for 29 Jan., beginning with the sentence 'I think the writer' (para. 3). It was subtitled 'Inevitability Inapplicable'.
52. Bertrand Russell, 'The Philosophy of Pacifism', 9.
53. '*Environment* for *world*'.
54. Alfred North Whitehead (1861–1947), English mathematician and philosopher, who collaborated with Bertrand Russell on *Principia Mathematica* (1910–13).
55. Bertrand Russell gave a series of lectures under the title 'Principles of Social Reconstruction' in London for eight consecutive weeks from 18 Jan. to 7 Mar. 1916. Hulme discusses Russell's views in some detail in his Notes for 3 Feb. 1916.
56. A condensed version of this instalment was published in the *Cambridge Magazine* for 5 Feb., with the subtitle 'The Kind of Rubbish We Oppose'. It provoked a reply from Russell in the *Cambridge Magazine*, 5/13 (12 Feb. 1916), 305–7. Reading Russell's reply, Hulme wrote to Ogden:

I am glad that Russell has replied, particularly as it's a letter that quite gives him away. It came too late however for me to say anything this week. But next week I will send you a careful reply. It will be next week's article. I shall print Russell's letter in next week's New Age Press Cuttings so that I can refer to it conveniently.

Hulme replied publicly to Russell in his *NA* 'War Notes' for 24 Feb. (reprinted in the *Cambridge Magazine* for 26 Feb.).

57. 'What is certain is that to end the war it is necessary first to understand it.'
58. Series of lectures in Boston in Mar. and Apr. 1914, published as *Our Knowledge of the External World* (Chicago, 1914).
59. 'It seems that as soon as one leaves the domain of mathematics, his thought falls prey to a sort of bewilderment made worse by a lack of knowledge of human nature.'
60. A slightly edited version of this instalment appeared in the *Cambridge Magazine* for 12 Feb. under the title 'Why We Are in Favour of This War: The Case Against "Another Cucumber Sandwich"'.
61. Probably Robert Peel Glanville Blatchford (1851–1943), journalist, author, and socialist.

62. A slightly edited version of this instalment appeared in the *Cambridge Magazine* for 19 Feb. under the title 'The Framework of Europe: "North Staffs" on the Distorting Effects of History'.

63. Max Scheler. For Hulme's discussion of Scheler's book, see his 'War Notes' for 20 Jan.

64. Added on to the end of the last paragraph was the following passage, not included in *NA*:

> But we ought to get rid of this distorting effect of history on our minds. We, ourselves, have not had for centuries any desire to conquer any part of Europe, and we find it difficult to grasp the fact that other nations are really moved by this desire. This particular difficulty is considerably increased by the malign influence of school histories. These books so consistently represent our own acquisitions as the accidental and undesired results of the triumph of virtue over vice, that we remain ignorant not only of the amount of calculation and brute force that went to the making of the *colonial* empire, but also find it difficult to realise the fact, that at the present moment others may be thinking of creating a *European* empire by similar methods.

65. An edited version of this instalment was published in the *Cambridge Magazine* of 26 Feb. under the title 'North Staffs Resents Mr. Russell's Rejoinder'. The two versions are almost identical except for the ending.

66. Hulme is probably referring to William MacDougall, *Introduction to Social Psychology* (London, 1908).

67. 'The Elements of Ethics', in *Philosophical Essays* (1910; New York, 1966), 52, 20.

68. Hulme rewrote the last few paragraphs for Ogden, beginning just after the quotations from Russell's *Philosophical Essays*. The *CM* version ends thus:

> I may, perhaps, make the course of this argument clearer by putting it diagrammatically. I claim that the dispute is presented by Mr. Russell as one between
>
> Pacifist Ethics and Warlike Impulses,
> whereas it ought to be between
> Pacifist Ethics and Warlike Ethics.
>
> Mr. Russell replies that *Warlike* ethics are merely quasi-rational grounds for indulgence of *Warlike* Impulse.
> I reply that the same may be true of *Pacifist* ethics.
> He then says the dispute is between
> Pacifist Impulse and Warlike Impulse.
>
> If he merely means this as psychology, then it may be true, but is irrelevant. If meant literally it leads to complete ethical scepticism.
>
> *   *   *
>
> It seems, then, as if Mr. Russell had entirely abandoned the *objective* conception of ethics; but I think it is possible to show that this is a change that might have been expected. The essay referred to above expresses agreement with a certain reaction against hedonist and utilitarian ethics. Now a *complete* reaction of this kind would accomplish two things.
>
> (1) The establishment of the *objective* character of ethical values.
> (2) The establishment of a *new* hierarchy amongst particular values.

I say 'new' for I regard it as demonstrable that there is some connection between the view of the nature of value we take and the order in which we range different values, so that a change in the first is likely, *when it is thoroughly realised*, to produce a change in the second. Now the criticism I should formerly have made of Mr. Russell is that, while he had completely broken with the utilitarian tradition in the first matter, he continued it quite uncritically in the second. This is perhaps clearer when put more concretely. The utilitarian view of the nature of the good is accompanied by a hierarchy amongst the values, and an *ideology*, which follow naturally from it. If you refuse to look on any values as objective and absolute, and can only give them meaning in relation to *Life*, then you are naturally led to a pacifist ethic. I admit this entirely. Herbert Spencer's pacifism, for example, was a perfectly logical development from his conception of the nature of the 'good'. But Mr. Russell used to hold a very different view of the nature of ethical values. It is then somewhat surprising that the account he gives of war as an atavism is almost identical with that given by Spencer in his Ethics. It is possible, then, to look on this combination of an acceptance of all the utilitarian values with a rejection of utilitarianism itself, as unstable and bound to lead to either (1) the course apparently taken by Mr. Russell. Perhaps suspecting instinctively that the *objective* conception of ethics might lead to the establishment of values he would call reactionary, and knowing the *liberal, pacifist, progressive* values to be in this region, the things about which he felt most certain—he dropped the *objective* conception. Or (2) the abandonment of the pacifist utilitarian hierarchy of values.

I postulate here, without proof, that there is a connection between the view held about the nature of value and the order in which the values are ranged; and that consequently the conviction that certain values are *not* relative to life might lead to an ethic which was by no means necessarily pacifist. Without proof this must necessarily appear unconvincing. But for my purpose here, all that it is necessary for me to do, is to make it clear that the difference between my view of war and that taken by pacifists does (rightly or wrongly) spring from a difference about ethics—a difference about the order in which values should be placed. What I also want to make clear, later, is that this difference is extremely important in matters which have nothing to do with the war. It lies at the root of the objections we should make, for example, to all the proposals in Mr. Russell's other lectures—on education, marriage, etc. Most important of all it leads, as we see in the case of Proudhon and Sorel, to a profoundly different conception of democracy.

The piece provoked another reply from Russell. Entitled 'North Staffs' Praise of War', it appeared in *CM*, 5/17 (11 Mar. 1916), 368. Both Russell's rejoinders have been reprinted in *FS* and in Bertrand Russell, *Prophecy and Dissent, 1914–16*, ed. Richard A. Rempel (London, 1988), 324–6.

69. An edited version of these Notes was published in the *Cambridge Magazine* for 4 Mar. as 'North Staffs Continues Where He Left Off'.
70. Alexander Bain (1818–1903), Scottish philosopher and psychologist.
71. Jean Henri Fabre (1823–1915), French entomologist who made many interesting discoveries about insect life.

A Notebook

1. Pierre Loti (1850–1923), pseudonym of Louis Marie Julien Viaud, French naval officer, novelist, and author of travel books. *Pêcheur d'Islande* (1886; trans. as *An Iceland Fisherman*) was a novel about the life of Breton fishermen.
2. From Pascal, *Pensées* (Brunschvig edition), fragment 233.
3. Hulme seems to have borrowed 1 vol. of Husserl's 2-vol. *Logische Untersuchungen* (Halle, 1900–1) from his friend C. K. Ogden, but to have had the other vol. already in his possession (undated letter from Hulme to Ogden, courtesy of the late Frank Ogden).
4. The full title of Scheler's work is *Zur Phänomenologie und Theorie der Sympathie-gefühle und von Liebe und Hass* (Halle, 1913).
5. 'Into your eye I gaze, O Life!'
6. In *Logos*, 1 (1910–11), 289–314.
7. Alexius Meinong (1853–1920), Austrian philosopher and psychologist, remembered for his *Gegenstandstheorie*, or theory of objects, and for his contribution to axiology, or the theory of values.
8. Hermann Cohen, *Die Logik der reinen Erkenntnis* (Berlin, 1902). It is not clear when Hulme heard Cohen lecture; it does not seem to have been at either the 1911 Philosophical Congress in Bologna or the 1913 Aesthetics Congress in Berlin; it would probably have been during one of Hulme's two visits to Germany, in 1912 or 1913.
9. See notes to 'Notes on Bergson' above.
10. Giordano Bruno (1548–1600), the most famous of the Italian Renaissance philosophers, who travelled widely in Europe to escape persecution for his cosmological beliefs.
11. Justin Martyr (*c*.100–*c*.165), foremost second-century Christian apologist.
12. Marcus Minucius Felix (*c*.260–300), Christian apologist.
13. Porphyry (*c*.232–304), Greek philosopher and student of religion.
14. Jacob Böhme (1575–1624), Protestant visionary and theologian.
15. Husserl's 'Philosophie als strenge Wissenschaft', in *Logos*.
16. From 'On Scientific Method in Philosophy' (1914; repr. in *The Philosophy of Logical Atomism and Other Essays, 1914–19*, ed. John G. Slater (London, 1986), 57, 64, 72–3).
17. From 'Philosophie als strenge Wissenschaft', in *Logos*, 1 (1910–11); repr. as *Philosophie als strenge Wissenschaft* (Frankfurt, 1965), 61.
18. Hulme began his studies at St John's College, Cambridge, in 1902, having received an Open Mathematics Exhibition. He did not graduate, however, because he was sent down in 1904 for rowdy behaviour. It has been suggested that he continued to travel to Cambridge between 1904 and 1906 to attend, unofficially, lectures in philosophy. He was readmitted to St John's in the spring of 1912. Though his life was quieter upon his return to Cambridge, and he was more devoted to work, questions over his supposed sexual interest in H. Wildon Carr's daughter resulted in his not returning that autumn to finish his degree.
19. 'The Nature of Judgment', in *G. E. Moore: The Early Essays*, ed. Tom Regan (Philadelphia, 1986), 67. Essay was first published in *Mind*, NS 8 (Apr. 1899), 176–93.
20. Bernard Bolzano (1781–1848), Czech philosopher and mathematician.
21. Pico della Mirandola.

22. Lorenzo Valla (1407–1457), Italian humanist, whose early work *De Voluptate* (*On Pleasure*) gave him a reputation for hedonism.
23. Girolamo Cardano (1501–76), Italian physician and mathematician. His autobiography was published by Gabriel Naudé as *De propria vita liber* . . . (Paris, 1643; 2nd edn., Amsterdam, 1654).
24. Juan Luis Vives (1492–1540), Spanish humanist, tutor to William de Croy, the boy Archbishop of Toledo, and to Mary of England.
25. Bernardino Telesio (1509–88), Italian scientific philosopher and author of *De rerum natura iuxta propria principia* (Rome, 1565).
26. Jean-Baptiste Greuze (1725–1805), French painter who won enormous popularity with his sentimental and melodramatic genre scenes.
27. Fate.
28. Probably James Frederick Ferrier (1808–64), Scottish metaphysician.
29. Hulme did not in fact publish any more on the subject. He was granted a commission in the Royal Marines Artillery on 20 Mar. 1916, and was killed in action a year and a half later.

A BIBLIOGRAPHY OF HULME'S WORKS

1909

'Autumn' and 'A City Sunset', in *For Christmas MDCCCCVIII*, by the Poets' Club. London: Women's Printing Society, [Jan. 1909].

'Belated Romanticism', *New Age*, 4/17 (18 Feb. 1909), 350. [Letter]*

'The New Philosophy', *New Age*, 5/10 (1 July 1909), 198–9.

'Bergson and Bax', *New Age*, 5/12 (22 July 1909), 259. [Letter]*

'Searchers after Reality—I: Bax', *New Age*, 5/13 (29 July 1909), 265–6.

'Searchers after Reality—II: Haldane', *New Age*, 5/17 (19 Aug. 1909), 315–16.

'A Note on "La Foi"', *New Age*, 5/27 (28 Oct. 1909), 482–3. [Letter]*

'Searchers after Reality—III: Jules de Gaultier', *New Age*, 6/5 (2 Dec. 1909), 107–8.

'A Conversion' and 'The Embankment', in *The Book of the Poets' Club*. London, Christmas 1909.

1910

Bibliography, in *Time and Free Will*, by Henri Bergson, trans. F. L. Pogson. London: Swan Sonnenschein, 1910; New York: Macmillan, 1910. [Unsigned]

'A Metaphysics Group', *New Age*, 7/8 (23 June 1910), 187. [Letter]*

1911

'A Note on the Art of Political Conversion', *Commentator*, 2 (22 Feb. 1911), 234; (1 Mar. 1911), 250; (8 Mar. 1911), 266–7. [Signed 'Thomas Gratton']

'The Art of Political Conversion', *Commentator*, 2 (19 Apr. 1911), 357–8. [Signed 'Thomas Gratton']

'Notes on the Bologna Congress', *New Age*, 8/26 (27 Apr. 1911), 607–8.

'The International Philosophical Congress at Bologna', *Nature*, 86 (18 May 1911), 399–400. [Unsigned]

'Bergsonism in Paris', *New Age*, 9/8 (22 June 1911), 189–90. [Letter signed 'T. E. H.']*

'On Progress and Democracy', *Commentator*, 3 (2 Aug. 1911), 165–6; (9 Aug. 1911), 179–80. [Signed 'Thomas Grattan' [*sic*]]

'Bax on Bergson', *New Age*, 9/14 (3 Aug. 1911), 328–31.

[Review of] *L'Attitude du lyrisme contemporain* by Tancrède de Visan, *New Age*, 9/17 (24 Aug. 1911), 400–1.

'A Metaphysic Group', *New Age*, 9/24 (12 Oct. 1911), 575. [Letter signed 'E. Belfort Bax, E. T. Hulme, and J. Stuart Hay']*

'Notes on Bergson. I', *New Age*, 9/25 (19 Oct. 1911), 587–8.

'Notes on Bergson. II', *New Age*, 9/26 (26 Oct. 1911), 610–11.

---

* Not included in this volume.

'Bergson Lecturing', *New Age*, 10/1 (2 Nov. 1911), 15–16. [Signed 'Thomas Gratton']

'Theory and Practice', *Commentator*, 3 (8 Nov. 1911), 388; (15 Nov. 1911), 404–5. [Signed 'Thomas Gratton']

'Mr Balfour, Bergson, and Politics', *New Age*, 10/2 (9 Nov. 1911), 38–40. [Signed 'T. E. H.']

'Bergsonism', *New Age*, 10/2 (9 Nov. 1911), 46–7. [Letter signed 'T. E. H.']*

'A Personal Impression of Bergson', *Westminster Gazette*, 18 Nov. 1911, p. 2. [Signed 'T. K. White']

'Notes on Bergson. III', *New Age*, 10/4 (23 Nov. 1911), 79–82.

'Bergsonism', *New Age*, 10/4 (23 Nov. 1911), 94. [Letter signed 'T. E. H.']*

'Notes on Bergson. IV', *New Age*, 10/5 (30 Nov. 1911), 110–12.

1912

'The Complete Poetical Works of T. E. Hulme', *New Age*, 10/13 (25 Jan. 1912), 307. ['Autumn', 'Mana Aboda', 'Conversion', 'Above the Dock', and 'Embankment']

'Notes on Bergson', *New Age*, 10/15 (8 Feb. 1912), 359. [Letter]*

'Notes on Bergson. V', *New Age*, 10/17 (22 Feb. 1912), 401–3.

'A Tory Philosophy', *Commentator*, 4 (3 Apr. 1912), 294–5; (10 Apr.), 310; (1 May), 362; (8 May), 380; (15 May), 388–9. [Signed 'Thomas Grattan' [*sic*]]

'Bergson in English', *Cambridge Magazine*, 1 (27 Apr. 1912), 265. [Letter]*

'A Prophecy', *Cambridge Magazine*, 1 (4 May 1912), 293. [Letter signed 'One Who Is Very Sorry He Can Read'; repr. in *Cambridge Magazine* for 16 Feb. 1918]*

'Bergson in English', *Cambridge Magazine*, 1 (18 May 1912), 353. [Letter]*

'The Complete Poetical Works of T. E. Hulme', in *Ripostes*, by Ezra Pound. London: Stephen Swift, [Oct.] 1912. [Poems published in Jan. *New Age* with a few changes; Pound reprinted the Hulme poems in *Canzoni & Ripostes* (1913), *Umbra* (1920), *Profile* (1932), and *Personae* (1926, 1949, 1952)]

An Introduction to Metaphysics, by Henri Bergson, trans. T. E. Hulme. New York: G. P. Putnam's Sons, [Nov.] 1912. [On title-page: 'Authorized Edition, Revised by the Author, with Additional Material'. 'Translator's Preface' on pp. iii–iv]*

1913

An Introduction to Metaphysics, by Henri Bergson, trans. T. E. Hulme. London: Macmillan, [Mar.] 1913. ['Authorized Translation'. The 'Translator's Preface', pp. v–vi, has been slightly reworded from that published in New York in 1912.]*

'Mr. Epstein and the Critics', *New Age*, 14/8 (25 Dec. 1913), 251–3. [Epstein claimed in 1931 that his drawing *Rock Drill*, published on p. 256, was meant to accompany Hulme's article.]

1914

'Modern Art.—I. The Grafton Group', *New Age*, 14/11 (15 Jan. 1914), 341–2.

'Modern Art.—II. A Preface Note and Neo-Realism', *New Age*, 14/15 (12 Feb. 1914), 467–9.

'Contemporary Drawings—No. 1', ed. T. E. Hulme, *New Age*, 14/20 (19 Mar. 1914), 625. [*A Dancer*, by Gaudier-Brzeska]

'Modern Art.—III. The London Group', *New Age*, 14/21 (26 Mar. 1914), 661–2.

'Contemporary Drawings', ed. T. E. Hulme, *New Age*, 14/22 (2 Apr. 1914), 688. [Hulme's introductory note to the series]

'Contemporary Drawings—No. 2', ed. T. E. Hulme, *New Age*, 14/22 (2 Apr. 1914), 689. [*Chinnereth*, by David Bomberg]

'Contemporary Drawings—No. 3', ed. T. E. Hulme, *New Age*, 14/24 (16 Apr. 1914), 753. [*Study*, by William Roberts, with Hulme's note of explanation]

'Contemporary Drawings—No. 4', ed. T. E. Hulme, *New Age*, 14/26 (30 Apr. 1914), 814. [*The Chauffeur*, by C. R. W. Nevinson]

'Contemporary Drawings—No. 5', ed. T. E. Hulme, *New Age*, 14/26 (30 Apr. 1914), 815. [*The Farmyard*, by Edward Wadsworth]

'Contemporary Drawings', *New Age*, 14/26 (30 Apr. 1914), 821. [Hulme's notes on the drawings in the series]

'German Chronicle', *Poetry and Drama*, 2 (June 1914), 221–8.

'Modern Art. IV.—Mr. David Bomberg's Show', *New Age*, 15/10 (9 July 1914), 230–2.

Reflections on Violence, by Georges Sorel, trans. T. E. Hulme. New York: B. W. Huebsch, [Nov.] 1914. ['Authorized Translation'. Later published in USA, by Peter Smith (New York, 1941), by the Free Press (Glencoe, Ill., 1950), by Collier Books (New York, 1961), and by AMS Press (New York, 1975).

1915

'The Translator's Preface to Sorel's "Reflections on Violence"', *New Age*, 17/24 (14 Oct. 1915), 569–70. [Repr. with slight changes in *Reflections on Violence*, by Georges Sorel, trans. T. E. Hulme (London: Allen & Unwin, 1916)]

'War Notes', *New Age*, 18/2 (11 Nov. 1915), 29–30; 18/3 (18 Nov.), 53–5; 18/4 (25 Nov.), 77; 18/5 (2 Dec.), 101–2; 18/6 (9 Dec.), 125–6; 18/7 (16 Dec.), 149–51; 18/8 (23 Dec.), 173–4; 18/9 (30 Dec.), 197–9. [Signed 'North Staffs.' Continued in 1916]

'A Notebook', *New Age*, 18/5 (2 Dec. 1915), 112–13; 18/6 (9 Dec. 1915), 137–8; 18/7 (16 Dec. 1915), 158–60; 18/8 (23 Dec. 1915), 186–8. [Signed 'T. E. H'. Continued in 1916]

1916

'War Notes', *New Age*, 18/10 (6 Jan. 1916), 222–3; 18/11 (13 Jan.), 246–7; 18/12 (20 Jan.), 269–70; 18/13 (27 Jan.), 293–4; 18/14 (3 Feb.), 317–18; 18/15 (10 Feb.), 341–2; 18/16 (17 Feb.), 365–6; 18/17 (24 Feb.), 389–91; 18/18 (2 Mar.), 413–14. [Signed 'North Staffs.']

'A Notebook', *New Age*, 18/10 (6 Jan. 1916), 234–5; 18/13 (27 Jan.), 305–7; 18/15 (10 Feb.), 353–4. [Signed 'T. E. H.' An edited version was reprinted in *Speculations* (1924) under the title 'Humanism and the Religious Attitude'.]

'War Notes. On "Liberty"', *Cambridge Magazine*, 5/10 (22 Jan. 1916), 221. [Signed 'North Staffs.' Abbreviated version of 'War Notes', *New Age*, 20 Jan.]

'War Notes. Inevitability Inapplicable', *Cambridge Magazine*, 5/11 (29 Jan. 1916), 242–3. [Signed 'North Staffs.' Abbreviated version of 'War Notes', *New Age*, 27 Jan.]

'War Notes. The Kind of Rubbish We Oppose', *Cambridge Magazine*, 5/12 (5 Feb. 1916), 266–7. [Signed 'North Staffs.' Abbreviated version of 'War Notes', *New Age*, 3 Feb.]

'Why We Are in Favour of This War: The Case Against "Another Cucumber Sandwich"', *Cambridge Magazine*, 5/13 (12 Feb. 1916), 304–5. [Signed 'North Staffs.' Slightly edited version of 'War Notes', *New Age*, 10 Feb.]

'The Framework of Europe: "North Staffs." on the Distorting Effects of History', *Cambridge Magazine*, 5/14 (19 Feb. 1916), 329–30. [Signed 'North Staffs.' Slightly edited version of 'War Notes', *New Age*, 17 Feb.]

'North Staffs Resents Mr. Russell's Rejoinder', *Cambridge Magazine*, 5/15 (26 Feb. 1916), 352–4. [Signed 'North Staffs.' Slightly edited version of 'War Notes', *New Age*, 24 Feb.]

'North Staffs Continues Where He Left Off', *Cambridge Magazine*, 5/16 (4 Mar. 1916), 376–7. [Signed 'North Staffs.' Slightly edited version of 'War Notes', *New Age*, 2 Mar.]

Reflections on Violence, by Georges Sorel, trans. with an introduction and bibliography by T. E. Hulme. London: George Allen & Unwin, [Mar.] 1916. ['Translator's Preface', pp. v–xi, similar to *New Age*, 14 Oct. 1915. In a subsequent edition published by Allen & Unwin in 1925, Hulme's preface and bibliography were dropped.]

1920

[Fragments], in 'Readers and Writers', by R. H. C. [A. R. Orage], *New Age*, 27 (26 Aug. 1920), 259–60. [Quotations from Hulme's manuscripts]*

1921

'Fragments (From the note-books of T. E. Hulme, who was killed in the war)', *New Age*, 29 (6 Oct. 1921), 275–6. [Fragments from Hulme's poetry]*

1922

'The Note-Books of T. E. Hulme', ed. Herbert Read, *New Age*, 30 (19 Jan. 1922), 148–9; (26 Jan.), 167–8; (9 Feb.), 193–4; (16 Feb.), 207–8. [Reprinted with some differences in *Speculations* (1924), under the title 'Cinders']

'The Note-Books of T. E. Hulme', ed. Herbert Read, *New Age*, 30 (30 Mar. 1922), 287–8; (6 Apr.), 301–2; (13 Apr.), 310–12. [Subtitled 'Bergson's Theory of Art'; reprinted in *Speculations* (1924)]

1924

Speculations, by T. E. Hulme, ed. Herbert Read. London: Kegan Paul, Trench, Trubner & Co., 1924; New York: Harcourt, Brace & Co., 1924. [Contains 'Humanism and the Religious Attitude', 'Modern Art and Its Philosophy', 'Romanticism and Classicism', 'Bergson's Theory of Art', 'The Philosophy of Intensive Manifolds', 'Cinders', Hulme's preface to *Reflections on Violence*, a Plan for a Work on Modern Theories of Art,* and 'The Complete Poetical Works of T. E. Hulme']

1925

'Notes on Language and Style', ed. Herbert Read, *Criterion*, 3 (July 1925), 485–97.

1929

Notes on Language and Style, ed. Herbert Read. University of Washington Chapbook, Seattle, no. 25. [Reprint of 1925 item above.]

1938

'The Man in the Crow's Nest', 'Susan Ann and Immortality', and 'A City Sunset' [poems], and 'Lecture on Modern Poetry' and 'Notes on Language and Style' [prose], in *T. E. Hulme*, by Michael Roberts. London: Faber and Faber, 1938. [First publication of 'The Man in the Crow's Nest', 'Susan Ann and Immortality', and 'Lecture on Modern Poetry'. This version of 'Notes on Language and Style' is more complete than that published earlier by Herbert Read.]

1955

Further Speculations, by T. E. Hulme, ed. Samuel Hynes. Minneapolis: University of Minnesota Press, 1955; London: Cumberiege, 1955. [Contains 'Searchers after Reality' series, 'Notes on the Bologna Congress', 'Notes on Bergson' series, 'A Lecture on Modern Poetry', 'Notes on Language and Style', Mr. Epstein and the Critics', 'Modern Art' series, 'Diary from the Trenches', 'On Liberty', 'Inevitability Inapplicable', 'The Kind of Rubbish We Oppose', 'Why We Are in Favour of This War', 'The Framework of Europe', 'North Staffs Resents Mr. Russell's Rejoinder', 'North Staffs Continues Where He Left Off', and 'Poems and Fragments']

INDEX